HOW TO PAINT AND DRAW

HOW TO
PAINT AND DRAW

Bodo W. Jaxtheimer

**With 300 illustrations in colour and
150 in black-and-white**

**Weathervane Books
New York**

CONTENTS

PART II: PAINTING

Everything which can be seen or touched is originally experienced as something plastic in space. If you wish to formulate the experience of these two senses for yourself, or to communicate it to others, you note down what you have seen; you draw points, lines, and areas in contrasting colors onto a flat surface. The image thus created gives an illusion reproducing the experience; it may be stronger or weaker than or equal in force to the original experience, according to your ability and to the material you use.

The most direct representation of volume is, of course, sculpture, or modeling in three dimensions. A sphere can be held, whereas a drawn circle representing a sphere cannot. Thus, the picture is an illusion, which in life is often much more significant than what is easily tangible. But even sculpture can show only volume, not space. If the object represented is significant and expressive only by its position in space relative to other objects, then a sculpture of it is no more complete than a drawing.

The desire to formulate and to communicate an experience is as old as humanity itself. It may even be that drawing and modeling are older than the spoken word, in any event older than poetry. It is conceivable that before the perishable word there was the picture, the drawing, by which even the mute can express himself. Things which are hardly describable in words at all can be understood at a glance from a picture, although, conversely, words can describe feelings which cannot be expressed pictorially except in abstract pictures. This aside, a verbal description of an experience is always much more related to consciousness and the intellect than the pictorial description, which achieves its strongest impact when dealing with visions and ideas not explicable by logical formulation. This "inner" vision may be so strong that it can be reproduced as directly as something which is objectively present to the sight.

The vision, on the other hand, may detach itself completely from the memory of recognizable objects, abstracting from the external form, which is universally recognizable at all times, inner, subjective processes and reactions which are actually unreal and do not correspond to a common vision or feeling. These abstract representations may thus not be universally comprehensible; then words and explanations are again needed to guide the response of the beholder to the point from which the painter started. Without them, quite contradictory interpretations can be read into abstract pictures, as in a game of ink-blot reading. Properly, a picture should need no captions; its true nature is to create an unequivocal effect without words.

The first efforts of human beings to set down pictorially the visible and tangible world were aimed at achieving the closest imitation of the object with means precluding any misunderstanding or ambiguity. The most unequivocal of these means is an area of color. If a child is given the most varied materials for drawing and painting, he will always choose color and make colored areas. The image on the retina of the human eye is composed of these colored areas. The lines which we think we see are only the boundaries we feel between two colors. This would not need saying if we were not educated (or miseducated) from childhood by the example of others and by our own efforts to set down everything we see primarily as outlines.

The line is in itself a considerable abstraction of immediate experience. If the child does not want just to daub, but to ''paint'' something definite, he first draws the outlines of the areas and then fills them in with color. The practiced painter does essentially the same thing—he can do nothing else. He must first set down the outline without which no area can emerge, and every pictorial representation is made up of areas. When the outline has served its purpose it can be eliminated and covered over with gradual transitions of color. This is the characteristic method of painting. If the outline remains and its inner area is only shaded in or left without filling at all,

Dürer, Schelde Harbor, Antwerp. Line drawing of great purity

Monet, Houses of Parliament in Fog. Pure painting. Overlapping colors cause shapes to dissolve

the picture is called a drawing.

There is, in fact, no need to choose between the two alternatives. There is an infinite variety of intermediary stages between a pure outline drawing and a painting composed exclusively of areas of color merging and overlapping each other; hence, no clear division can be made between drawing and painting.

Pure painting, as opposed to drawing with color, did not in fact begin to develop until the discovery in the Italian Renaissance that many objects in nature cannot be separated clearly from their environment; that smoke and vapor, flickering or dappled light, cloud and darkness make areas merge inconspicuously into each other. Thus, the shapes of the areas are more felt than seen. Later this discovery led to a closer definition and separation of the concepts of drawing and painting. Thus, to compensate for the narrowing of the term "drawing" to "line drawing" the Greek word "graphic" is sometimes used as a more general word. Its precise meaning is "written," and there is, a very close relationship between writing and drawing.

Hals, Malle Babbe (detail). Painting with gently overlapping colors. A foretaste of Impressionism. Oil

P. Breughel the Elder, Massacre of the Innocents in Bethlehem (detail). Painting which is very nearly colored drawing. Oil and tempera

Writing has developed from simplified drawings of objects representing certain definite concepts. Symbols were derived from these drawings and from the symbols signs or letters, which now retain only the meaning of single sounds. Letters are made by combinations of lines. The term "graphic art" is now applied to all kinds of representations which accept the principle of an abstracting line. This principle can be expressed in a reduction of everything visible to black and white, sometimes extended to include intermediate ranges of gray. It is still graphic art if colors are used, provided that they are kept clearly separate, either with an enclosing line or by the avoidance of any over-painting.

Thus, it is wrong to describe a picture as a painting because it is in color. It is equally wrong to make painting dependent on the brush, which can be used both for painting and drawing, as can colored pencils. The pen is the only exclusively graphic instrument, for it cannot be disassociated from the principle of the line. This explains, too, how wrong it is to use the word "painting" for those techniques which are entirely graphic in character: mosaic, stained glass pictures, batik, and sgraffito. If you examine an Egyptian wall painting you will see at once that it is not painting but graphic art.

There is, however, no precise boundary between graphic art and painting. The range of examples shows every gradation between them. An unceasing war

Toulouse-Lautrec, colored chalk drawing. This is still drawing, but painterly in intention

Greuze, black chalk, lightened with white. The illusion of color is reinforced by the use of red chalk for lips and shadows

can be waged by pedants for exact terminology, but it is unimportant. No one wishes to produce mongrel work in any sphere, but what is important is the effect of the picture itself, not its category. Categories can be left for the pedants, whose theorizings need not spoil our enjoyment of a picture nor impede the pleasure of trying to make one. These pleasures can be increased by a closer study of the development of pictorial representation.

This begins about 30,000 years ago in the Old Stone Age, and with something of a flourish—with colored cave paintings. A dispute as to whether line drawing or graphic coloring came first seems totally irrelevant as we admire these first, highly artistic creations of the human imagination. As we have shown, areas

of color can hardly be set down without an outline, and the line drawing must have originated simultaneously with the graphic coloring. The outline is not there as an end in itself but as a starting point. A pure line drawing may be equivocal, the area it encloses may be either substance or space. For example, if you draw a circle no one can tell whether it indicates a hole, a raised plane, a column seen from above, or a sphere. A simple outline, even when it is unequivocal, makes greater demands on the imagination of the beholder than a shaded or colored representation, or one drawn in perspective. A picture which has all these elements is the least demanding.

At least until the second half of the last century one of the foremost aims of

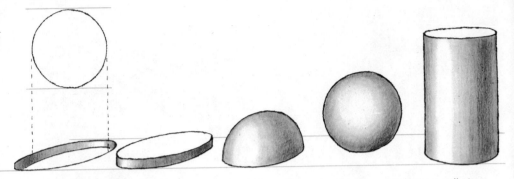

Seen from above, a circle may represent a hole, a disc, a hemisphere, a sphere, a cylinder

the student of painting and drawing was to create a perfect illusion of the impression derived from nature. In every age there were other no less important problems and aims, but teaching was based on the assumption that the true reproduction of nature was the aim of the accomplished artist, and that this formed the basis of his creative activity. Apelles, who worked as court painter to Alexander the Great, was the most famous painter in Antiquity. Among the many anecdotes concerning him is one illustrating this high regard for perfect naturalism. He once engaged in a public competition with a colleague; each was to paint a picture. Apelles' contemporary produced a picture of grapes which looked so real that the birds came to eat them. After due admiration of this feat the audience called on Apelles to unveil his picture. This he could not do, for the veil was all he had painted. Thus, Apelles succeeded in deceiving even the human eye.

The anecdote is, of course, apocryphal, and since no work by Apelles has survived it is impossible to know how closely naturalistic his painting was.

A few decades ago there were still theatre curtains which had to be studied for some time, before one could decide whether they were of draped material or merely painted linen.

Naturalistic representation ceased to be generally admired only with the advent of photography, when first black-and-white and then color photographs surpassed any drawing or painting in naturalism. Against this new invention painters and draftsmen had only one trump card, but it outplayed anything photography could do: even the best photograph is powerless against the artist's creative interpretation, against his intensified reformulation of his experience of reality. This does not imply that there was nothing more than unquestioning naturalistic reproduction in art until the advent of photography; the great artists have never been satisfied with that. If we study the bison painted (along with many other animals) in the cave of Altamira in northern Spain, perhaps 30,000 years ago, we can see such closeness to nature that the photograph could tell us little more of the animal's anatomy or proportions or of any important details; yet the drawing tells us something essentially more important even than this from the strong broad concept of the form. It is this which makes it impressive and imparts the menacing effect of the size and weight of the beast without any comparison with man or plant to give it relative scale. The drawing is by no means a mechanical, naturalistic reproduction but an all-embracing representation of its subject.

It would be interesting to know the circumstances which gave rise to this picture which is even today unsurpassed in its power and impact. There is no evidence remaining, but much can be deduced. It is certainly not painted from life. Apart from the impossibility of keeping the creature still while the artist drew it, the position in which it is depicted is composite and is not literally possible. Yet the picture is not untrue. Evidently the artist frequently watched these beasts in this and other poses and studied dead ones for all the details. Then, his mind full of all these impressions, he created the picture out of his head. This is in great measure why these pictures are so magnificent. An artist who always draws from a model cannot draw freely. The faculty of memory is not as objective as a camera, but it is truer in its ability to sift away the unessential, omitting incidental and fortuitous characteristics and revealing only the typical.

The traditional method of the classical Chinese and Japanese painters indicates, even prescribes, the way in which to arrive at a meditated, condensed representation which distills the utmost from its subject. We are repeatedly told in

Bison. Pastel on wall rock, Altamira Caves, Spain. Paleolithic Age, c. 30,000 to 12,000 B.C.

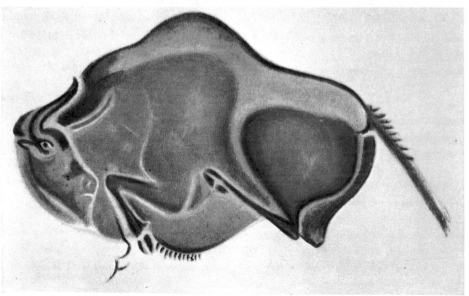

Sesshu (1420-1506, regarded as the greatest Japanese painter), Winter Landscape, India ink on paper. Clearly drawn from memory. Natural forms are made to appear crystalline (ice crystals)

written records how these painters wandered about in the countryside, deep in contemplation; and how only when returning home did they seize the brush and depict on the silk what had impressed them. Every triviality was forgotten, and a force more unconscious than conscious intensified the expression of the natural form to give it the subjective impact which the painter had received from the subject itself.

You can test how far a subjective impression differs from an "objective" reproduction by drawing a landscape, first from memory, then directly from nature, and lastly by photographing it from the same viewpoint. You will be surprised at how flat and insignificant the photograph appears against your drawing from nature, even when you have employed all possible mechanical aids for insuring an accurate record. This experiment does not apply when you put in clear detail and there is less space in the picture. Photograph and drawing then approximate more and more closely.

If we follow the historical development of pictorial art from the point of view of naturalistic representation we find two influences repeatedly at work against it. One is the human tendency to emphasize and exaggerate certain aspects, expressing itself in the form as well as in the content of the picture; the other is variations in ability.

Stylistic emphasis is most apparent in unusual proportions. Large eyes, heads, and hands are the most telling means of expressing the spiritual in Romanesque art. In the Gothic style they are elongated and narrowed. The Baroque expresses sensual enjoyment with colossal bodies; in the Rococo this robustness is transformed into an almost sickly sweetness, with the body acquiring an expression of languid decadence. Alternating with these periods are times when body and spirit achieve a harmony: the classical Greek and Roman, its rebirth in the Renaissance, and a later attempt at a revival of classicism. These three periods were concerned with the perfect proportion of all things and achieved varying success both in general concept and in particular example.

Greek vase (details). Example of well proportioned classical figure

Ability ebbs and flows to its own rhythm alongside these changes of style, generally expressing itself at the beginning of a period with monumental strength, reaching a perfection of balance at the zenith, and ending in decadence and decline, although at this final stage it often brings forth the most beautiful works of the entire cycle, like overripe, choice fruits from the last days of harvest.

Naturalistic representation reached its last and most trivial stage at the time of the advent of photography. The less gifted resorted to aids invented in an earlier time to obtain an "exact" replica of a model: the artist looked through a squared glass and mechanically transferred onto squared paper whatever lines filled each square; or used Lavater's silhouette maker, a piece of paper in a frame onto the back of which a candle threw the shadow of the model so that it could be simply traced around.

Meanwhile, everything which was known about pictorial representation was compiled into a categorical syllabus, and students in art academies were tormented

to the brink of despair with the copying of plaster casts, both whole and in detail, for a minimum of two years. In this way all their imaginative powers were completely numbed or destroyed for the rest of their lives. Many whose temperaments could not endure this stultification were dismissed from the academies as incompetent and went away to become important painters.

There may sometimes have been a few exceptions, and the author must beg indulgence for his sweeping generalization. At all events, the opposition of a full-blooded temperament to the fossilized, or better, "plasterfied," activities of the academies engendered something quite new: a painting direct from nature, but one in which the momentary impression was immediately transposed and interpreted. To put it crudely, the painter screwed up his eyes and painted only

Rape of the Daughters of Leukippos (detail). Baroque exaggeration of human proportions

21

the strongest colors which penetrated his sight. It was just this immediacy, rather than clarity of form, which inspired him. He saw significance only in the general impression which triumphed over the whirling mass of incidental detail.

In 1872 Claude Monet painted a sunset on the Seine at Le Havre; two years later he exhibited it under the title **Impression.** The influential art critic Leroy was incensed at this and other similar paintings and dubbed all the new daubers "Impressionists." Little did he know that he had coined the name for a style which now ranks among the highest in art.

The impressionist way of seeing and transposing was not entirely new. There are signs of it, as we have seen, in the Renaissance in the **sfumato** technique used by Leonardo, in which the air's haze is expressed by obscuring the unessential. This artificial haziness, in effect not unlike the work of the retoucher in photography, evolved increasingly into a sense of natural air, which is normally palpable in Rembrandt, still more enveloping in

Watteau, and with the Impressionists a mass uniting all things and beings.

This type of painting increasingly showed the atmosphere as a visible substance and added the new technique of color perspective to the already well-established linear perspective. Linear perspective as a set of mathematical formulae and rules was not discovered until the early fifteenth century in Italy, when it was immediately used in painting; but appreciably earlier there are suggestions of spatial perspective derived simply from observation. In fact, perspective appears wherever single objects overlap each other in a picture and thus show graduation in depth, and when objects in the background appear smaller than those in the foreground.

Perspective is also a means of making the illusion of space and volume more realistic. It is not essential to this illusion, for whatever one sees in a picture is unconsciously related to the aggregate of impressions seen in daily life. For example, there is not the slightest hint of perspective in the prehistoric drawing of

Leonardo da Vinci, background study to Adoration of the Magi. Construction based on middle perspective underlies this picture, to reappear in more austere form in Leonardo's Last Supper

Tiepolo, detail from the fresco on the ceiling of the imperial chamber at the Residenz in Würzburg. The bold perspective succeeds only from certain angles. From others, for example bottom left, it takes on a stucco effect

the bison, yet one feels that the head and legs are nearer than the body and not on the same plane. In Egyptian wall paintings, too, in spite of the characteristic combined view, part frontal and part profile, which takes no account whatever of perspective, there are foreshortenings of circles and spatial relationships which indicate perspective. In the later styles of ancient Greek art many elements of perspective had become a matter of course.

Giotto, the greatest painting technician of the fourteenth century, paved the way for the development of true perspective by his sheer artistic mastery of form in space; and by the time of Leonardo da Vinci perspective is often used according to established rules as one of the major constituents of painting. This new scientific acquisition stimulated tremendous enthusiasm among painters for several centuries to come, but it has never been able to increase the spiritual value of a picture. Ultimately the beholder is much more affected by the mysterious charm of a pervasive and perceptible plane in the picture from which depth or modeling seems to emerge momentarily. A plane broken by perspective has no more mystery and tends to distract from the sense of a concentrated visual experience.

Baroque and Rococo ceiling frescoes

Signac, Venice, Santa Maria della Salute (detail). The intended effect is achieved only by standing some way back from the picture. The artist makes use of a knowledge of light physics with regard to the additive and subtractive mixing of colors (See chapter on colors)

are examples of the extreme use of perspective. It is often impossible to see whether they are painted or moulded. This is intentional; the painters aimed at imitating the much more expensive work of moulding and at extending what plaster work was already there by painting moulded forms. Painted moulding looks completely chaotic when it is seen from the wrong angle; and the plastic moulding continuing on from it projects from the wall without any logic.

Lastly came the discovery and use of color perspective. There are no rules for its use, only a few principles which are always being questioned; thus it is difficult to say where and when it first appeared. Its first great triumph, however, was in Impressionism. Today the perspective-building qualities of colors are used for the most varied purposes. The many Post-Impressionist painters used them, for example, to bring back linear perspective into two dimensions and combined them with a conscious use of the psychological effects of color.

However exact and conclusive they may be, the facts of science are not absolutely indispensable to artistic creation. When they are used consciously, they operate as foreign bodies in art and obscure the artist's clarity of vision. They need first to be deposited like earth in muddy water to make a firm foundation in the artist's mind. Perspective founded on science was at first given an exaggerated importance and had a damaging effect on the work of many painters. The same is true of the speculations of Dr. Gall (1758-1828) on skull formation as an indication of character—which turned out, as it happened, to be untrue—and of the more correct theories on physiognomy of Lavater (1741-1801). In the same way the attempt of the Pointillists among the later Impressionists to work scientifically according to the physical properties of light soon came to an end.

Documentary naturalism lost its **raison d'être** with the development of photography. It had never in fact possessed one, artistically speaking, since it could never reproduce exactly what is seen. Before modern art turned sharply away from the directly recognizable, objective world it had already developed something which, though not contrary to naturalism, implied a critical attitude towards it. This was the stylization of accidental form into the typical. Here a very

human desire is at work: to survey and fit the surrounding world into a framework of the most generalized and simplified patterns and formulae possible; in other words the desire to see the species as an average and highly simplified form, a type, rather than as a multitude of individuals each with his own personal and different form. This desire has its parallel in other spheres: omnipotent nature is not concerned with the fate of the individual, but with the survival of the species.

Every stylization is simply the recognition of a common form behind many fortuitous related forms and the reduction of it to a geometric principle. This common form remains in the mind, making it easier to work back to its many individual variations. Once you have realized, for example, that the profile of a bellflower can be transcribed as a parabola, the frontal view of the human head as an ellipse, the contour of a young fir tree as a triangle, it will always be easy to start from these geometric shapes and to draw individual deviations from memory. Graphic abstraction from fortuitous natural shapes has led, among other things, to two independent offshoots of the art of drawing: ornamental pattern and writing.

Ornamental pattern, when it is fully

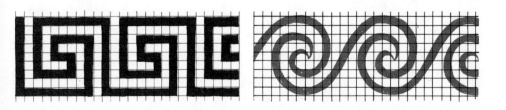

developed, always reflects some vital force of nature which is perpetually at work.

Perhaps the author may be allowed to describe an experience which relates to one of the most widespread of ornamental motifs: the meander, which is also called "wave-pattern," and sometimes "running dog." Meander was the name of a winding river, now called the Great Menderes, in West Anatolia. The term "wave pattern" recalls the profile of overturning waves at a shore; but "running dog"? One morning I looked out of my window onto a park covered with thick snow and saw a visitor approaching, a St. Bernard dog. Not seeing me behind the window, he ran across the snow and then lay down. Still I did not show myself, so he ran further and again lay down to wait. In the end he went away. Suddenly I saw how his tracks had made a perfect "running dog" pattern in the snow. The spiral curves each began and ended at the points where he had lain down. Then I began to understand something of the nature of this pattern: the symbol of the ever-repeated movements of a blind force perpetually

Irish manuscript, decorative animal motif. Example of almost abstract art, drawing on animal life for stimulus (eyes and beaks)

running against an obstacle, like constant drops of water, the rhythm of day and night, birth and death. The ability to extract meaning from a representation which has been reduced to a pattern or symbol and associate it in a flash with a whole chain of thoughts and feelings is very human. Writing is the most impressive example of this. While we read, we no longer think how the individual letters arose, even though the process is known by which they developed from representations of something in nature to fixed symbols. Besides the two branches of drawing which have taken on an independent existence, pattern and writing, every pictorial representation begins with a simplification, whether it aims at a naturalistic portrayal or at complete independence from the objective world. In short, it begins with a sketch.

We all know that frequently a sketch is more effective and impressive than a finished picture. This results in part from the simplification of shape and the absence of distracting detail. The most beautiful and splendid picture may at times leave the beholder unmoved at a superficial glance; he turns away with the feeling that demands are being made on him to concentrate his attention, to give himself up. The sketch holds him more easily, it invites him to linger. This is because a sketch leaves so much open to him; it stimulates him to complete in imagination what is fleeting and unexpressed; it is full of mystery. And mystery, as everyone knows, is always attractive. The fleeting, interrupted strokes that fade into the plane of the picture

Rembrandt, The Flight of Lot from Sodom. Pen sketch, obviously executed in a matter of minutes

are continued in the mind, an activity of which one never tires.

Another charm of the sketch is that one can see how it came into being and can follow the work of its creation. Everyone enjoys watching work being done, whether or not he himself could do it. It is often said that art should conceal art, and it is true enough that signs of the effort of creation can oppress or disturb the beholder's enjoyment. But in most sketches everything seems easy, since it arose without obligation, and everyone prefers a suggestion to a command.

Gradually a new conception was introduced into the visual arts, that of a work which has the nature of a sketch, which implies rather than formulates precisely, intended not as a sketch or study but as the finished work. This vagueness and evanescence brought yet another quality into the work of art: the idea of movement.

Until the beginnings of Impressionism it had not been possible, other than in sketches, to represent anything but a fixed moment of movement, like a still from a motion picture. But a strong gesture interrupted and frozen was less and less felt to be satisfactory. It is tolerable only when it is represented just before or after its climax. Lessing tried to develop from the Laocoön group a theory of the right moment of representation which would give the noblest expression of the inner event, but it had no practical outcome. Lessing's deductions could only be regarded by detached painters as a restriction of theme. The Impressionists, however, found an inspired solution to the problem of movement in the suggestiveness of the sketch.

The Impressionists also introduced a measure of movement into the principles of composition, which were gradually becoming ossified. By composition we mean the dividing up of the area of the picture. Composition began to develop as soon as an artificial and clearly defined area replaced the natural rock surface as the field of the picture: first the wall and later the support of wood or canvas, silk or paper. Even when a modern mural is freely placed on an empty surface its position is always re-

Above: Plan showing a selective composition based on self-portrait by Gauguin (Page 65). The slightest alteration in the selected field would destroy the composition

Left: Plan showing composition with a wide field of vision, based on self-portrait by Rembrandt (Page 65). This field could be somewhat extended or reduced without appreciably altering the effect of the picture

Right: Plan showing inharmonious composition, based on Van Gogh's picture Field with Fence. The spectator has an involuntary urge to move the frame upwards and to the left

lated to the edges of that surface, most closely, of course, when the picture occupies it completely.

Just as, before Impressionism, a depicted movement always seems checked, and rarely communicates the illusion of being inherent, so composition was fixed in a balanced arrangement, in a frozen, self-contained moment from life, employing the interplay of movement and rest, the forces and centers of gravity. To create the sense that movement is in progress involves an entirely different compositional idea. At first sight the harmony is missing which until then was usual inside the bounds of the picture. A dissonance has been introduced into the picture plane, requiring an alteration of the placing of the subject, a displacement of the conventional centering of balance. There seems to be an excess of unused space at the expense of the significant part which is the center of interest. The tension of movement in Impressionist composition (which, of course, continued in the following periods) is comparable to that in classical oriental paintings. In the latter the empty space is introduced, to a large extent,

as a field for movement, although these compositions are always harmoniously conceived.

It would certainly be wrong to regard Impressionism as a break in the development of art, although it contradicted so much that had gone before, including the tradition, vacillating but constant, which had aimed at naturalism. Impressionism is better regarded as the apex of a symmetrical curve which begins by turning away from naturalism. Impressionism is an end, a climax, and a beginning as well.

A considerable distance has been traveled since then, but the path seems to be leading into the desert. The objective world is more and more seen as a thematic and formal source, which then becomes a schematic memory, until even this memory vanishes. This is not to be seen only in finished works, for in many instances even instruction in painting and drawing is also turning away from the objective. One may ask what remains when the objective world is not used even for study and practice? Were there any other subject material it would not matter, but we have now to await the results of a pedagogic effort which causes the student to represent a horse so that a layman, after much puzzling, thinks it may be a squashed liver sausage. The question arises whether we can call training that which uses as a beginning what a few individuals found as the highly personal climax of their pictorial expression, a climax which cannot possibly be accepted as a universally valid starting point. Such training arrives at what it most wanted to avoid: academic restriction. It is a restriction greater

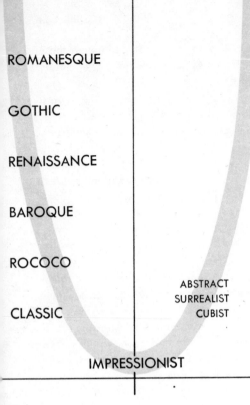

ROMANESQUE

GOTHIC

RENAISSANCE

BAROQUE

ROCOCO

                            ABSTRACT
                            SURREALIST

CLASSIC   CUBIST

         IMPRESSIONIST

painting technician, to be neither necessary nor durable. These are produced because they are in constant demand by the ignorant. The beginner is helpless in all this. He is guided by what he picks up by chance here and there; he has to rely on a few dusty old manuals which contain a mass of antiquated information, not to mention the plethora of wretched small tracts. At the same time there has been for many years no difficulty in reviewing and judging painting and drawing materials and their technical use.

Nowadays everything which has shown itself to be suitable over the centuries is used as support, from natural rock and wood to cloth, paper, and now artificial fibers. In the early history of painting the powdery pigment was transferred to the support by first making it into sticks; also, once the color was mixed with a binder so that it could be spread, the brush came into early use. Both of these processes have persisted. Only recently palette knife and airbrush have been added, although spraying is seldom used outside of commercial art.

The following sections of this book are written with the conviction that painters and draftsmen should be masters of their trade. We will deal, then, with the resources surveyed so far and attempt to explain a little their fluctuating importance in picture making over the centuries. This explanation should make a beginning possible for those who have as yet no clear idea of all the different factors involved in the making of a picture. They should then be able to see more easily which things they can themselves use most effectively.

than any yet if "abstract art" is the only admitted foundation and also the starting point.

This being so, it is not surprising that the material side of painting and drawing is so much neglected in the schools. Numbers of painters and draftsmen have no idea of the nature of the materials they constantly use, and this at a time when all materials have been thoroughly investigated and analyzed in their composition and qualities, their technical and artistic possibilites. Institutes and technical periodicals can give exact information, and manufacturers can supply materials of a quality never surpassed. Yet materials are ordered which the manufacturer knows, better than any

PART I: DRAWING

1. IN THE BEGINNING IS THE LINE

If conversation turns to judging a picture which is finally dismissed as worthless, one often hears at the end of the clever talk, "Well, anyway, I couldn't do it. I can't even draw a straight line."

The speaker, humbly sympathetic and respectful of the painter's ability, is usually speaking from a quite unfounded sense of his own incompetence. Even if he does not mean a literally "straight" line, the layman often credits the practiced painter with a mass of secret gifts, particularly the mysterious gift of "talent" for drawing. This awe is quite

unjustified. The average person at school and at work is assumed to have much greater ability to perform in several directions than what is needed simply to draw what he sees. Of course, **some** guidance is needed to acquire this ability, just as it is for writing, building, or cooking. A professional painter or draftsman naturally needs education and practice, just as does any craftsman, doctor, or administrator. Only very outstanding accomplishment is a matter of talent.

The famous straight line cannot be drawn without a ruler even by the great-

Left: Accompanying drawing magnified 12 times (left bell-tower). Right: ¼ actual size, pen

In the Beginning is the Line

C. D. Friedrich, Monastery Burial Ground in the Snow (detail), illustrating use of set-square for architectural drawing

est artist. If you test the lines in the drawings of great masters with a ruler you will see at once that no line is perfectly straight, that lines that seem parallel are not always, and that verticals are very rarely truly vertical. This is the case even with pictures of buildings which were themselves made with plumb line and level, and seem to be so in the free, unconstrained drawing, in spite of its demonstrably crooked and wavy lines.

In this connection let us see where truly straight lines are to be found in nature. There is, in fact, only one example: the sun's rays when they are made visible by the moisture in the atmosphere. Another example, the line of the horizon on the sea, does not generally appear straight because shadows and reflections are often concentrated near the horizon. They cause an optical curve, up or down, of the line.

One of the first rules of all picture making is to draw not what you know, but what you **see** at the moment. This is equally true of external sight and of interior vision, the "inner eye."

The straight rays of the sun, the only straight lines in nature, are often drawn with a ruler, which makes a delightful and natural contrast to an otherwise free representation. Apart from this, truly straight lines occur only in man-made structures, in architecture. Sometimes in a painting, buildings also are sketched in with the aid of ruler and protractor. But many artists are enraged at the mere mention of the ruler. In this matter you must not be influenced by the expression of other peoples' feelings, but do what you feel is right for you in your own work.

Straight lines also help in the construction of spatial perspective, but the artist will seldom use a ruler to make them; in any case he will eliminate them once they have served as controls, or scaffolding, for his structure.

Generally, a free drawing of a building by a practiced draftsman looks more natural and competent than the constructional drawing of an architect. No one can say with scientific accuracy why this should be so, since the mysteries of the human organism of sight are involved here. The way the human eye combines the impressions it receives is understood to some degree, but the significance the brain attaches to these combined impressions is a matter of psychology. Nothing differs so much from one individual to an-

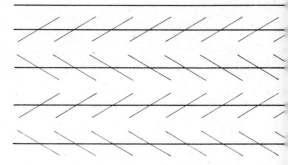

other as the eye's judgment, the ability to evaluate and judge measurements, angles, horizontals, and verticals. People do not react equally to the influence of optical illusion. These peculiarities of the process of sight, though not universally identical, have, like all other human senses, a constant tendency to equalize themselves, to work towards an average. This explains why, in the classic experiment we have illustrated, the heavier lines are seen to be true horizontals and parallel to each other only when one screws up one's eyes until the weaker sloping lines cannot be clearly seen. You may have noticed how painters often screw up their eyes while they are working. They do this in order to shut out confusing, peripheral impressions and isolate the essential effect, of color as much as of form.

We have explained from several points of view how every line is an abstraction. Scientifically speaking, a line exists only in the imagination, since it has no depth or width, and thus cannot be visible. Everything seen consists entirely of surfaces; they may be exceptionally narrow, but they remain surfaces. Pictures, however, are not concerned with mathe-matical reality but with practical vision, which accepts the convention that even a broad line exists only in the dimension of length. The mathematician, as well, must ultimately accept this convention, since he has to see his figures.

Nonetheless, the draftsman should never forget that a line is an abstraction, primarily the representation of a sensed but invisible boundary between two surfaces. The line thus becomes part of the mental equipment of the draftsman. It is irrelevant that he sometimes sees surfaces which can, with the best of intentions, only be felt as lines, such as telegraph wires, the highlighted edge of a table, the outlines of roof tiles — there are endless examples. In theory every abstraction is reversible, and there-

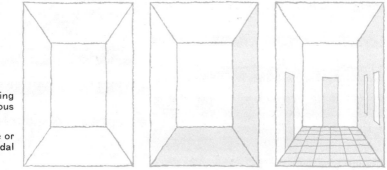

Left: Line drawing capable of various interpretations

Center: Concave or convex pyramidal frustum

Right: Unambiguous spatial effect

In the Beginning is the Line

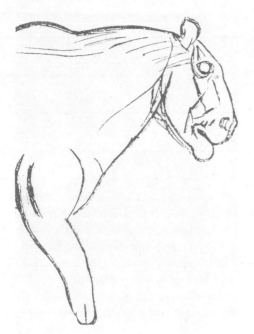

linear perspective is always ambiguous, indicating either space or volume until other elements give it definition.

The moment that the outline is doubled, not too closely, or the line itself evokes the illusion of shading and perspective by swelling and diminishing in width, all ambiguity disappears. This is equally true when the line is drawn not in one continuous stroke, but with numbers of small strokes. Either this produces an illusion of space or volume by implying perspective, or the line, especially if it is drawn with many strokes, is the beginning of surface texture which separates substance from emptiness and even leads to perspective.

Optical illusion makes one sometimes see a long, horizontal, straight line as though it had a downward curve. The idea of gravity is linked with it quite unconsciously, as though it were a rope which always sags slightly however tightly it is stretched. This fact was known

fore ambiguous: the mathematical equation ($y = x^2$), the wisdom learned from living (Where there is much light there is also much shadow), and equally so an outline. The ambiguity of the circle in the space which we invoked earlier (p. 17) can be applied further: for instance,

The white spaces on the left are equal to the black on the right, but the white look bigger

even in ancient Greece, and with interesting consequences, as the following example shows.

It was for long a scientific puzzle why the broad steps in ancient Greek architecture were not made with exactly horizontal edges and treads, but showed a slight curve upwards to the center. Practical comparison gives the answer: absolutely straight steps, when they are very wide, give the impression of curving downwards. The reason for this is that part of the tread, being above eye level, is not at first visible; only the edge can be seen. Being so long it appears to dip. When the treads are visible the light falls more strongly on them than on the risers. For the person climbing, the light is strongest ahead of him, and this is generally in the middle of the stairway. Here arises another phenomenon of optical illusion: a light line on a dark surface seems broader than an equally broad dark line on a light surface. Light stimulates the retina to spread its effect to a greater or lesser extent over the surrounding darkness. This makes the visible tread of the step seem to be broader in the middle. If it were absolutely horizontal it would seem to be worn away. For both of these reasons the steps were given a slight upward curve, imperceptible to the eye, which sees the steps as absolutely straight.

This effect of sagging is even more apparent if the straight lines are punctuated with something resting on them, like a pillar or a figure. Again an upward curve will set this to rights and go unnoticed. This is an adjustment which only the freehand draftsman can make. The technical draftsman would very soon

upset his whole construction if he attempted it. Now you can begin to see why it is that a freehand drawing of architecture can give a better effect of solidity and unity than an architect's drawing.

The man who protests "I cannot draw a straight line" naturally implies having to draw a relatively long line. Experience teaches that the longer the line, the wavier it becomes, and the humble protester thinks he should be able to draw a continuous, uninterrupted line by hand right across the surface of the picture. This is a task which no one can perform to perfection. It is a different matter to

Grossmann, Oswald Spengler (detail). The rhythmical lines heighten perspective and plasticity, and also add shadows

In the Beginning is the Line

[freehand pen strokes illustration]

Freehand pen strokes. From top to bottom: 1. Drawn in one continuous line 2. Strokes joined to give continuous line 3. Interrupted 4. Succession of short strokes 5. Line drawn with a ruler Compare this with freehand line

lay the edge of your hand down on the drawing board and draw only part of the line with a movement of the fingers, then move the hand and start a new bit. The junction of the bits requires a sure aim, which is always hazardous; thus, it is better to leave the joints frankly visible. Such a composite line is drawn with greater control, and besides being straighter in fact, it looks straighter, which is the most important factor in freehand drawing. Furthermore, it looks easy and sure.

The little imperfections at the breaks are attractive in themselves. Anything unfinished encourages co-operation and creative activity. This may sound some-

what high-flown, but the creative fantasy is fundamental to all men, and it is always satisfying to give it an outlet. Most children are much more quickly tired by a technically perfect toy than by one which does no more than stimulate them to imagine technical perfection. The imagination, too, is constantly changing its ground.

The ruler-straight line is only an ideal; the single-stroke straight line drawn freehand is a natural copy. Only the broken, composite, or repeated line can convey form. The idea of form can sometimes be heightened by letting the line extend beyond the outline of the figure. The artist can take his cue here from the tech-

Freehand drawing of building over plan drawn with ruler. The lines project at the edges

Constructive treatment of continuous and projecting vanishing and proportion lines

nical drawing, in which it is practical to fix angles more precisely by letting lines cross, for measurements, for instance, or to use compasses. This approach gives even technical drawings an indefinable charm, making them seem easy, almost sketchy. This charm is even more apparent in freehand drawings.

The artistic draftsman can carry the practice of working with overshot lines further, for in his first blocking out of the planes and masses he likes to find consistent combinations of lines which help in establishing and checking correct proportions. They are primarily guide lines, sections of which are then thickened where they form the outline of the surface to be depicted. This use of the line (drawn quick as lightning, not slowly and gropingly) comes from that positive attitude to the surrounding world and that manner of seeing it which may be called "constructive vision." Its opposite is naive impressionism, and between the

two extremes there are innumerable intermediate stages and styles.

The analytical, constructive way of seeing is directed primarily by knowledge and thought and a desire to see and understand the nature of things from the inside, to grasp reaity from within. Impressionistic vision, on the other hand, is entirely concerned with external form and surfaces, the inner structure is unimportant. It is essentially a painter's way of seeing. This does not mean that only painting results from it; a drawing, too, can be made in which every form is naively rendered. The impressionistic painter or draftsman is not concerned with understanding what he is representing at the moment, but only with catching the exact shapes of the various surfaces which compose the picture on the retina of his eye. From this may arise a mosaic of surfaces which need looking at for some time before the represented object emerges.

Preliminary drawing given additional detail by means of superficial sectional treatment

Use of geometric figures to reproduce the proportions of a restless model

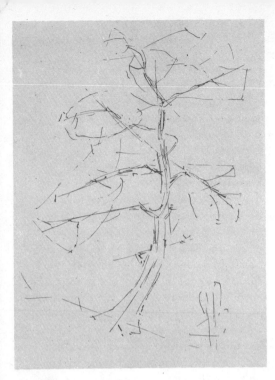

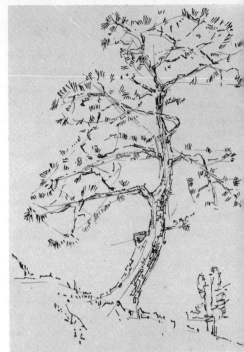

1. Impressionistic division of main surface, with little detail

2. Effect of solidity obtained by means of tinted surfaces, while shadows and individual shapes are outlined with restraint

3. The structural effect intensified and shadows heightened (chalk—medium and soft)

40

1. Preliminary drawing of constructive type, taking the shape of the tree trunk and branches as its starting point. Directional lines

2. Sketch showing which way the needles grow and the structural development of the bark

3. Final version, in which the shadows are lightly stressed by means of denser lines. (Pen; the preliminary sketch might be made with an erasable lead pencil)

1. Preliminary constructive drawing with perpendicular and vanishing lines as starting point. (The building's horizontal lines all lead to vanishing points on the horizon at sea)

2. and 3. Elaboration (Pen)

1. Impressionistic outline treatment of main areas of the background detail and architecture

2. and 3. Elaboration. The large areas already drawn serve as support for the elaboration of further proportions (Chalk—medium and soft)

1. Outline areas and proportion points

2. Outline with shadows and hair lightly hatched in

3. Darker areas treated as a whole using a combination of broad stroke, modeling, and detailed working

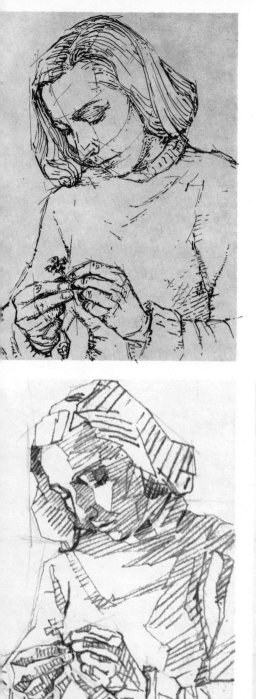

1. Here the posture and plasticity of the subject are set down by means of perspective and directional lines

2. and 3. Detailed work built up on Stage 1 (Pen)

In the Beginning is the Line

The serious student will progress most rapidly if in his practice he pursues both these extremes of vision to the utmost. He will then achieve confidence and certainty in seeing and reproducing and find most quickly his own personal means of expression. It is always wrong for a beginner to start with a one-sided program, with a preconceived notion of how to see and how to reproduce. It is equally wrong for the teacher to force his own individuality onto his students.

We have shown how in first attempting to make the ambiguous outline into an unambiguous representation, it is often the tone value that gives a thing substance. Tone value can also indicate the kind of material the subject is made of. The beholder always likes to know if he is looking at stone, wood, or cloth, whether the material is rough or smooth, soft or hard, dense or loosely assembled, etc. Lines, or strokes, can indicate material. Although it is not always ideal, the relatively stubborn "stroke" can give a peculiarly attractive rendering of material. However, color may sometimes seem a more suitable means of communicating fluid and other uniform surfaces. The simplest representation of a surface is made with parallel strokes, or hatching. But because a surface is seldom depicted parallel to the plane of the picture, parallel hatching will often throw the picture out of alignment. The lines of the hatching, like any strokes, tend to indicate a direction which is unconsciously associated with the vanishing point of spatial perspective. Either the hatching must take this into account or a different method of indicating surface must replace it: one conveying texture. Texture is essentially a means of representing a surface without implying any direction. The methods are innumerable. Even crosshatching loses any definite sense of direction, since it consists of four different directions, one pair perpendicular to the other.

It is possible to represent almost every material with textures of dots and lines. This can be practiced at every turn. **Once you can fill in textures, you progress to drawing the textured areas without any outline.** At first you need a guide: a thin pencil outline which is erased after the texture has been filled in with pen and ink. In time you will be able to achieve directly, without a guiding outline, the striking effect of textured areas which touch without outlines. These are the means of expression of impressionistic vision, of things seen as surfaces.

A uniform texture of equal tone value can be easily developed into one with gradations of tone which fades away. It can then be used for the representa-

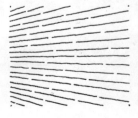 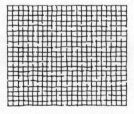 

tion both of receding perspective and of modeling in the round.

When talking of the sketch, we were constantly referring to broken and incomplete strokes. They do not generally end abruptly, but are faded out, either becoming narrower or lighter in tone, or both, according to the material used for drawing. If you use a pen which does not respond to alterations of pressure, the line disappears in dashes or dots. In the same way that gradations in the weight of the texture produce an effect of volume or of distance, so a heavier or lighter line can give the illusion of space or volume, even if the line is used only as a contour. It can raise the outlined object out of the picture plane clearly enough to make shading or complete rendering of the material by texture unnecessary. Thickening of the line conveys shadow or nearness to the beholder; a faint line betokens light or distance. In the strongest light, the line can disappear altogether.

If objects of equal size are placed side by side the one with the fainter outline will seem farther away. If you make the objects overlap so that the more faintly drawn ones are partly covered you have started creating the illusion of recession in space. This illusion can be considerably increased by reducing the size of the partly hidden objects.

1. Light and shade construction (positive-negative) Rhythmical construction
2. Use of line of variable thickness and broken line to indicate curve
3. Use of broken line to indicate curve in light; and line drawn several times over to indicate curve in shade
4. Foreground and background shown by use of heavy and faint outlines
5. Differences in size used in combination with heavy and faint outline to indicate perspective

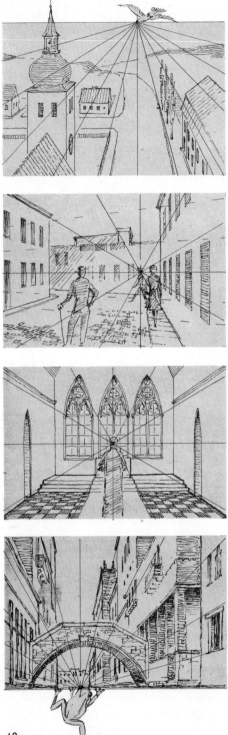

All these factors, heavy, light, and fading lines and dark, light, and fading areas, are the external media of perspective, of the art of conveying space and volume. This "art" rests on clear mathematical rules which make it possible to construct exact perspective. Every painter and draftsman should be acquainted with at least the main features of the construction of perspective. Even if in practice he does not wish to carry out these constructions exactly, he must support his subjective picture with constructional guiding lines if he is to avoid gross errors.

The easiest way to grasp the essentials of perspective is to look through a square of glass held directly in front of one eye, and copy onto it all visible outlines. If you then examine the lines, you will see that all the surfaces with rectangular outlines running parallel with the glass have parallel horizontal and vertical outlines on the glass. All lines leading into the distance, if they run perpendicular to your glass, meet like rays at one point. The outlines of surfaces which stand at an angle to the glass collect at other points. These points are called vanishing points. However many there are, these points all meet on a horizontal line, the horizon. This applies only to horizontal and vertical planes. If the planes are sloping, their vanishing points lie above or below the horizon. This horizon is always on **eye** level and is fixed. When one speaks of worm's or bird's eye view the eye level is simply unusually low or high.

1. Bird's eye view — 2. View with vanishing point in the perspective plane — 3. Central view — 4. Bottom view

If you stand in the center of a room which stretches in front of you with parallel and vertical walls, the vanishing point will lie on the central vertical line of your glass, and also of your picture. This is central perspective, frequently used for ceremonial and sacred pictures. You should now work from nature without a glass, transferring what you see directly onto your picture. This is easiest when you hold your drawing so that you can see above it, and your eye always meets it at a perpendicular, exactly as it did the glass.

Begin with a group of buildings whose receding lines are all parallel. You then have only one horizon line to find and two vanishing points. You find the horizon line by seeking architectural elements, such as window sills and ridges, which lie on a horizontal line right across the view. Put these horizontals, which are synonymous with the horizon, down on your paper, and from them fix the placing of the verticals. At first you will find it helpful to use a viewer, a frame of stiff gray board through which you can isolate any part of the subject, holding it closer or farther from your eye according to the scale of the subject matter in your picture.

In all these manipulations, especially when using a viewer, you should look only with one eye. If you use both eyes, you see the viewer double, since the separation of the eyes which is adapted to giving stereoscopic vision, presents a

Use of a viewing frame:
1. Two vanishing points — 2. Three vanishing points — 3. Uphill = three vanishing points, two points on the horizon — 4. Downhill = three vanishing points, two points on the horizon

49

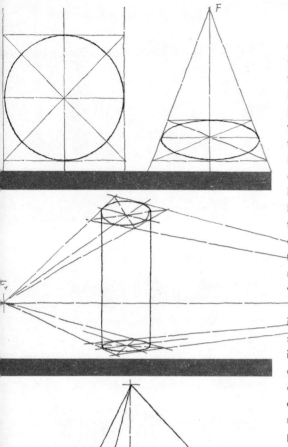

clear vision of near and far at the same time. Looking with one eye is thus better for seeing surfaces in one plane. Besides helping you to select your subject matter to the best advantage, the vertical edges of the viewer divide up the horizon, and you can transfer this important check on proportion onto your drawing. You must then find the vanishing points. Take several related receding lines, as steep as possible, and carry them as far as the horizon. They must all come together at one point. To find the vanishing point, you need only one receding line, but it is safer to check with several.

The second vanishing point is found in a similar way, but it often lies outside the area of the picture, as in the illustrated example with vanishing lines drawn in. Since it is not practical to extend the size of the drawing, the slope of the lines vanishing beyond the edge must be judged. Separate vanishing points have to be worked out for streets sloping up or down. If a sloping street runs parallel to one of the receding lines of a building, its vanishing point will lie on a perpendicular dropped from the appropriate vanishing point of the building. Then all that needs determining is its height above or below the eye-level horizon.

So far, perspective is fairly simple, but every perspective problem has difficulties which need special consideration and guiding lines for its solution. The per-

1. Circle and supporting figure. Aerial view and central view
2. Cylinder with two vanishing points
3. Slab with jutting pyramidal apex. Two vanishing points

spective of round or protruding or receding objects, for example, has its particular problems, and there are others in the rendering of reflections in water.

In the treatment of the perspective of round bodies, the sphere always remains a circle. A circular surface, however, has to be altered according to the same laws of perspective as employed elsewhere. Its alteration is best determined by surrounding it with a square. First draw the alteration in the square. Then join the center of the circle, which is also the center of the square, to the two vanishing points of the plane in which the circle lies. The two lines to these points will quarter both square and circle. They are thus diameters, which meet the tangents now to be made. These are each formed from two further vanishing lines which form the quartered square. From this it is not very difficult to draw in the foreshortened circle. It must always be an ellipse in the geometric sense and not the kind of egg shape which often appears! Mistakes are most easily spotted by tracing off the ellipse and examining it without its guide lines.

If you have to draw a pillar, imagine it to be transparent, and first draw the base and top surfaces before putting in the vertical joining lines. This is the best method for ridges too, such as the overhanging eaves on a house. It is best to imagine the main cube as transparent and draw the two diagonals onto the

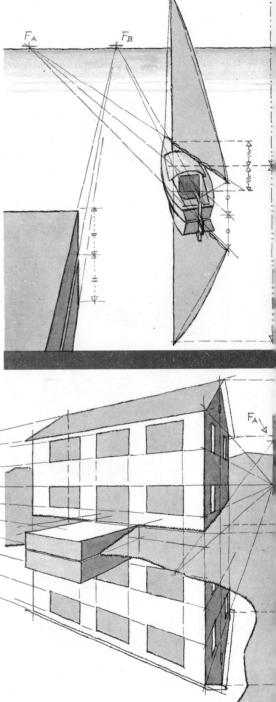

1. Reflection in the water, starting from the surface of the water

2. Reflection of a building raised above the surface of the water

51

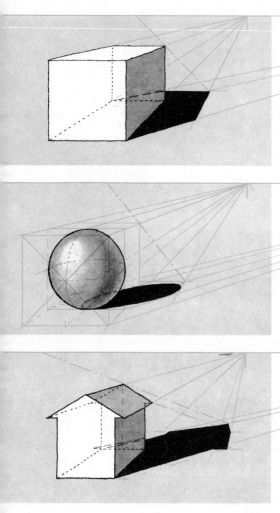

Above: Shadow perspectives (daytime) showing one vanishing point for the object and another for the shadow

Opposite page: Shadows in beam of artificial light (seen from above and side):

1. Cube in elliptic pool of light
2. Prism in parabolic pool of light with clearly defined shadows
3. Spherical objects in hyperbolic pool of light with parabolic shadow to infinity

wall, since you have to intersect the protruding corners. When you have judged the distance of the edge of the eave from the corner of the house, you find the points of the remaining corners with vanishing lines. The intersection of the diagonals is also the base line of the perpendicular to the center of the roof; for example, the apex of a tent roof or a steeple.

Reflections in water are always much admired by the layman and considered the mark of very great skill. Yet mirror perspective in a landscape is easily mastered with a little thought, since the reflecting water is always horizontal. Sloping mirrors, such as those hanging from a wall, make matters such more complicated from the constructional point of view, and require very close observation. Water reflections can easily be finished at home once the real object is taken from nature. The house in the author's drawing stands slightly above the level of the water, which you can then imagine as lying below the house. You continue the lines of the corners of the house to the water level and from there draw downwards the corner lines of the reflected house. In reflections all mirrored points lie vertically under the thing reflected, and the vanishing lines of the objects run to vanishing points which correspond with those of the reflection. The only difficulty is in judging the height of the building, or whatever the subject is, above the water surface, as there are rarely any definite control points.

Shadow perspective deserves a chapter to itself. Is is complicated for the beginner because it introduces two new sets of perspective lines, those of the angle of incidence of light and those of the direction of its radiation. There are few problems with sunlight, which consists of parallel rays. On the other hand, artificial light radiating from a virtual source point onto a nearby object is always radial or cone shaped. Furthermore, its strength diminishes the farther the illuminated surface lies from the source of light. Although the effect of shadows is simple enough to portray from observation and comparison with other lines of perspective, the phenomenon can only be rightly understood after a closer study of how it arises and how it can be constructed.

There are two kinds of shadows: the object's **own** shadow, in which any surface of the object lies that is turned away from the light, and the shadow **cast** by the object. Cast shadow is supposed to be always darker than the other, but this is not necessarily the case. A surface in its own shadow is generally lightened by reflected light; the cast shadow less so; the latter also looks darker by contrast, being surrounded by illuminated areas. These differences in tone can make an interesting contribution to perspective. The effect of depth is less if both shadows are of the same tone, which may well happen under certain lighting conditions.

The angle of incidence of daylight determines the breadth of a shadow, which always stands in a constant relationship to the surface throwing the shadow. One of its edges always runs parallel to the surface, and thus has the

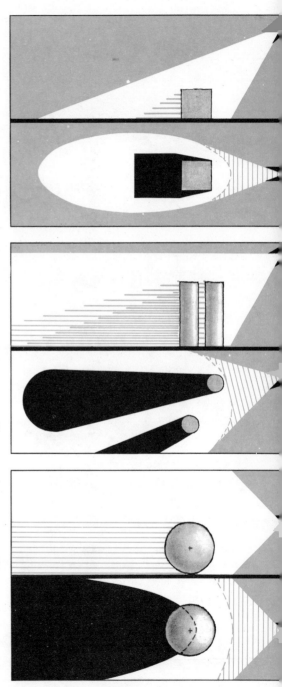

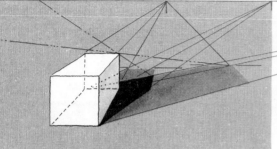

Slab with one vanishing point, two light sources, and two shadow vanishing points

same vanishing point. The other edge runs parallel with the line of incidence of the sunlight, and thus has its own vanishing point. It does not coincide with any other vanishing point of the perspective, except by chance. All the effects of daylight shadow are built up from its vanishing points and the angle of incidence of the light taken from the point of view of the draftsman.

Both circular surfaces and spheres always throw relatively circular, elliptical shadow. The general rule for other bodies or surfaces is that in daylight, they throw a shadow of a similar shape, geometrically speaking. Both the surface which throws and that which receives the shadow can be considered as the sections of a column with one common edge. This rule is of assistance when the light comes from an artificial source, that is to say, radiates from a point. It always throws an area of shadow corresponding to a conic section. The profile of this cone is determined by what shadow-throwing surfaces it meets.

The shadows made by artificial sources of light often have very strange shapes.

The best way to understand them is to study the sections of every type of conic profile. Circles and ellipses illuminated from a concentrated source will always throw shadows corresponding to the known stereometric curves of conic sections: circle, ellipse, parabola, hyperbola.

So far we have discussed light from a single source only. There is also diffused light, which can come as well from several directions as from one; for instance, in a room from several windows. Diffused light throws shadows as much as direct light. Generally, the shadows are weaker and their edges less clearly defined, and if the light comes from several different directions, there will be several shadows spread like a fan from each object with gradations in their density.

Shading to indicate rotundity was mentioned when discussing the filling-in of surfaces with fading texture. Spherical volume can be conveyed only by shading. An unshaded circle looks like a disc; a shadow on one side darkening to the periphery gives the impression of a hemisphere. The only way to create the illusion of a full sphere is to make a shadow running into a lighter band of reflected light near the circumference. This is very important for drawing and painting because natural shapes are generally rounded and do not have the sharp corners of cubes and rectangles. If a head or body, or a tree trunk, is to look convincingly three-dimensional the shading should never, except in a few extreme cases, be brought right to the edge of the outline, unless the effect is to be one of high relief.

2. AREAS, SURFACES, AND PLANES

First let us repeat: volume and space are registered by the human retina as a mosaic of surfaces. Every pictorial representation is concerned with arranging surfaces on a plane. The manifold means of perspective can recreate the illusion that these flat surfaces enclose bodies or that they surround space. Lines, in the mathematical sense, are invisible. Properly speaking, even the finest stroke is an unusually narrow surface. It is, however, felt as a line and can serve either as a means of delimiting the surface before it is given substance with pencil or paint, or as an outline which stimulates the beholder to imagine the substance of the surface.

The flat surface is thus the foundation of all pictorial art. Disregard of foundations always leads to catastrophe or to cheating. It would be reasonably consistent to consider as cheating those Baroque and Rococo frescoes which pretend to be plastic modeling. As you already know from working with a viewer, a picture can reproduce only the impression received by one eye. If we look with both eyes, their different viewpoints give us the feeling that we can see slightly around to the right and left of objects. This phenomenon is repeated in a stereoscopic photograph, which takes the appropriate picture for each eye. It is impossible for a painter or draftsman to reproduce this sensation. He draws as a one-eyed man sees. Hence, no picture

assumes depth of space or a sense of volume until it is looked at from some distance. The stereoscopic photograph, too, shows two practically identical pictures when the object photographed lies so far away that the difference in position of the two eyes or viewpoints is insignificant.

If you look at a wide landscape in which a telegraph pole stands about 15 feet away from you, and look at it alternately with one eye and then the other, the pole will seem to move back and forth against the background. If you move 100 yards from the pole and repeat the experiment it will move much less, and at greater distances it will not move at all. Thus, at great distances we do not see things in the round. It is only constant experience which gives us the impression of space, and it can give it equally when we look at a picture.

In pictures which are seen close up— near in comparison to the distance, say, of a ceiling fresco—the illusion of depth is most stimulating when the plane of the picture is not too drastically broken up. This breaking up is the result of a strong use of spatial shadow-and-color perspective, heavy dark areas which look like holes and light areas that jump out. If these resources are used only very sparsely so that they merely make suggestions to the beholder's imagination, then the almost unruffled plane of the picture does not distract from its con-

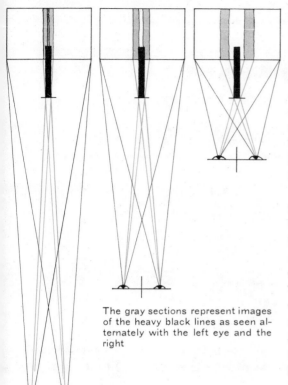

The gray sections represent images of the heavy black lines as seen alternately with the left eye and the right

as a phenomenon to be reckoned with. Even if the beholder is concerned primarily with naturalistic representation and responds first to the illusion of space and depth, he will be unconsciously aware of the picture plane. Excessive naturalism and the illusory depiction of what is known not to be there very soon becomes tasteless and tedious. Moreover, it is rare to find spiritual richness combined with exceeding virtuosity.

Emphasis of the picture plane is obtained by a number of so-called "artistic" means. The epithet is justified, for it is not enough here to follow the technical recipes unless they be combined with the extra "something" of real talent. The talent, however, can find no outlet without a mastery of the technical means. This is the precondition for any kind of art, if it is not to look amateur. How the means are mastered, whether in school or self taught, is a matter of little importance. Talent alone is not enough to produce a work of art.

The most important way of establishing the picture plane is by means of texture. It makes the surface felt as a uniform, tangible material. It is irrelevant whether this texture is achieved by means of drawing or painting, or arises from the substance of the picture's surface itself. Smooth white paper has no texture, nor has a smooth, polished, shiny painting surface, or smooth fresco plaster, whereas coarse paper, rough canvas and plaster have. If a textured material is available there is no need to trouble with graphic means of creating texture. On smooth surfaces, however, texture has to be created with appropriate pencil or brush strokes. Even the simple expedient

tent or theme. If, in addition, the plane of the picture is deliberately emphasized, it will, at a cursory, unconcentrated glance, seem devoid of any depth and arrest all the dynamic of color and movement. But if you really submerge yourself into a picture of this kind it can assume depth and volume as if by magic and perhaps only then be really understood. It would be interesting for physiologists and psychologists to study why this is so. For the practice of painting and drawing it must be simply accepted

of interrupting the line indicates that it is not intended to cut up the surface of the picture, but rather to work over it as though stitching a thread into the basic material of the picture.

Van Gogh in the course of his development as a painter, achieved the most uniform strokes possible for textural effect. With him it was certainly not a device, not an external matter. His pencil and brush strokes wind like eyeless serpents over the whole picture, an expression of the dreadful unseeing battle of all living things against each other. The texture gives exceptional emphasis to the surface, an impression which is again heightened by "false" perspective and a flattening of solid forms.

Flattening of solids and distances can also be used to transform all things depicted into a scheme of geometric figures. There is something of this in almost every sketch in which the artist has begun by linking up lines and shapes, seeking the way one curve or rhythm leads to another. This net of fine lines builds up into the effect of an expanding cobweb.

A uniform texture creates the quietest effect. But it can be carried too far, appearing mannered and so insistent that the subject of the picture becomes of secondary importance. A consistent texture is most effective on a rough surface. The original support may possess this, or it can be obtained with a thick application of paint from brush or palette knife. The rough surface gives

Left: Rough watercolor paper — Center: Canvas for painting — Right: Fine-grain sgraffito plaster

shadow effects, like a fine network of lines spread over all parts of the painted or shaded surface. A rough surface can also give a broken texture to a light, rapid brush stroke so that the basic color shines through everywhere, again emphasizing the picture plane.

Wherever a material creates a strong effect of texture or color by its substance, such as knotted carpet, tapestry, or varnished wood, it will give a strong suggestion of plane. Even the most brightly colored mosaic is absolutely flat in effect. Old book illustrations where the colors are outlined in black have the same flat look as stained glass with its black lead outlines.

Drawing with flat bristle brush (greatly reduced)

In all these different techniques, mosaic, colored drawing with black contours, and stained glass, the coarse net of irregular lines, which is both technically necessary and which determines the form, creates an effect of flatness.

If you look through a coarse-meshed net or curtain, its texture will hold the space behind it in its own plane, as long as you take care to look at both net and background together. If you look only at the distance, the net becomes blurred, and if you focus upon the net, you see it against a blurred background. This experiment can be repeated in front of a picture painted on coarse canvas; it shows how a picture can at the same time give an effect of flat surface and of living depth.

Besides the contour, which functions strictly as an articulation or outline, there is another method which is effective in stressing the plane of the picture: the black, cut-out silhouette. Black-and-white sgraffito (p. 212) has the same effect, although, unlike the silhouette, it can convey perspective. The effect of perspective is, however, reduced by the texture of the plaster. In fact, every method of drawing and painting can emphasize the picture plane simply by abandoning any kind of perspective, such as vanishing lines, cast shadows, or color dynamic. This results in the furthest remove from naturalistic representation. This approach is almost always seen in children's drawings, which are genuine, if naive, abstracts. Even an entirely naturalistic linear perspective can leave the picture all in one plane if the strokes used are very severe and uniform.

Line construction (subsidiary outlines erased)

brought into relationship with a second surface. The same thing occurs between volume and space, between two colors, or in life between two people. If more than two such entities or people are brought together, the dynamic of relationships becomes greater in number and more complex. The simplest demonstration of this is the fact that a white surface on a black ground always appears larger than the reverse, when they are placed side by side. This can be put in another way: light surfaces, or those with colors approximating to light and warmth (yellow and red), radiate and

K. H. Waggerl, Thistle (scissor cut-out)

This acceptance and emphasis of the picture plane is the artist's most important foundation, and out of it arises one of the most expressive factors in his work, the dynamic of the various separate surfaces or areas within the picture plane. A white or monochrome ground does not possess this dynamic, but it is created thereon with a single gray, black, or colored mark. This tension, relation, or discord, whatever you may like to call the dynamic between the mark and the picture surface, increases as more marks are added to build up areas of definite shape. It ceases if the entire surface of the picture is covered with identically shaped areas which make the whole into a texture plane.

Modern epistemology very aptly speaks of the "Gestik" which emanates from every surface as soon as it can be

Areas, Surfaces, and Planes

Van Gogh, Cypress Trees Beneath the Moon (Pen)

seem to grow, while surfaces related to the blue of shadow and distance seem to shrink. All darks and black belong with these latter. This rule does not hold when strong colors are brought together with dull ones, a radiant blue against a dull red, for instance. But color dynamic is a chapter to itself.

At present we are discussing the formation of areas. The most important element is the relation in size of two or more areas, both to each other and to the area of the picture. Naturally, a large area develops more power than a small one, yet a small, light dot can have a very penetrating psychological effect on a dark picture surface. This shows that surface "Gestik" is more a material circumstance or indication of what is being expressed by what the small dot represents.

Another factor is the shapes of the

areas. Regular figures of rectangular or circular contour show no tendency to movement, compared with shapes that are elongated or point to one side.

If two or more areas lie in the picture plane, a tension is built up between them. This magnetic field is an entity which creates its own relationship with the picture plane. It is destroyed if one of the areas has a shape that implies a direction—such as a very sharp triangle or a surface that contracts in perspective.

All relations between areas or magnetic fields and the picture plane are more insistent when the main point of interest is not in the center of the picture but moves away from it. If the composition is built symmetrically around the center line of the picture, the effect is always lifeless, peaceful, or solemnly ceremonial. Central perspective or a pyramidal composition has, thus, always been preferred for sacred pictures. The choice nowadays of emphatically asym-

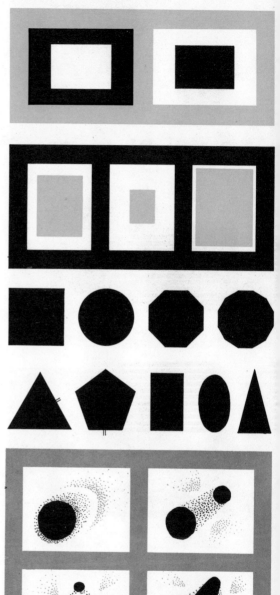

1. The area shown in black on the left is exactly equal to that shown in white
2. Left: These areas are equal
Center: The colored area is overwhelmed by the white area—or given added prominence
3. Shape without direction
4. Equilateral triangle and pentagon derive a sense of direction from the small stem. The rectangle and ellipse are two-directional vertically. The isosceles triangle has a single direction
5. Scattered dots in color indicate the direction of the white area; black dots, that of the black area (magnetic fields)

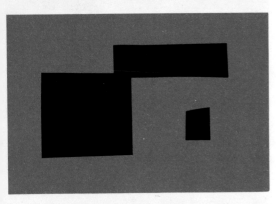

metrical arrangements expresses a desire to see Divinity more human and close to us. Symmetry, and especially central perspective, removes the Deity to the furthest imaginable distance.

You can now see how closely all matters relating to surfaces and areas are bound up with the composition of a picture. The illustrations given here are a modest attempt to encourage you to play, aimlessly at first, with areas and their shapes and arrangements, so that you understand something of the tensions and dynamics of their relationships before using them purposively to compose a picture. It is a serious, though frequent, mistake to compose only with pencil lines. If you cut out the appropriate shapes in paper and arrange them on the background you will have a much closer and clearer idea of how you want to compose your painting or drawing and what it will look like.

Experiments with balanced arrangement of plane on surface:
1. Two planes. No direction
2. Three planes. Both a pronounced and weak sense of direction
3. Three planes. Three different directions
4. Four planes, all of differing directions, sizes, and tone values. The placing of the equilateral triangle helps support the movement upwards and to the left

3. RHYTHM, COMPOSITION AND MOVEMENT

Rhythm in pictures results from spacing the lines and arranging the surfaces. Its possibilities are quite varied. Symmetrical, uniform spacing is monotonous and overemphasizes the plane of the picture, while a spacing which closes in or opens out leads out of the plane and evokes the illusion of flowing movement.

The rhythm of regular, parallel hatching is monotonous and inevitably stresses the frontal plane. If it swells and diminishes in the same stroke, it immediately suggests rotundity. If it does only one or the other it sets up a movement in one direction which seems to increase in speed where the rhythmic accents follow closer upon each other. The opposite effect may be felt also, depending on the sense of the whole composition.

If the accents giving the rhythm, here for the sake of simplicity portrayed simply by strokes, are made smaller as well as closer together, the effect of perspective gives a corresponding movement in depth. If the frequency is disproportionately increased, the movement seems to increase, and conversely it slows down

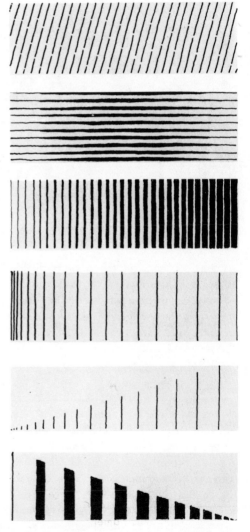

1. Monotonous rhythm and restful surface
2. Parallel lines of variable thickness, thickening in the center
3. Lines graduated in thickness, used to model a curve
4. Lines of equal thickness placed at intervals of increasing frequency create a speeding or a crooked effect
5. and 6. Lines graduated in size create perspective

Design for textile print

from pictorial representation, which is our theme in this book; yet both draftsman and painter should understand the nature of ornamental design, since it carries the elements of plane, rhythm, and composition to their ultimate conclusion. Composition begins to exist only when the area of the picture is clearly defined. The rock wall used by the prehistoric artist did not possess this defined limit. Once it exists, on the man-made wall or on canvas or panel, the artist has to show his mastery within this limitation and work out a strict utilization of space. The composition of a picture, however, unlike that of pattern, is not confined to a monotonous filling out of the available space. Contained by the edges of the picture area, it also strives towards a center of interest and a concentration of the essential, generally in a broadly geometric framework. Two or more geometric figures, acting as balancing weights, may be used to compose a picture; or one may act as a counterweight to the main center, with some sort of tension between them; or the figures may interpenetrate and overlap. None of this, though, is unambiguous, and the different solutions cannot be held to be universally applicable, for new answers to the problem of composition are always arising. Furthermore, a picture may begin either as a very tightly packed composition, a filled frame, or as a space in which the pictorial incident is the center of gravity but does not fill the whole area included within the frame. Just as we have defined two extremes of vision, the intellectual, constructive vision and the naive, impressionistic, we can define two extremes of composition. One is the

as the frequency of the accents diminishes. It is also possible to give a curved effect. The flattest effect is obtained from the rhythmic repetition of an ornamental pattern, on printed textiles or on carpets, for example, although the very movement of the eye itself gives some sense of pictorial movement as it unconsciously moves from one accent to the next, as though to make sure that the same unit is being repeated. If a cloth printed in a large, definite pattern is compared with a plain colored one, everyone will agree that the printed one is more lively; and that, conversely, it is peaceful in comparison with one that has a woven pattern or damask in it. Ornamental pattern, as we have already said, is quite different

Gauguin, Self-portrait. Selective composition

ined things. In any case, the isolated subject cannot prevent the beholder asking what happens beyond its borders. However full the composition and however detailed the rendering, however much it aims at being a slice of reality, it can give only a part, perhaps the essential part, of the incident it portrays but never the whole of it. On the other hand, a drawing may be placed in an empty space without arousing curiosity in the beholder, if there is nothing to awaken it.

It does not matter whether the picture is a drawing on white paper, grows in color out of a tinted ground, or, as so often happens in the work of Rembrandt, emerges as light against a dark ground; what is important is how the subject is placed in the "empty" space. This is for the most part the basis of composition in

Rembrandt, Self-portrait

"isolating" or "detail" composition, the other is "central" composition, which works from the center of gravity outwards. There are as many intermediate stages and links between the two as exist between pure seeing and pure understanding, since composition no less than vision is engendered by artistic feeling alone and scarcely depends at all on logical or technical considerations.

The subject isolated by the viewing frame is the most passive type of composition. The photographer has no other starting point, however much he may alter the aspect of the subject with the refinements of optical instruments. But the draftsman is not tied to an irrevocably inclusive subject; he can leave things out or introduce distant or imag-

Cimabue, Madonna and Angels. Pyramid composition

Apart from a few rare aberrations, the shape of pictures has always remained one of three regular geometrical figures: rectangle, circle, or ellipse. The center of gravity of these areas, the geographical center, is virtually never the right center of gravity for the pictorial composition, since it constitutes an indifferent balance. A hanging picture requires a stable equilibrium, which necessitates raising the center of gravity above the center point. It then forms the beginning of a symmetrical composition rather like the summit of the "figura pyramidale" so beloved in the Italian Renaissance. Central and symmetrical composition underlines ceremonial, sacred themes. It is often supported by a central perspective. Art historians have made great efforts to formulate a series of schemes of composition from the famous masterpieces, assiduously drawing diagonals and triangles, circles, ellipses, and arcs, not noticing in their zeal that linear construction alone can never fully render the effects of areas. Even if such analyses are carried out more realistically, nothing more emerges than certain similarities in the arrangement of areas which are hardly capable of explaining the individual peculiarities of the com-

modern murals which no longer fill the whole wall inside the architectural framework but leave large areas untouched inside these limits. On very large areas a small mural painting will act only as a center of gravity. The subject itself cannot then use the emptiness of the surface as a supporting field but must free itself from it.

Construction based on a stable focal point, both in the picture plane and central composition

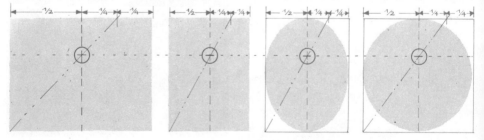

von Mieris the Elder, The painter and His Wife. The glances passing between the two figures and the dog form a triangle

seeks really to interpret a composition one almost needs a model in the round. Weight, movement, and projecting or receding effects of color cannot be understood through drawn lines and areas. The essence of a composition cannot be reduced to the formal arrangement of the plane of a picture, which is something very superficial. It is much more concerned with the dynamic of depth. The position and expression of the eye, for instance, is the only way of depicting which way a figure is looking. The path of the look cannot be represented, but, compared with the small dot representing the eye, it has a tremendous pull in the composition. This is proved by the well-tried rule that there must be much more free space within the field of a figure's vision than outside it. Perspective has the same pull, so do light and shadow.

Leibl, La Cocotte. Diagonal composition

positions. The artist can build only a very trite composition by constructing in this way. His feeling works more correctly and, in a higher sense, more logically for him. Besides, there are other centers in the composition that cannot be traced with areas and lines at all, such as, for instance, the empty space that takes up the turn of a body or a head which would otherwise jump out of the plane of the picture, or the high, wide expanse of sky which can express nobility, burden, menace, and many other sensations, according to what else is happening in the picture. The classical painters of the Far East were past masters in the art of using this empty space. When we discuss composition in color (p. 358) it will be seen that when one

Rhythm, Composition, and Movement

A flight of perspective can lead the beholder's eye to an imaginary point which is not represented but which nonetheless works as the center of gravity of the picture or as a counterweight to some clearly portrayed center. Light, again, does not make its only effect by the small patch represented but often by a path which may be merely indicated only by a few illuminated points rather than a continuous shaft. These are just a few samples of the endless possibilities. Another is shadow with its contribution of dark areas and indications of direction.

An entirely new concept of composition arose with Impressionism. Hitherto, the weight and stress of the composition had always been confined within the edges of the picture. Now there arose a disharmony between the incident in the picture and its borders. The beholder feels the urge to pull the subject back into position, and since he is unable to do this his interest is excited and held. It is the same sensation as that given by a piece of music ending on a discord.

Every picture conveys the feeling, often aroused by the composition itself, that at any moment some movement may begin. A simple experiment will show what this means. The illustration shows three identical male heads, schematically represented; yet, from left to right, the heads express first, active resolution on some reaction; next, moderation, patience, and self-possession; lastly, resignation to what is apparently seen. This is not the author's interpretation, but the opinion, formulated more or less exactly, of eleven out of fourteen people (two saw no difference, one thought they were three different heads). This makes it clear that the placing of the subject, that is to say the composition of the picture, can have a vital influence on its effect and character. It is equally revealing to tilt the subject instead of moving it from side to side; as the head is held at different angles, its expression alters. Expression is always made up of gesture and pose; both can be properly conveyed only by a relation to the hori-

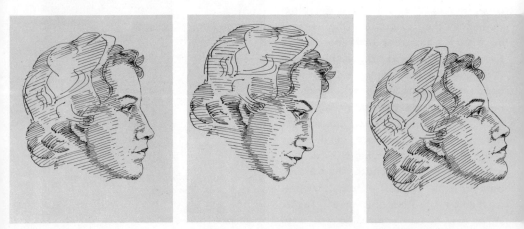

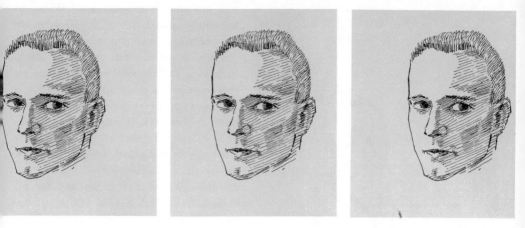

zontal and vertical axes, which are determined by the borders of the picture. The object's relation to the vertical and horizontal is the main indication of whether it is represented in movement or at rest. The determinant is the supposed line of gravity, which is always vertical; the base line is less important. An object can give a firm impression of rest even with a sloping base.

All bodies, which in pictures means all surfaces, fall down if their vertical axes fall beyond their base lines. The posture must express either helpless loss of balance or a willed movement. Whenever the line of gravity signifies a movement in progress, the picture gives the impression of arrested action, like the sudden stopping of a moving film. Sooner or later it becomes ridiculous unless some static rest can be felt; in other words, the figure should be able to remain in this position, at least momentarily, in reality.

This is a simple fact, easily proved. Here is an example taken at random. If you wish to represent a ball thrown up high, the only moment for represent-

ing it which is not ridiculous is when the ball has reached its highest point and for a fraction of a second stays there before it begins to fall. This is called the moment of rest. This rule applies equally to depicting a dancer, a discus thrower, or someone stepping forward. This is how Hodler represented his woodcutter: the axe has just reached the point of rest between swinging back and coming forward (p. 70).

If you look at the figure for a long time you can even imagine that the axe has passed the moment of rest. In an internal combustion engine it would be the moment of late firing (after the moment of rest), known to give more power than early firing (before the moment of rest), which is better for acceleration. This analogy fits the depiction of a movement exactly. The sense of speed is greatest if the movement is seized just before its completion; just after the moment of rest gives the sensation of greatest impending impetus. But to catch precisely the moment of rest itself may arrest all sense of movement.

Hodler, The Woodcutter (Charcoal). Movement frozen at top dead center

will feel that it has not only moved to a certain point but that it will move on or is already moving again. If you give it space at either end, the stroke seems to swing. In this way movement can be represented which really seems, for a few seconds, to be going on in the picture. It is a trick, if you like; but this is not a degradation of means. Every craft has its tricks and dodges. This trick for depicting movement was first used intentionally by the Impressionists, although it existed earlier. There is, for example, the famous, mysterious smile of Leonardo's **Mona Lisa**. The mouth, or, more precisely, the corners of the mouth, seems to be moving, which has never ceased to be impressive and astonishing. It is this sensation that gives the smile its expressive power. The trick resides in the vague **sfumato** painting of the corners of the mouth, which are given space to move up or down or outwards, and seem really to do so. How quickly, in contrast, one tires of a fixed, full smile which has no possibilities of altering! Mystery is the universal trick of all pictures which move us. The problem is how to achieve it. There is no doubt that in most cases it comes by chance. The artist's genius resides in his recognition of it, and in his not trying to alter or improve it. There is real art in omission, in implication, rather than complete statement.

The woodman would seem to be hanging by his axe handle, not swinging it.

The beholder likes to feel impending movement more than to see it, just as he likes to feel the depth and modeling of a picture grow on him and not have it thrust at him at first glance. If a stroke is given enough space to run on, you

We usually become acquainted with lead pencils in early childhood when we experience some of our earliest graphic pleasures in making lines with them. As we continue to use pencils we learn that the marks made with soft lead, although they cover paper well, smear and come off unless we are very careful. We learn, too, that hard pencils yield sharp, clear marks that hardly rub away at all. Why? We do not ask, really, because we have become so accustomed to these common tools for jotting down notes and making sketches that we hardly so much as think about the technical processes behind them.

If we were to give thought to these questions, the very term "lead" pencil might occasion some bewilderment, since ordinary pencils no longer have a trace of metallic lead. Since the fourteenth century, metallic lead—which can be used for drawing if pure enough—has come to be replaced by a crystalline form of carbon called graphite. In its pure form graphite is too soft for efficient use—although originally it was used pure. For the last 175 years, clay (a common earth formed chiefly of a mixture of oxides of silica and aluminum) has been mixed with it in order to make it harder. Before then, efforts were made to develop graphite sticks and blocks in which powdered graphite was held together by glue-like binders; results were less than satisfactory.

Pencil "leads" contain between 30 and 70 per cent of clay, according to grade of hardness. The clay is ground fine, mixed with the graphite, and formed under pressure into cylindrical rods. Such rods are extremely fragile and, therefore, are clinched between two pieces of wood glued together; in this way they can be held in the hand comfortably and sharpened easily. Cedar, a dark, smooth, aromatic wood, is used in the best quality pencils. There are 15 degrees of drawing pencils. The harder spectrum ranges from 10H, the hardest, to H, the least hard; F and HB are, respectively, hard-medium and soft-medium; and the softer spectrum ranges from B, the least soft, to 7B, the softest. Artists rarely use pencils harder than 6H or softer than 6B. HB is the most popular degree for ordinary use. Soft leads are thicker and more fragile than hard leads. A knife and piece of sandpaper are more satisfactory than a mechanical pencil sharpener for pointing them.

I recommend the increasingly favored practice of using refill instead of wood-clinched pencils, buying the different degrees of leads in boxes of a half dozen. Colored leads and chalks may be bought the same way.

Drawing Materials

So-called "chalks" have even thicker leads than soft graphite pencils, about one-eighth inch in diameter; they include all colors and carbon. The word "chalk" is misleading here, for the leads are not natural products, like charcoal, but materials artificially compressed like pastels, only more finely ground and purified. The leads of real chalks of natural derivation are, unfortunately, made only in black, from amorphous carbon, white, from a mixture of clay and baryta white, and red, or sanguine, from a clay reddened naturally by iron oxide. There are three grades of hardness: hard, medium, and soft, each differentiated by the admixture to the very soft raw material of corresponding quantities of binder instead of clay. If the chalks are thick or tough enough they can be used without a wooden or refill case; this is true particularly with the comparatively resistant Conté crayon and compressed charcoal.

You will remember from your school days how fragile chalk is. Binder must be used very sparingly or the color will not come off. White blackboard chalk consists of real chalk, or carbonate of lime, deposited as a sediment in the Cretaceous geological period by myriads of minute sea creatures. The chalk powder is obtained by grinding and then washing the chalk in water so that the particles which are still too large for use settle on the bottom. Prehistoric cave arists used chalk, presumably in its natural lump state. For black they used charcoal, a carbonized, not burnt, wood, the same used today for charcoal drawing. Charcoal sticks are made from thin, peeled twigs of the lime tree, which are made to glow without free access of air until they are completely carbonized. Lime wood, or willow, is best, as it is very soft and free of resin and gives a very even color. Charcoal made of hardwood is more uneven. Resinous pines and firs produce vegetable tar when carbonized, which would smear in drawing.

Colored earths are obtainable in red, yellow, brown, and dull green. The prehistoric artists evidently did not know the greens, but they used all the others. Colored earths are not found naturally in lumps, like natural chalks, which can be used as they are for drawing; and archeologists could not at first explain how the paleolithic artists applied their colors, for there is no trace of brush or pencil stroke in their cave paintings. All that could be found were pieces of hollow bone, the tibias of animals, containing traces of color on the inside. This discovery gave rise to the ingenious explanation that prehistoric man had blown colored powder onto the walls of the cave through these bone tubes. Presumably these archeologists had heard of spray painting, but it did not occur to one of them to try out this method which they had offered with such finality.

The experiment would be entertaining: someone takes a large marrow bone, scrapes out the marrow, sprinkles colored powder into it, and blows hard into one end. After the dust cloud has settled, a few grains of powder may be seen on the wall, but no one will be able to recognize any shape or form. To be effective, spray painting requires a strong blast of air through a narrow pipe which sucks thin fluid color from a second pipe and atomizes it in a cone. The only way to produce a definite shape with a spray it to use a stencil. Also, it would be impossible to make a satisfactory atomizer out of a marrow bone, which could function only as a very crude spray.

In the author's opinion, prehistoric man discovered and used a much simpler and more effective method: the color was ground between two stones and mixed to a dough-like paste with water and some binder—the sticky juice of spurge-like plants, milk, blood serum, or egg white—and then pressed into the hollow bones. The filled bone was put to dry in the sun or in warm ashes until a finished drawing pastel fell out. The damp mixture would not stick to the inside of the bone because the marrow would have left a lining of fat, and the

1. Charcoal — 2. Conté crayon — 3. Red chalk pencil — 4. Pastel chalk — 5. Graphite pencil — 6. Crayon holder for 6H to 2B leads — 7. Crayon holder for 3B leads and chalks (actual size)

Charcoal and chalk pencil holder

evaporation of the water in the mixture would make the paste contract as it dried so that it fell easily out of the bone holder.

There is no proof that this is the method used in prehistoric times, but anyone can make pastels in this way and draw with them. The applied color can be rubbed and spread with the fingers so that no trace of the strokes remains.

Modern pastels are made in exactly the same way. Gum tragacanth is used as a light binder, and instead of the marrow bone, metal or wood moulds are used. Color paste can also be prepared on a board and then rolled into shape by hand before it dries. In the section on Painting, techniques for which it is advisable to make one's own color sticks will be suggested. In general, pastels are more a painter's than a draftsman's material. However, if only one pastel color is used, such as red or sepia, or another discreet dark tone, the result is generally conceded to be a drawing. This, at any rate, used to be the rule. When the artist uses an additional color or two, the strict division between a drawing and a painting may become uncertain, as in some pastel works by Degas or Toulouse-Lautrec. However, painting is usually thought to begin when several colors are applied and overlap or merge.

Refill pencils are made to hold leads

up to a thickness of only about one-fifth inch, and a special chalk holder or "porte-crayon" is made for charcoal and pastels, since they are so fragile. The holder makes it possible to use short ends, and it is even more comfortable with longer, unbroken chalks. Three or four springy blades protrude from a handle, and a ring passes over them to hold them close around the chalk.

The drawing materials enumerated so far, lead or graphite pencils, chalks, charcoal, and pastel, constitute a group, as they are all erasable. The softer they are the more easily they rub out. Hard pencil is the least erasable; it has to be pressed quite hard onto the paper before it makes any mark, and even so the mark is never more than dark gray. Only the very softest graphite gives anything approaching a black line or mark, and there are some solid graphite pencils available nearly four-tenths of an inch

Lead pencil in four degrees of hardness, together with graphite pencil

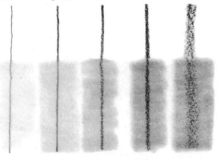

thick which can be used like pastels without a holder. They are useful for large-scale drawing and for the application of large areas of shading and for almost brush-like effects.

Some white, red, and black chalk leads are made which are nearly as hard as soft graphite pencils and give almost as firm a line. If a stroke is made in pencil or chalk with sufficient pressure it cannot be completely erased. Charcoal is different. It is so soft that the stroke can be wiped away completely into a gray smudge. Most pastels are the same, although their hardness varies. The factory aims at producing pastels with as near uniform hardness as possible, but some colors harden with time so that ultimately they will hardly mark at all unless the surface is very rough and hard, like wall plaster, or is primed with marble or pumice dust and size.

A drawn line is made by the surface mechanically rubbing something off the drawing instrument. The surface of even quite "smooth" paper is rough enough for drawing pencils and chalks, although it is much weaker than rough paper or the sandpaper used for sharpening

points. The rubbed-off particles of the pencil are held weakly and mechanically to the drawing surface. Only a few particles penetrate into the pores from pressure or rubbing. The smaller the particles the deeper they penetrate and the less easily they smudge or rub out. A rubber eraser is adequate to remove pencil marks from a firm paper which is not fluffy or fibrous. It removes the graphite particles which have penetrated the paper mechanically, but it always rubs away some of the paper, although a soft rubber does it less than a hard one. Plastic rubber, on the other hand, lifts up the particles of color by sticking to them. It is not made of rubber, but of just the right mixture of clay and vaseline to be malleable and not to leave either clay or vaseline when pressed onto the paper, and yet be sticky enough to pick up particles of graphite dust. Fresh bread crumb is even stickier and does not affect the paper; however, it must, of course, be completely free of fat or grease. It is the ideal cleaning material for restoring work, since it does not damage even the most delicate paper.

Chalk in three degrees of hardness, Conté crayon, charcoal

Soft and hard pastel chalks, with fine and broad points

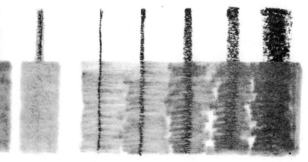

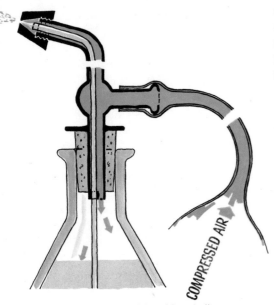

Spray attachment with rubber bulb

All pencil and chalk drawings are made without the third, binding element essential to a durable picture. Binder is therefore sprayed onto the paper after the drawing is finished, fixing the more or less loosely attached particles of color to the ground. All binders used in this way are called fixatives. In general, any adhesive material can be used as a fixative; the choice depends on the colors and ground.

The most usual, universal fixative is made from a two per cent solution of shellac in alcohol, as sold commercially. The basis of shellac is the resin of East Indian fig trees, which is extracted by punctures from plant lice, the **hemiptera** or **semi-aphides**. The resin contains some of the wax secretion from the insect, which reduces the brittleness of the resin. The wax is dissolved only in the alcohol

under heat, although the resin itself remains solid. If you wish to prepare shellac fixative yourself, you must warm the bottle of shellac and alcohol carefully in a water bath from between 140 and 158 degrees F. The bottle must not be more than half full, for some of the alcohol evaporates and could cause an explosion as it expands.

A simple blow pipe works quite well for spraying the fixative. If the drawing is large it is best to make a spray with a cork and rubber bulb. The spout and ascension pipe get encrusted in time with shellac; they can be cleaned with a thin steel wire and rinsed out by squirting a few times with pure spirits. It would be quite possible, theoretically, to brush on the fixative, but even the finest hair brushes rub off some of the particles of color and smudge the drawing.

Loose pigments used to be fixed in the following way: before drawing, the support was first primed with reversible glue, such as gum arabic, gum tragacanth, or carpenters glue. After the priming had dried, the drawing was done as though on ordinary paper and then steamed, so that the glue softened and fixed the particles of pigment onto the page from underneath. The advantage of this method is that the pigments are not embedded in the binder as they are when covered with a spray, and their surface is unaffected. The disadvantage is that the glue is sensitive to damp. This, though, is a disadvantage shared by all painting which contains glue, including all watercolors. Some experience is necessary to ensure the correct thickness of the glue; if it is too thin it will not hold the pigments sufficiently, and if too thick it tends to crack and scale off.

Colored pencils containing oil or wax and similar pencils are not erasable. They consist in principle of pigments mixed with oil and wax and a solvent which evaporates once it is exposed to the air in a thin layer. There are also non-greasy colored pencils which can be brushed with water after drawing. None of these is very pleasant in consistency or effect. They may have some justification for taking notes in sketching, but have nowhere near the beauty of the erasable colors.

Copying pencils are totally useless. Their coloring matter is aniline dye and ink which combines chemically to some degree with the fiber of the paper when it is at all damp. There is always some dampness in all "dry" paper, so that, practically speaking, precipitation always occurs. Direct moistening with water makes the drawing run and blot.

Ball-point inks are made on the same principle; their rather viscous fluid is not composed of particles. The color is a soap-like solution colored with aniline dye. The solution dries out very quickly by evaporation, leaving an indelible mark. These inks are very sensitive to alcohol and ethereal oils like benzine and benzole, and they run and fade if they come into contact with them. This can happen even if there are gases from these oils in the air.

Apart from this disadvantage, the ball point pen can be an excellent instrument for small sketches and can make very delicate marks on paper,

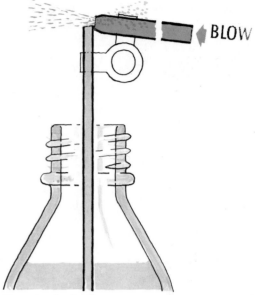

Blow-pipe for fixative

producing an effect like a pen drawing. It does not seem suitable for finished work, since the color appears not to be completely durable. If drawing inks, true inks, or liquid paints are used for drawing, pens or brushes are needed to transfer them to the ground. The classic liquid "color" for drawings is black drawing ink. We shall return in the section on Painting to deal thoroughly with the term "color," but we must here point out the many uses of the word. All attempts so far to find more precise terms and usages have failed.

Color means, first, that which is contrasted to black, white, and gray. Secondly, it can mean a pigment or coloring substance; this can include black, white, and gray. It also means pigment ready prepared for painting and drawing, either liquid in the form of a paint, or dry in the form of a pencil or chalk; and here, too, black, white, and gray are

included. Thus, one can speak of black watercolor or white tempera color.

Watercolor is also a vague term. Literally it should include all paints which have water as a medium. This would include tempera, distemper, gouache, and ink. In fact, it is used only to describe colors which have a gum binder and are transparent.

Watercolor is, technically speaking, halfway between paint and ink. The latter, being a true solution of organic substances in water, is quite different chemically and physically. Ink makes a chemical precipitation on the fibers of the paper and is virtually irremovable; it can, however, be chemically changed, on the paper, into something colorless and hence invisible. Watercolor differs from ink in that the fine particles of pigment can be filtered out of the water, whereas in a true ink the coloring matter is in molecular form and passes through a filter as well as the water.

Drawing ink consists of very finely ground carbon suspended colloidally in pure water, with a binder. When brought into contact with paper or cloth, the carbon coagulates into larger particles and adheres to the surface indissolubly.

The binder used in ordinary commercially prepared liquid drawing ink, or India ink, is a mixture of shellac and borax, which cannot be dissolved in water once it has dried, but which will dissolve in caustic soda. The carbon used is not ground to the infinitesimal fineness at which colloids begin, even in the finest makes. Carbon as used in genuine Chinese ink, which is a more complex mixture than the more popular India ink, is a very fine soot obtained by the incomplete burning of camphor oil. This soot is ground in water, a trace of glue, and various other materials of which the secret is not divulged, and pressed into a cake. The cake is pressed flat, ground down, and pressed again. This tedious process, rather like making flaky pastry, is repeated several times until finally the cake, still in a malleable condition, is pressed into oiled moulds, which often have appropriate characters carved into them. Lastly, the moulded cakes are dried very slowly until they are as hard as stone and absolutely durable. They are often covered with real gold leaf and are much prized by collectors and command high prices, particularly those of great age—perhaps nearly a thousand years old.

In use, the cake is rubbed down with water in a fine porcelain dish, an extremely tedious operation. The ink thus obtained must be used immediately before it thickens in the water. It is a much more expressive medium than ink bought ready prepared in liquid form.

It is worthwhile rubbing down real Chinese ink if one's first preference lies in brush drawing, and there are now small electrical machines to grind it down. Chinese ink cannot be used with steel nibs, as it begins to harden on the nib, but a reed pen can be used. The water must be distilled.

The brush is the most expressive instrument for ink drawing. It is erroneous to imagine that it cannot produce very fine lines; with the best brushes, both broad and hair-thin lines can be drawn, smoother and finer, perhaps, than with the finest nib.

The best brushes are of squirrel, ichneumon, or red sable (kolinsky) hair. They are round and must run to a needle point when wet. It is a professional touch when buying brushes to ask for water to test the point. It may look even more professional to lick the hairs to see if they form a firm point, but it is not very dainty and is no more effective. It is not enough simply to rely on well-known trade names when buying

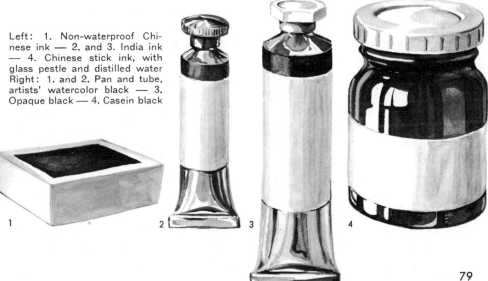

Left: 1. Non-waterproof Chinese ink — 2. and 3. India ink — 4. Chinese stick ink, with glass pestle and distilled water Right: 1. and 2. Pan and tube, artists' watercolor black — 3. Opaque black — 4. Casein black

1   2   3   4

brushes; even with the best of intentions brushes cannot be identical. A further indication of quality besides price and name is that the best brushes always have seamless ferrules. The brush size is measured in numbers, beginning at 0 and going up to about 20 or more. It is valuable to train oneself from the first to work with the thickest possible brushes. One works more quickly and with more expressiveness, and with the best quality, thick brushes it is perfectly possible to make fine lines. Thick brushes hold a great quantity of color, so there is no need to dip so frequently into the paint as with a fine brush. One can draw with fine strokes for much longer without the brush drying. Thin brushes under No. 6 are really suitable only for closely detailed work and corrections.

You will soon learn to judge and value a good brush if you try working with a poor one! There are some of badger and cow hair which are far from poor, but—you must ty for yourself and see the difference! Most brushes imported from China are of wolf's hair. They are certainly no better than sable hair brushes but perhaps more resistant. India ink and its soap solvent affects them all severely, and they soon become brittle. Perpetual rinsing is tiresome when one is at work and it does not help much. The caustic attacks the hairs as soon as they are wet. Rinsing in vinegar and water after use is helpful, as it neutralizes the alkali.

Genuine Chinese ink does not damage the brush, apart from the gradual mechanical wear inevitable for any brush. If it is not essential that the drawing be waterproof, black watercolor can also be used. It is much more pleasant to work with and a more expressive medium than India ink, and it does not damage the brushes.

There is a paint based on casein which is waterproof. It can be thinned with water, but once dry, it is not water-soluble. Casein is one of the nonreversible glues. Glues are called reversible if they can be dissolved again after they have set. Casein is soluble only in a caustic, however, and this damages the brushes. These waterproof colors are best used opaque, without making them transparent by thinning. They have a compact consistency which can be very attractive. Their black pigment is a fine soot.

All liquid paints can be used with a pen, as long as they are mixed to the right consistency. This requires experimentation. Ready-made inks naturally flow better from a pen and behave like writing ink.

Nowadays the draftsman is not bothered with sharpening his goose quill with a penknife. Steel nibs are sold in every thickness and degree of hardness, and there is a wide choice to suit all tastes. The most individual line, swelling and thinning as the pressure alters, is made with a soft nib specially designed for this purpose. Ball-points are primarily for regular, even lines without any appreciable differentiation from pressure. A wide nib gives two thicknesses of line according to the angle at which it is held. Other nibs are made for writing and do not produce a sufficiently sensitive line for drawing. Yet there are draftsmen who prefer these. There are people, too, who swear that there is nothing like an old goose quill or reed pen. Made from ordinary reed, the latter lasts only a few strokes. Chinese reed pens, however, are made of more suitable and durable material.

A drawing instrument with felt nibs has come into vogue recently. It is suitable only for very coarse and large-scale drawing. The color flows directly from a container located in the handle onto the felt tip. A practical reservoir pen for drawing ink has long been sought. Nothing so far has succeeded, for drawing ink is not strictly an ink but a mixed pigment which very easily blocks and encrusts the tubes leading to the nib, not to mention the nib itself. Reservoir pens with changeable nibs have been put on the market, however, but not everyone finds them satisfactory.

Color pens rather similar to ball-points are an improvement on this, and there are special colors made for them, but the lines do not respond to pressure. The special inks can be obtained either waterproof or water soluble. The waterproof ones require some hours to dry before they become indelible.

The author's advice at the end of this review of pens is first to take a perfectly ordinary writing or drawing nib and see if there is really anything which can improve on it.

All the pencils, brushes, pens, and colors so far dealt with are for work on ordinary unprepared drawing paper.

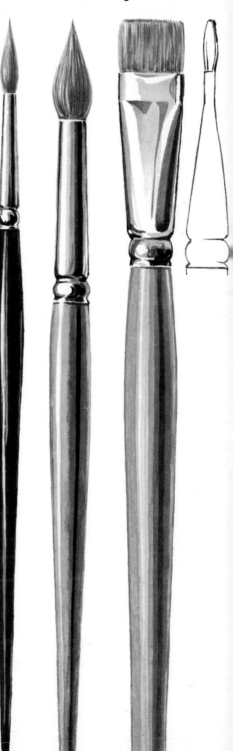

Round hair brushes Nos. 3, 6, 12; flat hair brush No. 18 (actual size)

Drawing Materials

Penholder and nib (actual size)

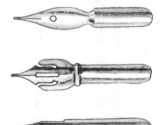

Smallest size drawing nibs

Round hand "steno" and "Ly" nibs

"Alto" and "Redis" nibs

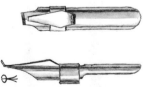

Prepared paper is needed for only one type of drawing: silverpoint. Pure silver is, like pure lead or tin, very soft, but it makes a barely perceptible mark on good drawing paper. Rag paper is not hard enough and must be given a ground. Bone meal used to be employed exclusively for this purpose. The best was said to be from the wing bones of capons. The bones were heated red-hot until they became bleached and could be ground to a very fine powder. The powder was also used for polishing parchment. Enough of the powder remained in the pores to cause the silver to rub off. On paper, the bone ash has to be applied very thinly with a solution of glue. A very fine chalk paste, not too soft, mixed with gum arabic is equally effective.

Silverpoint, which is like a very hard, sharp pencil, shows hardly any difference in tone or fluctuation in the thickness of line. Heavier tones and values have to be made by closer spaced strokes. Silverpoint line produces a silver-gray effect, which by oxidation soon turns to a dark brown.

Silverpoint has a very individual character, suitable mostly for small-scale drawings. It is the medium for a real craftsman who is after very fine detail. A silverpoint instrument used to be made by soldering a silver wire onto an iron or bronze handle and then sharpening it. The silver wears away very little. It is also possible to take a piece of fine silver wire about an inch and a half long and of the thickness of a pencil lead, notch the top end with a knife, and fit it into a refill pencil. The notches will make it hold.

There are many kinds of drawing paper on the market. They are not, unfortunately, always everything they are said to be. It is frustrating when paper expressly sold for pen drawing is so weakly sized that the ink runs. Handmade mulberry-leaf paper, which is entirely free of wood, is still the best. Rather absorbent papers can be used for brush drawing, especially with genuine Chinese ink, for which they should not be too heavily sized. The Chinese even primed their papers with alum in order to make the surface soak up the coagulating ink particles to some extent. It is quite easy to prepare a two per cent solution of alum, carefully cover the paper with it, and leave it to dry. The steeped paper is then thoroughly rinsed and allowed to dry again before the drawing is begun.

Japanese papers with prominent rice-straw fibers are very popular. They are especially attractive to the beginner, as their texture gives a good emphasis to the picture plane. But in time one tires of the effect, which can underline the bad as well as the good qualities of the drawing.

Good painting paper is always suitable for drawing, but the reverse is not true; a paper which is suitable for pencil or pen drawing may contain alkaline or acid ingredients which will affect certain sensitive pigments.

Mandarin injector with interchangeable nibs

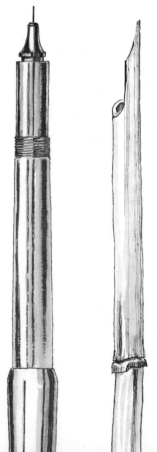

Spare nibs, 2 types

Small mandarin tube injector

5. DRAWING TECHNIQUE

After reviewing the materials available and the various uses to which they are best suited, the next step is the manipulation of the materials in order to produce a workmanlike drawing.

The first need is to provide a firm backing for the paper. The simplest way, of course, is to buy a drawing block which has the pages attached either at one side or all around. These blocks, however, are not made for all types of drawing paper, and the shape of the block dictates the format of every drawing; so it is better to buy the paper in separate, large sheets. The artist gets quite a different feeling for the paper if he is able to see and handle it on both sides, and

Drawing board, seen from above, front, and side

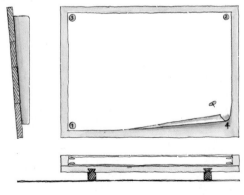

the financial outlay for individual sheets is not so great as for a series of blocks, some of which may not prove to his taste when he starts using them. It is much more interesting to choose one sheet each of different kinds of paper in a good shop. The make, specification, and price can be marked on the back of each, if there is no imprint or watermark by which to refer to it. It is useful to make one's own pattern book with cuttings, marking down comments on each example as it is tested, so that one becomes a real connoisseur.

A drawing board provides a good backing for paper. It should not be too large to begin with, about 2 by 3 feet. This will comfortably take imperial size sheets. The board should be of poplar wood, which, being one of the softest woods, makes it easy to pull out the drawing pins to remove the paper. It should have a hardwood border, which is intended to prevent its warping; however, it is advisable to make sure that the surface is quite flat before buying it.

Architects' drawing pins are the best. They are sold on cards instead of in boxes. These special pins have carefully turned, conical points and are easy to pull out of the board. If one of the points breaks off in the board in the course of time, a small pair of flat pliers should be used to pull it out. It is clumsy to hammer the point in to flatten it, as this inevitably makes dents in the board, which renders it useless for many types of drawing.

It is often better to use bands of adhesive tape instead of pins. If this is done, a board covered on both sides with white or light gray plastic can be used instead of the wooden drawing board, as it allows for greater ease in adhering and removing the tape. Care should be taken again to see that it is perfectly flat. These boards have the advantage of being completely resistant to water and India ink.

However the paper is mounted, the corners should always be fixed diagonally so that it lies quite flat: the paper is smoothed from one fixed corner, either with the edge of the hand or, better, with a dry clean cloth, down to the opposite corner before fixing it there.

It is important not to touch the surface of the paper any more than necessary, for even the cleanest hand leaves some grease, which can prevent watercolors from flowing evenly and also affect chalks. If there is any doubt about the cleanliness of the surface, it can be rubbed over just before work with diluted oxgall to remove any grease. This product is sold ready prepared in good art shops. The dry surface should also be brushed with a small clean brush, for no speck of dust must interfere with the strokes of the pencil, pen, or paint brush. The brush is also needed after using the eraser.

Paper should be quite dry, but not too dry, as it may be if it has lain too long

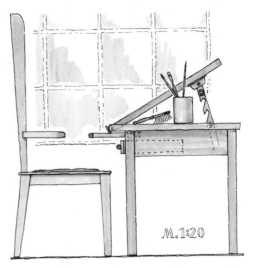

Adjustable table easel and working armchair

in an overheated room. If the sheets of paper have become too dry, they should be hung up with clothes pins in a cool atmosphere near an open window and left for a day or two so that they can slowly absorb the necessary moisture from the air. It is difficult to flatten paper when it has been wet, except by fixing it in a horizontal frame so that the air can reach it from both sides.

The paper must always be carefully placed with its edges parallel to the sides of the board so that in working you do not lose the sense of horizontal and perpendicular. From the beginning the habit should be formed of keeping the

85

Drawing Technique

Results obtained by using (from top to bottom): 1. Lead pencils 4H to 6B — 2. Different size nibs — 3. Regular drawing nib — 4. Brush

board still while working; it should never be turned around. Soon this becomes second nature. The stability of the subject is lost at once when the board is not kept in the same position.

It is usually best to set the board at an angle when working, rather than have it flat or upright. Most people who work at home need a table on which a board

can be raised to a slope. The whole table surface should not be sloping or there will be nowhere to put the drawing materials and eraser. The table must not be too high, about three feet is convenient If it is not at the right height for use with ordinary chairs, a revolving chair or stool that can be raised or lowered should be used, as it is important to sit correctly. The ideal chair to encourage both concentration and relaxation has a horizontal, not-too-deep seat, flat and relatively hard upholstery, and a very upright back.

Before the reader starts work, let us review the proper way to hold pencils, pens, and brushes. Most people manage more or less correctly, but many difficulties are due solely to a wrong grip. Pencils, pens, and brushes can be used in many different ways to express different things, but full freedom of expression is allowed only by a correct grasp.

Pencils and chalks are in themselves technically capable of a great variety of strokes, darker or lighter according to the amount of pressure with which they are used. The thickness of line can also be controlled to a lesser extent

Nibs filled with drawing ink do not allow any alteration of tone, but according to the kind of nib enormous differences of thickness can be obtained by different pressures. Ball-points and pens with a rigid, circular point are the only ones that give a completely uniform line, whatever the pressure.

The most expressive variation of stroke is obtained with the brush, and by diminishing the amount of liquid it holds, it can also be made to lighten the tone, an effect otherwise created by diluting the liquid. The brush, together with pencil and chalk, is best for filling in areas of color, a tedious business with a pen.

The variety of expression possible with the brush led the Chinese, and, hence, the Japanese, to adopt it for their writing. This use entailed the development of a very precise and disciplined system of hand movements which could be used equally effectively for drawing. It is natural that the brush became the classical drawing instrument in the Far East, for every literate Chinese who underwent the rigorous training in using the brush required to learn to write found himself in possession of a most expressive drawing technique as well.

In the West, brush drawing has always been purely a matter of personal choice, and with the absence of a traditional discipline it has never been used to much effect.

In the West the original close relationship of writing and drawing vanished long ago; nothing but the word "graphic" remains to remind us of it. It would be ridiculous here to try to use our writing as the basis of our drawing. Even the way a writer holds his hand is much too limiting and cramped for the draftsman. The edge of the writer's hand rests on the paper, while the pencil or pen is moved almost solely with the thumb and first two fingers. This position of the hand does not allow the writing

Japanese brush work, writing and designs

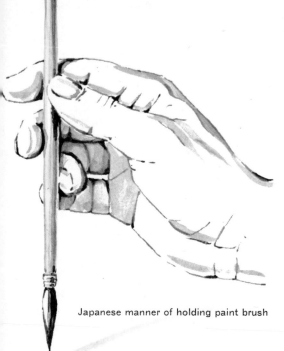

Japanese manner of holding paint brush

strokes downwards, one to the left, the other to the right. These eight strokes are composed of combinations of eight different movements of the hand: laying on, lifting, drawing, lingering, pressing, turning, returning, and finishing. The beginning and the ending of each stroke are especially important, for much of the personality of the stroke depends on them.

In the West no one has ever thought of working out a system of this kind, not even to the extent of devising a system of hand positions and movements. This is regrettable, for after the usual cursory instruction everyone has to fumble for himself, struggling with all the inadequacies and mistakes which have made trouble for even the most proficient of his predecessors. There are, of course, countless and immensely varied examples of their finished work, but without copying them exactly every student has to start from the beginning for himself. The Chinese draftsman, on the other hand, starts with an ancient tradition which has evolved to the greatest perfection and simplification. This tradition is based on the script. No one would be considered capable of drawing a good picture before he had developed a good hand in writing. This is understandable, for the same movements that are used for parts of characters are also used for depicting, for example, bamboo leaves, waves by the shore, pine branches, grass under snow, and meadows in morning mist. One could continue indefinitely to enumerate what can be done with the eight hand movements with their eight strokes, all with the one hand position.

even to flow; the hand has to be moved along after every few words. This primitive hand position is adequate only because our script is legible without any subtlety of line. Only with the introduction of modern shorthand have definite differences of thick and thin strokes produced a graphic symbol which functions in much the same way as the Chinese ideograph.

In oriental character writing the brush makes eight different marks: a dot, a horizontal stroke to the left and one to the right, a vertical stroke upwards and one downwards, a hook, and two short

This position has been so skillfully devised to use every subtlety of which the human hand is capable that all draftsmen would be well advised to try it. The thumb is turned slightly upwards and supports the handle of the brush against the first two fingers, which point slightly downwards. These three hold the brush. The nail of the third finger and the tip of the fourth finger guide the more delicate movements. The hand is suspended freely, and the brush always points vertically onto the horizontal paper or silk. Only the elbow is supported, and the forearm and wrist make the larger brush movements. The vertical position of the brush makes possible the finest subtleties of movement. When the brush is held at a slope, as is usual in the West, the resultant stroke is much less controlled and sure. Chinese classical painting countenances only this single hand position, and it cannot be improved upon.

Our constricted position for the writing hand permits several kinds of drawing strokes, but a flowing, broad drawing demands several other hand positions, which permit greater freedom of movement and free the hand from the drawing surface so that it is easier to see what it is doing. A child who has had no instruction in drawing will always squeeze his fingers around the point of the pencil and bend the first finger. When he draws, in little jerks, he can see nothing of what he is doing, and, as inspiration grows, misfortune soon comes: the point breaks and tears of frustration follow. The first rule then for all drawing is to watch the intended path of the line. This rule can be obeyed only if the drawing instrument is held as far away from its point as possible, and if the hand is held free. This makes it possible to obey the second rule as well, which is to draw lightly. If the pencil is held at the far end it is almost impossible to press hard and rigidly. A drawing should always be begun with light strokes, whether one starts with outlining surfaces or building structures. The first lines are a tentative groping towards the final ones.

The beginner is often not so careful. To give himself confidence, or to look confident to others, he haphazardly sets down a thick line, corrects it with an eraser, and as likely as not continues this alternation with growing discouragement. He is likely to enjoy his work more if he dispenses entirely with the eraser. Then every line he draws must be left; consequently, they must be laid

Wrong way to hold pencil, resulting in cramped handwriting

Drawing Technique

Ways to hold pencil for
bold, easy sketching

like a breath, like gossamer, onto the paper. Once a few correct lines have been strengthened, the others do not matter. They are hardly noticeable, and do no more than make an attractive fine texture on the white emptiness of the paper.

Competent draftsmen use the eraser sometimes to remove guiding lines if they are going to work later in another material—for instance, using watercolor or ink over a pencil sketch. Any other use of the eraser destroys the directness of the stroke. It is just this spontaneity which charms the beholder and arouses his imagination—not corrected, though absolutely "correct," lines.

There are two hand positions suitable for a light sketching stroke. With the first, the end of the pencil or brush points into the palm of the hand; with the second, the handle points past the edge of the hand while it is held by the tips of all the fingers. The latter is the typical grip for charcoal and bare chalks. The hand can use them on their sides, flat, without a change of grip, for putting in a surface in one stroke. The area covered depends on how steeply the pencil is held to the paper.

A stroke of stronger and more certain effect is obtained by holding the pencil closer to the point, either with the writing grip or the one described above for charcoal. The pencil must never be held so short that it obstructs sight of the line. A loose, long line is drawn from the shoulder and elbow, almost entirely without wrist movement. Strong and very sure strokes need a support for the forearm, wrist, or even the edge of the hand. Then the wrist can make the movement for the stroke. Very short strokes are made by the fingers alone. In this way one can draw with heavy pressure, as far as the firmness of the paper and the strength of the leads allow.

The question of strong pressure does not arise when using the brush. Only hair brushes are used for drawing, and they are so soft that it is almost impossible to tell with the eyes shut when the point touches the paper. The smallest touch with a filled brush makes a dot or a thin stroke. Greater pressure will give broader lines or areas. The finest and most regular stroke comes from a brush held perpendicular to the paper. The

The fist grip of pencil or brush, which, of course, is held loosely and not like a murderer clutching his dagger, is surest for horizontal and vertical lines. It leads directly to "building," that is, to a Cubist interpretation, however insistent curves and slopes may be. Extensive use of the fist grip is liable to become an affectation, but at least it forces the student to draw with broad, bold strokes. It should be practiced with discretion. A hand position is as indicative of character as is handwriting, and any affectation is betrayed in the finished work.

Without a traditional technique for holding the instruments and forming strokes, such as the Chinese learn, the Western student has to set about finding and developing his own personal technique as early as possible. It would be wrong to search out something quite new for the sake of originality alone, but it may be valuable to study the drawings of famous masters for an appropriate style of expression. Much of the individ-

Way to hold charcoal and chalk

hand needs support for fine brush strokes, using either the edge of the hand or the outstretched point of the little finger.

There is another grip which produces strokes of great individuality: the thumb points straight down the pencil or brush, while the fingers curl above it almost into the fist. This grip requires the use of a flat brush, and here we pass over the borderline from drawing into painting. Also, an almost upright surface is essential for this grip, whether using pencil or brush. With the other grips the slope of the surface was immaterial, except for the Chinese brush grip, which must have a horizontal surface.

Way to hold pens, pencils, and brushes when precise strokes are required

91

Way to make long strokes

dividual temperament. One artist may concentrate immediately on some detail, then add a second, then others, and carefully draw in the final lines, quite unconcerned about the "correctness" of the whole. He will see more cosmic significance in a grain of seed than in a tree or a whole forest.

To work from the small form to the large one certainly requires a touch and vision different from the reverse process. These suggestions are to indicate that the most suitable approach for a drawing is not consciously determined, but something which grows out of the artist's nature.

The development of technique is naturally closely concerned with a personal preference for certain drawing materials. This is a matter of individual sensuousness, which develops quite unconsciously.

uality of a work depends on the way the strokes are made. It is instructive to try to imitate the kinds of strokes in a chosen model. By this is not meant a true copy of a particular drawing, but a use of the other's manner in one's own drawing. An analysis of something perfect of its kind is a rapid means to self-discovery.

This, however, is not enough: the same motif should be drawn in different techniques. Especially valuable are those which the student does not like. His prejudice often turns out to have been misplaced, and he finds increased expression by mastering a new method. If not, he is reassured that he is already working along the right lines.

The mode of vision determines to some extent the way the strokes are made. Until now we have spoken of only two ways of seeing: an impressionistic and a constructive, or structural, mode. There are others, which differ according to in-

Way to hold brush for fine detailed work

Dürer, with his fine, precise lines, thought out everything in advance to the last detail. Kathe Köllwitz was more spontaneous; her broad, soft touch brings the deepest human qualities to light directly from her response to her subject. To draw a line with charcoal across smooth paper—some people cannot even endure the noise it makes—certainly evokes different feelings from drawing with pencil, pen, or brush. There is nothing to be gained from resisting or ignoring these physical stimuli and preferences, even though they seem to contradict the Chinese dictum, ''When you take ink you should not be taken by the ink, and when you use the brush, the brush should not use you.''

The beginner is not alone in being open to the temptation of filling in surfaces, especially shadows. Everyone has a natural desire for completeness, which is frustrated by empty spaces between wiry lines. It is as difficult to draw with pure lines alone as it is to paint a perfect watercolor. When drawing with a pen, the only way to fill in a surface is by hatching. You have to abstract once more, as you did with the line: you see contours which are in reality only boundaries between different colored areas. If the beginner uses charcoal or chalk, he is at once inspired by the softness of the material. He can rub and wipe with his finger to fill in surface and achieve wonderful gradations and the softest, smoothest rounding. But he should beware: this is only a hair's breadth from vulgarity.

The beginner must discipline himself firmly against mannerisms of this sort, or he will blind himself with cheap effects, which he seeks only because they are easy. Perhaps it will open his eyes if he attempts the same motif twice in the same material, once rubbed soft and once using more or less gentle strokes.

Above all, let the stroke be gentle! There is no difficulty in pressing hard and dashing down wild lines; this is not really the measure of a creative temperament. A better ideal is strength restrained by gentleness. A thoroughbred horse cannot be tamed by muscular strength, but by gentle guidance, behind which he can feel the iron will.

Drawing Technique

We do not wish to disguise the fact that problems arise when drawing a surface which appears more or less uniform. "Surface" refers not only to a smooth, paved road or a plastered wall, but to the surface of a field, the silhouette of a mass of foliage, mountains, water, sky, or a patch of dark shadow. It is all very well, say, in a pen drawing to deal with the problem of surface with parallel hatching. Suppose there are a rocky cliff, a field, and the sky as three different surfaces in the same picture. The three surfaces will have to be differen-

tiated from each other and, further, should awaken in the beholder the illusion of the substances of which they consist. The answer to this problem has already been touched on: texture can replace a mechanical copying of minute particles of the surface with a more impressionistic reproduction of the general effect. This gives as much, often more, than an "exact" picture.

The reason for this can be illustrated as follows: if a collection of various tree barks was shown to a group of people of average education, most of them would be able to tell the difference between a pine, a poplar, and a beech tree. But if these people were asked to draw the barks from memory, even just after looking at them, it is unlikely that they could do so. A general impression is much more important than individual details, and a texture can give this just as effectively as a painstaking copy. This is the principle behind oriental painting; which has a convention of textures to render different materials. Not only is it unnecessary for the draftsman to put in individual details instead of a texture, it is tedious both for him and the beholder if the texture fills the whole area. A mass of people need not be depicted by dozens of portraits, even though a texture of heads side by side is liable to be mistaken for a field of cabbages. The common spirit which has brought the crowd together can be expressed in one or two faces which merge into a massed sea of faces, each indicated by a few rapid strokes. Pictorially it is adequate, and, moreover, more attractive, to put in the texture fully over some parts of the

Design illustrating use of pen in landscape picture

area and let it fade off and disappear in others. The eye of the draftsman will see only the texture of a roof surface where his attention is concentrated. The rest of the surface he will see more as an indefinite patch of color, or in a drawing as an area of a certain tone. Thus, the whole area of the surface can simply be given a tone value, out of which the textural drawing appears at a few places or even at one place, in the direct path of the eye, on shadowed areas, or on the illuminated parts. If, for instance, the paving of a market place in sunlight is laid in with gray tone, and the bright patches where the light is reflected are left white, the texture of paving stones could perhaps be indicated in the bright patches. Though the picture is drawn in detail only in these places, which merge into the surrounding gray tone, the impression will be that the whole place is paved. The important thing is to find an appropriate way of making this tone.

Only one kind of tone should be used for brush drawing; it is laid on with the brush loaded with diluted color or ink. Chalk and pencil can make tone with broad, soft lines or by rubbing over the lines with the finger or stump. For ink drawing, one can make a wash of tone by brushing over the strokes with water, provided the ink previously used is water soluble. Sepia ink, once so popular, is water soluble; it comes from the ink bag of the cuttle fish. It is, however, notoriously sensitive to light, in contrast to modern materials which derive their coloring matter from pure carbon.

With the use of tone we are leaving the realm of pure line drawing. Tone

Tiled roof, repetitious design covering whole surface (brush)

Plaster, design in light and shade

Crowd, broken lines (chalk)

Drawing Technique

Drawing in non-waterproof Chinese ink applied with a mandarin injector

ter whether the line drawing or the wash is done first; but if soluble watercolor is used, the wash would dissolve and smudge what should remain as line drawing. Dark stroke accents cannot be put in until the end, and work must progress from soft lines and washes towards the dark values. This is always the correct mode of procedure for work on white paper, which, for this and other technical reasons is best for watercolor.

When working with pencil, chalk, or charcoal, it may be necessary to use the above-mentioned rubbing technique to make a toned surface, although very soft strokes done one on top of the other or with a broad point will always give a sharper effect. If the rubbed tone is preceded by a finished and strongly formulated line drawing it provides the material for stumping. Working in this order it is easier to decide where tone will enhance the picture and where it is unnecessary. Starting in the reverse order, with patches of tone which are afterwards defined with accents and contours, requires greater certainty, for there is no scaffold or framework from which to work towards the final idea. Whichever approach is used, tone or modeling must never show labor or anxiety. Its nature is to be flowing and easy, and it is better done with the fingers than with fine-pointed stumps, which carefully fill in every corner. Tone must show spontaneity. It is a very severe and impartial indicator of competence.

A drawing loses its freshness if it is fixed each time after work on it in order to avoid smudging. A drawing should never be fixed until it is finished. Eraser

increases the realism and plastic quality of the picture. Its use is a matter of choice, for it is impossible to say whether a tone drawing is "better" in principle than a line drawng, or vice versa.

Some forethought is necessary if tone is to be used. If one is working with insoluble, fast-drying ink, it does not mat-

and bread crumb should be left well alone, particularly when using chalks. With charcoal some final erasing and touching up can be done. Because it is so soft, charcoal has a very loose contact with the paper anyway, and it produces rather imprecise lines, which match the uncertain traces of the eraser.

A line and wash drawing on white paper is built up in the same way as a watercolor: working from light to dark. Starting with the wash and finishing with the accent strokes is more in keeping with an impressionistic vision. If the constructive approach is preferred, the reverse order is appropiate. It is possible, of course, to do both simultaneously, just as both modes of vision can be used together.

Black or white chalk drawing on colored paper is comparable to opaque color or oil painting. The artist works from the background color into the darks and puts in the lights at the end. This way of drawing is best done with lines alone; washing or stumping does not give good results. White strokes are best done with white pastel, not white pencil, which is too transparent on most papers. The greatest precision is obtained with a fine brush line of opaque white.

We have already shown why ready-made, bright colored paper is unsuitable for any drawing other than an explanatory sketch or a poster. It has more important artistic arguments against it, for the exact tone of color used is exceedingly important to the whole effect. Color laid on by hand can produce an exact tone and besides has an attractive surface quality. The background color has to

Tinted paper, black chalk, opaque white strokes inserted with a brush

combine well with the material used for the drawing, either by affinity or contrast. Some "black" inks have a brown tinge when diluted, others are colder, bluish or violet. It is rare to find a black that dilutes to a neutral gray, and when it does it is affected by the color of the paper and gives all kinds of nuances from the effects of color relationship. Even when undiluted, pure black inks do

the same. This must be kept in mind to avoid unexpected results. The Chinese, who are the greatest authorities on ink, used its hidden color qualities deliberately. More will be said on color relationships in the section on Color (p. 251). Without a close study, it is impossible to control effects with colored paper.

Despite the numerous varieties of colored paper produced since their manufacture began, the best artists have always tinted their papers themselves, aiming at an optical, colored gray by the exploitation of color relationships. Dürer laid a mat green over red ochre to make a sensitive brown or greenish gray. Sometimes he made a tone verging on violet and blue grays. But gray was always aimed at, not strong colors which are too noticeable, distracting from the drawing and the theme. Those who incline too much to strong colors should remember this.

Tinting of paper is best done with transparent watercolor. Opaque colors, besides looking dead, often make the ink stroke run because of their opacity, although they are tolerable for pencil or chalk. Even then the "heightening," as white shading for high lights is called, is unattractive on them. It is

Above: Rough white drawing paper, black chalk. A broad first application of Conté crayon is rubbed over flat; then more detail is inserted, and finally high lights are picked out with a soft rubber eraser
Below: White French Ingres paper, red crayon. The original line drawing is tinted in places by moving the pencil point lightly over the paper

thus advisable to keep to a thin glaze of watercolor; the whiteness of the paper behind it imparts a brilliance even to dark tints.

Corrections cannot be made on ink drawings on colored paper without spoiling the tint. Opaque white, too, cannot be corrected or washed off without smudging the ground. If pencil is used, then only opaque white can be used for heightening because white chalk does not combine satisfactorily except with black chalk or charcoal.

A drawing heightened with white pencil or opaque white cannot, thus, be attempted without some experience and competence. There is an easier technique on colored or gray tinted paper. It is, in the author's opinion, much safer, as it rests on uniformity of material. An eraser is all that is necessary; the rubbed out ground gives the high lights, as follows:

The light paper is colored all over with ground chalk, but not fixed. The drawing is then done in black or red chalk as required, as though onto white paper. A soft, pointed eraser is then used to take out all the high lights from the ground. It is possible then, if necessary, to deepen the darks with the chalk, or put in more detail.

Above: White French Ingres paper, red crayon. A soft drawing achieved by rubbing over the entire surface several times with a wad of cloth and finishing off with shadows added with a blunt crayon
Below: Light gray Ingres paper. 1mm. Rex nib used the wrong way round. A preliminary study for a portrait (no preliminary drawing). In one hour six sketches were done in this way

1. Drawing, black chalk on white paper — 2. The drawing traced through and corrected with red crayon rubbed over the wrong side — 3. The lines to be retained are pressed through onto

Another method is to draw with black chalk on white paper, almost without any shading. The drawing is then fixed so that it can be wiped and the tinting rubbed in, taking out the high lights again immediately with an eraser. The work can then be continued with the black chalk. This method has the advantage that all the thinner lines of the first sketching in are obliterated by the tinting, and the stronger ones are softened and gain in quality from the color of the chalk overlay. Subsequent working with black may stand out rather too much, however, unless all the lines are gone over again.

A technique used with immense success by Hans Holbein the Younger is almost unknown nowadays, although it requires a minimum of means. It em-

French Ingres paper with a hard pencil; this is then lightly tinted by pressing with a stump, then a few final touches are added directly onto the third sheet of paper (using a red crayon). Work carried out entirely in the presence of the model

ploys a tracing technique to eliminate every unnecessary or uncertain stroke, working down to the essential contours. All the work is done from the model. After the first sketching in, the back of the paper is rubbed over with powdered color and laid, right-side-up, over a second sheet. The correct lines are pressed onto the second sheet with a hard pencil or stick. This sheet is then worked on and again colored on the back and traced through. This process can be repeated indefinitely, until the drawing is quite perfect. The lower sheet picks up some of the color from the top sheet, especially where it is pressed deliberately, perhaps with a rounded stick, the back of a finger nail, or whatever seems appropriate. The soft, lightly spreading lines from the tracing give a very tender

101

Drawing Technique

Thin watercolors are used, then light gray opaque color is thickly applied. The whole is then covered with sweeping strokes of Chinese ink and bleached out under water

and subtle modeling. The powder used on the back of the paper must, of course, be of the same material as the drawing, red or lead pencil or black chalk.

Nowadays tracing paper could make the process simpler, white paper being needed only for the first and last drafts. The intermediate stages would not be pressed through, but traced onto the transparent paper.

Lastly, we shall describe a new procedure. It uses drawing ink which is indelible on paper once it has dried, but which cannot penetrate a thickish layer of glue-bound paint. Any thick drawing

paper or board can be used. All the surfaces and lines which are to appear white are painted in with ordinary poster white, preferably after a preliminary pencil sketch. This is not very easy, as the white paint does not show up well on the white paper, but unless it spoils the final effect the white can be tinted with color or black.

When the paint has dried, the whole page is covered with ink, using a broad hair brush, and left to dry again. The page is then laid flat in cold water, and the ink is washed off where it lay over the white paint. Then, the paper is held under running water and sponged or brushed with a bristle brush to remove all the white and whatever ink remains on it. Only the black ink and the exposed white lines and areas remain.

Most people enjoy this process immensely. All sorts of chance effects are produced by the varying thicknesses of the white layer, which in some places lets the ink through a little. Wherever the ink has got through it is held fast. The work looks like the most delicate brush drawing, and even quite clumsy work looks effective. Professionals who do not know the technique are often puzzled by what seem to be negative brush strokes, as though some mysterious substance had etched away the ink at these places.

This process can be elaborated in many ways; for instance, instead of white, opaque colors can be used, which by reason of their colloidal composition leave a hint of color behind on the paper when they are washed off. Colored waterproof inks or paints and even strongly diluted ink can be used instead of pure black ink. Again, it is possible to start by covering some areas with waterproof colors (casein colors, for example), draw over them with soluble white when they are dry, and then paint over that with ink or casein color; this will wash out where it covers the soluble white, producing a multi-colored effect. The design or picture still remains a drawing, since it is held together by a graphic texture, as in batik or mosaic.

A similar process, known as resist dying) has been used for centuries on textiles. Using wooden blocks, a design is printed in wax or paste onto the raw cloth, which is then dyed. The wax prevents the dye from taking on the printed areas.

How to enlarge a square grid. The colored lines indicate the procedure

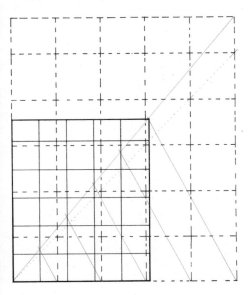

This review of drawing techniques does not exhaust the possibilities, and much can also be done with combinations of different techniques. Some materials do not go well together, such as pencil and chalk, nor is it possible to use a wash over charcoal. It is better, however, to experiment with the chance of finding interesting new combinations than to be too strictly confined by cramping rules as to what is "correct" or "allowed."

Drawing technique includes a knowledge of the purely mechanical processes of enlarging and reducing. Every draftsman and painter must at some time or other alter the size of a sketch or drawing to fit another format. The simplest method, which can be used even by quite an inexperienced draftsman, employs a network of squares.

The original drawing is conveniently squared up into a grid pattern, and correspondingly larger or smaller squares are laid over the paper onto which it is to be reproduced for the enlargement or reduction. It is comparatively simple to copy the lines in each square of the original onto the corresponding squares of the reproduction.

It is best to draw the new squares onto tracing paper, for once the new drawing is done, they are not wanted. The back of the tracing paper should be colored and the new drawing traced onto its paper. The flat side of a pastel is the best thing for this, for then the tracing can be uniformly wiped out. Carbon paper is not good because the "carbon," being generally an aniline dye, is indelible. Paper which has been rubbed over with chalk is suitable.

Drawing Technique

The pantograph is hardly ever used in freehand drawing, but a new copying instrument called a Bell Optican (antiscope) is very useful. It works on the principle of the epidiascope, but with greater precision. It reflects a well-illuminated image or drawing and projects it through an enlarging lens onto a surface placed at right angles to the original. Usually it does not enlarge anything above about six inches square, and cannot make above a six-fold linear enlargement. If the original is larger than six inches square, the enlarging has to be done piecemeal, which requires some practice and skill; and if an enlargement greater than six fold is wanted, the process has to be repeated in stages. This is liable to produce error, so that squaring up is really more satisfactory. The Bell Optican can also be used with a lens that reduces the size of the original, but its scope is rather limited. This machine should, of course, not be used for copying other people's drawings, which would be pure theft. Nor is it much less objectionable to use photographs as models for a drawing which could never be made freehand. Its use is quite justified however to bring up one's own small sketch to the required size or to enlarge a part of it to make a picture. Work can be continued on the enlargement, improving and adding, and being all one's own work there is no moral objection to it. Etchers, engravers, and miniaturists have used the reducing glass ever since it was invented; no one accuses them of dishonesty or lack of artistry for doing so. Art is not a game which must be played according to rules to make it more difficult. The purpose of technique is to remove material hindrances from the free expression of the spirit.

Anyone who does much drawing in a professional way and makes use of ruler and set square should consider investing

Diagram illustrating working of a Bell Optican (antiscope)

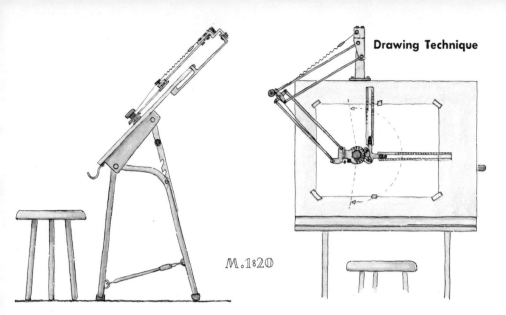

M.1820

Small drawing machine with adjustable board about 28 x 40 inches and hair-spring counter-balance seen from side and above

in a "drafting machine." It consists of a set square held in equilibrium by weights or springs, which can be moved all over the board without altering its angle. It is firmly mounted on a board and made in many sizes, from simple flat boards that lie on the table to the largest drawing boards which move by balancing weights or even hydraulic pressure. This elegant apparatus is intended for architects and technical draftsmen, but it makes work a pleasure for artists working on a large scale who use rule and square for guiding lines and need exact measurements, even though they work in freehand.

FORM

The following sections treat of the artist's subject matter from two points of view; first, investigating how natural and artificial forms have arisen and developed, reviewing the principles of growth and construction, and, secondly, indicating how these forms can be understood visually and transcribed onto paper. This artistic activity may involve leaving out some unessentials in order to stress the essential. The essential in turn is sometimes further enhanced by exaggeration, simplification, or elaboration.

It is clearly necessary to have a correct understanding of an object before reproducing it. Even deeper understanding is needed if the work departs from the external form, in an abstract representation, than if it is done from a model present in the flesh or in previous sketches and studies. To draw well we must be acquainted with the skeleton and surface anatomy of the human body and of animals, the principles of growth in plants, the methods of construction used in buildings, and the factors underlying the phenomena of landscape. Without this knowledge gross mistakes are inevitable. Even if we intend to draw what we see and feel rather than what we know, we need a basis of objective knowledge to give it significance. There is no need to cling helplessly to this knowledge, but without it we can never penetrate far into the nature of things.

The works of the old masters are full of distortions or alterations of form and shape, deviations from what the eye actually sees, but they are never biologically or structurally wrong. A beginner usually draws a movement incorrectly unless he has some idea of the anatomical structure of the body. It is not so much detailed information which is necessary as a comprehensive understanding of the biological or, in architecture, the structural, principles which constantly recur. These enable the artist to put onto paper forms taken either from nature or from his imagination. Whether in the constructive or impressionist style, a figure drawing is always begun in a different way from a landscape. The following pages aim at providing the basic knowledge from which an individual style of drawing can be developed.

The skeleton determines the proportions of the human body, especially its length. The bones are for the most part joined flexibly to each other. From this fact arises the mobility of the body and the changes in its shape.

The movement and position of the bones and joints are directed by muscles, which also affect the breadth of the body: a person with weak muscles is thinner than one with well-developed muscles. Muscles, too, determine to a large extent the contours and shape of the body.

Skin and the fatty tissues under the skin level off these contours, rather as a firm chalk drawing is leveled off by stumping. The fatty tissues have sometimes more effect on the breadth of the body than the muscles. For instance, if someone fifty years old has a waist measurement half as much again as that of someone of twenty five, it is due to the increase of fat tissue; the skeletal measurements of both ages are practically the same.

BONES AND JOINTS

Bones are rigid and unalterable in shape. According to a person's constitution some parts of the bones can be seen more or less clearly modeled under the skin. These places are where the artist starts fixing the proportions of the body. The shape and function of the whole bone must be understood in order to understand the shape of the body where it comes to the surface. Bones also determine the posture of the body, which is evident when the functions of the bones and their relations to each other are known.

The formal structure of a joint is unimportant for the artist; its **function** is what interests him. The simplest joints occur where two cartilaginous ends of bone meet without crossing and are held together with the fibrous cap which covers all joints. The most visible example is where the collar bone is attached to the breast bone. The cushioning discs between the vertebrae also allow a measure of movement to each bone against its neighbor. The spine as a whole is like a rod which can bend in every direction and twist around on itself. The ribs, with their cartilages and ligaments joining them to the breast bone and spine, build up the rib cage, which, thanks partly to the flexibility of the rib bones themselves, is a very elastic structure. The elbows and knee joints and finger and toe knuckles are like mechanical hinge joints, but, being organic structures, they are more elastic than rigid mechanical hinges. The knee joint as it bends also permits a twist to the lower leg down its long axis. The radius and ulna rotate against each other along the length of the forearm.

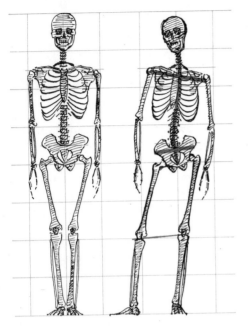

Chart showing alteration in axial skeleton in level upright position when weight is shifted to one leg only

ball of the hip joint that is to take the weight, and the resting leg has to move away; the spine bends to find a stable equilibrium and thereby causes an asymmetrical movement of the ribs. Shoulder and arm joints also unconsciously adjust themselves more or less visibly to maintain a balance. This will naturally involve a corresponding reaction of the muscles.

MUSCLES

The surface relief of the body is determined mainly by the muscles which are attached to the skeleton and move it and partly by the subcutaneous fat tissues. The muscles constitute the flesh of the body. There are also the vascular and intestinal muscles which are not externally visible and do not belong to surface anatomy. Every muscle is composed of small fibers which are bound together with tissue. Nervous stimulation causes the fibers to contract and this makes the muscle change its shape. If the nervous stimulation ceases so does the contraction of the fibers, and the muscle ceases to work. According to the demands on it the muscle grows in size or diminishes.

Muscles are attached very firmly to the bones by tendons. These are composed of strong, inelastic fibers, which can be seen and felt on the surface of the body when the muscles are tensed, for instance at the sides of the hollow of the throat, between the muscles of the forearm, wrist, and fingers, between the shin and toes, and at the sides of the kneecap when the knee is bent. The tendons running between the forearm and fingers and between the

The shoulder and hip joints are comparable to mechanical ball-and-socket joints. The shoulder can also rise and fall as a whole, and the entire shoulder girdle comprising collar bone and shoulder blade is attached to the chest in a way that allows some movement.

The hands and feet are composed of manifold systems of hinge joints and articulations. As units they can rotate at wrist and ankle with the mobility of ball and socket joints.

The movement of a large joint results in a series of movements in the smaller joints; for example, for you to stand on one leg, the pelvis must drop around the

shin and toes are appreciably longer than the corresponding muscles. Tendons, especially the largest, the Achilles tendon, which builds the contour of the heel, can easily be mistaken for bone, for they are tightly stretched and feel hard.

Except in sleep, the muscle fibers are always held slightly tensed, even when they are not working. They are like engines ticking over. This rest tension is called "tone." It influences the whole appearance of a person, and if the tone is too slack he looks, and probably is, slack, tired, or ill.

Every muscle can contract or relax either in jerks or very gradually. As long as there is any contraction the muscle is working, for there is no mechanism for maintaining it at a constant tension. If the muscle stops working, the limb which was held or moved by its power falls by force of gravity back to a position of rest.

Muscles only pull, they cannot push, and every muscle has its counterpart working in the opposite direction. If the extensor muscles of an elbow were cut, the arm would still be able to lift something towards the body by tension of the flexor, but, except by force of gravity, it would be unable to put it down again. Usually only the most important functions of muscles are given in anatomy books, but it is interesting to note that some muscles, particularly in the chest, back, and shoulders, have subsidiary functions; when a joint is bent to its fullest extent the direction of a muscle's "pull" may be changed and its function as flexor or extensor altered as well.

The area indicated in red is that part of the larger gluteal muscle which serves to move the hip

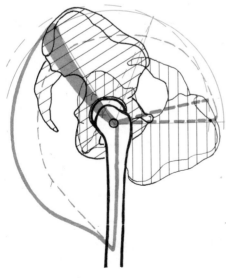

PROPORTIONS

Attempts have been made ever since Antiquity to submit the proportions of the human body to a canon or formula. In comparatively recent times Dürer made an exhaustive study of bodily proportions which is still valid as a point of reference for modern research. Since no two bodies grow to the same proportions, the search must start with an average of many measurements. From this it is relatively simple to find the individual character of a real body.

All research on this subject has concluded that the human body is constructed by and large according to the proportions of the golden mean. This proportion is a division of a given distance so that the smaller section stands in the same relation to the larger as the larger does to the whole. The algebraic formula is m:M=M:(m+M); where m= minor, smaller section, M=major, larger section. This division can be exactly found only in a geometric construction, but it yields an approximate figure of 0.618, which serves as multiplier for the value of the distance to be divided. The result gives the value of the larger section with sufficient exactitude.

This theory ought to be understood; though, since calculations and geometric figures are out of place in a freehand drawing, it is enough to judge by eye or to use the simplest measurements, with folded strips of paper or a pencil held out to mark off distances. This technique should be mastered, for it is essential to be able to divide distances. More

theory: the Fibonacci series in which each succeeding number is the sum of the two preceding ones yields increasingly close approximations to the golden section: (1:1, 1:2) 2:3, 3:5, 5:8, 8:13, 13:21 and so on. It is close enough to stop at the proportion 3:5, according to which 8 (3+5) can be divided easily according to the golden section. If a length is 176 inches, an eighth is 22 inches ($\frac{5}{8}$ = 110" + $\frac{3}{8}$ = **66**").

Of course, no figure drawing is started by making a series of measurements. All we need to do is to mark down the height from the standing line to the crown, and then to halve it. These divisions are halved again, and yet again until the height is divided into eighths. The third and fifth sections divide the whole height by golden section. Ever since Antiquity the following rules have been valid: the human head, measured from the under edge of the chin to the top of the crown without hair is an eighth the length of the whole height of the body. The navel is at five-eighths of the height of the body from the ground. If this distance is again divided according to the golden section in a relation of 3:2 it meets important lines of proportion on the shin. The diagrams show how divisions into eighths mark out other important points on the body.

The proportion 3:5 is not far advanced in the Lame series and is, therefore, not very exact. A multiplication of 176 by the index 0.618 arrives at 108.7. This makes a difference from the division into eighths of 1.4. The practical effect is that the navel has to come very slightly lower than the five-eighths line, a correction which can be made by eye.

From the left, the divisions of the colored vertical stripe are measured exactly, according to the golden section, while from the right the eighths are drawn freehand

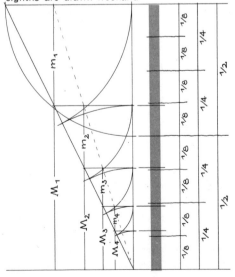

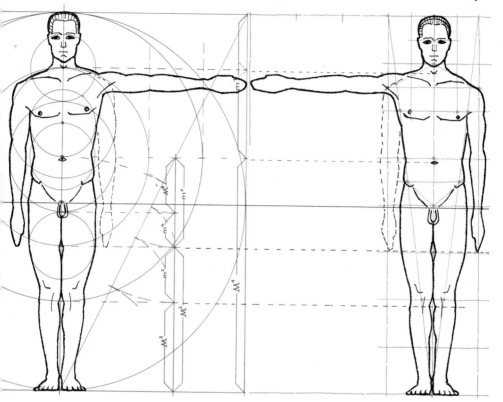

The radii are used to measure off sections according to the golden section. The circles then approximate to various body measurements. The hachures indicate the difference between constructive design and exact division into eighths

The drawings illustrated side by side show a comparison of the exact and rough schemes, demonstrating that the latter is perfectly adequate for freehand drawing. The exact scheme can be arrived at only with compass and set square, and these have no place in an artist's equipment. The difference is so small that a scaffold of 16 squares is perfectly satisfactory. It is quite sufficient to draw this scaffold freehand and by eye.

Some other measurements are of use. The two diagonals from the standing point to the corners of the complete double rectangle have been found to touch important points, though they bear no relation to the golden mean. Neither do the two outside lines of a rectangle formed by one-eighth squares on either side of the center axis; but these are easy to find and give useful indications for the breadth of the body. If the upper four squares are divided into sixteenths, the lines are valuable for finding the proportions of the head as a basis for the shoulder triangle and for the distance between the breasts. Another division into sixteenths in the fifth squares will give the triangle of the pelvis. Unlike many other guiding lines this one is not altered by movements of the body, as the pelvis is rigid within its own bone structure. No guiding lines can do more than give points of reference for comparing with the model.

The only generalization to be made about the adult human body, in view of the extraordinary differences of proportions from one individual to another, is that all healthy bodies are consistent: a thickset trunk has thickset head and limbs; short armed people generally have short legs as well. This harmony persists in the soft parts, too: the musculature, fat and skin tissues. There are, broadly speaking, three general types into which all the multifarious individuals can be divided:

1. The leptosome or slender type, tall and thin and long limbed, with a long, narrow trunk and correspondingly narrow shoulders and a long, narrow skull.

2. The athletic type with broad shoulders, a high solid skull, powerful trunk with large chest, firm abdominal muscles, little fat tissue, making the muscle contours clearly visible attached to large bones. The body has an overall wedge shape.

3. The pyknic or compact, thickset type, of medium height, with round skull, short neck, and a deep chest. A tendency to grow fat tissue inclines to make the muscle contours even out; the face is soft and plump and the body paunchy. This type loses its harmonious proportions if, through hunger or diet cures, an attempt is made to approximate it to an irrational ideal.

Fundamental differences between the male, female, and child's body structures also exist alongside individual differences. The male body is generally used for the study of anatomy as it shows the bones and muscles most clearly. Male and female differences are to be explained through their difference in biological function, the male being more adapted to work and the female to the demands of reproduction—hence, for instance, the greater breadth of the female pelvis. This in turn causes a strong curve inwards of the upper leg bones, which is why women tend to be knock-kneed. The pronounced narrowing of the female waist is in part due to the broader pelvis and in part to its stronger turn forward. The female rib cage is generally longer, deeper, and narrower than the male, and more rounded off at the top. The shoulders drop correspondingly lower and tend to be more rounded and sloping; sometimes the neck, too, seems longer and more slender.

On the female body the chest muscles are almost completely hidden by the breasts, which very enormously in shape with individuals. There is no biological nor aesthetic norm to be found for them.

The canons of earlier times maintained that on the whole the female body is smaller and gentler, shorter legged and armed, and with proportionately smaller hands and feet. A comparison of earlier representations of the female body, until the latter half of the nineteenth century, with photographs of modern sportswomen shows plainly how little these canons apply to the average modern woman. Rather do we see now that the proportions of the female body are not so different from those of the male, a reflection of the changed role which women play in social life. Sloping shoulders have become much rarer in women. A long leg is now the ideal of female beauty, and nowadays it is unusual to see such breadth of hip as used to be taken for normal in the old days.

It is biologically impossible that the skeleton should have altered so much in a century; the change can be explained only by the social tendencies of the modern age: women now hold themselves more upright and walk with more freedom and self confidence. Muscle tone, influenced by these factors, can disguise much and make the anatomy seem very different from what it really is, implying that there is still some mysterious chameleon-like quality in us that can even alter the shape of our soft tissues. Sport and uninhibited movement in sun and air with a minimum of clothing have become as usual for girls as for boys, and thus girls, too, develop their muscles at the expense of the fat tissues. Some medical opinion attributes a tendency to greater stature directly to the influence of sunlight on the body, particularly in early childhood.

It can be seen from the diagram of physical growth from birth to maturity how different parts of the body grow at different rates. In linear measurement the head, for example, only increases from between a half and a third, whereas the shin is four times as long in a man as in a newborn baby. All the other parts of the body increase in different proportions within these extremes. The five stages illustrated are not taken at regular intervals of age. Generally, a person grows most quickly between the fourteenth and sixteenth years, and often reaches full stature during this period. It is clear how important it is to observe the characteristic proportions when drawing children.

The oblique blue lines show the growth of individual parts of the body between 0 and 21 years

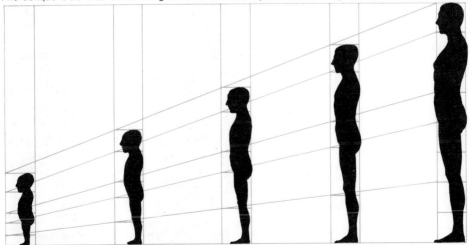

Human Anatomy

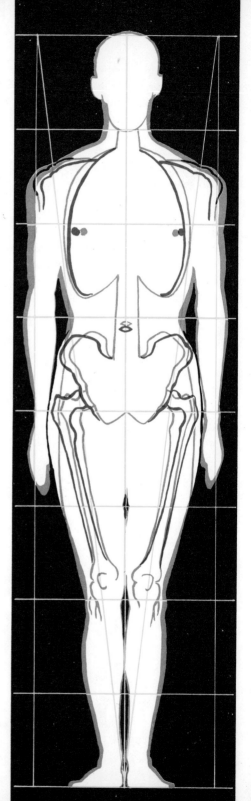

The white areas indicate the outline of the female body compared with a male of the same size. The red lines show the female skeleton, and the blue lines the male

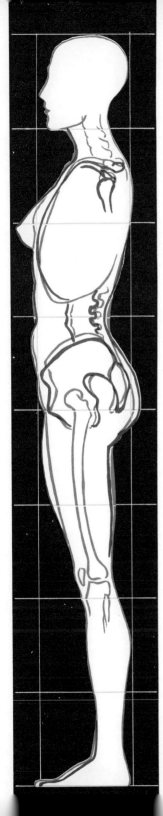
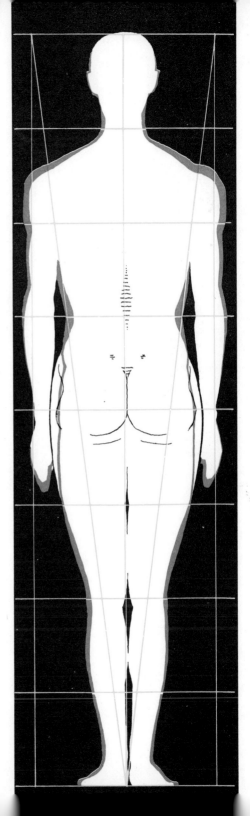

Skeleton and Superficial Muscles—Front View

		Sternomastoid	27
1	Cervical vertebrae (7)	Coicoid cartilage	28
2	Coracoid process (Shoulder-girdle)	Clavicular fossa	29
3	Collar-bone (Shoulder-girdle)	Acromion process	30
4	Greater tubercle (Shoulder-girdle)	Collar-bone	31
5	Shoulder-blade (Shoulder-girdle)	Deltoid	32
6	Sternum	Pectoralis major	33
7	Ribs (12)	Nipple	34
8	Humerus	Serratus anterior	35
		Biceps	36
		Rectus abdominis	37
		Radio-ulnar angle	38
9	Lumbar vertebrae (5)	Cubital fossa	39
		Obliquus abdominis externus	40
10	Radius	Extensor carpi radialis	41
11	Ulna	Brachio radialis	42
12	Iliac crest	(same as 13)	43
13	Anterior Superior spine of the ilium	Inguinal ligament	44
14	Iliac fossa	Mons pubis	45
15	Head of femur	Tensor fasciae latae	46
16	Greater trochanter	Femoral triangle	47
17	Neck of femur	Sartorius	48
18	Pubic bone	Gracilis	49
19	Femur	Quadriceps	50
20	Kneecap (patella)	Medial epicondyle	51
21	Head of fibula	Patellar tendon	52
22	Anterior fibial tuberosity	Gastrocnemius	53
23	Fibula	Tibialis anterior	54
24	Tibia	Anterior crest of the tibia	55
25	Medial malleolus	Soleus	56
26	Lateral malleolus	Malleolar angle	57

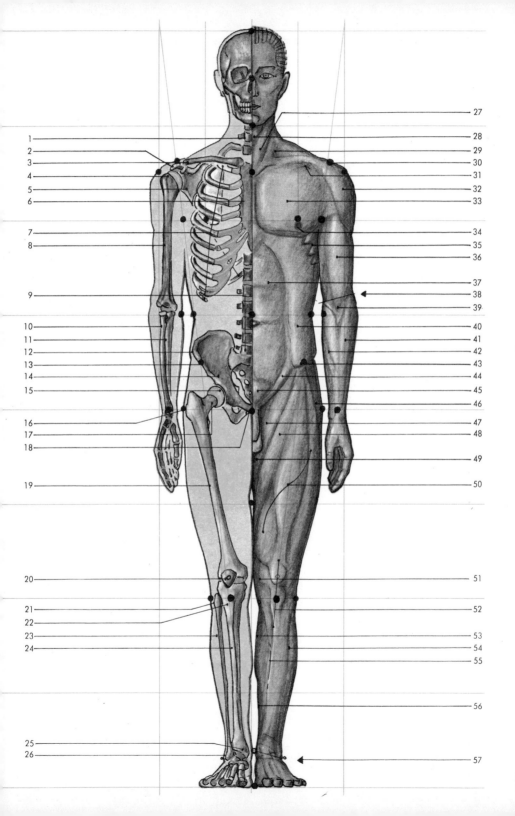

1

2
3
4
5
6

7
8

9

10
11
12
13
14
15

16
17
18

19

20

21
22
23
24

25
26

27
28
29
30
31
32
33

34
35
36

37
38
39

40
41
42
43
44
45
46

47
48

49

50

51

52

53
54
55

56

57

Skeleton and Superficial Muscles—Side and Back View

1	Clavicle	10	Cervical vertebrae (7)	Sternomastoid 31
2	Coracoid process	11	Spine of scapula	Acromion process 32
3	(Sternum)	12	Head of humerus	Trapezius 33
		13	Blade of Scapula	Infraspinatus 34
		14	Humerus	

4	True ribs (7)	15	Thoracic vertebrae (12)	Triceps 35
	(rib cage)	16	Floating ribs (2)	Latissimus dorsi 36
		17	Lumbar vertebrae (5)	Radio-ulnar angle 37

		18	Ulna	Obliquus externus 38
5	Iliac crest	19	Radius	Flexor carpi ulnaris 39
6	Anterior spine of	20	Ilium	Extensor carpi ulnaris 40
	the ilium	21	Sacrum	Tensor fasciae latae 41
7	Pubic bone	22	Head of femur	Gluteus maximus 42
		23	Ischial spine	

24	Ischium	Adductor magnus and gracilis 43
25	Greater trochanter	Vastus lateralis 44
26	Lesser trochanter	

27	Femur	Flexor muscles of the knee 45

8	Patella	
9	Tibial tuberosity	Popliteal fossa 46

28	Fibula	Calf muscles 47
29	Tibia	

		Achilles tendon 48
30	Heel-bone (calcaneus)	Malleolar angle 49

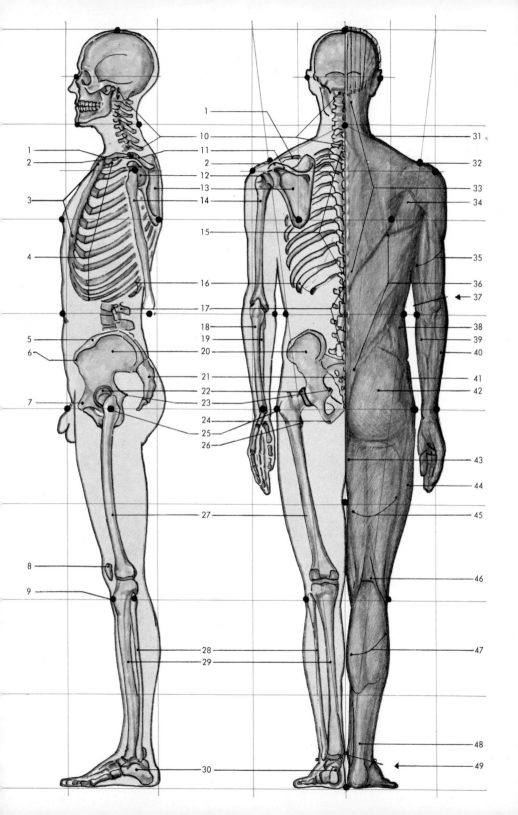

Musculature—Front View

1 Sternomastoid	Sternohyoid muscle 31
2 Trapezius	Levator scapulae 32
3 Deltoid	Subscapularis 33
4 Pectoralis major	Pectoralis minor 34

5 Triceps brachii (long head)	
6 Latissimus dorsi	
7 Serratus lateralis	Brachialis internus 35
8 Biceps brachii	Brachialis 36
9 Triceps brachii	Obliquus abdominis externus }37
10 Obliquus abdominis externus	(course shown schematically) }38

	Obliquus abdominis internus 39
	(broken lines show origin and insertion)
11 Brachioradialis	Flexor carpi ulnaris 41
12 Flexor antebrachii superficialis	Flexor carpi radialis 42
13 Rectus abdominis	Pyramidalis 43
14 Iliacus	Gluteus minimus 44
15 Tensor fasciae latae	

16 Pectineus	
17 Sartorius	
18 Adductor longus	
19 Gracilis	
20 Quadriceps (rectus femoris)	Adductor femoris 45
21 Vastus lateralis	Quadriceps 46

22 Vastus medialis
23 Patella
24 Sartorius aponeurosis

25 }Gastrocnemius	
26 }	
27 Tibialis anterior	
28 Soleus	Extensor digitorum 47

29 Extensor digitorum longus	
30 Cruciate ligament	Extensor hallucis longus 48

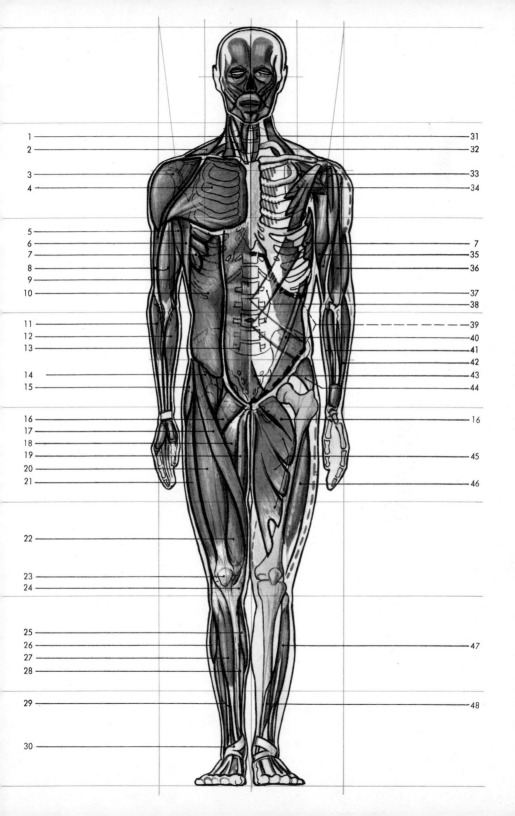

1 ———————   31
2 ———————   32

3 ———————   33
4 ———————   34

5 ———————
6 ———————   7
7 ———————   35
8 ———————   36
9 ———————
10 ———————   37
    38

11 ———————   39
12 ———————   40
13 ———————   41
    42
14 ———————   43
15 ———————   44

16 ———————   16
17 ———————
18 ———————
19 ———————   45
20 ———————
21 ———————   46

22 ———————

23 ———————
24 ———————

25 ———————
26 ———————   47
27 ———————
28 ———————

29 ———————   48

30 ———————

Musculature—Side and Back View

16 Occipitalis   Splenius capitia 33

1 Sternocleidomastoid   17 Trapezius   Levator scapulae 34
2 Pectoralis major   18 Deltoid   Lesser rhomboid 35
                            19 Teres major   Infraspinatus 36

3 Serratus lateralis   20 Greater rhomboid   Long head 37
4 Obliquus abdominis   21 Triceps brachii   Lateral head 38
   externus   22 Latissimus dorsi   Triceps brachii 39
5 Rectus abdominis   Intercostal muscles 40
                                                           Longissimus dorsi 41
                                          Extensor carpi radialis longus 42
                                          Obliquus abdominis externus 43

6 Tensor fasciae latae   23 Extensor carpi radialis   Anconaeus 44
7 Sartorius   24 Flexor carpi radialis   Flexor carpi ulnaris 45
                            25 Gluteus maximus   Deep muscles of the hip 46

8 ⎰   26 Greater trochanter   Quadratus femoris 47
10 ⎱ Quadriceps femoris   27 Gracilis   Adductor 48
9 Fascia lata   28 Biceps femoris

11 Kneecap   29 Semitendinosus   Semimembranosus 49
                                                                  Popliteus 50

12 Tibialis anterior   30 Triceps surae   Flexor digitorum longus 51
13 Peronaeus longus   Flexor hallucis longus 52
14 Peronaeus brevis

                            31 Triceps surae
                            32 Cruciate coural ligament
15 Tendons of the extensor
    digitorum longus

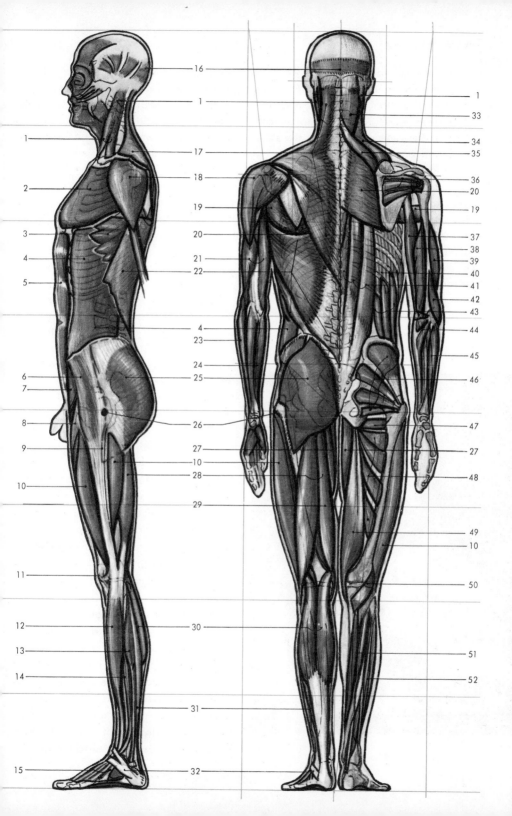

Human Anatomy

To make this review simpler, we have separated the anatomy of head, hands, and feet from the rest. Attempts have often been made to find scientific correlations between the shape of the skull, nose, and ear and the temperament or psychological characteristics of a person. The hand, too, has been studied in this light, and chiromancy even claims to read the individual's past and future fate from the lines on the palm. Science dismisses all these speculations; a sharp, aquiline nose reveals no more good of a person than a bulbous or flat one; an ear which according to our views is beautifully shaped is no more proof of musicality than one which has what looks like criminal characteristics. To think that joined eyebrows mean an unnatural death is a ridiculous superstition. The painting by Titian, however, which is only one of numerous possible examples, shows how much can nevertheless be learned of the mind and soul from the face and hands.

Titian, Tribute Money

THE HEAD

The shape of the head is determined first of all by the structure of the bones of the cranium. They can also indicate racial origins. The average shape of the long skull is enclosed frontally in a rectangle. Its height is an eighth of the whole height of the body of a full-grown man. The breadth is two-sevenths smaller than the height. The same head in profile fits into a square with sides corresponding to the height of the frontal rectangle, one-eighth of the total height. The muscles of the head have primarily technical functions; they open and shut the mouth and eyelids; they move the lower jaw for chewing and biting. For blowing, sucking, and speaking the mouth muscles regulate the flow of air.

The facial muscles, however, react to psychological stimuli as well, so much so that even small children and animals can understand clearly the momentary changes of mood of the person they are with from his face. Laughter, weeping, anger, and sorrow are universally understood expressions. They are all facial movements caused by muscular activity.

If certain stimuli are repeated frequently they become more and more impressed into the contours of the face, mainly by folds and lines in the skin. Constant cheerfulness or resentment, discontent, obstinacy, reserve or self-control create facial expression through the muscles of the face. A person's reaction to circumstances, rather than the circumstances themselves, determine the character of a face. Passing violent moods leave no trace.

As can be seen in the diagrams, there are few facial muscles, but an infinite variety of effects results from their interplay, providing all the changes of expression—even as the thirteen notes of the well-tempered scale can combine in every possible way to form the whole range of musical expression. The laughing muscles, for instance, are also the principal ones used in crying, but the difference is established by the intervention of the chin-raising muscle and the muscle in the brow. The eyes, even to the color of the iris, are fundamentally the same in all people, and of practically the same size, but their apparent size is considerably altered by the opening of the lids, which in turn is influenced by the formation of the upper lid and the cushion of fat surrounding the eyes at

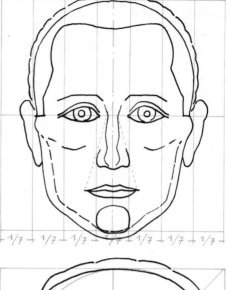

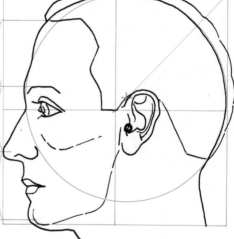

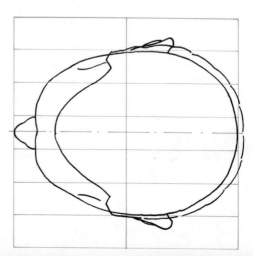

Above: The face divided vertically into seven. Center: The chin tip and the tip of the nose, nose and eyebrows, eyebrows and start of the hair are all an equal distance apart. Geometrically speaking, the central point of the skull lies on the diagonal and perpendicular lines, crossing the ear cavity.
Below: Head seen from above

the back. Fritz Lange, professor of orthopedics ("Die Sprache des menschlichen Antlitzes"), has distinguished six basic types of lid formation, a formulation which is of great use in portrait painting. The general tone of a person is often indicated by the eyelids. The eyes can be made large at will, but if the lids are usually rather dropped it is a sign of weak tone. The upper lid may, of course, relax momentarily with anyone—for instance, in moments of strong and passive sensual excitement, listening to music, or breathing in intense perfumes. Wide eyes have always been associated with a deep spiritual life, and there is a constant tendency to portray eyes larger than normal in relation to the rest of the face and body.

The width of the space between the lids does not differ much between in-

dividuals, but there is a much larger difference in the space between the two inner corners of the eyes. Here again the constitution is as much responsible as the position of the eye sockets in the skull. Deep-set eyes generally lie close together. The normal distance between the two inner corners of the eyes corresponds to the breadth of the visible eyeball.

The most important thing in drawing an eye is to establish the position of the eyeball from the placing of the iris and its pupil. The iris is immovable behind the cornea; the eyeball is moved by six muscles. The circular iris has a concentric circular opening in the middle, the pupil, which can be enlarged and reduced by muscular action to regulate the amount of light penetrating the eye. Emotion as well as light affects the size of the pupil. Depression, anger, and

Ear and nose, side and front view

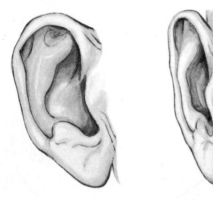

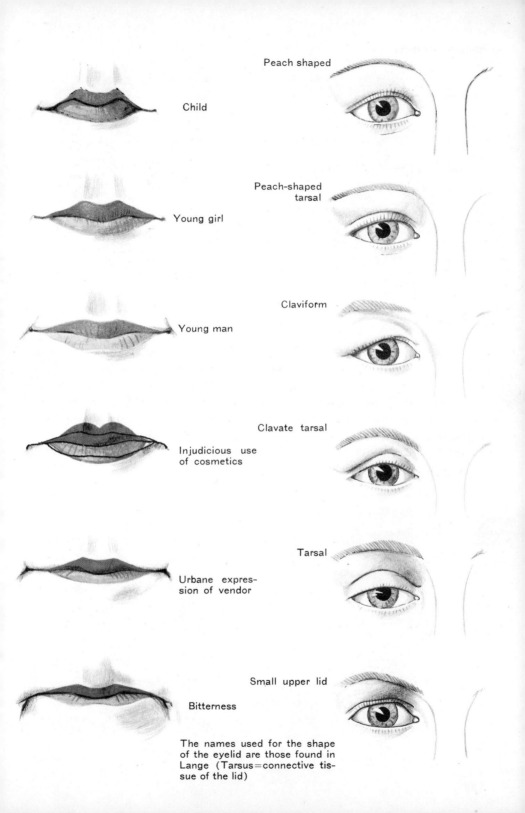

Child

Peach shaped

Young girl

Peach-shaped
tarsal

Young man

Claviform

Injudicious use
of cosmetics

Clavate tarsal

Urbane expres-
sion of vendor

Tarsal

Bitterness

Small upper lid

The names used for the shape
of the eyelid are those found in
Lange (Tarsus=connective tissue of the lid)

POSITIVE EMOTIONS

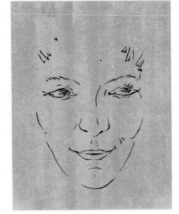

Smiles

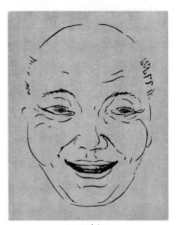

Laughter

sorrow make it larger so that objective vision is disturbed by excessive penetration of light. "To see things in a false light" is an apt figure of speech. Animation reduces the size of the pupil.

Focusing is operated by a lens lying behind the iris and moved by the ciliar muscle. The changes in it cannot be seen directly; yet it is always possible to know if someone is looking at an object or through it, or seeing in a "visionary" manner. There are no rules to help in drawing this; close observation is the only way. Shading and high lights, the

Worry

Tears

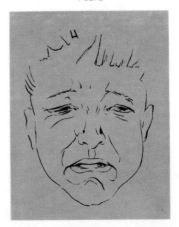

NEGATIVE EMOTIONS

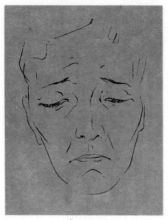

Sorrow

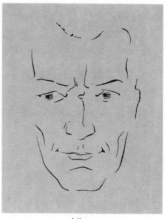

Vigor

path of the look of each eye, and their combined direction, which is parallel only when looking into the far distance, are the things to notice. The much admired portait which seems to look at the beholder from whichever direction it is viewed is achieved by the trick of making both eyes look straight out of the picture perpendicular to the picture plane. The color of the iris has no connection with character. The permanent expression of the eyes is related to the position of the iris in the eyeball and the position and shape of the lids. The "expression" of

Bitterness

Brutality

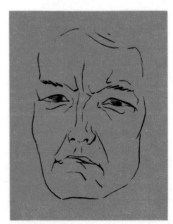

HEAD MUSCLES

No.	NAME	FUNCTION	POSITIVE EXPRESSIONS	NEGATIVE EXPRESSIONS
9	Frontalis	Wrinkles forehead, raises eyebrows, helps raise upper eyelid	Joy, attentiveness, surprise, meditation	Doubt, painful effort, resignation
10	Corrugator supercilii	Knits brows	Attentiveness, concentration	Indignation, anger, rage
11/24	Orbicularis palpebrarum	Closes eyelids (11 = upper, 24 = lower)	Powerful movement indicates all positive qualities (open eyes). Blinking: reflection, sailors' and painters' eyes	Open: stupidity, limp: fatigue, intoxication, sexual and other affectation. Blinking: cunning
13	Levator nasalis	Turns up and puckers nose	Criticism	Dissatisfaction, grumbling
14/15	Zygomatic muscles	Draw corners of mouth up and out, hard	Open laughter	Tears, disgust
18	Risorius	Draws corners of mouth up and out, gently	Gentle smiles	Tears
19	Triangularis	Draws corners of mouth downwards	Pain and sorrow	Bitterness, resignation, ill humor
20	Quadratus labii inferiorum	Depresses the under-lip		Vexation, disgust
22	Corrugator glabellae	As 9 and 10	As 9 and 10	As 9 and 10
23	Procerus nasi	Puckers the nose crosswise	Energy	Brutality
25	Nasalis	Depresses tip of nose	Pugnacity, energy	Irony
26	Caninus	Draws corners of mouth backwards	As 14 and 15	As 14 and 15
27	Buccinator	Draws corners of mouth outwards	Laughter between closed lips; obliging smiles. Self-control	Tears, resignation, exasperation. Insincerity obstinacy
28	Masseter	Used in chewing	Energy, self-possession (clenched teeth)	Doggedness, rage, repulsion, gluttony
29	Orbicularis oris	Closes and puckers mouth (as in whistling and kissing)	Self-possession, energy. Repressed tears	Resignation, rage, scorn, derision, sulking
30	Mentalis	Pulls up skin over chin (as in pouting)		Threats, anger, rage, brutality, contempt
31	Levator nasi et labii	Lifts nose and lips		Tears, disgust

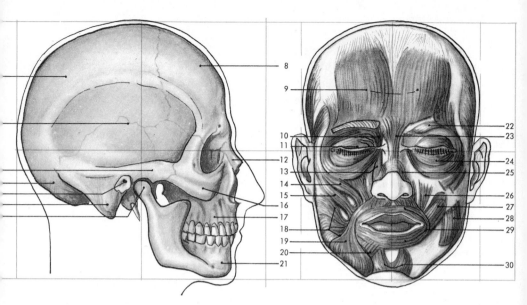

Bones of the skull:

1. Parietal — 2. Temporal — 3. Zygomatic arch — 4. Occipital — 5. External auditory — 6. Mastoid — 7. Ramus of the Mandible — 8. Frontal — 12. Nasal — 16. Malar bone — 17. Maxilla — 21. Mandible

Muscles of the head and neck with no power over facial expression

32. The Platysma — 33. Temporal — 34. Occipital — 35. Posterior auditory muscles — 36. Trapezius — 37. Splenius Capitis — 38. Levator Anguli Scapuli — 39. Annuent muscle

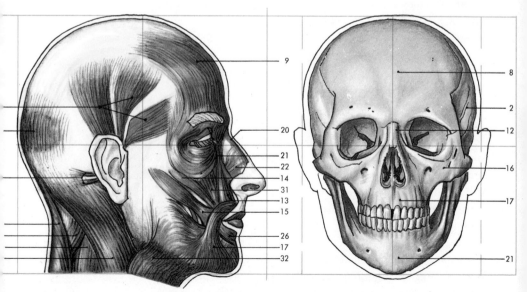

the eyes is, in fact, the general facial expression. Tears, or an increase of tear fluid, make the eyes shine more.

The original shape of the mouth is rarely to be found in older people. The movements of the mouth muscles affect the shape of lips and corners from childhood, for the mouth is the first feature to be moved by any change of feeling. In general, outward expressions of temperament make the lips turn out, while feelings held in and experience passively received make the mouth turn in and become narrower. A typical painter's mouth seems to belong to anyone— temporarily, at least, to anyone who looks, observes, and then reacts creatively to what he has seen. Purely receptive or acquisitive people, on the other hand, tend to have narrow, pulled-in mouths with regular, downward folds at the corners, the wrinkles of bitterness. Combinations of facial movement are a fascinating revelation of character, but there is always a harmony of expression even in melancholy people who are inwardly torn. Women's make-up is liable to substitute a mask for this harmony, inventing a new line of brow and broadening the lips to make a pretence of great sensuality; for portraits it is important only to let make-up underline the natural forms with color.

The folds of the cheek from nose to mouth corners run in about the same direction as the folds of a pulled-down mouth. They may, however, be due to heredity, and are sometimes seen, though not as lines, in children, as quite unrelated to their character. They are caused by smiling and weeping and by strain or discontent and are only exceptional if they look strange in the total build of the face, betokening some passion which is uncontrolled and not assimilated in the general character of the person. Lines of discontent are caused by the frequent puckering of the muscle which lifts the nose. Bellicosity causes a line to appear in the same way, one which is to be seen on the faces of almost all the great fighters of history. It does not appear on a face where the nose runs into the brow without an inward curve. Active concentration and combative effort may evoke activity of the frowning muscle, pulling the inner ends of the brows downwards and inwards and forming the so-called lines of thought. The middle part of the forehead muscle works against this frowning muscle, raising the inner ends of the eyebrows to give the expression of pathetic pain, the "Laocoön brow." This movement of the brows is rarely involuntary, it has to be practiced and studied and is a powerful means of expression for the actor.

A wrinkling of the whole brow, making vertical folds, is a natural movement and leaves its mark on all older faces, but it does not imply very much, for only someone who is controlled to the point of impassibility has none. Every passive effort uses it, astonishment, reflection, attention, and pomposity, too. The forehead muscles can replace those that lift the eyelids to some extent, if these are weak or do not function. Thus, folds on the brow have to be studied along with other expressions to be correctly understood.

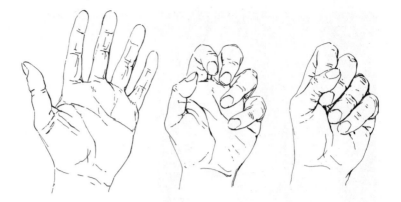

THE HAND

The length of the hand is equal to one-tenth of the length of the body. Its width is roughly in the relation of m:M of the golden section, measured with the fingers together, although it varies according to one's constitution. Women's hands are often less than one-tenth the length of the body, and correspondingly narrower.

The skeleton of the hand is composed of three sections: the carpals, metacarpals, and fingerbones, with three corresponding groups of joints. The wrist joint rotates against the radius (the ulna is too short to reach the wrist). The metacarpal joint lies between the carpals and metacarpals. It is not very mobile and serves simply to increase the elasticity of the palm. The two hand joints are moved by five muscles: ulna and radius flexor, ulna extensor, and one short and one long radius extensor. The fingers really begin with the four metacarpal bones, which are joined together in the carpas, or palm, by articulating muscles between them and by ligaments and skin. The separate fingers are formed

each of three bones continuing from the metacarpals. Between the finger bones are knuckle joints, which are moved by long tendons from the flexor and extensor muscles attached to the upper and lower arm. The first finger joint also allows rotation, which is worked together with a stretching apart of the fingers by the muscles between the bones.

The thumb turns the hand from a clamp into a holder. It is held opposite the fingers by a rotating joint between the wrist and the root of the thumb. It has a series of muscles, especially around the lowest thumb bone, to give it a strong counterpresssure to the fingers. The outstretched fingers move with an increased

Furthest possible hand movements

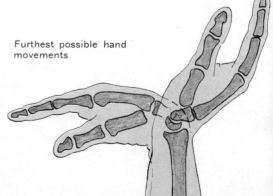

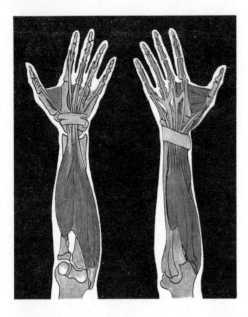

Muscles most used in flexion and extension of hand and fingers. Left: Left arm with flexors (palm of the hand). Right: Right arm with extensors (back of the hand)

fist, like a claw with concentrically approaching points. This movement is the key to many seemingly complicated positions of the hand. Its many bones and different muscles and tendons of different lengths make it into a splendidly sensitive instrument. Small wonder that it can reveal much about the nature of the person, with its gestures and positions, much of which can be reproduced by the artist. Often, characteristics such as grace, nobility, avarice, rapacity, or brutality are more easily seen in the hand than on the face. The reproduction of Titian's portrait should be examined once again in this light! A coarse hand should not immediately be accepted as a sign of coarseness, however. Quite often hands which look clumsy and ugly belong to sensitive and manually dexterous people. The author himself underwent an extremely painful examination of a wound by a doctor whose hands were classically beautiful; she was so unsuccessful in her search, however, that she handed it over to her senior, a surgeon whose thick, coarse, peasant-like fingers did all that was necessary without causing a twinge.

bend towards the end, as though to hold a sphere the size of a soccer ball. If fingers and thumb bend further the imagined sphere grows smaller and the finger ends begin to move. They can curl up until they are tight against the

Furthest possible hand movements

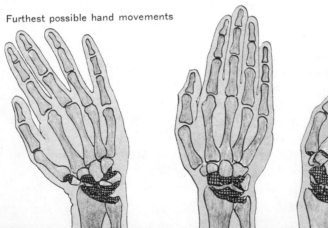

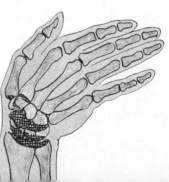

THE FOOT

The length of a man's foot is about one-sixth, of a woman's about one-eighth, the length of the body. Its widest part is about the same width as the widest part of the hand. A comparison of the structure of the foot with that of the hand is the best way of understanding it. It is built on the same principle as the hand, but it is placed at right angles to the shin instead of being a continuation of it; and the big toe, which corresponds to the thumb, does not stand in opposition to the other toes, so that the toes can only be used for grasping, not holding or manipulating. The foot has become exclusively adapted for walking and standing.

In this connection the foot has developed as a very efficient shock absorber. If one suffers a loss of this function—from too much motor driving, for example—considerable damage can result to the vertebrae and inner organs. The structure of the skeleton of the foot shows this function. Both lengthways and across, the bones are like conical vaulting stones, joined together into arches; but being organic, they are more flexible than stones and more like strongly bent springs. The sole of the foot is further cushioned with flexing muscles, fat, and skin tissue. This enlarges the tread area of the foot, but the double arch is still discernible in the characteristic print of the naked foot. These arches are higher if the foot is turned inwards, and sink if the foot turns outwards or after long periods of standing.

The ankle, like the wrist, can rotate, being worked partly by the muscles from the fibula and tibia, and more strongly by the largest extensor of the foot, the threefold peroneal muscle which works through the Achilles' tendon on the heel bone. Without this tendon it is impossible to walk or to stand. Its name refers to the Greek hero who was vulnerable only on his heel. Both flexors and extensors must be intact even for standing at rest, for a joint can be held firm only by the intertension of both sets of muscles.

The build of the third shin muscle, the soleus, together with that of the Achilles' tendon, determines the shape of the foot: the shorter the heel bone the shorter and thicker the shin musculature. Negroes, who have very long heel bones, have shin muscles extending long and thin almost to the heel.

The mobility of the foot is governed by the activity of the upper and lower ankle joint. The upper connects the ankle bone and tibia (the fibula, like the ulna, is not attached to the joint); the lower connects the ankle and heel bones. It is arranged so that it is bent inwards however far the toes point outwards: the typical position of dancers and jumpers. The toes, again like the fingers, are moved by long tendons which can be seen plainly when the right muscles are tensed. As in the hand, these tendons are held in their curving path by cross bands and projections of bone.

It is in walking that the continual and versatile co-operation of all parts of the body in the act of balancing becomes most manifest, since the foot has a relatively small bearing surface. In walking

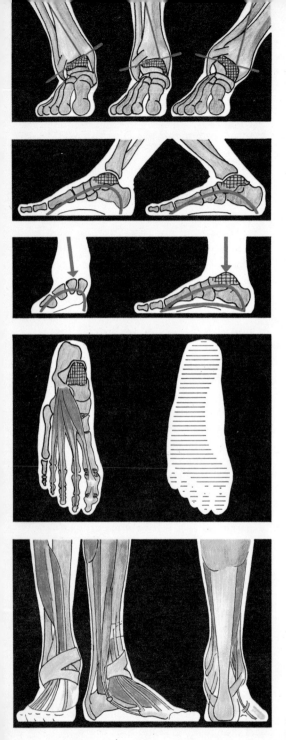

and in keeping one's balance, not only do the muscles of legs and trunk play their part, but the swinging of the arms also helps towards an easy gait. Thus, the swing of the arms is always opposed to the leg movements. If one side of the body is carrying a heavy weight, the arm on the other side instinctively lifts away from the body, but without discontinuing the swinging movement. Similar actions can be observed in athletics—javelin-throwing, for example, or the discus, or shot putting—where an explosively sudden weight shift has to be achieved.

Movement also shows up a person's general physical condition. Strenuous exertion of almost all muscles (even facial muscles are distorted in conditions of stress) presumes normal tone. One who is in poor condition betrays this by a dragging gait. And one's general condition depends to some extent on one's state of mind: you can see people walking along in bright and cheerful mood, self-assured and full of confidence, or sadly, with a depressed or care-worn slouch. If the foot is injured, even if only slightly, the gait becomes a painful limp; chronically unsound feet will permanently destroy the beauty of an upright gait, the most "human" of all man's movements.

1. (Right foot) Left: Outward tilt of the shank, showing flattening of the arch. Center: Normal upright stance. Right: Inward tilt of the shank, showing arching of the foot
2. Left: Extension of the foot, showing raised arch. Right: Flexion of the foot, showing flattening of the arch
3. Arch of the foot, cross-section and longitudinal section
4. Skeleton of the foot showing extensions of the toe, silhouette and normal foot print, seen from above
5. Formation of the most important adjuncts of the flexor and extensor muscles of the foot

THE NUDE

In portraying the nude figure, the principal requirement is a sound grasp of the plastic aspects of the anatomy and proportions of the human body. In teaching these proportions, a simple system of diagrams has been evolved, and these can be of practical assistance in drawing. Their use is largely restricted to the portrayal of the upright, motionless nude figure. Nonetheless, some adaptation to the needs of movement is possible. Generally speaking, nude and figure drawing become much more interesting when the body is portrayed in some position other than merely upright. The first task must be to establish whether the figure is at rest or in motion. Not only is this important to you, the artist; the spectator, too, will want to know whether your drawing relates to a completed movement or not. The use of a perpendicular line will clear up this point for you. Let us suppose that the subject is standing on one leg. In this case, the perpendicular will start just inside the leg which takes the body weight. If you find that the volume is evenly distributed on either side of the perpendicular, you will know that the body is at rest. If, on the other hand, it is unevenly distributed, the body is moving in the direction where the volume is greater. Draw in or visualize this perpendicular, and you will soon ascertain whether your drawing is accurate, or whether the figure you have drawn in motion is in fact in repose; or if the subject you have shown at rest is in fact in motion.

Whichever it is, at rest or in motion, you will always find directional lines which will plainly show where a movement begins, which way it points, where most weight is placed, its balance, counterbalance and rhythm. External outlines and variations due to the plasticity of the subject are indicated by means of directional lines touching each other. An example of this is to be seen in the variety of trunk postures which may arise from movements of the spine and shoulder. Two figures of great assistance in this respect have already been shown. The first is the pelvic triangle, which never alters; the second is the shoulder triangle, which may vary. In practice, yet another set of tangential lines will be found of help where the subject has his or her back to the artist. This is the triangle formed by the buttocks. Although the proportions of this triangle

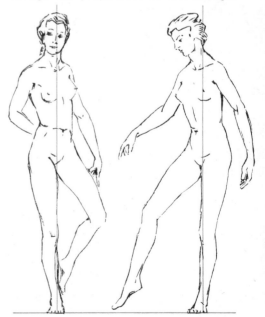

137

will vary among individuals, it is unaffected by movement, owing to pelvic support. This triangle can be expanded to form a square, should the exigencies of the perspective plane so require.

The safest way to determine the positioning of this triangle or square is to follow the cleft between the two buttocks, as this invariably divides both types of figure in half. This is a line reaching from the edge of the iliac blade at the top, right down to the larger upper thigh muscle when stretched.

If, as is often the case, one side is

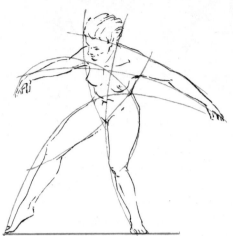

relaxed, then the tensed side should be used as the guiding line. Both sides can be relaxed only when the body is hanging or lying. The sides of the rectangle come where the buttock muscles are attached. The rectangle, or square, reveals two facts about the body, one relating to the bending and turning of the pelvis in against the middle trunk, the other about its constitution; one a matter of perspective in the picture, the other of its actual shape. Basically it is a rectangle lying on its side. In slender bodies it may become a square, and only in very thin ones an upright rectangle. Female bodies always have a wider rectangle because the pelvis is broader in women than men and there is a greater amount of fat tissue. A correct structure of all the guiding lines and figures provides a sure scaffold as a preliminary to drawing all poses, and the various strategic points and lines of proportion can afterwards be added to it without difficulty. Even a crouching pose which does not allow the height of the body to be gauged can be helped by a division into eighths. In the illustration only the arm can be seen

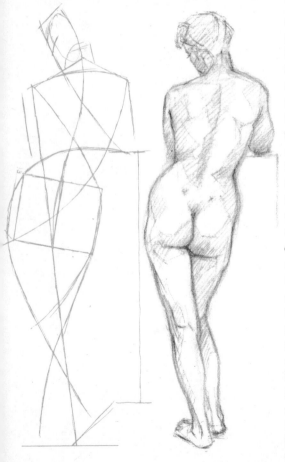

spective, by treating them as though they were transparent. This trick is the easiest way of making clear the relative positions of the parts of the body. It is usual to insist on the beginner's using cuboid figures for the human body delineated with a harsh, angular line, making him avoid sweet and soft, rounded contours.

This method has the disadvantage of making the artist turn people into robots, thereby losing his feeling for the roundness of the body. Severity of line is a discipline that can be practiced in other ways.

Exercise in perspective has taught us that the variety of vanishing points increases with the diversity of the shapes

at full length, but the face and shin are sloping in the same direction and thus have the same small degree of foreshortening. The length of the arms, shin, and head can be satisfactorily coordinated, and then the shoulder breadth, of which the foreshortening is rather restricted, can be fitted to it.

The more the body is turned away from a frontal view the stronger the foreshortening in perspective, which must be rendered with the help of geometric figures, not a linear scheme. If an arm is stretched out towards the artist, he needs to be very experienced to interpret it correctly at sight. The inexperienced artist should proceed by encasing the upper arm in a cylinder, the forearm in a truncated cone, the joints in conic sections, and the hand in a slightly curved rectangle with small truncated cones for the fingers. The same can be done with all other parts of the body: the head becomes an egg shape with meridians to indicate the features and the trunk a barrel describing an oval section.

It is a useful exercise to study these figures, with their foreshortenings in per-

Supplementary lines are used here to illustrate the division of the body into eighths, with and without foreshortening

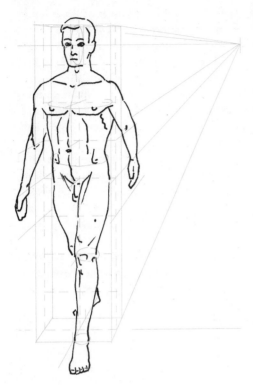

the space in which the body is contained. The only way of establishing the position of the body in relation to the artist is by enclosing it in a cubic structure. He imagines it in a glass box, the walls of which touch the outermost points of the body. This approach clarifies the foreshortenings and ambiguities caused by perspective. If this boxed man is approaching the artist, the reduction in size of the hinder parts of the body can be worked out from vanishing lines. The horizon and positions of the vanishing points provide a useful check on the direction and stability of the walking figure.

This imaginary guide is used not only by beginners but even by the greatest artists from time to time.

Life drawing should not be done at first from a posed model; it is much more instructive to make the first attempts in chance, natural surroundings, while watching sports or swimming, for example. If the artist is serious he will always find someone to hold a chance pose long enough for him to make a quick sketch. It is advisable not to plague this kind person by long searching after the perfect pose; better to flatter him by saying how delightful his momentary position is, and then he will stand like a statue. The advantage here is that awkward poses are avoided—poses which are too difficult to draw at first, and when once mastered are found undesirable.

of the individual bodies. The same applies to the guiding figures used now in life drawing. It is not appropriate to work out a large series of constructions for this work. Architectural studies are the best means of developing a feeling for perspectival relationships, and this feeling should be sufficient in life drawing. Architecture is closely allied to the structure of the human body. Nowhere else is man so much the measure of all things as in architecture, which is, therefore, at its best when based on the proportions of the golden mean.

Drawing architecture is useful for developing the sense of stability so necessary in life drawing. An understanding of the containment of space in architecture also develops a feeling for

At first, it will suffice to draw an outline of the whole figure, concentrating on correct proportions. Details are needed only where they are particularly obvious on the model. It is more impor-

Diagram of human body to help with the accompanying nude study

tant at first simply to gain assurance than to attempt a complete nude drawing. Enough experience should be gained before this attempt to impart individuality to the model, to give it the telling characterization that is half the charm and success of a drawing. It does not matter if your model is not an Aphrodite or Adonis. Even an "ugly" body can be beautiful if it expresses something, and this it will do only in a natural position. The dusty old academy poses, using horse tamers, bell ringers, amphora bearers, and such like, may be useful for showing anatomy but are no more desirable as a final picture than the silly affectations of mannequins or the well-tried repertory of pin-up girl poses.

Thus, it is important to know why, beyond the necessities of training, we draw figures. Two main reasons can be found: one is the purely formal beauty of the body, the other is its human expressiveness, although it seems that for many years beauty has caused distress in figurative art, and it is hard indeed to find a beautiful body in many modern exhibitions. Do all ugly poses really express something so essential? Would it not be a fine task to rediscover the beautiful body for pictorial art?

Nude studies from the studio

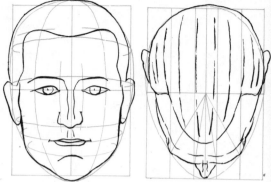

PORTRAIT DRAWING

In the section on the anatomy of the head we showed that non-physical factors like mood, temperament, and character are more important than biological functions in moulding the forms of the face and giving it individuality. These factors are thus at least as important to the draftsman as a correct rendering of physical proportions. A portrait must reproduce the personal character of the sitter's face and not just show a type of head. Nothing in the living world lends itself so easily to abstract drawing as a face. All our lives we read human faces into all kinds of living creatures, and indeed into inanimate things having nothing to do with people—in the graining of wood, flowers, the contours of hills. These phenomena can give as deep an impression of personality as the real faces of people and animals. There is great scope here for artistic expres-

sion, but this book is concerned only with the foundations of naturalistic representation as the basis for every kind of artistic interpretation. We learn drawing as we learn to write at school; how and what we write later is no concern of the teacher.

When fitting the parts of the body into a geometric scheme, we likened the head to an oval. This oval, like a bird's egg, can vary greatly in shape, from long and narrow to almost spherical.

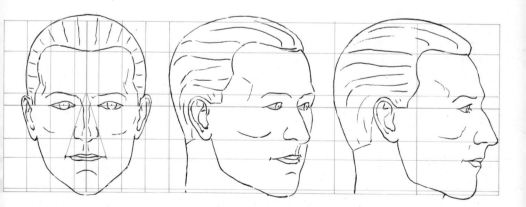

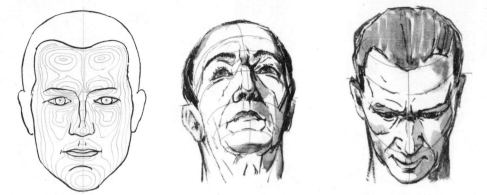

Facial contours. The middle line is shown foreshortened when the head is raised or inclined

The head is never a cuboid structure. The ever-present tendency to abstraction, a tendency quite independent of a deliberate stylization like cubism, often makes people forget this.

Students are often astonished, looking at a head for the first time from above, to notice that there is not a single flat frontal surface to be seen. Observed from above, the face, so often depicted far too flat, falls sharply away to the sides of the head, and the crown and brow build yet another oval. Awareness of this is an important step forward. For a deeper understanding of the shape of the head, and particularly of the face, it is useful to draw the chosen view as a relief map with contour lines. It is equally valuable to draw the head in many varieties of profile, both held erect and at various angles. All this helps to make the student more aware of the roundness of the head.

Apart from an external, formal resemblance to the sitter, a portrait is concerned primarily with finding a characteristic and consistent expression. There is no rule for achieving this, but it is helpful to know that the more the nonessentials are left out, the stronger and more determined is the expression.

A portrait drawing begins systematically from the linear scheme, from the relation of height and breadth in which the oval is contained. The slightest turn or bend of the head curves the straight lines into meridians, foreshortened by perspective: through the corners of the eyes, below the nose, through the meeting of the lips, the fold of the chin, through the eyebrows, and the beginning of the hairline on the brow. Into this scaffold of elliptical lines further points of measurement are marked: the width of eyes and mouth, the fold of the chin, the beginning of the hairline, the setting

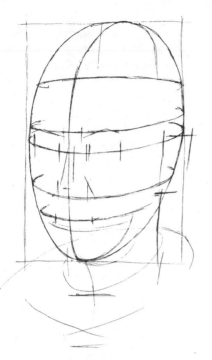

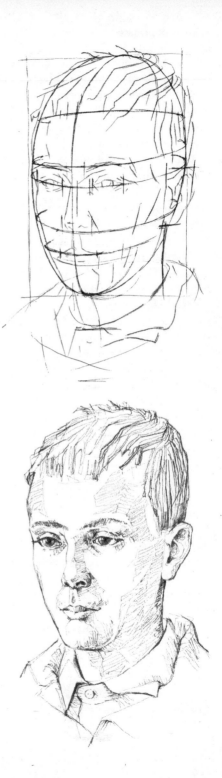

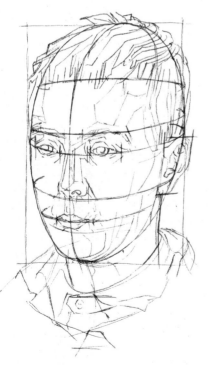

of the root of the nose, the nostrils and the breadth of its bridge, then the ear, its position and outline. The first working can also indicate the line of the eyebrows and the folds of nose, lips, and corners of the mouth.

The second phase of work starts with the main shapes in the regions of the eyes and mouth, and the lay of the hair. Ear, cheek surfaces, and temple can receive the broader details.

The third phase turns to greater detail, particularly the exact outlines which give individuality—but with the gentlest possible drawing. Preliminary softness in drawing the lines allows the fourth phase to pick out what is essential and characteristic until the portrait is worked up to the desired degree of finish.

This is the disciplined and scholarly way, and the way most certain of success in setting about to reach a "likeness," that desired goal which commands so much respect and which causes so much alarm among the inexperienced. It is a mistake to try to find the likeness right at the beginning instead of allowing it to grow out of the exact pursuit of the individual shapes and lines. However, this close attention to the individual shape must not become a routine which makes all the portraits from the same hand look as though the sitters were all relatives, a danger run by many professional portraitists. There is no need to treat every portrait as a first beginning, which would inevitably produce an academic aspect. Academic discipline is only a means to an end, which, with experience, should lead to a personal form of expression, in the same way that a personal handwriting grows from the school copybook.

The well-worn critical comment that much has been "put in" a portrait is misleading. A human face is much more significant than a cast and nothing needs or should be put in it, rather much should be taken out in order to emphasize what is essential and particular. The choice of what remains depends on the maturity of the artist and his temperament, his perception and ability to assess the significance of facial features.

The most easily accessible model is the artist's own reflection in a mirror. For study purposes it is quite unimportant that it is seen in reverse. But if one wants to make a true portrait, it is quite possible to train oneself to make a mechanical reversal of the reflection, altering the coordination of hand and eye to produce a mirror image.

Rembrandt, one of the greatest painters of all time, repeatedly studied his own reflection. He did not do this from vanity—he was by no means a handsome man. He painted himself because the sitter was always available, and he did it uncritically, for he was entirely preoccupied with the problem of light and shade. Over one hundred of his self-portraits survive and are among the most compelling ever painted.

Animal anatomy is best understood by a comparison with human anatomy, working from the idea that animals have adapted the structure of the human body to their own needs of existence. For artists, the idea that man is the measure of all things is always correct. The point of view of exact science would enforce him to be continuously rethinking instead of reacting primarily to his faculty of vision. The understanding of visible form is basically a matter of comparison, and for the human being the most accessible object of comparison is the human body, if he is trying to understand the structure of other living bodies.

We shall concern ourselves here only with vertebrates, and of these only those most conducive to pictorial representation: quadrupeds and birds. Their physical structure is very close to the human. It is composed of the spine, skull, thorax and shoulder girdle, pelvis, and four limbs.

QUADRUPEDS

The shape of the spine in quadrupeds is the first deviation from human anatomy because of the difference of posture. Its shape resembles a slightly curved arch, between the pelvis and shoulder girdle, and is not, like the human spine, S-shaped to balance the erect gait. Only the S-curve of the neck, composed with very few exceptions of seven vertebrae,

is repeated in quadrupeds. The sometimes considerable length of neck, in the giraffe, for instance, is due solely to the length of each vertabra. The vertebrae are never plastically noticeable in the neck, unlike those in the tail, which are a continuation of the spine beyond the pelvis. In human anatomy five vertebrae have grown together to form the os sacrum, but in most quadrupeds the more numerous vertebrae (many reptiles have up to 40) have remained mobile. The number of vertebrae in the back is greater in a number of animals; therefore the trunk is proportionately longer in animals than in humans.

It is important to study from the skeleton the line of the spine along the back in different animals in order to understand the arrangement and function of the pelvic and shoulder girdles. Unlike those of the human, their chest and loin vertebrae have very high projections. Thus, the outline of the back of an animal appears slightly S-shaped as it lifts over these projections at either end of the spinal arch. In felines this outline has a downward curve, like a span roof, which turns where the projections change in slope. The turn of this curve is again marked on the skeleton by a very short vertical projection. The peculiar alternation of slope in these projections prevents a reverse bend of the spine and gives a powerful spring mechanism to the back for jumping, worked by strong, straight muscles.

The typical conformation of the vertebral column in quadrupeds. Illustrated is the skeleton of a wolfhound

The fore- and hind legs of quadrupeds have different functions. The hind legs give the impetus and power to move forward; the forelegs primarily provide the main support for the greatest weight of the body, two thirds of which in the horse, for instance, rests on the forelegs. The mechanism of forward and backward movement in quadrupeds can be likened to a motor car with rear-wheel drive. Every quadruped begins a forward movement with a hind leg and immediately afterwards, almost simultaneously when running, moves the opposite foreleg forward to offset the change in gravity. A few animals move differently: the camel, for example, goes forward with both legs, first those of one side, then the other. This gait can be taught to horses in dressage, but is not natural to them.

The stance of animals at rest and mov-

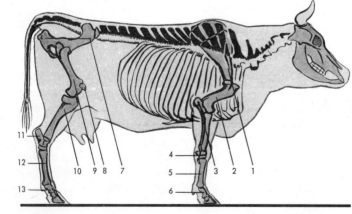

1. Scapula — 2. Upper arm — 3. Forearm — 4. Carpus — 5. Metacarpus — 6. Digit — 7. Pelvis — 8. Patella — 9. Thigh — 10. Shank — 11. Heelbone — 12. Metarsus — 13. Toe

Typical position of the spinous process in hoofed animals. Illustrated is the skeleton of a cow

ing is best understood by taking two lines of gravity, one running down the fore- and one down the hind leg—a system different from that of men and birds. Held for any length of time, it is un-natural if the two lines of gravity coin-cide. A horse's levade or a dog's up-right stance is a matter of training, but a horse that bucks or rears or a cat that stands up gives a momentary push to increase the weight of recoil against an obstacle which is thereby overthrown and whose resistance should, therefore, be taken into consideration as part of the equilibrium of the maneuver.

The position and build of the skeleton is naturally affected by the four-legged gait. Most quadrupeds walk on their toes, in contrast to humans, who walk on the soles of their feet, thus requiring a larger ground surface for balancing. It is an advantage for quadrupeds to touch the ground with the smallest pos-sible area, as this enables them to move off more quickly. Bears and monkeys walk on the soles of their feet and are much slower. The instep, affected by

this gait, has grown into a single bone. This, and the necessity to be always ready to jump in self-defense, has brought about the manifold bends, par-ticularly noticeable in the hind legs, which exist even in a position of rest. A sudden, powerful movement forward can be provided only by stretching the leg joints. A runner who needs to make a quick start waits in a crouched position for the starting gun. A frightened deer can give a bound from a position of rest. The beast of prey crouches for its leap, as will any cornered animal.

The bends in the foreleg are less visible from outside. At rest they are present only between the shoulder blade, short upper arm, and forearm. The upper arm lies inside the skin of the trunk, and the bends of the joints can be understood only by a study of the skele-ton. Drawings of animals often come to grief at this point. Elasticity of move-ment is much helped by the curve of the upper arm, which is much more flexibly attached to the trunk than the human arm, which, being used for work, re-

Typical position of the spinous process in animals of the cat family. Illustrated is the skeleton of a lioness

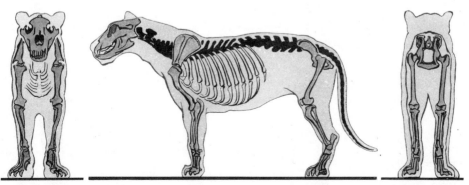

quires a stronger hold. The shoulder girdle in humans is still joined flexibly to the rib cage by the collar bone, but with very little mobility. Quadrupeds have no collar bone, which means that the shoulder blades are much more mobile. This is plainly visible in cats; at each step when they walk the shoulder blade rises as high as the withers. The collar bone is replaced by cords of sinewy muscle which are very supple and can act as brakes, like the springs of a shock absorber. Only animals which use their forelegs more for work than running have collar bones: monkeys, which climb, moles, which dig, and the kangaroo are among the few.

Where the forearm is more firmly attached with a collar bone, the joint of the limb is always more mobile, especially so in man. Quadrupeds who use the foreleg mainly for running and jumping do not need the rotary action of hip and shoulder; it would only require extra muscles to strengthen the scissor movement while they were running. Their shoulder and hip muscles work like hinge joints, and the limbs cannot move much sideways. This alters the structure of the pelvis. Herbivorous animals, which need to be able to run far, have a pelvis proportionally as wide as humans. Carnivores, which catch their prey by jumping, have a very narrow pelvis. The widest point is at the socket joints of the thigh bones. In horses and cattle the thigh sockets and hip bone knobs stand out equally. Beasts of prey also have much shorter necks than herbivores, which feed while walking and so are always bending their necks downwards.

In human anatomy we learned how a joint is held solely by muscular activity. It is tiring to stand for long, and even more so to remain with knees half bent. Quadrupeds, however, are in a position of rest with their knees half bent. Two other factors contribute to the tension of their joints: there are ligaments which hold them taut, and there is a slight

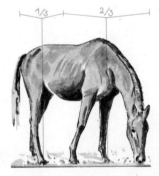

Left: Body balance shown by use of single plumb line

Right: Two plumb lines each with a different weight

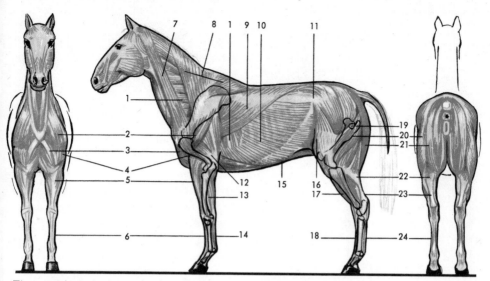

The most important muscles in a horse. In principle the same holds good for all quadrupeds. M = muscle.
1. Latero-serrak M — 2. Deltoid M — 3. Chest M — 4. Biceps — 5. Forearm (extensor) M — 6. Toe extensor tendon — 7. Annuent M — 8. Trapezius M — 9. Latissimus dorsi M — 10. Oblique abdominal M — 11. Anterior spine of the ilium — 12. Triceps — 13. Forearm (flexor) M — 14. Toe flexor — 15. Rectus abdominis — 16. Quadriceps extensor of the cannon — 17. Toe (foot) extensor — 18. Toe extensor tendon — 19. Greater trochanter — 20. Greater gluteal M — 21. Quadriceps flexor of the cannon — 22. Gastrocnemial M (triceps) — 23. Achilles' tendon — 24. Toe flexor

hollow on one side of the joint surfaces, and a corresponding convexity on the other, so that the two parts can rest against each other. The joints are held close by tendons, which are stretched only by muscular activity, causing the joint to move. This is why horses can stand all day without tiring, and why full-grown animals need never lie down and can even sleep standing up.

All animals, especially those with long necks, use the neck and head as a counterweight when walking. A horse nods its head constantly while it runs, both up and down and slightly sideways. The movement occurs mainly between the skull and the highest neck vertebra,

although the whole neck is brought into play to some extent. The tail also is used for balancing, although it is mainly a sort of rudder against wind resistance and serves horses and cattle as a fly whisk. Animals also give unconscious expression to their feelings with the tail. Dogs wag their tails when they are pleased, stick them up when they are aggressive, as do cats, and put them between their legs when they are afraid.

The pelvis of the elephant and giraffe falls steeply away from the horizontal backbone. It is flatter in the horse and flatter still in cattle. The drawings of skeletons show the differences of proportion and position of leg bones peculiar

Animal Anatomy

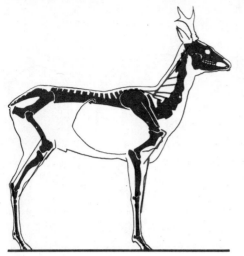

Skeleton of a roebuck. Example of braced tendons in extremities and neck

are in other respects similar to human feet. The soles of bears' feet are rough and grip the ground well, while monkeys' feet, which are adapted to tree climbing, developed like hands. The carnivore has to grip its prey; it developed thick pads which allow a quiet tread and protect the sharp claws from wearing away.

The front foot developed in a similar way. Only where there is some reason for the forepaw to twist around do the humerus and ulna exist and rotate around each other, as, for instance, in cats, which can give short side pushes. They can turn around only one eighth as much as the human forearm.

The human head rests its weight on the spine; relatively little muscular strength is needed to hold it in this upright position. But if the muscles are not working, the head drops to one side, as can be seen if someone falls asleep in a chair. In animals the head and neck must always be held stretched out, and this would entail vigorous activity and eventual fatigue if left to muscles alone. The head and neck are, therefore, held by a supple tendon running from the projections on the vertebrae of the chest to the back of the head. A plate of sinew runs from this tendon down to the neck vertebrae. If the animal bends its head down, it has to stetch the neck sinew by working the muscles; if it stops this muscular activity, the head springs back into its stretched out position. Old, work-worn horses sometimes hang their heads all the time because the sinew has lost some of its elasticity.

The shape of the skull is determined primarily by the relation between the

to each animal. In some animals the kneecap is grown together with the upper thighbone. Sometimes the shinbone has disappeared in part or completely. Both kneecap and shinbone are needed in humans for the twisting of the thighbone along its long axis. Where this is unnecessary in animals, these alterations, if we regard the human skeleton as the norm, take place.

In all toe-walkers the instep bones and heel bone have grown together or joined up, more completely in hoofed animals than in felines. The toes, too, have become one in hoofed animals, and a double hoof in cloven-footed animals. Carnivores still have all their toes. The double arch of the foot does not exist in any animals, not even in those which walk on their soles and whose feet

Gorilla

a profile line than in humans. The lower jaw has to adapt itself to the changed shape, and altogether the skull presents a profile roughly comparable to a pair of tongs. Animal skull shapes are widely varied according to their habits, particularly their manner of feeding. The position of the eyes is important. Monkeys and carnivores look straight ahead like humans. It can almost be said that the more defenseless the animal, the further its eyes are set to the side to enlarge the field of vision. A man, if he is concentrating, can see movement and color within a cone of about 90 degrees. He can see clearly only within an angle of 30 degrees. A rabbit when it rears up can see for 360 degrees—a complete circle.

brain case and the face, both in humans and animals. The brain case is relatively small in animals, and brow, nose, and upper jaw are in much less continuous

The aspect of an animal's head is much affected by the structure of its outer ear, and in some, too, by the formation of horns or antlers. The outer ear in

Brown bear

Head studies: Camel and striped gnu

humans and monkeys lies against the skull; most other animals have pointed, upright ears, although elephants, pigs, and some dogs have hanging ears. All outer ears are made of cartilage, but, unlike the human ear, they are very mobile. The ears of lynxes and squirrels have an added tuft of hair which makes them seem bigger.

Animals are far too different from each other to make a practicable scheme of proportions. The example given of the musculature of the horse can help the student to work out that of other animals. Parallels between human and animal skeletons and musculature should make understanding easier, for basically they are very similar, and a knowledge of their different requirements and habits explains the differences.

To draw an animal it is best to make a constructional sketch first, fixing the position of the backbone, leg bones, neck sinew, and skull, marking in the recognizable points of proportion: os sacrum, wither, knee and elbow, heel and foot. Next come the contours of the thorax and the straight stomach muscle, the hind leg, tail, and lower line of the neck. The sketch is finally developed with a more detailed outline of the head with the positions of the eyes and ears and the positions of nostrils and mouth, and, lastly, with a closer rendering of the structure and position of the feet (claws or hoofs).

Most animals are covered by a thick and relatively long fur, and unless the artist has an intimate and inborn knowledge of the animal's anatomy he will not get far using a purely impressionistic vision. The animal's coat should be described with texture-like strokes, unless paint is used, but even then the strokes should be made in the direction of the hair growth to give a realistic impression. The growth of the hairs is determined by the need for water to run off the animal as quickly as possible and to create the least wind resistance. In some places there are whirls and ridges or crests where the hair growth lies in different directions or meets.

The drawing and painting of animals has always been a subject of special interest, in the same way as portrait or flower painting. Even in modern art animals often occur and are frequently more attractive than other subjects treated. Perhaps the emphasis on the type in animal subjects has an appeal greater than the unnecessarily individual character of many other subjects.

Siamese cat

With modern zoological gardens, aquariums, and now underwater observation of animal life, the themes have increased in number. One group, however, seems to have been almost forgotten: birds.

Bengal tiger   Bison   Sea-elephant   Rhinoceros

Grecian tortoise

Young gorilla

Foal

BIRDS

The body of the bird, having only two legs, rests on a single line of gravity. The external shape of a bird is very different from that of its skeleton and soft anatomy, which make up its weight. Nevertheless, the external form has to be understood from the skeleton. The feathers are as important for flight as they are for a warm covering, and the wing and tail feathers, which serve to vary the weight distribution of the soft parts of the body to assist flight, do not follow the soft parts in their modeling as do the smaller down and covering feathers. The wing and tail feathers serve to continue the tensions of the thin muscles and tendons; hence the difficulty in reconciling the shapes of a live and a plucked bird. Only the beak, eyes, and legs are uncovered by feathers.

The usual mistakes made by children and beginners when drawing birds are due to the difficulty of seeing the position of the trunk, spine, and leg bones when they are all covered with feathers. In fact, the human skeleton is closer to the bird's than the quadruped's. The rest position of the bird is closely approximate to that of the human crouching on tiptoe, holding his arms close and bent, so that the hands are at the level of the armpits and hanging down. A bird's flight position can be imagined by the human spreading out his arms and pushing the edges of the hands backwards; a strong downward pull of the arms corresponds to a beat of the wings. Raising the arms is harder, but a bird is helped by air resistance against the fall of the body. A turn of the arms shows how the bird folds its wings.

The crouching position illustrated shows how the vertebrae, rib cage, and pelvis have become a single, though very elastic, bone structure in the bird. It does not need the flexible spine or shoulder girdle of the human skeleton, for the heavy work of the wings is better served by a firm support, and the strong beat downwards needs to lift the body as directly as possible, so that it is best rigid. The collar bones have become the solid forked wishbone, which has either grown into a single unit with the breastbone or is joined to it with strong sinew. The shoulder blades have become a narrow saber-shaped bone which often reaches as far back as the pelvis and is thus much restricted in movement. The breast muscles, the motors of flight, weigh as much in birds of flight as all the other muscles together. They are

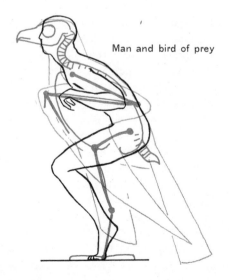

Man and bird of prey

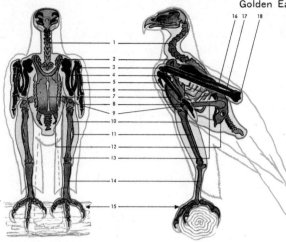

Golden Eagle

1. Atlas — 2. Furcula (collarbones) — 3. Carpus — 4. Upper arm — 5. Pollex — 6. metacarpus — 7. Sternal rib — 8. Forefinger — 9. Patella — 10. Tibia — 11. Fibula — 12. Pelvis — 13. Upper thigh — 14. Metatarsus — 15. Digits — 16. Radius — 17. Ulna — 18. Elbow joint

attached to a strongly protuberant piece of the breastbone, which is not present in birds which do not fly and which is smaller in swimming birds. All muscles other than those of the breast are very thin and model the trunk to an oval or teardrop shape which offers the minimum of wind resistance. The tail vertebrae do not need much mobility. The last of them have formed a flat plate to which the tail-steering feathers are attached, which, on the whole, point straight backwards. They, like all the feathers, are moved by skin muscles.

The neck vertebrae need greater mobility than in quadrupeds and humans. This is because the eyeballs are almost immobile in their sockets, and because of feeding habits. The number of vertebrae is greater: doves have 12, hens, ducks and birds of prey 13 or 14, geese up to 18, and swans sometimes have 25.

The vertebrae of the neck are surrounded by strong muscles, as those who eat game birds well know. The neck and head are not held with sinews, as in quadrupeds, but with muscles. This is why birds bend their necks in sleep or tuck their heads under their wings, so that the muscles are completely relaxed.

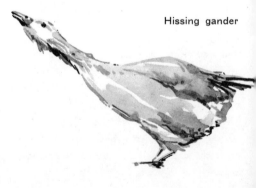

Hissing gander

The skull of the bird is unlike that of the quadruped or human. It consists mainly of eyes and beak. If a man had eyes of the same proportionate size as those of an eagle, they would be as large as tangerines; and of the great horned owl, even larger.

Bird's legs differ in the same way from human's as hoofed animals; only the toes remain. The very small thighbone when at rest is almost at right angles to the lower thighbone, and the shinbone is almost nonexistent. The instep has become a single bone, the bird's "leg." Generally, it has four toes attached to it, one of which points backwards. Climbing birds, like parrots, have two toes pointing backwards; in water birds they all point forwards. Many birds have only two toes; the African ostrich has three. The number of knuckles also varies. The toe pointing backwards has two, the inner, forward toe three, the second four, and the outer toe five. Whereas all the leg joints function like hinge joints, the two outer, forward toes have rotary joints, enabling them to be pulled towards the inner one.

The hip joint is still a ball joint, but it is so stiffened with tendons that an inward movement of the leg is possible to bring the leg under the line of gravity of the body, and in stepping forward the body can be moved in a straight line. More broadly built water birds cannot do this; they have to waddle, with inturned toes.

Head of peacock and turkey cock
Foot of webfooted bird, game bird, and song bird

The "arm" bones of the bird have been completely adapted for flight, but they still resemble human arms very closely, and even human hands. The humerus and ulna, however, have grown together at the ends and cannot rotate around each other but form a strong plate to which the arm pinions are attached. The wrist and finger bones have dwindled or disappeared completely, except for two extended bones of the first finger, which hold the hand pinions attached by a hinge joint which prevents the wing from bending too far either up or down.

The feathers present the draftsman and painter with a difficult problem if he does not wish to copy every detail naively and exactly. Basically, the feathers are a mass which, like a tiled roof, could be done with a texture; but this does not work, for the texture has to cover a relatively complex underlying form, and the difference of the feather's shape and its function must be made clear in places. There are two main types of feathers: the small, soft down feathers, which are indefinite in shape, and the covering, tail, and wing feathers, which are harder and clearer in shape. Down feathers, which provide warmth, correspond to the coat of quadrupeds. The covering feathers lie over the down and are more of a mechanical protection. Their size and definite shape make a clearly marked scaling which has to be reproduced lying correctly.

Every feather is composed of a quill and the feathering, which is made up of numerous small branches standing out flat to left and right of the upper part of the quill—symmetrically in the tail, covering, and down feathers, and asymmetrically in the wing pinions. The feathering of down is soft and curly, but on the others it is harder and cleverly toothed to form airproof plates. The narrower feathering of the wing pinions

Golden eagle in flight, showing disposition of feathers, seen from below. Feet omitted to make picture clearer. 1. Pinion — 2. Rudder-feather — 3. Down feather

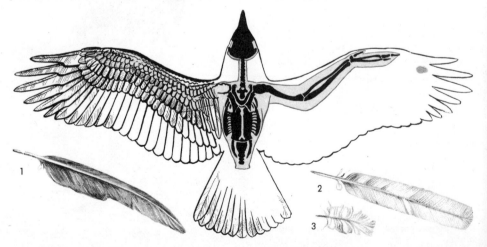

Bird of prey about to swoop

always points away from the body and overlaps like roof tiles, looking at the bird's back as a roof ridge. When the wing beats down, this layering causes the air to press the feathers together, and when the wing is lifted, they are opened, like the slats of a Venetian blind.

The wing and tail feathers serve to increase considerably the area of the bird's body when it is flying, without adding much to its weight. The shape of the bird when flying cannot be deduced from its bodily structure, but must be studied carefully in each case. Almost every bird has its characteristic flying shape.

The feathers are stuck at an angle into the skin at the lower end of the round quill and, like beak and claws, are extensions of the skin. They are moved by numerous small skin muscles, which can ruffle them and guide the movements of tail and wing feathers for steering.

Lastly, we should mention the decorative growth of feathers, crests, and unusually long tail feathers. They serve no practical purpose, but rather tend to restrict freedom of movement and flight. Other decorative skin forms are the strange combs and throat flaps on some birds.

Birds in all their variety of species have been used more than any other animals for ornamental stylization, especially emblems. The most interesting examples of naturalistic representation of birds are those of the ancient Egyptians, who solved the problem of reproducing feathers by drawing the most important tail and wing quills very exactly and leaving the others out, giving only the modeling or contour, but again putting in carefully observed details of eye, beak, and gait. Egyptian and Chinese wall paintings are full of fascinating, closely observed pictures of flight. In the Baroque and Rococo periods artists began to take an interest in the beauty of different species of birds and made delightful colored copper plate pictures of them, which are still the source of many lovely bird books. Might it not be a stimulating change from the eternal still lifes and bathing nudes to work on pictures of birds?

Cock

Kingfisher

Young sparrow

Crane

8. PLANTS

In drawing any plant, the principle of its growth must be understood in order to grasp the character of its outer form. No view of the whole is obtained from botanical analysis or the classification of small details, whatever wonders of nature these details disclose. In drawing a plant the most important thing is the first impression—what is seen at first glance—and the correct rendering of this characteristic appearance, whether it corresponds to a type-form or deviates individually from the type. Individual deviations are more quickly understood if the typical growths have been closely studied. This, of course, is most easily done with the largest plant structures, trees, rather than with the small ones. The principles of growth learned from the large plants are easily transferred to smaller ones, be they grass, flower tendril, or single leaf or petal. Thus, the artist, unlike the botanist, is concerned first with the large, immediately obvious form.

If we transpose our concepts of human anatomy to plants, then in trees and bushes the trunk, branches, and twigs correspond to the skeleton, and the leaves and flowers to the soft parts. The longer one considers this comparison the more fruitful it seems; the tree in leaf, like the human body, shows the shape of its skeleton only in part, although the peculiarities of its growth, called in plants "habitus," all derive from it. However, the foliage can alter the aspect of a tree much less than the soft tissues can change the appearance of a human. No tree suddenly becomes fatter or thinner; in a fixed position with a virtually constant climate and nourishment it will grow in the same way year after year, either strongly or poorly.

Yet, as always, comparisons should cease when they become lame, and principles should not be made too rigid. The life of plants follows rules different from those that govern mobile creatures. Their soft parts are organs, not muscles; their "skeleton" consists of vessels which have grown more or less rigid. These vessels naturally continue right into the organs, leaves and flowers, and they often repeat the same pattern of growth as the stem and its branches. The leaf simplifies this pattern to some extent and makes it an obvious ornament in a drawing. It is no wonder that leaves and flowers (which, in essence, are also made up of leaves) should have been so frequently used as subjects for decorative ornament. The type of leaf used often characterizes a whole style of ornament: acanthus for the Corinthian, vine and ivy leaves for the Gothic, and the water lily with its long, wavy stem for Art Nouveau. These are only a few examples, all of which used mainly graphic forms, even though they were carried out in relief. Plant forms were, of course, also used in the round; the most impres-

Plants

Acanthus   Vine leaf   Ivy   Water lily

sive example is, perhaps, the columbine shape used in the Renaissance.

The branch formation of a plant can be seen in a simplified, two-dimensional form in the veining of its leaf. The skeleton of a leaf is very similar in design to a bare tree, or to flowers and grasses which are stripped of their green. These general types of growth formation should be understood by the artist before he studies individual forms. Without this understanding two mistakes often occur: either both typical and individual shapes are bungled and what should be a tree looks like a birch broom standing upright decked out with cotton wool, or so much

Tree silhouettes

attention is given to the type-form each time that the characteristics of the particular plant being drawn are overlooked. In either case the result looks amateurish.

Drawing a tree means, up to a point, drawing its portrait, and the surest way to success is the "constructive," not the impressionistic, approach. First, there is the general line of the central trunk below the branches. As soon as a major limb branches off, however, the whole trunk usually changes its direction slightly. It bends away from the branch, just as the human body bends to adjust its equilibrium if the weight is put on one side. This is the rule for all trees with alternating branches, apart from a few individual exceptions, or where conditions of growth force a deviation from the rule. The majority of trees in the European and American landscapes grow to this pattern. The zig-zag growth of the trunk with alternating branches is always seen in saplings and is repeated in the leaf arrangement. The twigs do not grow on a plane with the bough or trunk but are grouped spirally around it.

As the tree ages and becomes thicker, the zig-zag tendency becomes less noticeable. Twigs break off or grow irregularly, so that a static symmetry is no longer necessary. As the trunk thickens, the distance between the offshoots

Copper beech

Fir trees

becomes smaller. Sometimes, too, the horizontal ground level develops a slope, and the trunk has to go with it; the upper part will tend towards the vertical again and give a general curve to the trunk. It may be that continuous washing away of soil around the roots makes the tree grow crooked from the beginning, and the weight of the trunk and branches prevents its righting itself to the vertical. This condition is often seen beside water, particularly in willows, some species of which have an additional tendency to grow strange bends and curves in trunk and boughs. If the main trunk is broken off while the tree is young, two or more main stems generally form, and it looks as though several trees were growing from one thick trunk. Through such ob-

servations much can be learned of the history of a tree from its growth and deviations from the normal habitus; it has to grow in situ, whatever changes occur in its environment, and adapt itself to these changes.

Among the commoners trees in Europe, only the maple, horse chestnut, and oak have paired branches, and, of course, the conifers, which each year produce a new whorl of twigs at the top of the main stem. For obvious reasons these trees all grow straight, especially the conifers. Their branches always remain relatively small compared to the main stem, whereas the oak, consistent with its compact shape and slower growth, forms branches hardly thinner than the trunk, and when the tree is full grown it

View of pine wood

cannot spread out, and there is not light enough for their leaves. If one of these trees remains standing when a wood has been cut down, it looks most unnatural. Constant strong winds from the same direction can also make a tree look unnatural, with branches growing only to the leeward side. This happens mostly near or on the tops of mountains or where the wind has a long unbroken run.

Even if trees are thickly covered in leaves, their trunks and branches are discernible to some extent. A general impression of a tree in leaf is best caught on paper by following through the branches where they can be seen. It is their growth that fixes the "likeness," for in a picture of a whole tree it will rarely be possible to reproduce the individual leaf shape of the various species. To help the student we have illustrated a few schematic renderings of particularly characteristic tree shapes. An understanding of how trees grow, be-

is often impossible to distinguish the trunk amid the maze of branches at the top. Another reason for this is that the main stem of a young oak breaks very easily; this is also the case with fir trees. As a rule the oak does not grow so straight as it gets older; also the trunk gets thicker, and the branches tend to grow more strongly than the trunk.

A thick wood is the best environment for straight, regular growth. The need for light makes the stem grow as vertically as possible, and as the top grows higher the lower branches die off. They

Japanese quince

sides preventing elementary mistakes in drawing them, will give the student a better sense of the character of a landscape. A tree, unlike a single flower, is hardly a subject which calls for isolated depiction apart from its surroundings.

Leaves or conifer needles can be seen only as a mass, best reproduced with a suitable texture. Both leaf shape and density of foliage are characteristic of a tree. An oak with its notched leaves is very different from a beech with elliptical leaf shapes, but both have dense foliage, in contrast to birch or willow.

It is very interesting to work out a texture suitable for leaves in varying light conditions. Photographs can be traced lightly by the beginner to help him see his way into the problem, although he should always devote most of his time to studies from life. As with all textures which render a mass of living or organic detail in three dimensions, it is best to use

Maple

Apple tree

the "trick" of picking out a few areas for exact delineation and merging them into a general toned surface. The beholder unconsciously associates the whole background texture with the part that is detailed. The bark is another area where texture is important. As with the texture for leaves, it must arise from individual observation, and once worked out is more effective if most of the area is merely indicated by shading rather than filled in pedantically in every corner. However, bark must be carefully observed; a vague, lifeless impression is not sufficient.

Lime tree

Grasses

As in politics and everyday life, the greater the understanding, the less the necessity for a display of knowledge. In drawing this is realized by a knowledge of the shapes and a mastery of expression. A quiet, discreet word with the authority of knowledge behind it is always more impressive than a full-scale explanation. Even if a wood is depicted as a whole it is well worthwhile putting in here and there a carefully observed leaf or patch of bark to give precision to the total effect. It is this approach which will make the larch wood seem satin soft, or the greenery of a pine wood clearing scrubby and prickly, so that the beholder will almost hear the wind in the tops of the trees, the rustle of birch leaves, or the sighing of the wind in the willows by the stream. This can come about only

if the artist's intention is precise. How this intention is communicated does not matter; it may be in terms of complete abstraction. Whatever the means, they are most effective when they are discreet and simple—they should never tell a tale of laborious toil. It will require a great deal of time for the student to make leaf textures like the Chinese with their thousand-year-old brush technique.

After studying trees, there will not be many problems in drawing bushes and shrubs. Many trees exist in the form of bushes, and other true shrubs, except for the difference in the proportion of branches to leaves, are like miniature trees or tree tops. To show the difference, a larger leaf texture is drawn on finer branches, emphasizing the smaller size of the plant.

Thorn apple

Oak

Artists have always paid much attention to the shapes of flowers and leaves. They should not be copied unthinkingly; each type should be studied for its basic form, especially in order to understand and interpret the perspective and foreshortening correctly. This is much more important with small plants seen at close range than with trees, which, at the distance necessary to see them, appear much more as silhouettes. If, for example, a drawing is made of a bluebell or a sunflower, it should not resemble a botanical study, which would display as much detail as possible frontally, but instead be a living picture characterizing the personality of the plant with all the grace peculiar to its nature.

It is not usual to draw flowers in their natural surroundings, unless, like Dürer's columbines and grasses, they are dug up in a great clump of earth. Then, the results seem less like pictures than botanical studies, even more so if the flower is left in its environment and rendered as a detail against surroundings which are represented by a texture. Photographers do this by showing a flower in its habitat and blurring the surroundings to emphasize the subject. To leave everything in focus would make the whole picture too dazzling. The eye itself looking at real flowers selects one on which to focus.

If a student is interested in flower drawing or painting he cannot do better

Martagon

Chrysanthemum

than take the Chinese as his model. He will learn from them how to give himself up completely to the particular individual form after having mastered the basic form of the type. There is an anecdote about a Chinese chrysanthemum grower which should be pondered in this connection: the Emperor heard of a famous garden and announced that he would visit it. When he arrived the garden had been flattened to a smooth gravel surface. But in the gardener's house, in a precious porcelain vase, stood one single chrysanthemum, the most beautiful out of the whole garden.

Unfortunately, there are many flower pictures which remind one of the dictum of Grünhagen, a tireless and delightful painter of the changing seasons: "Three primroses in a glass are shapely beings, spreading an aura of mystery, but three hundred are nothing but an amorphous blur."

Ever since man began to theorize about art he has assumed that the man-made dwelling place first made conscious artistic activity possible. This is true, for although the cave paintings were made at a time when men did **not** build dwelling places, prehistoric cave art is a solitary phenomenon. All pictorial and plastic arts are nowadays connected in some way with the man-built dwelling house.

Architecture forms a part of the subject matter of the great majority of paintings and drawings. More than this, a whole branch of painting has adopted the building itself as its subject. Although it had originally no other object than to reproduce the impression of splendor given by a town (splendid in comparison with untouched nature, then considered "raw"), the prominent architectural painters also included much of the at-mosphere of contemporary life in their pictures. Today, architectural painting has been almost entirely replaced by photography.

Some knowledge of building technique is indispensable for anyone who depicts architecture, whether as a primary subject or as a background for figures, just as he needs a knowledge of the surface anatomy of human, animal, and plant life if he is to understand the forms he observes and reproduce them intelligently.

Architecture deals with man-made structures, but its methods are based on natural laws and natural conditions, in particular the laws of gravity and the nature of the materials used. The measurements are man made, adapted to man's size and ways of movement. Thus, ancient classical architecture was based on the golden mean.

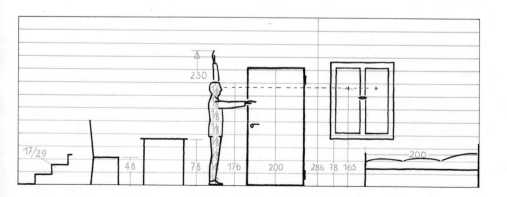

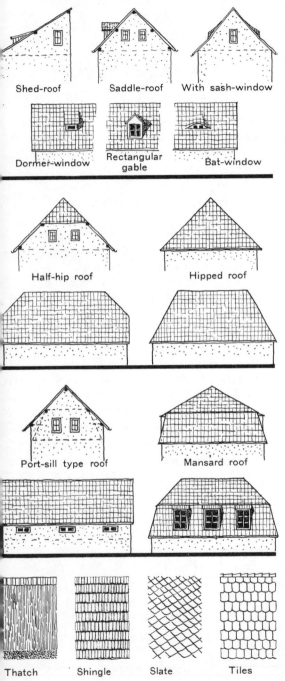

Shed-roof Saddle-roof With sash-window

Dormer-window Rectangular gable Bat-window

Half-hip roof Hipped roof

Port-sill type roof Mansard roof

Thatch Shingle Slate Tiles

When drawing buildings the human scale must be considered, or the figures will appear gigantic like Gulliver in Lilliput or minute like Gulliver in Brobdingnag. A few basic measurements should be remembered to prevent elementary mistakes; or, rather than relying on numerical figures, it may be easier to retain in the memory a scheme like the one illustrated as a reference to scale. If these few proportions are borne in mind, the building will turn out properly as a whole.

The building material by its nature dictates certain proportions. A wooden beam cannot extend farther than twelve or fifteen feet unsupported; beyond that it would bend or even break. Used as a pillar, wood must have a certain thickness in relation to its length or it will bend in. Other materials dictate other uses, but their peculiarities are much more obtrusive than those of the ideal building material, wood. Stone has a stronger resistance to pressure, but little tensile strength, and reinforced concrete is now used instead. Concrete gives resistance to pressure, and steel reinforcement adds resistance to strain. The material used also dictates the construction technique. The opposed diagrams in the illustrations show how each material must be used according to its nature. The roof needs special consideration; it is often drawn quite incorrectly. Naive observation is not always enough. When the main structural forms are understood, it will be easier to understand the peculiarities of an unusual roof or to follow the logic of its construction.

The general structure of a building is determined, according to the laws of gravity, by horizontals and verticals. A building with leaning walls must fall sooner or later. The eye feels this unconsciously and seeks out horizontal and vertical relations, even when they are not structurally necessary. The eye derives satisfaction if the axes of the windows lie vertically one above the other and the sills and lintels run in horizontal lines. If an architect disregards this convention he must introduce other optical lines of relationship to emphasize stability—for example, lines running right across the wall.

A building corresponds better with the laws of gravity if it narrows towards the top and the walls press together inwards rather than pulling apart outwards. This is also a matter of construction, for walls are built thinner as they get higher, as they have less weight to bear at the top, and also thus reducing the weight on the lower walls. This is seen clearly on towers and other high buildings. Another way of reducing the weight is to make larger or more windows on upper stories. On Gothic towers the roof-like spires become exquisite pierced filigree.

Much of the pleasure we derive from the best drawings and paintings of architecture is due to the workmanlike knowledge of the artists, who have not considered it beneath them to study the craft as well as the aesthetics of building. The views of towns by Bernardo Belotto (1720-1780), nephew and pupil of Canaletto and court painter to the King of Poland, are fully satisfying artistically, and, furthermore, they were technically adequate to be used alone for the rebuilding of some of the historic buildings of Warsaw, the plans having disappeared.

RIGHT WRONG

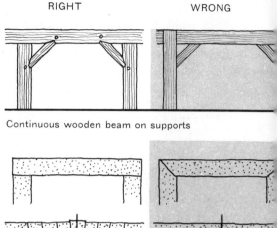

Continuous wooden beam on supports

Window or door frame of stone

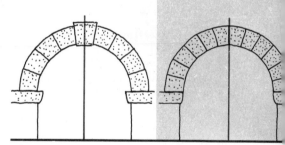

Round arch of beveled stone

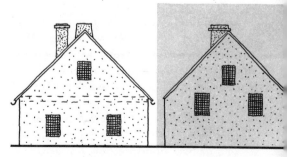

Arrangement of chimney stack and windows

173

Impressionistic effect obtained by applying Chinese ink with injector

Pen and brush

Of course the representation of a building as a picture has a purpose different from an architect's drawing. The picture need only create the illusion of the complete building, whereas an architect's scale drawing sacrifices illusion for exact detail and precise indication of forms. A picture will reproduce exactly only here and there, being concerned with an over-all impression; just as when we look at a building, even with great concentration, we do not see every detail with the same precision. The volute of a capital or the profile of a moulding or a gateway can merge into vagueness while the effect of precision remains. If the study were rendered in every detail, the general effect would be lessened, for the beholder can work out details in his imagination far more harmoniously than it could be done in fact.

Generally, old buildings are chosen for pictures which are primarily architectural in subject, but the picturesque appeal of modern buildings, cubist blocks of apartments with their bright colors and clean lines, should not be rejected out of hand. Surely the spirit of our time is fully expressed in these buildings. There is no dreamy atmosphere of contemplation, no coziness, but a challenging background to a life of restlessness, change, and activity. Yet modern forms have a charm of their own: driving through a town in a car as dusk falls on a wet November evening, the streets lie in a blue haze, the first bright lights are reflected in the wet asphalt, sulphurous clouds dissolve into the pink and gray haze of the horizon, and the car is nothing but an atom in all the bustle of the town. Here, surely, is an experience which can inspire the artist.

Architectural lead pencil study with touches of watercolor added

10. LANDSCAPE

In a landscape all the subjects we have studied in isolation are brought together: plants and animals, people and buildings; but the determining factors in a landscape are the form of the earth's surface, and the sky above it with its colors, clouds, mists and stars.

As with all solid things, the form of the earth can be made intelligible only through the medium of perspective. Linear perspective is the principal means, with its reduction in the scale of things as they approach the horizon. But a straight path with its sides running to a vanishing point indicates space and distance whether the land is rising or falling away. As in drawing buildings it must be related to other lines running parallel to it (cf. p. 49). If the path winds or rises and falls alternately it implies the rise and fall of the surrounding land. If it disappears and rises again the reduction in its breadth when it reappears shows how far away it has now run from the beholder, how far the landscape stretches. Fields and patches of woodland are useful in the same way because of the deviation from normal perspective caused by the undulations in the ground.

If a small tree is drawn near to a large one of the same kind, the effect will be to imply distance between them, although in fact trees of the same species can vary greatly in size. To make the real difference in size clear, the foliage of both trees must be given with the same texture and shown to be of the same size, for the size of leaves does not vary with the size of the tree.

Relative size modified by use of figures (duck, fishing vessel)

Landscape showing road and landscape divisions and indicating earth formation (Stabilo colored crayon)

Even though all the usual methods of perspective can be used to give an illusion of space and distance—gradations of size, heavy drawing against faint, dark areas against light—it is impossible for the earth formation by itself to give an indication of the scale of the scene. Even trees, as has just been shown, cannot always serve to do this. Only accessories of clearly defined size can perform this function unequivocally, such as people and animals, or buildings, which are always related to the human scale by the size of their windows and doors. Very often figures are added to a picture at the end to give the scale of the landscape. It is amusing to recall how in the Baroque period many landscape painters had to employ specialists to put in the figures for them, as they could not manage them themselves. Two examples in the illustration show the same earth formation with a different scale indicated by a single feature, the duck in one, reducing it, and the boat in the other, enlarging it.

Shadow perspective can also be ambiguous in a landscape. Cloud shadows are deceptive, and towards the horizon the haze of the atmosphere completely eliminates the modeling of mountain, tree or building. A mountain mass of great depth looks like a wall, trees become as flat as stage scenery, and the sea of houses in a distant town is nothing more than a flat silhouette. But the outline of a silhouette is sharpened by distance and the illusion of recession in space is associated with it. The same impression arises whenever these outlines

Misty winter's morning, paste and watercolor

become less clear, as through a mist or flickering light.

Color perspective in a landscape is much more reliable. What we have said so far applies principally to the graphic reproduction of landscape. Colors can give it a sense of breadth or of being closed in, without either figures to give a scale or vanishing points (color perspective p. 353). Usually, however, both linear and color perspective are used in a colored rendering of a landscape, as in all other types of painting.

To make the formation of the land in the picture really convincing it helps to imagine it first without foreshortening, spread out as in an aerial view. Children drawing an imaginary landscape do this, making the whole picture appear as

though it were on a steep slope facing the artist across a steep valley, but this is not what we mean! The artist should embrace the whole hill or tree in his mind just as he holds a vase or jug on the table, sensing its three-dimensional shape. Then when he draws his landscape with a normal position for the horizon he can better understand the implications. There must be a sense of space between the near and far objects. This is helped, for instance, by breaking the outline that joins something near and something far together on the skyline or nearer, either simply by broken lines in the drawing or by a color contrast. This may seem like a trick, and admittedly it is one. It is a trick used most often by the greatest of all landscape painters, the Chinese. There is all the difference between a trick used as a formula, and one which expresses a thought, or rather which is occasioned by a feeling—here the feeling of space. Space is the foundation of the landscape's being, just as a flat surface is that of a picture's, and once the artist has really felt the space in his landscape he can use well-tried conventions like those suggested without becoming mechanical; they will be something very different in his hands from an imitated trick.

The most intense way to experience a landscape is to walk alone and quietly, stopping whenever the eye is caught by something and noting it without any particular picture in mind, perhaps just memorizing it, like the classical Chinese and Japanese painters. Most of the great landscape painters of the pre-Impressionist era, such as Turner or the great German Romantic, Caspar David Friedrich, painted their landscapes in the

Study in pencil and watercolors, a landscape in the Giant Mountains

studio from quick notes made on the spot. These notes, made in pencil, chalk, or wash, did not attempt to render color or atmosphere; for this the artist relied on his memory. Though their landscapes are usually given exact topographical titles, none of the places is rendered literally; yet, as portraits of the landscape one feels that they are closer in "likeness" and atmosphere than if they had been copied exactly. The author has spent most of his life in the Riesengebirge in Sudetenland where Caspar David Friedrich worked, and although hardly a line tallies exactly, he can vouch for the atmosphere of the district in the pictures being unmistakable, and the impact of the pictures as strong as the landscape itself. For landscape in its highest artistic form expresses in the most absolute way a psychological condition, a mood,

closely comparable to the feelings experienced in hearing music. It hardly needs saying that this experience need not be "romantic" in character, a much abused word which has thus come into some disrepute. When Kokoschka painted Hamburg, or Monet painted the Houses of Parliament at Westminster the result is no less "romantic" an interpretation than that produced by painters who work more from their imagination, or in a romantic style (such as Friedrich in his **Die Sieben Gründe** of the Bohemian Riesengebirge).

The author used to live near a wild parkland which was a famous beauty spot. From early spring to late in the autumn painters could be met there. They set out on the day after their arrival looking for "subjects," stopping every few yards to find pleasing or striking views. They churned out whole series of pictures, often very able impressions of the subject, then hurried back to town and handed the paintings over with the paint hardly dry on them to the greedily waiting dealers, who, as the painters boasted without shame, sold them "like hot cakes." The pictures filled up empty spaces on the walls of the "best" houses, whose owners could then boast of having a "Nowak" or a "Vollmer," or whatever the name of the painter in vogue at the time might be. (In the same way they "went to the opera," never to Tosca or the Magic Flute.) This ham stuff was hardly more than enlarged picture postcards, copied views, with nothing in them of a creative vision, of impressions drawn from a real feeling into the landscape.

What a difference from Breughel's **Winter Scene** or Van Gogh's **Cornfield!**

It is strange, in this period of experiment and exploration of new subjects which lie beyond the boundaries of pictorial representation, that so few artists have attempted aerial views of landscape. Many people see it much more frequently today from the air than they do from walking in it. Nothing can be seen from a motor car, since the road ahead has to be stared at, and from a train it is rarely possible to achieve the quiet enjoyment that an airplane provides. From a height, the most broken landscape is flattened into a carpet; the picture plane is there already. Surely the airplane provides a great source of unexplored subjects, all strange and dreamlike.

Aerial view, chalk and red crayon

Pencil study of varied objects and shapes

11. STILL LIFE

Again in still life we bring together subjects which have already been treated separately: plants, animals, and objects. As in landscape, the separate objects are not there for themselves; the significance of a still life lies in their combination. The usual combinations of subjects in a still life are of interest primarily to painters, not draftsmen. The concept must be extended to include all the obviously chance combinations which are of constant interest to draftsmen, such as dented metal jugs in a corner, a hole in the ground, a dead bird.

The difference between the painter's still life and the draftsman's consists, without any inner reason, in the difference between the deliberate combination and the chance find.

Here arises the problem of the purpose of a still life. The French call it **nature morte**, which is less telling than the English concept of still, secret, and outwardly unmoving life. The term is derived from the Dutch **Stilleven** and was adopted by art historians in the eighteenth century. A still life is concerned with, one might say, the helpless, unconscious existence of things, whether they are really dead material or partake of the continuous life of a flower, a fruit, and, if we see more closely, of a dead animal, too.

The classical still life painting, pictures of flowers, hunting trophies, or fruit pieces, as they are called in dealer's parlance, arise from the painter's delight in his ability, his technical self-satisfaction. It is a piece of virtuosity, like elaborate compositions played by virtuoso pianists and violinists, or the florid passages sung by a coloratura, with nothing particular outside itself to communicate. In such pieces the artist at last finds the opportunity to show off his brilliant technique. It is no different with the purely painterly charm of the still lifes of the seventeenth and eighteenth centuries: a complete contrast to the **Piece of Lawn** of Dürer or the **Sunflowers** of Van Gogh, where all thought of the technique of the master is forgotten in sympathetic contemplation of the existence of these small things.

A composed still life is a useful way of practicing composition and studying painterly effects, different materials, the changes of color in light and shade, and their use for harmony or dissonance, and trying out combinations of different strong colors or emphasizing one dominant color with subordinate or complementary tones. Sometimes under the hand of a great master these technical exercises produce works of art.

The still life based on the chance find is something else. A pair of old shoes thrown away and forgotten may cause the artist to seize his pencil; and while the open seam, twisted leather, and torn soles may present interesting problems of form and interpretation, his imagination may be inspired by the amusing or tragic implications of the subject. The beholder of the drawing will certainly respond in this way. Thus, it is usually "ugly" things that interest the draftsman, what is forgotten and, for the former owner, long since dead. These things would probably mean nothing to the artist while they were bright and new with no patina of use and age. The charm comes not alone from what is picturesque, but also from a feeling for recording small things for their own sake,

Having thought of a still life in this way, the student may approach the incidental objects in a picture with a higher intention; in fact, a picture of quite a different subject often contains still life as an accessory. Dutch paintings of the seventeenth century should be examined for this. In the portrait of Georg Gisze by Holbein the loving inclusion of the many small still life objects enhances the extraordinary clarity of the face.

Same objects as in previous illustration, arranged for a study in color (glue colors)

Toulouse-Lautrec, Self-portrait (caricature)

12. CARICATURE

We have so far treated our aim in drawing as reproducing what we see as nearly as possible to nature. This is the only sure and secure foundation on which to branch out into exaggeration and distortion and on which to start artistic creation. This is a valid foundation for caricature as well, but here we have to move on to the second and last stage, that of creation.

First, we must explain what we mean by caricature. The word first brings to mind the witty drawing, which has so many uses: the illustration to a literary joke, social or political satire, advertisement. No academic training is necessary to produce this, as long as the drawing is not required to caricature a particular person. Many cartoonists, and by no means the worst, use the same figure again and again, of the kind that a child could soon learn to copy. Here the talent of the draftsman lies less in manual dexterity than in the brilliance of his literary concept. Even the satirical drawings of men of great ability like Goya, Daumier, Chodowiecki or Doré are not really caricatures, but very representative and typical figures with portrait-like features.

What we mean here by caricature arises from the portrait of a definite individual, portrayed as a person and not as a general type. Portrait caricature of this type demands great ability; it is also the clearest example of how something can be created out of a carefully understood natural form by the power of the artist to see into the essential nature of the person.

Many paths can lead to this insight, but its pictorial presentation depends on

Caricature

Portrait studies used in drawing the caricature on the right

two things: the most precise pinpointing of the characteristic forms of the face, and their exaggeration. Both of these can be emphasized with the pose and gesture of the whole figure. It can be approached from two extremes, as can nearly all artistic creation, either from the visual experience and impression of what is immediately seen, or from a knowledge of human peculiarities, weaknesses, and strengths, in short, an impression of the artist's psychological experience of the person. This portrait approach could arise without the artist ever having seen the person, and it is conceivable that a caricature could be made without ever having seen the subject, although it might then have to be provided with a title.

Here, however, we are dealing with a caricature portrait that can be recognized without a title. It is built on characteristic forms. If he starts from a visual impression, the artist will ask himself what this or that form or line signifies, whether this aspect is typical or not, whether the person's nature—helped here by his knowledge of anatomy and physiognomy—is to be found in this or that peculiarity, and what is essential, what subsidiary.

Starting from the psychological idea, the artist will seek formal structures which can express it. He must not alter forms consciously, but rather work with what is to be seen. His psychological impression will guide him in what he selects to emphasize and what he rejects. Usu-

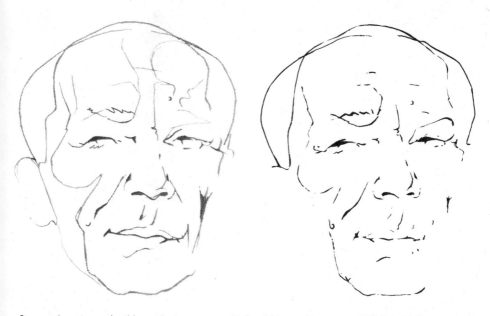

Successive stages in this caricature were obtained by tracing the portrait study seen from the front. It is that of an eminent surgeon. Like many great doctors, he employed sarcasm to ward off the absurdities of his patients

ally, of course, he will use both visual and psychological approaches. A significant caricature can arise only from an all-around idea, and it is irrelevant whether it appears immediately or grows slowly. This idea cannot be forced, but much can be done to help its growth.

Here the author illustrates a systematic reduction of a portrait to caricature as the idea takes shape. First comes a portrait study, or, better still, several. Over them he lays tracing paper and redraws the forms, already beginning to select and emphasize certain features. These tracings can be made again and again, or one can start at the beginning and draw a final caricature direct from the

model or from memory. Systematic work of this kind, which can be varied in a number of ways, is always of some value; it may result in a brilliant portrait or it may fail. Nothing can be won without trying, and systematic work is the best way to try. Even if the result is a failure, the practice is its own reward.

All this indicates that genuine caricature cannot be a sideline. It is a branch of fine art, demanding specialization and a grounding in straightforward portraiture which uncritically contains all that can be seen. Unless the artist can dominate nature, he will be unable to create, emphasize, or exaggerate.

13. LETTERING

Every artist must at some time or another come to grips with the problem of lettering, however little inclination he may feel for it. Lettering has little to do directly with artistic drawing, although, as we know, they were originally connected, since all writing derived from simplified pictures.

These pictures first signified whole words; they were then simplified and gradually came to represent abstract syllables, until in the final stage of development each individual letter represented only a sound. Apart from the Chinese, the writing of all civilizations has evolved in this way.

Roman capitals have been the basis for all writing in the Western world since about 500 A.D., at which time they were already over 1000 years old. They were used primarily for monument inscriptions which were incised into the stone after first being drawn on with a

SINEMATR

flat brush.

Alongside the Roman capital developed the faster and more flowing commercial hand. The small letters with their up and down projections (called "ascenders" and "descenders") evolved gradually from the habit of running the capitals together. The letters were sloped forwards to aid fluency, and the cursive script resulted.

The proportions of the Roman capital letter, the "capitalis quadrata," are based on a square. By turning the square into an upright quadrilateral the

porabar inmanib: fuif

"capitalis rustica," a narrow, cursive capital hand, was evolved. Numerous mixed alphabets grew out of these, which took on characteristic forms in different regions and countries. Among them was the special German or "black letter" alphabet which, following the usual Gothic stylization, broke up many of the curves

SUNTETSPIRITI

into angles, resulting in the Fraktur or "pointed" text. With the invention of printing, three basic ways of writing are differentiated: the printed alphabet composed of isolated metal letters, the drawn alphabet, and the written alpha-

Sat̃e Mihael arc̃hangele·De=

bet. The drawn is, of course, that which most concerns the artist and the one to which the other two owe their origin.

Every drawn alphabet derives from a group of geometric figures: a rectangle, which was originally always a square, a triangle, and a circle. The rectangle can vary a great deal in proportion, and the circle can become correspondingly elliptical, while the triangle also can vary in shape. In all good lettering these geometric figures remain in a definite relation to each other and can be combined into a basic skeleton shape, which we may call the prototype figure. Each style or alphabet has its characteristic prototype figure (from which the key letters O, H, and V are immediately derived and to which the remaining letters relate).

The prototype figure, however, does no more than determine the shapes of the individual letters and does not affect the word or line formation. The arrangement of letters in words, and of words in lines, has to obey a certain rhythm. It must be as monotonous as possible in order to emphasize the evenness of the lettering and at the same time give a compact unity to the text. Monotony in word and line rhythm also prevents the reader from being distracted from his subject matter and makes reading easy and fluent. Above all, the forms of the individual letters must be clear and simple.

Clarity results automatically from the prototype, which is based on the shape of the rectangle. This, without going to extremes and producing a hardly legible text, can vary from a square to an upright rectangle with a 1:4 width-height relationship. If this proportion is expressed as 2:8, it is easier to divide the proportions of the letters by eye according to the golden mean, as we learned when drawing the human body. In lettering, the golden mean is, once again, the most satisfactory proportion. Here we can only outline the elements of letter construction. Writing and lettering is a special field in which expertness is gained only by much practice. Real

mastery is a special gift, which, like every talent, reveals itself through an unusual predilection for the subject.

To make this exercise easier it is advisable to use squared paper. First draw an upright rectangle of 5 x 8 units, and divide it diagonally in both directions; then, as illustrated, draw in the ellipse. This is the basic proportion, the prototype, for capitals, which gives the construction of C, L, N, O, Q, and Z. By quartering the figure we get E, F, H, T, K, and Y. (E and F seem disproportionately broad, but in certain technical alphabets, which must be constructed with ruler, set square, and compasses, they are allowed to remain so. In the next stage it will be seen that they are normally altered to a more pleasing proportion. These mechanically constructed alphabets do not even use the ellipse, but instead join half circles with straight lines.)

Lines joining the centers of the top and bottom of the rectangle diagonally to the opposite corners give the two triangles which make A and V; and, when doubled, M and W. The C is made by cutting the ellipse where it meets the diagonals, and the G is made in the same way, both letters thus not filling the rectangle completely. All the other letters are narrower still. The E, F, and T can now be given their correct widths. The D is half the ellipse, plus an additional eighth, with a vertical. The other letters are formed using circles and half circles with a diameter of four units. Better proportions can be given to the R and B if they, too, have at least one added width unit; otherwise they would appear too narrow.

At this stage we are moving well

beyond the scope of rigid mechanical construction; creative lettering is more than measuring and logic. Nevertheless, the skeleton, the proportion of the golden mean, must not be forgotten. As we develop a more sensitively designed letter, it will be found that many have a center that differs considerably from the geometric center of the rectangle. In B, D, F, G, H, P, and R, the central horizontal is slightly above the geometric center, the lower part of the letter thus being rather bigger than the upper to give greater stability.

In K and Y the juncture of the diagonals is similarly altered. In S and B the two half circles are of different diameters. There remain J and U, which are made respectively of a half and quarter circle across five units.

We now must decide whether to keep each letter as a schematic shape built up of uniform elements, or whether to consider each letter individually. Experience teaches that individually designed letters are more quickly and easily read than those built up schematically. The latter emphasize the regularity of the rhythm, but other artifices can be used to recover this so that in artistic lettering one is able to concentrate on the individual shape of each letter. W and M are the most obvious examples. They are much pleasanter and more legible if they are narrowed by making the two outer strokes tend more toward the vertical than the inner ones. Two very simple and legible forms can be drawn directly from the basic rectangle, but their shapes are not attractive. The illustrations show how to find satisfactory proportions from diagonals within the rectangle, and other values from divisions according to the golden section. In the end we come to quite imponderable alterations, since no good writing is made from uniformly very thin lines. Either we make block letters with uniform thick lines, or we use a flat brush or broad nib to combine thick and thin lines. Serifs can be added to these. All these resources change the balance of the letters, so that the artist's sensitivity must be brought into play as the deciding factor.

A 3 x 5 unit rectangle for the small letters, in printing called lower case, can be derived from the original 5 x 8 rectangle. Ascenders and descenders, such as the "tails" of p and d, stand in a 3:5 relation to the average height. The 5:3 relation has already been used for the horizontal line in capital A, and small letters use the 3:5 relation in the same way as the 5:8 principle was used for the capitals. If necessary, the descenders and ascenders can be reduced to two units. The relation would then still be within the golden mean, though at the primitive level of 3:2.

Numbers, as the illustration shows, are developed on the same principle as letters from the prototype figure, but with more opportunities for variation. Which style is chosen is a matter of taste, but it should be constant for both letters and numbers and not mixed.

One should always aim for a regular rhythm in the structure of word, line, or paragraph. To be absolutely regular it would of course have to be composed entirely of strokes at the same angle and of shapes exactly similar and with regular spacing. But since writing is composed of letters of varying shapes and compositions, the only way to produce a rhythmic uniformity is to find an optical

abcdef ghijklmnopqrs tuvwxyz

bdef hi k mnst w

1234567890 38

Terra di Siena Odp.

regularity which will give the **impression** of a uniform amount of empty space between each letter. The shapes of these spaces vary enormously. There is a rectangle between H and N, a trapezium between N and A. The curves and openings which occur with most letters, such as E, C, and B, are seen mainly as part of the weight of the letter, and only partly as gaps between the letters. If L and T stand together, the free space seems to belong less to the letters than it does when L and N are side by side. In the seventh line of the illustrated development of capital letters the distance between the letters is dotted in at a constant two units. At a glance it is obvious that there is not enough space between T and B and between R and V, and that they should be set wider apart to make a satisfactory rhythm for the line.

It is a constant rule that, to make the text more legible, broad letters require close spacing and narrow letters broad. With a very narrow alphabet the separate letters are so compact that the spacing between the letters and the optical space can be regarded for practical purposes as identical.

The distance between words corresponds to the width of the letters; a two- or three-letter space between words is needed for clarity. The distance between the lines gives lettering its character. Generally, in a drawn block of text, a wide space between lines makes reading easier; a narrow one makes the block more compact. It is, thus, a matter to be decided according to the purpose of the text. In the block the spacing of the words must be determined line by line to fit them into the given length. Words can be crowded slightly if necessary, but it must not be noticeable or the unity of the block is destroyed. A drawn text should always look harmonious. The individual letters and their spacing must be built up on a consistent principle, so that their shapes are not more arresting than the content of the text. Mixed forms can be used, and sometimes even different prototypes can be combined. There are, for example, very attractive styles in which the letters are all narrow, except for the round shapes, which are drawn to a full circle instead of an ellipse. A mixture of ellipses and circles would destroy the harmony.

Many beginners try at once to develop a personal style of lettering. This is a mistake. As in drawing it is essential first to be able to control the stroke and learn to work in the usual styles with confidence and fluency. When this is accomplished, the student will generally find that he has, in fact, developed a personal style without having consciously sought it.

Really new alphabets arise from the unconscious work of many people and are always closely related to the style or taste of the period. All decisive developments in art arise from ideas which are much more objective and more a part of the whole spirit of the times than may at first appear.

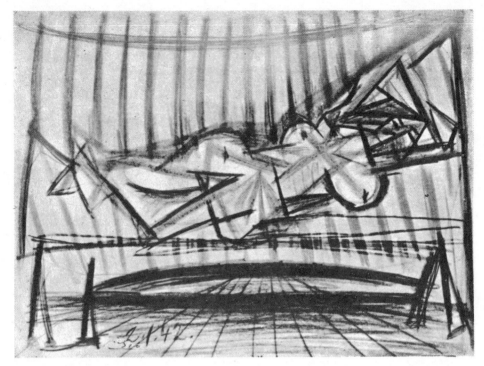

Picasso, Woman on the Divan. This nude study, possibly drawn in the presence of the model, shows a trend toward a near-abstract design

14. ABSTRACT ART

The great artistic problem of our time is to come to terms with abstract drawing, painting, and sculpture. The experience of the abstract presupposes in the artist a particular mental or spiritual attitude which is fundamentally the same for all branches of the visual arts. Only the means of expression differ, and the nature of the experience is of a particular kind, often expressible equally well in drawing, painting, or sculpture, though in some cases limited to one of the three modes of expression. In this respect abstract art has not altered the traditional situation.

What in fact is meant by "abstract"? There is hardly a satisfactory answer to be found from anyone. The etymological meaning of this word of Latin derivation is, more or less, "drawn out or extracted (from objective reality), unreal, conceptual, only thought." One can also say only felt, as against really seen; yet this is not quite accurate, insofar as we, when we set out to look for them, also "see" abstract forms and colors in the imagination. Painters and draftsmen must indeed do this, if they wish to reproduce abstract sensations.

This "seeing" is no more a deliberate thought process than the painter's poetic creative vision of impressions of real things. Part abstractions have always been associated with artistic vision. Medieval chimaeras and fabulous beasts which were never seen in reality in form or color express imaginary concepts, however naturalistically they are represented. They were the result of a desire to express some intangible, spiritual content of an imagined, or even of the visible, world. These attempts, which kept recurring, are the smallest and most remote rootlets of what has now become a rampant growth, spreading its tendrils over the whole of the objective world of the artist as "abstract art."

Böcklin represents the zenith of naturalistic representation of the imagined, and perhaps by self-suggestion, seen, world. He was about contemporary with Van Gogh, whose work represents what are basically the same natural forces; but while Böcklin was spinning out a mythological interpretation, Van Gogh saw more directly, more crudely, and his work speaks more forcefully: the dissolution of colors and forms into a seething blind mass of restless power. If we consider the work of Marc, we see that it is still concerned with realistic forms, but the color is not derived from the natural object, even though it may be thought and felt symbolically: blue horses' heads, and red horses. The colors here are by no means used with superficial decorative intent.

Thus we see that there have always been the means and the desire to represent in pictures feelings which are not

Klee, Flora of the South — an Echo. Watercolor. Klee's work often represents a preliminary step towards true abstraction

a part of the object, and to see in the things of the real world a second appearance which has no similarity to any recognizable object.

The intention of abstract art is to give pictorial form to feelings or sensations whether they arise from a mental concept or from an object. A program, one may say a dogmatic program, has been evolved which aims at drawing a clear division between objective and abstract representation. Michel Seuphor, one of the most outstanding interpreters of abstract art, defines the program in the following words: "I call abstract art every art that does not desire the memory or evocation of reality, in which it is irrelevant whether reality was the cause of the creative process."

There is also the common opinion that pure sensations independent of any known real object can be expressed only if the forms and colors of a picture are no longer associated with any recognizable object. If we hear the words "sorrow" or "joy" we many imagine situations from the past, but we do not undergo a direct experience of any definite shape or color, as we do if we say "spoon" or "house." A contradiction arises immediately in the pictorial reproduction of abstract visions: there are no abstract forms or colors in themselves. If we analyze an abstract picture we can always say that here we see a red triangle, this part looks like a blue rhododendron leaf, there the picture is reminiscent of a spiral nebula. It is only the combination of the forms which is unreal. We must also remember that there are no colors which we can imagine but cannot really see. What the human eye cannot perceive, like infra-red or ultra-violet, cannot be imagined either.

An abstract picture never gives the superficial likeness, even if it starts from a real object. It is trying, rather, to express how the painter felt as he looked at a thing, a person, or a scene. We all have these feelings, but we are not all inclined, or inwardly ready, to bring them to expression. Let us consider a few examples, which can, of course, elucidate

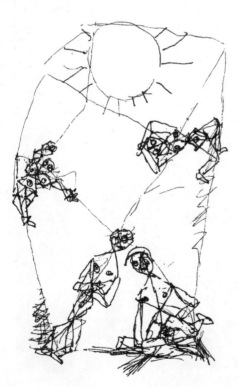

Klee, Human Weakness. Example of an illustration of an abstract conception which can yet be objectively comprehended

Gontscharowa, The Cats. This picture was clearly based on blinking cats' eyes

only the author's own sensations. It is certain that other people will feel quite differently, and it is precisely this difference or even opposition of sensations, natural among different people which explains why an abstract representation can never be generally understood.

If the author recites the days of the week he sees Sunday as orange-red, Monday as gray-blue, Tuesday as dark yellow, Wednesday white with gray shadows, Thursday violet, Friday gray-green, and Saturday a brassy yellow. He also see colors in numbers: one is white with gray, two is light yellow, three is blue, four is brown, five is light red, six light gray, seven orange, eight blue-green, nine red-brown, and zero is light blue. Combined numbers have yet other colors.

In these examples, which could be extended to include letters and even verbal concepts of feeling, the author reaches an abstraction only through color, and this seems natural: where there is abstract form or a concept which cannot be attached to a form, the abstraction can be expressed only in color. What awakens a sensation in these examples has already been formally abstracted. Numbers and letters consist of lines, and the line itself is, in drawing and painting and even in geometry, the abstraction of a surface. Where something is already abstract it cannot be abstracted further. How much the line is already an abstraction can be proved thus: there is no object which consists only of lines; it would have no substance. Objects are made up of surfaces, and

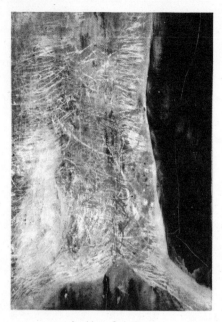

Jenkins, Solstice

Shinoda, Sorrow

surfaces in pictures are abstractions of the solid forms of which the whole universe consists.

Every artificially created form is an abstraction: a bottle, for example, but not a gourd or a pear. These latter growths clearly assume their form according to an ideal which could be expressed in universal terms by the outline of a white wine or champagne bottle. The formula for all these natural forms (let us refer to what was said at the beginning about aiding drawing from memory by using basic shapes) is, on a surface, a simple, symmetrical figure, described by continuous curves or straight lines, like the oval, parabola, or unequal triangle. Multiple symmetrical forms, like the circle, ellipse, or equilateral triangle, occur less often in the larger works of nature but are

more frequent in flowers, fruit, or smaller, almost microscopic things.

Every pictorial representation has always to deal with two problems of abstraction, one of color and one of form. Even color by itself must have some form definition or it could not be seen. All abstractions must ultimately be dominated by form and color as their means of expression.

Suppose we hear, or say to ourselves, words like "tram" or "nude" or "winter morning." The very sounds of the words, or the sight of them if we are reading, evokes something pictorial. It usually derives from something remembered, sometimes from something dreamed. If we set about painting or drawing this pictorial impression the immediate memory fades. Then we begin to think: "What was it like?" or "What belongs to it?

What is the **essence** of a winter morning? Which winter morning?'' This is not what is wanted here! As soon as we think and draw we seek the whole impression, the whole form of the object. With practice we can learn to fix the first idea without trying to complete it. This will produce something of the same effect we find in many of Picasso's pictures, an assemblage of fragments. Perhaps we first see a tram's buffer, the yellow of the seat, the knee of a passenger, the number plate on the outside, rails between paving stones. If we depict this assemblage it is still no abstraction; it is a stage towards it, in that we have learned to concentrate on what the memory unconsciously has retained from the whole. But abstraction also means selection.

We can look at it like this: we go a step further with our instant reaction to the word ''tram'' and retain only the colors; then, since the colors must have a shape, we put them down as square patches. We have continued our selection of impressions by eliminating all but the colors seen, which, although reduced to unmodulated patches, still have a relation to the objects. Blue and yellow can be expressed only by blue and yellow colors. If we were to put red, say, for yellow, and brown for blue, it would no longer be an abstraction, but just insanity.

If we study the reproduction of Klee's **Resonance of Southern Flora**, it is clear (with help from the title) that he made a selection on the basis of color, until nothing further could be transposed. The individual forms of the vegetation, unessential to the general impression, have been abstracted into a scheme of squares.

Let us imagine an ordinary brown enamelled milk jug. Milk is poured in and out of it. The milk flows into it in a line, spreads over the bottom of the jug, rises up and splashes out of the spout at the top. This we are doing, let us say, in a green tiled kitchen. We see the colors of the milk: yellowish and bluish. All this we see together at once, but this vision, although deriving from a natural-

istic scene, is as illogical as the colors of numbers. It is this illogical, but clearly sensed "seeing" that we reproduce in a picture.

In this example the author confined himself to noting down what he "saw" with his eyes closed. He named the colors of the natural surroundings in order to show how much had vanished in his interior sight, although what remains is in accord with the color seen with the open eye. It is possible to give here an impression of the process in time, which can never be done in an objective picture. A single picture can give what a filmstrip has to render in a series; here the author gave the idea of a milk jug with a linear representation. There are many other possibilities for the student to try!

The Milk Jug

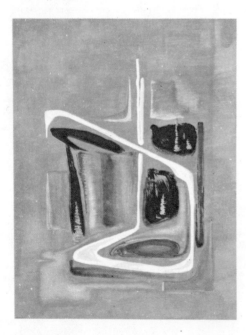

The impression could be reproduced, for instance, by color alone, without any clear, formal outline, for liquid has no definable shape, but depends on other factors: falling through the air it takes on a drop shape; on a surface it spreads out as far as its consistency and the nature of the surface allow; in a vessel it takes the shape of the hollow. The idea of milk can be expressed in color in any of these shapes, since it can take any of them. "Milk jug," on the other hand, is something different, for its form, color, and use are inseparable from it.

This simple example has been chosen deliberately to give an idea of the process involved in an abstraction. We also started out from an object, a tangible material, for how would it be possible to explain how to arrive at an abstraction taking as an example something like the working out of the concept "medieval poetry"? However, even a series of words only half understood (unless by chance our student is versed in Anglo-Saxon or Norman French) can leave an impression of shapes or colors. That, however, is an entirely subjective affair, **tot homines**. . . .

The second example begins with quite an ordinary acoustical experience, independent of any external natural forms or color impressions: rain falling on a roof at night. The author had here no need to investigate his "vision"; it came to him repeatedly on its own, and he noted it down as something valid only to himself which might one day be worked up into something.

We may read in the catalogue of an exhibition the titles **Solitary Walk** or **Sorrow** and wonder where the walk took

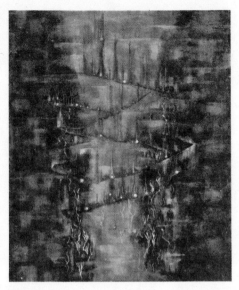

Rain at Night

things or the soul of something living the method is always the same: he must immerse himself in it until he feels something special about it, and then try to reproduce this feeling pictorially for others. The germ of it is in each one of us, but our training and upbringing does not direct most of us to function in this way. Two forms of art, music and dance, have always existed to prove that there are spiritual feelings in us to be expressed. We do not, of course, refer here to the infrequent naturalistic forms of these arts which imitate natural sounds or daily activities. Even with these it has never been attempted to identify specific emotions with definite scales or gestures and movements, except in the teaching of eurythmics, which has the admirable idea of expressing in dance emotions and musical sensations, words and sounds. In actual practice, however, this gets reduced to a sort of representational dumb language which can be understood perfectly objectively and is over-intellectualized.

place, what kind of sorrow it was, or whether it was just sorrowing in itself. We cannot know, but sometimes there is someone who can feel himself into it and find a related experience. Or the picture may simply be called **No. 76.** We are left to find something in it that speaks to us, or not, and it is no matter whether what we feel is at all related to the experience or feelings of the painter. A true abstraction can come only from meditation, from a state of deep sinking into oneself. It is rather a listening inwards or, better, looking inwards to the color or formal reflection of an experience which was once linked with a person, a landscape, or the exterior and function of an object. All these things, it is often said, have a soul; at least we use this same metaphysical concept for what we cannot explain in "dead" things. If someone wishes to represent pictorially the individualities of

The longer one considers the nature of abstraction and of abstract art the more one becomes convinced that it is the highest form of art. On the other hand, it offers every charlatan unimaginable prospects of success. There is the story of the unsuccessful painter who framed the portion of his friend's skirt where she had sat on his palette and called it **Chance**; he won first prize at an exhibition with his "painting." This story is far from abstract. Even today it can be successfully realized. The disadvantage of abstract art is that no one can recognize whether an inner necessity and a genuine experience led to the abstract picture, or an intentional or playful invention. Judgment is rendered more difficult because there is no need of any technical, professional proficiency to produce an abstract painting or drawing. Even a child can make curves, hooks, stripes, and geometric figures.

We have not yet developed an eye for sifting the wheat from the chaff in abstract art. This situation is not new in the arts. For centuries the art of primitive peoples was a closed book, an art that, in fact, has many abstract features. Today it is appreciated even by the man in the street, who has no interest in artistic problems. He may not be able to say clever things about it (thank goodness, one may say), but he may have a genuine love of these things. This may one day be true with abstract art.

Efforts to come to grips with abstract art are often hopelessly misdirected, however, and have created great confusion in art schools. It even happens that very "modern" teachers categorically forbid any tackling of objective form. These teachers, who may well be thoroughly serious artists, might as well ask someone to describe the atmosphere inside a great building while forbidding him to enter it. Starting from objective reality, we can only get inside it from the outside, or, more concretely, no one can interpret the spiritual content of a form and its color unless he has really studied it. Perhaps Goethe spoke the most tellingly about penetrating into the nature of things: "Nothing is inside, nothing is outside, for what is within is without."

Of course, it is not necessary to plague students until they are unconscious (in the truest sense) from exercises in copying flower pots or muscles to a photographic accuracy. What is at first just play with colors and invented shapes is equally important and can lead to new and great visual ideas, but these ideas can be fulfilled only with concrete formal structure. Teaching which includes this freedom leaves the field open to the most complete abstraction but does not lose its firm basis, which must always be in the external forms of things, about which no misunderstandings are possible.

15. THE DRAWING

If the student has studied the preceding chapters carefully and practiced faithfully, he will be able to produce a competent drawing. He now knows about the materials he needs and the formal problems that beset him as a draftsman and as a painter. It would require a lifetime and more to penetrate fully the structure and significance of all the forms in nature, but by now he has mastered some branches of this study and is able to learn the rest as special occasion demands. Yet even what we think we have mastered continues to pose new problems with the years. To take an example: even when the student has an exact knowledge of human surface anatomy, he will find himself gradually, or sometimes suddenly, seeing the forms he knows well in quite a different light. He discovers that he is no longer concerned with anatomically correct form alone; on the contrary, thanks to his knowledge, he may feel free to ignore it deliberately without committing any gross errors. With this freedom, he can now concern himself only with the over-all gesture, which, in certain circumstances, can best be expressed by the flow of lines rather than a precise rendering of the contours. The latter method only weakens his expressive powers. We have already referred to this practice—in life drawing by emphasizing the over-all rhythm, in portraits and caricatures by showing how only a few lines can capture an expression or mood. The objective forms of animals, landscape, architecture, and still life can also be treated in the same way. But the artist must know where to look for the central structural problem of every natural form and be able to draw it exactly as the need arises.

If the artist knows what is essential to master and has a general idea of the most important problems in other fields and subjects, he can then work according to a plan; he will not just sketch at random but will make studies. In other words, he will pursue a definite purpose in his drawing. The sketch is simply a note or memorandum, either of an object seen or of an idea that the artist wishes to remember. A study, however, has a definite aim in view: the fixing of some aspect of a subject required to carry out the idea suggested by the sketch. While the sketch is generally a quick view of the whole, the study is systematic work on a detail that needs mastering. One must always keep the details in mind in order to have a definite view of the whole picture.

The artist should never be in doubt as to whether he is making a sketch or a study. The sketch is always rapid and suggestive and leaves plenty of play for the imagination—that is its charm and its value. The study, on the other hand, sets a limit to the imagination by thoroughly investigating the subject.

Sketch

Study

We will now take a single example of how to approach a drawing with a very limited and definite purpose. Our model is a color photograph, which must serve here as a substitute for direct nature. We will imagine that we are in Engadin and that we see the chapel on a low hill surrounded by mountains. Why we choose to make something of this particular spot we leave to the reader's imagination. Our task, however, is to make the chapel recognizable, to draw its portrait. Any distortion of what we see must be used only to emphasize the essential features of the subject.

Of the many possibilities available we shall select three: an illustration of a story, a reminder of an occasion, and an outline drawing which contents itself with the external formal structure, its rhythm, accent, harmony, and dissonance. The drawing is to be black and white. A color photograph is chosen as a substitute for nature because natural models are always colored. A black and white photograph would already have translated the subject into values of black, white, and gray, and this is one of the problems we are to solve for ourselves.

We do not begin with a sketch but with a study. The aim is first to render the subject almost photographically. There are two reasons for this: working this way we make our first acquaintance with the given forms and learn to know them individually; also such a sketch will provide us with an exact note in the event, when we return home, we should wish to recreate something of our experience, reproducing it as it appeared to us without having to rely heavily on memory. The comparison between the

Motif for the set task

exact copy—the study—and the picture that we carry in our inner eye teaches us clearly what we can enhance or leave out. The alternative method would be to walk often by the subject and then to work only at home from memory. Nowadays, this is rarely possible.

As soon as we decide to draw a subject, we must determine how much of the surrounding area we wish to include. We can do this by shielding off what distracts us with our hands or by using a viewing frame, which is often a help to beginners. We quickly make our first decision, whether the shape will be a horizontal or vertical rectangle, or a square. It must include everything we think essential, not only the main object but all the accessories indicating place, position, space, and mood. We are not bound like the camera to a mechanical reproduction. We can crowd our motif or expand it, put in what is not there and leave distracting elements out. All of these considerations will influence the choice of format.

We are stimulated to draw this particular view largely because of the group of buildings, whose main attraction is their position on a hill among mountains. The left-hand group of trees seems rather fortuitous, but to leave it out would take away much of the charm of the view; moreover, the trees express an important movement toward the main subject.

The cast shadows show that it is a sunny day. If we wished to indicate that it were an autumnal landscape as well, we should have to use color or emphasize some accessories: for instance, half

First study

or completely bare trees beside leafy ones. But since color is not available and more trees would greatly alter the aspect of the view, we will ignore the season.

In the background, the left-hand mountain mass gives the character of the location. On the right, enough of the surroundings should be included to show that the chapel is not standing on an isolated hill top. Below, there must be enough space to show that the steps do not continue downwards indefinitely. A patch of sky above the top of the tower will indicate the breadth of the landscape. All of these considerations bring

us to a slightly elongated square as our format.

Now we take pencil and paper. The paper should be large enough not to limit our intended format, especially as there is no stongly outlined area to dictate it. To have plenty of paper space affects also our method of seeing and working. It is best to begin with the group of buildings, leaving enough space all around to allow us to adjust the scope of the picture after we have rapidly sketched in the surroundings.

We begin with the vertical lines of the towers and chapel walls. The width of the left-hand tower can then serve as a point of comparison for the various heights. We mark off this width by adjusting the distance of our thumb from the point of a pencil held toward the subject at arm's length. We can then determine how many width units make up the whole height of the building and how other elements, such as the bottom of the steps, the top edge of the breastwork of the wall, and the cornice lines of the towers, can be fixed against it. Once the width and height relation is secure, we fix the most important horizontal and vertical outlines with firmer lines. Putting in the window openings and some dark stones in the walls provides a further check on over-all proportions.

Next come the diagonals. The most insistent are those of the hillside, the steps, and the chapel roof. We hold the paper at arm's length, and gauging the slopes by sloping the extended pencil, we draw them in. The position of the right-hand vanishing point for the frontage of the building is found in the same way. The left-hand one is so far out to the left that we content ourselves with judging the slopes on the left. After this it is easy to find the correct angle for the slope of the tops of the towers and articulations of the walls. Another important diagonal leads to the highest tower along the tops of the left-hand group of trees. The main tree tops we already marked in at the beginning as vertical accents. Now they become the

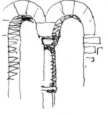

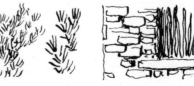

Above: First and second stages of study shown on left
Below: Attempts to delineate grass, masonry, and foliage; detailed study of window arches and breastwork

The Drawing

starting point for further lines of contact which outline the spaces between the trees.

We finish the play of lines with an allusion to the left-hand mountains, the outline of the surrounding walls to the right, and the background behind them. There could also be an indication of the lay of the clouds; often the direction and shape of clouds as they are blown by the wind is characteristic of a landscape.

A light diagonal hatching might tone in the building and the most important dark places, and a few last strokes can show the rough textures in the grass and the areas where details will be needed in the tree and mountain masses.

All this will have taken only a few moments. Now we must study our work from a distance and compare it with the original. We may, perhaps, make a correction or two with a heavier line and compare the drawing again with the landscape, this time through the viewing frame. Then, we finally decide where to cut off the picture with a penciled frame.

If the lines have been soft enough, the study can be given some sort of rounding off with stronger lines, behind

An essay in composition

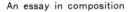

which the network of tentative strokes almost disappears. We now have before us an uncritical note. The closer it has come to the correct proportions, the better it is. If our practice and experience are adequate and the drawing large enough, we can now consider our preliminary work as done and go home with our study to work our information into the various final forms that will already have suggested themselves to us. Our aim should always be to keep the whole in mind and not get lost in detail too soon. A picture should grow altogether like a plant or a tree, so that whenever we stop work we should have reached some stage of completion.

When making this uncritical copy of the subject, we are certain here and there to have felt that something, either a detail or a more general area, seemed "awkward." The further we go with the drawing the clearer it becomes, until we gradually see how to enhance the character of the whole without giving it completely different features. In the final check to compare the model with the study, the viewing frame alone will show that we have made some unconscious exaggerations. Generally this is seen mainly in

Preliminary pen and wash drawing

the diagonals: the steep ones made too steep, the flatter ones too flat. This subjective and unintentional distortion is the beginning of real artistic creation. The next step is deliberate distortion or alteration, and a critical analysis of the original "copy," which leads to a creative composition.

Again we take a sheet of paper which allows plenty of free space. The reduction of a colored landscape into a structure of lines and light and dark masses is made much simpler if we first find the focal point, the center of gravity of the picture. In our example it is concentrated on the entrance to the surrounding wall, where the top of the hill is centered; all the main lines and movements lead to it: the verticals of the towers, the outlines of the areas of grass, and the steps. Even the far lines of the mountains and sky curve towards this point or bend in its direction. The walls of the building stand over it like a resting pyramid, towards which the slope of the pyramids of trees moves with a rising rhythm.

If we play about with this idea using the softest possible strokes, we shall soon see how to enhance the general impression; for example, the hill could be made steeper, simply by taking a more frontal view of the steps. This means moving our viewpoint a little to the left. The logical consequence of this is useful: the right sides of the buildings are more foreshortened by the move, and the right-hand vanishing point comes further to the left, towards the center of gravity of the picture. We know from our study of central perspective that the center of gravity has the strongest effect when it coincides with one of the vanishing

points. This is not the case here, but the points are close enough for the beholder's eye to be stimulated by the possibility of bringing them together. If we continue a line upwards from the tops of the trees on the left, it will nearly touch the highest point of the tower. This is right for the composition only if the buildings and trees are to be seen as a whole. But our task is to stress the buildings alone; the trees are to be included only as a foil to the main theme. This should be emphasized by making the line of tree tops at the left steeper, and, thus, the last tree taller, and letting the line fall down steeply to the right over the highest tree top. This gives a stronger rising rhythm up to the pyramid of buildings. Nothing is altered in the character of the picture by doing this; it is merely clarified.

The same is true if we alter the incidence of light so that the right-hand side of the buildings is in shadow. This might well have been the case, for this alteration does not contradict the natural course of the sun. The shadows added by this change will decidedly enhance the impact of the picture by emphasizing the main subject, the buildings. The main movement rising up from the left is nicely terminated by the vertical shadows of various shapes and sizes which repeat the general rhythm of rise and fall in the picture and offer a slight counter movement to the strong upward thrust from the left. Both movements meet more or less at a point that could be joined in a rising line with the center of gravity and the vanishing point of the right-hand side of the buildings. Concentrating around the center of the picture's gravity, the movements and tensions gradually support each other and lead to a static

Black pastel on glossy paper. Mural study

rest, without which the composition would seem uncomfortable and unbalanced.

At this point in our work we again look at the drawing through the viewing frame to test the balance of the picture. One small detail: the fir tree to the right of the entrance in the wall hides the door into the chapel. Either the tree can be left out altogether, or it can be moved to the right to show the door, which will further emphasize the center of gravity of the picture.

Now the composition is finished, and we have to decide what we intend to do with our work.

To proceed further, we trace the outlines of the composition onto a new sheet. In this way we isolate the skeleton of the picture and turn to the representation of the materials of which it is composed. We have masonry, with tiles and ashlar, curling beech leaves, soaring conifers; the hill is covered with a prickly coat of short grass, and the far-off mountain range must be given its crevices and

The Drawing

Contour study

sion in ink; so we can draw in first with a sharp, soft pencil, which can later be erased. If our first drawing is small enough, it is convenient to use the lucida to enlarge it. If the format is not very large, it is a good idea to draw with water-soluble ink, so that the shadows and other dark areas can be graded with a wash. Too many textures on a small drawing make it heavy, and broad shading with charcoal or chalk would only produce an indefinable smear.

The technique of a wash needs both care and a fluid hand. It lightens the strokes which have been gone over with the wet brush without letting them run. The process can be repeated several times until we have achieved the desired depth of shading or, if we are clumsy, until we are faced with a patchwork of black blurs. Even then all is not lost: damp blotting paper can lighten the color considerably. It is best to remember the adage, "When it tastes best, stop eating."

Our picture now shows very little evidence of our toil and tears. It will also have very little of the charm of spontaneity. This is not to be expected when we have worked stolidly at our subject as an exercise from start to finish. Yet dull, worthy drawings of this kind were produced by even the greatest masters. It may well be that someone will see the drawing and find it neither particularly attractive, nor exciting, but there will surely be someone to say, "Well, I couldn't do it. I can't even draw a straight line."

Yes, the **line!** It lies at the beginning of all drawing and it remains its substance. We can all go on learning how

strips of woodland. Clouds can be made with a play of fine lines, and a horizontal texture sparkles up from the stairway. We cover our new page gradually with a mass of surface textures without worrying about the general effect, but determining with sketch and study how to convey the separate details.

This may be thought rather pedantic, but it is fruitful: anything studied is a permanent gain, and it is dangerous to try to find imaginative short cuts before we understand the full story.

Until now we have used only part of our drawing sheet, so that our composition would not be constricted and we would be free to put our final frame where we thought best. Now that the composition is settled, we shall work right to the edges, using the whole area of our paper. If we are not content with calculating the rest from a few important measurements, we can use the squaring-up process to transfer our drawing to a bigger scale. We shall do our final version in ink; so we can draw in first with a

to use it better and more ably. First we struggled with a complete outline. Then we learned from sketching that there is more charm in an incomplete line. Now we leave out the line altogether around the large masses and let it be suggested by the mosaic of their textures; and even that is not required right to the edges of every surface. We know that the eye prefers to finish things off for itself; it is sufficient to start it off and support it here and there. The more we leave out, the better. In this way we reach back gradually to the picture plane, especially if we have some excuse to do without a window-like frame: drawing on a wall, for instance, or illustrating a book. A framing line would make a mural or book illustration unbearably rigid, cutting it off from the room or text. At any rate it seems so today. Perhaps we feel

this because human development, deliberately or unconsciously, is reaching out in every way, into every sphere, to extend space. The incentive to make this drawing came partly from the graphic interest of constructing the outlines. Let us therefore see what happens to the appearance of a picture if we do without any indication of material. This experiment means a new study, not this time to learn about the object, but to see how else to make a picture from it. Many painters close to the Impressionist school drew outline compositions (generally in blue) as a scaffold for their color surfaces. An example of this style is the picture by Gilman (p. 320).

16. SGRAFFITO, MOSAICS AND BATIK

Graphic art includes the techniques of sgraffito, mosaic, and batik. They are all three based on clear drawing. If color is used, it is in sharply defined areas without tonal gradations; the painter's way of merging and overrunning colors is technically impossible.

Each technique derives its particular charm from the effect of the material and the method of working it. In sgraffito it is wall plaster, in mosaic the small colored stones, or tesserae, in batik the cloth, generally real silk. Each of these materials has a pronounced texture which defines the picture plane strongly and, with sgraffito and mosaic, combines the design with the architecture. The **raison d'être** of both techniques is to decorate a wall, and batik, too, achieves its full effect only as a wall hanging.

All three techniques will succeed with anyone who can express a graphic idea clearly and simply on paper. These crafts can easily be learned and do not need much practice—much less than professional engraving or wood carving. Sgraffito and mosaic will, however, require the help of an experienced builder with the preparation of the plaster work. Useful hints can be picked up from watching his work, which may not be familiar from an acquaintance with only finished plaster. Batik, on the other hand, is a domestic occupation. The craft is easily learned if one knows a little about ironing and follows the simple directions for the use of cold dyes.

All three techniques require the design to be well thought out in advance. It is pointless to set to work with only a vague idea of what it should look like. Both design and procedure must be well planned.

Sgraffito

Sgraffito means "scored" or "scratched." The Italian term is always used in English.

The wall is prepared for sgraffito by giving it two or more coats of different colored plaster. The upper coat is either cut away to the shape of the design, or the design is scored out in line drawing, which then shows up in the color of the under layer. The process can be easily understood by smearing a slate or other dark ground with a chalk paste (without a binder) and, after it has dried, drawing into the white surface with a metal or wooden point; this scrapes away the white, leaving a dark line. The earliest sgraffito designs were made in this way: the wall was first rendered with a coat of mortar mixed with soot, and this was then masked with a layer of whitewash. The design was scored into the white with a metal or wooden stylus. At first this procedure was practiced only by ordinary builders for simple ornamental decoration or imitations of stone blocks.

The first sgraffito design of any artistic

value dates from the thirteenth century and is in the cloisters of Magdeburg cathedral. Strictly speaking, it is only a drawing scratched into the plaster while it was soft, and presumably afterwards colored with a brush, since it would not otherwise have been visible unless seen with side lighting to throw shadows. Today only a few traces of color remain. This attractive sgraffito medium is no longer used, but it would be worthwhile reviving its practice.

Sgraffito into lime wash over mortar mixed with soot was used to greatest effect during the Renaissance. Bohemia has the largest number of examples. Prints and engravings by famous artists were the most popular models. Enlarged on walls to monumental proportions, they look like rough pen and ink drawings. In the same period artists hit upon the idea of using calcareous earth pigments instead of soot to color the mortar, covering it with a thin coat of plaster in a contrasting color instead of the lime wash. It is difficult to make close hatching in plaster, so shadows and dark areas were cut out in solid pieces. The thickness of the top layer made the edges of all scorings and cut-out areas stand out in relief. This technique was at first used almost exclusively for the ornamental decoration of paneling, but it is now commonly used in all sgraffito work. The reader will be able later to judge to what extent it is worth his aiming at a professional standard in the mastery of this technique and how artistically rewarding it can be. To form an idea of the technique, the student must at least have a theoretical understanding of the composition of wall renderings and the

Sgraffito tools: 2 spatulas, screwdriver, 2 wire loops, stylus, scraper (side and front view)

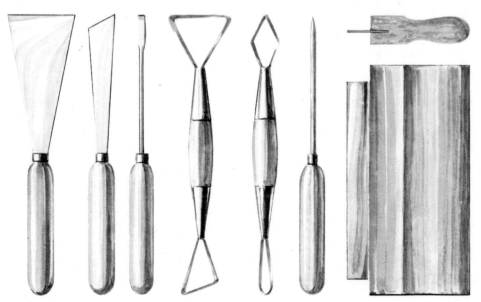

4-color sgraffito: dark green, red and blue plaster, a lime-washed sgraffito ground. Stage 1: Cutting through the drawing previously traced, scraping away the lime wash to the furthermost contour lines except where already cut deep. Stage 2: Provisional elaboration of the picture,

use of mortar or plaster as a wall covering. Its manufacture and application is, of course, the work of an experienced builder, but some acquaintance with the builder's work when he prepares the wall for an artist will give the beginner confidence, and make him feel less of an amateur.

Every mortar is a combination of three materials: sand, water, and a binding element. Lime, cement, or a mixture of both, serves as the binder, the choice depending entirely on the function of the rendering, which also determines the choice of the sand. Whatever its granulation, sand must be sharp and free of earth. Plaster, a harder preparation for

the top coat and containing more lime, is also a general term used for any wall coating.

The lime is obtained by heating broken-up limestone, such as marble, until it is red hot, and thus allowing the carbonic acid and water of crystallization to escape. When the burnt limestone is then brought into contact with water it generates great heat and forms a creamy paste which hardens immediately upon absorbing sufficient carbonic acid from the air. It never becomes as hard as the original limestone, however, and needs the addition of sand and grit to make it firm.

Cement is made in much the same way

working from top to bottom. The tools drawn in transparently are to be imagined vertical or at an angle of 30 degrees to the plaster surface

as lime, but clay, dross from smelting furnaces, and other materials are added in the heating; the product is then finely ground. Cement does not need carbonic acid from the air to harden it; it can set in an airless environment—under water, for instance. It is always harder than lime. If greater firmness is required, or there is likely to be insufficient air, cement is added to lime mortar, or replaces the lime entirely.

Besides making it harder, the additional material forms the main body of the mortar. The proportions vary between 1:5 and 1:3, the higher number being the sand content in relation to lime or cement, both measured dry.

"Fat" plaster has a lower sand content. In plastering a wall, the same principle applies as in oil painting: always put fat over thin, never the other way around. Water is added to give the right consistency. It does not require any special measuring, but plaster will not adhere to a wall if it is too wet. However, excess water evaporates. The mixture is too friable to take at all if it is not wet enough.

Even if he leaves all the plastering to the builder, the student must himself execute the actual work of scoring and carving. The plasterer would work in sgraffito with the same precision he has been trained to for cornices and mouldings;

The completed work

his training in the use of level and float would produce the same effect as a portrait drawn with ruler and compass. Even if at first the strange position close to the wall on a scaffold makes the student lose his sense of the vertical, and he has to use plummet and spirit level, he should put them aside after the first sketching in of the design. The cutting tools must be used freehand, except, perhaps, for work on large lettering.

A good outdoor wall plaster is composed basically of three layers. The first coat seals up any joints, cracks or seams in the wall and makes a rough but even surface, to which the second, finer coat can be keyed. The top coat forms a permanent texture and gives the wall the desired color. For sgraffito the colored layer is put in either as the second (middle) coat or as an extra coat above it. As each color requires a separate coat, it is technically impossible to do sgraffito in anything but a limited color scheme. If plaster is applied too thick to a wall it does not hold securely; it falls off of its own weight whenever frost or mechanical causes give it a chance. Polychrome designs are thus better carried out in a modified form of sgraffito, called plaster intarsia.

Sgraffito can be worked only while the plaster is soft enough to be easily cut and scored. If it has hardened so that it can be cut only with a mason's chisel and hammer, it makes lighter patches and the whole work will look faulty. The carving has to be done rapidly; there is no time to reconsider the design. Plaster is rarely in a condition suitable for sgraffito tools for longer than 24 hours, and then **only** if the under layer was well dampened before the application of the top coat, and the weather is dull or a screen of damp cloths protects the working surface from the sun. Hence, all preparation must be done beforehand so that the artist can concentrate on the technical execution of his design as soon as the top coat of plaster has been applied.

Like all work which is planned for a purpose, a sgraffito design begins with a preliminary sketch, which is gradually worked up into a working drawing. The technical demands of the medium dictate the first translation of the purely artistic idea into a suitable style. Besides using very definite lines and surfaces of uniform color, the shapes in the composition must be suitable for execution with a stylus and cutting spatula. Austere and angular drawing without much detail is the most effective, whether the work is done in the classical black and white or uses several colors. The cutting technique of sgraffito is best approached by making a cartoon from the first sketch, not with pencil or brush, but by building up the design from cut-out shapes of colored paper. This procedure is very useful for every kind of graphic decoration and will be dealt with more fully when we draft our batik design.

It is difficult to work out a well-balanced composition without fitting the sketched idea as soon as possible into a scale drawing of the whole facade. The scale may be chosen, according to the size of the proposed work, between 1:20, 1:10 and 1:5. The larger the proportion, the easier it will be to transfer the design to full size.

If several colors are used, it should be borne in mind that the strictness of the form makes each color much more insistent than in a painting. If a fresco on a facade were to be changed into a sgraffito, or a plaster intarsia, in as many colors, it could be done only by reducing many of the gradations and mergings, or overrunnings of tone, into one distinct color. This color would then stand out independently in its own right. To find a harmonious effect that does not break up the whole unity of the facade requires a thorough study of color problems, particularly as we are further restricted by the fact that many colors are not compatible with lime (see section on Painting).

To begin with, we are confined to a basis of one color, that of the top layer of plaster. In two-color sgraffito (a monochrome would be a colorless plaster-cut) the essential effect is the contrast with the top layer of plaster; in polychrome the combined effect of all the colors forms the contrast with the top coat. By attempting otherwise we risk the possibility of one predominant color destroying the unity of the design, unless the main color be used pervasively and more lineally.

It may be more enjoyable to color the sgraffito plaster oneself than to buy it ready-colored; however, ready-made colored plaster saves trouble and is guaranteed durable. It can be chosen from a color card to a specified granulation and comes ready for the plasterer to add water and apply it. Buying ready-made plaster is considerably cheaper than preparing it oneself because one does not have at hand supplies of the various sands needed to give the plaster its basic color. It is easy to make a stronger color by adding a small amount of pigment, but good pigments are expensive and it takes a large amount to color white plaster. Pigment also works like earth in the plaster and in large quantities reduces the binding effect of lime and cement. Furthermore, a lot of drying tests will be needed, since damp plaster is always much darker and more strongly colored than dry.

Sgraffito coats are always applied so that the darkest layer is lowest and the brightest color is on top. Over it all comes the finishing coat that covers the whole building. It is tempting to apply very thick layers in order to obtain as plastic an effect as possible with strong shadow outlines. This may look well at first, but the process soon becomes tedious, quite apart from the fact that deep cutting endangers the permanency of the work and destroys the formal unity of the design. In the long run a sgraffito worked in thin coats is more effective and professional looking than one which looks like an appliqué of fretwork.

The general effect depends on a good texture for the top layer of plaster. The sgraffito coats are better made of a fine plaster with little texture effect. The coat must be applied according to the size of granulation and should be about double

the thickness of the largest grain. Coarse granulation is thus possible only if there is to be no more than a single sgraffito layer. If the top layer of plaster is coarse, it is difficult to make subtle outlines; they will crumble, which looks unpleasant unless the design is done in very heavy drawing.

This consideration must be weighed against our desire for a coarse texture to stress the picture plane. It is particularly important in sgraffito to keep the design flat, as it must form part of the whole building. The sense of depth must embrace the whole architectural unit, not just the surfaces surrounding the design, and effects of perspective are totally out of place. At most, perspective should be confined to a simple arrangement of individual elements one behind the other as in a stage set, for which Egyptian wall paintings give the classical example.

There are three types of finish: one is

3-color sgraffito on the house of an employee at a large textile concern

rubbed flat with a float or felt, one is scraped, and one is thrown on. The strongest and most naturally varied texture is obtained with a float finish, mixing largish round pebbles into a relatively fine plaster. The pebbles make grooves and ridges and then fall off. It can be clearly seen how the float moved, in circles, up and down or horizontally.

The texture of scraped plaster is dependent entirely on the size of granulation. When the plaster is applied it is smoothed flat and then, when set hard, nearly scraped with a metal edge or a nailed board that works like a coarse brush. The result is uniform, without any direction in the texture, and is always darker in tone than a smoothed surface. The contrast is strong enough to be able to make a design recognizable if carried out in scraped against floated plaster.

If a finer plaster is smoothed with the trowel alone, not with a float, it falls into ridges and waves. This is certainly the most craftsmanlike of treatments. It has a mellow effect, especially on rural buildings when it is whitewashed every few years. After a time patches of earlier whitewash peel off leaving a natural looking relief patina. A two-color sgraffito looks very well in this technique, as long as the design does not get splashed with whitewash.

Thrown-on plaster, rough cast or wet dash, is the lowest grade of plastering and shows up—in contrast to a fine sgraffito layer—almost palpably for what it is, a thin skin covering the building. It is a comparatively coarse but watery plaster thrown on with a trowel, or more often squirted. It remains very rough and is rather fragile. While it is new it looks quite well, but it quickly accumulates dust.

Many cheap products have been developed in recent years to give a very smooth plaster finish. Any texture that

The light effects are obtained by leaving plaster unscraped with a smooth flat finish

Detail, taken with very oblique lighting. Top plaster is left to a depth of about $\frac{4}{10}$ inch

is put on them looks quite artificial and arbitrary. Sgraffito on these surfaces is reminiscent of an antimacassar on a plush chair.

The method of drawing out the design depends on the type of top coat. All plaster is exceedingly sensitive before it sets hard and retains indelibly any dust that falls on it or any lines used in blocking out the design. Fresco technique is, of course, based on this characteristic of plaster, but it has its dangers for sgraffito. Scraped plaster is the most convenient surface to work on. The surface is not scraped until after the work is finished, and unwanted lines and marks can be eliminated by it. What is often done is to make a full size cartoon of the outlines, lay it over the fresh plaster and press the lines through with a stylus, as for a fresco; but this is unnecessary. With sufficient experience of enlarging by squaring up, and a good feeling for the effects of engraving on a large scale, it is perfectly possible to work from a small drawing and draw directly onto the wall in freehand. It has the advantage that mistakes can be rectified at once, and sometimes an effect is very different on a wall from on paper. The freehand drawing does not lose spontaneity, as the traced one may well do.

Working on a surface which will later be scraped, it is possible to indicate the squares for enlarging onto the plaster by using string marks made with plumb line and level. If the top plaster is not to be touched afterwards, a lath frame can be hung up on hooks and a net of strong squares fixed to it. For rough cast the net must be hung on the scaffold so that it does not touch the plaster anywhere.

All the brass gravers and styluses and wire loops used by clay modelers can be used for cutting the lines and removing patches for the design, but the author has found screw drivers and spatulas of different breadths, some with sloping ends, to be more satisfactory. Lines can be begun very thin with a sharp steel screw driver and then thickened by turning the implement towards the flat side. The thickness of the line can be varied as it would be with a broad drawing nib. The outlines of the larger patches can be cut down first to just above the first sgraffito coat with a narrow, oblique spatula. They should be cut with a visible slope towards the surface. If the angle of the cut is too steep and is run along a ruler edge the effect is too metallic. All lines and outlines should be done freehand. It is better to make the patches too small at first rather than too big. It is easy enough to remove more plaster and make them bigger, but filling in is never wholly satisfactory and wastes a lot of precious time. The patches can be carefully removed with the flat of the spatula blade; generally the top layer comes away quite cleanly. Wire loops take much longer to lift out the plaster, and this is irritating because of the time factor, which makes the artist hasty and nervous. With a little practice the spatula can be used very neatly. A loop can never come cleanly to the edges and into corners, so that in any case the work will always have to be touched up with the spatula.

At first, the top coat should be removed only deep enough for the sgraffito layer to show through. Thus, one quickly gets an over-all impression of the whole design and allows time for the freed surface to harden slowly. If the patches were scraped clean at once it would take longer to get an over-all impression of the design, and the damp under surface would get smeared, while the top coat was hardening in other places more than necessary to be worked. Thus, it is best to remove the top coat quickly all over, and then start on the final cleaning up.

The same method applies if there is more than one sgraffito layer. The whole design is first cut down to show up the first sgraffito layer. Then the surfaces that are to be in the second and subsequent colors are drawn into the first and all cut down nearly to the second. The process is continued for the third and any subsequent layers.

When all the lines and patches are cut, the plasterer will decide when it is time to scrape them clean, though in time the artist learns to judge for himself. If you use a spatula blade held perpendicular to the surface, the plaster should crumble off almost dry. If it smears it is not dry enough; the surface would form waves and too much of the colored layer would come away. No more should be scraped off than leaves the surface clean.

It is obvious that this must be done from the top downwards or dust would collect in what is already cleaned, and the lines would have to be cleared again. If the top coat is also to be scraped it should be left to the plasterer, who will do it together with the rest of the wall. Unless you are experienced, it is easy to miss patches on a large surface, which will show up lighter and spoil the whole facade. The sgraffito layers, however, should never be left to the plast-

erer, even for touching up, for his whole training compels him to straighten off all the edges.

The beginner can start practicing on a board. There are cemented, pressed boards made from wood pulp, which can be treated as a rendered wall. In a smaller format, it is possible without the plasterer's help to cover hardboard with a mixture of fine scouring sand, powder color, and a slow hardening gum of some sort; wallpaper paste is the best. Each coat should be about $\frac{1}{12}$ inch thick. A pocket knife serves quite well as the cutting tool, both for scoring lines and cutting out patches. The effect of this work can be rather like a mistaken "refinement" of the scraping technique, in which the finest residue of top layer is used to shade in a design on the undercoat. It is neither painterly nor graphic in effect and is entirely opposed both artistically and technically to sgraffito. The thin residue of plaster is very insecure and soon weathers away out-of-doors. It looks rather like a wall pastel, but, with its easy but pointlessly carved edges, carries none of the conviction of a pastel.

Sgraffito and plaster intarsia must be intelligently related to the character of the materials.

Following page: sgraffito design for an agricultural college. Green top plaster and reddish brown sgraffito layer. White obtained with opaque lime

Mosaics

Mosaic is technically a more expressive medium than sgraffito. The number of colors used is not limited, nor is it any more difficult to produce a work in polychrome than in black and white. Only the preparation of the design and full-size cartoon take longer with many colors than with few.

The strength of a mosaic is not affected by the number of colors, nor does it reduce the graphic effect. The network of divisions between the colored stones always looks like a drawn texture enclosing each small fleck of color. If this were not so, mosaic could become a painting with the softest transitions of color.

Classical mosaic is made from colored tesserae all of the same size, between $\frac{1}{3}$ and $\frac{3}{4}$ of an inch square. Only occasionally, for lines running to a point or very curved, are the small squares sloped off or split. As a rule, a variation in the width of the joins serves instead; it does not matter how the joins run.

The work begins by giving the wall a first coat of coarse plaster. This must be absolutely flat, but should not be too smooth, as it must give a good grip to the next coat. Into this upper layer of plaster, while soft, the tesserae are pressed. Unless it is quite flat the surface of the mosaic will be uneven. Its thickness depends on whether the tesserae are all of the same thickness or not. If they are uniform the bedding layer can be thinner than if it has to even out differences of thickness so that the mosaic surface remains flat. The average thickness of mosaic, bedding layer and undercoat together, comes to about $\frac{2}{3}$ of an inch. The plaster must be rather fat and very fine so that the tesserae can be pushed into it easily and lie as close as possible to each other. Only very fine plaster can press up into the narrow cracks and hold the tesserae fast. The cracks average about $\frac{1}{16}$ of an inch if the edges of the mosaic stones are parallel. Very little plaster comes up into the cracks from underneath; after the mosaic surface is complete it is washed over with fine watery plaster. The attractive textured effect of the joins between the stones comes from the slight projection of each individual stone, and this is achieved by brushing away the plaster applied from above for about $\frac{1}{12}$ inch down into the cracks, a process which cleans up the surface of the stones as well.

Mosaic is most attractive when each stone is fixed directly into the wall, showing the natural irregularities of work done by hand, as was done in the past, as long as 2,000 years ago. Recently various methods have been evolved which enable larger sections to be composed in the workshop and then applied to the wall. These all produce a very smooth and close-packed surface which is technically perfect, but which loses much aesthetically. The result is even more negative when the artist sends his cartoon to be carried out entirely by artisans in the workshop which supplies the tesserae. However accomplished and tasteful these artisans may be, they cannot be expected to interpret the intentions of the artist exactly.

Nor can the artist be expected to exploit all the expressive qualities of the medium unless he has practical mastery of it, which means that he must carry out most of the execution himself. It is different if the design is purely decorative in intention and needs complete technical precision for its execution, for instance a tesselated pavement which has to be absolutely flat, or over-all ornamental decoration of walls and pillars. For these purposes the workshop can provide larger and closely shaped stones which can be fixed with scarcely any space between them. This is very different from the Early Christian mosaics, whose expressive and tectonic texture is not conceived merely ornamentally. Their technical "imperfection" has much more personality than the smooth elegance of the precision work from a factory.

This "imperfection" is the same quality we required the artist to seek in sgraffito: work which bears the imprint of the artist's own hand, not the impersonal touch of the plasterer's. In mosaic it is also the constantly repeated building up of the design step by step to the final creation. No technique gives a clearer sense of finality than this composition of a picture stone by stone.

Before tackling our cartoon we must acquaint ourselves with the material. It is stimulating to play about with a collection of colored stones on a tray and arrange them in different ways and patterns. Mosaic tesserae may be artificially made from fired clay, either colored right through or glazed with color only on the top: or there are colored glass pastes which are transparent and give a radiance to the work, and some with a layer of gold or silver leaf under glass. Many natural stones are used, cut to the right shape. Fragments of colored marble slabs and wall and flooring tiles of the right thickness are highly suitable. Even brightly colored pebbles from the seashore or the beds of streams can be used for a primitive, rather decorative style of mosaic.

The author once came upon a garden wall which was decorated with mosaics made from pebbles collected over the years. There were fishes, seagulls, wild boar and a series of other animals, an amusing record of the maker's holidays. He was entirely self-taught and had begun to collect the pebbles at random. Having decided on how to use them, he collected them more deliberately. Each year on his return from holiday he got a plasterer to cut out a space on the old wall surface about 3 x 5 feet in area and fill it in with a fresh, slightly prominent bed of plaster. He then worked from a rough drawing, pressing the stones, which he kept wet in a trough, into the plaster. The excess plaster was removed with a spoon and spatula and the stones wiped with a damp cloth. The plasterer gave a final touching up to the edges.

The stones looked very dull and pale when they dried, but once the plaster was quite dry and set they were brushed very lightly with hot linseed oil mixed with beeswax, taking care not to touch the plaster and mark it. The stones had first been heated with a blow torch so that the wax had time to penetrate the pores before setting. In a few days' time they were polished with a woolen cloth. This work had not, nor was it intended to have, any artistic pretensions; but far and wide the plaster garden dwarfs found the taste of the neighborhood had become too good for them, and they disappeared without a trace.

There are essentially four different mosaic techniques: odd stones or broken slabs pressed into thick plaster; builder's mosaic with strings of pebbles laid in horizontal lines; the almost joinless industrial mosaic; and classical freehand mosaic. We can deduce the methods of the others from a knowledge of the classical process. When properly done they are all very durable.

Once the theme and the size of the mosaic is decided in relation to the building we start work on a sketch. It can, and, indeed, should, be very small, so that a certain monumental quality arises from enlargement alone. This is a trick that can be used to some extent in all pictorial art. Nothing is so damaging in mural work, particularly in mosaic, as to lose the broad and simple effect in a mass of detail.

The sketch should be carried out in poster colors on paper the color of the plaster, without at first taking the texture of the joins into account. When a simple colored sketch is ready we place over it a sheet of tracing paper and divide up the areas of color into squares corresponding to the size of stones which will be used. This need not be done exactly; the aim here is to get an idea of how the design will look in mosaic.

To let the idea develop properly it is best to make an intermediate drawing before the full-size cartoon, about a half or third full size, again painted in continuous colored surfaces. In parts, at least, this can be divided up into the tessera squares, using a soft pencil directly on the drawing. If we feel there is no essential correcting to be done we proceed to an exact drawing of the most important outlines on good tracing paper. This page is to be kept for reference, and no more work is done on it at present. We now take thick drawing paper and color it to match the surrounding plaster, trace on the outermost outline of the mosaic—if it is to stand free on the plaster surface, and wash inside this outline with a neutral gray waterproof color to represent the shadows of the joins. Unless waterproof, it may run when the colors of the design are put on. Onto this we trace all the outlines of the design, a process best done with white chalk.

We now need a flat hair brush, or several if possible, of a width rather less than that of a tessera. With this we paint in the tesserae as square flecks of color. The brush has to be smaller than the tesserae, as it always spreads a bit. It is safest to experiment, before starting, to find the right thickness. We then mix the basic colors, if possible again in waterproof paints, such as casein poster paint, and then fill in the tesserae, carefully but not too rigidly, fleck by fleck, as close as they will lie. In this way we have an approximate idea of what the design will look like. If necessary, corrections can be made by covering over a portion with gray and rebuilding the color structure.

This draft shows only a few uniform tones of color. It is only now time to contemplate transitional colors by laying in the mixed colored over the basic colored squares. There is no point in fussing

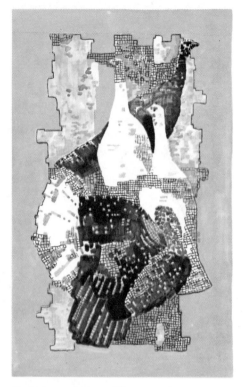

Preliminary design with some stone arrangement sketched in. The composition is not yet satisfactory

Design altered and somewhat enlarged. Right: detail of design in actual size. Final version 6 times magnified

with subtle mixtures of colors at the start. It is much more important to indicate the transitions broadly. Gradually as we work over the design again and again we shall achieve the desired subtlety. If we happen to blur some of the join lines in this process, they can be drawn in again in gray with a pointed brush, although this is necessary only if it is considered important to have an exact picture of the final effect. Next we see to the stones.

It is best to find out beforehand from the supplier what colors are available and which of them show up most clearly. We can now furnish the supplier with the design and ask him to put together the assortment of tesserae required. It is probably better to be present when the material is selected, for we are then better able to judge the possibilities open to us, and no doubt pick up a few good tips. It is worth finding out how the tesserae can be broken up and shaped, even if we intend to use them whole for the most part. One should always allow for a few more stones than the number that has been calculated, and a few of the lighter and darker shades than those scheduled. These extra pieces will certainly come in very handy.

In preparing the next stage of the work we draw the outlines of the original onto stout transparent foil, such as acetate, for checking later. The same drawing is copied again on soft oiled or waxed paper, which will later be laid on the fresh plaster for the outlines to be pressed through. While the bottom layer of rendering is laid on the wall in pure cement, or cement and sand, and left to set for a few days, we can again see to the stones. To ensure that no grease adheres to them they are washed in small lots in dishwashing detergent, rinsed with clean water, and left to soak. This treatment is particularly important when the stones are unglazed, for their porous clay body absorbs a great deal of water, and were they left unsaturated, the stones would draw off from the plaster the water which is essential for its hardening. The same is true of natural stone; only glass or glazed material does not need to absorb more water.

The student is well advised to keep his first mosaic to a size which can be executed in a small space. The work will go something as follows: the first fullsize drawing on transparent paper is placed on a board of suitable proportions; it is not needed for other purposes. It is covered with a sheet of thick transparent foil, and the colored original is hung up for convenient reference. Then the whole mosaic is set out on the transparent foil with the tesserae, using the underlying outline as guide. At a first attempt it will probably be necessary to

make a trial setting to see whether the sizes of the stones correspond to those assumed in the plan, or whether the plan has to be modified to accommodate the actual sizes of the pieces. In this preliminary setting some individual tesserae will be shaped with pincers and whetstone where it is absolutely necessary. The most important tool for setting is a pair of pincers, which can be conveniently used for changing over and moving the tesserae. One comes to realize that it is much more interesting to leave some accidentally set color as a means of enlivening the whole composition rather than to follow the model slavishly. Thus, there is no necessity at the start to root out from the assortment of stones the piece which fits exactly; it is better to get the forms approximately right in the first place and to revise them in detail afterwards. Of course, incorrect settings must not become too deliberate a habit.

Now the fun starts. The plasterer thoroughly wets the underlayer of plaster and puts in laths or screeds in order to spread a uniform bedding layer. Into this surface the tesserae are set, once the design on the oiled or waxed paper has been pressed or traced onto the plaster. The work is done from the bottom of the design upwards, a strong lath being inserted along the lower edge of the mosaic to support the first row of tesserae. If the design does not finish at the bottom in a horizontal line, the edge of the outline transferred from the oil paper drawing must be supported by a firm ridge of plaster. In this way the first line of tesserae is held firm from underneath and provides the necessary support for the stones above. The stones are picked up one by one and pressed by hand into the soft plaster. The best procedure is to start with the two or three lowest lines of tesserae from the composition and to set them complete, and then to continue to build upwards the main motif of the design, such as a figure in the middle of the picture. This enables us to follow the traced outlines and to check the progress of the composition against the outline tracing.

The setting of the stones should go forward as fast as possible so that the plaster is not given time to alter its consistency. Now and again, when a fairly large piece of the composition has been completed, the stones should be lightly tapped. A board about 6 x 12 inches, covered with thin felt or rubber, is laid over the mosaic and tapped or pressed with the hand to ensure an even surface.

This should be done as little as possible, for there is a danger of shaking the tesserae from their bed while the cement is still binding. In a mosaic built up in this fashion we do not aim at a completely even surface; with practice and experience the use of the board for flattening the mosaic can be given up. The irregularities which arise in the bedding of the stones by hand can be attractive in themselves.

Once we feel confident enough to undertake larger scale work, of the kind that is done on the front of a building from a scaffold, for example, it is no longer possible to transfer the pieces direct from a preliminary setting out. The method then is to divide the tesserae up in flat boxes of varied colors which are numbered conveniently so that the required color is easily found while working on the scaffold.

On large and complicated mosaics the plaster is likely to get too hard before the work is finished, and the stones will then not hold firmly. It is best in these cases to do only a section at a time, and where necessary to strip off the plaster and relay it, as has always been done with large frescoes.

If a mistake has been made and a few tesserae need replacing, it should be done at once. The tesserae must be carefully removed with the pincers, the space moistened slightly with a spray, the new stone given a touch of plaster on the bottom and pressed carefully into place. Corrections, however, should be avoided as far as possible.

Once the work is finished it is left until the plaster has hardened enough to give some hold to the stones. The ridge of plaster added to hold the bottom edge is cut away while it is soft enough to come off easily without shaking the whole composition. Once the stones are holding firmly, the whole mosaic is spread over with very fine watery plaster, which then is immediately wiped off the surface.

When this plaster is beginning to set in the joins the whole surface is brushed from top to bottom with a suitably hard nylon brush to clear the joins near the surface and let the separate stones stand out. Now the mosaic shows its characteristic texture for the first time. To finish off, each tessera is cleaned with a cloth moistened with an acid such as vinegar to remove the last traces of plaster from the surface.

Very old mosaics look now as though they had never been cemented from on top. The stones seem simply to have been fixed individually and to stand quite separate from each other. This relief texture is so attractive that we nowadays like to reproduce it, and it is possible to do so. In old mosaics the cracks are due to the decomposition of the lime plaster. This texture of empty cracks can be reproduced today by not placing the stones too close, and pressing them by hand into a very fine cement mortar without subsequently cementing them from above or pressing them smooth. It is the simplest process of all.

As a contrast we should mention how industrial mosaics are made. A mirror image of the design is drawn on sticky paper. The stones are arranged as close as possible onto this underlay with the top side down. The pieces are made to slope slightly in a cone shape towards the bottom edge, so that the plaster can run up higher and bind them firmer. The paper with the stones stuck on it is cut into convenient pieces which are set clean and flat into the plaster; the paper is stripped off when the plaster has set hard enough to bind the tesserae. A very fine plaster is smeared over the top into the thin cracks. This method is very efficient and sure, and is fully justified for floors and purely decorative purposes.

Second following page: Archbishop Maximian. Detail from mosaic in chancel of San Vitale, Ravenna. Example of great power of expression of portraiture in mosaic form

Batik

The word batik is a meaningless fragment of the Javanese word Ambatik, which signifies both writing and drawing. In a Javanese riddle describing the process of batik making, the answer contains the one special implement needed: the "tjanting."

A calyx with the beak of a bird of prey,
Five follow him across the empty field,
Wherever he goes he leaves his blood behind.

The answer to the riddle, the tjanting, is a small copper vessel, in shape rather like the calyx of a tulip. It has a thin curved spout which is likened in the riddle to a bird's beak. The five who follow it are the fingers which hold the vessel by a handle like that on a Turkish coffee pot. The fingers follow the jug as it moves over the uncolored cloth. In Java a smooth cotton is used, but we tend to prefer silk. Blood stands for the brownish yellow liquid wax which flows from the fine spout and leaves a trace of writing or drawing on the cloth.

What follows is quite mechanical: the cloth is dyed in a cold dip. After drying, it is ironed and the wax melts out, leaving a white design instead of the "traces of blood" against the colored ground. The wax prevents the dye from penetrating the cloth. This process is called "resist dyeing" and was used in the past for hand block printing, such as the famous Schwabian "blue printing," in which carved wooden blocks are dipped in a paste which does not dissolve in cold dye and pressed onto bleached linen, which is then soaked in a bath of dye. The places protected from the dye by the paste remain white.

The materials used in batik, then, are cloth and dye. We know that the pigments with which we paint or draw need a binder to fix them onto the ground. Textile dyes do not need this, since their coloring substance, which can also be called stain or ink, makes a true solution with water. That is to say, the inks are distributed in the water at a molecular fineness and cannot be separated by filtering. Seen through a microscope even the smallest particles of pigment are enormous, and they can be separated from water through ordinary filter paper. Being true solutions, textile dyes can penetrate the fibers of the yarn and often fix themselves there indissolubly. If this is so, the cloth will not discolor; the fastness of dyes can be increased by preliminary chemical treatment.

Unlike almost all painters' colors, cloth dyes are organic substances. They used to be extracted from plants, of which indigo and madder are the best known. Today the same substances—as well as a great many more, tens of thousands, that were not known as natural plant dyes—are obtained from coal tar in a chemically purer form. Their constant purity makes synthetically produced dyes much more reliable; that is to say, they are usually much purer colors and less liable to fade than vegetable dyes. Earlier, and often today as well, those dyes proved the fastest which do not evolve their true color until they have "developed" by combining with the acid in the air and setting fast in the cloth fibers as oxides. For instance, there is a

dye which comes out of the vat as yellowish green, and which turns to a lovely blue later when it has been in the air. A drastic example of how oxidation makes a dye fast is walnut juice on the fingers. A crushed green walnut gives off a pale green juice which soaks into the skin and after a few hours turns dark brown. The dye is so fast that it cannot be removed, and will grow out only as the skin scales off in the course of time. Skin is horn, like wool, and the same sort of substance as the fibroin of animal silks.

In dyeing, the difference between cloths made of animal and of vegetable fibers is important, as animal fibers resist acids better, and plant fibers resist alkalis. It is important to state which kind of cloth is to be used when buying dyes; some textile dyes are suitable for both.

Many cloth dyes take effect only in hot or even boiling water. These are, of course, unsuitable for batik work, as wax melts at well under boiling point. Cold dyeing produces, on the whole, much better colors on animal than on plant fibers. Animal fibers also hold the dye faster than vegetable ones with the primitive methods we are discussing. Wool is mostly too rough for batik; a smooth silk is the best choice, for the colors come out with greatest purity on silk, and its sheen and texture, especially if it has a linen weave, are added attractions. A great deal of work goes into a multicolored batik, which justifies the use of a good natural silk, even if other cloths are suitable.

Although today there is an inexhaustible selection of textile dyes with every imaginable nuance of color, the number of dyes that work out well under the primitive conditions of domestic dyeing is limited. Anyone intending to go in for batik should make a pattern book. It is important not to make the patterns too small, for colors look quite different on a large piece and on a small cutting. Different kinds of silk will need testing, so that the right weave is chosen for the right design. Taffeta weave is usually the most suitable; a delicate design should have the smoothest taffeta. This is woven from thread unwound from an undisturbed cocoon, unlike slub silk, which is taken from shed cocoons and cuttings, and thus consists of short fibers which have to be properly spun before they can be used. Slub silk is thus more fibrous and, like linen, has irregular thick knobs which are very attractive in the cloth, but which in batik make sharp line drawing impossible. Tussore silks look the same; they are wild silks taken from wild silkworms and are more difficult to dye. Silks are often dressed with metal salts to make them stiffer, and these, too, take dyes badly.

As we have said, batik is a process of resist dyeing. Only one color can be applied at a time, and when there are several colors everything which is to remain in the first color has to be treated with "resist" in the subsequent dips, while those exposed to the next must be protected afterwards from later colors. The more colors in the design the longer and more complicated the process. Some colors can, of course, overlap, so that every place where a later color is to come need not necessarily be covered every time, but some experience is needed to envisage the combinations of colors ahead. It is wise to make several

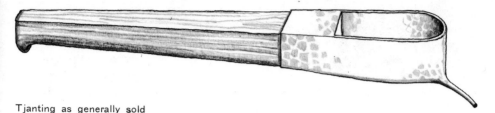

Tjanting as generally sold

test pieces of a given dye, say yellow, to test not only the pure color but also how it mixes with blue, red, and whatever other colors are to be used. Let us give a practical example: first we dye in yellow and cover everything which is later to be blue. For the second dip we cover everything that is to stay yellow, and dye blue; this will give blue where the wax was applied at the yellow dip, and green everywhere else. Thus two colors are given by one dip. If before or after the yellow there were a red dip, the blue could give not two, but three colors according to the waxing: blue, green, and purple.

It is not enough to know the theory of color combinations, every coloring substance reacts differently and must be tested in its combinations with cloth and other colors.

All this shows how important it is to prepare the work beforehand and not to make a first attempt with more than two or three dips. Even that can give five or six different colors. It should be borne in mind that overprinting always produces a darker tone than direct printing. In the example we discussed using blue and yellow, the blue will always be lighter in tone than the green. If the green is wanted as light or lighter than the blue it will have to be dipped in a separate green dye.

The graphic effect of batik is due equally to the manipulation of the tjanting and the fact that no gradual transitions of color are possible. As in sgraffito and mosaic each patch of color lies by the next without any modulation. To this is added a texture that cannot be either influenced or eliminated deliberately; it can at best be made closer or sparser. When the cloth is pressed into the dye the hardened wax breaks up and the dye, of course, penetrates into the cracks, making a fine veining of color. This is characteristic of batik, and in doubtful cases can determine the authenticity of the work. This texture emphasizes the picture plane in a very natural seeming way.

Another uncertainty must be reckoned with. After each dip it is practically always necessary to iron out all the wax; only rarely does the design allow one part to keep the wax through several dips. Thus, many of the lines and areas of the design are repeatedly waxed over, and it is unlikely that it will be done so exactly that the edges of the design remain sharp; a blurred effect is to be expected.

So far our cartoons have been made from a sketch, either in black or colors, using pencil or brush. For batik it is worth trying the method used by professional workers in many branches of ap-

233

plied art and one very suitable for sgraffito as well: the lines and surfaces of the design are cut out of colored paper and assembled. Whether this is first done directly full scale or smaller is a matter of patience. It should be remembered that small drafts are the best way of learning to make broad effects.

For the sake of simplicity we will assume here that we are working straight away with a full size cartoon. For simple batik the design is drawn against a single background color. Even if this is not what we have in mind we start by covering a sheet of drawing paper, rather larger than the format of the batik, with opaque color corresponding to the dominant color of the design. It would, of course, be more convenient to use ready-colored paper, but it can be bought only in a few primitive colors which hardly ever coincide with textile dyes, and furthermore the always rather irregular application of color by hand gives the work more character and personality. This sheet of paper is fixed to the drawing board to dry flat, and the same thing is done with other pieces of paper which we color according to the dyes to be used.

The background paper is cut to exactly the size of the batik and stuck onto a firm underlay. The design is sketched on it in white chalk, which can be easily wiped off, and the larger areas of the design are rapidly sketched onto the appropriately colored paper and cut out and laid on the background. The pieces can be cut out very roughly to begin with, as it is quite unnecessary to go into detail at this stage, and it will be easy to trim the pieces or replace them later.

The more freely the work is done at this stage the more spontaneous will be the final effect of the design when it is carried out. It may make the arrangement of the pieces easier if they are colored on both sides; they will not curl up, and the scraps can be more easily used. Once the general arrangement of the primary shapes and colors is roughly what is wanted, they can be lightly pasted on the background so that they can be quite easily taken off but do not move at every touch.

If the student finds it disturbing that the edges of his cutouts do not lie flat he can cover the whole composition with a sheet of glass. This gives the design finality and makes it possible to consider it from a critical distance. Then the composition can be improved by trimming the shapes and moving them about, and we can try cutting out thin lines, not necessarily all in one piece. This is better than painting the lines in. The cutout edges are needed to give their stark quality to the whole design, and should not be diluted with drawn-in elements, whose softening effect might be unconsciously transferred to the final execution.

Once the design is to our liking, we stick the different pieces down firmly and decide on the best sequence for the dyeing; light and pale colors are done first. For each dip we make a separate drawing on tracing paper. This is much simpler than trying to trace the outlines from a single drawing onto the cloth before each dip. The tracing is done with the blue used for embroidery transfers, which washes out very easily. If we have to trace onto dark patches, we can

Design prepared with colored adhesive paper. Intended for four tones, or for only three if the shadows on the red background are obtained by superimposing blue. Some imprecision arises from the wax stopping-out process

spread chalk powder over the back of the tracing paper.

A design coming right to the edge of the cloth produces an unfinished look, as if the piece had been cut out of a larger work. A frame around the edges looks better, made either by leaving a strip uncovered all around at each dip so that it is colored with every dye, or else letting the design run away unmistakably at the edge into the background color. A batik of any pretensions can hardly have any other purpose than a wall

hanging, and the theme and style should be appropriate.

For the application of the wax, the cloth should be held stretched on a frame so that the wax does not stick to anything underneath. When the cloth is ironed, care must be taken not to pull it out of shape, or the subsequent tracings will not fit over the design already printed.

The tjanting filled with wax is best warmed in a water bath. (It is better to have several tjantings with spouts of different breadths, or work is very slow when there are broad lines to be waxed.) As in sgraffito we begin with the outlines and fill in the larger areas afterwards. Techniques of working vary, depending on whether the artist needs to support his arm to steady it or not. For filling in the larger areas a flat bristle brush is used to spread the hot wax.

When all the lines and surfaces are sufficiently waxed we prepare the dye carefully in a vat, according to the maker's directions. It is important that a vat be chosen large enough to give ample room to spread the cloth. If it is too small the cloth will have to be crumpled too much, which will produce more cracks in the wax than is desirable. If the vat is large the artist can determine the amount of wax he wants to crackle. After dyeing and drying, the cloth is ironed between thick layers of absorbent paper. The iron should not be hotter than is necessary to melt the wax, and the paper should be changed frequently. Ironing should be continued until there is not a trace of wax left to be absorbed by the paper. This should be watched carefully, as specks of wax left in the cloth can spoil the whole effect of the subsequent dyeings, leaving ugly and quite permanent marks.

The work is made much easier if the design is so arranged that wax has only to be added and none removed between the dips. Then the wax will have to be ironed out only once, at the end.

It may happen, if the cloth is very thick or if the wax is too thinly applied or not warm enough, that the wax does not penetrate clear through the cloth fibers so that the back of the cloth takes the dye. To avoid this, a wax resist can be put on the back as well as the front, or, as is done by the sculptor doing fine modeling in plaster, spatulas can be heated in boiling water, dried and rubbed over the back of the cloth. This will melt the wax once more so that the cloth can absorb it.

The finished wall hanging looks best if enough cloth has been left to make loops at the top and a fringe at the bottom. It deserves a proper finish after so much work has been put into it. The most decorative effect is to hang the loops over a bamboo pole or rod of wrought iron, which, of course, should be hand-wrought.

Right: Munch, The Kiss, two-tone woodcut. This print was pulled from a plain soft woodblock (fir or larch)

17. PRINTING

Since the discovery of paper, artists have rarely been content to produce their drawings in single copies. They make prints by transferring the drawing onto a material which allows a more or less limited quantity of copies to be made. The principle of printing was used very early for textiles, before the beginning of our era, and it was known to primitive peoples before they came into contact with the more advanced techniques of modern civilization. Seals, or blocks, generally ornamental or with animal designs, were carved from wood, colored, and printed onto the cloth.

Practically the only material used for writing and drawing before the fourteenth century was parchment, which is unsuitable for printing. Not until paper was available were the possibilities of printing drawings investigated. Very

soon after the invention of the printing press, methods of "art" printing were evolved, making it possible even to surpass freehand drawing in delicacy and detail.

There are three different kinds of printing of the type in which the artist himself makes the block: relief, intaglio, and flat. In relief printing the design stands out, as on seals. This is the oldest technique, going back to textile block printing. In intaglio, such as engraving, the lines are cut into metal and filled with ink. The remaining top surface stays blank, that is to say, it is wiped clean after inking the plate. Moistened paper is pressed onto the metal plate and absorbs the ink from the grooves.

Flat printing exploits the mutual repulsion of water and grease. It is called lithography because a flat piece of stone

Kollwitz, Self-portrait, drawn on Ingres paper and lithographed

is used which can absorb both water and grease. The design is drawn onto the dry stone (often slate) with a greasy chalk and the surface is then moistened with water. Lithographic ink (a mixture of soot and linseed oil) is rolled onto it, and, being greasy, it adheres only where the grease pencil has drawn and transfers the design onto paper pressed onto the plate.

Lithography is the most recent of these printing techniques. It was invented by Aloys Senefelder of Munich in 1798. Lithography enables the artist to duplicate his work without any training in printing. He simply draws on the stone —in reverse image, of course—and leaves the rest of the work, which is quite mechanical, to the printer. If the artist uses transfer paper it is even simpler; he need not reverse his design but has only to draw onto it with a grease pencil. The lithographer prints off the original from the paper onto the stone, thus producing a reverse image of the drawing. The prints can reproduce the artist's drawing exactly. We say "can," because, as in all art, the artist should understand his medium and draw appropriately for it. However, anyone who can draw proficiently in soft lead or chalk should be able to do a lithograph transfer at first attempt. Care should be taken, as it should in any pencil or chalk drawing, not to draw too lightly or too heavily, to avoid blanks or black smudges. The student will best bring off a perfect lithograph by first making a visit to the workshop and watching the whole process through. He will no doubt pick up some good tips from a friendly craftsman.

The simplest method of relief printing is the linoleum cut. This requires a special linoleum, which can be bought in any art shop, where tools for cutting it can also be found. The simplest tools cost very little.

The linoleum chosen should be as light as possible in color. It is covered with a coat of opaque black paint before starting work. The design is first drawn onto a good tracing paper in black ink with pen or brush. The top side of the drawing is rubbed over with white chalk and the outlines traced onto the linoleum from the back, rendering the design in reverse. Everything which is to be white in the print is now first chalked over with white hatching on the black linoleum block and then cut out, so that the light color of the linoleum stands in contrast to the black surface, as it will in the print. A rubber brayer with a handle is rolled in the printing ink so that it is covered lightly but evenly all over, and then rolled over the block, causing everything standing out in relief to be covered with a thin layer of ink. The paper, which should be thin and preferably Japanese, is laid over the block and rubbed with the hand or with a burnisher, very gently at first and then more firmly. The back of a teaspoon makes a good burnisher. When the paper is removed the print can be compared with the drawing and further work can be done on the block, if necessary. Of course, this can consist only of cutting away more; there is no chance of putting anything back.

Some dexterity is needed, and, most of all, cleanliness; otherwise it will be painfully clear why printing is sometimes called the black art. The only way to spread ink properly on the brayer is first to spread it thinly with a brush onto a glass or plastic plate and then to roll it out until it is thin and even. A stack of newspapers and a pile of old rags should be at hand, and turpentine or spirits for cleaning the roller, block, and glass plate before the ink dries.

The woodcut is worked on in exactly the same way as a linoleum cut, but it requires more skill and much more practice; special wood and better tools—if possible sculptors' chisels—will also be needed. Lime wood is best for the block, which must be planed quite smooth. Watery paint cannot be used on it or the wood fibers stand up and make the surface rough. The chisel and gouge must always be used in the direction of the grain or the wood will splinter and tear.

Lucie ter Braake, Haydn. Simple linocut for a concert program (reproduced in actual size)

This danger is obviated by using cross-cut timber of hardwood like pear, maple, or even box. Generally, because of the size of the tree, this can be obtained only in very small single pieces; larger sizes are built up of several smaller pieces glued together. Woods cut down the grain generally show the graining and should be in one piece, but cross-cuts do not show graining and, of course, must be glued tight without leaving any gap.

Cross-cut blocks after being glued together are sawed into slices about an inch thick and polished mirror smooth with sandpaper, using several pieces, each one finer than the last. The slightest scratch on the surface makes a line across the design. The edges of the block should be cut into, to prevent the danger of splitting. Every art shop sells ready-prepared cross-cut blocks.

On an end grain or cross-cut block special engraving tools have to be used; the result is a wood engraving as distinct from a woodcut. A wood engraving is suited to finer drawing than a linoleum cut or a woodcut. A practiced wood engraver does not trace, but draws directly onto the wood. The drawing has to be done in reverse, of course, and perhaps the way to start is with a self-portrait, which can be drawn directly onto the block from the mirror, and which will come out the right way around on the print.

In all these techniques it is advisable to pull a print from time to time to see how the effect is working out. Relief printing differs from the usual graphic techniques in leaving untouched what will be seen in the drawing, whereas in ordinary drawing the artist makes the strokes that are to be visible. If the cutting tools were used like a pencil, it would produce an effect like drawing with white on black.

For intaglio printing, however, the normal drawing procedure is followed; in other words, the engraved lines come out positive in the print. The classic material for intaglio printing is a perfectly smooth and polished copper plate, which can be worked either with a graving tool or an etching needle. This is hardly a technique which can be self-taught, it needs to be learned systematically and with much practice. The following is intended as a description of the process, not as a course of instruction.

Etching comes closer to ordinary drawing than any other of the cutting or engraving processes. It is not so technically elaborate as copper or steel plate engraving. Even an etching, however, does not reproduce a drawing as directly as a lithograph.

The etcher covers the blank plate of copper with the thinnest skin of wax or a ready-prepared etching ground, generally a mixture of wax and asphalt. He then draws on this without special pressure with the etching needle, baring the copper with fine strokes. The drawing stands out against the ground in light copper color. Then the plate is placed in a dish and diluted nitric acid is poured over it. If the plate is very large, a border of wax can be built up round the edge, forming a tray on the plate itself to hold the acid. The acid bites into the copper where it has been uncovered by the needle for as long as it is kept in contact with the plate, working both downwards and sideways into the metal. Thus, all the lines made by the needle become thicker as time goes on. When the right time has elapsed, the acid is poured off and the plate washed. Then the ground is removed with paraffin or spirits. Next the etched plate is warmed, and printing ink is rubbed hard into it with a leather or cloth pad. The surface untouched by the acid is wiped clean of ink, first with a wad of fine muslin and finally with the hand, so that the ink remains only in the grooves. The plate is then put into an etching press, which is rather similar to a wringer, but has strong iron instead of rubber rollers, between which the plate is squeezed, together with the moistened etching paper and a piece of felt, which are laid over it. The

paper sucks the ink out of the grooves and emerges with a mirror image of the etched drawing—and a slight skin of the ink, which can never be completely removed from the top surface of the plate.

This first pull shows the etcher whether the drawing is to remain with all its lines of the same thickness or whether some parts need etching more deeply. If so, all the rest must again be covered with ground. New lines can also be added, and the whole etching process is repeated.

It is characteristic of an etching that the line is never as sharp as a pen stroke on hard paper. The acid cuts into the metal with branches and veins like ink into blotting paper, although this can be seen only under a magnifying glass. The etched line thus has a certain soft-

Woodcut, Gentian. One of a series of illustrations of protected plants (⅓ actual size)

ness. Another characteristic feature is the thin skin of ink over the whole plate, and the quite sensible and visible impression left by the plate on the paper when it was damp and soft. If a large plate has been given a border of wax, as described above, the picture will fade out towards the edges where the wax covered it over and prevented the acid from getting in.

A copper plate, like every printing block, can give only a limited number of prints, perhaps several hundred, even a thousand. The surface of the plate gradually wears away and the drawing gets fainter and fainter. For this reason the first prints are always considered the best. Experienced etchers used to make them recognizable by using a plate large enough to leave a band at the bottom. Sometimes inscriptions or signatures were engraved in these bands, but at the same time they scratched a soft drawing into the already etched plate with the needle (a leaf pattern, an animal, or some sort of emblem). This "drypoint" came out only in the first dozen copies or so, after which it vanished.

In the same way, whole plates can be worked in drypoint. No acid is used, and generally the prints are very faint, but if the scratching is done very forcefully the edges of the scorings stand up in a sort of fringed ridge. This makes the ink spread into a rather smudged line, as though the line had been drawn with a sharp pen on damp paper, making it blurred. Much experience is needed to know beforehand what the effect will be.

While etching and drypoint allow a fluid, free hand in drawing, as when using pen or pencil, the graving tool required for copper engraving has to be pushed with a strong pressure. The graver is sharpened into a point, with angular facets. The lines are not bitten into the metal with acid but cut directly into the surface with the graver. The line is made broader by pressing the tool deeper into the metal, and clear modulations in the thickness of the line are possible. It needs great skill to handle the tool correctly, and classical copper engraving has developed as an austere technique, demanding that the lines be drawn strictly parallel, whether they run straight or, corresponding to the perspective of the curves, are bent. Swelling of the stroke thus emphasizes shading. A dark area is best rendered by cross hatching.

The graving tool always leaves ridges, which have to be removed with a scraper to make a clear print. An incompetent engraving looks atrocious; the craft must be systematically studied, or left alone. This, however, is not the reason that there are so few engravers who can rank as artists. The stylization necessary to contain a free drawing in such precise lines has long since ceased to appeal to the taste of the times; yet it could be made to reveal some new and attractive sides.

Steel engraving is done in the same way as copper, except that a steel plate is used, which is engraved before it is tempered by heating and dipping in water. It gives many more prints than a copper plate, but steel cannot be kept for very long because it is almost impossible to prevent its developing patches of rust, which sooner or later ruin the whole plate.

Rembrandt, studies of Saskia for an etching (actual size)

Printing

Two more techniques come under the heading of intaglio printing: mezzotint and aquatint. Both work on the same principle: the copper plate is roughened, so that if it were printed from in this state it would give a uniform, satiny black surface. Scraper and burnisher are used to make smooth surfaces which print white, for the ink sticks only in the rough places. This makes possible the softest effects of transition and fading, like smearing chalk or charcoal in a drawing, or such photographic effects as bromoil.

The only difference between the two processes is in the method of roughening the copper: for mezzotint it is closely lined in both directions with a mezzotint tool (a sort of knife), and for acquaint resin powder is scattered evenly over the surface and fused onto it; the minute gaps between the grains of dust are bitten out by acid and so hold the ink and print dark.

Whereas linoleum and wood blocks need no special workshop, and lithographs can be handed over to the printer once the drawing is done, copper intaglio is an expert business, requiring a workshop and some training in the craft. The whole process with plates, ground and acids, inking and testing, and finally printing after the trial pulls needs a special room where the press figures as the first essential. Once the equipment is set up it is possible to try more complicated

Below: Goya, detail from aquatint. Right: Piazetta, detail, copper engraving (both actual size)

processes, such as colored etching. This is done by taking prints from the black etching onto further plates, which are prepared as for aquatint. Each plate is then etched for the separate color areas. The black print, which is pulled last, makes sense of the colored areas by printing the drawing over them.

It can be seen how carefully planned and precise the design must be for this process. There is no room for free drawing during the manual execution, and this is the reason why, although there are very tasteful and competent colored etchings, there have never been any of the artistic standard reached by the great etchers and engravers who worked only in black, like Dürer or Rembrandt.

Even in the less complicated processes of colored woodcuts and lithographs the color is never as important as the drawing. Toulouse-Lautrec was a real master of the lithograph and knew its every possibility, but even in his work the color is never more than an enhancing addition to his brilliant drawing.

Prints are generally priced lower than unique drawings, and this is justifiable economically from the artist's point of view, since he can certainly sell 100 etchings for more than he may be lucky enough to get for a single drawing. The technical consideration, however, is irrelevant to the artistic value of prints. They are unquestionably on a level artistically with drawings, and they are essentially unique in the same way, if the artist pulls the print himself and produces each one individually. We have only to think of Japanese color prints: no one else could print them in the same way as the artist himself intended, for as he cuts

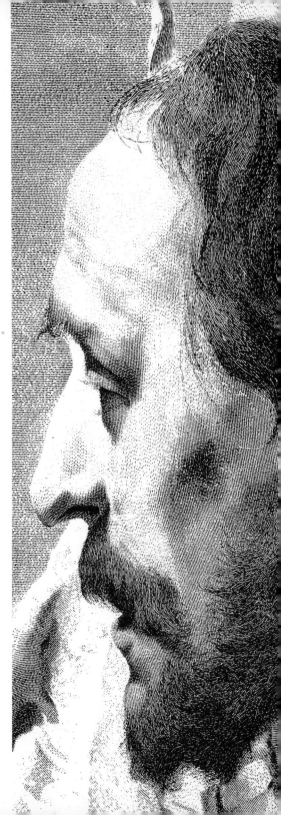

the block he is thinking how he will fade and merge the colors, so that the print has often almost the effect of a water-color. Apart from such manipulations, the technique of printing allows many effects which cannot be obtained at all with pencil, pen, or brush. It is worth seeing what happens if one tries to imitate an etching with a pen. What has already been said many times must once again be repeated for printing: every artistic medium has its own particular justification because each one has its own power of expressing something which cannot be said in a different one.

The monotype has only a superficial technical connection with printing, for it is a print which can be pulled only once, and on the face of it may sound like a highly unnecessary gimmick. But it is not! A monotype is a relatively simple process: the picture is painted in reverse onto a glass, plastic sheet, or polished stone slab and pressed off onto a sheet of paper while the color is still wet. Printing ink, oil, or watercolor can be used. For a second copy the painting would need to be done again entirely, and it would, of course, never come out exactly the same. The monotype is not the method to be used if something is required in several copies; it is in essence "unre-peatable."

The color on the plate can be scraped off and renewed as often as required; thus, the method of building up the composition is very fluid—quite the reverse of an ink drawing, in which every stroke is indelibly marked on the paper. Corrections and alterations can be made up to the last minute without their showing on the print. Many styles of work can be done in monotype, from a line drawing or a flat color mosaic to a composition in tonal variation or one using many colors. It is so variable that it belongs to graphic art hardly more than to painting, and the more elaborate uses of it require some skill and proficiency in painting. A black and white pen or brush drawing, however, is within the scope of anyone who can make a worthwhile sketch on a piece of glass, and if the color is laid on thinly and uniformly enough the result will always have a dangerously seductive individuality. In the hands of a practiced specialist it can become an incomparable vehicle of artistic expression. Unfortunately, most of the monotypes seen in exhibitions are only too obviously not by experts, but by someone quite unpracticed in trying his hand at a new medium. Then, indeed, the monotype appears to be no more than a highly unnecessary gimmick.

PART II: PAINTING

1. HISTORY OF THE TECHNIQUE OF PAINTING

A painting has three constituent materials: the pigments, the support, and the binder, which holds the pigments to the support. The painter's craft or technique consists in the correct combination and manipulation of these three elements. "Technique" in reference to painting is often confused with style, which is the personal use of the technique, or the painter's manner. This is a psychological, artistic phenomenon, as little to be taught as a style in drawing, writing poetry, or composing music. The craft alone can be taught, and this craft is called, for the painter, painting technique.

The problems which still today beset painting technique arise from uncertainties which can be explained partly by the imperfection of the materials, and partly by the historical development of the technique. From the beginning, painters have used materials which cannot be completely understood without a thorough grounding in chemistry and related sciences. In the old days this scientific knowledge did not exist, and even now it exists only among specialists who rarely have anything to do with the practice of the art of painting. Painters of earlier centuries used to be forever writing essays to expound their theories and problems concerning their material, unless they guarded their empirically found knowledge as a secret. An air of secrecy still surrounds painting technique, although it has been investigated scientifically since the end of the last century.

These investigations were for a long time centered around the world-famous Doerner Institute in Munich. It was named after a painter, Max Doerner, whose experimental work first made the problems of the painter known to scientists. After hundreds and thousands of years of uncertainty these unresolved questions could be answered with exactitude for the first time.

All this happened at a time when painting technique had reached its lowest depths. This had come about in the following way: in earlier centuries the apprentices in a master's studio were concerned solely with learning the craft, the only subject that can be taught. They learned to produce the colors from the natural or, sometimes even then, synthetic raw materials, to prepare the appropriate grounds, and to employ the methods needed to achieve durable and vivid results. Thus, they learned intimately the good and bad qualities of their materials. They learned also how to use these materials to carry out the ideas of their masters and of the period, and the most gifted developed new artistic resources from their thorough grounding in the material side of the art.

Towards the end of the eighteenth century, schools, or art academies, began to replace private studios, and at the same time the industrial production of ready-prepared painting materials increased rapidly. The production was not based on any systematic study, but on more or less uncritically adopted recipes, adapted to meet the widest requirements possible. Large sales were now the prime consideration; the quality deteriorated in consequence, and with it technique as well.

This situation is now quite changed. The research we referred to has resulted in the supply of excellent ready-prepared painting materials. It is nevertheless essential to be able to choose from among all the materials available, for there are still some very dubious products on the market. The demand from technically uneducated painters compels the industry to produce goods of inferior quality. The aim of the following pages is to explain enough about the character of the individual materials to enable the reader to choose them wisely and make appropriate use of them.

There is as yet no universal terminology for painting materials, due to an unfortunate gulf between scientists, who like to be systematic, and painters, who resist the new unmellifluous words, in spite of their exactitude.

Color, both generally and professionally, means two things: the phenomenon of color, and the coloring material ready prepared with its binder. Pigment means any colored material before it is in a condition to be used for painting. Painters do not react favorably to any attempts to discipline their vocabulary. However, the correct chemical names for different colors are coming into general use, instead of incomplete technical terms or names derived from outdated origins of the colors. For this reason the chemical and technically correct terms are always given first place in this book. The technically correct name is often helpful in indicating the correct use of the material.

Although we shall go more thoroughly into the properties of the different materials used when we discuss the various techniques of painting, it should be noted at once that the type of binder used always prefixes the reference to prepared paints: "oil color" means coloring material mixed with an oil binder, "watercolor" means that the thick glue binder is to be thinned with water. Thus, even here these terms are not quite consistent, although sufficiently clear for use by those concerned with the techniques.

2. COLOR

Color is the painter's means of expression—but color as **surface**. Thus he differs from the draftsman, who works with lines, the color of which is immaterial. The classical drawing is in black on a white ground, with possibly some intermediate grays. If sepia, red, or other colored chalks are used, the whole drawing is done in only one color and remains an abstraction of the natural model from the point of view of color, in the same way as the outline is an abstraction of the surface and of the volume. Black, gray, and white are abstractions of the color as is also the translation of the multi-colored natural impressions into a single color tone.

Black and white hardly ever occur at their purest in nature. Neither phenomenon can be designated as "color." Then what is color? For the painter it is first a powder which he spreads on his painting surface with something to make it stick. This says nothing about the physical or chemical properties of the coloring substance. If we look at color powders in the dark it is impossible to tell which is blue and which yellow. Colors can be recognized only in the light. Illumination alone creates them.

You were no doubt taught in school that white, colorless light can be divided up into a colored spectrum through a prism. Light is the radiation of a source of energy. The visible wave lengths of this radiation lie between 397 and 687 millionths of a millimeter. Each one of these wave lengths has a distinct color. These phenomena begin with violet and spread continuously over blue, green, yellow, and orange to red. Shorter light waves (ultra violet) and longer ones (infra red) cannot be directly perceived by the human eye.

If we say of a material that it is blue, it means that this material reflects only blue light waves; all the rest it absorbs and transforms into heat. This can be easily proven: if we touch a white object in the sunshine, it is scarcely different in warmth from the surrounding air. White reflects all light waves. A black object, on the other hand, can become so hot in the sun that it is too hot to touch, for all the light waves that reach it are absorbed, turned into heat, and then slowly given off again. If we cover an object of another color with a layer of blue, this layer gives the impression that the

Colored patches arranged according to the spectrum

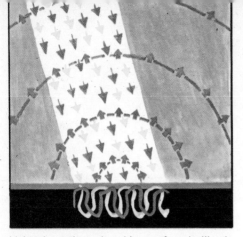

Light absorption when blue surface is illuminated

now divided into six colors. It becomes twelve-part if each pair of neighboring colors is again mixed. Further intermediate grades can be made by mixing yet again each neighboring pair, until by the time the circle is divided into 48 we have an almost continuous transition of color—a phenomenon which can be seen in perfect form in the spectrum or rainbow.

All these colors are called "pure," as each sector consists of only one or two primary colors, however fine the division of the circle, as against the impure, dull colors in which there is some of each of the three primary colors.

Just as light can be split up into its wave lengths and colors, it can be combined again. If three panes of glass in each of the three primary colors are superimposed, the light coming through them is colorless. Even the mixed color of two of these panes is lighter than the color of either of the two panes by itself, since two thirds of the visible scope of the waves is combined light. This combination of colors is called an "additive" mixture, in contrast to the subtractive, in which light is taken away.

whole object is blue. This property characterizes the substances which are called simply "color."

The color circle gives an optical elucidation of the properties of color. It is a scheme which includes first the three primary colors: blue, yellow, and red. These are called primary because they cannot be made by mixing other colors, and both by optical and material mixing they can give all other colors. If equal quantities of any two primary colors are mixed together they produce a new color; so there are three new colors: green, orange, and violet. The circle is

Three primary colors

6-part color circle

12-part color circle

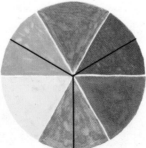

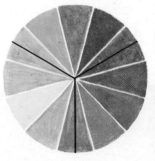

Subtractive mixture occurs whenever substances which reflect light are combined, as in all painter's colors. It can be understood in this way: imagine that colorless light is a whole made up of three thirds. Every patch colored with nontransparent, primary color reflects one third and absorbs two thirds. If we mix these patches of red, blue, and yellow together, then three times one third is reflected, and three times two thirds absorbed. Only one third of the whole light energy encountering the surface is reflected, and two thirds is absorbed; the combination of reflected light is no longer white but darker, which means gray.

In the color circle this subtractive mixture of equal parts of primary colors can be represented as a concentric section of the circle which is dark gray. If you take this section eccentrically from the original circle we produce not a neutral, but a colored gray. The color corresponds to the one or two dominant colors. In the illustration it is a brown, since red + yellow = orange predominate. Otherwise expressed you have ⅔ red + ⅔ yellow + ⅙ blue = ⅚ brown.

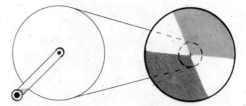

Optical color mixing by rotation

Subtractive mixtures can be made visible by the following experiment: paint a color circle (in three or more segments, it makes no difference) onto a disc of cardboard and rotate it quickly. The eye cannot separate the different color stimuli and they are mixed optically to gray. If instead of the complete color circle you paint an eccentric section on the disc, the result, when it is rotated, is a colored gray: blue-gray, green-gray, yellow-gray (beige or brown), and so on. All dull colors are made in this way, depending entirely on what section of the color circle, or what original colors are used. Gray would also result if only two colors were rotated, if they consisted of one primary color and a mixture of equal proportions of the two others, such as red and green (blue + yellow).

Additive mixing of the three primary colors

Subtractive mixing to give gray (concentric detail)

Subtractive mixing to give brown (excentric detail)

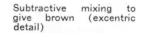
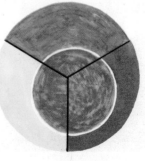

Color

Complementary color chart

It can be seen that green lies directly opposite red on the circle. Every pair of colors lying diametrically opposite each other adds up to gray. These opposed colors are called complementary colors. They and their effects are decisively important in all color sensations, and therefore in painting. This is due to the fact that the nearer two colors approach complementary relations, the more the eye is stimulated. It tries to combine them as gray, but since it cannot do so each color seems brighter against its neighbor than it would if it stood alone in a neutral weak-colored surrounding. If you look at a snow scene in the twilight everything looks gray on gray. If you light a lamp the landscape immediately looks uniformly blue. The blue increases in strength the closer the lamp light is to orange, the complementary color to blue.

The same thing happens on a cloudy winter's day if direct sunlight suddenly falls on the gray-white landscape. The shadows turn to pure cobalt blue, even though the glistening snow shows no orange, but a pure white, because many more of the long light waves, red and yellow, penetrate the thick blanket of air between the landscape and the low ly-ing winter sun. Where its direct rays do not fall, you feel all the more clearly the contrast, the weak blue reflection.

This does not occur only in winter light, of course, but everywhere and all the time; but it takes more observation and practice to notice it. This is what is meant in the art schools by the insistent exhortation to "see color in everything"; though often no further explanation is forthcoming for the innocent student.

An optical illusion causes the gray to appear to approximate to the complementary colors of the frame surrounding it

The Chinese express their advice more poetically: "In every colored picture one color should be queen. All other colors should be subservient to her so that she appears in all her splendor." By this is meant that all colors other than the "queen," the dominant color, should show a certain tendency towards the complementary, but should still appear dull and impure against the pure, dominant color. In this way the picture is given a unified effect, and is concentrated on the essential, marked in the dominant color.

If the surrounding color is only neutral gray it inclines in effect towards the color complementary to the dominant one. The well-known example is illustrated here: the red, green, and orange frames make the gray windows green-gray, reddish-gray, and violet-gray respectively. All this shows that the human eye cannot see colors "objectively"; it always sees one color in relation to at least one other color; in this it is unlike the ear, which in some musically developed people retains absolute pitch. Such people can define a bird call in the exactly right notes, whether they hear it quite isolated or through the bird chorus of a wood in springtime. It is impossible to register color independently in the same way.

Even the perception of cold and warm colors is subjective. It is like dipping a hand into water, first at 60 degrees, then at 50 degrees, when the latter feels cold; but if the hand is first dipped at 40 degrees, the water at 50 degrees seems warm.

Above: Winter Landscape at Twilight
Below: the same landscape after an orange-colored lamp is lit

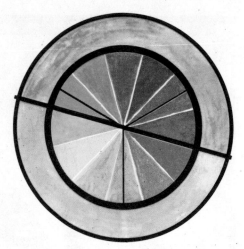

Cool and warm color chart. The cool colors range from blue-green to alizarin red; warm from yellow-green to cadmium red

The diagram shows the general division of the circle into warm and cold colors, but in practice they can work out quite differently. It is quite possible to talk of a cold yellow or red, although these are the colors of warmth and fire as against the blue of shadows and ice. Blue can look warm if it is mixed, and stands in contrast to a red bordering on violet or a light, greenish yellow or "cold" violet-gray.

The psychological effects of color work in the same way. Warm colors seem to approach the beholder, cold to recede and make the space larger. Red reduces space and has an oppressive effect, orange is aggressive and exciting, yellow is quieter and more cheerful. Green is the most neutral from this point of view.

None of these effects is noticeable except in large areas. A picture which is in one color tone can give its mood to the subject. A "lady in blue" has by its color alone quite a different effect from a picture of a woman done in tones of red. But all radiations of color change in relation to others and can turn into their opposites—or remain without any positive effect.

It may be questionable policy to construct a picture entirely on the psychological effects of color, but it is even more dangerous to do it according to preconceived theories, as is the practice of some artists. The adherents of some sects try to arouse spirituality by the use of pure colors, excluding any tendency towards gray. The effect does not work on people not spiritually prepared, and this is why such unworldly art is questionable. We expect a direct impact from all art; it should not require a special mental or spiritual education. This is not the same thing as using certain scientific facts about optics, as the Pointillists did. They built up their color surfaces according to fundamental optical laws out of small dots of pure color. The pictures of the greatest exponents of **pointillism**, like Segantini or Signac, have a direct appeal. Their scientific scaffold is not what the beholder notices, he sees merely the artistic effect.

3. COLOR AS SUBSTANCE

Every material has color. One might say that the whole world consists of coloring materials. The problem is to what extent they can be used for coloring or painting. First we must draw the distinction between coloring and painting, each a different activity using different coloring materials.

Whether you are going to paint a garden fence or a picture, you use color powders, which feel like flour to the touch. These are mixed with suitable binding material to make paints. Alternatively you buy the coloring material ready prepared in tins, boxes, or tubes, or in blocks which will dissolve in water, and which contain water-soluble glue. In every case the color can be seen as it will look after it has been applied.

If you intend to dye cloth or stain wood you are again given a powder or pieces of crystal, but it generally looks almost black. It dissolves completely in water, possibly with the addition of other chemicals, but even in solution it does not show its ultimate color. This it will not do until it has combined chemically, and without needing a binder, with the cloth or wood fibers.

Unlike paints, these dyes remain in true solution; they cannot be removed. Filtered infusions of tea or coffee are "inks" of this kind. But if a can of oil paint is left standing for some time the color powder sinks to the bottom in a thick ooze which has to be stirred vigorously to make it combine again with the

oil above it into a homogeneous paint.

The same is true of a glue solution, and it is even more apparent in powder which is mixed only with water for painting purposes. These are all pigment or solid colors, which form a more or less opaque layer or skin over the object treated. Pigment colors differ from inks, dyes, or stains both in being indissoluble solids and in their chemical composition: inks, dyes, and stains are organic chemical substances, while pigment colors on the whole are inorganic in nature. There is one exception among the materials used in worthwhile painting: alizarin red has an organic basis. No inorganic substance gives this color; the paint is prepared by giving an organic dye to white clay.

The inorganic pigment colors are for the most part metal oxides and hydroxides, either by themselves or combined

Left: dye-bath. Right: bath with deposit

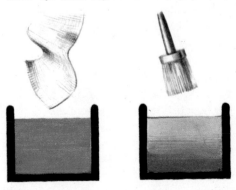

with clay. They exist in nature as colored earths and are thus usually rather dull, "impure" colors. Artificially produced pigments are on the whole purer; some approximate to the absolute purity of spectrum colors, but never attain it completely. The effect of complementary colors can make them seem so in a picture.

The nature of pigment can be understood from the following example: bricks are made of loam, a very yellow clay, and baked; yet when they come out of the oven they are red. While the heat of the oven fuses the clay into one piece, it causes the yellow in the clay, which is iron hydroxide (rust), to give off its water content, thereby becoming a red iron oxide.

If the unbaked loam is dried and

Loam (ochre). Very light, moderate, and well burnt

crumbled fine, or if baked bricks are ground to a fine dust, they can be used in that condition for painting. Böcklin did this, though it is much easier to purchase yellow and red clay, technically pure and uniformly ground, as ochre. If yellow ochre is scattered on a hot plate it will soon become red ochre. The extraction of the water content makes the powder specifically heavier and denser; it loses some transparency, the characteristic of the so-called glaze colors, which allows the ground to shine through. Opaque colors, which are often burnt

pigments, cover the surface completely with a relatively thin application, so that the color effect is constant whether the ground is light or dark.

Most metal hydroxides can be turned into darker and more opaque colors. Of synthetic paints the most striking example is the hydrous oxide of chromium, hydrous green chromic oxide, or viridian, as it is usually called, an extremely pure, transparent color. By burning or strong heating it becomes anhydrous green chromic oxide, chrome green, a dull color and very opaque. The specific weight alters from 2.74 to 5.21, and the granulation is finer. Not all pigments can be altered by burning, and some are destroyed by strong heat.

There are also pigments which make a chemical reaction when mixed together or with a calcareous binder. All pigments affect the drying time of oil binders. Oil with white lead dries to the touch in about 30 hours, whereas with umber it is still sticky after 100. To avoid these difficulties attempts have been made to use absolutely neutral pigments like ground glass pastes, but these are not satisfactory because they break up the light in undesirable ways. Modern painting technique has therefore to resign itself to using pigments which, like natural ochre and carbon, were used 30,000 years ago for the cave paintings, and which have thus proved their durability.

Both old and new pigments are chosen primarily for their tolerance to light. They are classified according to their ability to combine with binders, principally with lime.

A number of pigments are similar in

color but have quite different properties and prices; for example, the brightest and most light-resistant yellow is cadmium, but it is destroyed by lime. When painting on lime it can be replaced by uranium yellow, uranium oxide, which gives almost the same color; if it need not be quite so pure and bright, Mars yellow, yellow iron oxide, is usually preferred by painters, since uranium yellow is the most expensive of all colors.

The reader may ask, since all colors can be mixed from the three primary colors, why others are used at all. Some artists have indeed taken a pride in using only these three, but quite apart from the fact that it is impossible to maintain pigments of the three primary colors in a condition of absolute purity it is very tedious to be forever mixing colors, and other technical difficulties arise as well.

First let us see how another color is derived from two pigments—for instance, green from blue and yellow. The method is the same with dry pigments and those already mixed with a binder. The grains of color, each perhaps a hundredth or a thousandth of a millimeter in size, cannot be distinguished individually by eye; they combine on the retina in a unified color effect, or, more

Above: alizarin red—light, medium, deep
Below: medium alizarin red—with white, alone, with black

precisely, not they but the minute blue and yellow particles of reflected light rays. A pervasive green pigment, chrome green, for instance, is different. It does not reflect two different light waves, but one single green one.

In practice it is almost impossible to copy a definite color tone by mixing, so there should always be a series of colors ready in the box, even as there is in the mind, which are permanently there as original colors in the identical tone. These paints enable the painter to see the colors in his imagination as he works, just as the notes of the well-tempered piano live in the imagination of the musician, and from them he can imagine all the delicate nuances and intermediate colors and mix them in practice. Added

Left: chrome green (green grains)

Right: ultramarine blue mixed with ochre (blue and yellow grains)

Color as Substance

to this, a larger choice of paints makes him able to deal more easily with all kinds of technical difficulties.

It is almost impossible to vary the tone value of individual paints to lighter or darker than the original simply by mixing with white or black pigments. White makes the brilliance of pure pigments chalky, and black often has a dirty effect. With yellow it gives a smudgy green, with red an unattractive brown, and with orange also a brown. None of these colors has any brilliance.

There is no need to give an elaborate explanation of the properties of light absorption of the white and black pigments. A practical test is more to the point. Take three tones of alizarin red — light, medium, and dark — and paint a patch of each. Then beneath the dark tone paint a patch of medium tone mixed with black to correspond to the original tone, and beneath the light tone a patch of medium mixed with white. You will quickly see by the contrasting results how desirable it is to have every possible tone of the important pigments in your paint box. Most synthetic paints are produced in two or three tones. They are not mixed, but the pigment is treated physically or chemically during manufacture. Even so the tones are inadequate to reproduce all the variations of tone in nature.

To remedy this the transparent properties of pure, bright pigments can be utilized. A transparent layer in the complementary color over a dull colored under-

Glazes: Left: ultramarine violet over light ochre. Right: medium alizarin red over viridian

painting will provide the rich glowing darks which gave the mysterious depth and glow to the paintings of the old masters.

Whether or not to work with glazes is today an artistic question. Since the Impressionist period it has been rather out of fashion for technical reasons: pictures begun directly from nature, and if possible completed at one sitting, could not be built up on an underpainting, which has to dry all day, while its glazing requires repeated rest periods. Painters and art lovers, too, were enamored of the new effect of flat, opaque colors. However, that is no reason why glazing and its color effects should not be used today, when most pictures are again painted in the studio, and only the sketch is painted direct from the natural model.

At any rate, it would be a pity to be as narrow minded as Lenback, who is said to have turned from the work of a rival with the words, "I believe the swine still uses glazes!"

4. PIGMENT COLORS

The exigencies of printing allow us in our reproduction of the pigment colors to give only approximate values. This is no disadvantage to the reader, who must test the colors and mixtures for himself if he is to profit at all from these studies. The comparison of the real paints with the illustrations in this book will be an excellent test of the value of his purchases.

The following list shows which colors are needed for the first practical essays, while those entered in italics are desirable but not essential. The smallest pans of watercolor, but of first-class quality, are sufficient. Very little will be used, so that they will form the basis of a watercolor box for later work.

You will also need a sheet of best, smooth watercolor paper and at least one fairly large sable brush about size 16, with a worn point, since only broad strokes will be made.

Once again let us insist: there is no sense in beginning with second-rate paints and paper.

BLUE: Ultramarine fine ground/Prussian or Paris blue (iron cyanogen)/Cobalt blue deep, light/Cerulean blue.

YELLOW: Ochre Golden ochre/Mars yellow/Cadmium yellow light, medium and dark/Naples yellow (lead antimoniate), light and dark.

RED: Mars red/Cadmium red dark, light/ Alizarin red/Venetian red (iron oxide/ Pozzuoli red.

GREEN: Viridian (hydrous green chromic oxide/Chrome green, (Anhydrous green chromic oxide)/Terre verte (ferrous oxide and silicic acid)/Emerald green.

ORANGE-VIOLET-BROWN: Cadmium orange/Ultramarine violet/Cobalt violet /Burnt sienna/Cyprian umber/Burnt umber/Caput mortuum.

BLACK AND WHITE: Ivory black/Lamp black/White lead/Zinc white.

There are less varied tones of the different pigments in watercolors than in oil or dry powder colors.

BLUE is found in nature in only two forms: mountain blue, a compound of copper which is impermanent, and lapis lazuli, a blue semiprecious stone. Neither raw material is used today for making colors, although lapis lazuli is unaffected by light. It was used in old paintings as a costly glaze over modeled underpainting, and the stone was thus sometimes called glaze stone. The name ultramarine has also remained current, since it was brought from overseas, beyond the Caspian.

ULTRAMARINE BLUE is now made artificially from a combination of soda, alumina, sulphur, and silicic acid, and is an essential blue pigment for both art and commercial paints, being inexpensive to produce. (There are also ultramarine red and violet, but they are unimportant.) Ultramarine blue is the nearest of all pigments used to primary blue in the color circle. It has high tinting strength and is very pure. It can be mixed with green or red and gives the purest of mixed violets when combined with alizarin red. It gives only dull greens when mixed with yellow pigments, but it gives a pure blue-green with viridian. Since it has been made to resist lime, it has become the most important blue for murals and house painting. Even in the humblest school child's paint box it is found in a fairly pure form. The best kinds have no tendency towards either red or green. It is unaffected chemically by other pigments.

PRUSSIAN BLUE (iron cyanogen) is the second important blue and is essential to even the most limited palette. It is also known by its older names of Paris or Berlin blue. It is the strongest in tinting power of all pigments, the smallest traces make all yellow and even brown pigments a bright green. With red, however, it gives less clear mixtures, and with cadmium red a rich, deep black, so that the painter can dispense with any black pigment on his palette.

Unlike ultramarine blue (finest), which has strong covering power though it can also be used as a glaze, Prussian blue is a pure glaze color. In thick layers it assumes an unpleasant coppery tone and creates the effect of a hole in the picture plane. Mixed with ultramarine blue, however, both pigments lose their unpleasant qualities of color and become a very deep, pure color, which is most brilliant if the colors are glazed one over the other alternately. Prussian blue being cheap is in every ordinary

paint box. It is useless for murals, as it is destroyed immediately by lime.

COBALT BLUE is an expensive color. It is imitated in ordinary paint boxes by a mixture of ultramarine and zinc white, which never achieves the exceptional clarity of real cobalt. It is clear even when applied thickly. It is a pigment to be used by itself, as it is easily swamped by other colors when mixed; the best mixture is with viridian. It is not very strong in tinting power, and stands midway between a glaze and an opaque color. It looks very rich and has a fascinating effect, particularly in fresco but also in watercolor and mat tempera. Some of its charm is lost when it is mixed with a fat, shiny oil binder. Small additions of cobalt blue make oil colors dry more quickly. It can be obtained in two tones, and there are two exceptionally attractive variants as well: cerulean blue, the color of a cloudless sky and very valuable for atmospheric tones, and blue-green oxide (cobalt tin color), often used to reproduce the color of the winter sky close to the horizon. There is no sense in making any mixtures with these two. They must stand alone, like jewels.

Both these variants of cobalt are equally unaffected by lime and resemble cobalt in all other technical and coloring qualities, including resistance to heat. They are used for porcelain painting and pot glazes.

YELLOW is the most frequent color among natural pigments. The yellow coloring of earths is always iron hydroxide, or rust, precipitated on clays of varying degress of purity. These yellow or red-colored clays are called ochres. The color is purer the less the iron hydroxide

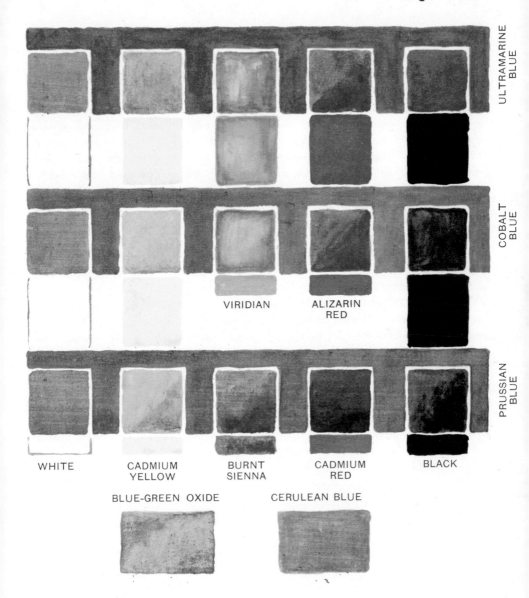

ULTRAMARINE BLUE

COBALT BLUE

PRUSSIAN BLUE

VIRIDIAN ALIZARIN RED

WHITE CADMIUM YELLOW BURNT SIENNA CADMIUM RED BLACK

BLUE-GREEN OXIDE CERULEAN BLUE

is dulled by other additions. Manganese combinations often occur in nature and to a varying extent change the yellow into brown.

Natural ochres are the cheapest of all good pigments. Synthetic ones are dearer; they are yellow iron oxides and are sold as "Mars colors." They are purer in color than the natural earth pigments, but they are still classed with the dull pigments. Ochres are the most widely used colors in painting, as they are often

263

employed as an underpaint for other dull color tones. They mix with all binders and pigments, and as colors constitute to some extent a reconciling element, quiet and soft, amid the strong, bright colors, like a calm person among a group of excitable temperaments. The same applies to any mixtures made with ochre or Mars yellow. They bring a harmony because of their dulling quality, a pervasive ground tone to the picture, especially when the ochres are used for monochrome underpainting. They are of medium strength, and can be used equally well for glazing and covering. They are chemically neutral and are found in every paint box.

CADMIUM YELLOW is the purest of all light-fast pigments. It corresponds, in its medium tone, to the primary yellow of the color circle. It can be produced in an endless number of tones, from the lightest lemon yellow to orange and even a deep red. Combination of cadmium with sulphur does not alter its chemical structure, but only its physical character, from crystalline to amorphous. The best of all yellows to be bought are light, medium, and dark cadmium.

All cadmium colors are considerably more expensive than ochres and all are affected by lime. They must not be brought together with lead colors, such as white lead, either, as this darkens them. The only whites suitable for mixing with them are the completely neutral zinc white or titanium white. For painting on lime, uranium yellow is substituted for cadmium as far as its high price allows, uranium being the most expensive of all pigments. Cadmium loses its original lightness and transparency as it loses

its crystalline form. Deep cadmium and chrome green are the most opaque of all pigments on the painter's palette. Cadmium yellows are pure and can be used in many bright color mixtures. They give the most radiant warm greens when mixed with Prussian blue and viridian. They also mix well with all red pigments. Cobalt yellow, which often has a slight green tinge, can be used as a substitute for cadmium lemon on lime.

NAPLES YELLOW, or antimony (lead antimoniate), should have its place in every well-ordered palette, although it and its reddish variant are not classed among the pure colors. It has another limitation: having strong covering power, it can ruin the transparent character of a rapid watercolor painting, and should therefore only be used very sparingly or not at all in this medium. On the other hand, both in color and consistency it is very attractive in tempera and oil, giving the whole coloration of the picture a misty solidity, something of the tangibility of air, as though a bright yellow were shimmering through fog and cloud. Its stability in lime makes it a valuable addition to the palette of the mural painter. Naples yellow has a very different consistency from other pigments, showing how individual a character a pigment can have. The use of the tactile quality of pigments, apart from their color, is one of the aspects of painting technique which should form part of the equipment of every able, experienced artist.

RED comes mainly in natural earth colors. Most of the nuances of red ochre are named after their original sources: Venetian, Pompeiian, and many more.

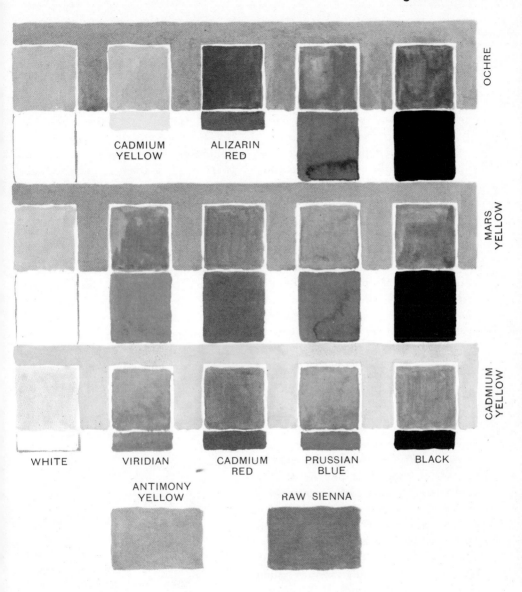

OCHRE

MARS YELLOW

CADMIUM YELLOW

CADMIUM
YELLOW

ALIZARIN
RED

WHITE

VIRIDIAN

CADMIUM
RED

PRUSSIAN
BLUE

BLACK

ANTIMONY
YELLOW

RAW SIENNA

Iron oxide is the coloring matter in the clay. Red oxides are little more expensive than yellow oxides, and on the whole the observations on naturally colored yellow clays apply equally to the reds. In mixtures they are not very friendly, the red base remains dominant. As burnt colors—there are burnt colors derived either naturally or artifically from yellow ochre—the red ochres and Mars red are more opaque than the yellows. Laid on thickly they can be too in-

265

sistent unless care is taken with the surrounding color.

One of the best known red ochres is that used in red pastels and pencils. An ochre called "red bole" was favored by the earlier Italian masters as a ground color. They always used it as an underlay for a gold ground.

Two classic red pigments have been eliminated from the modern, trouble-free palette: mountain cinnabar and carmine. Neither is fast to light. They will be dealt with in more detail in a chapter on obsolete colors. Their colors, however, were so unique that permanent substitutes had to be found for them. CADMIUM RED and ALIZARIN RED were the answer. All that has been said about cadmium yellow applies to cadmium red, and it should be remembered that, like cadmium yellow, the red cadmium colors must remain unmixed if they are to retain their brilliance. Unfortunately, they are totally unsuitable as glazes; although the granulation is generally finer than in the yellow sorts, the pigment will not spread in a thin layer. The artist must find the right compromise between a transparent and an opaque application. Neither cadmium nor alizarin red gives a true primary red, but a mixture of the two comes close. This works well because alizarin red is as excellent a transparent glaze as Prussian blue, and almost equally strong in tinting power. It is a dye made from coal tar and the only organically colored pigment on the trouble-free palette. It was found while trying to produce a permanent madder red. Red madder, which is very similar to carmine, was for centuries an important textile dye, extracted from the root of the madder plant which was grown in large fields. Its most important coloring constituent is alizarin, whose resistance to light is destroyed by other organic substances. It can be extracted pure from coal tar, and after the experience of 50 or 60 years may now be considered fast to light. The organic dye can be precipitated indissolubly onto white clay and thus create a workable pigment. This color is quite indispensable, for there is no other inorganic color even approximating it; whereas cadmium red and cinnabar can be replaced to some extent by Mars red (iron oxide).

ALIZARIN RED, like the cadmium colors, can be produced in an endless variety of tones. They range from orange to violet. The darker tones are the most resistant to light. It achieves its brightest effect as a glaze over opaque red and opaque green underpaintings (red and red-brown earths, green earth, and chrome green). In a direct mixture it gives only one really distinguished color: the purest violet of the palette, a mixture of alizarin red and ultramarine blue.

Neither cadmium nor alizarin red is unaffected by lime. Venetian red (iron oxide), Mars red, and cobalt red have to be substituted for them. All of these, however, need to be surrounded by complementary colors to enhance their brilliance. Alizarin red is an example of how the technical peculiarities of a pigment are not to be ignored: in a thick layer the decidedly transparent color loses its deep glow completely.

GREEN can be mixed from the blues and yellows already listed to every shade likely to be required, but a few

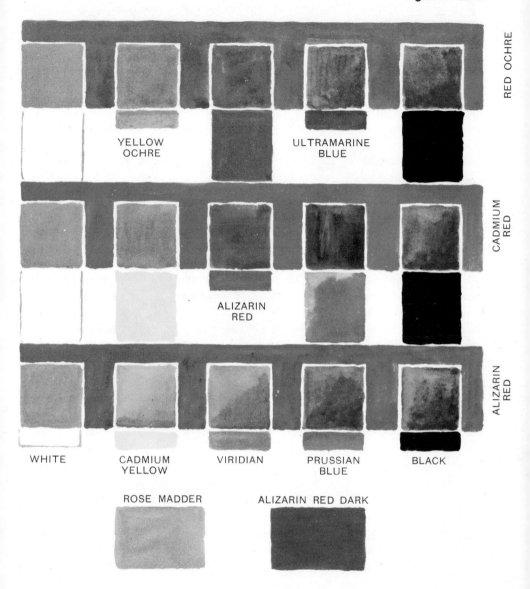

RED OCHRE

YELLOW
OCHRE

ULTRAMARINE
BLUE

CADMIUM
RED

ALIZARIN
RED

ALIZARIN
RED

WHITE

CADMIUM
YELLOW

VIRIDIAN

PRUSSIAN
BLUE

BLACK

ROSE MADDER

ALIZARIN RED DARK

pure and cold tones are difficult to achieve; it is practical, therefore, to use independent green pigments. Moreover, there are among them two materials which both technically and as colors are unsurpassed by any other pigments: the

two green chromic oxides, brilliant and opaque.

If I had to make up a serviceable palette from a minimum of colors it would include ultramarine and Prussian blue, cadmium and alizarin red, ochre and cad-

267

mium yellow, umber and burnt sienna, and the two chromic greens just mentioned.

OXIDE OF CHROMIUM (hydrous green chromic oxide brilliant), or VIRIDIAN, is the most important unmixed green pigment, with a cool, very pure tone very close to a spectrum color. We have described how removal of the water of crystallization by heating results in anhydrous chromic oxide, opaque. Both pigments are unaffected by light. The hydrous oxide, viridian, is a decidedly transparent color, which keeps much of its great brilliance even when mixed with white. Combined with cobalt blue it makes nearly the same tone as the costly blue chromic oxide, and also provides useful mixtures with ultramarine and Prussian blues. The richest scale of greens, including nearly all the warm brilliant greens, comes from combination with cadmium and Mars yellow.

CHROME GREEN (anhydrous green chromic oxide) is a pronouncedly soft and warm green and an opaque color. It is less suited to strongly altered mixtures than to slight tinting, and looks well when used pure. Being one of the colors with the greatest covering power, it is very uncertain for glazing. Terre verte, to which chrome green is otherwise similar as a color and technically superior, is better for this purpose. Both chromic greens are found in a fairly pure form even in cheap paint boxes. They can hardly be varied in tone. They are very cheap and are unaffected by lime, and thus are much used for house and industrial paints and for printing and ceramic painting and glazes.

TERRE VERTE (green earth) is produced in cool and warm tones named after the two most important early find-places, Verona and Bohemia. (Veronese green earth is not to be confused with vert Paul Véronèse, another name for emerald green.) All the variants are essentially combinations of magnesium, aluminium, and silicic acid (augite). Terre verte used to be the most important pigment for underpainting. Being a dull transparent color, it held the lightness of the white ground for the subsequent overpainting. It was also the ideal cool and discreet basis for complementary effects with all red pigments. Terre verte is insignificant for direct mixtures, and equally so for thick application. Deep tones in unmixed terre verte are best when it is laid in several glazes one over the other—an affect which cannot be achieved with chrome green.

This example shows once again how different the characteristics of pigments can be even when their colors are nearly identical. Much subtlety can be gained by playing these different characteristics off against each other, but only if each one is known and felt on its own, just as a cook must know the separate taste of each of his ingredients, a composer the quality of each instrument, or a sculptor the tactile quality of stones and woods in themselves before he begins to carve them.

Lastly, a green should be mentioned which is found in almost every color assortment: permanent green. It is generally a mixture of viridian with zinc yellow or cadmium, and is not a separate pigment. It may be useful and give no

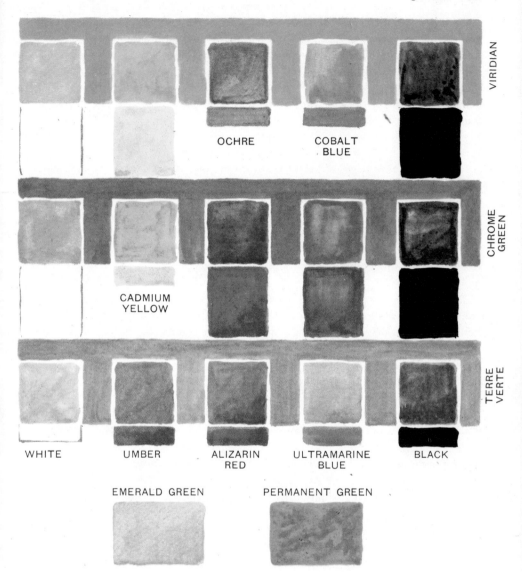

VIRIDIAN

OCHRE   COBALT BLUE

CHROME GREEN

CADMIUM YELLOW

TERRE VERTE

WHITE   UMBER   ALIZARIN RED   ULTRAMARINE BLUE   BLACK

EMERALD GREEN   PERMANENT GREEN

trouble, but I would never advise you to buy ready-mixed colors. They tend to standardize your sense of color and make you more dependent than is desirable. There is, on the other hand, an arsenic green sold as EMERALD, Schweinfurt, Smaragd, or Véronèse green, which is a good, stable pigment. It cannot be imitated by mixing and is essential for cold, light green tones. It replaces the verdigris and other copper colors which were formerly used.

Pigment Colors

ORANGE, VIOLET, and BROWN are the remaining color groups combined from the primaries. These, unlike original green pigments, are easily mixed and thus are not needed in the palette as independent colors. This is particularly true of orange and violet. There is, however, an orange in the cadmium range. Pure violet, as made by mixing alizarin red and ultramarine blue, does not exist as a pigment. Ultramarine and cobalt violets should be mentioned for work on lime grounds; the latter, cobaltous oxide arsenate, is one of the few really poisonous substances in the palette. Their intensity or tinting strength is not very high.

There are, on the other hand, several valuable original browns derived from natural earth colors which can be made darker and redder and at the same time more dense by burning.

BURNT SIENNA is the most important brown pigment. The purest form of iron oxide is the coloring agent; its reddish color is very difficult to copy in a mixture. Raw Sienna, the hydrous iron oxide of Sienna earth in its natural state, is much less important as a color. Although it has covering power, it remains a transparent color which is unpleasantly obtrusive when laid thick and is hardly ever to be used unmixed. Over underpainting in other colors, however, it is a brilliant and light glaze. Direct mixtures are possible with most pigments for subtle, dull nuances.

UMBER is the darkest original brown pigment. The best natural kind, Cyprian umber, acquires a very dark, reddish tone when burnt. The active agent in this is the iron particles in the earth, which owes its characteristic color mainly to compounds of manganese.

Umber, both burnt and raw, is the classical shadow color. Burnt umber certainly has a shady character in some respects! It is heavy in tone and opaque, and in spite of its high tinting strength it tends to make "holes" in the picture and, like almost all dark pigments, it delays the drying time of oil binders. Nevertheless burnt umber is valuable for darkening all colors, much better in effect than black, and it makes a good rich black when mixed with Prussian blue. Without umber Rembrandt would hardly have succeeded in painting his mysterious shadows.

CAPUT MORTUUM derives its strange name from the color of the skulls in the Roman catacombs, though in fact it has little in common with them coloristically, and nothing at all as material. It is a synthetic compound of manganese which can be produced in a great variety of nuances, based on two varieties, one a deep red-brown and one violet-brown. Being already very unclear colors and lacking in intensity, they are not good mixers. The violet variety gives the shadow tone of newly ploughed earth or, when used as a half-glaze, the color of young swelling buds in springtime, that mauve haze that seems to hover in birch trees or shrubs before the buds have burst. It is a useful addition to a modest palette.

All brown pigments are easy to handle technically. Even the slow drying effect of burnt umber can be helped by a small addition of cobalt or lead pigments.

Brown pigments show most clearly the convenience of having a series of con-

CADMIUM ORANGE

COBALT VIOLET

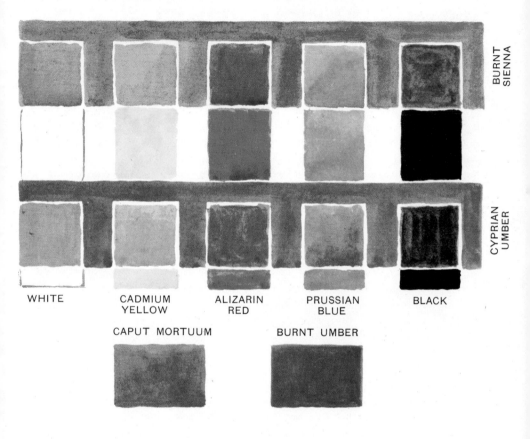

BURNT
SIENNA

CYPRIAN
UMBER

| WHITE | CADMIUM YELLOW | ALIZARIN RED | PRUSSIAN BLUE | BLACK |

CAPUT MORTUUM   BURNT UMBER

sistent, mixed tones on the palette. Although it is easy to mix these unclear colors from strong brilliant ones, it saves a great deal of time to have the original pigments for them, and it helps the visualization of color effects to have the mixed tones ready at hand. Thus, it is rational neither from the point of view of time, nor of technique—nor financially—to have too few basic colors. It is best to make use of all the available pigments which are valuable for color and are technically uncomplicated; they are not so very numerous.

You should be warned against fancy trade names, however, and, once again, be advised against the ready-mixed paints offered for sale.

Pigment Colors

Although BLACK and WHITE pigments have nothing to do with color, they both, particularly white, play an important role in painting. The mixing tests we have illustrated show that all pigments mix with white in their own way. It lightens them but dulls them at the same time. This is an effect contrary to a glaze, in which the white of the underpainting lightens the color without altering its character.

White is quantitatively the dominant pigment in all painting, unless the work is done primarily in transparent color, or glazes. Only watercolor and fresco use hardly any white. Watercolor in particular loses all character if much white is used.

The natural white pigments are chalk, gypsum, heavy spar (sulphate of baryta), and clay (white bole). They can be used only as a priming or as a filling material for "cutting" other colors, not for painting proper. They go gray with all oil, resin, and wax binders, and keep their lightness only in glue. For house paint and pastel chalks the color pigments can be "cut" with natural white pigments in large quantities without reducing the depth of color of the "cut" substances—but only if glue is used exclusively as the binder or fixative. This is why some house paints are recommended for use only with glue; a limitation which does not exist for pure, uncut colors.

The most usual white pigments for pictures are white lead and zinc white, although they may soon be replaced entirely by titanium white.

WHITE LEAD (basic lead carbonate), generally called Cremnitz white in its finest varieties, has strong covering power and is thus the main constituent of all opaque whites. It has a warm tone, hardens quickly in oil, and would be the only white used in painting, except that it tends to blacken in combination with many sulphur colors (cadmium pigments, for example). For these pigments the wholly neutral ZINC WHITE is the only possible choice. It has weak covering power, little coloring strength, is cold in tone, and delays drying.

To counter the properties of both whites there are ready-prepared mixtures of the two, but as with all mixtures it is not advisable to buy them, as mistakes can be made in their use. If they are needed they must be mixed by the artist himself.

TITANIUM WHITE (titanium dioxide) occurs naturally, but for the quantities required is generally made artificially. It has a very strong covering power, is neutral in tone and as unaffected by light as the two other pigments. Little is known as yet about how it behaves in pictures, but there seems no reason to fear that its excellent qualities will have to be paid for in the course of time. It may well make lead and zinc white superfluous.

BLACK is totally unnecessary in the painter's palette. The two most important black pigments, ivory black and lamp black, mix disagreeably with colored pigments. If they are used solid they make "holes" in the picture, and as tinting they have a deadening and muddy effect; used as a glaze, they produce an equally dead, gray effect. Much more subtle grays are obtained from mixtures of complementary colors, and the colored darks that the layman will always see as black. Gray does not exist as a pigment. Black pigments are needed only for graphic work and to some extent in watercolor. They are often considered as organic substances, but in reality they are pure carbon, which is obtained by burning organic substances. An element is never really an organic substance, from whatever natural compound it is extracted. Ivory black is prepared by charring defatted bones; the finest sorts are from ivory chippings.

LAMPBLACK is soot from carbonized oils. Genuine Chinese ink is made from camphor oil. It is deeper and more velvety in tone, almost "colored," in contrast to ivory black, which is colder and grayer. Black made from charred twigs (vine or plant black) is a very light pigment tending to brown tones. All black pigments are difficult in oil, as, being of very low specific weight, they need 200 per cent oil to bind them. This makes drying very slow. Thus, there are sufficient reasons for eliminating black from the palette.

Obsolete Coloring Materials

We have already mentioned several pigments which, though famous for centuries for their coloristic qualities, are highly dubious from the technical point of view. A good craftsman should know, however, why these and some more recently discovered pigments are better not used. Of them all, only carmine has not yet found a fully satisfactory substitute in color. All the others are easily mixed from the pigments already recommended. Do not be persuaded to use them on the grounds that they have retained their color in pictures many cen-

turies old. This is a matter of chance, on which it is safer not to depend, or of very artful and elaborate treatment. Nowadays, as we have said, it is unnecessary to tackle these complicated processes, since there are better pigments which are easier to use.

The old, strong-colored pigments were almost all without exception organic inks of vegetable or animal origin, precipitated more or less loosely onto clay. They are classified under the heading of substratum colors, or lakes, since they became pigments only when combined with a base or substratum. Such, for example, are alizarin red, called madder lake, and some inorganic colors like the iron reds and yellows. Most of these organic precipitations are soluble, particularly in alcohol. They "bleed" if fugitive solvents and thinners are contained in the oil, which soften the oil after it has hardened. The colors, which have also dissolved, run into the softened oil layers and "strike through." This does not happen with alizarin red, as the precipitation is indissoluble. In the old days the organic pigments were used simply because there were no corresponding inorganic ones. They fell into disuse more and more as the chemistry of color progressed and found new colors for the painter, though many of these, too, were unstable.

No more revolutionary discoveries are to be expected in the field of inorganic pigments. This has been proved by the systematic research of Ostwald into the coloring properties of all elements. An increase of painter's pigments can now be made only on the basis of organic compounds, once they are made absolutely light-fast. All the "brilliant" colors have this aim. Among them are colors of a radiance which is rarely found in inorganic pigments; yet they are still very uncertain, and it is foolish to use them, even for purposes of study, because the color imagination of the student would be diverted from the basic colors of the palette and undermine his foundation in the permanent, light-fast pigments. We shall now briefly consider the characteristics of the most famous historic colors.

INDIGO is a blue ink. It is obtained from the indigo root, or woad, and was used for centuries primarily as a textile dye. It was practically the only blue. A synthetic product was ultimately discovered which was an improvement but not completely light-fast. The color, something between ultramarine and Prussian blue, soon becomes a dull, dark blue when it is a pigment, and is sold even today in this tone as an imitation or as "genuine" indigo. The color tone is thus the result of fading.

INDIAN YELLOW is the main yellow pigment of ancient times. It is an ink extracted from the urine of Indian cows that have been fed on mango leaves. The color is exceptionally beautiful and radiant, but is easily imitated by a mixture of middle cadmium yellow with traces of burnt sienna.

GAMBOGE was always in the palette of the eighteenth and nineteenth century painters. It is a yellow gum resin which fades quickly and even when fresh has no particular tonality.

It was, of course, recognized that neither Indian yellow nor gamboge is

fast to light; so the painters of the nineteenth century turned with great enthusiasm to the newly discovered CHROME YELLOW, which seemed to be the answer to all their requirements. Unfortunately, time has told against it, for it has been found to turn greenish and finally almost green-black. Nothing has yet been found to prevent this, and even Van Gogh's famous Sunflowers is deteriorating irretrievably. The strange, macabre yellow tone in the picture is the first stage of decomposition of the chrome yellow he used. Cadmium yellow was still unknown in Van Gogh's time. In spite of this, chrome yellow is still found in several tones in every assortment of paints, and is still bought out of ignorance in large quantities, especially as it is much less difficult to use than cadmium yellow, which dulls easily in mixtures.

Among the red pigments of doubtful stability is RED CHROME, a similar variant of the yellow pigment as is the red of yellow cadmium.

CINNABAR, or vermilion, is produced in a synthetic variety which is claimed to be fast to light, though this cannot be relied on. Cinnabar has on occasion remained unaltered for over 500 years, but in other cases it has blackened in a few weeks.

CARMINE is again an organic ink, precipitated for painting purposes onto clay. The ink is an extract from the female cochineal insect found on certain kinds of American thistle.

MADDER LAKE is a dye from the madder root, similar in color to carmine. Alizarin red serves as a substitute; it can at best replace only madder lake and, unfortunately, cannot achieve the brilliant red of carmine.

The term "lake," quite wrongfully attributed to the pigments synthesized today, alludes to the strong transparency of a pigment. Lake refers either to a substance which colors a substratum or to a binder which is transparent and has a sheen or lacquer.

DRAGON'S BLOOD is a genuine lake, a red resin which is both unimportant as a color and very sensitive to light. It is bought occasionally by the ignorant on account of its romantic name.

One sometimes reads grisly stories of demoniac painters who painted with their own blood. It is even told of Domenico Theotokopuli, "El Greco," that in his ecstatic and mysterious painting he deliberately drew blood from his fingers, since he was said always to have his hands bandaged. If this is true—and very little is known of the life of this painter—it is more likely that he suffered from the effects of turpentine on his skin, a trouble which has forced some people to give up painting altogether. Blood blackens after a few days, and is useless for painting.

Famous ancient green pigments are all copper compounds and all sensitive to light; moreover, one of them, VERDIGRIS, has the fatal characteristic of dissolving in the acid of linseed oil and "bleeding." The old masters laid verdigris as an unmixed glaze in egg white between isolating layers of varnish in order to be able to use the lovely green tone which became obsolete only with the discovery of viridian. Used as described, the organic substance (copper acetate) is also unaffected by light.

The famous, infamous EMERALD, or Schweinfurt, green was as necessary an evil as verdigris as long as there was no nonpoisonous, stable, strong green pigment. Emerald green (copper arsenate) is one of the few really dangerous poisons used as a pigment, and still used today as an insecticide. It can be deadly to men as well, whereas most of the poisonous qualities of pigments are rather the exaggerations of romantic horror, being dangerous only to small children who are at the stage of consuming everything they see.

The well-known VANDYE or CASSEL BROWN has a good brown tone but was never necessary, as umber was known earlier. It is simply brown coal, a mixture of organic substances, and thus sensitive to light. It is still much used, out of ignorance.

ASPHALTUM, or bitumen, on the contrary, has fallen out of fashion. It is a natural organic substance and was used in the last century mainly for underpainting, as its gray-brown tone ideally suited the taste of the period as an underlay for glowing glazes. In the course of time, however, it was found that this underpainting either began to "bleed" or the thick layers of paint above it literally peeled off as they lost all hold on the underpainting. Some of the "black Madonnas"—that from Czenstochau, for instance—turned black not from heavenly intervention but because the asphaltum underpainting was striking out.

SEPIA is extracted from the ink bag of certain species of Mediterranean cuttle fish. It was favored as a substratum color and as ink in the Romantic period and gave an antiquated coloration to pictures. It soon turns gray, however.

In the color assortments of many stores you still find a great number of names which, in the great majority of cases, disguise only half-usable pigments or mixtures.

Surfaces on which you can paint directly are called grounds. First, however, a firm base is required, such as paper, cardboard, pasteboard, artificial boards of various kinds, wood, or cloth. Masonry and stone, even glass and metal, can also be used. These bases are called "supports." With the exception of paper, they are unsuitable as direct painting surfaces. Some would affect the paint chemically and alter it, others are impermanent in color or darken in contact with binders, or do not give sufficient hold for the paint. These supports must be given a ground.

Grounds function mainly as isolators between the support and the paint; they can also act as a sort of underpainting, when they are tinted, for instance, and give the picture a foundation color. In all cases the ground must be appropriate to the type of painting technique used.

PAPER is the simplest painting ground. It takes all glue and pastel colors without any priming, but it must be protected with size against the penetration of binders containing oil or wax. Good quality paper, free of cellulose and as white as possible, is one of the most durable painting grounds if it is properly cared for. Its quality depends on the materials and methods of its manufacture.

Paper as we know it now was preceded historically in China by sheets made from bamboo pulp and in Egypt by papyrus. At about the beginning of the second century A.D., the first paper production began in China from cloth rags, which are still today the basis of all the best varieties of paper. Europe did not produce paper until about 1200, in France. Until then the only known writing surface was parchment, which can also be used for painting. Parchment is the undressed, smoothed skin of sheep, goats, donkeys, or calves, with the hair removed.

Most paper manufactured today is no longer made from rags but from wood, which is reduced to the finest dust and mixed to a paste with water, glue, and fillers (kaolin). This mixture is finely sieved and laid on broad felt moving belts in the paper machine. The water is squeezed out and after pressing and smoothing, the thin sheet of paper is wound at the end of the machine into great rolls. Any wood content lessens the quality of paper, as can be seen particularly in newspaper, made entirely from wood pulp, which quickly yellows and goes brittle.

Today there are very few papers made entirely of rag. One example, however, is good quality, handmade watercolor paper. It is made one sheet at a time and is rather thinner and irregular at the edges, which can be observed, together with the watermark, when the sheet is held against the light. Watermarks in the paper are not necessarily a guarantee of quality, however. They are made by raised patterns or lettering woven into the sieve. In these places the pulp is rendered thinner and more transparent; the same process can be used in machine-made paper.

A famous brand of paper, made especially for watercolor, is the English Whatman paper, made from pure linen rags. It is sold both in sheets and in painting blocks. Similar good papers are made in other countries as well.

Every paper is sized to prevent the ink or color from running; unsized papers react like blotting paper. The type of size used affects the quality of the paper; good papers have animal glue size, and inferior sorts are sized with resin. The material of the size can be tested by dropping ether on the paper; if it is resinous the ether leaves a brown mark around the edge of the drop.

Most good papers can be used on both sides. In doubtful cases the top of the usable side shows the watermark or stamp the right way around. The surface texture has nothing to do with the quality of paper; more important for painting is the thickness, for if it is too thin, paper does not take the paint well.

The strength of paper is measured by its weight per ream. Painting papers weigh between 72 and 140 lbs. per ream. 210 is a thick card. Still heavier weights produce pasteboard, which is hardly ever made today solely from pure, white rag pulp, and therefore must always be given a proper ground.

Smooth paper for painting

Hammered watercolor paper

Handmade Whatman paper (with rough edges)
A thin coat of watercolor is used to show up the texture

Some papers are manufactured already colored right through. We have already spoken of the disadvantages of these tinted papers; the artist should always prepare light-fast tinting for himself.

All papers swell with moisture; they stretch and buckle, which is very inconvenient for painting. Paper should, therefore, always be thoroughly dampened and stretched. To do this, soak the paper in water and lay it flat until it assumes a dull surface, being sure to turn it over frequently. Then smear the edges with flour paste or strong gum arabic and smooth the paper flat onto a drawing board. A wooden frame made for the purpose can also be used. As it dries, the sheet becomes as smooth as a drum and buckles very little if it is dampened again. After the painting is finished, it is cut away from the pasted edges; so the sheet chosen must be larger than the finished picture to allow for the waste margin.

Although the texture of paper is no indication of its quality, the surface texture greatly affects the finished painting. Paint looks quite different on smooth, cloudy, and rough, cloth-like papers. Smooth papers can be given a texture with fine sandpaper, which if rubbed first up and down and then across gives a linen or canvas-like effect that shows up especially where it is painted.

Pastel requires a certain roughness of surface. A good ground to roughen the paper is made from skim milk mixed with a little starch flour. The addition of a small amount of pigment will produce a colored ground, but only very small amounts should be added or the pastel will smear. Larger additions of pigment require stronger binding glues, such as gum arabic or capenter's glue.

Carpenter's glue is most frequently used for priming on all surfaces: wood, canvas, pasteboard, or paper. The following recipe is suitable for all of them: soften 70 gr. carpenter's glue (hide glue, which is a transparent yellow-brown) in one quart of water until it is completely absorbed; glue in beads is the best. It swells in a few hours and is more easily weighed than slabs, which take twenty-four hours or more to soften. When soft, the glue in its container is put into a water bath and heated to 158 degrees F., at which temperature it dissolves completely. It should never be boiled or it will lose much of its binding power. Therefore a glue pot should be used, which also avoids the problem of its sticking to a pan, which it does readily if heated directly. The fillers, or thickening, and pigments are added after it has dissolved and while it remains in the glue pot. Chalk, baked gypsum (analin), kaolin, or marble dust are used in making a gesso priming. Chalk is for the softest, marble dust for the hardest, roughest surface.

Both the priming and the surface must be warmed when the priming is applied or the paste begins to coagulate and cannot be spread evenly and thinly. A good, even ground must be built up of many thin coats and not one or two thicker ones.

Papers and thin boards, such as cardboard, must be primed on both sides or they curl. This can also happen with hardboard and composition boards which are only primed on one side. The backs require only light priming, or cheap cloth or paper can be stuck on them to prevent the tension being on one surface only.

Glue in bead and sheet form

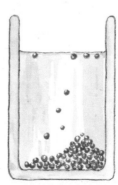 

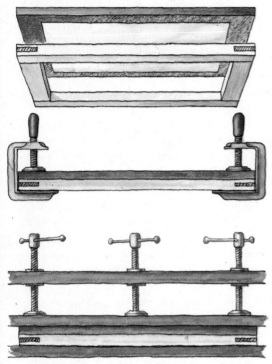

Method of mounting a frame in a clamp or press

Mounting large sheets of paper is a specialist's job. It is inadvisable to attempt it without training in bookbinding and the appropriate equipment, including the press. Badly mounted paper comes unstuck in places, causing blisters and loose corners, mistakes which cannot afterwards be rectified and which can ruin the whole effect of a picture. Mounting is thus better left to a bookbinder or mounter. The small expense involved is preferable to the losses sustained from spoiled material.

Sized and primed boards of large size must sometimes be stiffened with a frame glued onto the back. To make the wooden frame stick securely, the priming or backing must be removed from around the edges where the frame is to be glued. This is most easily done with a tooth plane.

The construction of the frame and the mounting is a carpenter's job. After mounting, the frame and board must be put in a veneer press for at least half a day; no glue holds permanently without pressure. With a sufficient number of clamps and some experience of carpentry you can do the mounting yourself; it is not as difficult as mounting paper.

Even the best paper containing no wood pulp will yellow if exposed constantly to sunlight and will become as fragile as when it is stored in perpetual dry heat. Continuous damp causes mildew, which results in permanent stains. Damp storage also softens the glue of both ground and paint; it may begin to rot, at which point the picture cannot be saved. If these dangers are avoided, paper is very durable. There are papers which have survived in good condition from the time when paper was first invented. The best quality paper thus provides both an ideal surface for all glue and pastel colors and, with a suitable ground, a good covering for inferior boards.

Hardboard sheets, which are obtainable in many varieties, are very similar in character to good rag pasteboards. They usually have one rough and one smooth side. The rough side generally has a rather disagreeable wire grating texture which must be entirely eliminated by the priming if it is not to spoil the effect of the picture. The smooth side always has a slight residue of the paraf-

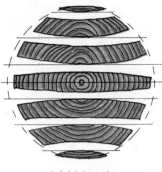

Inlaid boards

fin which is used in the press to prevent the board from sticking to the metal. Since paraffin prevents the priming from adhering, it must be removed with sandpaper. Smooth surfaces are rubbed with a wooden block with mitered edges, covered with sandpaper .

A board thus prepared provides a very good support, especially for backing paper or canvas. Unlike plywood or massive panels of glued planks, it does not warp.

Wood is a living material, and even after centuries it never quite comes to rest. Absorbing moisture at different rates it always warps in quite unforeseen ways. The illustration shows how various are the pulls in each board cut from the same stem. This pull never quite ceases. Wood must season for at least ten years in the air before it can be worked into boards for painting. And apart from this fact, not all woods are suitable, particularly those which are resinous. Only de-

ciduous woods are to be considered; walnut and pear are the best.

In earlier centuries painters used wood frequently, simply because they had nothing better. In spite of the fact that boards were prepared according to all the rules of the art, every old painting on wood is now a problem for the restorer. The board must be protected from warping by inlay, which is the only way to counteract the constant working of the wood.

Plywoods have definite advantages over boards made from planks glued together. There are basically two kinds. One consists of laminations glued together so that the grains run in different directions, the other of veneer surfaces with wooden bars between them. The latter, called "block board," is less likely to warp. Avoid plywoods having round-cut veneers as their outer layer. These always develop fine hair cracks which cannot be hidden even by the thickest priming and painting. The round-cut veneer can be recognized by its unnatural graining. Only **plank-cut** veneers can be used for painting.

Diagrammatic representation of the natural pull of wood

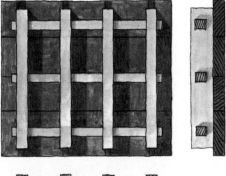

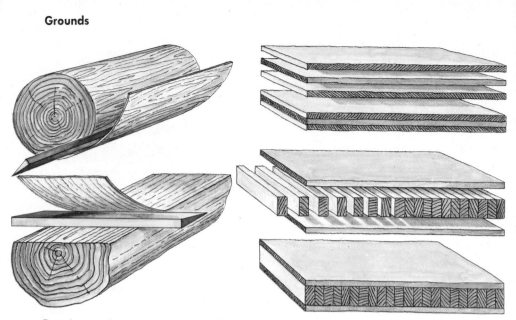

Round-cut and plank-cut veneers; block and plywood

A ground is easily applied to wood without using a lining, and this is about the only convenience that wood has to offer. Boards of synthetic fiber are much more suitable as supports for painting.

Canvas has been the classic painting support for oil and tempera since about the sixteenth century. It, too, needs priming before it is painted, to prevent the oil or other binder from soaking into the fibers of the cloth. The priming also provides a durable white surface, which is needed because even bleached canvas darkens considerably in contact with glue or oil. Other textiles of vegetable fiber, such as cotton or jute, can be used for painting, but none of them are in any way comparable to pure linen canvas.

Linen is woven from the spun fibers of the flax plant. It is sown in springtime and quickly sends up thick, light-green shoots which, in June, produce flowers of a color you would now, as a color specialist, identify as light cobalt blue. The seed cases develop out of the flowers. The fibers come from the woody stalks, which grow more than a yard high. The wood content is dissolved by rotting (steeping) it. It is then broken up and hackled or combed away from the yellow-gray silky fibers. Linseed oil is extracted from the seeds. If painters were to adopt a plant as an emblem of their profession it would have to be the flax.

The spinning of the flax fibers first produces the single-strand yarn. Double or multiple yarn is then twisted from the single strands. The best texture of linen is obtained from untwisted yarn, for it best shows the characteristic thickenings arising from the constantly newly added fibers. They give the finished linen or canvas its typical surface texture. This texture shows to best advantage when the yarn is woven with a plain cloth weave (rather than the twill weave or its fancy variants) or the satin weave, which is generally used only for fine household linens. For these only the finest yarns are used. Coarser linens are used for painting.

All this, however, is, like the type of weave, a matter of taste; there are no differences in quality.

The quality of the linen depends entirely on the flax used, and the fineness and length of its fibers. Linen with knobs in it, which is often recommended as painting canvas, still contains remnants of wood from the flax stalk; it is this which forms the lumps. Apart from being very noticeable in the surface of the picture, these knobs or lumps show that the linen is second rate. Sail cloth can be used if a very coarse texture is desired. Gauguin was fond of painting on it, and the flat effect of his pictures is strongly emphasized by the coarse texture of his support.

If the canvas is held against the light it is easy to see if the warp (longitudinal threads) and weft (horizontal threads) run equally close together. Good machine weaves are always regular; handwoven linen is not. There is no particular advantage in handwoven linen as such, unless it comes from a good studio where handspun yarn is used, as this shows up most strongly the attractive, irregular thickenings caused by the spinning. Since every bleach injures the fibers somewhat, it is better to use unbleached linen, particularly as it will in any case be covered by the ground.

Every linen receives a dressing in the factory. It makes a better "feel" and makes the cloth shinier when it is pressed. The dressing is usually tragacanth or starch and is harmless. Resulting folds and wrinkles, however, are tiresome, for they show through even the thickest priming. Some linens are as broad as 25 feet (theatrical canvas for scenery) and, of course, must be folded. The folds can be removed only by boiling the cloth and ironing it when it is still damp. The canvas can then be stretched on a frame, or, better still, stuck onto hardboard.

Plain cloth   Twill weave   Herringbone pattern   Satin weave

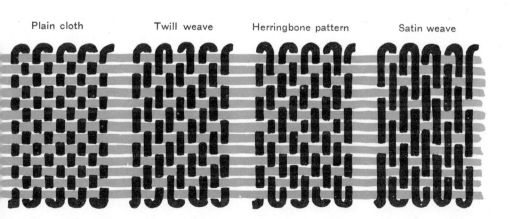

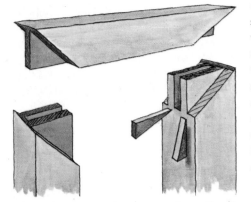

Placing wedges at the corners of a mitered stretcher

The general lay opinion seems to be that a picture has no technical worth unless it is painted on canvas held by the proper stretcher bars. This is, of course, a fallacy, a survival of old fashioned techniques as outdated as painting with fatty oils of unknown constitution. The stretcher is made of four pieces of wood fitted together with double mortices at the mitered corners. For a large stretcher, cross pieces are fitted to keep the frame rigid against the pull of the canvas. The wood is supplied ready-prepared to standard lengths graded to inches and is obtainable in any art shop.

To make the stretcher, the corners of the wood bars are joined as tightly as possible and adjusted with a set square. A piece of thin wood may be lightly nailed across the corner to keep the correct angle until the stretching is completed. The canvas should be at least an inch and a half larger on all sides than the stretcher, and care must be taken to keep the lines of the canvas weave parallel to the sides of the stretcher, for

a slanting weave upsets the painter's sense of the perpendicular when he is working. The canvas is first fixed to the stretcher provisionally with large architects' drawing pins, and thus temporarily stretched, it is given its preliminary two coats: a glue size solution first, which is allowed to dry, and then the first coat of the primer, such as gesso. Once the latter has dried, the canvas can be restretched. The pins should be removed in the same order in which they were put in and replaced by special rustless pins.

Stretching large canvases requires at least two helpers and is even easier with four. The work is always begun from the center of each side, pulling the cloth across from the middle of the opposite side. For heavy canvas and large pictures special canvas pliers are used.

Next, the priming of the canvas has to be completed. The first coats were given **before** the stretching because, unlike paper and wood, linen crumples and shrinks as soon as it is damp. The fibers swell when they are wet and shorten and stretch again when they are dry. Thus, if the linen were placed untreated on the frame the excessive stretching of the fibers when it was wet would make it very slack after the first coat of priming had dried. But if the first coat of glue hardens in the fibers before the cloth is stretched, it prevents it from swelling and shrinking much afterwards; although in fact the canvas always gives a little when it is primed again and has to be given a final stretching before the actual painting begins. The stretcher is so made that the edges can be forced apart by wedges. The wedges are placed in pairs into the corners; the laths hold-

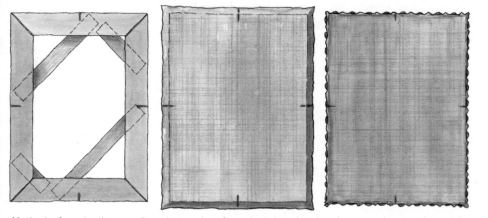

Method of protecting a mitered stretcher from knocks, showing how to place and stretch a canvas

ing the angles are removed, and the wedges carefully hammered in as far as necessary, while keeping the frame rectangular, to make the canvas taut.

A stretched canvas is always sensitive to knocks, and the priming makes it difficult to remove dents once they have been made; so it is much better not to stretch canvas but to stick it down. This gives the most solid painting support while keeping the attractive woven texture and hiding the unnatural smooth surface of the board. Even a very thin canvas has a texture that looks like something that has grown naturally, and in this it is superior even to paper.

It is best to hand over the mounting of the canvas to a competent framer or bookbinder, although the process is less difficult than mounting paper. The board should be free of grease and slightly roughened; the paste must be of a good quality which can be used cold, like starch paste or dextrin. Carpenter's glue works equally well, except that the work has to be done very quickly and in a warm room, and the board and canvas both have to be warmed beforehand or the glue will not take.

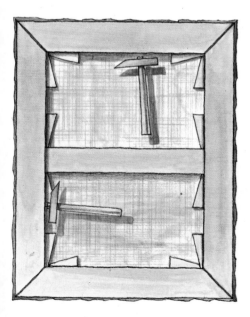

Driving a wedge into the corner of a stretcher protected from bending by means of a crossstrut

Grounds

A cold glue allows more time to lay the canvas carefully according to the markings, and if a mistake has been made the canvas can be lifted off and stuck again.

Both board and cloth are covered with paste. Once the cloth is laid correctly on the board it is rubbed over with a straight-edged, rounded block; the movement is always from the center towards the edges, following the lines of the thread. Lastly, the overhanging edges of the canvas are bent under and stuck to the back of the board. The whole back is covered with cheap muslin or brown paper, concealing the turned edges of the canvas.

The painting board prepared in this way is better in quality and appearance than a canvas on a stretcher and is more easily handled, both for painting and framing. It cannot go slack and is virtually invulnerable.

You already know that there are many reasons for priming: it prevents the binder from soaking into the cloth fibers, glue and filler being less absorbent, and with its white or colored pigments it gives a durable background which is unaffected by light or binder.

Only paper is given just a single light priming; boards and canvas must have several coats. Generally, three applications are needed:

1. Size without filler—one coat.
2. Priming with filler—two or three coats, which will darken, however, especially in contact with oil binders thus necessitating:
3. Pigment priming—one or two coats, which can be white or colored, and will not darken with oil.

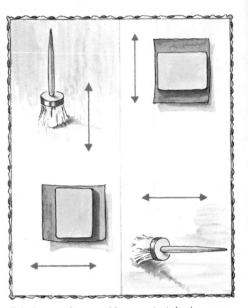

Priming and smoothing a stretched canvas. The left half shows the first part of this process, and the right half shows the second

The second and third categories need more than one coat to make the covering quite uniform. A single thick coat will always spread unevenly, causing the ground to absorb the paint unevenly. Moreover, a thick coat of priming hides the texture of the underlay too completely. A ground painted on in thin and frequent coats is more uniformly absorbent than one thick coat.

After each coat is dry, it is rubbed over to remove the skin of glue that forms, which would prevent the following coat from holding well. Smooth surfaces can be rubbed with a piece of sandpaper mounted on a wooden block; for canvases it is best to use a hard nylon or soft wire brush. Brushing penetrates the hollows in the cloth, whereas sandpaper would begin to smooth down the canvas itself. To ensure even distribution, the priming is always put on with the brush strokes running at right angles to those used on the previous coat.

The final coloring or whitening coat is left untreated so as to be least absorbent. In all, a maximum of eight priming coats is sufficient. Each one must be applied very quickly in order not to soften the previous coat which has been allowed to dry thoroughly before being covered.

This priming used to be called "chalk ground" as distinct from a ground of equal parts of chalk and oil. The use of the word chalk is quite misleading, for what is meant is actually a pure glue ground, irrespective of whether chalk, bole, analin, or other filler is used. A ground of equal parts chalk and oil would be better called glue and oil ground, the upper coats being given an oily binder, while oil grounds use oil alone except for the first sizing.

The two oil grounds have been mentioned only because they are often the only ones found on the ready-prepared panels and rolled canvas offered for sale. They are very convenient, especially for amateurs and painters with little technical experience, but they have no other advantage. Oil grounds are responsible for the unfortunate habit of rolling primed, and worse, painted, canvases, because the elastic oil film seems to suffer no harm from it. In fact, even a fully oxidized oil film cracks or crumples when it is rolled up, and cracks when it is unrolled. A mixed glue and oil ground suffers even worse. Old pictures which have been left rolled for a long time or are rolled up after many years generally crack right through to the canvas and are a great problem to picture restorers. It sometimes takes weeks to scrape away the canvas from the picture layer and stick on a new canvas—a process called in the trade "relining."

Oil grounds absorb no binder, but this is a dubious advantage. There are excellent technical measures to be taken against excessive absorption by soft glue grounds. Pure glue grounds cannot be bought on the market, for they are very sensitive, and primed canvas must be already stretched, which is impossible on a commercial scale with all the varied sizes in demand. It is better not to try to buy ready-primed supports; no one can, or will, say what has been used on them.

METAL remains alien to any painting with pigments and binder. Although

The paint layer (blue) is shown reacting to the rolling and unrolling of canvas (gray)

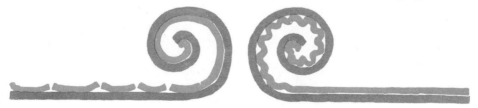

paintings on thin sheets of copper survive in good condition from the eighteenth century, it is totally inadvisable as a support. Only enamel colors will hold securely on metal, and they are only really secure when fused on in patches, separated into little cells formed by soldered-on wire, a technique far removed from the character of painting.

NATURAL STONE, on the other hand, forms a good support, both on facades and indoors. Either wax colors can be used, which are made to penetrate the pores of the stone by heating (encaustic), or watery pigments can be made to petrify with the stone by means of waterglass, which is sprayed over the painting. Stone is not primed, although sometimes for mineral painting it is etched.

BRICK WALLS and any other similar artificial stone must be primed for painting. Plaster is generally used for this. At least three coats are applied before it is painted: an undercoat or rough rendering, an upper coat, and a top coat. Each layer contains finer grit and sand than the one below, whether the work is done in pure lime plaster, lime and cement, or pure cement plaster.

Plaster containing cement is suitable only to be painted on when it is quite set and dry. Casein or silica paints can be used on it, and glue colors are suitable indoors. **Fresco-secco** was done with egg yolk as a binder. True fresco, **fresco-buono**, is done only on pure white lime plaster while the plaster is still quite wet. The pigments are mixed exclusively

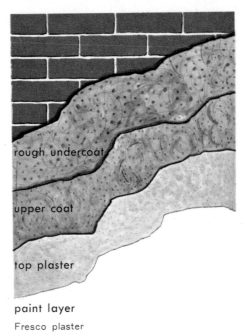

paint layer

Fresco plaster

with water and bound into the top plaster by a coating of crystalline calcium carbonate, the "sinter skin," which exudes from it. As soon as the fresco plaster begins to set, the pigment no longer takes on it. Thus, large frescoes are always painted piecemeal; the fresh plaster is added to the brick wall for each section as needed.

We can see that there is no universal support for all painting techniques. At any rate the priming must be suited to the subsequent technique, and the technique is determined primarily by the binding material.

6. BINDERS AND READY-PREPARED PAINTS

"Binder" is the technical word for a substance that enables pigments to be fixed onto the ground. Lenbach's opinion was that "one can paint with anything that sticks." This remark is typical of the indifference of the later nineteenth century to technique. Lenbach was at that moment thinking only of those binders which work as adhesives, and, mixed with pigments, become "colors," that is to say, ready-prepared paints. No one can paint with pigment powder; it must be made suitable for application with either a brush or pen or made into a pencil. The kind of binder chosen depends on the painting technique in view. The terms used for ready-prepared paints, like "oil colors" or "watercolors," give some indication of the binder, but closer examination shows that it is not quite as simple as it seems.

Colors which are petrified onto the painting ground by some chemico-mineralogical process, as in fresco, or are fixed by some material sprayed after their application, such as mineral paints, do not contain a binder. Pastel colors, which are bound by the application of a fixative, also contain no binder.

Adhesive binders are basically of two sorts. There are those which have a more or less constant natural consistency and have to be dissolved and liquified for painting purposes, hardening again after the evaporation of the solvent. All kinds of glue, resin, and wax belong to this group. The others are naturally liquid and do not harden by the evaporation of some constituent but by the absorption of acid from the air. Certain oils have this property—but not all! If even the smallest trace of olive or lubricating oil (neither of which oxidizes to a hard substance) is mixed with a hardening oil it will prevent that oil from oxidizing. The oil layer becomes more voluminous when hardening, but after long periods of time it shrinks again. This is due to the oil giving off carbon dioxide, which is in fact a sort of very slow burning. This can be seen on any very old oil painting. The surface is cracked and split and shows what might be called "late crack formation."

There is also an "early crack formation" which may arise even a few hours after the paint has been applied. This is due to mistakes in technique. Forgers cause them intentionally to imitate late crack formation and make the picture look old. The crackle of ceramic glazes is due to similar "mistakes."

Since late crack formation has been found to be an inevitable evil of pure oil painting, attention has been turned again to tempera, which is a much older binder. True tempera consists of bringing together two substances which generally repel each other: water-soluble glue and oil. This is done in such a way that the two substances form a completely new, inseparable liquid to which, within

Late crack formation in a picture 150 years old

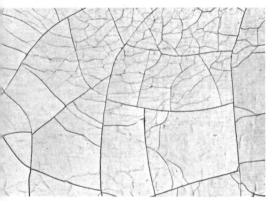

Late crack formation in a picture 100 years old

Early crack formation in a picture 20 years old
(Macro-photograph by Hans Roth)

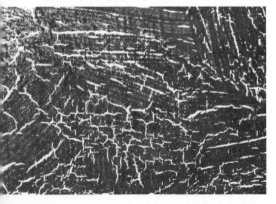

limits, either water or oil can be added. The general technical term for this true mixing of substances is "emulsion."

Milk is a well-known example of a natural emulsion, mayonnaise an artificial one. If the reader is versed in the art of making this delicacy he will know that it can succeed only if an egg yolk is stirred constantly while oil and vinegar (the watery element in this case) are added to it alternately in small drops. The egg yolk functions as the emulsifying agent. Egg yolk is itself an emulsion of egg white and egg oil. Pharmacists seem to have the special gift of making emulsions without an agent. If you want to use tempera frequently you should enlist the kind aid of a member of this esoteric profession to see that your emulsion comes off! When it crackles and clicks in the mixing bowl, the magic has worked. The word "tempera" comes from the latin **temperatio,** meaning a proper compound, as against **mixtura,** which means any ordinary mixture. Unfortunately, color merchants are not so precise in their use of the term "tempera colors," as you will soon discover! The technical advantage of genuine emulsions is that neither the glue nor the oil can form a hard film as it dries. A honeycomb of each substance contains minute droplets of the other, although these are too small to be seen with an ordinary microscope. This structural parceling of each constituent enables additions of one or the other to be made without their showing when the emulsion is spread as paint. The surfaces are multiplied; thus, both evaporation and oxidation occur much more quickly.

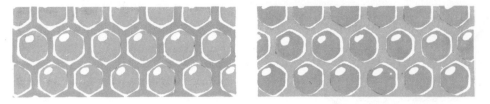

Diagram showing structure of O-W emulsion (oil in watery element) and W-O emulsion (watery element in oil)

In past centuries the preparation of paint was a long and tedious process. The pigments came to the painter in large lumps or in coarse irregular powders. They had to be ground with pestle and mortar and then further rubbed down on stone or glass with a muller, while at the same time being mixed with the binder.

Nowadays the pigments are bought already ground so fine that no further grinding is possible, for every pigment has a definite fineness suitable to it. The figures, in thousandths of a millimeter, are as follows: ochre .5 to 30, iron reds 1 to 80, Prussian blue .3 to 10, white lead 2 to 5. If pigments are ground too fine their colors tend to go muddy, and in a colloidal condition can change color entirely. Grinding by hand can reach a colloidal state, as you know from Chinese ink. The lamp black "takes" indissolubly only when it becomes a colloid. Pigments are bought today fine enough to mix with the binder when stirred with a stiff bristle brush. As little binder as possible is used, just enough to make a stiff paste. A few hours, or at most a day, give the binder time to penetrate through the powder and show whether the paste is too dry and needs more

binder or is too soft and can take more pigment. Pigments vary in their reactions to binders; some repel water, some oil. Alcohol helps to make a uniform paste in these cases, as it combines equally well with water and oil.

In most ready-made colors the pigments are generally finer than the dry powder. The mechanical rollers between which pigments are mixed with binders grind the pigments still further. This is not always an advantage, as a coarser granulation prevents too smooth a film of oil from forming and reduces the danger of early cracking by making the surface larger. The painting layer is also more solid if the granulation is coarser. For both these reasons the old painting instructions always warned against excessively long and fine grinding of the pigment with the binder.

While most materials are best bought in art shops, it is advisable to go to a druggist for some others, notably cold pressed linseed oil, balsams, double rectified turpentine and gum arabic. The druggist has to follow specifications established by the Federal government, so the products are fully reliable, and their methods of extraction guaranteed. The

Tools formerly used to grind colors: mortar, stone slab for grinding, agate and glass mullers

painting material industry, on the other hand, carefully guards its processes as a trade secret, which unfortunately does not help the acquisition of a solid painting technique.

Glues are the easiest binders to handle. They are dissolved in water, which evaporates sufficiently after the paint has been put on for the work to feel dry after only a few moments. The surface can be painted over immediately, if the artist is a fast worker, but it should not be gone over too often with the brush.

Some of the water takes a few days to evaporate, during which time the glue remains swollen and can easily dissolve again. The glue can also be dissolved again even after the paint has dried fully, but it takes longer. All glues which act like this are called "reversible," as distinct from the irreversible glues which cannot be dissolved once they have set. The most important of these in painting is casein, a milk product. Glues can also be divided according to their animal or vegetable origin, but this is of no practical importance to the painter. Carpenter's glue, prepared from the boiling of skins, behaves no differently from plant glues like gum tragacanth or gum arabic.

TRAGACANTH is gum extracted from bruising the branches of the tragacanth bush. It provides the most important binder for watercolors and for gouache and other opaque colors generally sold as tempera paints, although in fact they do not contain an emulsion. The more exactly named "egg tempera" and "oil tempera" are emulsions.

You already know how painting techniques and their appropriate colors are named according to the binder employed. Watercolors are an exception to this. They are named after the water, used so copiously and noticeably in the technique, which dissolves them and thins them. It is never worthwhile to prepare watercolors oneself. We shall describe only how the colors we buy are produced. Tragacanth is the binder, but other substances are added:

1. Ox gall, or rather its salts. This facilitates a fine dividing up of the pigment, which thus allows a very thin application.

It has the property of neutralizing the smallest traces of grease. Ox gall can be bought in every art shop for the purpose of neutralizing the surface of paper, which often becomes marked with grease on its way from the factory to the user. It may not be visible, but it will prevent the paint from taking evenly; thus, it is a worthwhile precaution to rub ox gall over otherwise untouched paper.

2. Honey, sugar syrup, or glycerine. Substances which prolong the drying time of watercolors—particularly those in porcelain pans—so that they are more quickly soluble.

3. Boracic or benzoic acid salts. They act as preservatives. Without them all glues in solution putrefy.

The characteristic smell of watercolors is often given by oil of bitter almonds, added solely to disguise the rather unpleasant smell of the glue.

Watercolor pigments are often so finely ground that they act as colloids. This is noticeable if an attempt is made to wash off the color. Some colors, although they become fainter, will stay in the paper. Genuine watercolor painting was made possible only by this fine grinding of the pigments. The method was evolved in the seventeenth century and was developed to its full perfection by the English painters Girtin (1773-1802) and Turner (1775-1851). Until then only "gouache" colors had been obtainable as finely ground pigments. Unlike true watercolors, the latter are not fully transparent and require the addition of white to make them lighter. Gouache colors as now sold are an unnecessary halfway house between water-colors and opaque colors. The pigment of the latter is hardly finer than that of all the rest, including the finest sorts of powder color. Opaque colors can be prepared at home and should be used within a few days of mixing. They generally use tragacanth as a binder, but can also use gum arabic, cherry gum, or egg white.

CHERRY GUM is extracted from the cherry laurel. It was used in earlier centuries as a glue for cherry gum tempera.

GUM ARABIC is extracted from Arabian and Indian acacias. Both gums are very light and almost colorless in solution.

ALBUMEN is the main constituent of egg yolk, which was, before the development of **fresco-buono**, the most frequently used binder for mural painting. The fat content of the yolk makes it less liable to dissove after it has dried than egg white, and its color soon fades in the light. If egg white is used it should be whipped and then strained, so that it loses its coagulated, sticky consistency and mixes more easily with water.

I would caution you against mixing glue colors for yourself from the usual trade powder colors unless you are going to use large amounts in a short space of time. Too much preservative can have a deleterious effect, and it is difficult to judge the right quantity for small amounts of paint. It is best to avoid preservatives altogether. The advantage of mixing glue colors oneself is that they are then certain to be pure pigments, for bought opaque colors, especially the so-called poster colors, are often mixed with other materials to give them body and density. Fillers are added to make the paint more uniform and solid, and also to make it cheaper. This reduces the intensity of the color, and is particularly noticeable in mixtures, which rarely have the brilliance you would expect from the brightness of the constituent colors. Complementary juxtapositions, too, are less strong in effect because all fillers have a dulling effect.

If opaque glue colors are used only occasionally it is best to buy what are sold as "artists' tempera colors," as they are most likely to be undiluted pigments, if they are made by a reputable firm. The binder used is only glue, not an emulsion. These incorrectly styled "tempera" colors give an optical effect similar to that of a genuine mat tempera or oil painting.

Since few artists today prepare their paints themselves, it is difficult to buy the

Mixing oil paint with a round bristle brush in a glass container

right jars to keep them in. We therefore illustrate the type of jar provided for the author by a glass factory at small cost. It can also be used for mixing up the paints, and will save you the trouble of trying to fill tubes once the paint is mixed, a procedure fraught with difficulties and waste. Once the paint is kneaded in the jar, it should be rolled together to form a smooth lump and covered with a close-fitting plastic disc. A piece of ordinary adhesive tape can be made into a handle for lifting it. The jar itself is closed with a close-fitting rubber lid. The plastic disc will keep the paint from contact with the air and is especially necessary when there is not much paint left. It can easily be lifted out with tweezers. A stiff plastic spatula can be used to take out the paint. The jars are easily cleaned: they should first be wiped with a paper towel, and then washed out with water or white spirits, according to the binder used. Jars such as these can be obtained from firms supplying cosmetic factories, or a druggist will get them for you.

There is the danger with all glue colors you make yourself, and especially with casein, that you will put in too much binder. Even if it is thinned with water, it will make a skin over the painting. Carpenter's glue, tragacanth, gum arabic, and cherry gum should all be mixed in the proportion of 100 cc. of water to 7 gr. of dry substance. If the solution is stronger than this, because of careless measuring, the paint may scale or crack. It is therefore advisable to make trial strokes with the brush to see if the paint is just firm enough. Better too little binder than too much! If the color does not hold firmly on the painting, it can be sprayed with a very dilute solution of glue. A glue solution can be tested by smell. If it is beginning to go bad it is useless.

CASEIN is the best irreversible glue for painting purposes. It is derived from sour skim milk. It must contain no fat, as this prevents it hardening. It is not heated, but strained through butter muslin for 24 hours until all the whey is removed. The remaining curd is called casein. It swells a great deal in water, but is not soluble. To make it dissolve, an alkali, such as lime in solution, must be added.

A glassful of pure powdery white lime can be obtained from a builder's yard. It is best taken from the top stratum of the pit. It should be added to the curd in pea-sized quantities, one at a time, until a glassy, uniform, and sticky mass is obtained. For 70 gr. of this dissolved casein only a few gr. of lime will be needed; one quart of water is poured on and stirred to make a uniform solution, producing a glue which is probably still too strong, depending on the consistency of the curd. If it is very dry it may need twice the quantity of water. A test can be made with a cheap pigment: the brush stroke should dry hard in two or three hours, but must not scale off the paper, which should be firmly stretched, even when several coats are laid one on the other. Casein takes about a week to become completely insoluble in water. Paintings done in casein colors can thus be considered weather-proof, but only in so far as the support is weather-proof too!

Naturally, only pigments unaffected by lime can be used with casein. This is true also of the casein powders that can be bought ready prepared, as they too need a lye to make them dissolve, generally borax, potash, or soda. Casein, except in dry powder form, is as liable to attack by bacteria as any glue, and must thus be used immediately after it has been dissolved. Formalin converts it into a stable horny mass (galalith), and if a solution of formalin is sprayed on the finished painting it may cause the paint to come away from the ground. Undiluted casein is a strong emulsifier, making other materials emulsify very quickly. It functions at the same time as a glue.

RESINS and **BALSAMS** behave in the same way as glues for painting, except that they are soluble not in water but in volatile oils; spirits of turpentine (generally called simply "turpentine") is the most usual one used in painting. This is mainly a distillation from balsam, a natural secretion of conifers. Balsams can be considered as resins which occur in nature in a heavy solution with turpentine. French turpentine, which is twice distilled, is considered the best. Doubly rectified French turpentine can be bought both in art shops and drugstores. Ordinary turpentine contains unevaporated resinous elements. If it is dropped onto a glass plate it should leave no trace that can be seen or felt as sticky after it has evaporated. Resins and balsams dissolved or thinned with turpentine take much longer to dry than water-soluble glues. When dry they form a hard, glassy skin which is very brittle.

Resins, like reversible glues, remain soluble. If overpainting is done with resin essences there is a danger of taking off the underpainting, at least superficially, and smearing. An addition of beeswax can afford some protection, and this also modifies the brittleness of the resins. Resin, like oil, "burns" slowly over a long period. This makes it crumbly and dark, especially if it has been used without pigment as a finishing varnish. Finishing varnishes play an important part in oil painting, because resins do not yellow and can at any time be softened and removed with turpentine, as long as they do not contain too much wax.

Perished resin varnishes can be regenerated by the famous method developed by Max von Pettenkofer: the picture is exposed to alcohol or petrol vapor in a closed container, thereby giving the varnish back its firmness and transparency.

SHELLAC shows that a small amount of wax can prevent the deterioration of resin. As you already know, the basis of shellac is the resin of tropical trees which is secreted when the trees are punctured by insects. This resin contains animal wax derived from these insects, and this makes it an ideal painting medium, though it is, for some unknown reason, very little used. It is sold in thin sheets and is used mostly as a polish for wood and as an insulator in the electrical industry.

For painting, light colored sheets that have not been artificially bleached are the best because shellac loses some of its solubility from the effects of light. It is dissolved in 95 per cent alcohol under mild heat to melt the wax in it. In a 2 per cent solution it is the most usual fixative for spraying on chalk drawings and pastel paintings. In thin coats it is also very useful as an insulator against absorption on glue grounds. Paints take badly on thick layers of shellac, and glue colors even scale off.

MASTIC is the most important resin used in painting. It is obtained in the tropics and sub-tropics from the mastic bush in the form of pale yellow balls or droplets which still have the earth and bark adhering to them. It is easily soluble in turpentine. A standard essence of one part (weight) resin in two parts of turpentine is the most practical. It is made in the following way:

A glass vessel which can be hermetically sealed is half filled with spirits of turpentine, and the drops of mastic are hung in a piece of gauze over the liquid without touching it. The vapor from the turpentine, which quickly develops in sunshine or warmth, gradually dissolves the resin, which then drips through the gauze into the turpentine. The bottle is shaken now and again to wet the gauze and accelerate the solution. All impurities will be held by the gauze, and the liquid will be clear and light yellow. Mastic can be added to the bag until the required concentration is reached. This can be gauged by weighing; the contents of the jar should increase by 40 or 50 per cent, assuming that the turpentine has not evaporated to any marked degree. Mastic dissolves much more quickly if heated with turpentine, but it turns brown and is thus rendered unsuitable for painting. Reaby-made mastic varnishes may contain admixtures of other substances such as poppy oil, which looks just like mastic

Dissolving mastic in two parts rectified spirits of turpentine

but delays hardening considerably; a thin application of mastic essence on a glass plate will dry completely to the touch in 24 hours, while poppy oil takes several days.

DAMAR is generally mentioned in the same breath as mastic, and in fact the two resins act in much the same way as far as painting is concerned. Damar solutions are as clear as water, which is an advantage, but damar is considerably more brittle than mastic, and also less fast to air and damp. Thus, varnishes made of damar sometimes cause a milky-blue "bloom" on a picture, which will disappear once the damp has been expelled. Mastic is therefore a better binder, its slight yellow tinge being hardly noticeable in combination with pigments.

TURPENTINE is a balsam secreted by conifers. The following kinds are differentiated for painting: Venice turpentine (larch), Strasbourg (silver fir),

Canadian turpentine or balsam (Canadian fir) and the olio d'Abezzo from stone pines. Many of these cannot now be bought except at drugstores, but it is not really very important which tree the turpentine comes from. It should simply be as clear and transparent as possible and viscous, not crumbly and dry. Dropped into spirits of turpentine it should become thin. Good turpentines are as good as resins for binders; they do not yellow, but they are slower to exude the spirits of turpentine in which they are dissolved and thus stay sticky longer. Balsams, particularly Venice and Strasbourg turpentine, are some of the best substances for quick drying emulsions.

There is a whole series of resins, such as copal and amber, which used to be in favor with artists. They are, however, dubious in effect in the picture, since they give such a brilliant shine that, in general, it is better today to avoid them.

WAX has so far been mentioned only as an additive to oils and resins. It is also a binder on its own and was much used in antiquity when it was the most weather resistant of all binders. Surprisingly enough, modern science has not yet been able to discover how wax was made sufficiently fluid in those days to be used at ordinary room temperatures for painting. It is known that in preparation the wax was melted on the fire and the pigments added to it, but the hot wax color does not remain liquid on the brush, and thus could not be applied to the picture. Even at a temperature of 104 degrees F., when the sweat is pouring from you, you will find that the wax stiffens on the brush between the pan on the fire and the picture, making it quite impossible to spread on the canvas. Brush marks on old wax paintings make it quite certain that wax colors were put on with a brush. Moreover, so-called "Punic" wax was used, which does not melt below about 212 degrees F., whereas unprepared beeswax needs only a temperature of about 147 degrees F.

Probably the solution to the problem lies in using a slowly evaporating medium which is liquid when cold, something like turpentine oil or petroleum. But if you try to keep wax liquid in this way at a bearable temperature it needs about 15 or 20 times the amount of medium as of wax; since the wax alone is the binder, it could in this solution only make very weak colors, and they would not hold very firmly to the ground. This could be helped by warming afterwards, which would at the same time accelerate the evaporation of the liquifying agent. This was certainly done in antiquity, for there are traces of marks from iron spatulae to be seen on antique "encaustics" (wax paintings are called after the Greek word meaning "to burn in"). The brush marks show, however, that strong colored paints were applied at one time, rather than a long series of weak coats built up by overpainting.

I have tried this method, using wax thinned with turpentine, and found that sufficiently strong color effects could be achieved, which the transparency of the wax made very attractive. I would rather you did not ask, however, how long it took to put on the innumerable coats!

Certainly the antique encaustics were not painted in this way! Perhaps you can solve the riddle.

There would be no need to make such a fuss about this accursed wax were it not of such a perfect consistency, almost unalterable and of unlimited durability. Wax has been found unaltered after 5,000 years. It does not yellow nor crack and is not sensitive to acids in the air nor to weathering nor water. It shrinks a great deal in high frosts, however, and would crack in high latitudes on an outside facade in winter weather. It can be seen how durable wax is from the paintings done on marble, where the areas surrounding the pictures have weathered, leaving the wax paintings themselves unaltered and standing out like a flat relief on the surface of the stone. If anyone succeeded in making wax usable for painting under normal conditions it would make all resins, oils, emulsions, and water-resistant gums superfluous; we should have a single, uniform, and completely unproblematical binder.

All this refers only to pure beeswax. The best kind is the so-called "virgin wax" from cells not yet used for hatching grubs, which is ivory white in color. This can rarely be obtained, except by lucky chance from a beekeeper. But even ordinary pure beeswax is good. It can be bought at good hardware stores. If it comes from a beekeeper it has to be purified in boiling water. All dirt sinks to the bottom of the cake of wax that forms over the water as it cools, and which can be scraped off.

Punic wax was obtained by boiling up the wax with sea water. When hartshorn salt was added, the calcium and magnesium salts combined with the wax and caused its higher melting point. If you wish to make Punic wax yourself there is no need to go to the expense of a trip to the Mediterranean, it can be done easily as follows:

Boil 50 gr. purified beeswax in 500 cc. distilled water and add 5 gr. soda which has been dissolved in a little water. This forms a kind of soap with the wax, into which is stirred enough of a 10 per cent solution of magnesium chloride to make the Punic wax fall out in more or less firm crumbs.

In antiquity this wax, under the slogan "punica est optima," was used as widely as linseed oil varnish is today for painting of all kinds. The underwater surfaces of ships were protected by coats of it. The few encaustics of an artistic kind which have come down to us are as fresh in color as though they had just been painted.

LINSEED OIL over the years has proved itself relatively the surest of all oils used. Therefore it alone will be treated here. The much prized nut and poppy oils have the fatal drawback of occasionally softening without apparent reason, or even of never hardening.

Linseed oil is extracted from the seed of flax. For painting and medical purposes it is pressed out cold, for although more oil can be obtained by pressing it under heat this darkens the color and alters it in other ways. Care must be taken that the seeds are not mixed with those of any other plant or wood, as the oil will then not harden. The raw oil contains a watery slime which has to be removed. In old painters' manuals many recipes, some very strange ones, are given for the extraction and purification of linseed oil. Painters had then themselves to press and purify the oil. With today's science and technology it is, of course, hardly a part of the painter's art to extract oil from flax.

Opinions still vary on whether the oil is best if used when quite fresh or after it has matured. It is certain that newly pressed oil oxidizes more slowly than an oil which is six or nine months old. Rancid oil cannot be used; it is easily recognized by its smell and taste.

The oxidation of oils can be very much influenced. It can be accelerated by pre-oxidation, for instance, by blowing oxygen into it. This produces linseed varnish, which is used, instead of untreated linseed oil, exclusively for commercial paints.

For the artist's use "stand oil" is made in the following way: Linseed oil is exposed in an open container to the action of air and sun in contact with lead oxide which always forms on the surface of lead plates or rods. This thickens the oil, because the hardening process has already begun, and it gives a very shiny, fat effect when applied. It hardens quicker than untreated oil.

A number of pigments have the same effect, especially the cobalt and lead compounds. They act as catalysts, accelerating the rate of the reaction, in this case the absorption of oxygen by the linseed oil. If a pigment is said to be a "good drier" this always refers to its effect on oils, which harden by the absorption of oxygen.

Leonardo da Vinci, The Last Supper. The picture was given a final coat of oil paint on a fresco ground and is shown here after restoration. The plaster had become mouldy in places, and was spotted out with gray-brown local color

Some pigments delay oxidation; lamp black is one of the worst of these. It may contain remains of nonhardening oils, and, in any case, like all dark pigments it requires much more binder to make it adhere than do light pigments. All these matters are related to the formation of cracks while the paint is drying, what we have called "early crack formation"; if quick drying oil colors are painted over those which harden slowly, particularly if these have not completed this process, the upper surface will soon break. Thus, in oil painting the rule is always to use slow hardening colors over quickly oxidizing ones. If the composition demands otherwise, then traces of "quick dryers" are added to the slow-drying colors and painted over only when the under layer has become quite hard. The old masters managed in this way to lay thick layers of white lead over dark and slow hardening colors without causing any cracking, except the inevitable late crack formation.

If you examine old pictures carefully you will often see that the surface is not uniformly covered with splits and cracks, but that there are large cracks in some places and none at all in others. The reason for this is the variation in thickness of the paint and the different behavior of the pigments.

Linseed oil, like all painting oils,

bleaches in the light and yellows in the dark. For this reason it is pointless to use bleached oil; it yellows and discolors all the more on the canvas. A thick layer of oil which reduces the penetration of light through to the bottom, yellows more, and more permanently, than a thin one.

It is also a great mistake to think that oil colors cannot absorb moisture. This can be demonstrated by spreading linseed oil on a glass plate and leaving it to harden for as long as a month or two. If the plate is then laid in water the oil film can be seen to swell and ultimately to come away from the plate entirely. A similar experiment with casein would have a contrary result: the casein would not be affected by the water. Transitory moisture does not damage oil paintings, and this may be why the layman imagines that an oil painting on strong canvas is the most durable and solid of techniques. He needs to revise this conception. The fact that the great masters succeeded in painting pictures which have withstood the test of several centuries is a tribute to their care and attention, but it does not make the technique in general any more certain.

Oil painting is quite useless on a wall. The film of oil seals the pores of the plaster, which then starts to rot, bubble up, and finally crumble away. It is amazing that there are still house painters who recommend washable oil plinths in buildings. A tragic example of the dangers of oil painting on plaster is the famous **Last Supper** of da Vinci. Always experimenting with new methods, Leonardo painted over his picture in oil colors. Its deterioration continues relent-lessly, defying the most highly developed techniques of conservation and restoration.

Although pure oil colors are still produced in great quantities, many good paint factories now have reduced the content of fatty oils in paints and produce the so-called "resin" oil colors. They contain a large, unfortunately unspecified, percentage of resin and some wax, which is also added to pure oil colors. Wax both protects resin varnishes from perishing and prevents pigments from separating from the oil in the tubes or forming a sort of jelly which is impossible to paint with. Resin oil paints harden more quickly than pure oil colors. Both evaporated solvents for resins and wax reduce the amount of binder and accelerate the absorption of oxygen by the oil.

In addition to bought oil colors, which are nowadays always resin oil paints, a suitable resin oil color can be obtained by carefully warming together 100 cc. of linseed oil with 5 gr. wax melted at about 158 degrees F., and adding, when it has cooled and been placed in a jar, 100 cc. mastic essence (of a proportion 1:2). Shut the jar immediately and shake it so that both substances are well mixed together. The pigments are kneaded with this binder into mounds of paste and left to rest at intervals to test the amount of binder required by the different pigments. These mixed pigments can be thinned with turpentine, just as watercolors can be thinned with water, without affecting their adhering to the ground. After the turpentine spirit has evaporated, 100 parts of linseed oil, about 30 of mastic, and 5 of wax will be found in the hardened paint.

Our list of organic binders is now at an end, for all other oils, lacquers, varnishes, and such like, though they may be usable, are no better than those already listed and tend to muddle the painter and involve him in technical difficulties.

To avoid the difficulties of oily binders it is better to use emulsions instead. They provide the advantages both of oily and watery substances, while the disadvantages are rendered harmless by the emulsion texture. A simple emulsion is obtained by combining an egg yolk with glue (tragacanth or gum arabic) and linseed oil, to which an essence of resin is added later. The method is the same as for making mayonnaise.

The emulsifying properties of an egg yolk are, of course, limited; it will function for about 75 cc. of gum solution and 150 cc. of oil, depending on the size of the yolk. It is best not to try to use it to the saturation point.

Before making any emulsion it is wise to measure out the various constituents carefully, as the bit-by-bit method makes it difficult to remember exactly how much has been used. An emulsion is most easily made by mixing it in a water bath at about 75 to 85 degrees F., and then stirring it until it has cooled to room temperature to prevent its separating.

An emulsion can be made even without an emulsifier—for instance, with gum arabic and essence of resin (and with linseed oil). It is a sleight of hand possessed by chemists as part of their professional equipment. A successful result is announced by a sort of clicking sound in the mixture as it is stirred. The sub-stance making the "honeycomb" formation should always be double in quantity to that which is being mixed in and, when necessary, thinned only with the substance which combines with it. Otherwise too much of the enclosed material would break the cell-like structure of the "honeycomb," and the mixture would curdle.

If you make your tempera colors yourself it is sufficient to make a paste only of a selection of the pigments which you intend to use. If a pigment is to be used only for a nuance in a mixture it can be taken from the watercolor box or the collection of oil colors, according to whether the tempera reacts better to an addition of water or of oil and turpentine. But, as we have said, this addition of other types of paint can be used only for mixtures, not for putting on by itself! This method saves much trouble and rightly used does not affect the technical quality of the tempera painting.

Once a layer of tempera color has hardened completely it is less sensitive to the solvent of the following layers than glue or oil colors necessarily are, but it does remain sensitive to some extent. The only paint which for practical purposes is completely insoluble to the following coats is a resin oil emulsified with casein—a relatively easy emulsion to make without an emulsifier.

LIME and **WATERGLASS** are inorganic binders. They are never used directly together with pigments; at most they are added, in a very dilute form, to the water in which the colors are ground. This is, however, not sufficient for fixing the pigments onto the ground.

Lime in the form of thick lime water can be used in a limited manner as a binder mixed with the pigment, but only for light colors much dimmed by white, and even they can be used only in a single layer, which is rarely sufficient in painting. If more than one coat is put on, the paint flakes off either as a whole or in separate layers.

True fresco, **fresco buono**, is very different. The pigment is ground up with water or lime water, or is bought ready mixed in bottles. It is painted onto the fresh plaster and the hardening lime covers it with a thin transparent skin.

We have already dealt thoroughly with lime plaster in the section on sgraffito. The use of pure lime (without cement) which alone gives fresco plaster its binding power is the reason why today paintings on facades in **fresco buono** technique can no longer be durable; for lime in every form reacts strongly to all acids, however weak they be. The author experienced this first as a young boy: he left a half lemon on the marble rim of his washstand and found a few hours later that the pretty star pattern of the fruit section had eaten into the "eternal" stone. His mother was less impressed with the charm of the design, since it was quite indelible. Lime plaster is equally sensitive even to the sulphurous acids in the air from the smoke of coal fires. In a few years they can destroy the crystalline lime layer over the fresco and bring about the deterioration of the paint as well. This is the situation in northern latitudes—at any rate since the introduction of coal firing. The greater moisture in the air is an added enemy,

making even the carbonic acids in the air destructive. The only hope of preserving fresco in northern climes is to use it indoors.

The only really weatherproof binder is waterglass, which has only recently been used by artists. It was first tried as a binder for painting in 1842 in Germany. It was at that time used mainly as a protective coating against fire for stage scenery, the stage then being illuminated by open lights. In 1880 A. W. Keim began to study and improve the technique of painting with waterglass. He called the technique "mineral painting"; it is nowadays sometimes called silica painting.

There are three kinds of waterglass: potassium, sodium, and double waterglass, which is made of a combination of the other two. The formulae are simple: K_2SiO_3, and Na_2SiO_3. Potassium waterglass is the only one suitable for painting purposes. The pigments must contain a certain percentage of zinc oxide (zinc white) and magnesia in order to petrify with dry plaster or natural stone through the agency of the waterglass. They are painted on the ground, as in fresco painting, with only water or with very dilute waterglass. The waterglass is sprayed on afterwards like a fixative. It then combines with the carbonic acid in the air to make potassium carbonate and silicic oxide. The potassium carbonate is water soluble and is removed by washing or simply by the rain. If sodium waterglass were used, sodium carbonate (soda) would be produced, which does not wash off easily and would veil the painting.

7. TECHNIQUE OF PAINTING

The technique of painting, as I have already said, is not to be confused with the style of painting or personal touch of the artist. Technique is the artist's trade, which he must master in order to be able to express himself. Technique, however, is closely connected with the artistic idea: a painter who is master of many techniques will not only interpret an experience or visual impression into a formal composition, but will also immediately translate his vision into a definite technique. Some people go about it the other way: they have devoted themselves to a single technique and only let themselves receive visual experiences which correspond to it.

Rembrandt, for example, was never, from all we know of him, inspired to a picture by a tender balmy spring landscape which would require the soft transparent coloring of watercolors. Rembrandt had to use oils in order to achieve his mysterious deep darkness from which he could then draw out the light only with thick layers of paint. Perhaps one could say more correctly that his motif dictated this particular technique, which could only be oil painting; and from this technique, the famous chiaroscuro, he never deviated.

Titian also often painted on a similar principle, i.e., bringing the light out of the darkness, but he used a less heavy painting for the light and gave an essential role to a light underpainting, letting it shine through the thinnest glazes, sometimes using 30 or 40, one over the other, and at the end putting in a few opaque lights. Titian's pictures often stayed in the studio for months, as each layer had to dry out before he went on to the next; so he had several pictures under way at the same time. Monet or Cézanne would not have got very far with such a procedure. They painted mostly outside from nature at an intense tempo. The picture was begun in a few hours and often finished without a break. The Impressionists used the so-called **alla prima** oil technique which can be executed only with the most consistently behaved tube oil colors.

Value judgments are irrelevant to a painting method insofar as it is a means of expression, but a picture can be judged from the technical point of view with absolute standards. The best technique is that which maintains the picture permanently in the condition in which it was left by the artist. Permanent is a strong word, for ultimately all material is perishable. Experience shows, however, that paintings which have not altered after a few years or decades can last for centuries without traces of decay.

You already know what the different factors are which contribute to this problem: the three components, pigment, ground, and binder. The most problematical is the binder, the least complicated, the color. The ground or surface stands in reliability between the two. But even the best technique is uninteresting if its materials are wrongly or imperfectly used. And the picture is uninteresting if it speaks to no one and provides no experience. However, whoever has taken the trouble to learn painting properly will surely have something to say with it.

The whole wide range of techniques stands between the two poles of watercolor and oil painting. All the rest are intermediate modes of expression, to be recognized externally from the depth of color obtainable. It can be theoretically imagined thus: watercolor works from a white ground into the color and dark and soon reaches its limit there; oil painting grows from the depth of darkness into the light, which can extend through colors to pure white—white put on and not achieved by leaving out, as in watercolor.

This, at any rate, is the broad principle of technique, which can, of course, be varied, particularly in oil, where it is possible to work with the thinnest transparent paints of which watercolor consists entirely. With these transparent paints it is possible to achieve a glow of color comparable to the stained glass of a cathedral when the light is shining through it.

The many techniques are best understood by experimenting with the tendencies and styles of the two opposed methods, both in seeing and execution.

The similarities and differences in painting can perhaps be best explained by a comparison with music, for both arts have many ideas in common, even many common terms—for instance,

"tone," "color harmony," "tone color." A painting can be compared to the many-colored sound of a full orchestra, a solo song to a drawing. As in musical technique there are in painting many Italian terms which cannot reasonably be translated: **al fresco, fresco-secco, alla prima, sfumato** are words familiar to every painter and art historian. A comparison with instrumental music will make the qualities of watercolor and oil technique quite clear: the watercolor begins with a soft and gentle note and ends with a full deep concord. Everywhere at the same time the greatest depth of which it is capable should be enveloped in the fluidity of the lighter colors.

The oil picture begins with a mild deep sound of solo wind, grows in the many colors of the full orchestra, over which stand out the trumpets and horns with the brightest tones; violins and flutes draw light contours, and the high lights resemble the echoing cymbal.

Even if an oil painting is performed in the hurried pizzicato of Kokoschka the mark would be legato and the time andante. Watercolor can only be prestissimo; the technique allows of no exception.

Technically speaking, watercolor is the simplest way of painting. (This you know already from what has been said about water paints and paper.) When it comes to ability, however, and sureness, it is one of the most demanding of all techniques on the painter's ability.

Oil painting requires a thorough knowledge of the materials, and the way the picture is built up technically needs to be well thought out if it is to last. The old masters knew their job so thoroughly because they produced, or at least prepared, everything themselves: the grounds, pigments, and, most important of all, the binders. The Impressionists (and not they alone!) relied on the products of industry which were just coming on to the market and were by no means perfected. They worried very little about the technique of mixing and putting on paints, and the result is what one would expect: very many pictures of the second half of the last century are deteriorating irretrievably. A consistent oil color has never been found which will stay unchanged in both upper and under layers. Added to this the different pigments influence the setting time of oil binders. For this reason oil colors cannot be worked with so unconcernedly as watercolors. On the other hand, with oil colors you can, if you go the right way about it, work at the same picture either at one sitting or after weeks or months, glazing and repainting solidly.

If you are equally conversant with the principle of watercolor painting and with the various ways of painting in oils you can proceed with all the other techniques. A painting with reversible glue as binder can be done as quickly as a watercolor, but it also allows as leisurely work as oil colors. This depends entirely on what you wish the final effect to be. Fresco on damp plaster requires the same speed, and as far as possible single-coat painting, like watercolor, while with fresco-secco you have plenty of time and can overpaint as you wish. Painting with genuine tempera and the mixed techniques of mineral painting allows both the thin transparent texture of watercolor and the opaque, even-modeled effects of oil color. Pastel is the only exception; it is made up of fine or broad lines, but this you already know from the section on drawing.

First you need either a single sheet of paper or a watercolor block. Directly before starting work, the paper is well dampened and stuck or, if necessary, pinned down. If you have a painting block you must thoroughly dampen the top sheet with a sponge cloth several times, though not so much that it forms uneven patches of wet, which would make it ripple. A single wetting is not enough. It takes quite a while for dry paper to soak up enough water; once it is soaked through it will hold the moisture for some time.

During this process, while the paper is relatively dry before another wetting, you can lay in a few pencil outlines of your intended picture. Wet paper will hardly take pencil at all. The lead should not be too soft—H is about right. The drawing should be done so lightly that the lines can be left without spoiling the effect of the finished painting. After the drawing, dampen the paper again and leave it to dry while you get the paints ready. If you work with semi-permanent pan colors, drop a little water onto each with a pipette so that the paint will come off more quickly later. Always keep two jars of water at hand: one for washing out the brushes and the other, rather smaller, filled with clear water for the pipette or for clean brushes. Ordinary tap water is often very hard and full of lime, which makes watercolors flake; for painting you should use boiled water, at least.

Right from the start get used to working only with thick brushes of the best quality. An average size is No. 6, with which you can make the finest lines, if it can be drawn to a fine point when damp. This point, of course, wears away after a dozen pictures or so—according to size —but even then the brush is excellent for less fine work. Even when it has grown

The best artists' watercolors in tubes and chinaware in the sizes usually obtainable; and students' and scholastic watercolors

quite blunt it will still take up a good quantity of paint, and this is important: in watercolor painting the brush must always be full, whether you are doing fine detail or large surfaces.

To paint freely with watercolor you must expect a certain waste of paint; wash the color quickly and broadly onto the paper with a full brush. This will give enough color, probably too much. Rinse the brush thoroughly, press it out in an absorbent cloth, and use it to remove the excess from the wet painting. Do not color frugally and tediously; do not add a little again and again until the color is dark enough; it makes a wretched daub.

The paints are best kept in a large tin box, which can be bought for both pans and tubes. It is, of course, beneath you to buy a box ready filled with paints. Select them to your taste according to what you now know about pigments. Tubes or pans—it is all one, but take note:

Pans are more economical, for you use only what you need, but it takes longer for pan colors to soften. To take out paint from the pan, use cheaper brushes or old blunted ones that are no longer fit for painting. Never use a dirty brush on a pan! You will never again get a really pure color, and that is one of the essentials of watercolor. More than in any other technique muddy colors are to be avoided.

Tubes are simpler. You simply squeeze the quantity of paint required onto the tin palette and take from it for mixing or painting direct. Do not imagine that

Watercolor artist at work. His equipment consists of a container with water to wash brushes and solvent, a pipette, jars of used and unused brushes, pencil, eraser, damp sponge, a rag. He is using a watercolor box fitted with pans and a folding lid forming a palette

a collection of colors mixed in a disorderly smear will be an inspiration! If you want to experiment with mixtures it will perhaps help to have several palettes ready. Watercolor palettes are made of white enameled tin and have shallow hollows to hold the fluid paint. Generally, the lids of paint boxes are made to serve as palettes, but they can also be bought separately. It is not very practical to have several porcelain dishes, especially if working in the open.

If you use pans the palette needs only the largish hollows into which plenty of the liquid paint is placed and mixed. For tube colors there is a palette with a row of smaller hollows into which the contents of the tubes are squeezed in small quantities, and from there moved onto the larger hollows as the paint is required.

Since watercolor must be painted broadly and fast and since every new shade must be mixed clearly on the palette, we shall soon fill up all the space on it. It would take far too much time to clean a section for each new mixture, so it is best to use a second palette and even a third if necessary. Unused left-over paints are then still available, and this can be very convenient if a first application has been too thin and needs going over again. This often happens as the work progresses. Watercolor can be done quite well with one brush, but three are better: one for yellow, orange, and cadmium red, one for alizarin red to violet, and one for

Detail (1:1) from a watercolor study using rough Whatman paper, once slightly wetted

Watercolor

better to have two brush jars, one for blunt brushes for taking out paint and mixing it and one for painting brushes. If the brushes stand spread out like a sparse bunch of flowers it is easy to see which one you want.

Often even several palettes get filled up, and sponge-rubber cloths or rags are needed to wipe them clean. A whole stock of these should lie ready to wipe away paint that is finished with. Dirty cloths can be thrown into a box, and after the artistic side of the work is done they must be carefully washed out under the tap. These cloths are also excellent for removing unwanted paint from the picture.

Later, when the paper has dried out too much from the first painting, it cannot, of course, be dampened with the cloth again. A fixative spray filled with clear water is then used—but be careful! Not more than a breath of water should be sprayed on—perhaps to be repeated again later—or the colors will run into each other and all over the place.

For painting with watercolors you should sit at a table supporting the block or board at the edge with the left hand. Then you can hold the surface flat and at the correct angle. The more fluid your painting is the more the color will tend to run down and be darker at the bottom. This has to be prevented. The palette, too, should lie on the table. If it is held in the hand the fluid colors will spill into each other in the heat of the

green to blue. If you want to work in the really grand manner, use one more for gray and one for brown. If you work with only one brush it must be very carefully cleaned before each use. This takes time and is never quite certain. If, for instance, you use yellow after blue it is more than likely that a trace of blue will stay in the brush and give the yellow a greenish tinge.

It looks very fine to hold all the brushes in the left hand, and the palette too, but it is not really very practical. It is much

Stage reached when work stopped about an hour later. The end was precipitated by approaching mist, and as a result the shadows were overworked and too dense

moment. Easels and palettes held in the hand are used only with thick, not liquid, paints.

However much you try to get the final tones at once, you will very rarely succeed. As you work, the effect of the picture evolves only gradually, and you see how to heighten it with darker depths and alterations in the colors; also you will need to put on two or three layers of color. Provide yourself, too, with a few strips of paper for testing colors, particularly mixtures; watercolors always look different on paper and on the palette.

In watercolor you are working only with transparent paints. The white or tinted ground shows through all the painting. If you want to hide it with an opaque color, then give up watercolor altogether. If your painting has the effect of one done in opaque paint, however cool and clear the color may be, the spontaneous, fleeting and watery character, the tenderness of its nature would be lost. Opaque paint or paint too much overlaid produces "holes" in the picture, particularly if in other places there is no more than a single layer of paint.

You know by now, of course, that white should never be found among watercolor pigments. White should be created only by untouched paper, at most gone over with a clean brushful of water. If a patch of color is too dark it can be moistened with a clean brush and some of the paint removed. Natu- rally, the paper will never be quite white again where paint has once been on it.

The nature of the paint allows the following method to be tried: let a first draft in not-too-heavy paint dry completely and then lay the whole sheet of paper in water. As soon as the colors are dissolved, rinse it. This must be done quickly and thoroughly to prevent the runny paint from sticking in new places where it is not wanted. The paper is then dabbed dry with a series of clean cloths;

this removes still more paint. A very faint image will remain, its strength depending on the kind of paper and the paints. If the pigment is colloidal in fineness, more will stay in the paper than if the coarser pigment powder was used. Differences in the granulation will thus affect the depth of color left by the different paints. You can then paint further on the paper while it is still damp or has been dampened again.

This method gives you a sure foundation for a carefully thought out, detailed composition; but, of course, it loses the rapid, unfinished charm of a spontaneous painting and, as has been explained, the pure white of the paper.

Another method gives a similar effect: you work over the whole picture with very weak colors and put in deep, full colors only when you are certain of everything else. The final effect is more brilliant and harder than with the washing-out method, because some places on the paper can be left untouched.

At first every watercolorist tends to make a number of technical mistakes due to a lack of sureness in putting down form and color. One of these mistakes, or faults, is working too slowly. If the paper dries too much, the paints, particularly the very fluid ones, dry with a dark rim round them which is very hard to take out, even by washing over with water. It would be wrong to give up using liquid paint because of this, as the animation of the work would be lost and the temperamental effect of the picture with it.

If you want to begin more gently, more tentatively, then start with cool, light colors. This is done for a tentative begin-

ning in any technique. The natural model provides a parallel: the distance is always cooler in color than the foreground and tends to blue. Warm, close colors come last. If you paint with the reverse procedure, the picture becomes heavy and without contrasts, which is especially unfortunate in a watercolor. Every picture should be built up from weak to strong colors, not vice versa. In watercolor painting this means omitting the strongly colored areas until the cool, duller colors and weak shadow tones can be seen.

When discussing pigments we mentioned that black has its place in watercolor, if it is transparent. Otherwise it would be an alien element among the colors. Black should always either stand alone or under a color. If transparent black is laid over other colors it kills them completely and makes them colorless and dirty, but as an underlay it can, particularly in a very thin gray application, give the illusion of substance and solidity. The limits of depth are reached in watercolor when the application of a dark color begins to be opaque. It may be that you sometimes put on a light yellow or green or blue so that it is almost opaque,

This picture of a stream quite familiar to the artist was painted one misty spring morning. Light conditions remained constant for some hours, allowing time for greater deliberation, and enabling him to achieve the gentle tones without overpainting. Whatman paper was used, and as it was continually drying, had to be partly wetted again (detail, $\frac{1}{2}$ actual size; the surrounding landscape was shaded off)

but if the color becomes darker it is permissible only if it lets through a shimmer of the color of the paper. An impression of great depth can be achieved in watercolor even with very light colors. Like a drawn sketch, the watercolor which most stimulates the beholder to co-operation arouses his imagination and thus can affect him more than an oil painting. The oil painting has to formulate more unambiguously with its depth of color and the technical manner of reproducing exact detail, or else be consciously indistinct. The fortuitous does not suit it.

Illusion or suggestion, inviting the collaboration of the beholder, is the essence of the watercolor as an art form. For instance, the illusion of twilight and darkness can be obtained not only from depth of color but from tone: you can paint a twilight scene in the lightest colors if the characteristic color harmony, the dominant tone of the hour, is rightly caught. This matters more than depth.

I said, earlier, that watercolor is composed of "pure" applications of color. This does not mean that you must, for instance, make green by putting pure yellow and pure blue onto the paper. By "pure" is meant clear and definite mixtures made on the palette. (In no painting is it permissible to mix paints on the picture itself.) Correction of a color can be done only by overpainting with a transparent wash or, if that cannot help, by washing out the wrong color with water. Overpainting requires great

speed so that the color underneath does not smudge. It cannot be done while the paint is too wet. A feeling for the correct moisture of the paper is a matter of experience and ultimately, too, of personal taste. Some artists produce their best effects with absolutely liquid colors which even run into each other; others can work only if the paints dry clear, without a rim, next to each other.

Every painter has his preferred technique, but there are some effects which can be expressed only in watercolors: cool light, misty springtime, soft autumn, and, ever and again, water—rain, streams, lakes, melting snow. It seems that anything that is wet calls for a technique that uses water profusely as its elixir.

You can see how difficult watercolor painting is. Even if you prefer painting in oils and find yourself more at home as a beginner seeking out the right coloration by trial and error with oil paints, watercolors are still the best teacher and ultimately the best criterion of ability, for you have to define your form and color at the first stroke, practice speed and concentration and work broadly and simply. Thus it is quite right that watercolors are used almost exclusively in the schools, although a good painting is so difficult. It is, besides being the simplest technique, of the highest educational value.

Watercolor is the beginning and the crown of all painting technique.

If all the principles of watercolor painting are turned upside down we get those of oil painting. This is most plainly seen in a technique developed since the beginning of so-called "plein-air" painting: work in the open air and not in a studio. It is called alla prima and implies an application of paint without underpainting or glazes, enabling the artist to finish his picture in one sitting, directly from the object.

Factory-made oil paints in tubes are essential for this; they do away with the need for preparing the paints and allow the painter to complete his work directly in the open air instead of working in oils in the studio from a watercolor or gouache sketch. One can safely say that without factory production of paints in tubes the development of plein-air and impressionist painting would have been impossible. The method of working is so simple that any tyro can cope with the technique once he knows something of the fundamental principles involved in the use of the materials. If he is lucky enough to come by first class paints and a semi-serviceable painting surface (there are no first-class surfaces to be bought!) then his oil painting may last for a long time in a satisfactory state of preservation.

There is no need to spend time in lengthy instructions; you can have a try straight away:

Buy painting board (card) prepared with a half chalk ground, some flat bristle brushes, one each of sizes 2,3,4,7,9, and some oil paints (these will, in fact, be resin oil colors, but today they are simply termed oil colors in the trade). The choice of colors can be the same as those recommended on p. 261 for the first attempts in watercolors. Added to these you now need white pigment—either titanium white or lead and zinc white. A ready-made assortment of paints always contains a few undesirable colors. You will also need some turpentine (genuine spirits of turpentine) and white spirit (turps substitute) for cleaning the brushes. If you have only one palette you will need a palette knife to scrape off unwanted remains of paint and make space for new ones—an old table or kitchen knife will do the job. Finally, plenty of old rags for squeezing out the brushes and cleaning the palette knife must lie ready at hand.

Showing still more clearly how oil is the opposite of water painting, the painting surface must not be white. You can choose any dull color which fits in with the color scheme you have in mind. The most suitable is either a pervasive shadow tone or, if you are going to work with glazes, its complementary color.

The coloring of the ground can be done in several ways—for instance, by painting in ordinary water or glue paint (sold as "artists' tempera color"). If you find this rather fluid paint too risky, because it may soften and smear the priming, you can adopt one of three courses:

1. Mix dry powder color to a liquid with mastic varnish in the proportion of 1:2 and thin again with spirit of turpentine.

2. Dilute oil paint with turpentine until it is runny.

3. Rub over the white surface with pastel, wipe in circular motion with a thick wad of rags, pressing quite hard, and then fix with solution of shellac until it will not smear—no harder—as though it were a chalk drawing. This method of coloring the painting surface is the best under the given conditions; it contains no dangerous binder, the coat of shellac prevents it from being too absorbent, and the subsequent painting cannot dissolve the priming. It also has the advantage of being dry in a few moments after application. With a priming of oil color you will have to wait at least a day before beginning to paint. Priming with glue paint takes an hour or two to dry,

Flat brushes Nos. 4 and 16, with short, medium, and long bristles

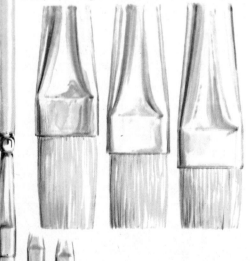

or longer unless it is exposed to heat or the sun. Furthermore, a coating of glue paint leaves the surface more absorbent than shellac fixative or resin oil, and the painting method to be described requires a surface as little absorbent as possible.

The painting should be done standing, and the surface should be almost upright. This gives the painter the greatest freedom of movement and accustoms him from the start to step back to check the effect of the picture from the distance of a few paces. An easel is therefore required. Advice on choosing an easel is given in the section on The Studio and Its Equipment.

After these initial preparations, you can begin. First comes the drawing in on the panel. Unfortunately, it is still considered "professional" to draw in with charcoal, although the black from the charcoal immediately takes away the purity of the colors put on over it. Pencil is equally unsuitable. It is best to draw with a fine brush and very thin color. If you are still uncertain, use a pastel or red chalk, according to which color best suits what will follow. On a foundation of terre verte green, for example, it is best to draw in with terre verte pastel; of course, a harder pastel would be more convenient and more delicate, but unfortunately it exists only in red, black, and white.

The rule is to draw lightly for the blocking in and to rub out with a rag as many of the wrong lines as possible, blowing away any chalk which lies too thickly.

Do not on any account attempt detailed drawing at this stage! The drawing in is only intended to divide up the painting surface and settle the composition, and this in not too-definite a manner; after all, you are painting now, and in painting the color is as much a determining factor as the form. In any case, all details will be covered over with paint again. If you were embarking on a largish painting, a sketch of the composition in color would be part of the preparation.

Now take the paints. The first selection which you squeeze, but not too lavishly, onto the palette should not be all the brightest colors. The darker colors should predominate at first; they will give a rather neutral colored mat, and broad indication of the picture. Even if you have to paint large areas, say, in cad-

mium yellow, you should underlay them first with a "rub-in" in medium ochre. Parts of this underpainting will, perhaps, be able to remain at the end as half-shadow, particularly if it has been applied as it should, not aggressively and thickly but lightly, with thinned, almost transparent paint. "Blunting," "granulating," or "dimming" are the rather outmoded painter's expressions. Instead of thin, transparent painting the laying-in can be done in separate touches, or scrubbed onto the panel with a rather dry brush and unthinned paint. This is a matter both of personal taste, of your now developing personal touch or way of painting, and of practice. In this first

Painting in oils. In addition to the colors, the equipment includes cleaning materials, diluent, spatula, and palette knife

stage of painting you begin to model the forms, for you are, as Rembrandt kept saying to enlighten others and remind himself, "a painter, not a colorist." "Coloring" you do only once: when you tint the ground. In the first mat stage of painting you put in the shadows and other dark areas and lighten with colors mixed with white where form or color require it.

The first selection of paints on the palette has included white pigments, among them white lead, which causes the colors mixed with it to harden quickly. Pigments sensitive to lead, such as cadmium sulphide, are hardly likely to be needed at the beginning, but when they are used they must, of course, be lightened with zinc or titanium white. For this is the characteristic of the **alla prima** technique, and indeed of all body paint techniques, at any rate in the top layers; white is added to all colors to lighten them. Even were the ground white it would not be used as it is in watercolor. This use of paint gives quite the opposite effect both from watercolor and from a glazing technique in oils.

You started modeling the forms slightly at the first painting. In the method presently under discussion darks and lights which give the sense of relief should now be indicated in the many colors suggested by the natural model, not merely modeled in dark and light of the local color. This method of work would require a modeled monochrome underpainting in the complementary color finished with glazes of the local color.

Although the color is built up gradually, the picture is completed in one sitting. This is technically necessary, for the paints must be laid on one after the other, "wet in wet," before the binder begins to harden. It is dangerous to continue working on a half-dried painting because fast-drying paints on the top would break and form early cracks. In **alla prima**, the oxidation of the oils and resins proceeds as though all the paints were put on in one application.

The convenience of oil painting is that the colors, even when thinned, cannot run into each other unless they are so fluid they run from the palette too. Thus, although the paints are put on as a more or less soft paste, they make no hard rims as does watercolor when the paper is too dry. And though here, as everywhere, it is much frowned upon to mix colors on the picture itself, the consistency and long hardening time of oily binders do allow a little working together of paints lying side by side.

When the work has taken shape from

Ph. O. Runge, sketch for a portrait of the artist's mother. Oil colors on canvas. This sketch gives an exceptional insight into the proper organization of the alla prima method. First came a thin underpainting in unobtrusive colors, so that in the shadows the green ground partly showed through. The high lights were then painted in opaque directly onto this layer, as were patches of reflected light in the shadows. Runge used the green ground which shimmered through as a complementary color for the reddish glaze which covered the whole, thereby rendering the skin tone in all its lifelike freshness and engendering the most varied shades of optical gray.
With unique application, Runge extracted the utmost from color mixing as well as from transparent overpainting (glazing) and also direct opaque shades. By combining these two effects he gradually attained an outstanding plastic and almost glassy look. He might well have revolutionized the handling of color, but he died at the age of 33.
The sketch reproduced here was obviously kept for a long time rolled up. The cracks running through paint layer and primer all the way across show clearly the damage caused when the picture was unrolled

H. Gilman, Mrs. Mounter at the Breakfast Table. The underpainting for this picture seems to have been applied boldly with very little detail. Completely opaque color areas are juxtaposed without over-lapping, like a mosaic built up of patches of oil paint

the form and color point of view it is worked up with stronger colors and lights until the last high light adds the finishing touch.

If you have done it well then the painting can be considered truly finished. In some places the tinted ground stands almost untouched, and the more neutral-colored ground work shines through the upper painting, though in places this may be so thick that not even a black ground would show through. Thick painting gives the surface a pleasing, tactile, plastic texture. Carried to extremes this

manner of painting has led to painting with the knife.

The method described above is that used by the majority of painters since the beginning of Impressionism to the present day. Technically it is preferable to make one's own glue ground, rather than to use bought ones; the best are on hard-board with glued-on canvas. The texture of the woven cloth corresponds to impasto **alla prima** technique much better than a smooth board. The surface should be protected with shellac sufficiently to prevent its absorbing the binder from the bought tube colors; for this produces both yellowing and the so-called "sinking in" of the colors. When this occurs the absorption of the binder allows the colors to harden without any sheen, and as this never occurs uniformly it gives a blotchy effect to the whole picture. The paint sinks again, however often these mat areas are repainted, unless the area is first allowed to dry thoroughly and then given a coat of varnish. This process, however, would bring an entirely unwanted binder into the painting. A finishing varnish gives the surface a uniform sheen and protects the penetration of dust into the unevenness of the paint. It must not be put on too soon. A good varnish is 1:2 or 1:3 mastic essence with at least 2 per cent addition of wax.

You can also dissolve wax alone in turpentine with a small addition of mastic to give a paste which is just spreadable. This varnish is the surest protection against damp; it should be applied very thinly with a soft bristle brush. The drawback is that it remains soft for a long time, unless you expose the picture surface, after careful brushing, to warmth until the turpentine has evaporated. The surface begins to sweat, and some water evaporates along with the spirit of turpentine. Strong heat should never be used with oil because this browns it rapidly. Gentle warmth, from 140 to 160 degrees F., is unharmful.

Another reason why coating varnishes should be put on very thin is so that they will not arrest the oxidation of the oils. It probably takes 60 to 100 years for a thick oil paint to be fully oxidized. This is when late crack formation sets in.

We can make one final comparison between watercolor and thick **alla prima**

oil painting: both methods are technically easy to manage. Both require ideally that the work be completed at one attempt in front of the subject.

But whereas watercolor painting entails no technical risk to speak of, oil and resin oil painting are the most dubious of all methods. However, corrections are always possible with oil paints. They allow the artist to work as long as he wishes at a painting to gain the greatest effect of form and color. Any error can be rectified without aesthetic damage to the painting, or covered over, scraped out, and repainted, and even made pure white right at the end. On the other hand, a watercolor is ruined if it is corrected or lightened with white.

Both techniques have one good thing in common: they show hardly any difference between wet and dry colors, whereas all glue techniques and fresco paintings suffer from a very great alteration. Opaque oil paints and watercolors are thus the best techniques for the beginner and should both be practiced.

Lastly, we must consider a branch of **alla prima** technique much used at the present time in abstract painting: palette knife painting. The paint is not put on the canvas with a brush but with spatulae of the most varied sizes, even some small trowels like those used by builders for laying bricks. The paint is used unthinned, straight from the tube, as though it were putty or mortar. A palette knife cannot at once give such precise form as a brush, and modeling is done after the paint is put on with the edge and point of the knife. The character of the picture surface thus painted is rather like a low relief. The shadows of the solid paint are part of the effect and often constitute

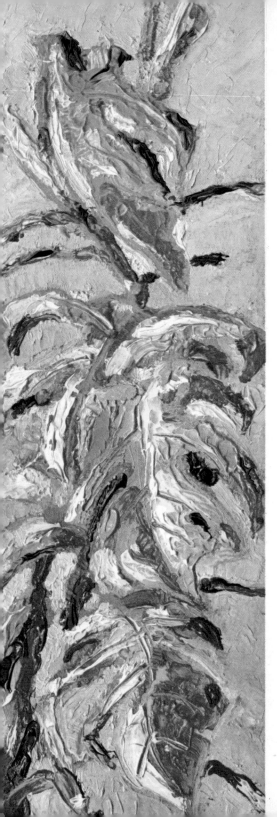

the picture's only charm. Spiritual content is often in short supply when so much seeking for effect is involved. For if anyone thinks he needs the texture created by the shadows for realizing his artistic concept, he can paint it in with thin paint, and probably give thereby a better idea of whether he has something significant to say or is simply covering the surface with a colored texture which is more or less all there is to be expressed. Many, however, go a step further: they model a low relief in gesso and cover it with thin paint, or they squeeze the paint straight from the tube onto the surface and develop great virtuosity in spinning out the ooze in the finest threads.

I will offer no opinion as to whether with methods of painting such as these there are other, hitherto unrealized ideas to be expressed. But it is certain that such a use of paint by the pound in this way implies a great lack of respect for it. Its charm as a substance can be thoroughly enjoyed only by using the whole range between softest glaze and a thin body color. Again, there is the question of the technical dangers of putting on paint inches thick at a time. Only in lucky cases will the compact layers remain without huge splits until late crack formation occurs. Thereupon, when the thoroughly oxidized oil begins to "burn," enormous cracks will be accompanied by the shrinking up of lumps of paint, and much of it will fall off. Even were this not to happen, the inevitable coarse splits will ruin the intended effect of the picture—quite apart from the fact that the thicker the paint is, the more the oils yellow and brown.

Knife technique. Detail, actual size

10. GLUE COLOR PAINTING

A medium which is handled in much the same way as impasto **alla prima** oils is opaque glue paint. Glue colors produce a dead mat effect, however, and can never rival the depth or luminosity of oils.

The difficulty here is that glue colors look distinctly darker wet than dry. This aspect is most pronounced in the medium hues, and means that the artist while still at work on a picture cannot know with certainty what the final effect will be. It requires some experience to use glue colors without spoiling a picture by constant retouching. There are, moreover, technical limits, even where use can be made of impasto overpainting; glue paint applied too thickly is liable to break away from the ground, develop cracks, and crumble. Properly bound glue paint should be indelible when dry (but on no account contain too much glue). Assuming that such paint is used, it will adhere well, and hide the ground without caking.

Glue colors have greater hiding power than oils applied equally thinly. The reason for this is that oil holds the color particles permanently congealed, as it were, while glue solutions shrink noticeably in volume in the drying; when this happens on a big scale, the particles cling to the under layer like fine pebbles. Only when they are wet, therefore, can glue colors equal oils in depth. Once the water contained in them has evaporated, leaving only the glue, the pebbled surface is left considerably enlarged and capable of reflecting more light. The color is almost as vivid as pigment in powder form, and its hiding power is correspondingly enhanced. A study of seventeenth and eighteenth century gouache still lifes with flowers, painted on a dark ground, demonstrates the truth of this. For oil colors to have the same hiding power, they must be applied much thicker. If you apply a little glue color to a glossy paper and then draw a hard pencil line across both the paper and the patch of color, you will find that whereas the pencil only leaves a faint mark on the shiny paper, it shows up clearly on the color patch, because the

Half varnished patches show the difference in color between wet and dry glue paint

Glue Color Painting

The theme was a travel sketch in watercolor. For the glue color version, white watercolor paper was primed with cobalt blue and cadmium red watercolors. To give an accurate rendering of this scene, high up over the Adriatic where pirates once nested, as it was imprinted on my mind, I compressed the composition somewhat, reducing the big shadows on the right and leaving out the bushes on the left

rougher surface of the pigment acts like sandpaper. Conversely, a patch of oil paint would become even glossier than the paper, and the pencil would give off hardly any particles of graphite at all.

To learn to judge how much glue colors will lighten in drying, you should try making a number of brush strokes in glue color, then half cover them with a thick coating of a varnish composed of pyroxylin and amyl acetate.

This experiment should not lead you to suppose that you can impart a darker hue to a finished glue painting by varnishing it over. What occurs in this case cannot be gauged in advance, nor can it

by any means be regarded as a comprehensive painting technique. The picture is robbed entirely of its essential charm, and with it a large part of the artist's inspiration. The same thing happens to watercolors when they are varnished. Conversely, the chalky tone of an opaque glue painting can render effects which are virtually unobtainable in any other medium, although not altogether unlike a certain type of pastel.

Glue painting, then, has its own characteristics; but quite apart from this, it is well suited to sketching and to preliminary sketches for oil and true tempera painting—far more so than watercolor,

Stage 1: The background and light areas were covered with titanium white, lightly tinted. This resulted in greater brilliance for the luminous colors to follow. The priming color was mixed from the start in the main shadow tone, and this was largely left. It could be further varied, as necessary, by the use of pale glazes

for example. It should be noted that while watercolors must be applied on a wet ground, glue color, which is equally direct in its application, has the advantage of always being painted on a dry ground, so that, despite rapid execution, the paint underneath never runs or smudges.

The most suitable support for this medium is cardboard. Paper that is less than 14 ply buckles when painted and remains buckled even after the paint—which varies in thickness—has dried out. This may occur with cardboard, too, and depends on the quality of the board and the way the paint is used. For this reason,

pasteboard, or a synthetic fiber board with good quality paper of the required thickness glued to it, provides a better support. In addition, any support which is good for oil painting will serve the purpose, as long as it is properly prepared to receive glue color. The final choice of a support is determined by the format and by the artist's aims.

Similar considerations determine whether to leave the ground white or to tint it. The best and easiest way to tint paper is to apply a very runny watercolor with a flat brush from two to four inches wide, known as the blending brush, moving it back and forth over the paper. To

Stage 2: The colors are everywhere uniformly intensified, and it would have been possible to complete the work boldly at this stage
Stage 3: Too much elaborate detail at this stage marred the artistic effect. This shows that one can never stop too soon; and also that watercolor work does not transpose

do this, the support must lie flat to avoid collecting paint at the bottom edge, thus ensuring that the surface is kept fairly even.

It is also possible to tint the glue ground with pastel chalk. When this is done, however, shellac should not be used for fixing, as glue colors do not adhere well to this fixative and flake off with repeated overpainting. A weak glue solution, such as gum arabic, tragacanth, or skim milk, makes the most satisfactory fixing agent; carpenter's glue is not good, as it cools down too much in the spraying and sets prematurely. The glue must be thin enough to travel up the blowpipe.

The spraying calls for particular care, since water stays on the paint surface longer than the alcohol in shellac, which evaporates more speedily. As soon as the medium has been rendered indelible, work can proceed as with **alla prima** oil painting. The same palette and brushes will do, and water may be used for thinning and washing.

As mentioned earlier in connection with ready-made colors, "artists' tempera," as it is called, will prove fairly safe; but it is better to obtain pigment in powder form and make it up for yourself, using an appropriate glue solution. In this way, you will be sure of painting

into other media. Despite the exaggerated shadows, the white from the previous sketches shows through and loosens the whole composition. The correct way to obtain this effect in glue colors would have been to paint directly on to unprimed white cardboard. Ordinary bought tempera colors were used for this picture

with pure and unadulterated colors.

Deciding whether to use a white or a tinted ground will be determined by your particular aim; and whether white or tinted, it should play a part in the picture as a whole. A delightful effect is achieved when a tinted ground is left to show in places. Using glue colors, and carrying out the underpainting in watercolors, the color can be made to darken very gradually so that the tinted ground is distinctly preserved. On a white ground, the underpainting has a naturalness and delicacy which looks wonderfully fresh against the overpainting. The final coat may also be applied more thickly, if this

is in keeping with your aims and methods. From a technical viewpoint, this is quite safe, provided that the layer of paint is less thick and cakey than it is with **alla prima** oils. The technical possibilities of glue painting are increased if casein is used in place of nonreversible glue. This can hardly be done, however, without restricting color choice, since it means that no coloring matter sensitive to either chalk or lye may be used. Even when casein has been left to set for a full week and is completely insoluble in water— and the water used for thinning has evaporated—it will be all but impervious to simple overpainting. Prolonged wash-

Glue Color Painting

ing is the only method. Hence, the best use for glue colors is for really extensive and time-consuming work. For instance, pictures requiring glazing are difficult to do well because the layer beneath the nonreversible glue dissolves so rapidly. With casein, too, the colors lose rather more of their brightness than with the glues previously mentioned. When a mat painting is completely dry, it can be given a sheen by brushing or by rubbing with a woolen cloth. This makes the colors appear somewhat deeper and is a procedure which thoroughly suits the medium. If the paint is laid thinly onto a white ground it will look like a genuine fresco. Naturally, it is a prerequisite that either the untreated sheet of paper or the glue ground should be prepared with casein-bound pigment before painting begins so that, even when the ground is untreated, it is given a layer of casein.

If you try applying this undercoat on cardboard not treated with glue, you will find at once that the cardboard will roll up with great force. Fresh casein is a powerful binding agent, and it is often insufficiently thinned. When this happens, it rolls off in broad flat cakes, taking even the primer with it. For this reason, the paint layers should barely go beyond the point of indelibility. If this point is not reached, a very strong dilution of casein can be used afterwards as a fixer. The most risky procedure is the impasto use of a casein color containing too much glue. It detaches itself stubbornly from the ground. Abstain altogether from impasto work with casein colors. However, if this is the very effect you want, but at the same time you wish to avoid the yellowing and browning which often accompany oil painting, then you are better advised to use true tempera.

The same bristle brushes should be used for casein colors as for oils. For large-scale work, such as mural painting, it is better to use correspondingly larger round brushes and to reserve the usual flat brushes for fine detail. Round brushes always take up more color, and naturally induce a different brush technique from flat ones, which are best suited to the juxtaposition of rectangular patches of color. When using both types of brushes in the same picture, you will find the best way is to start with the larger round brushes and then paint in the details with flat brushes, so that ultimately the entire work is painted over. This is the only way to achieve any unity. Otherwise, if you leave one part of the picture as painted with round brushes, while another exhibits the cubist style which comes of using a flat brush, this unity will be lost.

You can also follow this method with glue colors, for which both round and flat hair brushes are indicated. As a rule, flat bristle brushes are too stiff for malleable glue colors, even in relatively thick applications. They are also apt to scrape off the water-soluble underpainting.

In summary, the four methods of approach enumerated below should make it easier for the reader to grasp the countless ways in which thick glue paint can be used:

1. Simply cover a white ground on prepared or unprepared paper, using flat hair brushes and opaque color.

The paint is laid on in the same way as with **alla prima** oil colors, contriving an immediate and complete opaqueness. An underpainting may be executed using opaque color thinned in water.

2. Begin with a light coat of watercolor on unprepared white paper using a round hair brush, and then finish it off by painting the picture over a second time with opaque color alone, using a flat hair brush. Your first attempt will show, however, that you must be more familiar with this working method before you can extract from it all the lovely effects of which it is capable: the thin layer of watercolor shines a good deal brighter than the opaque color which follows it. Since underpainting is justified only when its effect is still discernible in the finished picture, leave the lightest and brightest parts untouched, and apply the opaque colors only to those of medium, dull, and dark hues. The same is true of the two types of paints as of the two types of brushes: you will obtain a satisfactory effect only when, even leaving a few spaces, every part and every object in the picture is painted over with opaque color. To take just one concrete example: if one were painting a landscape with a watercolor undercoat, it would be a big mistake to leave the sky untouched, solely because in nature it stands out so brightly against the colors of the

Detail from illustration on page 327, actual size

earth and vegetation. To give just one possibility: the picture would gain greatly in depth and breadth if at its zenith the darker colors of the sky were overpainted in opaque color, the foreground in the same way, while on the horizon the opaque color were most sparingly used for both sky and earth.

3. Proceed as with No. 1, but on a tinted ground. This is undoubtedly the easiest and most direct way of using opaque color.

4. Proceed as with No. 2, but on a tinted ground. In this way, the tinted ground takes on some of the luminosity of the underpaintings, so that the colors look restrained and at the same time related to one another. Using this method, complementary values of gray can be obtained very nicely: for example, by using predominantly red tones over a green ground; or by laying ultramarine blue dark patches over yellow ochre. The most luminous colors and the high lights can, of course, be brought out only by applying completely opaque paint. Reference has been made so far to water-soluble glue colors, but the same remarks apply to casein colors. When a watercolor is intended for glazing, underpaintings will be carried out in well-diluted casein color, and light-colored plaster may be substituted for white paper. Using casein, a possible variation on procedures 2. and 4. is to glaze the opaque layer, a process which seldom succeeds if watercolors are used over a layer of opaque paint,

as the watercolor all too easily causes the opaque layer to run and smudge.

For the beginner, glue and casein colors are the least problematical materials with which to obtain experience of practically the entire range of painting techniques. Their range includes the use of watercolor for glazing, as well as the relatively primitive **alla prima** oil technique, the different types of fresco, as well as the balanced build-up of a multi-layer painting in tempera, using a resinous solution or a mixed or alternative technique. An attempt may even be made to achieve the characteristic shades of pastel work, without doing violence to the materials, for the chalky tone of opaque glue painting comes very close to that of the pastels. And all this can be done without the long waits for the paint to dry out and without having to come to terms with the catalystic peculiarities of the pigments. As soon as the water has evaporated, both with water-soluble glue and with casein, the paint layer is ready to be worked over again. Lastly, glue colors are less trouble for the artist to prepare himself than, say, the preparatory ground, and require less in the way of study and experiment. Carefully executed, glue color painting holds its own, from a technical standpoint, with any other kind of painting; but we must remember what it is intended for. A picture painted in permanently water-soluble glue color should be placed behind glass and framed; and casein colors are the right medium for wall painting in a room or for a large-scale panel with a dead mat surface.

11. PAINTING IN TEMPERA

If the binder used is an emulsion, a somewhat more advanced painting technique is required. All the methods dealt with so far have been such that, provided the ready-made materials were of the finest quality, the resultant picture would be as durable as if one painted with homemade painting materials. Any deterioration observed in following the methods so far described should be attributed to inexpert handling rather than to the materials themselves.

If the ground and paint layers contain a good deal of oil, the picture will yellow and blacken and develop cracks. Colors which contain too much glue are apt to fall off. Both phenomena accompany the use of a fatty medium or a solvent containing too much glue to thin the colors, in place of turpentine or water.

Admittedly, genuine tempera colors are also to be found on the market, but only an experienced chemist can say how the emulsion used was compounded. The names "egg tempera" or "oil tempera" merely tell you that you have an "O-W" (oil-water) emulsion in egg tempera, which you can dilute only with water, and which, when painted, will remain soluble in water; an oil tempera color, on the other hand, will be a "W-O" (water-oil) emulsion, and can be diluted only with turpentine. You now know enough to guard against the mistake of adding oil to a fatty oil tempera

to make it more runny, a process recommended in many old art textbooks. With the exception of casein colors, which are deliberately kept short of binder, all homemade colors should contain just enough binder to make the pigments adhere.

Experience shows that all bought colors contain too much binder. The reason for this is that the purchaser would find fault with a margin too narrow to guarantee indelibility. He would not know what to do, and on the next occasion would buy a different make.

Thus, it is a mistake to add extra binding agent to bought paints. Solvents which evaporate are the only ones to use. If, despite this, the makers continue to market every conceivable "art material," with no more precise indication of the drying time than "slow drying" or "quick drying," it is because over-fatty colors can be smeared on with such gay abandon. Due to their fatty oil content they take on a sheen when they harden; and, when a glaze is used, they do not attack and dissolve the underpainting. In principle, therefore, bought colors have no place in the supplies of the artist who wants to develop a really good technique.

This fact should be particularly borne in mind in handling true tempera. Bought materials only deprive a compound with this type of binder of the advantages peculiar to it. The advantages of the

Painting in Tempera

lean "O-W" emulsion and of the fatty "W-O" tempera are, as you know, their ability to dry rapidly and the fact that normally they do not crack or turn yellow. Their drawbacks are the need either to use up the tempera colors made with egg or a casein within a few days, or else to substitute a preservative to forestall deterioration. Materials of this kind, to be found at any art supplier's, are very difficult to measure accurately for oneself; they also diminish the binding power of the medium, and this in turn entails the use of more binder than is strictly called for. However, the inconvenience of frequently making up easily perishable tempera should not deter you, once you are convinced of the abiding artistic value of your work.

The easiest ways to handle lean or fatty tempera are much the same as for oil or glue colors. But even with lean tempera, such as the commercial egg tempera, you will not obtain the best results on paper without a primer. After a while the oily constituents seep through the paper. You may test this for yourself by studying the back of the unmounted sheet of paper, some weeks after a painting is completed. It will be seen, too, that the whole effect of the picture is grayer and yellower, as the luminosity of the originally white paper has been lost. When using lean tempera, therefore, such as those containing vegetable gum or resinous oil, the paper must first be given at least one or two coats with a glue-bound preparation. Conversely, fatty tempera should only be used on the same sort of ground as oil painting. In using tempera, one principle which we have so far only referred to in passing

Jan van Eyck, The Lucca Madonna. On the left, the whole picture; on the right, a detail from it. The brothers Hubert and Jan van Eyck were long regarded as the inventors of oil painting. However, recent research has established that most of their pictures were painted in alternating techniques, with layers of oil and resin between layers of tempera. They are in an outstanding state of preservation, which would hardly be possible with pure oil paint. After over 500 years, they are almost entirely free of cracks and not yellowed. The faint late crack marks noticeable on the detail clearly result from too thick an application of lead white

now presents itself: always paint fat on lean. So far, this has been implicit in the instructions themselves. It is irrelevant to the use of glue colors, and with the **alla prima** oil technique described, it is precluded by the use of any strongly diluted underpainting. If a very diluted oil paint is used to give a glaze-like tint to the ground, this should show through. Both fatty and lean tempera colors can receive the same treatment if you start with a light shade of underpaint.

The position is different when it comes to large and protracted works of art. Then the last layers will consist of undiluted fatty tempera colors with, if required, the admixture of a wax mastic to make them flow better. Thus, you begin with a lean tempera diluted with water. Over this place a coat of undiluted tempera. Continue with fatty tempera, first thinned with turpentine, then undiluted. Lastly, use super-fatted undiluted tempera colors. This not only obviates the need for a varnish to seal and protect your surface, but also gives a depth of color as rich as that of pure oil painting. The colors harden without any perceptible lightening in shade.

The technical significance of fat on lean is quite clear: the ground should dry or, it may be, oxidize as quickly as possible, so that if delayed-action oxidation occurs it will cause no increase in volume which might make the upper layer split or give rise to early crack formation. This is not really as elaborate as it may sound once you are used to the fat on lean principle in all painting; you will then find that you conceive of the construction of a picture in the appropriate artistic terms. Note that even though while painting in lean tempera the result looks like glue painting, and in fatty tempera more like oil paint, the tempera color always results in a slightly brighter and chalkier tone. This does not altogether hold true when the upper layer is super-fatted, however. Tempera color laid on a shiny surface, like casein painting, can be brushed and rubbed. Naturally, the less fat it contains, the weaker it will be. When applying a protective top layer which will preserve the colors' luster and depth, then it is pleasanter and more in keeping with the materials to apply the sheerest coat of wax rather than a greasy resinous varnish.

Within reason, there is unlimited scope for the impasto application of exceptionally fatty tempera, and certainly more so than for pure oil painting (with the exception of palette knife painting). Thick applications of tempera color always remain spongy and porous, owing to the inner structure of the binder; and the result is a picture at once transparent and, when exposed to the air, able to dry right out and oxidize through and through, and become exceptionally hard. Tempera hardens to such an extent that it takes considerable force to remove a paint layer from its ground, while a layer of oxidized oil paint remains softer and more sensitive after oxidation.

A tempera painting attains its greatest degree of hardness and permanence, however, when from the ground up its construction follows its own special rules. This is a method known as a mixed or alternating technique, and is only relevant to studio conditions. As against working in **alla prima** oils, this tempera technique starts from a completely different visual concept, a creation in the true sense of the word, in which the model or impression is received but not copied from nature, and remains a more or less distant memory.

If yet another comparison with music may be made, this technique corresponds somewhat to the final and most polished of interpretations, perhaps of a piano sonata, played by an artist who has long since committed the sequence of notes to ear and finger and can apply himself more to tempo and touch.

This mixed technique is the one used by the true master of his craft; it belongs to work in the studio based on thorough and constructive thought, where the very slightest potentiality of the paint can be used to its maximum. Every single operation can be broken down to the smallest detail. If you wish to sustain your attempt and achieve its object, you must be clear in your aims, in command of your medium, and skillful in execution. You cannot hope to work as you would with the **alla prima** technique, developing color effects of formal designs from a vague idea while you are painting.

Mixed techniques are built up in the following way: on a carefully prepared white glue ground, make a rough sketch in red chalk. Next, go over the firm outlines in watercolor. At this stage, considerable detail may be included, since the drawing will not receive a thick coat at the beginning; subsequently, however, every part of it will be used.

For tinting, use a 1:3 mastic solution, or a light balsam solution with the addition of the pigment powder, possibly terre verte, to give a nice spreadable glaze. If the ground is too absorbent, it needs a preliminary coat of shellac as insulation.

This glaze is also known as the imprimatura. This concept is derived from a method of chalk drawing used by Holbein the Younger (already mentioned in the section on drawing). In tracing from life, a little of the red chalk was pressed from the back of the tracing paper onto the new sheet of paper, leaving a faint red outline. The idea of "imprimatura," then, comes from the "impression" made by the tracing chalk. Here the purpose is very much the same as that of the imprimatura in drawing, but achieved with the brush; it gives a monochrome underlying tone on which to obtain a moulded effect by lightening with white. This means that using white lean tempera directly on the imprimatura while still wet, you now paint in your brighter tints over a line or color drawing, so that the drawing shows through. Thus, the picture begins to take shape as a tone monochrome chalk drawing. This lightening with white should allow the color of the imprimatura to show through even where it is brightest, and should go lightly over the darker parts of the picture, so that in the end the entire imprimatura receives a coat of lean tempera.

A notable characteristic of this method is that the resinous solution takes up the watery tempera so well—tackily, it must be admitted, but with great power of absorption. The two layers dry out rapidly, at least superficially, and are quite hard and free from tackiness within a few hours.

A second characteristic, and one which becomes clear only when the whole process is repeated, is that when using lean tempera direct on the wet imprimatura you can draw lines finer than any you could achieve with oil paint, for example. The old masters portrayed the delicate lines of beards and furs and chased work in jewelry in this way, using marten-hair brushes.

When all the paint has dried and no sticky patches are left, a second imprimatura should be laid on. This time, concentrated essence can be used for mixing; furthermore, the different parts of the picture can now be colored in in their appropriate local color. Here you will see why the first imprimatura had to be entirely covered with tempera; the tempera protects the second imprimatura from possible running and smudging.

In the areas of wet local color you should next lay either lean tempera (white) alone, or paint with all the colors in your palette (this is far from the final layer in your picture)—in a very unobtrusive hue, at first an intimation of what is to come. At this stage your picture will correspond somewhat to the rapid sketch, well-diluted in turpentine, which serves as the underpainting in **alla prima** oils. If in the course of the second application of tempera the

imprimatura dries off somewhat, you may continue to paint over it. If the watery tempera colors run, however, you must again apply resinous varnish. The expert way would be to paint the whole picture in this manner; in other words, continue painting further coats onto resinous glazes. On the principle of fat on lean, you will use fatty tempera in the upper layers, particularly when you wish to paint direct onto a layer of tempera without a resinous glaze when you complete the picture. It is not so usual to lay a final coat of over-fatty tempera as it is to varnish the whole picture over when it is completely dry, using a waxy mastic essence or wax alone. This imparts a smooth, hard enamel-like surface to the picture. There is no sense in using impasto painting in mixed technique, which in any case is unsuited to the artistic concept involved. This is a technique which extracts the utmost from binding agents and pigments, or, to put it differently, which entails no waste of material.

The artist who uses the mixed technique must feel drawn toward it and be willing to forego the somewhat facile charm of impasto paint with a plastic texture. He must also use a smooth ground. As only the best ground will do

Pure red sable brush

This study, designed to illustrate alternating technique, shows, from bottom to top:
1. A glue ground, with drawing in watercolor — 2. Imprint (the imprimitur — see text) in a 1:4 mastic and chrome oxide solution — 3. Lightening with white, using titanium white egg tempera — 4. Diluted resinous oil used to render local colors — 5. Final coat of egg tempera varnished over with wax

for such meticulous work, you will undoubtedly take canvas-covered board. The canvas must be finely and smoothly woven, however, and the primer must be polished with sandpaper, producing a ground as smooth as paper, whose linen texture will in time be completely obscured.

Hence, the mixed technique is absolute painting, the method which rejects any external material appeal. It is the method which gives precedence to content, what the picture is about, over means, how it is done. The tendency to value these nonessentials at the expense of the subject is one found in all fairly recent paintings.

The subject matter of a picture painted in mixed technique is brought out by rich color effects, not by striking mannerisms. The color effect is based on a gray brought about partly by optical color mixture, which in turn consists partly of an additive light mixture. The glaze is like colored glass through which reflected light shines strongly at different angles of refraction; this brings out interfering colors such as exist in genuine pearls. Thus it is impossible to copy a picture painted like this in oils, using **alla prima** technique. Anyone who has attempted to do this will have discovered how primitive any kind of **alla prima** technique is when compared with mixed technique.

So far as scientific research into painting methods has been able to ascertain, mixed technique was discovered by the brothers Hubert and Jan van Eyck, and they are among the select few, the greatest painters of all time. They do not owe this to their technical ability alone, to which the amazing state of preservation

of their works bears such eloquent testimony.

If the mixed technique is out of favor at the present time, one does not need to be a prophet to predict that in the changing cycle of fashion it will again play a great part. That is, of course, unless technical progress provides us with a further simplified medium with all-embracing artistic potentialities. The first step would be the discovery of a completely foolproof binding agent, capable of making the paint layers into a homogeneous whole and liable to no further change. Synthetic materials are constantly being improved and might in time make such a discovery possible. From a technical viewpoint, the mixed technique rests essentially on the contrast between the use of resinous glazes and lean tempera colors thinned with water, i.e., an "O-W" emulsion: it lies embedded like trellis work between the films of resin.

When once you have grasped this notion, you will see how worthless would be the use of a fatty "W-O" emulsion in mixed technique. An unnecessary layer of fatty paint would result. The same is true of casein tempera. The strong binding power of its glue constituent renders it unsuitable for painting in several layers. Casein tempera is a good binder for a weather-proof "O-W" tempera applied in a single layer.

An artist can tackle these problems only against a background of wide practical experience, and he must know what his aim is. He will then find his way by means of systematic experiments. All that can be given here are basic ideas, but these can be subtly adapted to any and every form of painting.

12. THE USE OF COLOR WITHOUT BINDING AGENT

Another lasting medium of artistic expression is color used without a binder, such as pastels, true fresco, painting with waterglass, and silica painting.

PASTELS are technically the simplest medium to use. The only requirements are suitable paper, pastel crayons, and a fixative with a diffuser. No palette, brushes or vehicle are required. Drying offers no problems, and once you have chosen your materials correctly, you are unlikely to make any technical mistakes. Instead, we encounter difficulties of quite a different kind.

What is most awkward is that colors cannot be mixed in advance, an unbreakable rule in all other media. With pastels you have no choice but to use each crayon as it stands, and then to blend them in. This fact led to boxes of pastels containing many colors. If you try to get along with a modest assortment of possibly 20 or 30 crayons, you will soon discover the technical limitations of the medium: you will need so many superimposed colors that it will become impossible to fix the powder firmly to the paper. The only way to manage with a very few pastel colors is to adopt the pointillist method; but this scientific manner of picture building is not for everyone. When you have at your disposal not less than a hundred or so crayons, however, a fresh difficulty arises: you forfeit the contact with the pigment which you are used to with any other medium. The chalks remain purely objective and external to you. It is true that with pastels the properties of the individual pigments are virtually inexhaustible. Their glazing and hiding power and their richness and ability to blend well are largely offset by the manner in which the powder is applied. As a rule gradations of brightness are produced by white pigments. Those sold commercially are usually chalks, earth pigments and gypsum, which can also be used as fillers. It is true that these pigments cloud the colors, but by this very clouding they emphasize the special characteristics of the medium: the hazy, nebulous colorings and a soft, tender expressivity. "Pastel color" is a widely used term.

It is a term which recognizes the pastel's peculiar power of expression, which, like every medium, has its own range. The logic of this will possibly become more apparent if you imagine a violin concerto played on the trumpet, or military music played on the harp. The art of pastel painting marked the style of a particular epoch, the rococo, and this could hardly have been otherwise. For although pastels were already known at the close of the Renaissance, it was not until the eighteenth century that the medium reached perfection, above all in portraiture. It was immediately abused, for ultimate refinements such as high lights could not be added firmly or precisely enough with the crayon, especially in miniature work; therefore the artists resorted to the use of fine brushes and opaque colors.

The Use of Color Without Binding Agent

Crosshatching, rubbed and not rubbed

Apart from this, the use of some type of crayon is older than the hills, and by far the oldest method of painting. The cave paintings were carried out with crayons, although admittedly not in the manner of a pastel. If prehistoric men had thought of applying their earth colors, chalks and coals, with brush and binder, they would probably not have gone on using crayons. Crayons were very keen for rendering shapes with precision, and the results are models of figurative representation. It is fortunate for us that prehistoric man remained loyal to his crayons, as it is unlikely that any cave art would otherwise have survived. The only conceivable binding agents of the time were adhesive plant sap, blood serum, and animal size, all of which, after so long a period closed up in the caves, would have perished.

So you see that, aesthetically, the binding agent is the root of all evil, at least where contemporary pastels are concerned. For the pastel can maintain its singular, misty effect only until it is fixed, and the effect is often damaged by fixing. Without fixing, the powdered pigments are held together in loose strata like the scales on butterflies' wings. Fixatives cause the color particles to

stick fast and the light is then reflected off a level surface, as when color is applied with a brush. The picture will take on an appearance reminiscent of normal glue paint technique. The only way to avoid this effect is to leave your pastels completely unfixed. The rococo pastel artists did exactly this. In any event, since pastels are so sensitive that they must be framed behind glass, they can in fact last quite as well unfixed, especially on a velvety surface which improves the adherent qualities of the particles. The rococo painters used roughened parchment.

Today, velvety "pastel paper" may be bought ready-made. However, only a master will succeed in using this type of paper without producing tawdry color effects. A further point is that these velvet-type papers are always tinted, but not always with light-fast colors. Thus, they are best recommended for use with completely opaque chalks.

The most sympathetic paper is a rough white, such as a first-class Ingres paper. To give it a tinted ground, rub it lightly downwards and across with a broad pastel chalk. Then, with a soft wad of cloth, merge the chalk strokes in an even, circular motion over the surface. However carefully you do this, some irregularities will still remain, almost a texture which has a lively charm similar to that of an imprimatura. As with the latter, you can begin with a drawing underneath, which must, of course, be fixed before the paper is tinted.

Fixatives tinge the colors with gray, particularly if fillers rather than pure white pigments are used in the composition of the crayons, as they are apt to darken in the binder. This is almost the rule with ready-made pastel colors. As a matter of fact, manufacturers often use coal tar for pastel colors, which are seldom if ever light-fast. After a time, the picture becomes progressively paler; only inorganic permanent pigments retain their effect. You can imagine how extraordinary a picture will look then. Happily, the coal tar colors in use are partly soluble in alcohol. I say happily, because this enables you to make a test. On a sheet of thin paper, such as French Ingres, draw a line with each of your pastel colors, one beside the other, and then spray them with alcohol. The soluble colors will at once penetrate the paper and make runny blots on the reverse side. Unfortunately, this does not mean that·all the colors which do not go through will prove satisfactory. Certain coal tar colors are not soluble in alcohol, among them alizarin red (which is intrinsically satisfactory) and such dubious, impure pigments as chrome yellow, Cassell brown and cinnabar. The graying of pastel paintings due to fixing can be obviated by the exclusive use of zinc white, flake white, and titanium white instead of chalk and analogous white pigments. But to be quite sure, you should make your own pastel colors. Only then will you be certain of working with worthwhile pigments.

Pastel artist: His equipment consists of a box containing 80 colors, a bottle of fixative with spray diffuser, a stump, and a rubber eraser

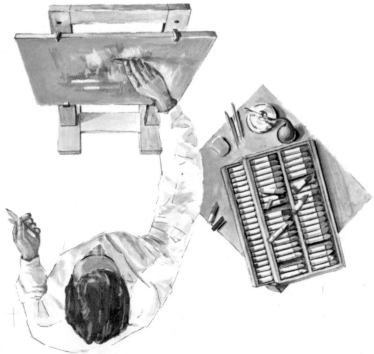

The Use of Color Without Binding Agent

You should set about preparing your pastel chalks more or less as follows: using a small trowel, knead your powdered pigment with water and a trace of tragacanth gum. This dough-like paste should be left for a day or two with a damp cloth over it to allow the pigment to become saturated with water and gum. When it has been left in this way, you will see whether to add more water or more pigment. When your mixture has reached the right consistency, take some pieces out and roll them on a tray to a uniform thickness. The crayons can then be placed on a baking sheet lined with parchment and placed in an oven. They should stay there on a low heat, with the oven door open, for a few hours. To dry them in the air takes too long and gives the glue time to go mouldy. Unfortunately, the exact quantity of glue cannot be laid down; it is simply a matter of finding out for oneself. Just enough glue is needed to hold the crayons together, but several pigments cohere without glue at all, with nothing but water.

To obtain a mixed color or a tint lightened with white, you should proceed as follows: first make long, thick crayons of equal size out of the appropriate pure pigment and white (preferably titanium white), and keep them really moist. Next, cut one tenth of the length off the end of the colored crayon, and substitute a piece of the white crayon for it. Blend the two together, and you have a new crayon. This affords a clear-cut and reliable means of obtaining any mixed or whitened tint.

As each crayon dries, place a strip of thin parchment around it, with appropriate remarks. If you take the trouble to make crayons out of all the important pigments, say 20 of them, preparing each in its pure, mixed and whitened form, you will soon have a set of 100 or more crayons, which should last you quite a long time. This gives you an intimate contact with your colors, and is a new and most rewarding experience which amply repays all your labor. Apart from this, a pastel painting is built up on the same principle as an **alla prima** oil painting. Thus, you proceed from medium tints to darker ones, with the cool colors predominating. Next, paint in the brighter and stronger colors, rendering the deepest and warmest shadows, and last of all the high lights.

This should be gone over lightly, not pressed or rubbed, and for this reason corrections should not be made to the lines, but whenever possible and needful it is better to erase the wrong lines with a soft rubber eraser and go over them again. However, supposing the wrong color adheres as a result of repeated fixing, all you can do is to prepare and fix a fresh white ground to receive clean, bright colors again. The colors will stand out best on a white ground.

The nature of your craftsmanship will determine whether you obtain individual mixed tints and delicate fusions by rubbing with your fingers or with a stump, or whether you prefer to shade the colors lightly into one another by hand. The second of these methods is the best way to steer clear of an effect of meretricious

This nude study was painted on white cardboard to bring out the individual paint layers. The ground was lightly rubbed in with the finger; the lines applied over it were not rubbed

sweetness. As with drawing in chalk or with a lead pencil, so with the pastel: beginners are all too ready to stump and smear their work, delighting in the delicate way the colors run into each other, and not realizing what a sugary mess they are producing. The discipline entailed in shading in, however, would speedily bring about a notable improvement. Only the artist in command of his materials will be sure of enhancing his effects by blurring his lines. With this in view, study the pastel paintings of the rococo.

We have already noted that pastels must be kept framed behind glass if they are to be hung on the wall. Unfixed pastels must also be treated in this way, since in a portfolio, for example, they will leave marks even on the smoothest interleaf. The glass must not be in direct contact with the painting. A simple way to prevent this is to give the pastel a mat cut to a suitable thickness. There is a danger, however, that when the glass is polished on the outside with a woolen or silk rag, the color particles will be drawn to the inside of the glass by electromagnetic action. This is a frequent phenomenon with the modern pastel, but rare in old ones. Possibly this may be due to the use of flake white (white lead) as the white pigment in old works, and the fact that its use is no longer allowed in pastel chalks sold commercially. Surely a somewhat exaggerated precaution? For even if white lead is poisonous, who is likely to breathe it in fatal amounts? It would not be at all easy to kill oneself with it; and anyone who wanted to could find surer methods. At all events we have in titanium white

(RN 56) a wholly innocuous substitute for flake white.

The pastel medium has latterly branched out, chiefly under the stimulus of W. Ostwald, to bring mural painting within its range. A painting of this kind bears no comparison with a small-scale pastel, but with a pastel mural this is not the point. The point is rather that the use of pastels on the wall is straightforward and makes for an effect which is aesthetically most in keeping with modern notions of wall painting. This prompts us to the following reflection: a mural should not resemble a picture stuck on or cut into the wall, as they all used to; instead it should liven up a plain wall without attempting to disguise it. The wall must still be an integral part of the architecture. Figures and similar objects should be apposed directly on the wall and not be separated from it, as formerly, by anything in the nature of a background or a frame. A brief glance in passing cannot take in the background graduations. Yet on closer study, they create an illusion of depth and breadth, an impression that the background suddenly recedes; and this can be all the more delightful if no attempt has been made to indicate perspective. A moment later the design appears to return to the surface. The total effect is strengthened by the roughness of the plaster. Naturally, it does not lend itself to the application of a close, opaque color; the use of porous colors, however, causes the texture and shade of the plaster surface to extend to the whole design and underlines the nature of the wall surface.

We can, of course, make pastel completely opaque, by stumping or brushing in the color, for example. But this is wrong and, indeed, does violence to the material—just as it does to lay on porous colors with a half-dry brush. Obviously, pastel murals must be extremely thoroughly fixed. Shellac solution is not really suitable. However, the binding agents used for liquid wall painting, foremost among them casein solutions and waterglass, are well worth considering. Nonreversible glue solutions can also be used indoors, though they must be given a dressing of formalin, and protected against the effects of humidity. A further prerequisite for the stability of a pastel on the wall is the right type of plaster. It must be thoroughly dried out, and care must be taken, when tinting the surface all over, to use only a binder which will suit the fixative to be used later.

The artist who wishes to execute a painstaking mural will accordingly prepare his own primer on fresh, dry plaster not treated in any other way. Where casein is used as a fixative, priming is best carried out with the weakest possible casein bound color. This need not dry indelibly instantly, since a further casein solution will be sprayed on later. Hand sprays rather like air sprays are sold for this purpose. Immediately after use they must be thoroughly washed out in water. The safest way to test indelibility and make sure that not too much glue is used is to try out the same plaster on a piece of board. For casein pastels, bought pastel chalks will do.

Details (1:1) from study on page 343

13. FRESCO

Fresco painting is the most famous of all mural techniques. People who should know better misuse the term "fresco," using it to describe every type of wall painting. However, it means only a picture painted on a freshly plastered wall while still quite wet. It is more correct to speak of "fresco buono." The Italian word "buono" (good) is used to distinguish authentic fresco technique on fresh plaster from "fresco secco," in which the plaster, though fresh, is quite dry.

The latter process is actually the more ancient. It was known to the Egyptians, Greeks, and Romans; and its technical peculiarity is the admixture of a binder, in this case, size. Byzantine and Late Roman paintings in fresco secco are celebrated for their use of egg yolk; their work was often given a protective coat of wax varnish, but this was possibly not until a later date.

There are many fresco secco techniques, but all require wall plaster specially prepared for the purpose which led to the discovery of the fresco buono process.

Lime was known as a thin liquid binding agent at a very early time. After a number of intervening developments, the

Michelangelo, detail from the Creation of Adam in the Sistine Chapel. Note the emphatic contours, corrected in places in the course of painting first attempts were made, in Italy about 1300 A.D., to paint "al fresco" on fresh plaster with unbound watercolor. The first to appreciate this seemingly modern technique and to make brilliant use of it was Giotto.

The technical preparations center around the production of suitable plaster, capable of taking up the colors from underneath. The reason for this is that the colors are mixed with water alone, or with lime water, which binds them better. For the mortar, only pure lime mortar will do. Cement or diluted cement mortar is quite unsuitable. Fresco mortar is always made out of burnt lime slaked in the quarry. It must stand in the quarry in at least four inches of water for a minimum two months, and much longer if possible. The mortar is composed of this quarry or bog lime, mixed together with sand and water. Spiky river-grit and sand are suitable, but for the best fresco mortar, marble grit or marble sand is used, as they produce the whitest and hardest plaster. You may like to think of lime plaster as a primer on a brick wall. This primer holds the colored pigment, but it will do so only as long as it is quite fresh, which, in practice, means soft and wet. Thus, one of the chief points is that the brick wall should be thoroughly wetted before the plaster is laid on it; if possible this should be done some days previously. To give a better hold, the joins between the bricks may be scraped out about half an inch.

Maulpertsch, a cartoon for a fresco painting. Note in what detail this design was worked out, to be transposed later with a quick sure touch to the fresh plaster

Fresco

The first layer of plaster consists of about four to five parts grit and coarse sand and one part lime. It should set very hard indeed and if need be can be made thicker still by beating it with a stick. It should be about one inch thick. If beating makes the surface too smooth, it should be roughened to provide a good hold for the next layer; this consists of about three parts finer sand and one part lime. Lastly, a layer known as the fine plaster, consisting of two parts fine and finest sand and one part lime, is applied. Rub this surface down with an emery board to make it really smooth.

This kind of plaster will be dry on top in at least three days. When the colored pigments have been applied with water, a thin transparent film of crystalline carbonate of lime is formed. The pigments become more or less petrified together with the plaster. At least this is the aim, but it succeeds only if the carbonic acid in the atmosphere penetrates the entire layer of plaster by about one and one-half to two inches. The carbonic acid in the atmosphere can reach the lowest layer only if the plaster is sufficiently porous. The consistency to aim for is one which appears to contain too much water. Some of this water will be used up in crystallization and the rest will evaporate, thus inducing a certain porousness.

The success of these hardening and evaporation processes depends on factors which can be neither predicted nor regulated with accuracy. What tips the scales is the composition of the limestone and the atmosphere after the application of the plaster. Heat causes the water to evaporate too fast, so that it is no longer

Lead palette for mural work with liquid paint. Work will be brisker if more than one palette is kept in use

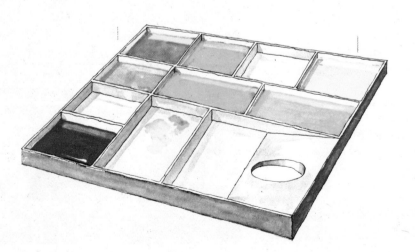

available for crystal formation. The most favorable conditions are an average temperature of about 60 degrees F., as this enables the evaporation and the absorption of acids from the atmosphere to proceed together. It is worthwhile providing artificial means of supplying these acids, as the air contains only a small percentage.

In the Middle Ages, and sometimes even in the baroque period, little hairs, such as those from calf's skin, were incorporated in the plaster to make it more porous. For one thing the capillaries helped the water to rise to the surface; and for another, the hairs were partially destroyed by the corrosion of the lime, thus creating a system of very fine air holes. This enabled the acid more easily to penetrate the furthest layers.

We know of fresco plasters which

Dry pigment in tin, prepared color in glass, round brush for painting, and circular brush to cover large areas in local color

today, after over 600 years, are almost as stable as modern cement plaster. Others again have been found to be so brittle underneath that the limestone carbonate can never have been properly formed. This suggests that the water evaporated too quickly and that the brickwork was not as wet as it should have been.

The outward sign that the plaster is being formed is that at first the plaster looks wet and shiny, but after an hour or two it turns mat. This tells you that it is time to start applying the paint. This stage appears to last for about 48 hours, but in reality as soon as the surface looks mat, the process of carbon intake has begun, though slowly at first. The watery layer of paint delays this process, until a certain stage is reached. After that it cannot be halted, and the plaster surface becomes shiny again. In appearance it is almost as if a very fine film of ice had formed over it, rather like the gleam of a polished egg shell. When this stage is reached, no more pigment can be taken up, and the picture should have been finished several hours previously.

Thus, the fresco painter's allotted working period, from start to finish, is very short indeed. It goes without saying that the great masters of the art of fresco could not complete their gigantic mural and ceiling paintings in this space of time. Accordingly they used to do their work in sections. They would carry on until they reached as clear an outline as possible, such as that of a figure. Up to this outline, the surrounding layer of plaster was marked out, right through to the wall fabric. When the artist com-

pleted his first figure, the plaster could again be applied to another part of the painting.

This difficulty, together with the impossibility of seeing a monumental work **in toto** from the artist's scaffolding, makes it essential to work from a detailed design.

The first step is the small-scale sketch, followed by individual studies such as whole figures, heads, hands, and drapery. Next the sketch proper. This may be on the same reduced scale as the first sketches, or somewhat larger, or very occasionally, even at this stage, full size. As a rule, glue colors will be used on white cardboard paper. At this point the cartoon known as the "tracing" is drawn, a full-size sketch of the most important outlines, which is pressed into the wet plaster. This cartoon obviously must be made on soft paper only. The outlines are marked through with a blunt metal graver or any other suitable tool. It is also possible to perforate the outlines, and then to trace them onto the wall by filtering pigment through a bag of powder. Any falling particles will be held by the plaster, so this method cannot always be used. Moreover, you may wish to use pigments which would be destroyed by the lime, thus disappearing after a time, such as the cadmium and alizarin colors and cyanide blue. A colorless outline lightly pressed into the plaster will not be inconvenient when painting, and it leaves the artist free to work. Fresco painting is carried out on the same principle as watercolors, that is, proceeding from light to dark. Glazing is likewise used without adding white pigment. In monumental works, however, these principles are followed less strictly. It may be necessary to mix in some white pigment, and if so, white lime is the only sort to use. There is little use for black, but if it is used, carbon should be avoided. Even though the lime does not destroy the carbon, it binds it only temporarily; in the end it decays together with a thin surface layer of plaster. Manganese black is better. As with all monumental painting, simple and large-scale use of color is alone appropriate and impressive. This accounts for a fundamental difference between fresco and other media as regards planning the picture; we must also remember that relatively little correction is possible while work is in progress. The ideal is to do all the painting at a stretch, for too much over-painting interferes with the process of binding the colors to the ground.

The color is best applied with a sort of soft round watercolor bristle brush of gigantic proportions. The brush should not be too stiff, as it would tear away the soft surface layer of mortar. Hair brushes would be too quickly spoiled by the lime. Once the fresco is finished, no further treatment is called for. On the contrary, to overpaint it or varnish it in any way would utterly nullify the special effect of a fresco painting, which is of exceptional beauty. As a painting medium in the truest sense, it does not belong on the face of a building, but in a large room. Only there is there a guarantee that the fresco will suffer as little as possible from attack by acids in the air.

For an external wall face, the only satisfactory method is to paint with waterglass, known also as silica or mineral painting. Once the technical process of binding has been fully dealt with, there remains little to be said about the actual method of painting. As it is hardly possible to make one's own materials, a description of these processes must read rather like an abstract from the printed instructions of the manufacturer. The colors are thinned with water or waterglass and applied with a fresco

H. Weidner, Augsburg Market. Silica painting on facade, covering a broad area (Lohwald Works)

brush to dry plaster previously scraped; or alternatively they may be laid on in crayon form, like pastel chalks. All the pigments must be tempered with zinc and magnesia. The binder, waterglass, is usually sprayed on after the picture is painted, or it can be used as an intermediate fixative where a heavier application of paint is desired. That is all. The build-up of the picture depends on whether you use a dark-tinted plaster, a special facing plaster which is colored in a block, or a light-colored plaster. This determines whether the picture is built up like a watercolor, an oil painting, or a pastel.

Compared with the marked individuality of other media, the total impression is not very striking. To quote from Wilhelm Busch, we might say that it is nicely colored, and therefore good. This criticism is not merely derogatory. The outstanding durability of silica paint assures for it a future of great promise and leads us to suppose that some great artist will use it to achieve effects never before thought of; especially as it is not abso-lutely essential to have a plaster wall surface underneath. The manufacturers of silica paint also sell primers which can be applied on any support to give a good enough hold, and these make a satisfactory foundation for silica colors. On a ground of this type you will be able to experiment in your studio.

When you come to reflect on everything that has been said about the most important painting techniques, you will see that all techniques are good when they are properly handled and all are bad if you make mistakes. None is perfect. Your choice must depend as much on your personal inclination as on the use you intend to make of your work. Any artistic experience can be transposed into any medium; though it is a fact that some seem to call for one kind of medium and others for another. Thus, it is most revealing, particularly for a beginner, occasionally to carry out the same motif in a variety of media. It is dauntless zeal which will achieve the goal, and not irresolute musing.

In painting, the surface area counts far more than it does in drawing. You know the principle, which is that there are no colored lines, only colored areas. The line, as a means of abstract graphic expression, can only enclose spaces and separate them from one another; it is color which sets off the surface.

In drawing, the line is about the only way to contrive a convincing illusion of space. The line can be used with similar effect in painting too, but it is not a specifically pictorial means of expression. Apart from the fact that a polychrome picture is always more effective than a colorless or monochrome one, color can be used to render the illusion of space much more clearly than lines or tinted surfaces.

Whether you are doing a pure line drawing or a drawing with tinted surfaces, you must adjust the scale of objects to their diminishing size as they approach the horizon or vanishing point, if you are to create an illusion of space. This is not the case with color, but you can conceive light or dark areas to the point where the colors vanish. It is entirely a matter of circumstance whether you fix on light or shade; looking outwards from a woodland glade, the colors vanish into light, while looking inwards from the edge of the wood, they seem to vanish into darkness. Furthermore, strong colors push weaker ones into the background, just as pure colors appear nearer than impure ones. Where shades are of the same strength, red and yellow advance more than blue, and warm colors before cool ones. The following

Illustration of the color vanishing point (looking into the wood and out of it)

Color Perspective

instance arises out of the different degrees of pervasiveness of the light rays, and it also determines the effect of color perspective: Imagine you are driving along a street with a clear view towards a traffic signal. You will hardly notice the green light from a distance, while the amber light will seem suddenly to leap unmistakably out at you, and the red light to recede. The red glass acts as a filter for the red rays from the white incandescent light which shines farthest, but as a color comes closer to a blue than to a yellow, so accordingly its effect is less aggressive. On the other hand, drive along the same street in a really thick fog; from a corresponding distance away you will probably see neither green nor amber, but you **will** see the red light, and probably brake too soon. This is because against a dull gray background, the red seems to advance so much more —in the absence of any other strong colors to judge by—that you are likely to underestimate appreciably your distance from the lights.

Color dynamism: the nearest is orange, the furthest is blue. Green and violet are not particularly dynamic

Hence, it follows that you cannot produce an effect of perspective if you use only one color without any modulation, for instance, an even gray tone. You need the contrast with other colors. Similar contrasts will determine whether the foregoing should be reversed: pure in-

Colors lose their dynamism progressively as they grow lighter and grayer

tense blues can on occasion produce an effect of greater proximity than dull yellows and reds.

We may substitute "bright" for "dull." In the present context it is practically the same thing. Think back to the difference between additive and subtractive mixtures: a subtractive gray contains the same color components as an additive white. The differences are merely due to a loss of light through absorption.

The farther away an object is from you, the more the variegated reflections of white light from a distance will cover up the colors reflected from smaller objects and shadows. An additional factor is reflection from the atmosphere itself. For example, if you gaze into the entrance to a tunnel, the darkness at the entrance will lessen in intensity the farther you go from it. The air between you and the tunnel reflects white light, and the greater the humidity, the more light is reflected. To the human eye, the absorption of red and yellow rays seems to be correspondingly greater when blue rays are reflected. Thus it happens that in humid conditions landscapes appear bluer and more spacious than they do in a dry atmosphere and sunshine: clear colors come forward toward the onlooker. This is a phenomenon which a landscape painter must fully appreciate if he is to depict what he perceives just as he perceives it. The Chinese were masters of the art of conveying a sense of space by suggesting a darkening atmosphere, particularly in graphic work painted in thinned China ink, with a near color effect. In classical Chinese art, linear perspective played a very minor role, if any.

Alongside this atmospheric darkening, the plasticity of silk, which reflects the light in tiny particles, also serves to achieve depth of perspective. Coarse canvas can be used in the same way. Pictures executed on canvas whose texture remains visible have more atmosphere to start with than those painted on a smooth support. This also applies to watercolors on rough paper. Where the texture of the support has its own light and shade, the picture not only

Pure green and pure blue advance more than darker and more opaque yellow and red

Gauguin, Horsemen on the Beach. The blue of the sea recedes sharply against the red of the beach

gains a surface, but also produces an impression of several planes graduated in depth. Moreover, the texture helps to some extent to avoid crude and blotchy shadows which look like holes.

The Impressionists were the first artists in the western world to "see" the atmosphere overcast with all shades from gray to white in a bright light. They achieved an effect of depth and flatness simultaneously in their pictures by the appropriate mixture of grays and whites in their colors. The plastic thickness of the paint also helped, resembling as it did a woven fabric. Here the effect is even more forceful and conspicuous, however. The Italian artists of the Renaissance had already discovered and rendered a shadowy atmosphere instinct with mystery (you will recall the comparison with the entrance to a tunnel). This was the celebrated **sfumato**, the smoki-

ness, quite different from atmospheric humidity. They saw it not only in open landscapes, but indoors too, in the rooms where they painted their portraits and figures. This **sfumato** enabled them to banish from their pictures the harsh contours which had previously marred the pictorial effect. Over the main parts of the painting, they set the light flowing forth in a gentle glow against the dusty obscurity. Analogous aims and effects are attained in photography by placing a soft-focus attachment in front of the lens. Leonardo da Vinci and Titian were exceedingly enthusiastic about the phenomenon of **sfumato**, but they used it with the subdued grace of their day. They were, of course, among its most glorious exponents. Then came Rembrandt, who shattered this sobriety, carrying the trend relentlessly to its utmost limits. He rendered darkness and shadows with an intensity to be found nowhere else in the history of painting: and yet he did not create "holes." The black of the **The Man with the Gold Helmet** is shot through with a riot of color; the air becomes palpable, suggesting that one is feeling one's way through a room utterly devoid of light. One senses vaguely what is concealed in the shadows. Rembrandt produced this effect by using countless glazes. He is understood to have used 30 to 60 of them, and Titian is known to have worked in the same way. In all probability the glazes were carried out in complementary colors, and these produce shadows which no longer appear to be colored. How different from the workaday black which stares up at you from a tin of shoe polish! The discovery of the visible atmosphere and the first attempts to use **sfumato** in painting it mark the beginning of something which can properly be called "painting." Until then, artists had colored rather than painted; a single object was rendered in local color and distorted in the process. Color perspective was used only by accident, not consciously. Linear perspective was almost the only means employed to give an impression of depth.

To penetrate the mysteries of color perspective, while bearing in mind that the ever-changing exceptions and special cases far outweigh strict rules such as those of linear perspective, you can hardly do better that follow the main stages of its development; after Leonardo and Rembrandt, Watteau marks just such a stage before the Impressionists, and among present-day artists, Kokoschka has given it fresh significance.

The alpha and omega of the study of color perspective lies in the perpetual observation of nature. This will reveal that when colors are blurred for purposes of perspective, the result is not neutral gray, but a variation of tints on the original color, accompanied by a blurring of outline.

The tinting and brightening of the original color (or its darkening, for that matter) is liable to alter at any moment. For example, red does not always turn to gray-pink; the nearer the color is to the horizon, the more dependent it becomes on light conditions. You may have occasion to observe a tiled roof in widely differing circumstances: in the sunlight, rain, and under a cloudy sky, in the morning and in the evening; each time it will look completely different; and to paint what you see, on each occasion, you would need every color you have.

15. COLOR COMPOSITION

We have already seen that the effect of perspective can be created by the exclusive use of color or of lines and other graphic methods; or by a combination of the two. The same holds true for pictorial representation.

You will easily discover whether a composition is executed by means of color alone, or graphically, or the two together, if you make a black and white photographic print. If the composition was drawn graphically, the black and white picture will be clearly defined; if color was used, the monochrome reproduction will have no clear lines. With sufficient knowledge and experience, you should be able to visualize this without bothering to test it. The same means can be used to distinguish between perspective achieved by line or color. The fact remains that the principles of color and line are much more closely related in respect to composition than to perspective. A composition is not built up in the same way as linear perspective, and "rules" in the strict sense do not apply. Composition is far more a matter of sensibility than of logic. Let us review the various means by which a picture can be composed:

First, the "selective" picture; by this is meant the best picture a photographer can obtain, given the size of his camera. It is an entirely passive exercise in the art of composition, as the photographer can only select his composition, neither

adding to nor subtracting from it. What he can do is to use special lenses which will bring near objects nearer, or make distant ones appear more distant—in other words, alter the depth of perspective. The photographer is also bound by the size of his plate and his film, and the most he can do afterwards is to crop it and adjust the size of the picture accordingly.

On the other hand, draftsmen and painters alike are able, if they so wish, to decide on the best size for their pictures by using an adjustable finder. But there is a good deal more to their art than this passive function, for by bringing objects closer together, or placing them wider apart, they can give the

358

picture content an appearance of greater depth, urgency, or breadth, or otherwise alter it entirely. In any selective composition the edges of the picture itself are fixed immutably. When these confines are pushed back, fresh, possibly disruptive elements are introduced into the picture. If they are later made to contract, something essential may be left out, spoiling the whole effect of the composition. What is left may be not a picture, but merely a detail. A conscious, active composition does not cling fast to the edge of the picture.

Less haphazard than a selective composition, which resembles a view out a window, an "active" composition grows out of a relatively ill-defined expanse,

rather like spotlighting a particular scene on a darkened stage, or a landscape at night. The darkness is less of a factor in the event portrayed and serves more to set the tone; here we have life itself, the world, the cosmos. A composition

Color composition

Left: One color (yellow): light, medium, dark cadmium yellow — burnt sienna — yellow ochre — Naples yellow (reddish) — raw umber — gray (ultramarine blue, ochre, and alizarin red mixed)

Center: Two contrasting colors (blue and red): light, medium, and dark cobalt blue and oxide of chromium blue — burnt sienna, cadmium red, caput mortuum

Right: One main color (green) and several duller subsidiary colors: hydroxide of chromium (green), with traces of pale cadmium yellow — Naples yellow (antimony) reddish, mixed and painted over with ultramarine blue, alizarin red, ochre

like this does not make one want to look farther, as a selective composition may well do.

Picture framing is also to be considered from the outset. A selective composition inevitably calls for a frame to shut it off, and a mount is often used. The type of composition which grows out of the surface does not need one, however. In other words, you cannot alter your selection once you have decided on it without interfering with the effect of the picture itself. On the other hand, you will find that you can enlarge the area of a picture with ill-defined limits, without altering the effect of the picture.

Contracting the surrounding area is rather a different matter. The design will lose its urgency and become more commonplace. This may not affect the composition of the scene itself, but it will affect the picture's spiritual content. To take an example: if you stand on a broad plain, the effect of the expanse, solitude, and so forth is largely due to the immensity of the heavens above. If you view this same landscape through a finder, which takes away a good deal of the expanse of sky, much of its grandeur will also disappear. There was an academic maxim which would seem very much to the point here: it laid down a ratio of 1:2 or 2:1 between earth and heaven. To construct their pictures so that the "empty" space was left in all its glory was one of the masterly achievements of the classical Japanese and Chinese painters and has never been surpassed. If hitherto we have been concerned solely with the surrounding shadow, this should not be taken to mean that it is a sort of inevitable constituent

of an "active" composition. The reverse is true! The surround may equally well be bright, but what it must do is to stand in some kind of relationship to the picture content, whether by reason of its texture or its color.   The surrounding area may be white, especially in a watercolor; and in a watercolor this will usually be the white of the paper, or support. In other media, a gray or tinted ground can also be very delightful, particularly when the tinting is not tonelessly smooth and dead but shows the irregularities of the brush strokes. It is then that it really contributes to the picture. Modern mural painting exploits the support to similar effect. The texture and color form a lively continuation of the picture itself, and act as a unifying element with the architectural limits and joins, which in their turn are underlined by a representation focused on one spot. This spot then becomes an animated center in a fixed surround. This manner of composing a mural painting undoubtedly marks an advance over the rigid framing of murals practiced in earlier times. It is an advance which enables us to achieve as much or more, with limited means, as in a painting which utilized every available space between joints in the building, and released a shower of shapes and colors. Even the most receptive onlooker will feel no more than this, and even he will probably not take away much of the detail of the picture, however often or searchingly he looks at it. A modern, simple type of mural, with its greater economy, makes a more lasting impression. Just try to reproduce from memory at home something you have seen in, shall we say, a baroque church. You have scant chance of success. If you try with a sgraffito, a mosaic, or a painting on a modern building, you are certain to draw a fair reproduction.

This indeed is the aim of composition. We aim to produce a picture at once forceful and memorable; a picture which will be at its most commanding when the boundaries of the surface are not too rigidly adhered to, depended on, leaned on; a picture which remains the focal point of an expanse, quite apart from its own centers, tensions, and rhythms. As there is no book of rules for composition such as there is for linear perspective, we shall not attempt here to translate into terms of color precepts which you have already learned about composition in drawing. It is more instructive to seek out, brush in hand, what exactly constitutes the composition of this or that well-known painting. The following may be found relevant:

The a posteriori analysis of any work of art, or of an artistic era for that matter, is open to question, whatever its purpose. Were the old masters to be told all that later generations have read from, or into, their works, they would be beside themselves with astonishment. It has become an absurd parlor game in art history to don the armour of immense learning and clap a completed work of art in the steel frame of rigid logic. Those who do this fail to notice that they have a gyrocompass in their head fixed at "Just you rhyme, or else. . . , !"

Apart from the fact that it is of no importance anyway, no one can state afterwards why and on what basis an artist suddenly felt impelled to alter his conception. A correction is unlikely to

spring so much from pondering as from the artist's sensibility. Painters and sculptors, if they are worthy of the name, do not think; they see and feel, just as a poet hears and feels what he writes, and as he goes by sound and not grammar. Turn back if you will to the detail from the Michelangelo fresco. Art critics will be ready with cogent explanations as to why Michelangelo colored over the marked contour, which he had drawn in so vigorously on the cartoon. But I feel certain that if he had altered nothing, the same critics would explain why not with no less cogency.

With this in mind you will know better than to regard the following analyses of two compositions as infallible. We are groping after the truth, not expounding it!

One thing is certain, however, and this is that the usual test, which is to try to convey a surface composition by means of schematic lines, is preposterous. Movement can never be interpreted as line, but only as surface area, and even direction lines describe a path of vision rather than a line of vision. Add color, and the design will be composed mainly of colored areas, which it is quite absurd to express in terms of lines.

Lines used to analyse a color composition can only be regarded as a plan, a framework or pointer to indicate the general trend or feeling of movement.

The two pictures on the pages that follow are placed side by side because both have the horse as their ostensible subject. Their artistic aims are otherwise quite dissimilar. The picture by Marc is a well-balanced, selective composition, which leans heavily on the picture's

Marc, The Red Horses. Right: Composition analyses (linear pattern and surface impression)

boundaries. These boundaries can neither be contracted nor enlarged without significantly altering the true sense of the picture, which hinges on the three horses. They are intercepted in the course of motion; and taken on its own, the scene is like a high-speed photograph. This motion, as it were, frozen, is stretched across a network of horizontal and vertical lines, facing left, and is emphasized by a triangular link between the focal points of the picture, that is, between the three heads. The marked bias of this network in a leftwards, downwards direc-

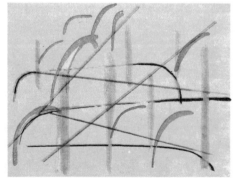

tion is taken up by a set of lines leading downwards to the right, but this is revealed only on closer study. The result is a returning sense of repose and delightful harmony. These lines weave the animals and the landscape into a whole. The diagram shows that the true motif of the picture is a series of planes which whirl around, wind about, and finally settle as they were. The three horses are

Reuther, Horses. Below left: Composition Analyses (surface impression and linear pattern)

treated as a whole, and the potentially unwelcome effect of frozen movement is thus offset.

The color likewise brings out the motif. An intense red impels the scene forward, and the violet of the middle horse is seen as a connecting shade of red. This is the keynote which shines brightly and is everywhere repeated, both in the foreground and in the background. The yellows and blues produce the same effect, and as a result a web of colors may be discerned in addition to a web of lines. The green is the only color to appear in the background and nowhere else, but in this way it impels the main motif forwards, but this again is modified by the clear blue with its warmer effect.

Although the picture is exceptionally gaily colored, it is seen at first glance as a colored fabric, a gay material. Closer inspection brings out its amazing vitality.

Whereas Marc applied his colors in thin coats, and exploited to the full their chromatic potentialities, Reuther used the palette knife to produce a porous effect. He does not treat his colors as "absolute" and costly paint to be carefully husbanded, but as a palpable material, reminiscent of a granular whirl of lines on a dark stone. Reuther's picture has two-color planes. The first, the foreground, holds the true picture content, horses and riders, in dull, grayish-pink-violet tones, with many gradations of black; the second, the background, is a bluish-green and conveys an impression of indeterminate distant expanses with a glassy look about them, in spite of the fragmentary porous paint layers. The shadows, which seem to keep breaking through, weld the foreground and background together into one plane, even though the shapes and color surfaces of the motif itself stand out much more unequivocally against the background than they do in Marc's picture. It is doubtful whether the connecting lines which we reconstruct were used at all in visualizing and planning the work. The painting does not depict any motion in progress. Animals and riders alike are impassive and at rest; but the whole is instinct with the possibility of an imminent departure—at a gallop. A springy rhythm built up of arcs points upwards to the right, where it is intercepted and balanced by an arc which rears up toward the left-hand portion of the picture like some massive bridge thrown across slender supports, calling to mind an audacious construction in reinforced concrete. Nevertheless, this picture, which is difficult to explain in detail, has some of the formal elements of the prehistoric cave paintings: massive bodies on thin, fragile legs, which accentuate the fleeting, fugitive nature of animals. This tendency has become almost a stylistic commonplace among present-day artists to whom the subject matter serves as a starting point. The two principal lines of the composition are intercepted by a swirling movement starting in the direction of the horses' heads. The circumference ravels itself into a knot over against the two heads, and as with all live animals it is problematic whether the imminent wild movement which one senses will proceed from flight or from a bitter struggle. The riders' function is accentual; they stress the element of tranquility, but rather than taming the animals' primitive force, they are at its mercy.

16. THE CARE AND PRESERVATION OF PICTURES

There are overzealous housewives who, in a fit of frenzy, will clean the life out of an oil painting with soap and water. "This bit must be done too. Look!" they will say, showing you the dirty finger tip they have just run over the picture.

A given oil painting may appear to survive the cleaning process once or twice unharmed. It will depend on whether the paint is in thick layers or thin, and whether the ground is bound with glue or with oil. In any case, the picture will develop premature flaws and cracks, for the soap and water are bound to penetrate it somewhere, turning the oil to soap or soaking into the ground. What may also happen is that some of the oil paint is "cleaned" right away at once; the mitered frame over which the canvas is stretched will press through; the top layer may go mat. It goes without saying that by then the picture is worthless!

Even if the determined cleaner is warned not to use soap and water, pictures will still be dusted. The trouble is that the dust is rubbed in rather than out. If you find this hard to believe, take a picture down after dusting and remove it from its frame. If the picture is painted on canvas and has a mitered inner frame, you must put something in to fill the empty space at the back. Place a suitable object, a book or folded cloth of the right size, on a firm base which may be a smooth paper base. Next, turn the picture upside down so that the back lies

like a close-fitting lid over it all. Work on the front, applying careful pressure, and do not allow the beveled edges of the mitered frame to press through. Then, take some white bread, preferably still warm, and on no account more than a few hours old; scoop out the soft crumb, and form it into little balls which you can roll lightly over the surface of the picture. You will hardly believe how much dirt adheres to the bread crumbs. Throw this away, and take a fresh piece. Apply very little pressure to start with, then more. Try the complete process on only one part of the picture, and you will soon see that the portion you have cleaned is very much brighter and new looking than the rest of the picture.

A soft rubber eraser removes the dirt equally well, but it might leave traces of vaseline behind, so that you would have a nondrying fat on your picture. Thanks to its fat-free adhesive properties, the bread leaves no trace. Naturally, you should not use a milk loaf or one made with fat.

This is the finest method and the one always used by picture restorers before they do anything else to a painting. No one without first-class professional skill and experience should ever attempt to do more. A picture not protected by glass should never be cleaned with a duster or a feather mop. On the other hand, the use of a vacuum cleaner with a metal attachment is permissible. It may be moved over a picture lying flat,

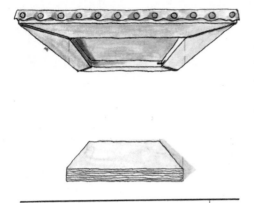

Filling in the empty space behind a wedge-framed picture to clean its surface

but should not actually touch the surface. With care, it is also possible to blow the dust off, provided the stream of air is not so strong that it blows the dust **into** the pores of the picture. Even the most sensitive watercolor, in fact any painting, will tolerate cleaning with bread crumbs. This method is also the only one that can be used to clean a simple glue color painting on the wall. All oil paintings lose something of their brightness in time, it may be only in places, and this makes them look patchy. When this happens, a protective varnish is applied. However, no very recent painting should ever be treated in this way if you do not know exactly what the binder was made of. Surface resinous glazes are easily ripped off, and then the picture is past saving. For a year or two after application, resin undergoes a process of oxidation and then is no longer so easily dissolved. In any case, mastic should be laid on as swiftly as possible, preferably in a single stroke. Repeated applications with a hard brush will take off even an old layer of resin. The least

dangerous process is that of varnishing on top of pure oil paint. After two years' oxidation, neither turpentine nor mastic will do any harm. Daily professional dealing with these matters alone can give you the experience you need to be able to say at a glance what was used for binding. An expert will also know the most appropriate way to test doubtful cases. All painters are occasionally asked to undertake to restore a damaged picture. In principle, they should refuse to do this, even if they have the necessary technical ability; for special experience, over and above sheer knowledge, is required to restore a picture. Unfortunately there are more dabblers than craftsmen in this field. A painting of particular artistic or historical merit should not just be handed over to a picture restorer, even one of some repute. It should be entrusted to a public institution specializing in art restoring, which has the means to assess the extent of the damage, and can say who is the best person to go to under the circumstances. This method usually gives the best value for the money. Small picture restoring firms are prone to recount awful stories, in order to get as much money as they can in return for sketchy, shoddy work. Above all it is only too easy to spoil a picture completely.

The explanations that follow should not in any way be regarded as a guide to picture restoring, but are meant to supplement your knowledge of painting techniques and enable you to view the subject with confidence.

Any picture in need of restoration should first be treated on the wrong side. Any broken or otherwise damaged canvas, or holes, cracks, or rents in paper, split or warped boards should so far as possible be put right before the real work of restoring and preserving begins.

Severely damaged canvas is usually glued onto a new canvas, after removing any rough parts or paste which may have been applied for protection. In former times, weeks were spent in detaching the whole canvas from the reverse side of the picture, while the front of the painting was temporarily fixed to a firm base. This was a risky way to care for a piece of art, and has been abandoned. The process of affixing a new canvas behind a painting is the restoring process most frequently undertaken today. Any cracks and flows can be ironed out at the same time. The adhesive used must be one which will not cause the canvas threads to swell. Old canvas, which has been kept taut and over-stretched for a very long time, may shrink by as much as 5 per cent or more, squeezing the layers of paint together so that they fall off.

Sometimes a board of a special aluminum alloy is used instead of canvas. Very large wooden boards must be inlaid from the outset, as already described, to halt any tendency to warping. Rents and cracks are repaired with glue. Rents and cracks in a paper support are dealt with by pasting underneath, ironing out, and pressing. If parts of the picture are damaged, the golden rule is never to paint over the faulty parts in an attempt to imitate what you imagine the original painting to have been. Experience has shown that it is best merely to fill in the faulty parts in a plain color, to tone in with the surrounding area. The bad parts

will then not be too jarring, but will remain recognizable. Any attempt to match up and disguise these parts is taboo; this is little short of forgery.

A knotty question is the renewal of yellowed or tarnished paintings, or those which have darkened through chemical changes. Little can be done for a painting which has gone completely yellow, though you may try placing it in the light, as this sometimes bleaches out the yellowed oils to some extent.

There is no help for a painting in which the pigments have changed because of chemical reaction. This is a process of decomposition almost always present when chrome yellow has been used. In the initial stage a strange unhealthy shade appears, which turns to a kind of green (this is apparent in the present condition of Van Gogh's **Sunflowers**, and this is the "mysterious" quality for which this picture is so admired). In time chrome yellow becomes a greenish black. Coal-tar colors go gray.

If it is merely a question of a surface oil varnish, applied by an experienced painter or restorer, which has gone yellow or brown, the varnish is merely removed. This is done meticulously, bit by bit, by spotting out with turpentine, alcohol, or similar means. A responsible restorer will constantly use his microscope to check whether the varnish removed contains any grains of pigment. If so, whether or not he has already removed a glaze, he must at once suspend his work. As a rule, when a yellowed varnish has been removed, "the golden tone, the glory of the old masters" which spectators may have raved about, is shown up in a harsher and candidly disappointing light. This, however, corresponds to the artist's intention. If he had wanted the golden tone, he would have used ochre or some other yellow pigment for his final coat of varnish. Resinous varnishes, which we call "dead," that is, varnishes which have begun to crumble and have lost their transparency, are not handled directly. Pettenkofer's now celebrated method is to expose them to a steam bath of turpentine, alcohol, or petroleum in an enclosed tank to restore lost cohesion to the layers of paint.

Mildew will always put in an appearance if there is enough moisture and nourishment for this type of fungus. Dust may contain suitable nourishment and help it to grow on the front of an oil painting where it could not otherwise hope to live. More often it is the back which is attacked, and the glue in the primer is eaten away. This unhappily also shows in the front, which seems to puff up and later decays.

Pictures which have gone mildewy should first be dried until the fungus and its spores can be removed, like dust, with bread crumbs. Then alcohol is applied several times to kill the germs. That is all. Damp stains are very hard to remove. They are due to the matter secreted by the fungi. Bleaching with hydrogen peroxide is not without its dangers because of the risk of attacking the paint layers in the process.

The restoration of pastel paintings whose colors were either not fixed at all or whose fixative has lost its binding power is a subject apart. A good deal can be done by very patient dabbing on the places which have become affected. The picture will lose something, of course, but will still be recognizable. If powder

pigment has stuck to the glass itself, the only thing to do is to remove the picture carefully from its frame and clean the glass, and if necessary put back a new one instead. It is risky to apply a fixative after the painting is finished. Old pictures were painted without the aniline colors, which were not yet known, but they are likely to have used gum substances, which are every bit as sensitive, if not even more so. The least that can be said is that no fixative with an alcohol content should be used. Glue, or skim milk, would certainly not make the colors run, but it might give a delicate painting a hard, brittle appearance.

To sum up, a painting of any value should be entrusted only to a fully qualified restorer. But how is one to tell if the picture in question can properly be considered valuable?

All painters constantly find themselves in the dilemma of having to act as assessors in their friends' homes. They are led before some futile work by its proud owner. One has only to describe this monstrosity for what it is to offend him mortally. But because a picture looks bungled, this does not mean that it is worthless, for a painting of the highest order may lie beneath. "Suspect" paintings of this kind have long been X-rayed. The individual metal ingredients of the pigments show up quite differently when X-rayed, and it is easy to see if there is another painting under the top layer. Many a celebrated painting has been uncovered when a worthless painting was washed off. On the other hand, under some worthless modern overpaintings all that has been found was a forgery. It is extremely difficult to prove the authenticity of an old master. The very greatest

Revealed by X-ray. Left: Saint Monica. An artistically undistinguished 17th century painting. X-ray photography revealed the far more valuable portrait of Magdalena Wittich by Christopher Amberger, who lived in the 16th century (X-ray photograph by Hans Roth)

experts are often taken in. A signature is no guarantee, as it may be forged just like the rest of the picture. When an expert examines a picture scientifically, he first tries to ascertain whether by any chance it was painted with pigments unknown at the time of the painter in question. Examination of the pigments under the microscope provides further information. The grains of old pigment are less uniform than those produced today. The age of the canvas, wood, or other support is a further clue. It is frankly no easy matter to give an accurate assessment of an old support. A professional forger will always find means of obtaining old boards, canvas, or paper. Nevertheless, if enough of the paint layer can be spared for the expert chemists and physicists, they should be able to unmask any modern forgery. Contemporary copies or forgeries, if well executed, are almost impossible to detect; if badly executed, however, the expert will spot the forgery

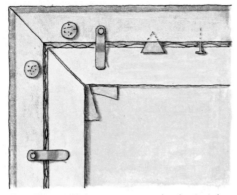

Framing a picture on a wedged stretcher (back view). Spring clamps, triangular chips or tacks driven in are used to secure the frame. The stretcher itself is not touched. Cork discs keep the picture from touching the wall

by the signature, which, if exposed to infra-red rays, will show the original signature underneath.

This is all intended for your information, rather than for practical use. On the other hand, the framing and preserving of your own pictures are matters which it is essential for you to know something about. The worst enemy of all works of art is humidity. Constant extremes of heat and dryness are likewise

undesirable. All pictures with a mitered inner frame or fixed on a board should be placed in a picture frame with a broad enough rebate to keep them from being jolted or from falling out. All types of material shrink or stretch to some extent, depending on the degree of humidity in the air. Mitered inner frames and boards should never be nailed directly to the picture frame. The right way to attach them is either to drive in suitable pegs or small metal plates, or to fasten on small steel spring brackets to hold them firmly but flexibly. The use of brackets on the back of the picture also has much to recommend it. When the painting is so sensitive as to need glass to protect it, the painting and the glass must not touch; this applies to watercolors and glue color paintings as well as to pastels.

It is best to use a mount not less than about one tenth of an inch thick. In many cases, even if no mount is used a frame with a double rebate is the answer. The frame puts the finishing touch to the picture; its shape and appearance must be chosen to match the aesthetic impact and style of the whole.

Above left: cross section of frame with spring clamps
Below left: with tacks or metal chips (triangular); spring clamps are best

Above right: The glass and picture divided by strong passepartout
Below right: Here the glass is separated from the picture by inserting a strip of framing felt

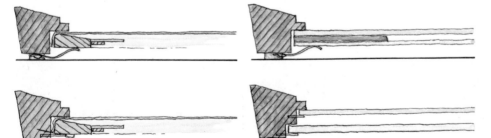

17. THE STUDIO AND EQUIPMENT

Anselm Feuerbach averred that the use of a good brush was half the battle for a good picture. We know from Goethe that the sight of a pad of clean paper and a handful of well-sharpened quill pens stirred in him an irresistible craving to write. And the most callow novice feels his fingers itching when a fresh white watercolor block lies before him, a splendid paint box open in front of him full of bright colors, and water and first-class brushes all stand ready. If this novice can in addition be left in peace and quiet there is no holding him, however little he knows.

Take this same beginner into the studio of a great painter, where ill-treated tubes of paint, empty vodka bottles and bedaubed palettes lie scattered in wild confusion, not forgetting the dirty window panes, the dust and unfinished paintings everywhere, and he will certainly put his hands in his trouser pockets and never speak of touching a brush again. Without being a Philistine, all he will take away from his visit will be, not to put too fine a point upon it, a feeling of condescension.

Listen to what the son of a Chinese painter, Kuo Hsi, wrote, a good 900 years ago: "On days when my father decided to paint, he would sit down before a bright window, tidy his desk, and burn incense on either side. Then he would take a fine brush and the best China ink, wash his hands, and clean the ink stick, as if making ready to receive an honored guest. He would gather his thoughts together, and then set to work. . . ."

The same spirit animates the studio of C. D. Friedrich, as conveyed in Kersting's picture. Anything simpler or more modest it would be hard to imagine. Nor is it conceivable that Friedrich's painting could have taken shape in either a sumptuous or a slovenly studio. Vermeer van Delft's picture of a studio conveys, again, a serene, cheerful, solid middle-class atmosphere. One hardly expects this pleasant, tasteful room to be an artist's studio.

Compare this sight with that which appears to be **de rigueur** in every film containing a studio scene, and you will ask which comes closer to the truth. It may be a question of taste how and where one works. But it is certain that simplicity, tranquility, and orderliness are more conducive to concentrated work than grandeur, distracting in its smugness, or shambles where one can work only in one mad rush. This makes impossible any sensitive, creative work. A room in which one spends a great deal of one's time has an imperceptible influence, first on oneself, and in time on one's work. When arranging your studio, you should bear this in mind. One last point: the studio does not exist to impress your visitors.

The first thing to decide on for a studio is the lighting. It is beyond doubt most practical to face north, as this keeps out the direct sunlight, which would make work impossible; but it is usually cold, and many people find that it weighs on them. To face in any other direction means bringing at least some sunlight into the room. If curtains are used to screen it off, the light is no longer uniform and untinted. It is best then to face north; but with an overhead light source which can be screened, or with a window facing south, but far enough away from the work bench, ideal conditions can be contrived, free from any hint of gloom or oppression.

The window by which you work can scarcely be too big. As a screen and for nighttime, it is best to use plain white curtains; the room should indeed be white all over. An artist who expresses himself constantly in color feels restricted if he has always to contemplate the same color sources. Gray walls make for a cheerless light and benumb the imaginative faculties. White walls will most easily enable you to create the light conditions in which the picture will ultimately be seen. These are the light conditions under which it should be painted.

The most favorable light is that coming from the left, preferably from above and behind, so that the right hand in working does not cast a tantalizing shadow over

Kersting, C. D. Friedrich in His Studio. It is interesting to note the presence of a ruler and set-square as indispensable equipment. (See text and illustration on Page 34

the surface of the picture. However, you can easily become accustomed to having your light source on your right, if the lighting and positioning of your model call for it. Supplementary overhead lighting is particularly useful in this case.

It is always risky to paint by artificial light, for there is none which corresponds exactly to daylight. Many of Rembrandt's light effects lead us to believe that he painted by candlelight, but beyond doubt he confined this to underpaintings and in-between stages. The final coat of color he certainly laid on during the day, carrying the nighttime appearance of the scene in his mind. Artificial light if used should not be cold or harsh, nor should it be too warm or gentle, and it is best to avoid light from a single source.

The size of the room will be determined by the size of the picture which you intend to paint. This consideration apart, one artist will choose to work in a small room, and another in a spacious hall. What matters is that the artist should be able to step far enough back from his work to take it all in in one single glance at an angle of 30 degrees. For purposes of ready reckoning, this means that the distance from which the painting is to be seen should be twice the length of the picture's longest side. A picture which measures 5 by 7 feet should be seen from a distance of 14 feet. With the exception of watercolors, all picture surfaces should be placed perpendicularly, or very nearly so. For this you must use an easel. Unfortunately you will find nothing on the market between the antediluvian model, such as that in Vermeer's picture, constructed on a shaky tripod,

and portable frames of the most complicated design. Yet it is a simple enough matter to construct a movable easel with a counterbalanced weight. A drawing board can be obtained, however, equipped with a counterbalanced weight or with a hydraulic adjusting device. It is useful for painting if your drawing board has a block which compensates for the table's perpendicular tilt. An easel with a counterbalanced weight will help you to work a great deal more smoothly. With it you will be able to adjust the height of your board to the nearest fraction of an inch, and vary the position of the easel to suit the lighting.

Unfortunately, again, there are no artist's trolleys available. Of course, you may use an everyday service wagon, but it is worth the trouble to make one to measure for professional studio use. Many types of work require the use of a table. The usual height of about 30 inches is far too uncomfortable; a height of about 23 to 27 inches, depending on how tall the artist is, is very much better. This gives you a better view of the table top, whether you are engaged on a sketch or painting a watercolor which must be kept horizontal to catch the excess paint. For drawing you will often find a table with adjustable beveled board comfortable to work at. This has already been illustrated on p. 85, together with its chair. At one time, dining room chairs were made like this, so that it was possible to remain seated at the table for hours on end, upright, yet at ease. Front lighting is best if you are working at a table.

You will find it extremely useful to cover one or two studio walls with fiber

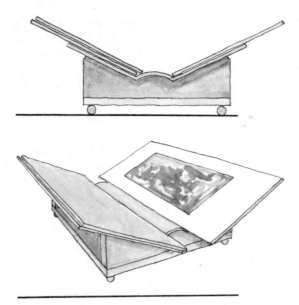

Homemade trough for easy reference to studies and pictures

boards about one half inch thick, to a height of about 6½ feet, or to the ceiling. The exact material you use is unimportant, so long as it is soft enough for a pin to go in and out easily. Here you can put up sketches as necessary from time to time.

These boards are less expensive, even if they occasionally need replacing, than wall plaster, which you would be constantly repairing, as you would be forever hammering in nails, and fragments of the plaster would keep falling out. The boards should be given a coat of white commercial emulsion paint. The usual size for the boards is about 5 by 8 feet; but it is best to use the biggest you can, so that they can on occasion be used for rough drafts and sketches. Use good drawing pins and you will easily be able to put up and take down large pieces of stiff paper. Naturally, they will not do for heavier paintings, but for this

purpose long enough nails should be used, driven right into the wall. This enables you to drive the nail home properly without an unsightly mark from broken plaster. You may in addition fix a guide rail at the top to take wire cable or screen rod on which to hang heavier pictures, as is usual in museums everywhere. In any case, you would need a very large studio indeed to have a well-lighted wall free on which to do this, as there are still a good many other things to be fitted in.

To begin with, you will need a cupboard for your designs; and if it is to take the largest size of paper, this is bound to be a monster. Metal cabinets are the most useful. Wood ones are slightly cheaper, but in either case, since each drawer is only about 1½ inches high, and there are several of them, this is an expensive item. Papers, sketches, and pictures on paper can also be kept

Jan Vermeer van Delft: The Artist in His Studio. This splendid studio may be regarded as wishful thinking by the artist, for as far as we know he was badly off. Nor does the primitive easel fit in very well with the sumptuous surroundings

Easel-board on castors

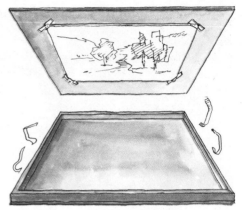

Portable case for wet oil paintings

in portfolios, but these are eternally to be found leaning up against the walls, where they fall down, encourage the dust to settle, and jostle sensitive sheets against one another. These are always a makeshift affair. On the other hand if you have pictures which are to be looked at more often it is most useful to arrange them in a book trough, where the pages can be turned over like those of a book. The portfolios too should have thick, firm, stiff, hinged spines.

The way you store your paints, brushes, crayons, bottles of fixative, binder, and cleaning agent, as well as a thousand and one oddments, depends on what you like, what you can afford, and what you have room for. Roller-shutter cabinets are very practical, and if suitably painted over give the room a pleasant look.

If you do a lot of large-scale work, and always have a good many rolled sheets of paper lying about in the studio, it is far more convenient and economical to keep them horizontally, rather than to have them standing about in dusty corners, where the edges and exposed

areas of the picture get crumpled and dirty. Various kinds of metal and wood roll-shutter cabinets are to be found, but, though practical, these are expensive. However, the most rudimentary type of bookshelf can be converted to this use if it has a curtain in front and is not less than 62 inches wide, as the largest size of paper is about 60 inches wide. Suitable rods, like those used in wardrobes, can be obtained at any furniture dealer. Slide the rolls of paper over these rods, cut to the required width. Ready-made cabinets have built-in paper cutters.

Other furniture and fittings depend on the sort of work to be done: raised platforms for models (figures in action and portraits), more tables and seating accommodation, cupboards and bookcases. It is a studio tradition to make one's platforms and seats out of chests, but as these are not sold in the shops, they have to be specially ordered. In doing this, it will be found more practical, if less usual, to order chests suitably graded to fit one into the other, rather than equal-sized coffers open on the one side, with hand-holes. They must all be of the same height, however, to keep the platform level. Chests all of exactly the same size take up a great deal of space.

It goes without saying that every studio must have running water, and facilities for washing and rinsing. The basin for rinsing must be acid-proof, made of rust-proof steel or a suitably glazed ceramic material.

One can go much further, and make a studio delightful, as if it were a home with several rooms. However, this presupposes a large storage space. This makes it easier to maintain a peaceful and orderly atmosphere in the studio, without losing time over superfluous details. If you work out of doors a great deal, you must be able to improvise and set up your equipment as the occasion demands. The first Impressionist painters went into the countryside laden like packhorses. A modern, fairly successful artist will drive out in his roomy motorcar, taking with him everything he needs to make himself at home; not forgetting a large sunshade, folding table, camp stool, paint boxes, and palettes.

For a watercolorist, the most important requisite is a bottle of pure water; for an artist in any other medium, it is his easel. Recently, several models of telescopic tripod easels have come on the market, which are very suitable and handy. For watercolor work, a lightweight folding table will serve both as support and as a place to rest the box and palette.

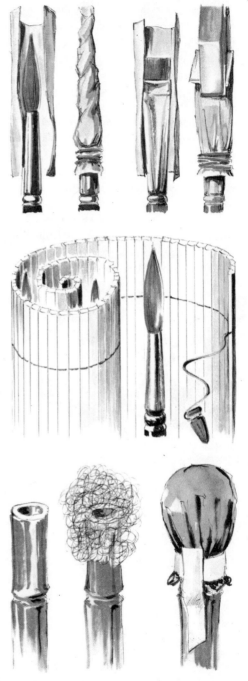

Top: Redressing a brush that has become too difficult to handle
Center: Rod-mat to carry brushes
Bottom: How to stuff a maulstick (painting stick)

377

The Studio and Equipment

If you paint in oils out of doors, you will want to provide your painting board or canvas with a well-fitting lid so that you can move your work while it is still wet. If you cannot buy a suitable one, fix four clamps to the edges of the support so that they project a little, and make a lid of stiff pasteboard or thin hard fiberboard.

To carry your brushes about, you should get a number of small mats, of the kind illustrated, made of little wooden slats. Make a mat yourself for your long brushes. This is the most elementary but safest way to protect brushes from dirt and damage, even if they are still wet and not thoroughly cleaned. Tie them up

Simple studio easel with two pegs for height adjustment. The oldest but still the most useful type

Fully adjustable metal folding tripod with poplar board

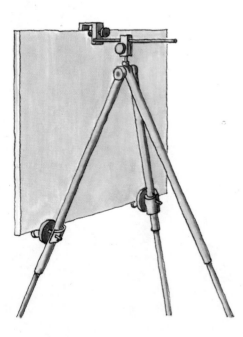

tightly, and no harm can come to them.

You may find you are bothered by the light out of doors. The only answer is to use a large sunshade with a jointed stick, which will always give you shade. Never use a colored parasol, however, always a white one. Trying to paint in the blazing sun is always upsetting. The blinding light deprives you of your ability to judge colors. You may try to sit inside your car and work from there, but the windshield will get in the way and you will feel cramped, so this can be only an unsatisfactory makeshift.

This glimpse of the proper way to organize an art studio on a professional footing will give you an insight into what is needed. You cannot limit your equipment to what you would need for work in one particular medium—for instance, watercolor painting; even if you are a complete amateur, it is useful to have an idea of what is absolutely indispensable.

You may find some comfort in the thought that even the grandest and best equipped studio carries not the slightest

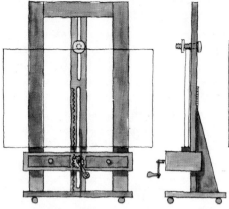

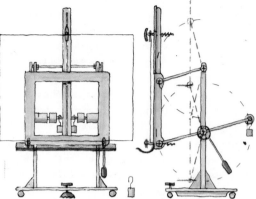

Large mobile studio easel with shelf and tool-box. Rack and pinion drive for height adjustment

Mobile studio easel with counterbalanced weight, fitted with dragwheel and lock, grooved ledge and additional balances (designed by the author)

guarantee of success—all it can do is to lighten the task. Many a work of art has originated in the most miserable setting. Even with the most modest means at hand, given flair and imagination, somewhere to work can be found in every home. The one thing which cannot be skimped is the purchase of first-class materials.

It is simply a question of discipline always to take watercolor paint out of the pan with a perfectly clean brush. You will soon realize which colors rapidly become firm in their pans, colors such as chrome hydroxide and ivory black. Always buy these in the smallest possible quantities, while for other colors the larger sizes are more economical. The pans dry up easily once the tinfoil is removed, so always take care to close the box well; also always be sure to keep the box horizontal, as many colors which appear to be firm, such as the cobalt compounds, do in fact gradually run. Possibly it is better to buy the cobalt colors in tubes for this reason.

If you work almost daily with watercolors, it is worthwhile to place a moistened sheet of blotting paper of the right size over the pans each time you close the box. This prevents the colors from ever becoming completely hard. If you do not use your watercolors for long periods at a stretch, the constant damp will ultimately cause mildew to appear on some paints, despite the preservative. Look at them from time to time, remove any paints attacked in this way, wash off the mildew and leave them to dry.

All tubes of paint must be closed with care after use. Inside the cap there is a tiny cork disc; do not lose this, for it will enable you to re-open the tube easily. For this reason you should always leave it unscrewed by half a turn. Any paint left over will stick to the thread so hard that you will have to use force to open the tube again, and usually it gets broken in the process. It is often a help to leave oil points standing upside down in turpentine, so that both cap and thread bathe in it. It also helps if you place size and watercolors in the same way in warm water. After the tube is closed it should always be rolled up carefully from the bottom. It is well worth the extra trouble. If you work more often in pastels, you will find that worn down and broken bits of chalk soon spoil the look of the finest pastel crayon box. Sort out these pieces and put them in a small empty box, and clean all your pastel boxes very thoroughly, so that useless left-over and broken pieces do not crumble still further and discolor the good crayons.

Usually it is the brushes which receive the worst treatment. Valuable watercolor brushes should always be cleaned only by rinsing in plenty of water; they should never be left standing in the water, as this makes them crooked. Should this happen, swirl the brush around in the water, squeeze it out, then wind a strip of thick paper around it, secured with a rubber band, and twist the ends around carefully so that they overlap. Hang it upside down to dry. Make sure it is quite clean by pressing it out with a white cloth or a scrap of cellulose. "Collars" for flat brushes may be pressed together with a clothes pin. In this way brushes which have become cross-grained can be made as good as new again.

After cleaning an oil paint brush in gasoline or a turpentine substitute, squeeze it out well, and rinse it out in pure turpentine to make sure that no cleaning agent is left on the brush. All brushes dry most speedily and satisfactorily hanging upside down.

When working in tempera colors, wash the brush thoroughly before the paint has had a chance to dry; otherwise there will be no way of removing all the binder and scraps of paint. If you are working out of doors, and cannot do this, wrap each brush in aluminum foil to keep it moist before you put it away in the brush mat. This, of course, applies equally to oil paint brushes. It is better to throw away a brush on which casein color has been allowed to dry, rather than carrying the useless object about with you. After washing casein and fresco brushes in water, rinse them out again in vinegar diluted with water in order to neutralize the alkaline, which is harmful to hairs and bristles. Leave the brushes for a while before squeezing them out, then give them a last rinse in running water before drying.

Moths appear to regard hair brushes as a delicacy, so when they are quite dry you should keep them in an airtight container or plastic bag. On no account leave them for any length of time in their jar, where they would also collect dust.

Cheap plastic palettes are not yet in mass production, so you should get a carpenter to cut you a variety of palettes from odd pieces of thin, hard fiberboard or plywood, covered in synthetic foil, to a cardboard pattern. These are no trouble at all to keep clean with ordinary household cleaners. They are a good deal better and cheaper than palettes made of expensive pear wood or plum wood, and are also more pleasant to use than tin or china. For studio work, you can also stick stiff, transparent foil to fiber boards with adhesive tape and keep this on your trolley; then, by sliding white or colored paper underneath, you will see at a glance what the shade in question will look like against a colored ground. This practice can naturally also be extended to palettes. Foil is cheap and expendable. No attempt should be made to clean it.

For fine work and anything which calls for precise brush movements, a painting stick is indispensable. This gives you a restful support for the hand holding the brush. You will need both shorter and longer ones, and it is best to buy a number of bamboo sticks, cut them to suitable lengths, and wind cotton wool around one end fixed on with a rough material or chamois leather and bound on firmly with adhesive tape.

The beginner who goes into a shop selling artists' materials may be put off by the choice before him. Before starting, haltingly and confusedly, to buy the wares recommended, first ask to see all the sales brochures and catalogues of paint vehicles and mediums, brushes and other equipment available, preferably from several first-class firms. Go through all this literature very carefully at home, and compose a well-thought-out shopping list. When you go back, you will discover to your astonishment that now it is the salesgirl who is at a loss, for much of what you have marked as essential is not stocked at all. She may try to persuade you to buy materials that are "just as good," but you should be very wary of doing this; it is better not to give in at all, but to insist on ordering what you want. Tubes of paint should be tested before you buy them to make sure that they are still completely flexible. Tempera and size colors which have been kept a long while are especially difficult to squeeze out, and the most expensive pigments are particularly given to premature hardening.

If the day comes when you can install or even build a proper studio for professional work, you should be absolutely clear as to what you want and why. For example, studios are often placed on the top floor. But is this really practical? The older ones belong to the days when artists painted only enormous pictures; but apart from this, their ceilings were so high and the windows so unpractical, that unless the artist was constantly attending to the fire, he was bound to freeze.

We hear so much today about the "dream house." I presume in the same spirit to put forward plans for the studio of my dreams. The basic structure is very simple, and I have from the outset foregone the romantic winding stairways, dim corners, and partitions which visitors find so appealing. A light, functional room, protected against outside noises, is alone conducive to the creation of works of art, precisely because these works themselves are often so cut off from the logical and functional.

The most important thing seems to me to be the division of the studio into three parts. For my own purposes the studio must have relatively high ceilings, as I am most drawn to wall painting. There must be room for storage and preparation and a living space where one can rest, read, and write, as well as receive visitors—who, in principle, have no business in the studio, except when it is necessary for them to come and look. Nothing puts one off more than discussion of half-finished works, whether captious or flattering.

The Studio and Equipment

1:100

Arrangement of north wall of studio, showing large windows and recess for washing

Right above: Ground plan of the studio, with ante- and adjacent rooms

Right below: Section A-B showing arrangement of studio and living room

(Scale 1:100 expressed in meters)

I   Studio, 40 sq. m. (130.4 sq. ft.)

II Adjoining room for preliminary operations, 18 sq. m. (59 sq. ft.)

III Living and reception room 21.75 sq. m. (71.30 sq. ft.)

IV Vestibule containing WC, hall cupboard, and landing with access through double doors to studio and also to private residence (V).

1   Easel with counterbalanced weight

1a Display wall

2   Easel board (see page 376)

3   Picture trough (see page 374)

4   Work table, 70 x 200 cm. (27 x 78 in.) covered in gray or green synthetic fabric or foil, about 65 cm. (25 in.) high

5   Cupboards with shutters or doors, 30 or 40 cm. (12-16 in.) deep for small items of equipment, liquids, pencils, etc., and small stretching blocks and paper

6   Cupboards or drawers for equipment such as rolls of paper, canvas, boards, stretchers, completed pictures, etc.

7   Large cupboard 80 x 130 cm. (31 x 60 in.) to hold designs and other pictures on paper

8   Bookcase with hinged flap for use as writing desk

9   Extra space, may be used as cloakroom, etc.

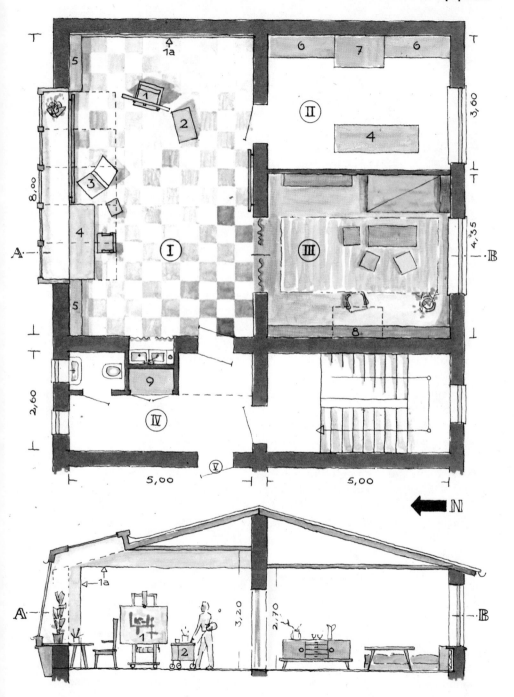

18. THE PAINTING

As a pendant to the section on The Drawing, we shall now describe how a color painting is made and how to achieve a mature and definitive work of art—to use the most ambitious term for a painting.

The extreme opposite of a painting is a drawing, in particular a sketch or impromptu study. Yet a rapid drawing is likewise the starting point for a painting. Drawing consists in fact of the division of the picture area, the composition, and later on the details. It makes no difference whether these drawings are executed with charcoal, crayon, or paints and brushes; nor does it matter whether the painting is accompanied by drawing. Color is the element from which a painting is made; but even the smallest speck of paint is also a shape and must be put down somehow. It is a question of technique, whether you begin with an outline and work up from that, or with a brush mark which you expand on all sides until it reaches the outlined shape. In any case it is a question of draftsmanship. The same is true even if the color surfaces merge with one another.

The dividing line between the individual colors is felt to be present even if it can scarcely be seen. Remember Monet's picture of Parliament in London (p. 15). Here you can hardly point out a single boundary between the buildings and the sky, but in spite of this you are fully conscious of the shapes of the buildings. It would be perfectly possible to produce a drawing without the use of color, but a colored representation cannot do without drawing. Without drawing, all that you are left with is a shapeless mass of colors running into each other. It is important to bear this point in mind, for the paragraphs which follow aim at the elaboration of a systematic procedure of universal validity. Here we have a clear distinction between line and color, which is absolutely necessary if one is to proceed in a workmanlike way.

We must be sure that we know why color always has greater impact than a black line or tinted areas. There is always something unequivocal about color. Red, after all, is red, and cannot very well be regarded as green or blue. Differences of tone between areas drawn side by side leave you at liberty to conjure up any color you wish. A patch of sky left plain white in a line drawing will be automatically felt to be in a different shade from the equally white strip of roadway—assuming that the drawing is objective and unmistakable. Now look back at the Dürer drawing opposite the Monet picture we have just referred to (p. 14) and you will see that the Dürer contains three empty spaces: sky, water, and quayside. The moment you have grasped the picture content, you assign to each identical bright surface a different color concept.

It follows from the unequivocal statement which is implicit in the use of color that every time you paint, you not only can but must express your ideas in more downright terms than when you draw.

Huber, St. Anne's Altar (detail). Left: preliminary drawing revealed by infra-red photography (Photo Hans Roth)

Once you begin to paint, you begin to move towards something which, when completed, will leave little unsaid as to form, and nothing whatever as to color. If anything is left plain—if, for example, the ground is left untouched in places— the picture will always have an unfinished look. The fact that this unfinished look has a singular charm in no way affects the issue. Dürer's outline drawing, on the other hand, despite its many spaces, seems anything but unfinished. Imagine these spaces given additional treatment, filled in, perhaps, and you will see that this would not make the drawing any more "finished."

However, a mature painting will come into being only where there are a deep purpose and a clear aim. An artist must have become fully aware of the absolute limits to his attainment before he can achieve this. Naturally, these limits are narrower in drawing than they are in painting. For this reason monochrome can be said to offer greater scope to the imagination than color work. Color, the element which cannot be used in drawing, must be rendered uncompromisingly in painting, and from it there is no way back into the realm of individual imaginings.

It is also in the nature of drawing for

The Painting

it to say what it has to say once and for all, whereas painting gropes its way progressively toward its final form. This is simply due to the way colors affect each other. You learned long ago that a blue may at first appear correct, but appear to change when its complementary color, orange, is placed beside it. The blue will appear to be more intense; but place another blue beside it, and the first one will weaken it. The artist may, for technical reasons, occasionally endeavor to produce the definitive shade at a first attempt, relying on his imagination and experience, as in watercolor or true fresco work. As a rule, however, it will suit him better to begin by indicating his color faintly, and to arrive at his final shade step by step. It is equally important to make a workmanlike distinction between draftsmanship and painting. As a rule the painter utilizes his line drawing as a starting point, a scaffolding which

will gradually be lost to sight. He may choose to erect this scaffolding with great care, or he may prefer to sketch it in very rapidly, just enough to support the first structure. From then on he must use paint, however. Isolated masters of the craft may work without preliminary drawing of any kind. Lovis Corinth, for example, would often start with an eyebrow or a nose, and would draw on from there, or some similar feature, in color, until the portrait was done. But most artists would go aground if they tried to do this. One must have supreme command of the rules to be able to lay them completely aside. You know well enough that from a technical point of view it can never be done with impunity. The same holds good for the distribution and sequence of individual processes: depart from the well-tried rules, and you will imperil the artistic impact of your work.

Before you begin, you need to visual-

Cézanne, pencil head study

Spitzweg, The Bookworm
Right: Macro-photograph by
Hans Roth
Below: Detail, actual size

ize clearly and deliberately how you mean to put your artistic aims into effect. You will find simply that if you take whatever ground comes to hand and attempt to express an idea or a vision, however clearly you see it, without technical and workmanlike preparations, with no sketches or concentrated spadework, a true work of art cannot possibly emerge. An exceptionally skillful artist may possibly bring this off, relying on experience garnered throughout his working career, but as a rule it is precisely the greatest masters who adhere to well-tried rules of procedure, modified over the years to

suit their own needs. They know only too well that this is how they will get on fastest. The accepted blueprint for the creation of a painting in its final form is to divide up all the technical and artistic processes so far as humanly possible.

At the outset of a new work, a painter must make up his mind on two fundamental points: what he wants to paint, and how he wants to paint it. Unless the idea behind the picture is a mere passing impression, in which case all the work can be done in front of the subject, and will usually be in the nature of a sketch or study, the question of

The Painting

what to paint entails a lengthy process of familiarization. While it is true that, apart from some small corrections afterwards, the great Impressionist painters completed whole works at a stretch with the subject before their eyes, it should not be forgotten that what the Impressionists were interested in was after all not **what**, but **how** they painted. For the Impressionists, preparation meant grappling, incessantly and intently, but still more visually, with this question of how to paint. They painted countless studies at one sitting and the subject was a matter of relative indifference to them, so long as the color harmony or textural quality stimulated them. They might find this quality in a misty sky, a ferment of limitless greens (herbage, copse, or meadow), or the dusty glare of a hot day, with its shimmering light, which at first glance seems to be just gray and more gray, but which is in fact built up of thousands of the most subtly differentiated specks of color. They painted all this, then, as background preparation for such works as Monet's **Sunrise**, or Cézanne's **Mont Saint-Victoire**. To show how indifferent the Impressionists were to the subject of the picture — in the intellectual sense — you have only to imagine that instead of London's Parliament, Monet's painting depicted an old harbor shed down by the water. You will surely agree with me when I assert that this would make the same impression on us.

Van Gogh's attitude is in some respects the opposite of this. He is generally reckoned among the Impressionists, but he was by no means always preoccupied with the manner of his painting. To take his portrait of **Le Père Tanguy** as an

Picasso, Portrait of Vollard, painted in 1910

example: it is difficult to imagine it as Duke X, or to substitute an orchid for **Bottines.** For his sailor, Van Gogh carried out numerous detailed studies to arrive at the exact expression of the face, hands, and striding demeanor of his subject, and to discover how to set these things down finally on his canvas. So he divided his work up, concentrating one after another on little details, and went on working at them until they took their place in his idea of the picture as a whole. An artist can develop this intense preoccupation with detail to such a pitch that he sees it before his eyes and feels it in his fingers. When this stage is reached, he must carry out his final work without a single glance at the studies. This is essential, because to refer to the preliminary work now would result in copying, not creating. It is better to close one's eyes and conjure up the idea, rather than to copy what one has already painted. If you cannot do this, it means that your work was not thorough enough.

Picasso, Portrait of Vollard, painted in 1915

Picasso, Portrait of Vollard, painted in 1937

An actor who is not sure of his lines ceases to play his part and is reduced to mouthing the words with the help of the prompter.

To sum up, before tackling a given subject, the artist must sketch out his idea with the help of countless line and color studies. How many he must make depends on his skill in general and on the degree of difficulty of the particular motif.

Leaving aside any universal search for a new mode of expression or a new way of looking at things, as with the Impressionists, the question of how to paint also brings us to consider the craft and the technicalities of building up a picture. As a rule this is a concept which emerges clearly even as early as the first sketches, and later on, in the effort to overcome difficulties of line and color. You are well aware that in watercolor no opportunity occurs to heighten the color progressively; that the rendering of fine detail cannot help looking contrived,

that in certain cases depth of color can be achieved only by the use of glazes, and that this is not possible when using **alla prima** technique—to mention but a few such difficulties. A further factor is the degree of skill of the artist and, finally, the nature of his expression as a whole, the way he paints. All this has its technical importance even in the preliminary sketch.

For this reason, the old masters went to great pains to divide their work up properly. First, using means akin to drawing, they marked out the form their picture would take. Often this meant a monochrome underpainting, usually gray in appearance, but containing within it every detail graphically portrayed. The second process, an elaboration in color, may be understood as roughly comparable to coloring a black and white photograph. In fact, as you know, there is more to it than this. While some of the greatest masterpieces of painting were created in this way—Van Eyck's **Ma-**

389

donna, for instance—Rembrandt would have nothing to do with it, saying that he was a painter, not a dyer. In his eyes, his underpainting gave him a far better foundation to work on than explicit form which only needed coloring.

Rubens worked in yet another way. Neither in Van Eyck's nor in Rembrandt's work does a trace of the underpainting as such show in the finished painting. In Rubens' work, on the contrary, some hint of the hatching look of the gray primer he used shines right through to the top surfaces; thanks to the effect of color interference, this creates the wonderful mother of pearl luster seen on the skin of his female subjects. Rubens used powdered charcoal bound with size and applied it in broad sweeping strokes obliquely over the white primer, thus producing an original tinted effect. The great Flemish artist employed every process, however insignificant. We might say that he never did the same thing twice over. By virtue of his deft hand, his sovereign artistry, and, if we may be permitted to say so, his serene and nonchalant attitude to life and choice of subject, thanks too to the inner harmony of the times he lived in, from the artist's standpoint, he was spared the need to grapple agonizingly with problems of color and line. Show anyone a Rubens in an art gallery, and you will invariably see a happy smile on his face. Show the same person a Rembrandt, and his face will take on an earnest, respectful expression even before Rembrandt's most cheerful picture, the one known as **Rembrandt and Saskia**. He may be totally lacking in expertize, yet he will sense that a battle was fought over the question, "How?"

As you strive to achieve your own manner of painting, you are doing more, therefore, than studying mere techniques. Above all, your manner must come from self-knowledge. This depends on your degree of maturity, on whether you are honest and disciplined enough not to founder on the reefs of vanity, which will tempt you to strain your talents beyond their limits.

It is sheer madness to take it upon yourself "to paint like Titian," or "to paint like Kokoschka." If among the numerous paths which lead to maturity in art there is one which you feel to be particularly sympathetic, then by all means regard a painter who has already trodden a similar way as your master; but your work should never be a copy of his. If at any time you engage in that most instructive activity, copying other men's work, it should remain copying, and should be done in front of the original. This is the best way to find out what you would choose to do differently, and why.

The work of a painter whose style is markedly original reveals its manner even in sketches and studies. Their penciled lines are admittedly an indication of form, but when they come to shadow and detail, they are thinking not so much of drawing as of the color to be laid on with paint and brush. Cézanne's head studies are a case in point; essentially he was a painter, and nothing but a painter. On the other hand, Van Gogh's brush strokes are always graphic in effect, although his paintings are certainly not graphic in the sense that Toulouse-Lautrec's colored drawings are.

People often think that the spiritual

Design for a mural on light green plaster surface

greatness of a painter is more or less bound up with the size of his pictures. In a general way, this attitude may appear ridiculous, yet there is a grain of sense in it. An artist has to take a very deep breath indeed to encompass works as gigantic as those of Rubens or Makart. The majority of the historical painters of the past century failed to bring this off, as they lacked the human dimension of a Rubens or the unbelievable skill of a Makart. The second-rate fresco painters of the Baroque and Rococo periods were spurred on by the intoxicating mood of their day, and not least by the pace at which a fresco must be executed.

An artist who is not ruled by an inner apprehension of magnitude, and who works on a picture for years or decades, as oil painting will enable him to do, may all too easily find he has produced merely one square yard after another of scenes, though each one may be reasonably well painted. For this reason, every artist should discover beyond doubt what size picture suits him best, the size to which he is constitutionally suited. Even in the smallest works an

391

artist cannot do without a certain bold-
ness of design and color. Leaving aside
the attitude of mind which may induce a
certain monumentality even in the minia-
turist, this quality evinces itself in a rough
and ready treatment of form and an
exaggeration of the most important dimensions in the picture. It is always a
surprise to see a large magnification of
a miniature. The same is true of a master-
piece of small genre painting, particularly if behind a cheerfully descriptive
style there lurks a gift for caricature,
which is the case in the work of Spitzweg.
Whereas in former days an artist's work
revolved around the creation of a single
style which persisted throughout his
working life, there are many modern
painters whose work has changed so
strikingly over the years that an impartial
spectator would hardly suppose works
belonging to different periods of their
careers to have been executed by one
and the same person. Much current criticism is wrong, however, in assuming that
this indicates lack of character on the
part of the artist; on the contrary, a determination to gain by increased awareness is proof rather of strong-minded-
ness. This awareness is the fruit of a far-
ranging familiarity with the work of other
men and with the men themselves. Nowadays, you may read in your morning
newspaper of a picture which has caused
a sensation and by the same evening
already have seen it, even if it is several
hundred miles away. Previously, the
journey alone would have taken weeks.
So now that one style no longer lasts
for generations, it is not to be wondered
at that several may take place in one
man's lifetime and may be practiced by

one and the same man with a perfectly
free conscience. As a most illuminating
example of this, we have three portraits
of Vollard by Picasso. The subject is the
same in all three pictures, and although
each of them shows him older than the
previous one, they do demonstrate how
a totally different means of expression
may be used to render the same external
image.

As you have seen, the **way** you paint
may be determined by **what** you paint;
the converse may also be true. It is
equally possible for a work of art to
develop without the artist having had
to come to grips with the problem as
such. You will seldom be able to tell how
a work was created by looking at a
finished product, nor can you by any
means rely entirely on what you are told.
What an artist records in his correspondence and diaries reveals more of the man
than it does of the purely technical
aspects of creation or the real motive
behind it. Accordingly, I shall take the
ideas underlying three of my own pictures, and with their help try to indicate
a possible—but by no means the only—
route from individual impulse to actual
creation. At best, we can speak of hints
and parallels; there are no hard-and-fast
rules.

Let us assume you have learned the
craft of drawing and painting, and that
you set out to portray an inviting motif;
a certain amount of artistic rearrange-
ment is inevitable, and it is far from
certain that your handiwork will have the
compression and finality of a true work
of art. You will learn nothing from the
artist of genius who occasionally brings
this off, however, because perfection is

inviolable and uninstructive. For this reason the designs I shall give are not completely worked out, as they would then express only a personal point of view and not be worth discussing. I would urge you rather, if you feel like trying your hand at any of the motifs, to work out your own solutions for them. The illustration on page 391 shows a design for a wall painting. It was inspired by a child's drawing, which may have conjured up some episode on a journey by its resemblance to a souvenir postcard. This by way of parenthesis. The real inspiration came from the drawing, because it showed such feeling for color and form. This, combined with the gaucherie of the representation, led me to simplify and reduce the data to the form of a mural drawing. It also meant dispensing entirely with the linear perspective which is "false" in any case, and giving the picture breadth and depth by graduating the dimensions and tone values.

The design is now ready to be transported into the mural technique, the easiest of which in this case would be a mural painting. The individual color areas could be hatched in lightly with pastel crayons, but not so as to shade into one another. Instead, local color should be laid on lightly, heavily, or more or less solidly to achieve an effect of modeling. To carry out the same design in sgraffito, you would need to restrict your colors very considerably, and the result would be more like a plaster intarsia. The simplest way to proceed would be to hollow the individual areas out of a top plaster laid on rather thicker than usual, as if doing a monochrome sgraffito. Next, use a trowel to spread the colored mortar over the hollows. There is no limit to the colors that might be used. Finally, the entire surface

Landscape in the Giant Mountains on an April morning. Pencil and watercolor (Compare illustration on page 179)

Evening in early spring in the Giant Mountains. Left above: first watercolor study. Left below: provisional version in alternating technique. Above: design for a new version in watercolor and tempera

should be treated like sgraffito plaster. The loveliest effect is obtained if—as in the design—the light background color forms a kind of linear grid.

The best way to carry out this design in mosaic form would be to assemble it out of large fragments. They should be fitted in compactly and precisely so that interrelated color areas are matched, and where joins are visible they should be made to look like lines separating colors from one another in a drawing.

This design would also look well in batik. Four shades would suffice, and the darkest tone should consist of all the colors painted one over the other.

What this means is that a single design can be realized in several different ways, and that the clearer the underlying graphic concept, the richer and more challenging these potentialities will be.

The second motif depicts an evening in early spring in the foothills of the Giant Mountains in Czechoslovakia. It is one of a series of twelve pictures in which I endeavored to catch the culminating points of this landscape through the four seasons. The mainspring for this project lay in more than 20 years spent in these parts, and in the crucial experiences which of necessity accompany one's development from childhood to maturity. The landscape was always there in the background, and in the end it became more firmly fixed in my memory than the people or the material events concerned. When one lacks either the desire or the ability to sublimate spiritual states, events, and emotions by means of abstract expression, one finds them best expressed in the form of landscape.

At the same time I wanted to set down a permanent record of the face of this landscape, and this meant anything but a pleasant view in bright sunshine. Seen like that, the scene was much like any other in many parts of the central European uplands, and this is how it was invariably painted by those who hoped to make a profit out of the many tourists on holiday there. For me, the emphasis lay elsewhere: on the haze-shrouded day, veiled in mist, the time before sunrise in late October when the trees stand skeletal and gaunt and the pond is a smooth mirror; on afternoons in August with a storm brewing over the naked hill forest; the mornings in April, damp with rain; the quiet twilight that follows a snowstorm; on midday in June when a vapor hangs over the dusty rye fields, and so many more.

After I had been drawing for many years and produced more than a thousand sketches and studies without anything particular in mind, these were my abiding impressions. I started making deliberate studies and from them pictures which were wholly dictated by the actual scenes. At the same time this brought into play much of the technical knowledge and experience I had acquired. For instance, the color effects were unattainable except by the use of homemade paints. Many years later, seen from afar, both in the physical and intellectual sense, my attitude to it all changed. Then what I wanted to do was to leave only essential shapes and colors, and to omit entirely all the secondary emotional factors which had at one time been all too acutely bound up with my memories. Compare the first study with the "final" picture which followed, and with the design for the later **Evening in Early Spring** picture, and you will appreciate the evolution I have traced and which took the same course in all twelve pictures. If my main concern hitherto was with **what** to paint, now, while keeping to the plan, I was more concerned with **how** to paint. In **Evening in Early Spring** I sought to banish the dull brown tone entirely to make way for a cooler, more silvery rendering of the atmosphere. This was achieved by hatching lightly over a light ground with bright outlines and cool, gentle colors. My idea was to convey the feeling of twilight by keeping everything luminous, rather than by actually showing it darker. One color only, the most intense and significant of the whole picture, was to show up boldly, and that was the yellowish green of the sky. I did not attach undue importance to the formal aspect of the multiplicity of branches, placing more emphasis on the curving lines and shapes. The plain, too, had to be stressed, giving an impression after a while of space and depth.

The intermediate stage had been a lean tempera painting on a white ground with bright grayish blue tones, but for the final version mixed technique was to be used. Naturally, neither the underpainting nor the imprimatura was to be laid on in continuous areas, but in little, short brush strokes. This was done to achieve the wavering light of dusk. There is not a sharp contour anywhere in the picture, which keeps its open, light, silvery look. The painting itself is made up chiefly of thin glazes, and the brush technique employed makes this into a well-knit fabric. This is a style which allows for the subtlest shades, the most brilliant light, as well as great depth of color without the dead weight of a—to my mind—primitively thick application of paint. The support used was not too

coarse a canvas, whose natural fabric showed through the primer.

As for the third picture, this originated in a commission I was once given to do a painting of an operation. I was to make a point of doing a lifelike portrait of the operating surgeon. The whole setting was quite unfamiliar to me, so I started by doing a series of sketches and studies of other operations, to get the feel of the situation. When I first went in to look on, dressed as a doctor, I received one surprise after another. Apart from the fact that the scene was unexpectedly picturesque, I had to revise my conception of what one might call the spirit of the place. It is neither as solemn nor deadly serious as I had imagined it from what I had seen in books or films. The proceedings were matter of fact and prosaic, the atmosphere was brisk, and only after work had begun did it change to one of extreme concentration for those concerned, dictated by the need for

Study from the operating theater, watercolor

Left above: Study for the picture sketched above right. Left below: Study from the operating theater

speed. I found I quite forgot the patient, who was completely covered up. The scene of the operation might have been prepared with the aesthetic effect in mind. As a whole it had nothing of the grisly quality we associate with bleeding from a wound or even the slightest accident.

I came to the conclusion that the whole composition was made up of relatively simple shapes, but that a certain tedium in the posture of the figures was a real problem. Lighting was another matter. In the University Clinic, where I was working, the operating theaters were alll green tiled, while the overalls, caps and masks all looked a faded green, as did the cloth and covers. On the other hand, the main lamp cast a very warm light over people's faces, making them look an unreal tomato red, while the clothes looked ochre and pink, with occasional cobalt blue shadows. The light which, despite all attempts at concentration, was very scattered, combined its complementary color, green, to produce fluffy, palpable, shapes, which seemed literally to smoke with toil, heat, and smell. The contours were very vague in places. Elusive flickering lights and self-shadows everywhere. The mainstay of the composition must be the distribution of very colorful

The Painting

light and the green, which, while homogeneous, contained diverse modulations.

I was lucky in that the scene portrayed in the final picture was one which could well be transferred to canvas without substantial alteration. Unfortunately, the operation (plastic surgery of the hand) did not last long, so that all I could do was to indicate the most important colors for the main figures. Altogether, however, the studies provided a satisfactory basis for the final version. I planned to do it in **alla prima** oil paint on fairly coarse canvas, with a thin layer of underpaint in broad areas on a terre verte tinted ground, the light patches laid thickly in titanium white or white lead, with a little Indian red for added emphasis. Over this coarse underpainting went a cobalt blue semi-glaze in short brush strokes for the shadows, and the reddish parts of the light in pale cadmium red, then last of all the elaboration of all the colors and details.

I hope that what I have said about the genesis and realization of these three pictures has shown that it is fruitless to wait for, or even to chase after, inspiration: methodical work, however, will always bring you nearer to your goal,

and is less of a disappointment if success does not come immediately. Whatever point you reach may serve as a springboard for a new start made in the light of all the experience gained. For this reason, I should also like to advise you never to throw your work away because it seems to have gone wrong. You will often discover later on that from other points of view it is a success.

Possibly you, too, once expressed your feeling of helplessness in the face of your desire to paint or draw, in the one sentence: "I cannot draw a straight line." You now know that the reason you shied away from artistic creation was that you misunderstood it entirely, and that everyone can acquire enough technique to produce a presentable picture.

To turn this into a real work of art, no very great technical skill is needed. But what you must have is a real desire to succeed and a recognition of your particular artistic bent. Everyone has some ability. The best way to find out where your talent for drawing and painting lies is by working hard in the relevant media. The technique which really suits you will be your key to stirring achievement.

Nulla dies sine linea!

Line Perspective, see Perspective
   (Graphic)
Linen, see Canvas
Linoleum Cut 239, 240*
Linseed Oil 224, 291, 299 ff.
Lion 149*
Lithographic Ink 238
Lithography 237 f., 238*
Local Color 318
Lumps (in Linen) 283

M

Magnesia 303, 351
Maple 165, 167*
Marble Dust 75, 279
Marc 193, 361 ff., 362*
Martagon 170*
Marten-Hair Brush 336, 336*
Mastic **296 f.**, 316, 321, 366, 297*
Maulpertsch 347*
Meander 26, 25*
Metal (Ground) 287
Mezzotint 244
Michelangelo 361, 346*
Mieris, von, the Elder 67*
Mildew 368, 379 f.
Milk 73, 295, 326
Mineral Painting, see Silica Painting
Mixed Technique 306, 330, **334 ff.**, 338,
   397, 337*, 394*
Mona Lisa 70
Monet 22, 179, 304, 384, 388, 15*
Monkey 149 f., 152, 153*, 156*
Monotype 246
Monumentality 392 f., 387*
Mortar **213-215**, 347 f.
Mosaic 16, 58, 103, 212, **223-229**, 226*,
   227*, 231*
Mount 370
Mounting (Canvas, Paper) 85, 285 ff.,
   84*, 285*
Mouth 70, 127, 127*
Movement 27 ff., 63 f., 68 f., 137, 364,
   69*, 362*

Movements of Animals 148 ff., 159
Mulberry-Leaf Paper 83
Munch 237*
Mural 344, **346-352**, 209*, 300*, 391*
Muscles (Animal) 147, 150 f., 154, 158,
   161, 151*
Muscles (Human) **107 ff.**, 113, 120, 122,
   124 ff., 126 fl., 132, 135, 109*, 121*,
   123*, 131*, 134*, 136*

N

Natural Stone 288
Naturalism, Naturalistic 13, **18-21**, 29,
   56
Network of Squares **103 f.**, 210, 220,
   103*
Nude **137-142**, 137*, 138*, 139*, 140*,
   141*, 142*, 192*, 343*
Nut Oil 299

O

Oak 165, 169*
Objective World 29
Oil Colors 301, 304, 306, 379
Oil Ground 287
Oil Painting (Technique) 97, 289, 296,
   299, 300, 305, **315-322**, 324, 15*,
   16*, 199*, 300*, 317*, 319*, 320*,
   322*
Oil Painting (Treatment) 365 f.
Oil Tempera 292, 331
Oils 287, 289 f., 300 f., 331, 365
Opaque Color 97 f., 293, 323, 329 ff.
Opaque White 97 f., 102
Optical Illusion **35 ff.**, 254, 35*, 36*,
   254*, 255*
Ornament, Ornamental 25 f., 64, 161,
   163 f., 25*, 26*
Ostwald 344
O-W Emulsions, see Emulsions
Ox Gall 85, 293

Also by ANTHONY F. C. WALLACE

Religion: An Anthropological View   1966

Culture and Personality   1961

King of the Delawares: Teedyuscung, 1700–1763   1949

THE DEATH
AND REBIRTH
OF THE
SENECA

The history and culture of the great

Iroquois nation, their destruction

and demoralization, and their cultural

revival at the hands of the Indian visionary,

Handsome Lake

_____

THE DEATH
AND REBIRTH
OF THE
SENECA

Anthony F. C. Wallace

WITH THE ASSISTANCE OF SHEILA C. STEEN

Alfred A. Knopf · *New York*

1 9 7 0

THIS IS A BORZOI BOOK
PUBLISHED BY ALFRED A. KNOPF, INC.

Copyright © 1969 by Anthony F. C. Wallace

All rights reserved under International and Pan-American
Copyright Conventions. Published in the United States by
Alfred A. Knopf, Inc., New York, and simultaneously in Canada
by Random House of Canada Limited, Toronto. Distributed by
Random House, Inc., New York.

Library of Congress Catalog Card Number: 79-88754

Manufactured in the United States of America

First Edition

TO BETTY

PREFACE

THIS BOOK TELLS THE STORY OF THE LATE COLONIAL AND EARLY reservation history of the Seneca Indians, and of the prophet Handsome Lake, his visions, and the moral and religious revitalization of an American Indian society that he and his followers achieved in the years around 1800. It is not intended to convey in a formal manner my theoretical views on social movements, although the case of Handsome Lake originally led me to consider the subject in a comparative frame of reference. For my general writings on revitalization movements, and for studies of special aspects of the Handsome Lake religion, the reader is referred to the several books and papers listed in the bibliography. Nor does the book attempt to describe in close detail the Iroquois cultures. The interested reader may consult the works of Morgan, Speck, Fenton, Shimony, Lounsbury, and others listed in the bibliography for further ethnographic information.

Library and field research in preparation for the book were begun in 1951 and largely completed by 1956; writing and analysis have been done on and off during subsequent years. Thus the dates of reference for "recent" events on the Allegany Reservation are the early 1950's. Much of the reserve, however, is now gone, covered by the water behind Kinzua Dam; the people—and the religious center—have been moved to new locations. Several persons have been of great help in collecting materials and in achieving interpretation. In particular I want to express gratitude to Mr. Merle H. Deardorff, who gave freely of time, wisdom, and extensive files of notes and photostats, all of which have been invaluable both in the accumulation and in the understanding of data; to W. N. Fenton, C. E. Congdon, Oscar Nephew, and Paul A. W. Wallace, for illuminating discussion; to the Social

Science Research Council and the University of Pennsylvania for, respectively, a Faculty Research Fellowship (1952–3) and a research grant (1953), which permitted the collection of data and much of the writing; to Sheila C. Steen for loyal and creative research assistance; and to Josephine H. Dixon and Marilyn Crill for patient and careful secretarial work. To my wife Betty I extend thanks for typing, discussion, and for helpful encouragement. And to many unnamed Iroquois people go my gratitude for instruction and hospitality and my admiration for their creation—the religion of Handsome Lake.

ANTHONY F. C. WALLACE

Philadelphia, Pa.

July, 1967

CONTENTS

PART III / *The Renaissance of the Iroquois*

ILLUSTRATIONS

(following page 144)

CORNPLANTER, BY F. BARTOLI (*circa* 1796).

RED JACKET, AGED SEVENTY, BY ROBERT W. WEIR (1828).

JOSEPH BRANDT, BY GEORGE CATLIN, *from an original by E. Ames.*

HENRY ABEEL, BY CHARLES B. KING (1825).

THE CHIEF READ JARET, BY BARONESS HYDE DE NEUVILLE (1807).

CHARLES AND HENRY ABEEL (sons of Cornplanter), *from a photograph taken prior to 1868.*

PETER, A SENECA, BY BARONESS HYDE DE NEUVILLE (1807).

THE FAIR INDIAN OF THE BUFFALO TRIBE, BY BARONESS HYDE DE NEUVILLE (1808).

SENECA WOMAN AND CHILD, BY BARONESS HYDE DE NEUVILLE (1808).

AN INDIAN FAMILY (probably Oneida), BY BARONESS HYDE DE NEUVILLE (1807).

MARY, SQUAW OF ONEIDA TRIBE, BY BARONESS HYDE DE NEUVILLE (1807).

AN INDIAN AND HIS SQUAW, BY BARONESS HYDE DE NEUVILLE (1807).

SETTLER'S COTTAGE AT ANGELICA, NEW YORK, BY BARONESS HYDE DE NEUVILLE (1808).

Unfortunately, there is no known portrait that can be identified as that of Handsome Lake.

A Map of the Iroquois Country in the 18th and early 19th centuries and a map of the Seneca Reservations in 1797 appear on the two pages following.

(xiii)

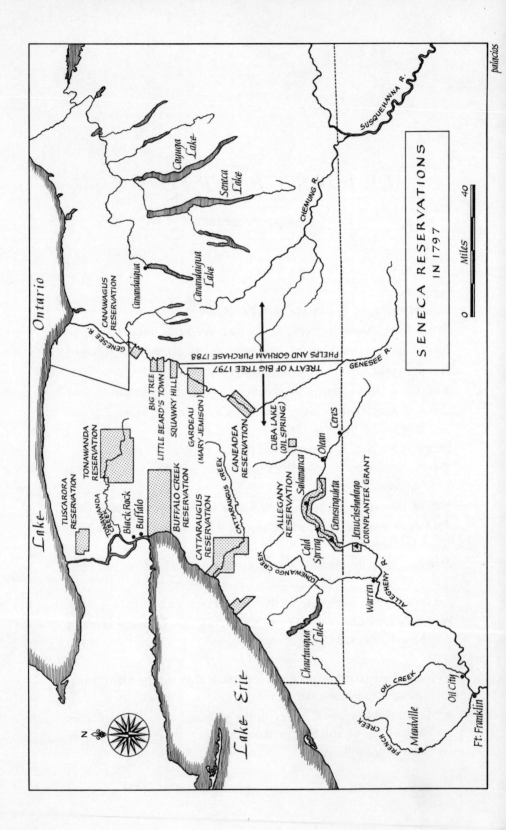

palacios

SENECA RESERVATIONS
IN 1797

Miles

0   40

Ontario Lake

Cayuga Lake

Seneca Lake

Canandaigua Lake

Canandaigua

CHEMUNG R.

SUSQUEHANNA R.

CANAWAGUS RESERVATION

GENESEE R.

PHELPS AND GORHAM PURCHASE 1788

TREATY OF BIG TREE 1797

GENESEE R.

BIG TREE

LITTLE BEARD'S TOWN

SQUAWKY HILL

GARDEAU (MARY JEMISON)

CANEADEA RESERVATION

CUBA LAKE (OIL SPRING)

Ceres

Olean

Salamanca

ALLEGANY RESERVATION

Genesinguhta

Jenuchshadago CORNPLANTER GRANT

TUSCARORA RESERVATION

TONAWANDA RESERVATION

TONAWANDA CREEK

Black Rock

Buffalo

BUFFALO CREEK RESERVATION

CATTARAUGUS CREEK

CATTARAUGUS RESERVATION

Cold Spring

CONEWANGO CREEK

ALLEGHENY R.

Warren

Chautauqua Lake

Lake Erie

OIL CREEK

Meadville

Oil City

Ft. Franklin

FRENCH CREEK

N

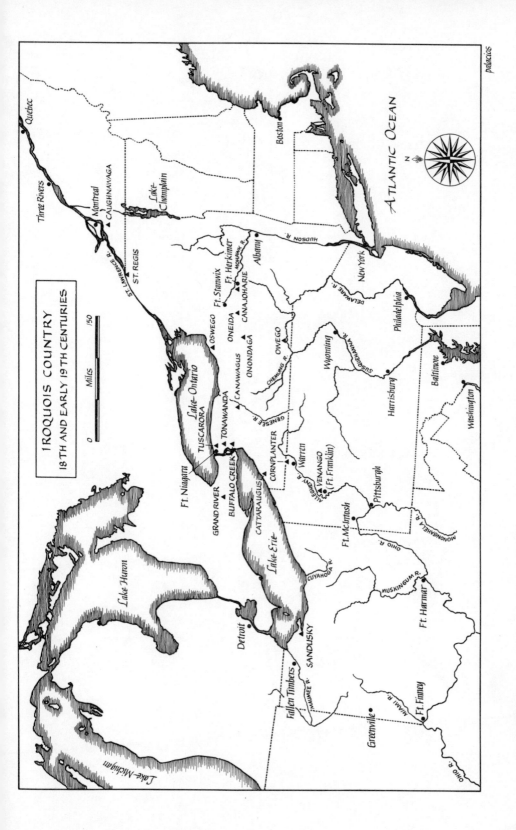

IROQUOIS COUNTRY
18TH AND EARLY 19TH CENTURIES

Miles
0   150

ATLANTIC OCEAN

N

Quebec

Three Rivers

Montreal
CAUGHNAWAGA

Lake Champlain

ST. LAWRENCE R.

ST. REGIS

Boston

Ft. Stanwix
Ft. Herkimer
Oswego
ONEIDA
CANAJOHARIE
ONONDAGA
CANAWAGUS
MOHAWK R.
Albany
HUDSON R.

New York

OWEGO
CHEMUNG R.
Wyoming
DELAWARE R.
SUSQUEHANNA R.

Philadelphia

GENESEE R.

Lake Ontario

TUSCARORA
TONAWANDA

Ft. Niagara

GRAND RIVER

BUFFALO CREEK

CORNPLANTER
Warren
VENANGO
(Ft. Franklin)
ALLEGHENY R.

Harrisburg

Baltimore

Washington

Pittsburgh

CATTARAUGUS

Lake Erie

Ft. McIntosh

MONONGAHELA R.

OHIO R.

CUYAHOGA R.

MUSKINGUM R.

Lake Huron

Detroit

SANDUSKY

Fallen Timbers

MAUMEE R.

Greenville

Ft. Harmar

Ft. Finney

MIAMI R.

OHIO R.

Lake Michigan

palacios

INTRODUCTION

THE RELIGION OF
HANDSOME LAKE TODAY

THE OLD WAY OF HANDSOME LAKE IS AN AMERICAN INDIAN
religion that is still practiced on Iroquois reservations in the
United States and Canada. It is not Christian, although it includes
some elements borrowed from Christianity; it is essentially an amalgam
of ancient tradition and the innovations of the Seneca prophet named
Handsome Lake. It was developed by several tribes of Iroquois who,
a century and a half ago, felt a need to lift themselves from defeat,
demoralization, and despair and to revitalize their communities. This
book tells the story of the origin of their religion: how the Iroquois
lived before catastrophe befell them; what the disaster was like; and
how Handsome Lake and his disciples designed for themselves and
their people a new way to live and brought about a renaissance of
Iroquois society.

· The Old Way of Handsome Lake ·

AMONG THE TWENTY THOUSAND or so Iroquois Indians living on the
several reservations in New York State, Quebec, and Ontario today,
there are perhaps five thousand followers of the Old Way of Handsome Lake.[1] It is impossible, however, to obtain an accurate census

of "Handsome Lake followers," or "longhouse people," or "the pagans," as they are variously called. The Handsome Lake religion does not demand that its communicants rigorously avoid all other denominational affiliations. Thus many "Handsome Lakers" attend church or mass at times, and at times the longhouse, deriving benefit from both, each in its proper season. Many Baptists, and Mormons, and Episcopalians, on occasion—particularly at the high festivals of New Year and Green Corn—drop in at the longhouse to listen gravely to the *Gaiwiio* (the "good word," the Code of Handsome Lake), to partake of strawberry juice and corn soup, and to smile gratefully at the antics of the False Faces soliciting tobacco. There is good in both, they say, in the Handsome Lake way and in the Christian way. Some of the Seneca prophet's followers even aver that Christ was one of the four angels who taught Handsome Lake the *Gaiwiio*, but doctrine is not settled on this point.

The Handsome Lake religion now, more than one hundred and fifty years after its conception, is embodied in an organization that has no formal name or address, as a Christian denomination might have, but that nevertheless functions in almost every way as a church. Its headquarters is on the Seneca Reservation at Tonawanda (near Buffalo, New York), where are kept the wampum belts of Handsome Lake himself—belts so sacred that, according to legend, no white man has ever seen them, so sacred that even the preachers may read them only once every two years on a sunny day when no fleck of cloud, even so big as a man's hand, can be seen in the sky. On each of the New York reservations (except Tuscarora, near Niagara Falls) there is a longhouse. The term "longhouse," used in its religious sense, includes the council house itself, where the Handsome Lake meetings (in addition to other community functions) are held; the general congregation of Handsome Lake followers; and the specific organization (including preachers and lay functionaries), which arranges the annual calendar of services. There are longhouses on the Allegany Reservation (near Salamanca, New York), on the Cattaraugus Reservation (near Gowanda), at Tonawanda (near Buffalo), at Onondaga (near Syracuse), at Oneida (on the Thames River in Ontario), at St. Regis (along the St. Lawrence River), at Grand River (near Brantford, Ontario), and at Caughnawaga (near Montreal). Handsome Lake himself did not design the organization that now carries on his work. He founded the religion; his followers organized its practice.

The Seneca Reservation on the Allegheny River, where Handsome Lake once lived, extends in a long, thin strip along the oxbow from the New York–Pennsylvania state line, east almost as far as Olean, and encompasses the city of Salamanca, whose white inhabitants lease their land from the Indians. It is about forty-two miles long and contains forty-two square miles. Driving through it in 1950, before the Kinzua Dam flooded much of the low-lying area, on a good macadam highway, one would see a scattering of old farmhouses, log cabins, and brightly painted prefabricated "ranch-style" bungalows with television antennas stretching skyward here and there to escape the mountain screen that rises on both sides of the river. At Onoville, Quaker Bridge, and Red House there are country stores, filling stations, and small clusters of houses. Many of the men divide their time between working for the Erie Railroad, which runs through the reserve, cultivating their gardens, and working around the house. The women are housewives; some of them serve as domestic servants, secretaries, and factory workers in Salamanca, Olean, or Jamestown. Many of the fields are growing up in weed and wood because farming, a century ago the economic mainstay of the people, is less profitable today than wage work. There are no real-estate taxes to pay. About eleven hundred Seneca people live on the reserve: white men in respect to their names, their manner of dress, and means of earning a living; Indians in their view of themselves as a minority group, separated from the surrounding world by the legal and economic arrangements that make up the reservation system, and identified with an Indian past. Great events in their history are not Columbus, and Plymouth Rock, and the Declaration of Independence. Rather, they remember, dimly and often not too accurately, the founding of the League of the Iroquois, the days of glory when an Iroquois hunter could walk safely from the Atlantic Ocean to the Miami River in Ohio, the dark days of Sullivan's Campaign, when their villages were burned, the disastrous treaties at Fort Stanwix and Big Tree and Buffalo Creek, the treaty at Canandaigua, which guaranteed their lands and which was overturned by Congress in order to build the dam, and the great revival led by Handsome Lake.

Thus, while to the casual eye these are only an American minority group, no darker in skin color than many southern European immigrants, and equipped (many of them) with television, cars, refrigerators, plumbing, central heating, and a high school or college education, the discerning eye sees a separate cultural world more ancient than memory.

The symbolic hub and pivot of this Seneca world is Cold Spring Longhouse: a one-story rectangular frame building, about fifty feet long and twenty wide, its long axis paralleling the road. It is of clapboard painted white, with a shingled gable roof, and it stands in a treeless field close to where Cold Spring Creek joins the Allegany River. Off to the side are an old log kitchen—said to be the remains of a much older longhouse that once stood near Carrollton, up the river—and a frame shed used as a dining room. The longhouse interior is sparsely furnished. At each end are two tiers of raised, grandstand-like benches, and two similar tiers stretch along the sides. Movable wooden benches, anciently painted and now almost bare, stand in front of the fixed seating tiers. These are arranged in various ways depending upon the use to which the longhouse is being put. In the center of the floor is a bench where drummers sit when there is dancing. Two iron stoves, one at each end, face each other; their stovepipes extend to the chimneys at the back walls. Six windows light the room, and two doors face the road: the one on the left, to the west, for the women; the one at the eastern end for the men. An invisible line separates the male and female halves of the longhouse, men and women entering separately by their proper doors and sitting apart. (But a newly married couple may be seen to separate as they enter and later on to sit touching one another across this sexual equator.) Special ritual equipment is kept in a loft, which can be reached by upending a bench and hoisting oneself from it through the trapdoor. In ground plan a longhouse looks like the drawing on the next page (the basic plan, with minor variations in the location of doors and windows and type of seating equipment, is to be found in all longhouses). This simple plan is little modified from aboriginal times, when instead of stoves there were firepits, and instead of chimneys a slot in the roof; when roof and walls were sheathed with elm bark, and there was no glass. As far back as the Seneca can remember, there has been a longhouse of one sort or another, where the people could assemble to discuss politics and war and peace or to worship the Great Spirit in thankful or penitent mood.

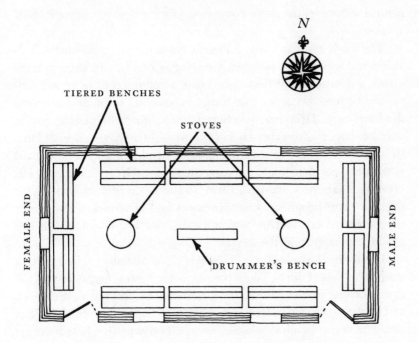

The heart of the Handsome Lake religion is the *Gaiwiio*, the "good word." This is the gospel—a gospel transmitted by word of mouth from preacher to preacher and memorized so that it can be chanted by a man standing in a longhouse filled with the noise of bustling people, slamming doors, and rattling stove grates, hour after hour, for the mornings of four days. Each preacher repeats a slightly different version, depending on which old man or woman he learned it from and on his own predilections and memory. Some of the preachers rattle off the *Gaiwiio* in a language so archaic that many of the words are meaningless to their own and their listeners' ears. Some tell the story of Handsome Lake's death—he was murdered by witchcraft—in awesome detail; others pass over it lightly out of consideration for the Onondaga tribe, on whose reservation he met his end as the victim of Onondaga witches. There is extant a verbatim translation of one preacher's version of the Code, edited by the anthropologist Arthur C. Parker and published by the New York State Museum. But this version has not supplanted the independent, parallel scriptures that have come down orally through other lines of speakers.[2]

The Code itself is many things: a narrative of Handsome Lake's vision and travels as a prophet, a catalogue of sins and their punishments, a description of heaven and hell, a definition of the good way of life, a prescription for the proper ceremonies to be performed in the longhouse. Drinking, witchcraft, theft, quarrelsomeness, gossip, wife-beating, adultery, abortion, jealousy—these things are evil. Husbands and wives are to love one another; children are to be treated with kindness; man must be reverent to the Great Spirit and His creation. Like the Christian's Bible, so the Code of Handsome Lake is history and prophecy, commandment and exhortation, and above all, a chart of conduct by which a man may live honorably in this world and happily in the next.

Handsome Lake followers hear this Code partially recited twice a year. This "short form," delivered by a local preacher, occupies the first morning of the Midwinter Ceremony in January or February and of the Green Corn Dance in August or September. In the fall of alternate years at each longhouse (except Tonawanda, where it occurs annually, and Sour Springs, which has an irregular schedule) the Code is recited in full by professional speakers at a religious "Six Nations Meeting." The full recitation occupies the mornings of four days. On the two former occasions the abbreviated Code has been grafted onto an ancient rite, but the Six Nations meetings are pure Handsome Lake and date from about 1845.

In October, 1951, a friend and I drove up from Philadelphia to see the "doings" at the Six Nations Meeting at Cold Spring Longhouse on the Allegany Reservation. We ate supper with an Indian family who were expecting us and had prepared a room in their comfortable old frame farmhouse. After supper we walked a couple of hundred yards to the longhouse to see what was going on. Visitors (the "comers") from the other reserves—Tonawanda, St. Regis, Caughnawaga, Cattaraugus, Onondaga, Grand River—were checking in. They had parked their cars in the field by the longhouse. As they entered, they were announced by the head of the reception committee and assigned a place to stay. (The delegates were asked their clan, and if they had not made other arrangements, a clan member was always ready to take them in.) Outside their end of the longhouse the women were running a food sale to raise money for the doings, which cost about five hundred dollars.

The first day of a Six Nations Meeting is called the handshaking. This is a formal reception for the visiting delegates. "There are no eats," as my informant said, "and only the faithful attend." The visiting delegates, after a few welcoming remarks by the head of the local reception committee, present their credentials—strings of wampum, consisting of half a dozen or so beads strung on a thong and attached to a notched stick, which identify the holder as the delegate from a particular longhouse. As each string is presented, the delegate in a long speech tenders the good wishes of each and every one of the congregation back home and details the composition of his party: the number of delegates, speakers, feather dancers, singers, and drummers. After all the strings are lined up on a bench, the hosts walk around the room, shaking hands with each of the twenty-five or thirty visitors. In the evening everyone, young and old, men and women, participates in social dances.

The next morning the real business of the meeting begins. The first part of the Code of Handsome Lake is recited by a guest preacher from another reservation. The preacher stands between the two fires in the longhouse. He is a middle-aged man, stocky, with a farmer's heavy hands and brown, lined face. Lank black hair straggles over his left eye. He is dressed in a baggy, threadbare, dark blue business suit with a blue workshirt and a brown string tie. On his feet, planted solidly and far apart on the pine flooring, are black, highly polished workshoes. As he speaks, his eyes are half closed and his head is tilted back, and he holds cradled before him in both hands a thick rope of white wampum strings. Behind him on a bench sits his assistant, holding the brown deerskin bag to which the wampum, carefully wrapped in a white handkerchief, will be returned when the preacher finishes speaking. The congregation are seated around the four sides of the longhouse: the women on his right, the men on his left. While he speaks, the men's heads are bare; but there is no ban against tobacco, and most of the men are chewing. Tin cans are scattered about on the floor as spittoons, and old-timers with expert eye use the hot shelf of the stove. From time to time men and women step outside to chat, to smoke, to visit the outhouses. Children are running in and out all the while, banging the doors. There is the constant rustle of feet, of whispers, of blue jeans sliding along wooden benches. A baby gurgles and is given the bottle. A man ticks reflectively on an "I Like Ike" button in his lapel. One of the deacons stamps over to the stove and rattles the grate. Someone begins to cough and cannot stop coughing and has to go out. But the speaker chants on, hour after hour, with eyes half closed, standing alone in the middle of the longhouse, holding in his hands before him the big shock of Handsome Lake wampum strings that serve as his credentials. The noise does not bother him, for it is no sign of irreverence. Now and then he stops to drink from the tin dipper of water his assistant fetches him. He finishes before noon, which is the meridian between sacred and profane time.

The first morning's recital tells the story of the death and rebirth of Handsome Lake. The Code has drifted, here and there, a little way off from the true relation. In one hundred and fifty years, tradition has accumulated small errors and illusions, and different preachers recite different versions. The preacher does not try to find and search through the old, mildewed diaries and letters of the Quaker missionaries or to compare differing versions of the tale in order to tease out the bare bones of history. "The beginning was in Yaikni [the lunar month in which the strawberries ripen], early in the moon, in the year 1800," he intones, and it does not matter that the year actually was 1799. For, in truth, it happened substantially as it is told: The early documents, the diary notations by one Quaker, the statements dictated by Handsome Lake himself, confirm most of the contents of the Code. The preacher repeats what old men remembered their prophet having said to them; the sayings, hoarded like jewels in the memory, have been only a little polished as they passed from hand to hand. Dozens of times have the listeners heard the same Code, delivered now by one, and now by another, of the many Handsome Lake preachers. Each one says it a little differently, but the substance is always the same, for the Seneca have cultivated, for hundreds of years, the techniques of verbal memory. An officially recognized speaker must have an almost phonographic memory: an ability to repeat, with proper inflection and emphasis, not only the sense, but even the exact words of treaties, of council decisions, of ambassadors— and of prophets. And so an aspiring preacher may, under the guidance of ambition, close his eyes and achieve almost total recall of the mumbled words of an old man reciting the Code by the fire, heard on winter evenings in his youth, forty years before. The speaker holds the *Gaiwiio* in his memory entire and plays it off for the people. In this way, even without benefit of written record, something approaching an imprint is handed down. One can even identify the "edition" of a particular speaker and trace it back through previous holders to the original disciple. This preacher is speaking from the "Blacksnake Edition," the version basically derived from Handsome Lake's nephew Blacksnake, who preached at Cold Spring on the Allegany Reservation and taught what he knew of the prophet's life and words to Owen Blacksnake, who taught it to Henry Stevens, who taught it to Edward Cornplanter, who taught it to the man now speaking.

After the *Gaiwiio* has been spoken, the Great Feather Dance begins. Two men straddle a bench in the middle of the floor where the preacher had been standing and hammer out the tempo on the bench with large turtle-shell rattles. The bench itself has been pounded by the sharp edges of turtle rattles for years; the wood is split and battered, and a ragged trough is hollowed out; soon it will need to be patched. The two men who lead the dance, which honors the Great Spirit, are dressed in elaborate, colorful Plains Indian headdresses, beaded shirts, trousers, and moccasins. They stomp and twirl, prance and rear and spin, while their followers—who include some of the most important men and women in the community—usually just shuffle.

After the Great Feather Dance everyone eats in the cookhouse dining room, where long tables and chairs borrowed from an undertaker have been set up with regular tablecloths, knives, forks, spoons, and china. The meal is substantial: salt pork, boiled potatoes, cold beets, cole slaw, applesauce, white pound cake, and green tea. It is paid for by the receiving longhouse, which for the last six months has been raising the money at cake-and-canned-goods sales, raffles, teas, and other "doings" where contributed items are sold.

In the afternoon there are two orders of business: the "interpretation" of portions of the text of the morning by various visitors who are responsible for the sacred part of the services, and "confession." In preparation for the confession two benches are arranged in front of the stoves, one for the women and one for the men. On this first day the visitors confess the local longhouse officials, first the three men, and then about six women.

This public confession is not a perfunctory matter, nor is it an ecstatic, "holy roller" kind of thing.[3] Each man begins confessing loudly, almost defiantly; then his voice subsides until it is almost inaudible; and then after a deep, shuddering breath he starts again. It is obvious that the participants are deeply moved. Cheek muscles twitch; sighs are heavy, spasmodic. As they speak they wheeze, they cough, they rub their eyes. Tremors course through the arms and legs of one man; he shivers as if with cold. They have publicly confessed their sins: one drunkenness; another quarreling with his wife; a third, the least upset, apparently, merely announces that he is sorry for the evil things he has done and is resolved to do them no more. They sit down, looking sheepish and relieved.

The women confess—most of them—more demurely, simply repeating the formula of admitting sin without specification, and repentance, and resolution to sin no more. One woman, however, is in the grip of a severe struggle. She waits until the longhouse matrons have all confessed and then climbs down from the spectators' gallery and sits with shoulders bowed on the confessional bench. She is silent for perhaps ten minutes, apparently unable to talk. She is a stolid-looking woman, but her face is turgid, almost blue in color. She looks at the floor, her face twitches, and she seems deeply depressed. When at last she takes hold of the strings of white wampum handed to her by the confessor, her whole body quivers. She speaks slowly, almost inaudibly, while her fingers stroke and caress the wampum as if it were her sole support. She confesses that she left the longhouse to become a Catholic; now she repents and wants to return to the longhouse. Tears roll down her cheeks; from time to time she dabs at her eyes with a handkerchief. The spectators listen very quietly, almost as if so much emotion were embarrassing to watch. After she stops speaking, the confessor, who had been standing in front of her, leaves and goes to the visitors' benches. She sits down trembling. A preacher from another reserve gets up and stands in front of her and harangues her for ten minutes. She slumps exhausted on the bench, her shoulders sagging. Then all the officials, local and visiting, and many of the congregation come up to shake hands with her. She goes back to her seat; two more preachers speak, and the meeting ends for the afternoon.

In the evening there are traditional social dances, consisting of the usual shuffling line winding around the singers' bench, always counterclockwise. There is a good crowd for this, and the mood is lively and jovial.

The remaining three days of the Six Nations Meeting follow the same pattern: the preaching of the *Gaiwiio* in the morning, sermons on the text, confessions and exhortations in the afternoon, social dances in the evening. During the morning *Gaiwiio*, on the second, third, and fourth days, strawberry juice in a bucket is handed around to the congregation and drunk from a dipper. There are several current explanations for the serving of the strawberry juice. Some say it is because the prophet's first revelation occurred at the time when the strawberries were ripe. Others say it is because there is a spring in heaven from which strawberry juice constantly bubbles forth. It is just a form of "blessing" on the people, according to a third view.

But the true reason is deeper than all these. Strawberries have been since ancient times, before the coming of white men, a special plant among the Seneca. The three angels first came to Handsome Lake during "the month of strawberries." In their first message they instructed Handsome Lake to call a council of the people, at which he was to tell them of his vision; and those who assembled to hear him the first time were to eat dried strawberries. This was shortly after the strawberries had ripened. The council was held, and the strawberries were eaten; and according to the story as it is told in the *Gaiwiio* today, every spring since that time there has been a Strawberry Festival, when the juice of the berry is drunk by old and young, and the Creator and His spirit-forces are thanked for the first fruits of the year and implored to allow all growing things to reach fruition. Whether or not Handsome Lake originated the Strawberry Festival, the sacred quality of strawberries is certainly older than Handsome Lake. The earliest of the wild strawberries are traditionally believed to have medicinal value and are searched out and devoured. Strawberries are said to sprout along the road to heaven, and a person who has come through a severe sickness will say, "I almost ate strawberries." In all probability, the fact that Handsome Lake's angels spoke to him of strawberries reflects the influence of the strawberry season on the content of his dream, and his subsequent endorsement of the Strawberry Festival probably emphasized a custom already old.

On the morning of the fourth and final day, the preacher completes his recitation of the *Gaiwiio*. When he comes to the part describing Handsome Lake's final agony and death, faces flush, and a few women weep and men dab their noses with handkerchiefs as the preacher sits down. Slowly and reverently the preacher's assistant folds the wampum and places it in the deerskin pouch. Men get up and stamp out. The Great Feather dancers peer shyly through the door. Someone comes up and shakes the preacher's hand. Two singers move a bench into the middle between the stoves. In the afternoon, after the last of the confessions, the "comers" turn the meeting back to the local hosts, and the chief of the Faithkeepers delivers a speech summarizing the doings. In the evening the last social dance is held; this is called "shoving off the canoes." And on the next day the comers depart, on their way to another longhouse, where the same ritual will be held.

Thus it is ended until the next time.

The doings of a longhouse are under the management and direction of four persons: a man and a woman from each of the two moieties, or "sides." These are called the Headmen and Headwomen. They are responsible for setting the times of ceremonies; for appointing persons to perform certain tasks such as preaching, managing the evening social dances, serving food, and carrying messages; and for arranging board and lodging for visitors. They function as a committee, and during a meeting one may frequently see one of them get up and cross the floor to hold a whispered conference with another. They combine the roles of the board of trustees and the minister, in his purely business administrative capacity, of a Protestant church. They are not usually civil chiefs or clan matrons; the religious longhouse organization is distinct and separate, in principle, from the political organization.

The terms "clan" and "sides" require some definition before further use. The population of many American Indian tribes is divided into anywhere from three or four to twenty-odd groupings which are technically called "sibs." The Seneca refer to them as "clans" in English. All the members of a clan are supposed, by tradition, to be descended from a common ancestor, even if available genealogical records cannot show a connection. But no one among the Seneca is very much concerned about the fancy of common ancestry. Clans almost always have animal names like Wolf, Bear, Heron, Sturgeon, Eagle. Among the Seneca there are eight clans: Wolf, Bear, Beaver, Turtle, Hawk, Snipe, Deer, and Heron. The newborn infant is automatically a member of his mother's clan unless he is "borrowed" or "adopted" by another in a formal ceremony. Men and women of the same clan ought not to marry, and still rarely do. Clan members are expected to maintain a generally friendly attitude toward one another, as if they were all members of one big and more or less happy family. When he is traveling, a Seneca may look first for lodging or food to other clansmen on a strange reservation where he has no particular friends. The clan, where the old order of chieftainships is maintained, is represented in national and confederate councils by its own chiefs, who are nominated by the clan matron, its oldest and most venerable woman.

Among the Seneca, the clans are classified into two "sides," or in technical jargon "moieties": Wolf, Bear, Beaver, and Turtle on one side, and Deer, Hawk, Snipe, and Heron on the other. The sides are not named; nevertheless they are extremely important in the structure of many ceremonies, for it is customary on many ritual occasions for one side to "give" the ceremony to another. The theme of reciprocal benefices between the two sides threads through all Seneca ritual arrangements. The Handsome Lake preacher and his assistant (the man who sits behind him on the bench holding the wampum, ready with a glass of water, available to prompt him if his memory fails) must be from opposite sides. The two sides literally sit on opposite sides of the longhouse on some reservations. At condolence ceremonies the bereaved moiety is condoled by the other side. Games like lacrosse and the Sacred Bowl Game may be played with moieties contesting. Whatever its origin, the moiety principle now provides a ready tool for the organization of reciprocal behavior on almost any ritual occasion.

Serving under the direction of the Headmen and Headwomen are the Faithkeepers. These men and women serve as the deacons of the longhouse: they fetch and carry, cook, serve at table, contribute money and labor, and generally perform lay services essential to the practice of ritual. Theoretically, the Faithkeepers should include a man and a woman from each clan, but there are usually some positions vacant. These assistants are the nucleus of the congregation, the most persistent in attendance, the most dutiful in confession, the most faithful participants in dancing, singing, and game playing.

The Headmen and Headwomen, and the male and female Faithkeepers, may also call upon persons who have no formal status in the longhouse organization to do minor jobs like waiting on table, lending equipment, drumming or singing, and dressing up as False Face dancers. The performance of these tasks merges gently into devout participation in the ritual itself, and in this sense every participant comes under the direction of those officials who are responsible for the proper conduct of this or that part of the ceremony.

The preachers—always men—have relatively little administrative responsibility. In this their role is very different from that of the priest or minister in a Christian church. The Handsome Lake preacher, a "holder of the *Gaiwiio*," has no other responsibility than to know the "good word" and to preach it effectively when he is called upon. Such men hold themselves somehow apart; they often strike the observer as a bit temperamental, tending to be a little vain of their knowledge, jealous of other preachers, somewhat patronizing in manner. They are the stars of the longhouse. Every longhouse has a string of these preachers, usually three or four, each of whom may know a slightly different version of the Code, varying according to the identity of the earlier preacher from whom he learned it, and to idiosyncrasies of memory, interpretation, and emphasis. Some of these men preach only before their own congregation; others have recited their version before a council of preachers at Tonawanda and are officially authorized to preach at other longhouses during Six Nations Meetings or on special invitation. The personal lives (including scandal) of these preachers, their manner of delivery, the peculiarities of their versions of the Code, are constant topics of discussion and comparison among the faithful. Since preachers are qualified by knowledge of the Code and not by purity of past—or even present—conduct, a famous preacher lives in a glare of sensational gossip. But it is also noteworthy that sometimes, by report at least, weak and wavering men who possessed a knowledge of the Code and were appointed preachers have through their identification with this role of great responsibility become transformed personalities, putting away such weaknesses as drunkenness, extreme shyness, or lecherousness to stand before the people as new men. The wampum of Handsome Lake does not rest lightly in a preacher's hands.

In addition to the organization of the local longhouse, there is an association of all the longhouses in a united religious body whose "head" is the longhouse "down below" at Tonawanda. Here are kept the wampum strings that Handsome Lake himself held as he preached; here the best preachers are qualified for interlonghouse speaking; and here, every fall, in September or October, delegates from each of the other ten longhouses (Cold Spring, Cattaraugus, Sour Springs, Lower Cayuga, St. Regis, Caughnawaga, Onondaga, Oneida, Grand River Onondaga, and Grand River Seneca) assemble to arrange that fall's itinerary of Six Nations meetings. Starting each time with a meeting at Tonawanda, the chosen delegates, led by an Onondaga master of ceremonies, spend a month or more on the road, visiting five long-houses where a Six Nations Meeting is held. Thus, in theory at least, each longhouse except Tonawanda has a meeting every other year; Tonawanda has one every year. And by the same token, every other year a delegation from each longhouse is supposed to take to the road and make the circuit of the others.

The annual calendar of the Old Way, however, includes much more than Six Nations meetings. In each longhouse there is also a round of much older ceremonies, long antedating Handsome Lake, which have been continued with only minor modification. Most of them are still performed in substantially the same manner as they were in pre-Columbian times. This cycle begins with the great festival of Midwinter, in January or February, five days after the first new moon following the zenith of the Pleiades. Next comes, by tradition, the Thanks-to-the-Maple, in early spring, when the sap rises and the maple sugar is running. In May or June, at corn-planting time, the seeds of garden vegetables are blessed, "our Grandfathers the Thun-ders" are asked to water the crops, and "our Elder Brother the Sun" is begged to be careful not to burn the young plants. June is the time of the Strawberry Festival, the first fruits ceremony. Late in August or September the second great festival is held: the Green Corn Dance, which rivals the Midwinter Festival in length and solemnity. And later in the fall, when the corn is dried and put away and the nation is pre-paring for winter, the cycle closes with a Thanksgiving Ceremony, which renders thanks to the Creator for the harvest and bids the corn rest for the winter while the people hunt.

These ancient pagan festivals, revolving around the universal themes of birth and death, love and hate, food and hunger, health and disease, were old when Handsome Lake was born. In their embrace he found solace, and theirs is the Old Way that his "new religion" recommends to the faithful. There is matter enough in them to give meaning to life. The drums beat in high, quick pitch; the dancers twirl and stamp the floor; the masked men cavort about the fire, sifting hot coals through their hands as if they were playing with cool dust; and the ancient words drone on, words about the deepest human hopes, longings, fears, and pain, words spoken by those spirit-forces that men may see in dreams, the elder brothers and fathers and grandfathers, even up to the Creator Himself....

Let us now see how it all began, this new religion, which in itself was not all new, and which now is called the Old Way of Handsome Lake.

I

THE HEYDAY
OF THE
IROQUOIS

2

THE SENECA NATION
OF INDIANS

THE WORLD IN WHICH HANDSOME LAKE GREW TO MANHOOD, AND IN which he took his place as an active hunter and warrior, was the world of an unvanquished Indian nation: the Seneca, the most populous and the most powerful of the confederated Iroquois tribes. They numbered about four thousand souls, and their tribal territory extended from the upper waters of the Allegheny and the Susquehanna rivers, on the south, to Lake Ontario, on the north. The western marches of the Seneca territory were the shores of Lake Erie. On the east, beyond Seneca Lake, were the Cayuga people. The other Iroquois tribes—Onondaga, Oneida (and Tuscarora), and Mohawk—lay successively eastward almost to the Hudson River. The whole area occupied by the Iroquoian confederacy between the Hudson River and Lake Erie was compared by the Iroquois themselves to a longhouse compartmented by tribes; and in this longhouse the Seneca were "the keepers of the western door." They were guardians of that portal from which Iroquois warriors traditionally issued to attack the western and southern nations, through which Iroquois hunters passed to exploit the conquered lands along the Allegheny and Ohio, and on which other nations, in friendship or in war, must knock before entering the home country of the confederacy. Their warriors ranged from Hudson's Bay to the mountains of the Carolinas, and from the

Atlantic to the Mississippi, fighting against members of alien tribes and, on occasion, against the French and the English; their chiefs and orators sat in council, year after year, with Europeans in the colonial capitals, working out a *modus vivendi* with the invaders. To be a Seneca was to be a member of one of the most feared, most courted, and most respected Indian tribes in North America.

· *Villagers, Warriors, and Statesmen* ·

A SENECA VILLAGE in the eighteenth century was a few dozen houses scattered in a meadow. No plan of streets or central square defined a neat settlement pattern. The older men remembered days when towns were built between the forks of streams, protected by moats and palisades, and the dwellings within regularly spaced. But these fortified towns were no longer made, partly because of their earlier vulnerability to artillery and partly because times had become more peaceful anyway after the close of the fifty-odd years of war between 1649 and 1701. Now a village was simply an area within which individual families and kin groups built or abandoned their cabins at will; such focus as the area had for its several hundred inhabitants was provided by the council house (itself merely an enlarged dwelling), where the religious and political affairs of the community were transacted. Year by year the size of a village changed, depending on wars and rumors of war, the shifts of the fur trade, private feuds and family quarrels, the reputation of chiefs, the condition of the soil for corn culture, and the nearness of water and firewood. The same village might, over a hundred years' time, meander over a settlement area ten or fifteen miles square, increasing and decreasing in size, sometimes splitting up into several little settlements and sometimes coalescing into one, and even acquiring (and dropping) new names in addition to the generic name, which usually endured.

The traditional Iroquois dwelling unit was called a longhouse. It was a dark, noisy, smoke-filled family barracks; a rectangular, gable-roofed structure anywhere from fifty to seventy-five feet in length, constructed of sheets of elm bark lashed on stout poles, housing up to fifty or sixty people. The roof was slotted (sometimes with a sliding panel for rainy days) to let out some of the smoke that eddied about the ceiling. There was only one entrance, sometimes fitted with

a wooden or bark door on wooden hinges, and sometimes merely cur-
tained by a bearskin robe. Entering, one gazed in the half-light down
a long, broad corridor or alleyway, in the center of which, every
twelve or fifteen feet, smoldered a small fire. On opposite sides of each
fire, facing one another, were double-decker bunks, six feet wide and
about twelve feet long. An entire family—mother, father, children,
and various other relatives—might occupy one or two of these com-
partments. They slept on soft furs in the lower bunks. Guns, masks,
moccasins, clothing, cosmetic paint, wampum, knives, hatchet, food,
and the rest of a Seneca family's paraphernalia were slung on the walls
and on the upper bunk. Kettles, braided corn, and other suspendable
items hung from the joists, which also supported pots over the fire.
Each family had about as much room for permanent quarters as might
be needed for all of them to lie down and sleep, cook their meals, and
stow their gear. Privacy was not easily secured because other families
lived in the longhouse; people were always coming and going, and the
fires glowed all night. In cold or wet weather or when the snow lay
two or three feet deep outside, doors and roof vents had to be closed,
and the longhouses became intolerably stuffy—acrid with smoke and
the reeking odors of leftover food and sweating flesh. Eyes burned
and throats choked. But the people were nonetheless tolerably warm,
dry, and (so it is said) cheerful.

The inhabitants of a longhouse were usually kinfolk. A multifamily
longhouse was, theoretically, the residence of a maternal lineage: an
old woman and her female descendants, together with unmarried sons,
and the husbands and children of her married daughters. The totem
animal of the clan to which the lineage belonged—Deer, Bear, Wolf,
Snipe, or whatever it might be—was carved above the door and
painted red. In this way directions were easier to give, and the stranger
knew where to seek hospitality or aid. But often—especially in the
middle of the eighteenth century—individual families chose to live by
themselves in smaller cabins, only eighteen by twenty feet or so in
size, with just one fire. As time went on, the old longhouses disinte-
grated and were abandoned, and by the middle of the century the
Iroquois were making their houses of logs.

Around and among the houses lay the cornfields. Corn was a main
food. Dried and pounded into meal and then boiled into a hot mush,
baked into dumplings, or cooked in whole kernels together with beans
and squash and pieces of meat in the thick soups that always hung in

kettles over the fires, it kept the people fed. In season, meats, fresh fruits, herb teas, fried grasshoppers, and other delicacies added spice and flavor to the diet. But the Iroquois were a cornfed people. They consumed corn when it was fresh and stored it underground for the lean winter months. The Seneca nation alone raised as much as a million bushels of corn each year; the cornfields around a large village might stretch for miles, and even scattered clearings in the woods were cultivated. Squash, beans, and tobacco were raised in quantity, too. Domesticated animals were few, even after the middle of the century: some pigs, a few chickens, not many horses or cattle. The responsibility for carrying on this extensive agricultural establishment rested almost entirely on the women. Armed with crude wooden hoes and digging-sticks, they swarmed over the fields in gay, chattering work bees, proceeding from field to field to hoe, to plant, to weed, and to harvest. An individual woman might, if she wished, "own" a patch of corn, or an apple or peach orchard, but there was little reason for insisting on private tenure: the work was more happily done communally, and in the absence of a regular market, a surplus was of little personal advantage, especially if the winter were hard and other families needed corn. In such circumstances hoarding led only to hard feelings and strained relations as well as the possibility of future difficulty in getting corn for oneself and one's family. All land was national land; an individual could occupy and use a portion of it and maintain as much privacy in the tenure as he wished, but this usufruct title reverted to the nation when the land was abandoned. There was little reason to bother about individual ownership of real estate anyway: there was plenty of land. Economic security for both men and women lay in a proper recognition of one's obligation to family, clan, community, and nation, and in efficient and cooperative performance on team activities, such as working bees, war parties, and diplomatic missions.

If the clearing with its cornfields bounded the world of women, the forest was the realm of men. Most of the men hunted extensively, not only for deer, elk, and small game to use for food and clothing and miscellaneous household items, but for beaver, mink, and otter, the prime trade furs. Pelts were the gold of the woods. With them a man could buy guns, powder, lead, knives, hatchets, axes, needles and awls, scissors, kettles, traps, cloth, ready-made shirts, blankets, paint (for cosmetic purposes), and various notions: steel springs to pluck out disfiguring beard, scalp, and body hair; silver bracelets and armbands and tubes for coiling hair; rings to hang from nose and ears; mirrors; tinkling bells. Sometimes a tipsy hunter would give away his peltries for a keg of rum, treat his friends to a debauch, and wake up with a scolding wife and hungry children calling him a fool; another might, with equal improvidence, invest in a violin, or a horse, or a gaudy military uniform. But by and large, the products of the commercial hunt— generally conducted in the winter and often hundreds of miles from the home village, in the Ohio country or down the Susquehanna River —were exchanged for a limited range of European consumer goods, which had become, after five generations of contact with beaver-hungry French, Dutch, and English traders, economic necessities. Many of these goods were, indeed, designed to Indian specifications and manufactured solely for the Indian trade. An Iroquois man dressed in a linen breechcloth and calico shirt, with a woolen blanket over his shoulders, bedaubed with trade paint and adorned with trade armbands and earrings, carrying a steel knife, a steel hatchet, a clay pipe, and a rifled gun felt himself in no wise contaminated nor less an Indian than his stone-equipped great-great-grandfather. Iroquois culture had reached out and incorporated these things that Iroquois Indians wanted while at the same time Iroquois warriors chased off European missionaries, battled European soldiers to a standstill, and made obscene gestures when anyone suggested that they should emulate white society (made up, according to their information and experience, of slaves, cheating lawyers with pen and paper and ink, verbose politicians, hypocritical Christians, stingy tavern keepers, and thieving peddlers).

Behavior was governed not by published laws enforced by police, courts, and jails, but by oral tradition supported by a sense of duty, a fear of gossip, and a dread of retaliatory witchcraft. Theft, vandalism, armed robbery, were almost unknown. Public opinion, gently exercised, was sufficient to deter most persons from property crimes, for public opinion went straight to the heart of the matter: the *weakness* of the criminal. A young warrior steals someone else's cow—probably captured during a raid on a white settlement—and slaughters it to feed his hungry family. He does this at a time when other men are out fighting. No prosecution follows, no investigation, no sentence: the unhappy man is nonetheless severely punished, for the nickname "Cow-killer" is pinned to him, and he must drag it rattling behind him wherever he goes. People call him a coward behind his back and snicker when they tell white men, in his presence, a story of an unnamed Indian who killed cows when he should have been killing men. Such a curse was not generalized to the point of ostracism, however. The celebrated Red Jacket, about whom the "Cow-killer" story was told, vindicated his courage in later wars, became the principal spokesman for his nation, and was widely respected and revered. But he never lost the nickname.[1]

Disputes between people rarely developed over property. Marital difficulties centering around infidelity, lack of support, or personal incompatibility were settled by mutual agreement. Commonly, in case of difficulty, the man left and the woman, with her children, remained with her mother. A few couples remained together for a lifetime; most had several marriages; a few changed mates almost with the season. Men might come to blows during drunken arguments over real or fancied slights to their masculine honor, over politics, or over the alleged mistreatment of their kinfolk. Such quarrels led at times to killings or to accusations of witchcraft. A murder (or its equivalent, the practice of witchcraft) was something to be settled by the victim's kinfolk; if they wished, they might kill the murderer or suspected witch without fear of retaliation from his family (provided that family agreed on his guilt). But usually a known killer would come to his senses, admit himself wrong, repent, and offer retribution in goods or services to the mourning family, who unless exceptionally embittered by an unprovoked and brutal killing were then expected to accept the blood money and end the matter.

Drunkenness was perhaps the most serious social problem. Two Moravian missionaries who visited the Iroquois country in 1750 had the misfortune to reach the Seneca towns at the end of June, when the men were just returning from Oswego, where they had sold their winter's furs, and were beginning to celebrate the start of summer leisure. Hard liquor was dissolving winter's inhibitions and regrets. At Canandaigua, the missionaries, who were guests at the house of a prominent warrior, had just explained the friendly nature of their errand when the rum arrived. "All the town was in a state of intoxication, and frequently rushed into our hut in this condition," complained the white men. "There was every reason to think that fighting might ensue, as there were many warriors among those who were perfectly mad with drink." After a sleepless night the missionaries traveled on, reaching the outskirts of Geneseo on the second of July. "The village," said the observers in surprise, "consisted of 40 or more large huts, and lies in a beautiful and pleasant region. A fine large plain, several miles in length and breadth, stretches out behind the village." But the kegs of rum had anticipated them. "When we caught sight of the town we heard a great noise of shouting and quarreling, from which we could infer that many of the inhabitants were intoxicated, and that we might expect to have an uncomfortable time. On entering the town we saw many drunken Indians, who looked mad with drink. . . ."

Alas, poor Christians! They had to hide in a stuffy garret, without food or water. David, their devoted Indian convert and servant, stole out toward evening with a kettle to fetch his masters some water and was seen. "A troop of drunken women came rushing madly toward him. Some of them were naked, and others nearly so. In order to drive them away he was obliged to use his fists, and deal blows to the right and left. He climbed up a ladder, but when he had scarcely reached the top they seized it and tore it from under his feet." David barely managed to escape "in safety" from these playful Amazons. The missionaries decided not to wait the two days until the liquor ran out to meet the chiefs in council; they bent their prayers to an early departure. They finally managed to escape at dawn by jumping down from an opening in the gable and tiptoeing away. "The Lord watched over us in such a manner that all the drunken savages were in their huts, not a creature to be seen. Even the dogs, numbering nearly 100 in the whole village, were all quiet, wonderful to relate, and not a sound was heard. A dense fog covered the town, so that we could not see 20 steps before us. A squaw stood at the door of the last hut, but she was sober and returned our greeting quietly."[2]

But such drunken debauches were only occasional rents in a fabric of polite social behavior. Other missionaries were more favorably impressed than the Moravians. The Seneca, said a Quaker scribe, "appear to be naturally as well calculated for social and rational enjoyment, as any people. They frequently visit each other in their houses, and spend much of their time in friendly intercourse. They are also mild and hospitable, not only among themselves, but to strangers, and good natured in the extreme, except when their natures are perverted by the inflammatory influence of spirituous liquors. In their social interviews, as well as public councils, they are careful not to interrupt one another in conversation, and generally make short speeches. This truly laudable mark of good manners, enables them to transact all their public business with decorum and regularity, and more strongly impresses on their mind and memory, the result of their deliberations."[3]

· *The Iroquois "Matriarchate"* ·

DURING THE SEVENTEENTH and eighteenth centuries Iroquois men earned a reputation among the French and English colonists for being the most astute diplomatically and most dangerous militarily of all the Indians of the Northeast. Yet at the same time the Iroquois were famous for the "matriarchal" nature of their economic and social institutions. After the colonial era came to an end with the victory of the United States in the Revolutionary War, the traditional diplomatic and military role of the Iroquois men was sharply limited by the circumstances of reservation life. Simultaneously, the "matriarchal" character of certain of their economic, kinship, and political institutions was drastically diminished. These changes were codified by the prophet Handsome Lake. As we shall see later in more detail, the changes in kinship behavior that he recommended, and which to a considerable degree were carried out by his followers, amounted to a shift in dominance from the mother-daughter relationship to that of the husband-wife. Handsome Lake's reforms thus were a sentence of doom upon the traditional quasi-matriarchal system of the Iroquois.

The Iroquois were described as matriarchal because of the important role women played in the formal political organization. The men were responsible for hunting, for warfare, and for diplomacy, all of which kept them away from their households for long periods of time, and all of which were essential to the survival of Iroquois society. An expedition of any kind was apt to take months or even years, for the fifteen thousand or so Iroquois in the seventeenth and eighteenth centuries ranged over an area of about a million square miles. It is not an exaggeration to say that the full-time business of an Iroquois man was travel, in order to hunt, trade, fight, and talk in council. But the women stayed at home. Thus, an Iroquois village might be regarded as a collection of strings, hundreds of years old, of successive generations of women, always domiciled in their longhouses near their cornfields in a clearing while their sons and husbands traveled in the forest on supportive errands of hunting and trapping, of trade, of war, and of diplomacy.

The women exercised political power in three main circumstances. First, whenever one of the forty-nine chiefs of the great intertribal League of the Iroquois died, the senior women of his lineage nominated his successor. Second, when tribal or village decisions had to be made, both men and women attended a kind of town meeting, and while men were the chiefs and normally did the public speaking, the women caucused behind the scenes and lobbied with the spokesmen. Third, a woman was entitled to demand publicly that a murdered kinsman or kinswoman be replaced by a captive from a non-Iroquois tribe, and her male relatives, particularly lineage kinsmen, were morally obligated to go out in a war party to secure captives, whom the bereaved woman might either adopt or consign to torture and death. Adoption was so frequent during the bloody centuries of the beaver wars and the colonial wars that some Iroquois villages were preponderantly composed of formally adopted war captives. In sum, Iroquois women were entitled formally to select chiefs, to participate in consensual politics, and to start wars.

Thus the Iroquois during the two centuries of the colonial period were a population divided, in effect, into two parts: sedentary females and nomadic males. The men were frequently absent in small or large groups for prolonged periods of time on hunting, trading, war, and diplomatic expeditions, simultaneously protecting the women from foreign attack and producing a cash crop of skins, furs, and scalps, which they exchanged for hardware and dry goods. These activities, peripheral in a geographical sense, were central to the economic and political welfare of the Six Nations. The preoccupation of Iroquois men with these tasks and the pride they took in their successful pursuit cannot be overestimated. But the system depended on a complementary role for women. They had to be economically self-sufficient through horticulture during the prolonged absences of men, and they maintained genealogical and political continuity in a matrilineal system in which the primary kin relationship (not necessarily the primary social relationship) was the one between mother and daughter.

Such a quasi-matriarchy, of course, had a certain validity in a situation where the division of labor between the sexes required that men be geographically peripheral to the households that they helped to support and did defend. Given the technological, economic, and military circumstances of the time, such an arrangement was a practical one. But it did have an incidental consequence: It made the relationship between husband and wife an extremely precarious one. Under these conditions it was convenient for the marital system to be based on virtually free sexual choice, the mutual satisfaction of spouses, and easy separation. Couples chose one another for personal reasons; free choice was limited, in effect, only by the prohibition of intraclan marriage. Marriages were apt to fray when a husband traveled too far, too frequently, for too long. On his return, drunken quarreling, spiteful gossip, parental irresponsibility, and flagrant infidelity might lead rapidly to the end of the relationship. The husband, away from the household for long periods of time, was apt in his travels to establish a liaison with a woman whose husband was also away. The wife, temporarily abandoned, might for the sake of comfort and economic convenience take up with a locally available man. Since such relationships were, in effect, in the interest of everyone in the longhouse, they readily tended to become recognized as marriages. The emotional complications introduced by these serial marriages were supposed to be resolved peacefully by the people concerned. The traveling husband who returned to find his wife living with someone else might try to recover her; if she preferred to remain with her new husband, however, he was not entitled to punish her or her new lover, but instead was encouraged to find another wife among the unmarried girls or wives with currently absent husbands.[4]

· The Ideal of Autonomous Responsibility ·

THE BASIC IDEAL of manhood was that of "the good hunter." Such a man was self-disciplined, autonomous, responsible. He was a patient and efficient huntsman, a generous provider to his family and nation, and a loyal and thoughtful friend and clansman. He was also a stern and ruthless warrior in avenging any injury done to those under his care. And he was always stoical and indifferent to privation, pain, and even death. Special prominence could be achieved by those who, while adequate in all respects, were outstanding in one or another dimension of this ideal. The patient and thoughtful man with a skin "seven thumbs thick" (to make him indifferent to spiteful gossip, barbed wit, and social pressures generally) might become a sachem or a "distinguished name"—a "Pine Tree" chief. An eloquent man with a good memory and indestructible poise might be a council speaker and represent clan, nation, even the confederacy in far-flung diplomatic ventures. And the stern and ruthless warrior (always fighting, at least according to the theory, to avenge the death or insult of a blood relative or publicly avowed friend) might become a noted war-captain or an official war-chief. The war-captain ideal, open as it was to all youths, irrespective of clan and lineage or of special intellectual qualifications, was perhaps the most emulated.

In the seventeenth century an Onondaga war-captain named Aharihon bore the reputation of being the greatest warrior of the country. He realized the ideal of autonomous responsibility to virtually pathological perfection. Let us note what is told of Aharihon in the *Jesuit Relations*.[5]

Aharihon was a man of dignified appearance and imposing carriage, grave, polished in manner, and self-contained. His brother had been killed about 1654 in the wars with the Erie, a tribe westward of the Iroquois. As clansman and close relative, he was entitled—indeed obligated—either to avenge his brother's death by killing some Erie people or by adopting a war captive to take his place. Aharihon within a few years captured or had presented to him for adoption forty men. Each of them he burned to death over a slow fire, because, as he said, "he did not believe that there was any one worthy to occupy his [brother's] place." Father Lalemant was present when another young man, newly captured, was given to Aharihon as a substitute for the deceased brother. Aharihon let the young man believe that he was adopted and need have no further fear, and "presented to him four dogs, upon which to hold his feast of adoption. In the middle of the feast, while he was rejoicing and singing to entertain the guests, Aharihon arose, and told the company that this man too must die in atonement for his brother's death. The poor lad was astounded at this, and turned toward the door to make his escape, but was stopped by two men who had orders to burn him. On the fourteenth of February, in the evening, they began with his feet, intending to roast him, at a slow fire, as far up as the waist, during the greater part of the night. After midnight, they were to let him rally his strength and sleep a little until daybreak, when they were to finish this fatal tragedy. In his torture, the poor man made the whole village resound with his cries and groans. He shed great tears, contrary to the usual custom, the victim commonly glorying to be burned limb by limb, and opening his lips only to sing; but, as this one had not expected death, he wept and cried in a way that touched even these Barbarians. One of Aharihon's relatives was so moved with pity, that he advised ending the sufferer's torments by plunging a knife into his breast—which would have been a deed of mercy, had the stab been mortal. However, they were induced to continue the burning without interruption, so that before day he ended both his sufferings and his life." Aharihon's career of death continued without interruption, and by 1663 he was able to boast that he had killed sixty men with his own hand and had burned fully eighty men over slow fire. He kept count by tattooing a mark on his thigh for each successive victim. He was known then as the Captain General of the Iroquois and was nicknamed Nero by the Frenchmen at Montreal because of his cruelty.

The French finally captured him near Montreal, but even in captivity his manner was impressive. "This man," commented Father Lalemant, "commonly has nine slaves with him, five boys and four girls. He is a captain of dignified appearance and imposing carriage, and of such equanimity and presence of mind that, upon seeing himself surrounded by armed men, he showed no more surprise than if he had been alone; and when asked whether he would like to accompany us to Quebec, he deigned only to answer coldly that that was not a question to ask him, since he was in our power. Accordingly he was made to come aboard our Vessel, where I took pleasure in studying his disposition as well as that of an Algonquin in our company, who bore the scalp of an Iroquois but recently slain by him in war. These two men, although hostile enough to eat each other, chatted and laughed on board that Vessel with great familiarity, it being very hard to decide which of the two was more skillful in masking his feelings. I had Nero placed near me at table, where he bore himself with a gravity, a self-control, and a propriety, which showed nothing of his Barbarian origin; but during the rest of the time he was constantly eating, so that he fasted only when he was at table."

But this voracious captain was not renowned among the Onondaga as a killer only. He was, on the contrary, also a trusted ambassador, dispatched on occasion to Montreal on missions of peace. He was, in a word, a noted man. He was a killer, but he was not an indiscriminate killer; he killed only those whom it was his right to kill, tortured only those whom he had the privilege of torturing, always as an expression of respect for his dead brother. And although his kinfolk sometimes felt he was a little extreme in his stern devotion to his brother's memory, they did not feel that he was any the less a fine man, or that they had a right to interfere with his impulses; they were willing to entrust the business of peace, as well as war, to his hand.

A century and a half later Mary Jemison, the captive white woman who lived for most of her life among the Seneca on the Genesee River, described her Indian husband in not dissimilar terms. "During the term of nearly fifty years that I lived with him," she recalled, "I received, according to Indian customs, all the kindness and attention that was my due as his wife.—Although war was his trade from his youth till old age and decrepitude stopt his career, he uniformly treated me with tenderness, and never offered an insult. . . . He was a man of tender feelings to his friends, ready and willing to assist them in distress, yet, as a warrior, his cruelties to his enemies perhaps were unparalleled. . . . In early life, Hiokatoo showed signs of thirst for blood, by attending only to the art of war, in the use of the tomahawk and scalping knife; and in practising cruelties upon every thing that chanced to fall into his hands, which was susceptible of pain. In that way he learned to use his implements of war effectually, and at the same time blunted all those fine feelings and tender sympathies that are naturally excited, by hearing or seeing, a fellow being in distress. He could inflict the most excruciating tortures upon his enemies, and prided himself upon his fortitude, in having performed the most barbarous ceremonies and tortures, without the least degree of pity or remorse. . . . In those battles he took a number of Indians prisoners, whom he killed by tying them to trees and then setting small Indian boys to shooting at them with arrows, till death finished the misery of the sufferers; a process that frequently took two days for its completion! . . . At Braddock's defeat he took two white prisoners, and burnt them alive in a fire of his own kindling. . . ."[6]

With this sort of man serving as an ego-ideal, held up by sanction and by praise to youthful eyes, it is not remarkable that young men were ambitious to begin the practice of war. All had seen captives tortured to death; all had known relatives lost in war whose death demanded revenge or replacement. The young men went out on practice missions as soon as they were big enough to handle firearms; "infantile bands, armed with hatchets and guns which they can hardly carry, do not fail to spread fear and horror everywhere."[7] Even as late as the middle of the eighteenth century, Handsome Lake and his brothers and nephews were still busy at the old business of war for the sake of war. Cornplanter became a noted war-captain; Blacksnake, his nephew, was one of the official war-chiefs of the Seneca nation; and Handsome Lake himself took part in the scalping-party pattern as a young man. But Handsome Lake became a sachem and later a prophet, and he never gloried in the numbers of men he killed as his brother Cornplanter (somewhat guiltily) did. "While I was in the use of arms I killed seven persons and took three and saved their lives," said Cornplanter. And Blacksnake, in later life, told with relish of his exploits as a warrior. "We had a good fight there," he would say. "I have killed how many I could not tell, for I pay no attention to or kept [no] account of it, it was great many, for I never have it at all my Battles to think about kepting account what I'd killed at one time. . . ."[8]

The cultivation of the ideal of autonomous responsibility—and the suppression of its antinomy, dependency—began early in life. Iroquois children were carefully trained to think for themselves but to act for others. Parents were protective, permissive, and sparing of punishment; they encouraged children to play at imitating adult behavior but did not criticize or condemn fumbling early efforts; they maintained a cool detachment, both physically and verbally, avoiding the intense confrontations of love and anger between parent and child to which Europeans were accustomed. Children did not so much live in a child's world as grow up freely in the interstices of an adult culture. The gain was an early self-reliance and enjoyment of responsibility; the cost, perhaps, was a lifelong difficulty in handling feelings of dependency.

The Seneca mother gave birth to her child in the privacy of the woods, where she retired for a few hours when her time came, either alone or in the company of an older woman who served as midwife and, if the weather was cold, built and tended a fire. She had prepared for this event by eating sparingly and exercising freely, which were believed (probably with good reason) to make the child stronger and the birth easier. The newborn infant was washed in cold water, or even in snow, immediately after parturition and then wrapped in skins or a blanket. If the birth were a normal one, the mother walked back to the village with her infant a few hours afterwards to take up the duties of housewife. The event was treated as the consummation of a healthful process rather than as an illness. The infant spent much of its first nine months swaddled from chin to toe and lashed to a cradle-board. The child's feet rested against a footboard; a block of wood was placed between the heels of a girl to mold her feet to an inward turn. Over its head stretched a hoop, which could be draped with a thin cloth to keep away flies or to protect the child from the cold. The board and its wrappings were often lavishly decorated with silver trinkets and beadwork embroidery. The mother was able to carry the child in the board, suspended against her back, by a tumpline around her forehead; the board could be hung from the limb of a tree while she hoed corn; and it could be converted into a crib by suspending it on a rack of poles laid horizontally on forks stuck in the ground. The mother was solicitous of the child's comfort, nursed it whenever it cried, and loosened it from the board several times a day to change the moss that served as a diaper and to give it a chance to romp. The children, however, tended to cry when released from the board, and their tranquility could often be restored only by putting them back. Babies were seldom heard crying.

The mother's feeling for her children was intense; indeed, to one early observer it appeared that "Parental Tenderness" was carried to a "dangerous Indulgence."[9] Another early writer remarked, "The mothers love their children with an extreme passion, and although they do not reveal this in caresses, it is nevertheless real."[10] Mothers were quick to express resentment of any restraint or injury or insult offered to the child by an outsider. During the first few years the child stayed almost constantly with the mother, in the house, in the fields, or on the trail, playing and performing small tasks under her direction. The mother's chief concern during this time was to provide for the child and to protect it, to "harden" it by baths in cold water, but not to punish. Weaning was not normally attempted until the age of three or four, and such control as the child obtained over its excretory functions was achieved voluntarily, not as a result of consistent punishment for mistakes. Early sexual curiosity and experimentation were regarded as a natural childish way of behaving, out of which it would, in due time, grow. Grandparents might complain that small children got into everything, but the small child was free to romp, to pry into things, to demand what it wanted, and to assault its parents, without more hazard of punishment than the exasperated mother's occasionally blowing water in its face or dunking it in a convenient river.

The years between about eight or nine and the onset of puberty were a time of easy and gradual learning. At the beginning of this period the beginnings of the differentiation of the roles of boys and girls were laid down. The girls were kept around the house, under the guidance of their mothers, and assigned to the lighter household duties and to helping in the fields. Boys were allowed to roam in gangs, playing at war, hunting with bows and arrows and toy hatchets, and competing at races, wrestling, and lacrosse. The first successes at hunting were greeted with praise and boasts of future greatness. Sometimes these roaming gangs spent days at a time away from the village, sleeping in the bush, eating wild roots and fruits, and hunting such small game as could be brought down by bow and arrow, blowgun, or snare. These gangs developed into war parties after the boys reached puberty. Among themselves, both in gangs and among siblings of the same family, the children's playgroups were not constantly supervised by parents and teachers, and the children governed themselves in good harmony. Said one close observer, "Children of the same family show strong attachments to each other, and are less liable to quarrel in their youthful days than is generally the case with white children."[11]

The parents usually tried to maintain a calm moderation of behavior in dealing with their children, a lofty indifference alike to childish tantrums and seductive appeals for love. Hardihood, self-reliance, and independence of spirit were sedulously inculcated. When occasion presented itself, fathers, uncles, or other elder kinfolk instructed their sons in the techniques of travel, firemaking, the chase, war, and other essential arts of manhood, and the mothers correspondingly taught their daughters the way to hoe and plant the cornfields, how to butcher the meat, cook, braid corn, and other household tasks. But this instruction was presented, rather than enforced, as an opportunity rather than as a duty. On occasion the parent or other responsible adult talked to the child at length, "endeavoring," as a Quaker scribe gently put it, "to impress on its mind what it ought to do, and what to leave undone."[12] If exhortation seemed inadequate in its effect, the mentor might ridicule the child for doing wrong, or gravely point out the folly of a certain course of action, or even warn him that he courted the rage of offended supernatural beings. Obedi-

ence as such was no virtue, however, and blows, whippings, or restraints of any kind, such as restriction to quarters, were rarely
imposed, the faults of the child being left to his own reason and
conscience to correct as he grew mature. With delicate perception
the adults noted that childish faults "cannot be very great, before
reason arrives at some degree of maturity."[13]

Direct confrontation with the child was avoided, but when things
got seriously out of hand, parents sometimes turned older children
over to the gods for punishment. A troublesome child might be sent
out into the dusk to meet Longnose, the legendary Seneca bogeyman.
Longnose might even be impersonated in the flesh by a distraught
parent. Longnose was a hungry cannibal who chased bad children
when their parents were sleeping. He mimicked the child, crying
loudly as he ran, but the parents would not wake up because Longnose
had bewitched them. A child might be chased all night until he sub-
mitted and promised to behave. Theoretically, if a child remained
stubborn, Longnose finally caught him and took him away in a huge
pack-basket for a leisurely meal. And—although parents were not
supposed to do this—an unusually stubborn infant *could* be threatened
with punishment by the great False Faces themselves, who, when invoked for this purpose, might "poison" a child or "spoil his face." "I
remember," recalled a Cayuga woman of her childhood, "how scared
I was of the False-faces; I didn't know what they were. They are to
scare away disease. They used to come into the house and up the
stairs and I used to hide away under the covers. They even crawled
under the bed and they made that awful sound. When I was bad my
mother used to say the False-faces would get me. Once, I must have
been only 4 or 5, because I was very little when I left Canada, but I
remember it so well that when I think of it I can hear that cry now,
and I was going along a road from my grandfather's; it was a straight
road and I couldn't lose my way, but it was almost dark, and I had to
pass through some timber and I heard that cry and that rattle. I ran
like a flash of lightening and I can hear it yet."[14]

At puberty some of the boys retired to the woods under the
stewardship of an old man, where they fasted, abstained from any
sort of sexual activity (which they had been free to indulge, to the
limit of their powers, before), covered themselves with dirt, and
mortified the flesh in various ways, such as bathing in ice water and
bruising and gashing the shinbones with rocks. Dreams experienced

during such periods of self-trial were apt to be regarded as visitations from supernatural spirits who might grant *orenda*, or magical power, to the dreamer, and who would maintain a special sort of guardianship over him. The person's connection with this supernatural being was maintained through a charm—such as a knife, a queerly shaped stone, or a bit of bone—which was connected with the dream through some association significant to the dreamer. Unlike many other tribes, however, the Iroquois apparently did not require these guardian-spirit visions for pubescent youths. Many youths were said not to have had their first vision until just before their first war party. Furthermore, any man could have a significant dream or vision at any time. Girls too went through a mild puberty ritual, retiring into the woods at first menstruation and paying particular attention to their dreams. With the termination of the menstrual period the girl returned to the household; but hereafter, whenever she menstruated, she would have to live apart in a hut, avoiding people, and being careful not to step on a path, or to cook and serve anyone's food, or (especially) to touch medicines, which would immediately lose their potency if she handled them.[15]

The Europeans who observed this pattern of child experience were by no means unfavorably impressed although they were sometimes amazed. They commented, however, almost to a man, from early Jesuit to latter-day Quaker, on a consequence that stood out dramatically as they compared this "savage" maturation with "civilized." "There is nothing," wrote the Jesuit chronicler of the Iroquois mission in 1657, "for which these peoples have a greater horror than restraint. The very children cannot endure it, and live as they please in the houses of their parents, without fear of reprimand or chastisement."[16] One hundred and fifty years later, the Quaker Halliday Jackson observed that "being indulged in most of their wishes, as they grow up, liberty, in its fullest extent, becomes their ruling passion."[17] The Iroquois themselves recognized the intensity of their children's resentment at parental interference. "Some Savages," reported Le Mercier of the Huron, "told us that one of the principal reasons why they showed so much indulgence toward their children, was that when the children saw themselves treated by their parents with some severity, they usually resorted to extreme measures and hanged themselves, or ate of a certain root they call *Audachienrra*, which is a very quick poison."[18] The same fear was recorded among the Iroquois, including the Seneca, in 1657. And while suicides by frustrated children were not actually frequent, there are nevertheless a number of recorded cases of suicide where parental interference was the avowed cause. And *mutatis mutandis*, there was another rationalization for a policy of permissiveness: that the child who was harshly disciplined might grow up, some day, to mistreat his parents in revenge.

This theory of child raising was not taken for granted by the Seneca; on the contrary, it was very explicitly recognized, discussed, and pondered. Handsome Lake himself, in later years, insisted that parents love and indulge their children.

· *Iroquois Polity: The Philosophy of Peace* ·

THE POLITICAL ORGANIZATION of the Iroquois—the system by which decisions were made about problems affecting village, tribe, or confederacy—had three levels. The town or village itself decided local issues like the use of nearby hunting lands, the relocation of houses and cornfields, movement to another site, the acceptance or rejection of visitors, and the raising of war parties. There was a village chiefs' council, numbering up to twenty men, formally organized with a chairman and one or more representatives for each clan. These chiefs were influential men and women, who might be League sachems, warcaptains, warriors, or simply old men who were looked up to and consulted. The council generally met in the presence of the warriors and the women, and rarely diverged in its decisions from the popular consensus, or at least the majority view. This council met in the village's ceremonial longhouse, which usually was merely a large dwelling.

The tribes, or nations, had only an uncertain coherence in political matters, and readily split into factions, which might even remove geographically from one another and become permanent subdivisions. The Seneca, in particular, were divided into two groups: an eastern, pro-British group, and a western, pro-French group (the Geneseo Seneca). The Seneca national council met only occasionally, in the great council house at Caneadea or at another of the nation's towns as circumstances at the time might dictate. The membership of these tribal councils seems to have been simply the sum of all the chiefs of the village councils. Thus the Seneca tribal council might include as many as a hundred chiefs, and the membership changed as the composition of the village councils changed. The chairman, or speaker, of this council was elected by the council itself. The tribal council debated major issues of external policy such as war and peace, and sale of land; its recommendations, however, were contingent upon the willingness of the individual villages to carry them out, and in matters where agreement in the council was difficult, or an agreed-upon decision was expected to be unpopular, the whole nation might be presented with the problem at a mass meeting where anyone had the right to speak. The chiefs then waited for a consensus. Some of these tribal (i.e., village) chiefs and council speakers were chosen as perennial liaison men for dealings between colonial officials, like Sir William Johnson, and their village, factional, tribal, or even Six Nations constituencies. They were in this role sometimes referred to as "chiefs to do business," and most of the practical work of administration of policy and formulation and communication of issues was handled by these men rather than by the councils themselves. They were often better known to the whites than the hereditary, or sachem, chiefs. Still, the tribe was essentially not a political organization but a group of villages that spoke the same language.[19]

The only indigenous political structure that effectively coordinated communication and decision at a level above the individual village was the confederacy itself. In the Great Council of the Confederacy at Onondaga, voting representatives of each of the five original nations, together with nonvoting delegates from affiliated tribes like the Tuscarora, met annually in autumn, and at other times if called together by a member nation, to discuss crucial issues affecting the welfare of all the tribes: major wars and peacemakings and alliances; the sale of confederate territory; policy in matters of trade, religion, and relations with the whites; internal disputes that might threaten peace and good order. There were regular procedures for investiture of the sachems, and the strings and belts of wampum that were handed across the fire to emphasize the official nature of important statements were carefully preserved. One of the speaker's main responsibilities was to remember, word for word, what was said when each string or belt was handed across the fire. A well-trained speaker could relate with precision the transactions of the confederacy for a period of several generations into the past and could, moreover, present a diplomatic argument or a tribal council's decision with as much animation and eloquence as a European statesman addressing sovereign or parliament. The League also depended heavily upon "chiefs to do business" in the periods between meetings of its council.

Of the forty-nine sachems who sat around the great council fire at Onondaga, eight were Seneca. Each sachem had a special name, which was actually an official title, assumed when his clan matron appointed him and the council accepted the appointment. One of the Seneca titles was Ganeodiyo, or Handsome Lake, of the Turtle Clan. Although the tribes were unequal in numbers, no tribe had a greater voice in decision than any other, because the representatives of each tribe voted as a unit and decisions had to be unanimous. The Onondaga, whose principal town was usually the meeting place of the Great Council, were responsible for keeping the official wampum of the confederacy. The Seneca, the westernmost tribe, were known as the Keepers of the Western Door, because two of their sachems were appointed to inform the confederate council of embassies of peace or threats of war from the western nations and to keep a watchful eye over tributary tribes. These two chiefs had executive assistants whose formal duty it was to coordinate the normally small and individualistic war parties in the event of a major threat to the confederacy. In practice, however, military activities were organized by zealous and reputable warriors irrespective of title. The League was not an organization for more efficient warfare, and its contribution to military effort resided largely in its success in keeping domestic quarrels from becoming so bitter that they might prevent cooperation among villages and tribes. Although the fame of the Iroquois was based chiefly on their ruthless destruction of other nations, although much of the pride of each man resided in his personal accomplishments on the warpath, and although war was almost the constant condition of national existence, the Great League itself was in philosophy and in practice an inward-looking, harmony-maintaining body. Herein lay another paradox: The warlike Iroquois conceived the normal and desirable way of life to be a peaceful, quiet one and bent much energy toward the maintenance of peace among themselves and their near neighbors.

The League had originated many years earlier (about 1450) in a successful endeavor to revive an even more ancient, but less formally constructed, ethnic confederacy among the Iroquois. Ethnic confederacies were common among Indian tribes in the Northeast. Villages, bands, and tribes speaking similar languages, holding similar customs, and sharing a tradition of common origin usually combined into a loose union that at least minimized warfare among themselves. The Illinois Confederacy, the "Three Fires" of the Chippewa, Ottawa, and Potawatomi, the Wapenaki Confederacy, the Powhatan Confederates, the tripartite Miami—all the neighbors of the Iroquois were members of some confederation or other. But the Iroquois League was to them as ice is to water: a rigid crystalline form of a normally shapeless substance. The Great League, with its forty-nine chiefly titles representing most of the clans of the five tribes, its council fire at Onondaga, and its archives of wampum, was called Kanonsionni, the Longhouse, and the people of the Five Nations considered themselves, for many purposes, members of one family. "We bind ourselves together," had said the mythological founder, Dekanawidah, "by taking hold of each other's hands so firmly and forming a circle so strong that if a tree should fall upon it, it could not shake nor break it, so that our people and grandchildren shall remain in the circle in security, peace, and happiness." The chiefs were consecrated men, disqualified from taking part in war except as common warriors, and expected to have skins seven thumbs thick so as to remain untouched by gossip, envy, and criticism. "Be of strong mind, O chiefs!" they were charged. "Carry no anger and hold no grudges. Think not forever of yourselves, O chiefs, nor of your own generation. Think of continuing generations of our families, think of our grandchildren and of those yet unborn, whose faces are coming from beneath the ground."

The minimum purpose of the League was to maintain unity, strength, and good will among the Five Nations, so as to make them invulnerable to attack from without and to division from within. The native philosophers who rationalized the League in later years conceived also a maximum purpose: the conversion of all mankind, so that peace and happiness should be the lot of the peoples of the whole earth, and all nations should abide by the same law and be members of the same confederacy. "The white roots of the Great Tree of Peace will continue to grow," the founder allegedly announced, "advancing the Good Mind and Righteousness and Peace, moving into territories of peoples scattered far through the forest. And when a nation, guided by the Great White Roots, shall approach the Tree, you shall welcome her here and take her by the arm and seat her in the place of council. She will add a brace or leaning pole to the longhouse and will thus strengthen the edifice of Reason and Peace." But should a nation, after being invited three times to become a prop to the Iroquois Longhouse, persist in an obstinate refusal, it was supposedly incumbent upon the Five Nations to attack and conquer them, and thus bring the survivors into the circle by main force.

Thus the chiefs, tranquilly sitting about the fire at Onondaga, puffing on their long cane pipes, were easy in their minds about the forest wars. They could say that despite all the quarrels over beaver and boundaries, they themselves had always had in mind the extension of the Great Peace. Even with the French they had tried to live at peace. To the Jesuits, those cold-blooded, black-robed men of great courage but little tact, they had said, "If you love, as you say you do, our souls, love our bodies also, and let us be henceforth but one nation." They had restrained themselves, many times, from fully annihilating the French and their Algonquian allies at Montreal and Quebec and Three Rivers. "I heard the voice of my Forefathers massacred by the Algonquins. When they saw that my heart was capable of seeking revenge they called out to me in a loving voice: 'My grandson, my grandson, be good; do not get angry. Think no longer of us for there is no means of withdrawing us from death. Think of the living—that is of importance; save those that still live from the sword and fire that pursue them; one living man is better than many dead ones.' " And again and again they had proposed peace and union under the Great Tree. "Not only shall our customs be your customs, but we shall be so closely united that our chins shall be reclothed with hair, and with beards like yours." Again and again they had paddled up and down in canoes before a recalcitrant town while an old sachem cried in a loud voice: "Listen to me! I have come to treat for peace with all the nations in these parts . . . the land shall be beautiful, the river shall have no more waves, one may go everywhere without fear."

And the warriors, hidden in the bushes overlooking the stream, watched anxiously to see whether the foreigners made peace and agreed to share the fur trade with the Iroquois, so that they themselves might go home, or whether their deadly service would be needed after all. . . .[20]

· Iroquois Warfare: The Strategy of Threat and Retaliation ·

WHATEVER ITS PHILOSOPHICAL rationalization and economic consequences might be, the actual mechanism of Iroquois warfare was the traditional process of blood feud. A family, one of whose members had been killed by an alien (i.e., a person who was not one of the five or, after about 1722, Six Nations or their allies), was morally obligated to avenge the death by killing, or capturing and adopting, one or more members of the "enemy" tribe. Friends of the injured family could help in the satisfaction of the score, but the feud was fundamentally a personal matter between the injured family and the alien group. Such a feud could begin from various incidental circumstances: a chance encounter with a trespassing stranger; a drunken brawl; involvement in a military campaign initiated by a third party. Over a period of time, however, a sequence of mutually vengeful killings could occur, involving an increasing number of members of the two groups, until finally there were so many unsettled scores left on both sides that a state of chronic "war" could be said to exist, justifying an endless exchange of forays, some of them involving large numbers of vengeance-seeking warriors on both sides. Inasmuch as these forays were technically intended by the participants not to acquire territory nor to establish political sovereignty but to even the score in a feud, good tactics required minimal loss of life by the avenging party. A victory with heavy casualties was, in effect, a defeat, since the score then remained uneven.

This mechanism was partially controlled by political policy, particularly as expressed and maintained by the Great League. The League itself had been explicitly designed to prevent the proliferation of blood feuds within and among the various member nations; this purpose was clearly stated both in the Dekanawidah myth, which described the origin of the League, and in the rituals of condolence that were held whenever one of the forty-nine members of the council died. Indirectly, no doubt, the League's ethical position on intra-Iroquois blood feuds influenced Iroquois warfare by maintaining a climate of mutual confidence among the tribes. In this climate it was more feasible to organize large-scale military enterprises than in an atmosphere of mutual fear and suspicion. But it should not be supposed that Iroquois warfare was merely the military activity of the League. The League—and probably tribal and village councils also—functioned more as a restraining than as an initiating body. The League as an entity and its several chiefs could urge upon the warriors the wisdom of holding back their striking arms; and their influence was such that raids could be postponed or put off indefinitely while diplomats negotiated issues for the common good. Conversely, the League organization could deliberately sit silent while the war captains prepared their campaigns. Furthermore, the council organization served as an information center, receiving, discussing, filtering, and disseminating news and opinion that could influence the military passions of the warriors and the women. Thus, while the League was in itself not a war-making body, it could aim and time the unleashing of the war potential that, because of the wide ramification of the kinship-revenge motif, was always straining to burst into active hostilities. This process of control by restraining, directing, and timing the ever-ready mechanism of revenge operated most conspicuously in relations between the Iroquois and white groups, because the records of negotiations and of fighting are here more satisfactory; but the same process governed the relations of the Iroquois to other Indian tribes.

The major functions of Iroquois warfare—its consequences, both intended and unintended, for the Iroquois way of life and their situation in the world—were, in the early part of the century, threefold: to maintain an emotional equilibrium in individuals who were strongly motivated to avenge, or replace, murdered kinfolk, and thereby to maintain the social equilibrium of kinship units; to extend, or at least maintain, Iroquois political influence over other tribal groups, and thus to provide access by trade or hunting to land rich in peltries; and to perpetuate a political situation in which the threat of retaliation against either party could be used to play off the British and the French against one another. Territorial immunity, military support, trade advantages, and outright gifts of food, dry goods, and hardware could be extorted from both sides under the asserted or implied threat that the Iroquois and their allies would abandon their neutral role and would join the generous party in an attack on the stingy one if their wants were not satisfied.

The equilibrium-maintaining function of Iroquois warfare requires some amplification. Certainly the Iroquois were not unique among Indian tribes, or even primitive peoples generally, in the importance of kinship in establishing the individual's social rights and obligations and in defining his image in his own eyes and the eyes of others. Such discipline and security as the individual enjoyed tended to be provided by his family (and by "family" we mean not merely the immediate household but the various and widely ramifying connections of the kinship system). In such a setting an injury to an Iroquois Indian's relatives became doubly significant, not only because it disturbed the integrity of the group with which he was identified, but also because the affected individuals could not depend upon obtaining redress through police and courts. It was thus a matter of honor for kinfolk to protect one another and, if necessary, to avenge injuries. In the case of a killing, the most immediately affected parties might well be women—mother, sisters, and wife of the lost person—who could demand either the torture and death of the offender or the adoption of a captive to take the departed person's place. (In a fundamental sense, even the dead offender was adopted, since the scalp torn from the slain foe was often ritually adopted into the bereaved family, and the bodies of captives who had been tortured to death were sometimes eaten ceremonially.) While women could hold the initiative in demanding redress and could determine the fate of captives, men were responsible for risking their lives to bring back scalps or prisoners. Joining a war party thereby became a test of manhood, conducted under the watchful eyes of bereaved women, and failure to participate in the revenge process would prejudice the reluctant youth's standing in the eyes of his own family and the community generally.

The effectiveness of the League in partially blocking the free exercise of the revenge process among the five participating tribes may therefore have been partly responsible for the implacability and ferociousness of the Iroquois in pursuing external enemies; with the intrusion of political influence into the revenge motif locally, it became even more essential for warriors to validate their moral stature in the eyes of kinsmen and community by allowing no slackness in the settling of external scores. If this interpretation is sound, then the Iroquois reputation for pertinacity and ruthlessness in fighting with their external enemies may be regarded as an indirect consequence of the blocking of the blood feud among the participating members of the League. The *pax Iroquois* resulted in the displacement of revenge motivations outward, onto surrounding peoples, Indian and European alike.

But this displacement brought new difficulties in turn, perhaps more clearly recognized by the sachems of the League than by the warriors. The intensification of external warfare—augmented in the seventeenth century by the abrasive circumstances of competition in the fur trade—meant ever more costly raids and counter-raids, in what seems to have been a rising crescendo of violence. The strain on the Iroquois themselves was great: serious loss of manpower, the need to replenish the population by mass adoption of captives, and the development of something like a chronic combat fatigue, the symptoms of which—preoccupation with death and misfortune, persistent nightmares of captivity, of being burned alive, of attack by enemy warriors—were vividly described by the Jesuits. Paradoxically, the League of peace had become a facility for destruction. Thus the League, lest the revenge process get out of hand, perforce had to expand so as to embrace under its sheltering branches, which precluded the blood feud, ever more of the Iroquois' traditional enemies. Each accretion to the League required the warriors to go farther and farther away to settle a score, and thereby reduced the total frequency of raids and their cost in terms of lives and human suffering. By the middle of the eighteenth century a rough equilibrium had been established: The nearby Indian nations had been brought by various mixtures of conquest, threat, and diplomatic persuasion into some sort of affiliation with the League. While killings and counterkillings still occasionally occurred, they no longer threatened the survival of the tribes; and there was still sufficient opportunity, in the raid exchanges with the southern Indians, for the revenge motif to exercise the kinship devotions of the warriors and women.

The social interests of the League sachems, on the one hand, and the warriors and the women, on the other, conflicted. Warriors and women formed a bloc composed of complementary roles in the revenge process, each dependent on the other for validation and fulfillment of status. The sachems, however, *as sachems* had to view the revenge process as potentially destructive. Thus one repeatedly finds sachems, or their representatives in contact with Europeans, com-

(47)

plaining that they could not control their young men, that the warriors were apt to heed the women rather than the chiefs. While such statements were certainly true, for reasons given above, the situation that they reflected was also fruitful in insuring the successful fulfillment of the third function of Iroquois warfare. The chiefs of the League, or of any particular tribe, could at any time say that the warriors and the women could no longer be restrained from striking a blow against some enemy to gain revenge for some recent or ancient injury. Thus, while the League as such, by the treaties of 1701, remained committed to neutrality between the French and the English, groups of warriors—acting according to the code of revenge—could, if offended, at any time assail either party. It was always possible, of course, for the British to seduce some Mohawk into service against the French, and the French to persuade some Geneseo Seneca to strike the British, but these breaches of contract served more as an ever-present reminder of the importance of keeping the League itself neutral than as an excuse for terminating the agreement. Thus, without more duplicity than was characteristic of either the British or the French themselves, the League chiefs were able to orchestrate the revenge mechanism of warfare into the contrapuntal melody of extorting political and material gifts from both the French and the English. The importance of this theme in Iroquois life from 1701 to 1755 can hardly be overestimated: It gave them territorial security, a relatively high material culture, a continued ascendancy over neighboring peoples, and an enormous sense of their own importance.[21]

◄| 3 |►

THE RITUALS OF HOPE
AND THANKSGIVING

I N THE COURSE OF TRYING TO LIVE UP TO THE RIGOROUS IDEAL OF autonomy and responsibility, Iroquois men hunted, traded, fought, and negotiated at a high cost in loneliness and discomfort. They too on occasion yearned for someone's help to relieve pain and hardship, felt rage at insult and neglect, were jealous of others' success, were miserable when a loved one died. Even though their public behavior was stoic, they were underneath not nearly as insulated from one another, as self-sufficient and indifferent to human contact, as the overt fulfillment of the ideal of autonomy seemed to imply. Indeed, the severity of the ideal guaranteed an equal intensity of desire for its converse—dependency and lack of responsibility.

In general, Iroquois religion tended to be a means by which the disappointments and sacrifices entailed by living up to the ideal of autonomous responsibility could to some extent be compensated. Its rituals and beliefs were cathartic, satisfying the desperate needs for nurturance that could not be expressed, and might even be feared, in daily life. But the religion did its work in disguised, symbolic, and ceremonially insulated forms so that acting out normally disallowed wishes did not threaten self-respect. In the opinion of the Iroquois themselves, these rituals prevented both mental illness and social disorder.

The set of issues to which Iroquois religion addressed itself was unlike that to which contemporary European religions were oriented. European methods of social discipline in the main produced adults who were relatively tolerant of external restraint and whose typical problem was guilt, particularly over wishes for aggressive, dominant independence in matters of sex, politics, and human relations generally. The religious antihero of the Europeans was proud, independent Lucifer; of the Iroquois, it was the infantile, beggarly False Face. European religions provided a rich variety of ritual prescriptions for the management of guilt by confession, atonement, forgiveness, and absolution. Early Iroquois religion did not pay much attention to guilt of this kind because Iroquois people were not much bothered by it. But their religion did concern itself explicitly with cathartic ways of handling existential frustration. In general, these ways can be analytically separated into rituals of thanksgiving and hope and rituals of fear and mourning. The former—including particularly the communal thanksgiving festivals and the cult of dreams—worked to provide reassurance of continued protection and support from supernaturals and of ultimate impulse gratification, especially of desires for nurturance, within an indulgent earthly community. The latter—notably witchcraft, the masked medicine ceremonies, and the condolence rituals—attempted to cope with the consequences of loss: loss of love, loss of health, and loss of loved ones by death. Ultimately, of course, the two categories merge, for impulse gratification itself was believed to be prophylactic or even curative.

· *The Calendar of Thanksgiving* ·

IN THE EIGHTEENTH CENTURY, as now, most of the important communal ceremonies of thanksgiving were performed at fixed times through the year and were relevant to seasonal subsistence activities as well as to general themes of belief. Villages differed, then as now, in the number of such ceremonies and in the details of their execution. Among Handsome Lake's people, there were probably six: the Midwinter Ceremony, in January or February, which marked the beginning of the Seneca year; Thanks-to-the-Maple, in late February or March, when the sap started to rise; the Corn Planting Festival, early in May or June; the Strawberry Festival, in June; the Green Corn Ceremony, late in August or September; and the Harvest Festival in October. The Midwinter Ceremony lasted nine days and the Green Corn four; the remainder were one-day affairs. The nucleus of all the ceremonies (with the possible exception of Thanks-to-the-Maple, about which little information has been recorded) was a morning-long ritual that constituted virtually the entire external form of the one-day ceremonies and occupied one day of Midwinter and of Green Corn. This archetypal ritual day began with the Faithkeepers notifying the people to assemble at the longhouse. When the people had gathered, a speaker opened the meeting by reporting any sickness in the village. Then he proceeded to give thanks to the pantheon in the standard Thanksgiving Prayer, starting with the spirit forces on earth and going on to more and more sacred beings: in the lower pantheon, the people (categorized as civil chiefs, religious chiefs, ordinary men and women, and children), the waters, the herbs, grasses, and other small plants, the saplings and bushes, the trees, the staple agricultural foods (corn, squash, and beans), the game animals, and the birds; in the middle pantheon, the thunderers (who made the rain), the winds, the sun, the moon, and the stars; and in the upper pantheon, the major deities and the Creator. Then the speaker announced the special purpose of the day's meeting, gave instruction concerning the forthcoming rituals, and announced the singers for the Feather Dance. The Faithkeepers, men and women, now performed the Feather Dance. Next he announced the names of the singers and dancers for the Women's Dance. The women danced, carrying ears of corn, while the male chorus described in song the life cycle of the corn. The speaker thanked the participants and announced the Great Feather Dance, which now included everyone who wished to join in. At morning's end the speaker concluded the proceedings by thanking on behalf of the chiefs all of the participants and announcing plans for the succeeding day (or, if the ceremony was over, for the next festival on the calendar). Everyone now left the longhouse and joined in a midday feast.

The theme of this basic ritual sequence was thankfulness and hope: thankfulness to the spirit beings for past benefits to the community and hope that they would continue to provide them. Paralleling this ritual address to the gods, there was a similar communication from the speaker to the human participants, who also had to be thanked for their help in order to ensure their continued interest in the communal ceremonies.

The Midwinter Ceremony began the ceremonial year. This ceremony regularly took place five days after the first new moon following the zenith of the Pleiades. This event, which occurs late in January or early in February, was observed by the two ritual Headmen, who had charge of the Faithkeepers. Midwinter was the longest festival of the annual calendar. Its main theme was a testimonial to the Creator, of thankfulness for the blessings and indulgences of the past year, and of supplication to Him to permit man to enjoy yet another spring.

On the first day of the festival there occurred the "boiling of the babies." This ceremony was the public naming of the babies who had been born since the Green Corn Ceremony. The "boiling" was not the fate of the babies even symbolically; what was boiled was the corn soup the participants ate after the naming ceremony.

The New Year began officially at dawn on the second day, when the Big Heads woke the occupants of the houses and notified them that the New Year had begun. The Big Heads were two men wearing shaggy bearskin coats and masks of cornhusks; they were not permitted to dress themselves and accordingly were fitted out by two women attendants. They received gifts of food and returned to the council house to reveal their dreams. If they did not attend, the Big Heads warned, the lazy dreamers would get their heads "stuck to the ceremonies." Having one's head stuck to the ceremonies was a miserable condition in which any dreamer who had failed to reveal his dream and to act out the ritual it indicated was obsessed by the desire that generated the dream. Later some False Face dancers went out to the houses, accompanied by female attendants, to stir the ashes again and to begin songs of thanksgiving. They returned and blew ashes on sick people. Finally, two Faithkeepers carrying paddles came to the houses to stir the ashes on the hearths visited earlier by the Big Heads and False Faces.

On the third day, called "ashes stirring," small groups of people carrying paddles made the rounds of houses in the village, again stirring up the ashes in the individual cabins. On their return to the council house, a singer sang the song of thanksgiving to the pantheon. After the thanksgiving, additional groups of persons walked from house to house, in response to dreams, asking that their dreams be guessed.

The fourth day was the day of the rituals of the secret medicine societies. A speaker and a singer, leading a party of men who danced the Great Feather Dance in the council house and in the circuit of private houses, exhorted the people to attend the rituals of the proper societies. The Great Feather dancers were followed by a party of women who danced the Women's Dance. Then the various medicine societies—the False Faces, the Buffalo Society, the Otter Society, and so on—performed brief curing rituals for those sick persons whose dreams indicated a need for their membership in a particular society and for those who needed a "booster" ritual on this anniversary of a previous cure. Men and women also on this day propounded their dream-riddles, and the guessers offered miniature talismans representing the tutelary revealed in the dream. That night bands of young people dressed up as False Faces roamed about the village, begging or, if rebuffed, stealing food.

On the fifth morning occurred the burning of the white dog. This dog, a spotless animal, had been strangled (its blood could not be shed) on the day of the Big Heads, and its body, garlanded with ribbons, beads, and metallic ornaments, hung on the wooden statue of Tarachiawagon, the Creator, before the longhouse. Now it was burned in the longhouse as an offering to the Creator, and the Thanksgiving Dance was performed, and people sang their personal chants. On this day also the medicine societies continued their curing rites in the longhouse, and, in the afternoon and evening, in private homes.

On the sixth day the Sacred Bowl Game was played briefly, a traveling team proceeding from house to house to contest with the occupants to make levies of food. In the afternoon again there were medicine society dances on behalf of the sick. The Buffalo Society dancers, for instance, butted their covered heads together and devoured corn mush; the leftovers were thrown out of the door for the "animals outside." In the Bear Dance, everyone ate a jam of preserved strawberries. The evening of this sixth day was the comedy hour of the festival. The evening started in the crowded council house with social dances and leftover medicine-society rituals. Then the False Face dancers—men dressed in ragged clothes, carrying huge turtle-shell rattles and wooden staves, and wearing grotesque wooden masks—burst into the council house, incoherently gobbling and cooing, rolling on the ground, and dancing the awkward, pompous False Face Dance in return for gifts of tobacco. The people laughed uproariously at their crude antics. After them came the Husk Faces. With them, the humor was more subtle. The Husk Faces, wearing round, popeyed, friendly looking masks made of braided cornhusks, arrived at the council house during a period of social dances. They announced their arrival by a great din of banging and scraping the bark walls of the council house with hoes and wooden shovels. Two heralds burst in, shoved the dancers aside, and seized some elderly gentleman as an interpreter. He was taken outside to interview their leader, who was supposedly a woman. He returned with his captors and delivered her "message," but part way through suffered from forgetfulness and excused himself, saying that he had to go outside once more to see the Great-Wet-Woman, whom, he said, he had not seen for a year. At last he came back and carried on an animated dialogue with himself, alternately as Great-Wet-Woman and her interpreter. The Husk Faces now revealed (as they did every year) that they were a race of supernatural agriculturists who lived on the western rim of the earth, whither they were now hurrying to cultivate their corn, which grew to vast heights, bearing prodigious ears, in fields filled with high stumps. Also their babies were crying and their women had to get home to tend them, so they could only stay and dance for a little while. Then the Husk Face women (actually men in women's dress) did the Women's Dance in honor of the "Three Sisters," corn, squash, and beans.

The seventh day followed the basic ritual sequence described above; the eighth focused on the singing of personal songs of thanksgiving. The ninth and last day was devoted to concluding the ceremonies. Adults who had changed their names were presented, new council-house officers were inaugurated, and there was a final performance of the Great Feather Dance. Personal chants of thanksgiving were held, and the sacred Bowl Game (symbolizing the struggle of the Good with the Evil Twin over control of the earth in the days of creation) was begun again. During the one or more days of the game's continuance, social dances were held in the evening, and the daylight hours were devoted to feasting and to the enactment of dream commands, lest those whose heads were still "stuck to the ceremonies" delay by their preoccupation the coming of spring.[1]

After the Midwinter Festival, toward the end of February, when the sap started to rise in the trees but before the ground had thawed and the ice and snow had run off the mountains, most of the people left the village to camp near family-owned groves of sugar maples. They spent several weeks in the woods, the women chiefly occupying themselves with sugar-making, while the men, in addition to helping in this process, hunted to support the camp and trapped the small fur-bearing animals, particularly the beaver, whose meat was regarded as a luxury and whose fur was a valuable article in trade. Everyone returned to the village before the spring thaw.

The sugar-maple season was also the occasion of the religious ceremony called Thanks-to-the-Maple. On the morning of the chosen day individual families returned thanks to the maple trees and burned tobacco as an invocation. Afterward there were social dances, and in the evening the people sang the songs of the Chanters for the Dead (the *ohgiwe* cycle). The Chanters for the Dead was a society, headed by a woman, which owned certain songs that, in addition to being sung at Thanks-to-the-Maple, were sung as occasion required throughout the year for persons (thereafter members) who were troubled by dreams of departed relatives or friends. At an *ohgiwe* ceremony the songs were sung to the accompaniment of a large water-drum; a diviner identified the troubling spirit, and a feast was held at which food was set aside for the restless ghost, to satisfy the needs that made him plague the sick man's dreams. These songs were supposed to have been revealed to a good hunter from a grave beneath a hard maple tree.

When the snow melted on the mountains, the ice became soft and crumbled over the lakes and streams, and small creeks swelled into brown frothing rivers, bearing the winter's watery debris down to the sea. This was the time when human life came almost to a standstill: Hunting, travel, even war were impossible because of the sogginess of the ground and the impassability of the fords; it was too early to plant, and the last year's store of dried corn was almost used up; clothes and cabins were worn and shabby, and the people were hungry, waiting for the renewal of warmth and sunshine and green things. They waited in their villages for the world's rebirth for which they had prayed at the Midwinter Festival a month or two before.

After the thaw, the pace of life accelerated. There was industrious fishing: men, women, and children armed with fish spears assaulted the cool creeks and lakes; weirs were emptied; nets of cord or brush were dragged up small streams. In April, when the passenger pigeons nested, the whole village took part in a hunt for squabs, knocking the young birds down from the trees and gathering them in baskets. Parties of women planted the corn in hillocks row by row, and other important plants—tobacco, squash, and beans in particular—were set at the same time, to grow in the carefully hoed and weeded gardens. Men and youths repaired old cabins or built new ones and busied themselves in the woods near the village, hunting for deer and small game. Toward the beginning of June small groups of women, with children and sometimes with menfolk, made picnic parties into the hills, picking wild strawberries and carrying them home in baskets of woven splints, to make into a syrupy tonic beverage and to dry and preserve for later seasons. These berry-picking excursions provided occasion for much merry and malicious gossip about who was seen with whom and about the supposed philanderings of certain men and the wantonness of certain women.

At the time of the planting of the corn, the Corn Planting Ceremony was held. One morning the Faithkeepers went about the village to the various houses, collecting corn, squash, beans, and other garden-vegetable seeds. These were taken to the longhouse and soaked. The Creator and all the spirit forces were thanked for their mercies in the past and asked for continued support. The Thunderers, "our grandfathers," were requested to water the crops, and "our older brother," the Sun, was implored not to burn them with too-fierce rays. And again in June, when the berry moon was five days old, the Faithkeepers called the people together for the Strawberry Festival. They thanked the spirit forces for permitting them to live to witness still another festival and for bringing the fruits, of which the strawberry is the first, to ripening; and they asked that the spirit forces permit all things to reach fruition. At some day during the spring, also, there was a great hubbub and to-do in the village. On the day of the exorcism of disease and witchcraft, two companies of men and women, boys and girls, wearing red and black wooden masks, marched through the village. They stopped at every house and rubbed turtle-shell or bark rattles over the cabins, brushed disease spirits out from under bunks, and collected tobacco, which was burned at the council house where the two companies, proceeding from opposite ends of the village, joined at last. There the Thunders and the Winds and the

False Faces themselves were implored to keep disaster, in the form of tornado or pestilence or witchcraft, away from the village.

Summertime in the Genesee Valley was a warm, dry season; the hills in the distance were soft in the misty air and a warm brownness mantled the earth. Thunderstorms and sudden showers from time to time broke over the villages, but the countryside was never watered well enough to achieve the lush greenness of regions farther south. The women were at their busiest in the summer, with the duties of agriculture added to the perennial chores of tending the children, cooking, making and mending clothing, and manufacturing pottery, baskets, and other housewares. By contrast, summer was of all the seasons the easiest for the men. There was casual hunting for small game near the villages and occasionally longer summer hunting and trading trips. There were, for the older or invalided men, various arts and crafts to be carried on now as in winter—the making of wampum, the carving of masks, ceremonial canes, and drumsticks, the fashioning of wooden spoons and ladles. Sometimes men went to war in the summer, but fall was preferred as the time for military adventure. Summer was, however, the best time of all for politics and diplomacy: for meetings of tribal councils, for councils of the Great Confederacy, for councils with representatives of other Indian nations, and for treaties with the whites. At such council and treaty occasions, not only the chiefs, speakers, and prominent warriors attended, but also (depending on the availability of food at the council site) hundreds of ordinary warriors, women, and children. The winter's catch of trade furs would be exchanged at forts and trading posts for hardware and dry goods. Summer was a time for visiting, for sociability, and for the renewal of friendships and alliances. During the summer there were no fixed religious festivals. If drought threatened the crops, the Thunder Rite was held: tobacco was burned, the game of hoop and javelin was played, the people danced, Elder Brother Sun was implored not to burn the corn, and the Grandfather Thunderers were requested to bring rain. A Condolence Council had to precede any formal treaty involving chiefs of the League if one of them had died during the winter or spring and his successor had not yet been installed.

Autumn was inaugurated by the Green Corn Festival, which among the Iroquois, as among the other tribes of the eastern woodlands, marked the middle of the year. When the corn was ready for eating, some time late in August or in early September, the community gathered at the council house to give thanks for the ripening of the crops for another year. The festival required four days. The first was for the naming of children born since the Midwinter Ceremony. The second was for the Great Feather Dance. The third was for the singing of personal chants (*adowe*), a performance of the Thanksgiving Dance including boastful recitations of war exploits, and the burning of a white dog as an offering to the Creator Tarachiawagon. And the fourth was for the Bowl Game, the sacred game of chance, which continued, if it was not decided on the morning of this fourth day, on as many succeeding mornings as were required for one moiety or the other to win all of the 102 beans. Although most sacred ceremonies ended at noon on each day, the afternoons and evenings were devoted to other rituals: social dances in the evenings, the Women's Rite (*towisas*) on the last afternoon, and the appearance of the False Faces. In form and content the Green Corn Ceremony was substantially the same as the first day and last three days of the Midwinter Festival, which was the longest ritual of all in the Iroquois calendar.

After the Green Corn came the time of harvesting. The winter was on its way now, and the surplus of vegetable stuffs had to be put away for later use. Corn and other vegetables were taken in from the fields; some corn was husked and hung up in braids to dry, and the rest was shelled and buried in baskets in bark-lined pits or stored on the ear in elevated cribs. Tobacco was hung for curing, beans were dried. In this work both men and women participated, for any failure to make maximum use of what the earth had yielded might mean hardship or even starvation later. When the harvest was in, and before the people moved out for the fall hunt, they devoted one day more to the Harvest Festival, thanking the Creator and His spirit forces for permitting them to reap a full harvest, and testifying to the happiness of the corn now that it had again been returned safely into storage to rest for the winter.

The late fall and winter was the prime season for the hunters and warriors. Some departed on the trails through the forest on forays against nearby tribes, like the Mahican, or on occasion against such distant peoples as the Cherokee and Catawba south of the Ohio River, and the Montagnais and Cree in Labrador and around Hudson's Bay, or even to the Illinois on the Mississippi River. Others, often taking with them wives and children, or sweethearts, traveled by canoe and afoot to favorite hunting grounds where beaver, otter, marten, elk, bear, deer, and other animals valuable for food and peltry might be found. Some moved to the region watered by the Ohio River, and northward about Lake Erie; others remained closer to home, along the Allegheny, and on the streams of western New York (although by 1700 these grounds were almost empty of the trade furs like beaver and otter). On occasion a large party of hunters would drive a herd of deer between converging lines of fire into corral or ambush, but most of the hunting was done individually. Some of the meat was cured by drying and smoking over fires and was briefly stored in underground pits. In the evenings the older people sat about the fires in the bark hunting lodges and told the sacred old legends and myths, which according to their belief should not be recounted in the summer lest the teller be assaulted by snakes.

By the end of January most of the hunting parties had returned to the village, and the reassembled community prepared for the celebration of the next New Year.[1]

· Dreams and the Wishes of the Soul ·

WHEN THE BLACK-ROBED Jesuit fathers began the preaching of the gospel to the Seneca nation in the year 1668, they quickly found that the Seneca were rigidly attached to Iroquoian religious traditions. Particularly obstinate were they in looking to their dreams for guidance in all the important affairs of life.

"The Iroquois have, properly speaking, only a single Divinity," wrote Father Fremin "—the dream. To it they render their submission, and follow all its orders with the utmost exactness. The Tsoanontouens [Seneca] are more attached to this superstition than any of the others; their religion in this respect becomes even a matter of scruple; whatever it be that they think they have done in their dreams, they believe themselves absolutely obliged to execute at the earliest moment. The other nations content themselves with observing those of their dreams which are the most important; but this people, which has the reputation of living more religiously than its neighbors, would think itself guilty of a great crime if it failed in its observance of a single dream. The people think only of that, they talk about nothing else, and all their cabins are filled with their dreams. They spare no pains, no industry, to show their attachment thereto, and their folly in this particular goes to such an excess as would be hard to imagine. He who has dreamed during the night that he was bathing, runs immediately, as soon as he rises, all naked, to several cabins, in each of which he has a kettleful of water thrown over his body, however cold the weather may be. Another who has dreamed that he was taken prisoner and burned alive, has himself bound and burned like a a captive on the next day, being persuaded that by thus satisfying his dream, this fidelity will avert from him the pain and infamy of captivity and death,—which, according to what he has learned from his Divinity, he is otherwise bound to suffer among his enemies. Some have been known to go as far as Quebec, travelling a hundred and fifty leagues, for the sake of getting a dog, that they had dreamed of buying there. . . ."

Father Fremin and his colleagues were appalled: Some Seneca might, any night, dream of their deaths! "What peril we are in every day," he continued, "among people who will murder us in cold blood if they have dreamed of doing so; and how slight needs to be a offense that a Barbarian has received from someone, to enable his heated imagination to represent to him in a dream that he takes revenge on the offender." It is small wonder that the Jesuits early attempted to disabuse the Seneca of their confidence in dreams, propounding various subtle questions, such as, "Does the soul leave the body during sleep?" and "Can infants in the womb dream?" either affirmative or negative answers to which would involve the recognition (according to the Jesuits) of logical contradictions in native theory.

But Jesuit logic did not discourage Seneca faith. The Quaker missionaries who reached the Seneca 130 years later found in them much the same "superstitious" respect to dreams that their unsuccessful predecessors had discovered. "They are superstitious in the extreme, with respect to dreams, and witchcraft," wrote Halliday Jackson, "and councils are often called, on the most trifling occurrences of this nature. To elucidate this—in the winter of 1799, while one of the Friends was engaged in instructing the children in school learning, a message came from a confederate tribe, eighty miles distant, stating that one of their little girls had dreamed that 'the devil was in all white people alike, and that they ought not to receive instruction from the Quakers, neither was it right for their children to learn to read and write.' In consequence of this circumstance, a council was called, the matter was deliberated on, and divers of them became so much alarmed, as to prevent their children from attending the school for some time."[2]

The Iroquois theory of dreams was basically psychoanalytic. Father Ragueneau in 1649 described the theory in language that might have been used by Freud himself. "In addition to the desires which we generally have that are free, or at least voluntary in us, [and] which arise from a previous knowledge of some goodness that we imagine to exist in the thing described, the Hurons [and, he might have added, the Seneca] believe that our souls have other desires, which are, as it were, inborn and concealed. These, they say, come from the depths of the soul, not through any knowledge, but by means of a certain blind transporting of the soul to certain objects; these transports might in the language of philosophy be called *Desideria innata*, to distinguish them from the former, which are called *Desideria elicita*.

"Now they believe that our soul makes these natural desires known by means of dreams, which are its language. Accordingly, when these desires are accomplished, it is satisfied; but on the contrary, if it be not granted what it desires, it becomes angry, and not only does not give its body the good and the happiness that it wished to procure for it, but often it also revolts against the body, causing various diseases, and even death. . . .

"In consequence of these erroneous [thought Father Ragueneau] ideas, most of the Hurons are very careful to note their dreams, and to provide the soul with what it has pictured to them during their sleep. If, for instance, they have seen a javelin in a dream, they try to get it; if they have dreamed that they gave a feast, they will give one on awakening, if they have the wherewithal; and so on with other things. And they call this *Ondinnonk*—a secret desire of the soul manifested by a dream."

But the Hurons recognized that the manifest content, or emptiness, of a dream, might conceal rather than reveal the soul's true wish. And so, "just as, although we did not always declare our thoughts and inclinations by means of speech, those who by means of supernatural vision could see into the depths of our hearts would not fail to have a knowledge of them—in the same manner, the Hurons believe that there are certain persons, more enlightened than the common, whose sight penetrates, as it were, into the depths of the soul. These see the natural and hidden desires that it has, though the soul has declared nothing by dreams, or though he who may have had the dreams has completely forgotten them. It is thus that their medicine-men . . . acquire credit, and make the most of their art by saying that a child in the cradle, who has neither discernment nor knowledge, will have an *Ondinnonk*—that is to say, a natural hidden desire for such or such a thing; and that a sick person will have similar desires for various things of which he has never had any knowledge, or anything approaching it. For, as we shall explain further on, the Hurons believe that one of the most efficacious remedies for rapidly restoring health is to grant the soul of the sick person these natural desires."

Disease or bodily infirmity could, according to Iroquois theory, arise from three sources: from natural injuries, such as the wounds of war or physical accident; from witchcraft, by which were projected magically into a victim's body certain foreign articles such as balls of hair, splinters of bone, clots of blood, bear's teeth, and the like; and from "the mind of the patient himself, which desires something, and will vex the body of the sick man until it possesses the thing required. For they think that there are in every man certain inborn desires, often unknown to themselves, upon which the happiness of individuals depends. For the purpose of ascertaining desires and innate appetites of this character, they summon soothsayers, who, as they think, have a divinely-imparted power to look into the inmost recesses of the mind. These men declare that whatever first occurs to them, or something from which they suspect some gain is to be derived, is desired by the sick person. Thereupon the parents, friends, and relatives of the patient do not hesitate to procure and lavish upon him whatever it may be, however expensive, a return of which is never thereafter to be sought. . . ."

To the soul, the Huron, Seneca, and other Iroquoian peoples ascribed several faculties not unlike the faculties that European psychologists of the day (i.e., the theologians) recognized. The Huron considered that the human body was inhabited by a single soul with several functions, and depending on the function that was being alluded to at the moment, a different name was used. There was a name for the soul in its capacity to animate the body and give it life; in its capacity to have knowledge; in its capacity to exercise judgment; in its capacity to wish or desire; and in its capacity to leave the body, as it might during dreams or after death. The soul occupied all parts of the body, and so had head, arms, legs, trunk, and all the rest of the anatomy (in ethereal counterpart) of the corporeal body.

Intuitively, the Iroquois had achieved a great degree of psychological sophistication. They recognized conscious and unconscious parts of the mind. They knew the great force of unconscious desires, were aware that the frustration of these desires could cause mental and physical (psychosomatic) illness. They understand that these desires were expressed in symbolic form, by dreams, but that the individual could not always properly interpret these dreams himself. They had noted the distinction between the manifest and latent content of dreams, and employed what sounds like the technique of free association to uncover the latent meaning. And they considered that the best method for the relief of psychic and psychosomatic distresses was to give the repressed desire satisfaction, either directly or symbolically. It would be fair to say that the seventeenth- and eighteenth-century Iroquois' understanding of psychodynamics was greatly superior to that of the most enlightened Europeans of the time.

The dreams reported by the Jesuit fathers and in the ethnological literature up to the present time provide a measure of the range and types of manifest content, and to a degree of the latent content, of Iroquois dreams. Dreams involving overt sexuality were not rare, and since they were freely reported and often acted out in therapeutic orgies, they gave the fathers great concern. Normally the Iroquoian peoples were modest in dress, often rather shy in public contacts with the opposite sex, and although premarital affairs were freely permitted to the young people and divorce and remarriage were easy for adults, chastity and marital fidelity were publicly recognized ideals. The fulfillment of dream wishes, however, took priority over other proprieties.

In 1656, at Onondaga, three warriors came to the village during the Midwinter Ceremony. They had been absent for a year in an unsuccessful campaign against the Erie nation. One of the warriors "was as wasted, pale, and depressed, as if he had spoken with the Devil. He spat blood, and was so disfigured that one scarcely dared to look him in the face." This man, when he arrived, announced that he had a matter of great importance to communicate to the elders. When they had assembled, he told them that during the campaign he had seen Tarachiawagon, He-who-holds-up-the-sky, the Good Twin and Creator, in the guise of a little dwarf. Tarachiawagon had addressed the warrior thus:

"I am he who holds up the Sky, and the guardian of the earth; I preserve men, and give victories to warriors. I have made you masters of the earth and victors over so many Nations: I made you conquer the Hurons, the Tobacco Nation, the Ahondihronnons, Atiraguenrek, Atiaonrek, Takoulguehronnons and Gentaguetehronnons; in short, I have made you what you are: and if you wish me to continue my protection over you, hear my words, and execute my orders.

"First, you will find three Frenchmen in your village when you arrive there. Secondly, you will enter during the celebration of the Honnaouroria. Thirdly, after your arrival, let there be sacrificed to me ten dogs, ten porcelain beads from each cabin, a collar [belt of wampum] ten rows wide, four measures of sunflower seed, and as many of beans. And, as for thee, let two married women be given thee, to be at thy disposal for five days. If that be not executed item by item I will make thy Nation a prey to all sorts of disasters,—and, after it is all done, I will declare to thee my orders for the future."

The dreamer's demands were fulfilled.

The Jesuits noted also, among the Huron, a formal ritual of gratification for sexual wishes expressed in dreams. In 1639, among the Hurons, Father Le Jeune met an old man ("in the common opinion of the Savages, . . . one of the most respectable and virtuous men of the whole country") who was dying of an ulcer that had spread from his wrist to his shoulder and finally had begun to eat into his body. This man's last desires were "a number of dogs of a certain shape and color, with which to make a three day's feast; a quantity of flour for the same purpose; some dances, and like performances; but principally . . . the ceremony of the 'andacwander,' a mating of men with girls, which is made at the end of the feast. He specified that there should be 12 girls, and a thirteenth for himself."

During the dream-guessing rites at Midwinter and, on occasion of illness, at other times of the year, persons propounded riddles in a sacred game. Each person or a group announced his "own and special desire or 'Ondinonc'—according as he is able to get information and enlightenment by dreams—not openly, however, but through Riddles. For example, someone will say 'What I desire and what I am seeking is that which bears a lake within itself'; and by this is intended a pumpkin or calabash. Another will say, 'What I ask for is seen in my eyes—it will be marked with various colors'; and because the same Huron word that signifies 'eye' also signifies 'glass bead,' this is a clue to divine what he desires—namely, some kind of beads of this material, and of different colors. Another will intimate that he desires an Andacwandat feast—that is to say, many fornications and adulteries. His Riddle being guessed, there is no lack of persons to satisfy his desire."

Nightmares of torture and personal loss were apparently not uncommon among warriors. In 1642 a Huron man dreamed that non-Huron Iroquois had taken him and burned him as a captive. As soon as he awoke, a council was held. "The ill fortune of such a Dream," said the chiefs, "must be averted." At once twelve or thirteen fires were lighted in the cabin where captives were burned, and torturers seized firebrands. The dreamer was burned; "he shrieked like a madman. When he avoided one fire, he at once fell into another." Naked, he stumbled around the fires three times, singed by one torch after another, while his friends repeated compassionately, "courage, my Brother, it is thus that we have pity on thee." Finally he darted out of the ring, seized a dog held for him there, and paraded through the cabins with this dog on his shoulders, publicly offering it as a consecrated victim to the demon of war, "begging him to accept this semblance instead of the reality of his Dream." The dog was finally killed with a club, roasted in the flames, and eaten at a public feast, "in the same manner as they usually eat their captives." In the period 1645–49 Father Francesco Bressani saw a Huron cut off one of his fingers with a seashell because he had dreamed that his enemies had captured him and were performing this amputation. In 1661–62 Father Lalemant describes three similar cases among the Five Nations. One man, in order to satisfy the dictates of his dream, had himself stripped naked by his friends, bound, dragged through the streets with the customary hooting, set upon the scaffold, and the fires lit. "But he was content with all these preliminaries and, after passing some hours in singing his death song, thanked the company, believing that after this imaginary capitivity he would never be actually a prisoner." Another man, having dreamed that his cabin was on fire, "could find no rest until he could see it actually burning." The chief's council in a body, "after mature deliberation on the matter," ceremoniously burned it down for him. A third man went to such extremes of realism, after a captivity nightmare, that he determined "that the fire should be actually applied to his legs, in the same way as to captives when their final torture is begun." The roasting was so cruel and prolonged that it took six months for him to recover from his burns.

Some dreams were violently aggressive. One Huron dreamed that he killed a French priest. "I killed a Frenchman; that is my dream. Which must be fulfilled at any cost," he yelled. He was only appeased by being given a French coat supposedly taken from the body of a dead Frenchman. A Cayuga man dreamed that he gave a feast of human flesh. He invited all the chief men of the Cayuga nation to his cabin to hear a matter of importance. "When they had assembled, he told them that he was ruined, as he had had a dream impossible of fulfillment; that his ruin would entail that of the whole Nation; and that a universal overthrow and destruction of the earth was to be expected. He enlarged at great length on the subject, and then asked them to guess his dream. All struck wide of the mark, until one man, suspecting the truth, said to him: 'Thou wishest to give a feast of human flesh. Here, take my brother; I place him in thy hands to be cut up on the spot, and put into the kettle.' All present were seized with fright, except the dreamer, who said that his dream required a woman." And a young girl was actually adorned with ornaments and, unaware of her fate, led to the dreamer-executioner. "He took her; they watched his actions, and pitied that innocent girl; but, when they thought him about to deal the death-blow, he cried out: 'I am satisfied; my dream requires nothing further.' " And during the Feast of Fools, the annual *Ononharoia* or "turning the brain upside down," when men and women ran madly from cabin to cabin, acting out their dreams in charades and demanding the dream be guessed and satisfied, many women and men alike dreamed of fighting natural enemies. Dreams in which hostility was directed at members of other nations were properly satisfied by acting them out both in pantomime and in real life; but bad dreams about members of the same community were acted out only in some symbolic form, which had a prophylactic effect. Thus, for instance, someone on the Cornplanter Seneca Reservation (during the nineteenth century) dreamed that a certain young woman was alone in a canoe in the middle of a stream without a paddle. The dreamer invited the young lady to a dream-guessing ceremony at his home. Various people gathered, and each one tried to guess what the dream was. Finally the dream was guessed. A miniature canoe with a paddle was thereupon presented to the girl. This ceremony was expected to forestall the dream-disaster from happening in real life.

Dreams in which the dreamer met a supernatural being who promised to be a friend and patron, and to give his protégé special powers and responsibilities, were very common. They were experienced often by boys at puberty, who deliberately sought such guardian spirits. One case was described in some detail by the Jesuits. At the age of fifteen or sixteen the youth retired alone into the woods, where he went sixteen days without food, drinking only water. Suddenly he heard a voice, which came from the sky, saying, "Take care of this man, and let him end his fast." At the same time he saw an old man "of rare beauty" descend from the sky. This man approached, gazed kindly at him, and said, "Have courage, I will take care of thy life. It is a fortunate thing for thee, to have taken me for thy master. None of these Demons who haunt these countries, shall have any power to harm thee. One day thou wilt see thy hair as white as mine. Thou wilt have four children; the first two and the last will be males, and the third will be a girl; after that, thy wife will hold the relation of a sister to thee." As he concluded speaking, the old man held out to him a piece of raw human flesh. The youth turned aside his head in horror. "Eat this," then said the old man, presenting him with a piece of bear's fat. When the lad had eaten it, the old man disappeared. On later occasions, however, the old man frequently reappeared with assurance of help. Most of the old man's predictions came true: the youth became a man, had four children, the third of whom was a girl; after the fourth, "a certain infirmity compelled him to . . . continence"; and as the eating of the bear's meat augured, the man became a noted hunter, gifted with a second sight for finding game. As an old man, looking back, he judged that "he would have had equal success in war had he eaten the piece of human flesh that he refused." This man in his last years became a Christian and was baptized. Dreams of supernatural protectors (or persecutors) also came often to sick persons, and from the identity of the spirit, the identity of the appropriate therapeutic ritual was deduced. Thus dreams of false faces call for the curing rituals of the Society of Faces; dreams of birds (in recent years, particularly of bloody or headless chickens) indicated that the Dew Eagle Ceremony was required. Sick persons often dreamed of someone (or a relative of the sick person dreamed), and the dream was interpreted to mean that the sick person "wants a friend." During the Eagle Society Ceremony, the sick person is given a "ceremonial friend"; thereafter the two treat one another as kinfolk, and the relationship of mutual helpfulness is life-long. If a boy's friend, for instance, is an older man, that man "must help the child to grow up to be a man. He must advise the boy, acting as his counselor. . . . When one is ill, they choose a friend for him from the other side (moiety). It is believed that the ceremony of making friends merges the relatives of the two principals into one kindred unit: the relatives of the man are linked with the relatives of the child. The older man must act as an example to his junior friend. The older man's conduct shall be observed by the younger boy who considers the older friend a model of behavior. The creator has ordained that these two be friends and it is hoped the younger one will grow up to be the fine man his older partner is supposed to be. Whatever he observes the older man doing, he shall do it. The old man bears the onus of the child's future. As a reward he will see the Creator when he dies. When the two meet on the road, the older person speaks first. 'Thanks you are well my friend?' The younger one answers, 'Truly thank you I am well my friend.' Every time he sees me, he calls me 'friend.' "[3]

The force of the unconscious desires of the individual, which are so compelling that "it would be cruelty, nay, murder, not to give a man the subject of his dream; for such a refusal might cause his death," sometimes was reinforced in native theory because the dream might be the vehicle for the expression of the desires and commands of those supernatural beings whom his wandering dream-soul had met. Some of these supernatural dreams have already been mentioned. Those involving powerful supernaturals like Tarachiawagon were apt to achieve great currency, and (if the chiefs considered the dream ominous) the whole nation might exert itself to fulfill the dreamer's demands; neglect invited national disaster. In the winter of 1640, during an epidemic of smallpox among the Huron, a young fisherman had a vision: a demon appeared to him under the form of a tall and handsome young man. "Fear not," said the being, "I am the master of the earth, whom you Hurons honor under the name of Iouskeha. I am the one whom the French wrongly call Jesus, but they do not know me. I have pity on your country, which I have taken under my protection; I come to teach you both the reasons and the remedies for your misfortune. It is the strangers who alone are the cause of it; they now travel two by two through the country, with the design of spreading the disease everywhere. They will not stop with that; after this smallpox which now depopulates your cabins, there will follow certain colics which in less than three days will carry off all those whom this disease may not have removed. You can prevent this misfortune; drive out from your village the two black gowns who are there." The demon continued with prescriptions for distributing medicinal waters to the sick; but after a few days, apparently, the popular disturbance subsided, and the priests were not expelled. In the winter of 1669–70 a woman at Oneida was visited in a dream by Tarachiawagon, who told her that the Andaste (southern enemies of the Five Nations) would attack and besiege the Oneida village in the spring, but that the Oneida would be victorious and they they would capture one of the most famous of the Andaste war-captains. In her dream she heard the voice of this man coming from the bottom of a kettle, uttering wailing cries like the cries of those who are being burned. This woman became for a time a prophet; every day people gathered at her house to hear her pronouncements, and she was believed absolutely in all she said. Prophetic dreams of this kind, of course, derived much of their impact from the conviction of the community that while some dreams expressed only the wishes of the dreamer's soul, others expressed the wishes of his personal guardian spirit or of various supernatural beings, particularly of Tarachiawagon, the Holder of the Heavens, the Master of Life, He who decided the fate of battles, the clemency of the seasons, the fruitfulness of the crops, and the success of the chase.

The effectiveness of the Iroquois dream-therapy was admitted, in some cases, even by the Jesuits, who had neither formal psychological insight nor religious sympathy for the primitive dream-theory. Father Le Jeune described the case of a woman who had gone to live with her husband in a strange village. One moonlit night during a feast she walked out from her cabin with one of her baby daughters in her arms. Suddenly she saw the moon dip down to earth and transform itself into a tall, beautiful woman, holding in her arms a little girl like her own. This moon-lady declared herself to be the "immortal seignior" of the Hurons and the several nations allied to them, and announced that it was her wish that from each of the half-dozen or so tribes she named, a present of that tribe's special product—from the Tobacco Nation, some tobacco, from the Neutrals, some robes of black squirrel fur, and so on—should be given to the dreamer. She declared that she enjoyed the feast then being given and wanted others like it to be held in all the other villages and tribes. "Besides," she said, "I love thee, and on that account I wish that thou shouldst henceforth be like me; and I am wholly of fire, I desire that thou be also at least of the color of fire," and so she ordained for her red cap, red plume, red belt, red leggings, red shoes, red all the rest.

The moon-lady then vanished and the mother returned to her cabin, where she collapsed "with a giddiness in the head and a contraction of the muscles." Thereafter she dreamt constantly of "goings and comings and outcries through her cabin."

It was decided by the chiefs that this was an important matter and that every effort should be made to give satisfaction to the sick woman: not only *her* wishes, but those of the moon-lady, were involved. She was dressed in red; the disease was diagnosed (from the symptom of giddiness) as demanding the Dream Feast or *Ononharoia* ("turning the brain upside down"); and messengers collected for her the articles she required. The Jesuits sounded a sour note, refusing to contribute the blue blanket she wanted from a "Frenchman," but the lady went through the five-day ritual, supported most of the way on the arms of sympathetic friends. She hobbled in her bare feet through over two hundred fires; she received hundreds of gifts; she propounded her last desire in dozens of cabins, relating her troubles "in a plaintive and languishing voice," and giving hints as to the content of her last desire, until it was finally guessed. Then there was a general rejoicing, a public council, a giving of thanks and congratulations, and a public crowning and completing of her last desire (which Father Le Jeune, exasperatingly, does not describe or even hint at).

An honest man, the father was compelled to admit that all this worked. "It is to be presumed that the true end of this act, and its catastrophe, will be nothing else but a Tragedy. The devil not being accustomed to behave otherwise. Nevertheless, this poor unhappy creature found herself much better after the feast than before, although she was not entirely free from, or cured of her trouble. This is ordinarily attributed by our Savages to the lack or failure of some detail, or to some imperfection in the ceremony. . . ."

Not all therapeutic dream-fulfillments ended in even a partial cure, of course, but this was not felt as any reflection on the principles of dream-therapy. The whole village vied to give the sick person his every wish, for any frustration was a threat to life. A dying man might be seen surrounded by literally thousands of scissors, awls, knives, bells, needles, kettles, blankets, coats, caps, wampum belts, beads, and whatever else the sick man's fancy, or the hopeful guesses of his friends, suggested. And if he died at last, "He dies," the people would say, "because his soul wished to eat the flesh of a dog, or of a man; because a certain hatchet that he wished for could not be procured; or because a fine pair of leggings that had been taken from him could not be found." And if, on the other hand, he survived, the gift of the last thing that he wished for during his illness was cherished for the rest of his life.

The material on Iroquois dreams can be divided into two major types of dreams or visions recognized by the society and separately institutionalized (although in many dreams the two types are blended). These two types may be called *symptomatic dreams* and *visitation dreams*.

A symptomatic dream expressed a wish of the dreamer's soul. This wish was interpreted either by the dreamer himself or by a clairvoyant, who for a fee diagnosed the wish by free association in reverie, by drinking a bowlful of herb teas while chanting to his guardian spirit, by consulting his guardian spirit in a dream or trance (sometimes going to sleep with a special herb under his head), by water scrying, and in later days by reading tea leaves and cards. Anyone, man or woman, could become a clairvoyant, and there were many in each community, some occupying roles of reputation—like famous doctors —and others of more humble pretensions helping their immediate families. These diagnoses served as signals for the execution of various more or less conventional patterns of acting out the wish, either literally or symbolically. Some of these acting-out patterns were prophylaxes against the fate implicit in the wish—for example, the symbolic or partial tortures and the abortive cannibal feasts. This sort of acting out seems to have been based on the idea that a wish, although irrational and destructive toward self or friends, was fateful, and that the only way of forestalling the realization of an evil-fated wish was to fulfill it symbolically. Others were curative of existing disorders, and prophylactic only in the sense of preventing ultimate death if the wish were too long frustrated. The acting-out patterns can also be classified according to whether the action required is mundane or sacred and ceremonial. Thus dreams of buying a dog, and then traveling a long distance to obtain the dog, involve no particular sacred ceremony revolving around the wish itself, nor would a dream of going on a war party require more than participation in the normal course of military enterprise. But most of the symptomatic dreams of mentally or physically sick people demanded a ceremonial action, often not only at the time of the dream, but periodically thereafter during the dreamer's whole life span. The annual festival at midwinter not merely permitted but required the guessing and fulfillment of the dreams of the whole community. There were probably several dozen special feasts, dances, or rites that might be called for at any time during the year by a sick dreamer: the *andacwander* rite, requiring sexual intercourse between partners who were not husband and wife; the *ohgiwe* ceremony, to relieve someone from persistent and troubling dreams about a dead relative or friend; the dream-guessing rite, in which the dreamer accumulated many gifts from unsuccessful guessers; the Striking Stick Dance, the Ghost Dance, and many other feasts, dances, and games. The repertoire could at any time be extended by a new rite, if the dreamer saw a new rite, or a nonsacred rite, in a dream, or if his clairvoyant divined that such a rite was called for; even ordinary "social" dances became curative when performed for someone at the instigation of his dream. Some rites were the property of "secret" medicine societies, membership in which was obtained by having received the ministrations of the society upon dream-diagnosis of its need. Visions of false faces called for the rituals of the False Face Society; visions of dwarf spirits indicated a need for the "dark dance" of the Little Water Society; dreams of bloody birds were properly diagnosed as wishes for membership in the Eagle Society; dreams of illness were evidence of need for the Medicine Men's Society Rite. The relationship of dreams to ritual was such that the repertoire of any community might differ from that of the next because of the accidents of dreams and visions, and from the annual calendar of community rituals any element might at any time be abstracted and performed for the benefit of an individual.

The symptomatic dreams described above displayed in their manifest content relatively humble and mundane matters: wanted objects, like dogs, hatchets, knives, clothing, etc.; familiar dances and rituals, and their ceremonial equipment; familiar animals, birds, and plants. The second category of dreams, however, showed powerful supernatural beings who, in the dream, usually spoke personally to the dreamer, giving him a message of importance for himself and often also for the whole community. Sometimes these were personality-transformation dreams, in which the longings, doubts, and conflicts of the dreamer were suddenly and radically resolved, the dreamer emerging from his vision with a new sense of dignity, a new capacity for playing a hitherto difficult role, and a new feeling of health and well-being. Such experiences were particularly common among boys at puberty. Retiring alone to the woods, fasting, and meditating in solitude, the youth after a week or two experienced a vision in which a supernatural being came to him, promised his aid and protection, and gave him a talisman. The guardian spirit, in a sense, took the place of the parents upon whom the boy had hitherto depended, and from whom he had now to emancipate himself emotionally if he were to become a whole man. Guardian spirits varied in character and power: Some gave clairvoyant powers, some gave unusual hunting luck and skill, some gave luck, courage, strength, and skill in war. Clairvoyants possessed particularly potent guardian spirits that enabled the shaman, simply by breathing on a sick man's body, to render it transparent. Prominent shamans claimed the power to foretell coming events, such as approaching epidemics, and other great public calamities. A few such men became known as prophets and were "apt to acquire great influence and their advice [was] usually followed without much question." This gift of prophecy was the endowment of a particularly good, and powerful, guardian spirit.[4]

In Iroquois theory a dream thus could reveal the wishes not only of the dreamer, but of the supernatural being who appeared in his dream. Frustration of the wishes of the supernatural was dangerous, for he might not merely abandon or directly cause the death of the dreamer, but bring about disaster to the whole society or even cause the end of the world. Hence dreams in which such powerful personages as Tarachiawagon (culture hero and favorite dream-figure) appeared and announced that they wanted something done (frequently for the dreamer's welfare) were matters of national moment. Clairvoyants were called upon; the chiefs met and discussed ways and means of satisfying the sometimes expensive or awkward demands of the dreamer (representing the powers above) or of averting the predicted catastrophe. Not infrequently this type of dream also bore elements of personality transformation for the dreamer, who in his identification with the gods assumed a new role as prophet, messiah,

and public censor and adviser. Such prophets might make highly detailed recommendations about the storage of crops, the waging of
war, diplomatic policy toward other tribes and toward the French or
the English, measures to avert epidemics or famine. Rarely, however,
did such prophets maintain a lasting influence; but on the rare occasions of their success, a prophet, basing his message on a visitation
dream, might bring about a radical transformation of the Iroquois
way of life.

The theory of dreams among the Iroquois was in evident accord
with the theme of freedom in the culture as a whole. The intolerance
of externally imposed restraints, the principle of individual independence and autonomy, the maintenance of an air of indifference to
pain, hardship, and loneliness—all these were the negative expression,
as it were, of the positive assertion that wishes must be satisfied, that
frustration of desire is the root of all evil. But men are never equally
aware and equally tolerant of all their desires; and dreams themselves,
carefully examined, are perhaps the quickest portal to that shadowy
region where the masked and banished wishes exist in limbo. What
then, if anything, can we learn about the unconscious of the Iroquois
Indians from scattered dreams recorded by the Jesuits and other casual
observers?

The manifest content of Iroquois dreams was as various, probably,
as the wishes of mankind: There were dreams of love and hate,
pleasure and pain, of lost loved ones and longed-for guardians; incon-
sequential and absurd things happened, and incidental objects were
transfixed by the arrow of desire; abhorrent actions and repulsive
thoughts plagued the restless sleeper. Dreams as reported in the
literature seem to have held a prevailing anxious tone, ranging from
nightmare fantasies of torture to the nagging need to define the unconscious wish and satisfy it before some disaster occurs. The most
dramatic and most frequently mentioned dreams seem to come from
three groups of people: pubescent youths (who must renounce childhood's indulgences); warriors (who feared capture and torture); and
the sick (who feared death). These were, perhaps, the stress points
that generated desire. Adolescent conflict, dreams of battle, and the
silent panic of the sick; these are things of which many men of many
cultures, including our own, have experience.

The manifest content and the conscious rationale the Seneca gave
to dreams themselves were mainly in the active voices, and such

passivity as showed itself was laden with pain unless it occurred in visitation dreams, where a man might be passive in relation to a god. But the latent content, representative of the underlying wish, may be seen in the *acting-out*, which was so often passive or self-destructive. Dreams were not to brood over, to analyze, or to prompt lonely and independent actions; they were to be told, or at least hinted at, and it was for other people to be active. The community rallied round the dreamer with gifts and ritual. The dreamer was fed, he was danced over, he was rubbed with ashes, he was sung to, he was given valuable presents, he was accepted as a member of a medicine society. The man whose dream manifested a wish to attack and kill was satisfied by being *given* a coat; the man who dreamed of sleeping with a woman did not attempt to woo his mistress, he was *given* an available female by the chief's council. Only in the personality-transformation dreams of pubescent boys and adult prophets was passivity accepted in the dream, and these were the dreams of men *in extremis*.

This observation suggests that the typical Iroquois male, who as a matter of fact in his daily life was an exceedingly brave, generous, active, and independent spirit, nevertheless typically cherished some strong, if unconscious, wishes to be passive, to beg, to be cared for. This unallowable passive tendency, so threatening to a man's sense of self-esteem, could not appear easily even in a dream, and when it did, it was either experienced as an intolerably painful episode of torture, or was put in terms of a meeting with a supernatural protector. The Iroquois themselves unwittingly made the translation, however: An active manifest dream was fulfilled by a passive receiving action. The arrangement of the dream-guessing rite, indeed, raised this dependency to an exquisite degree: The dreamer could not even *ask* for his wish; like a baby, he must content himself with cryptic signs and symbols, until someone guessed what he wanted and gave it to him.

The culture of dreams may be regarded as a necessary escape valve in Iroquois life. Iroquois men were, in their daily affairs, brave, active, self-reliant, and autonomous; they cringed to no one and begged for nothing. But no man can balance forever on such a pinnacle of masculinity, where asking and being given are unknown. Iroquois men dreamed; and without shame they received the fruits of their dreams, and their souls were satisfied.[5]

❧ 4 ❦

THE RITUALS OF FEAR
AND MOURNING

THE INTENSE INTEREST OF THE INDIANS IN LOVE AND FRIENDSHIP WAS not always apparent to early observers, who were apt to be more impressed by the mask of stoicism. But numerous incidental comments confirm the existence of a tender side of Iroquois character. Far from being so autonomous emotionally that social slights were matters of indifference, behind the impassive façade the Iroquois were often agonizingly shy, sensitive, and vulnerable both to flattery and to insult. A visit from a great man delighted whole villages, for—as a successful negotiator said—"Indians have a great idea of personal importance."[1] Neophyte chiefs were warned that they had to develop a skin "seven thumbs thick" in order to endure the disappointments and malicious gossip in which a political life was bathed. Insulted persons silently nourished grudges for years and in secret sought the help of witches to punish their enemies. Elaborate rules of conversational etiquette, designed to preclude interruptions of speech and face-to-face criticism, worked to avert the too-frequent chafing of tender sensibilities. But neighbors feared neighbors, and kinsmen their relatives, who might nonetheless be responsible through witchcraft for all manner of misfortune. Death aroused the most violent reactions: severe anaclitic depressions or moods of paranoiac suspicion, which in native theory (and it was a theory based on exact intuition) could only be forestalled by replacing the lost object with an adopted substitute upon whom could be lavished, depending on the character of the mourner, either the most extreme love or the most vicious hate (tortured victims also were adopted), or in some cases both alternately. Descriptions of Seneca mourning behavior read like psychoanalytic essays on the dynamics of depressive states, and the paranoia of bereavement, which generated the blood feud and fears of witchcraft, was regarded by the Iroquois themselves as a continuing threat to the solidarity of the community.

· *The Importance of Love and Friendship* ·

THE SUPERFICIAL RESERVE between the sexes, the avoidance of public embraces, the apparent casualness of marriage unions, the cool acceptance of divorce, gave some early observers the idea that the Seneca were deficient in romantic feeling, or even in animal passion, and others that they were extraordinarily licentious. Neither impression was close to the truth: Avoidance at first, and disillusionment later, public reserve always, were inevitable, precisely because of the extraordinary height of emotional aspiration. The Seneca legendry was full of romantic tales of young men who braved incredible dangers to win their beautiful brides. The theme of sexual jealousy was recurrent in folklore. Love magic was almost a profession. Guy Johnson, the son-in-law of Sir William Johnson and his successor as Superintendent of Indian Affairs, summarized the matter as a kind of emotional dialectic between romantic enthusiasm and spartan reserve. "Although the Indians appear to be little attracted by personal beauty, yet they are no means defective in the Animal Passion for their Females or in Constitutional Vigour, but thro' Education and Habit they do not manifest them to Superficial Observers . . . the Indians being all Warriors whilst young, & valuing themselves on the Reputation, affect a Coldness of Character, however Amorous, there being no Reputation derived from the latter, by which, and the uncommon affection of Modesty in their Women, when sober, Strangers are easily deceived; besides which Indians, who naturally are very Jealous, assume a Seeming Indifference for the Sex in order to Satisfy their Doubts by rendering those whom they Suspect more ungarded in their Actions.—Therefore the Indians are by no means chaste, but being naturally of a cold Behaviour, rather than Disposition, they Spartan like, avoid the outward appearance of an Attention to that, which derogated from their Military Merit."[2] And Governor Blacksnake in his old age described in nostalgic detail a romantic episode in his youth that illustrates this ideological conflict between love and duty. Blacksnake was traveling with his uncle Cornplanter to Sandusky, in the Ohio country, in order to negotiate with the Indians there. They hoped, by serving as diplomatic middlemen, to avert a war between the western Indians and the United States. Along the way they fell in with a band of displaced Osage Indians, and Blacksnake "took a liken" to a young woman who was "the Handsomest that I ever See among my own people." Although they could not speak each other's language, Blacksnake managed to make his interest known, and she hers. Eventually he discovered that she had no husband. He wanted to marry her, but his uncle Cornplanter, the head of the Seneca party, said no. "I then said no more about it marriage," he recalled. "I have felt sorrow."[3]

The concept of "friend" also was vested with an extraordinary degree of interest. The guardian spirit was the "friend" par excellence; there was the ceremonial friend chosen in a dream, particularly in connection with the Dew Eagle Dance, whose comradeship was believed to cure and prevent serious illness; and individual men (often warriors on the same expedition) not uncommonly entered into a compact of mutual loyalty and service. This bosom-friend relationship could be very close. Stone, in his biography of Joseph Brant, remarked on Brant's "lamentations" when a white officer who was his friend was transferred to Jamaica. "Those unacquainted with Indian usages are not probably aware of the intimacy, or the importance attached to this relationship. The selected friend is, in fact, the counterpart of the one who chooses him, and the attachment often becomes romantic; they share each other's secrets, and are participants of each other's joys and sorrows."[4] But in friendship as in love, the exigencies of war and travel made such relationships insecure.

· The Faces of the Gods ·

THE PROMINENCE OF MASKS in the rituals and supernatural beliefs of the Iroquois Indians implies that they embodied an idea of peculiar importance. False Face dancers performed dramatic pantomime at the New Year's and Green Corn ceremonies; they drove out witches and disease in the spring and fall; and they cured illnesses at any time of the year. Cornhusk masks were worn by other ritual dancers at New Year's and Green Corn. Some of the more secretive medicine-societies employed special, rarely seen masks. Even the mythology dealt with beings who went by the name of False Faces and who possessed a curious dual character, compounded of strength and shyness.

The wooden False Face masks were by all odds the most conspicuous. These masks were not called false faces or masks by the Seneca themselves, but simply *gagosa* ("faces"), the same word that was used for the human face. They were somewhat larger than life size, twelve to eighteen inches from forehead to chin, and broad in proportion. Although no two masks were identical (as one old Seneca put it, there are as many types of faces as there are different people), they had with few exceptions certain common features: They were painted black, or red, or black and red; they had large, staring eyes made of pieces of copper or brass sheeting pierced for pupils; long, protuberant, and frequently bent noses extended from brow to lips; the mouths were open and dramatically distorted. The mouths were the bases of native classification. There were wide mouths, upturned at the corners in a sardonic leer, sometimes with huge teeth showing; mouths rounded into a wide funnel for blowing ashes, sometimes with tongue sticking out; mouths puckered as if whistling, the lips everted into two flat, spoonlike disks; mouths with straight, swollen, shelflike lips; mouths twisted at one corner to accompany the bent nose, as if the face had been twisted by paralysis. Each was crowned with long, flowing hair, anciently buffalo mane, more recently horse tails. The antiquity of these concepts is considerable. Archaeologists have dug up miniature stone replicas in prehistoric cemeteries and villages. Champlain first saw them among the Hurons in 1616; a Dutch traveler found them among the Mohawk and Oneida in 1634. Masks were not mentioned by observers among the Seneca before 1687, but there is no reason to suppose that they had not a similar antiquity there; the Seneca were less thoroughly missionized than the Hurons and the Mohawks. Probably the earliest wooden masks go back at least into the sixteenth century. Their origin is obscure, but they probably originated as individual icons, representations of personal guardian spirits revealed in dreams, and came to be institutionalized as their peculiar suitability to religious and psychotherapeutic practice led more and more persons to dream of them. Indeed, the legend of the origin of the Society of Faces, who own most of the wooden masks, has it that the Faces were indeed revealed to a lonely hunter in a dream; they taught him their songs and their rituals, and no doubt in his dream he discovered what they looked like.

The wooden masks were made to fulfill a dream. Whoever dreamed of a Face instructing him to make a mask was obligated either to make one himself or to employ a craftsman to make one. The mask-maker first carved the outlines of the face in the bark of a living basswood (or other soft wood) tree, and then released the living Face by notching the trunk above and below and splitting it away. The mask was completed carefully, its back hollowed out to receive a wearer's face, and finally "baptized" by being placed briefly in the fire at a council-house meeting, while the great False Face, of whom it was a living likeness and deputy, was supplicated by the burning of powdered Indian tobacco thrown onto the embers. Once thus baptized, a mask was alive and charged with a power that could do almost limitless good or ill. It must be carefully kept, when not in use, either hanging with face to the wall or neatly wrapped in a clean cloth and placed in a drawer, or box, or other safe storage place. A little bag of tobacco must be tied to the inside of the mask, because the Faces loved tobacco, and on occasion (if the mask fell or if the owner dreamed of it) a little tobacco must be burned as an offering; it must be fed "False Face pudding" on occasion, by smearing a thick gruel of parched cornmeal and maple sugar (the warpath diet) on its lips; and its face must be wiped with sunflower-seed oil to keep the "skin" soft and clear. Old masks developed a lustrous patina from repeated applications of the oil. Masks had names and personalities, even whims; they liked to be talked and sung to and caressed, to have their hair arranged and their foreheads stroked; they were addressed as "grandfather." If one were to be transferred to another party, or perhaps sold, the transaction must be explained, the owner's regret expressed, and assurances given that the new owner would continue to feed, anoint, and supply tobacco. A neglected mask might sweat or even cry; large tears could be seen rolling from its eyes. Such unhappy Faces might ultimately avenge themselves by bringing a fatal illness on the owner; but Faces were rarely mistreated. They were loved and indulged like children; childless owners were even known to request that favorite masks be buried with them.

Although the Faces thus normally lived a passive, happy life, they did have on occasion very important, if not onerous, duties to perform. Most of them belonged to, and all were at the disposal of, the members of the Society of Faces. The membership of this society included a large share of the community, for all those persons, old and young, male and female, who had ever been saved from the ravages of disease through the kindly interference of the Faces or who had ever dreamed of membership in their society were automatically members. The society had no clubhouse, and its leadership was informal: a pair of women, representing the moieties, who were generally responsible for the care and assignment of the masks to ritual duties, and some men who on ceremonial occasion led the expeditions of the Faces and from time to time instructed the membership in the origin legends associated with the masks and the beings whom they represented. Without the ministrations of the society, a Seneca community would (in theory) have faced extinction.

As we have seen, in the spring and in the fall the Company of Faces conducted a public exorcism of disease, tornadoes and high winds, malevolent witches, and ill luck of all kinds from the entire village. The Company of Faces divided into two groups, starting at opposite ends of the settlement. Preceded by heralds wearing masks of braided cornhusks and augmented by recruits as they went along, the Faces visited every house. Stripped to the waist, masked, bearing rattles, the young men shouted terrifying cries as they moved along. As they approached the house or any member of the society, the leader chanted:

> *A long voice, a long voice*
> *Yowige, yowige, yowige*

and when they returned to the council house whence they had started, he sang a song suggestive of an ancient song of thanksgiving to a guardian spirit:

> *It might happen, it might happen*
> *Hai ge hai*
> *From the mighty Shagodyoweh*

(81)

Hai ge hai
I shall derive good luck
Hai ge hai.

During their patrol the masked visitors crawled into each house on hands and knees, prowled through every compartment, swept under the beds, and peered into dark corners. They jostled the sick to their feet and played practical jokes on lazy people. The horseplay was high-spirited. "Once," comments a recent observer, "a leader was about to gather his company of exterminators and depart for another house when one turned up missing. They heard a most terrifying racket in the loft. They ascended to discover him violently shaking an old straw bedticking, from which bedbugs were fleeing by the score. This fellow, . . . possessed of an extraordinary sense of the ridiculous, was shaking his rattle and crying in the most orthodox manner."

At last the company assembled at the council-house, where the Faces rubbed their rattles on the windows, banged on the doors, and finally burst into the room and crawled toward the fire. Now the Faces had to be paid for their work; and they had to be paid quickly, lest they assault the stoves and scatter hot coals about the room. The speaker thanked all the spirit forces and burned tobacco (collected at the houses just visited), imploring the Faces to protect the people against epidemics and tornadoes.

Partake of this sacred tobacco, O mighty Shagodyoweh, you who live at the rim of the earth, who stand towering, you who travel everywhere on the earth caring for the people.

And you, too, whose faces are against the trees in the forests, whom we call the company of faces; you also receive tobacco.

And you Husk Faces partake of the tobacco. For you have been continually associated with the False Faces. You too have done your duty.

Partake of this tobacco together. Everyone here believes that you have chosen him for your society.

So now your mud-turtle rattle receives tobacco.

Here the Faces scraped their rattles on the floor in delight.

And now another thing receives tobacco, your staff, a tall pine with the branches lopped off at the top.

So presently you will stand up and help your grandchildren, since they have fulfilled your desires. Fittingly, they have set down a full kettle of mush for you. It is greased with bear fat. Now another thing is fulfilled: on top there are strops of fried meat as large as your feet.

At this news, the Faces rolled over in ecstasy on their backs and seized their feet, staring at them and trying to put them in their mouths.

Besides, a brimming kettle of hulled-corn soup rests here.
Now it is up to you. Arise and help your grandchildren. They have fulfilled everything that you requested should be done here for you to use. Arise and make medicine.

Now those sick persons who had dreamt of a False Face, or whose illness had been diagnosed by a clairvoyant as produced by the Faces, came forward and stood by the fire, or if they were not well enough for that, sat on the bench in the middle of the floor. The Faces swarmed over them, blowing ashes on their heads, rubbing ashes in their hair, manhandling them with roughly tender, kindly hands. Then they danced around the council house to the music of a turtle rattle and a singer. The Doorkeeper's Dance, which followed, was for the Great World Rim Being (Shagodyoweh). And finally all persons within the council house joined in a round dance. Dancing was compulsory, for those who resisted were said to become possessed by the Face, falling to the floor, crawling toward the fire, and shuffling the hot coals.

The Faces treated the sick again in public rituals in the council house at midwinter and at the Green Corn in late summer. Most of their curing rituals were not public at all, however, but private affairs, conducted in the home of the sick person by the Order of Common Faces. These ceremonies were performed, on a request being made to a leader, whenever they were needed in response to a patient's dream or the diagnosis of False Face Sickness made by a clairvoyant. In characteristic fashion, masked beings banged on the house with their rattles and rubbed their staves up and down the door frames, burst in howling and babbling incoherently, danced, blew ashes and laid on hands, received hot mush and tobacco, and departed.

But probably the most widely noticed occasions of the appearance of the Faces was on sixth night of the Midwinter Ceremony. At this time the Faces were known as Beggars and Thieves. Worn by little boys and youths, they had been going about from house to house begging for tobacco and stealing food if not given tobacco. On the sixth night they repaired to the council house to beg again for tobacco from the people congregated there. There were the usual rattling, bumping, and scraping noises outside the building; then the door banged open and in crawled a ragged company of men, dressed in ragged, patched, torn clothes, and wearing False Face masks. Some carried the big turtle rattles, some the smaller horn rattles, some staves with which they hammered incessantly on the resonant floor. A ripple of delighted laughter swept around the congregation, now and then interrupted by an exclamation of mock terror as a Face thrust its leering visage close to a pretty woman. A few pirouetted clumsily; one rolled around hugging its knees; a third walked up and down the rows of benches, peering hopefully into each face and cooing like a mourning dove. At last some young man handed over a handful of Indian tobacco; this is what the Face was waiting for, and he immediately began his dance, solo, with the tobacco-giver beating out the tempo with the sharp edge of the rattle on the scarred floor. Soon all the Faces had found kindred spirits with tobacco to exchange for a dance, and the floor was creaking under the clumsy feet of the capering Faces, until at last they all suddenly departed, their appetites for tobacco satiated.

The vast powers that the False Faces were able to control on man's behalf shared the uncanny quality known as $utgo^n$. Witches were $utgo^n$, as were disease, storm, and other evil or mysterious things. In witchcraft, perhaps, $utgo^n$ took its most dramatic form. Witches, both men and women, were universally feared, and people suspected of witchcraft were hated and avoided. The fear of inciting a witch or his client to take revenge may have dissuaded some from expressing hostility openly and from aggressive acts of insult, theft, mayhem, and murder. But the other side of the coin was the persistent fear that any accident, illness, or death in one's kin group was the work of a secret enemy. Witch fear thus served both to suppress overt acts of rudeness and aggression and to nourish an endemic suspicion of one's neighbors. Some witchcraft was performed out of the witch's or his clients' private malice against the victim, to make him sicken and perhaps die. Magical poisons could be blown on the intended victim, concocted from arcane matter like the decaying flesh and bones of corpses;

foreign objects could be magically projected into his body; a doll might be hidden near a longhouse against whose lineage revenge was sought; a peg representing an enemy might be driven into a tree to rot; or the witch could simply wish the victim to death. Professional witches were supposed by some to be leagued in a coven, membership in which had to be obtained by the sacrifice of a kinsman, and to be able to transform themselves into were-animals, such as owls, turkeys, dogs, and pigs. Some of the services of legitimate shamans or curers might also be classified as witchcraft, for such persons, although not lending themselves to murder, could use their arts to cure the sick, to confuse and terrify the enemy in war and opponents in sport, to induce abortions, and to control the sexual desires and capacities of persons in whom a client was interested, causing uncontrollable lust in one, impotence in another. The traffic in abortion- and love-magic was active although it was considered to verge on the unethical.

Protection against witchcraft was best secured from the benevolent protecting power (*orenda*) of a guardian spirit, whose influence could shield one against *utgo*[n] and could ensure good luck in the hunt, warfare, love, and other important interests. Circumspection in behavior could avert the jealousy and wrath that might prompt others to turn to witchcraft. Shamans used poultices, sucking, and massage of the affected part to remove introjected objects and poisons. And if all else failed, a known witch might be killed with public sanction and without fear of retaliation from his kin. Also, the False Faces worked to protect the whole community against witches, as we have seen.[5]

The central myth that explained and identified the power over witches and other evils possessed by these alternately comical and awful Faces was the creation myth, in which the prototype of all the Faces, the Great World Rim Dweller, is no other than the Evil Twin, the brother of the Creator. Thus the Faces are party to the inmost secrets of the cosmos. Although Handsome Lake himself did not leave any known document narrating the story of the creation and of the origin of the Faces, several of his contemporaries and descendants on the Allegany Reservation have done so, and we can be reasonably sure of what his own belief was concerning these matters. His own brother, Cornplanter, dictated to a white man through an interpreter a brief account of the Seneca cosmogony in 1821; and about 1843 either his nephew Governor Blacksnake or Brooks Redeye, the

Handsome Lake preacher at Allegany at that time, dictated a longer version of the creation myth. These, with other texts from Allegany and elsewhere, provide a complete and coherent story, which accounts for and identifies, among other things, the Faces.[6]

In the beginning, before there was any earth, there was a world above, in the sky. This sky world was all alive: the land was living and the waters were living and there was an abundance of delicious animals and fish and fruits. There were manlike beings there, too, who were never sick, or in pain, or too cold, or too hot, and who never had to work. There was no sun or moon or stars; instead, there was a great tree that shed light half the time and half the time kept dark, so that the sky-beings had a kind of night and day.

Now in this sky world there was a family with five sons, and the youngest son was preoccupied with his love for a young woman. He loved her so much that he became weak. So he told his parents to go to this young woman and tell her of his love and of his weakness, which was the consequence of prolonged passion, and to tell her also that if she would come and attend him and be his wife, he would become strong again. This they did, and she consented to become his wife; he soon became strong again. But not long after this he became sick once more with the same weakness; for several days he grew weaker and weaker, and all the while he complained of his weakness. At last he called his oldest brother and said, "I have been complaining of weakness for several days. Now I am willing to tell you the instructions I received in a dream during the last sleep I had. I dreamed that the youngest of my brothers said, 'The living tree, The-Tree-That-Is-Called-Tooth, must be plucked out by the roots, and by the hands of the four brothers; otherwise you will die.' Also in my dream the living tree said, 'There is another generation coming out of the living tree. It will sprout out of the ground beside that living tree which gives light and control over the land.' "

The four brothers understood what he said, but they did not know what to make of it. Finally they asked him, "If the living tree should be plucked out by the roots, what shall we do for light?" He answered, "There is a young tree growing beside the old tree, and this will give light forever. The first one will be done away with for the sake of the new creation of the world, and the other will grow on solid ground and will stand and live forever. This will come to pass."

So they went to the tree to see whether a new tree was growing, as he said, or not; and they found that a young sapling was indeed grow-ing on top of the ground. The youngest brother then said he would go forward and take hold of the living tree and pull it down by hand, as the dream dictated. But the oldest brother said again, "Why do you think you will die if we do not pluck out the tree of light?" And the sick man said, "It is a true dream that has power by itself. It must be done; if not, I shall die for cause of disobedience."

And so at last the four brothers consented to pull the old tree down. The oldest brother took hold of it first and pulled and worked at it until he wore himself out; then the next younger brother took hold, and so on, until the youngest of the four brothers at last pulled the tree down to the ground. Then the whole tree, roots, trunk, branches, and leaves, plunged through the hole.

The sick man got up at once and went to the falling tree, calling his wife to come with him. When they came to the place where the tree had stood, they saw only the hole in the plain. The man-being stood at the edge of the pit and looking down saw a light. He called to his wife, "Come and look. Sit close by me." So she did. Then he blessed the tree that had fallen through the earth for the sake of the new creation and he blessed the young tree that remained. While they sat there and gazed at the light below, an air came up through the hole in the earth, very tender, and they heard the sound of the south wind, which is the air of life. And from this air she conceived a child.

He said to her, "Do you see plainly the light below?" She an-swered, "Yes." "There shall be your new home, on a new-created earth below, and you shall be the mother of the earth-beings," he said. And he pushed her off the edge of the pit and she fell through the hole in the sky.

She was not worried but rather contented. For a long time she fell slowly through the hole in the sky-plain, but when at last she had passed through, and looked back, she could see nothing; it looked blue as far as her eye could see. Then she saw a white bird flying; the bird noticed her and went away to notify other birds. Then it came back and said, "Are you afraid, being cast away like this?" And she said, "Yes," and she looked at the bird, and the bird turned into a man and he said to her, "You shall be saved, and it shall be fulfilled accord-ing to the instructions from above. You shall be assisted. You shall inhabit a place on the great waters below." Then he left, and another one came and said to her, "You will see tens of thousands of the inhabitants of the air and the waters below. They are preparing to take care of you."

And, indeed, as she looked down to see where she was going, she saw a great multitude of fowl flying in the air and heard a loud sound amongst them, because they were talking to one another. When she came near them, they all assembled and flew up toward her. Then they stopped her fall a little distance above the water. Then they held a council to decide who would be strong enough to bear her upon his back. But all the fowls of the air and even the water birds excused themselves; they were not able to remain long on top of the water. Then they asked themselves whether any of the creatures that live below the surface of the waters might be able to hold her up forever. Everyone had something to say and someone to suggest. But in the end only the mud-turtle remained as a candidate. While all the other species excused themselves, the mud-turtle said, "I never tire out or die without my father's consent." So he swam up on top of the water, and then the birds let her down upon him, and she stood upon his back, and there she rested. And all the fowls lighted upon him to rest themselves too.

The turtle grew very fast. The water fowls flew in every direction and the water creatures dived under the water, all to find earth to put on the turtle's back. And when they came back, each one had a little bit of ground with him and laid it on the turtle's back. Soon the earth was large enough for her to walk about and exercise herself. Then the mud-turtle spoke once more and said, "I will stand forever under you, for you to live upon. And there will come a great race that will build upon this earth, for it was given to me to have the power to do this and it shall be fulfilled according to the dream from above. I shall stand under the earth until the Great Spirit calls for me." Now Mud-turtle is the foundation of the earth. And all the animals rejoiced upon the earth, where forever they might find rest, and they praised Mud-turtle, the foundation.

Not long after this the woman gave birth to the child who had been conceived in the world above. This child was a female, and the mother called it "daughter." Soon the daughter was able to talk with her mother, and soon after this she could stand up and walk around at her mother's side. Then she got to be big enough to walk out of the cabin, and she became very fond of going to the water. The mother always forbade the child's going to the water, but the child always replied, "I want to go to the water to catch the young fowls that are on the shore." Still the mother forbade the child; and still the child wanted to know why she was not allowed to go where she wanted. But the mother did not want to tell her what would happen if she went into the water. After a while the girl grew up to be a young woman and to have her monthly periods, and now she was even more desirous of playing in the water. But the mother still forbade it.

At last the young woman disobeyed her mother; she did go to the water, she did play with the water, she did go into the water. And soon afterward the mother discovered that her daughter was pregnant, and she knew that she had conceived by going into the water. The daughter was pregnant with twins, the Evil Twin Tawiskaron and his brother Tarachiawagon, the Good Spirit. The twins came into conflict even before they were born. Their mother heard them disputing in the womb over how to emerge. One of them said, "Let us go out the regular way and save the mother." And the other one said, "Let us go out the nearest and quickest way." But the first one said, "I will go out the right way to save the mother." And again the other one said, "I will go the nearest way and the cleanest way because I can see the light under her arm on the left side of her body."

The Good Twin was born in the right way. But the Evil Twin came out under his mother's arm. She immediately called the grandmother, for she knew that she was going to die. She gave directions on what to do, saying, "Mother, you must take my body and bury it under the ground. Lay my head against the wind, so that the sun will rise at my feet and go down toward my head and the moon likewise. And also build a fire at my head upon the grass every night till the ten days are up. After a while you will see two cornstalks growing from my breasts above the grave, and they will bear corn that will be good for seed. Keep it and plant it here, for generation after generation of my children will live here forever. One of my sons shall be called the Good Spirit, and he will place good things upon earth and will regulate it. And the other you shall call the Evil Spirit, and he will place all the evil things upon the earth." So the grandmother took the children and laid them aside, and then she took the dead body and buried it under the ground and laid the head toward the wind. Then she went to the children. They were in good health. And then it became dark and she went to sleep.

When she awoke it was light, and the twins were talking to one another and smiling happily because the night was passed. The Good Spirit said, "It is good. Let the sun be created and rise against the wind to shine and make light." And the sun did so, and it went down at the head of the wind and it became dark again. Then the Good Spirit said, "Let the moon be created and rise against the wind." And the moon rose and shone with the light of the night. And the Good Spirit was pleased at what he had done.

But the Evil Spirit made fun of it and contradicted his brother who was creating the world.

The Good Spirit formed man out of the dust of the ground and breathed into his nostrils the breath of life, and man became a living soul. The Good Spirit said, "Let the vegetables grow upon the land, and every kind of herb." But they did not grow because he had not yet made the rain and because there was not a woman to till the soil and to multiply the earth. So the Good Spirit made a woman, and he called the man and the woman together and said to the man, "That woman shall be your wife," and to the woman he said, "This man shall be your husband. And you shall enjoy yourselves upon the earth in order to multiply from generation to generation. And here are vegetables and herbs to sustain life from the fruits of the earth, which shall grow forever."

Thereafter the Good Spirit busied himself with completing the creation. He made rivers and streams, with double currents so that men would always paddle downstream; he scattered and improved the corn that grew from his mother's grave so that this corn was fatter, oilier, and easier to grow than any corn known today; he created the deer, elk, bear, beaver, and other game animals. But the Evil Spirit, his twin, always trailed after him, jealously undoing the good his brother made and, in his attempts to equal his creative elder twin, creating all manner of annoying and evil things, like bats, frogs, owls, worms, snakes, and carnivorous monsters. He changed the streams so that they flowed only one way, and broke them up with waterfalls, rapids, and whirlpools; he blighted the corn, so that ever after it grew smaller, was harder to raise and less tasty, and sighed mournfully in the wind; he made caves, and spread disease, storms, ice, and death. Once he even stole the sun, and he and his grandmother ran away with it to keep it for themselves, but the Good Spirit brought it back. Although the Good Spirit was not able to reverse all the damage his brother did, he was able to counteract most of it.

At last, one day, the great work was nearly completed, and the Good Spirit began a tour of inspection, walking westward around the earth. Far to the west, on the rocky rim of the world, he met his brother the Evil Spirit, who now was in the form of a giant. The Creator asked the stranger, as he had asked all the others, what he was doing. "Looking over my creation," said the giant. "It is *my* creation," said the Good Spirit. Finally they agreed to settle the dispute by a contest of magical power: each one would try to make the Rocky Mountains move. The Good Spirit said, "You try first." So the giant took a whole hickory tree as his cane and rubbed a snapping turtle across it. The mountains trembled but moved only a little way. Then the Good Spirit said, "Now it's my turn." He made the giant turn around with his back to the mountains, and while the giant's back was turned, he moved the mountains close up behind him. "Now turn around," he said. The giant turned and bashed his nose against the side of the mountain.

Then the giant said, "You are the Creator. I submit and beg to be allowed to live." The Good Spirit granted the request, on condition that he would help the people and take them as his grandchildren. So the bargain was made: If the people would wear masks representing the giant, and would burn tobacco for him and give him a little cornmush, he would give them power, through the masks, to handle hot coals without being burned, to withstand the cold without shivering, and to drive away disease, witches, and high winds.

So the Faces represented a being, the powerful giant Shagadyoweh, who dwelt on the rocky rim of the world and who was defeated by the Creator in a contest to decide who had created the world. The twisted nose of many of the masks was a memento of the event. But behind the bent-nosed giant stood, in shadowy file, other images who could be alternately (or simultaneously) invoked by the same masks: Tawiskaron, the Evil Twin; the sea-father of the twins; the Four Brothers (the "Mystery Masks") who control the winds; the Whirlwind Spirit; and He-Whose-Body-Is-Riven-in-Twain (the spirit, half Tawiskaron and half his good brother, who is half winter and half summer). And also represented by the masks were a whole legion of forest spirits, huge, shy, featureless heads who flitted from tree to tree on spindly legs, with their long hair snapping in the wind, and who sometimes visited lonely hunters, begging for food and tobacco.

Shy and querulous as these Forest Faces were, they were also power-ful: the unexpected sight of them could cause paralysis, or nose-bleed, or possession, but properly fed and placated, they brought luck to the hunter. Logically, the same mask could hardly be an embodiment of all these beings; but this was not a matter for logic. The Faces were the faces of many gods.

On the various occasions when men wore the Faces the triangular interaction among maskers, masks, and audience ran the gamut of human feelings. The adult masker, wearing the Face and impersonat-ing the Great World Rim Dweller or the Forest Faces, vented atti-tudes and feelings that were not permitted him in sober social life. He might gurgle and coo like a baby, crawl on the floor, suck his toes, and beg for things to eat. He might thump with sticks on walls and windows, bang open doors, throw fire and ashes around, dance uninhibitedly. He might throw people out of bed, smear them with human excrement, upset the furniture, and frighten the timid with wild cries. And at the same time he controlled mighty matters, hav-ing the power to cure incurable disease, avert deadly tornadoes, cast out malevolent witches, and bring order to a whole community. The Seneca, as masker, could recapture the fancied omnipotence of in-fancy, doing the impossible with ease and the infantile with im-punity, indeed even to the applause of spectators. The beings whom he represented were the very prototype of the infant: ambitious beyond their years, desirous of emulating their betters, mischievous and destructive, quickly enraged at neglect or frustration, careless of their parents' welfare, yet hopeful of forgiveness if their dreams of stolen glory were discovered. And at the same time the omnipotent infant was the omnipotent parent, able to cure disease, avert thunder, and scare away evil people.

It is hardly to be wondered at, then, that not infrequently Seneca men and women—normally so reserved, so self-sufficient, so hardy and independent—were seized with an irresistible and terrifying urge to be like the Faces. Some resisted it, refused to join the dance, tried to get out of the council-house, but once touched by the doorkeeper in a great "doctor" mask, they might fall to the floor in a fit. As far back as 1616 Champlain saw women possessed, walking "on all fours like beasts," and cured at length by the masked company who blew ashes on them and pounded out raucous music with turtle rattles. Sometimes people were obsessed by the idea of the masks: They experienced repetitive nightmares in which they saw faces peering out of bushes in the twilight and heard the long drawn "Hoo-oo-oo!" Such disorders were specifically cured by the Society of Faces, which manhandled the victim, blew ashes, and inducted him into the society so that he too came to possess and recognize a Face, fed and anointed it, and wore it to cure others. The ministrations of the Faces also were helpful in a wide variety of difficulties, many of them, in the language of a later day, "psychosomatic" in large part, such as intractable aches and pains, paralyses and tics, and nosebleeds. Induction into the Society of Faces, identification with one or another of the legendary figures represented by the masks, and the acting out of infantile roles (modified by good taste, and in the name of socially desirable goals like the curing of disease, the averting of witchcraft, and the like) logically should, and indeed often did, produce a cure or at least give benefit.

The Faces of the gods, then, were really the faces of the Seneca themselves. They represented that strange and forgotten part of the self where repressed and disallowed desires of various sorts, often childish or infantile in form and content, normally subsisted in silent turmoil. Rage and fear, lust and hate, boundless ambition and abject passivity, cold cruelty and noble altruism, were all forever ready to emerge; and depending on time and place and person, they emerged in various ways. With unconscious wisdom the Society of Faces found a means of venting these emotions, of bleeding them off harmlessly, without too much frightening the patient. As with the cult of dreams, membership in the Society of Faces made it possible for the poised, independent, self-controlled, self-sacrificing Seneca to express what he did not allow himself to feel: a longing to be passive, to beg, to be an irresponsible, demanding, rowdy infant, and to compete with the Creator himself; and to express it all in the name of the public good.

· *The Cult of Death* ·

THE IROQUOIS were deeply affected by death. As they put it, the Being That Is Faceless, the Great Destroyer, roamed night and day with his club uplifted over the peoples' heads, waiting to strike down all men, and boasting, "It is I, I will destroy all things. . . ." But death could come in many forms: by violence, in war at the hands of an enemy, in peace at the hands of a drunken friend, by stealth at the wishing of a witch, by accident or disease. Death came to the mighty, the chiefs, upon whom the people leaned; death came to the weak and insignificant; death came to the proud captive. And what the people did in the face of death depended both upon who died and upon how he died.

"There is something peculiarly pathetic," wrote missionary Asher Wright, "in the attachment which these interesting people [the Seneca] cherish for their patriarchal sepulchres. The feeling of reverence for the graves of their ancestors is universal among them. Tis a national trait."

He described affecting instances. "Bury me by my grandmother," said a little boy of seven a few minutes before he died; "she used to be kind to me." And "Lay me by our mother," said a little orphan girl under the missionaries' care, when she knew she would not get well. An old woman of eighty, speaking of a planned tribal migration, lamented, "I am sorry for I had hoped to be laid by Mother in yonder graveyard." A chief complained also of the same removal: "We can not go to the west and leave the graves of our fathers to the care of strangers. The clods would lie heavily on our bosoms in that distant country should we do it." Wright spoke of seeing middle-aged men and women "weep like children" when the least allusion was made to dead loved ones, and he wrote of the solicitude with which the grave goods were placed beside the bodies: a chief's best clothes, guns, traps, and knives; almost the whole of an infant's wardrobe; even the poorest people would scrimp and borrow to buy for departed friends a respectable robe. Mothers often visited the graves of their children and noticed the least change in the appearance of the enshrouding earth; sometimes they identified the spot of an unmarked grave after years of absence.[7]

The death of a League chief, one of the forty-nine *royaner*, was symbolic of group calamity. When such a great chief died, it was as if the Great Faceless had kicked apart the burning brands and, exulting in destruction, stamped out the council fire with dancing feet. No business could be done; the people were (at least metaphorically) dismayed and appalled at the havoc. The universe itself seemed to be shaking.

The death of a chief was considered to be serious, not only because it formally interrupted council procedure, but also because grief was a principal cause of derangement. The death of a League chief, bereaving the entire moiety of the departed (i.e., roughly half of the Five Nations' population), was expected to produce catastrophic grief-symptoms in whole nations. It was a "calamity . . . hopeless and dreadful." The nations, personified as individuals, were thought of as lying alone in a darkened house, weeping and withdrawn from reality, unable to hear "the sounds made by mankind, nothing of what is taking place on earth," and unable to speak.

The description of the melancholia of bereavement is almost clinical in its detail and insight, as it is recited in the monotonous intonations of the Requickening Address of the Condolence Council. "The organs within the breast and the flesh-body are disordered and violently wrenched without ceasing, and so also is the mind. . . . Verily, now, the life forces of the sufferer always become weakened thereby. . . . The disorder now among the organs within [the] breast is such that nothing can be clearly discerned . . . when a direful thing befalls a person, that person is invariably covered with darkness, that person becomes blinded with thick darkness itself. It is always so that the person knows not any more what the day light is like on the earth, and his mind and life are weakened and depressed . . . the sky is lost to the senses of that person . . . such a person knows nothing about the movement of the sun [i.e., night and day and the passage of time are not noticed] . . . invariably the mind of that person is simply tossed and turned on the grave of him in whom he fondly trusted. . . . Verily, it is a direful thing for the mind of him who has suffered from a grievous calamity to become insane, [for] the powers causing insanity are immune from everything on this earth, and [insanity] has the power to end the days of man. . . ."

In order (theoretically) to prevent the consequences of extreme grief, when a League chief died a Condolence Council was held at an early opportunity and before the chiefs undertook any new business. At this council the mourners were cleansed of their despair, and a new chief was installed to replace the old. Little was said about the departed: It was the survivor, not the dead, who was the object of compassion.

The Condolence Council was "given" by the "clear-minded" moiety to the mourning moiety. The clear-minded ones came through the forest to the village of the dead chief, singing the *Hai Hai,* or Roll

Call of Founders of the League, as they walked along. It was a mournful song, recounting the glorious names of the original founding fathers, still preserved as titles of office, but lamenting that their work had grown old and that their successors were a weaker race. Then at the wood's edge, where the cleared fields began, the clear-minded and the mourners met and sat down together across a fire, to exchange greetings and the Three Rare Words of Requickening. The Three Rare Words were: Eyes, Ears, and Throat. The clear-minded, perceiving that the mourners' eyes were blinded with tears, their ears clogged and unable to hear, and their throats choked with sadness so that they could not speak and could breathe only with difficulty, wiped away the tears with the white fawn-skin of pity, cleaned out the ears, and removed the throttling obstructions from the throat. Then the mourners reciprocated, and the two parties marched in procession to the longhouse, where the Twelve Matters were dealt with, one by one, by the clear-minded on behalf of the mourners.

The Twelve Matters—each endorsed by a string of wampum passed across the fire—were the therapeutic or "requickening" ritual that delivered the melancholic mourner from the toils of his depression and paranoid suspicion. The first matter rearranged the wrenched internal organs by pouring in the water of pity. The second wiped clean the bloody husk-mat bed where the wretched one sat cross-legged. The third let daylight into the darkened house of grief. The fourth pointed out that the sky was still beautiful; the fifth that the sun still rose and set. The sixth leveled the rough ground over the grave and placed a little roof of wood and thatch over it, so that the heat of the sun and the wet of the rain would not disturb the corpse. The seventh reminded the mourners that if their kinsman had died by murder or witchcraft at the hand or instigation of another Iroquois, they were not to seek blood revenge but should accept the traditional twenty strings of wampum as were-gild. The eighth gathered together the scattered brands of the council fire and convened the council to do business again. The ninth exhorted the warriors and the women to be of strong heart, to help one another to do the work of life, and not to be listless and indifferent—for that mood of mind should properly prevail only when the earth is at last split asunder and the doom of all things impends. The tenth matter forbade the chiefs to neglect the mourning people lest their minds become insane from grief. The eleventh instructed the people of the

League, in case of another death, always to run with the Torch of Notification through all the villages of the League. The twelfth and final matter was the request of the clear-minded that the mourners point out the man who was their candidate to be the new chief.

After a return of condolences by the mourners to the clear-minded (who also were grieving, although less wretchedly) the new chief's face was shown. He was examined, and if the condoling moiety accepted him, the antlers of office were placed on his head, and he was charged to show henceforth the proper qualities of a chief: to have a skin seven thumbs thick, immune to malicious gossip and cantankerous criticisms; to act always in the best interests of the people, not only those living now, but also the generations to come; and to lead a good, clean personal life.

Then there was a feast for all in the longhouse, and finally an evening of dancing in which the chiefs "rubbed antlers" and the crowd of common people had a good time in a series of social dances. The clear-minded visitors were granted access to the mourners' women, with humorous appeals for self-restraint. "I now let escape from my hands our womenfolk. Accordingly you shall use them properly. Don't anyone treat them too roughly!" announced the master of ceremonies.

And he added, "So now another thing. Time may also be devoted to something else. Perhaps one of you may have had a dream. Then in that event let us amuse our minds with dreams."

And with clear minds the erstwhile mourners began life anew, feasting, dancing, flirting, and telling one another their dreams of the previous year.[8]

The origin of the Condolence Council was, according to Iroquois mythology, the result of an act of divine intervention in human affairs; in fact, it was the occasion of the founding of the Great League itself.

According to the Dekanawidah myth, there was a time when the five Iroquois tribes were not united in a league. They constantly warred and feuded among themselves, and were continually being warred upon by neighboring Algonquian tribes, so that no man, or woman, or child was safe. At last a man named Hiawatha, depressed by the death of his wife and family, fled into the forests, where he lived as a cannibal, waylaying and devouring luckless travelers. One day the god Dekanawidah, who had been born of a virgin and who had come across the lakes in a white stone canoe, found Hiawatha's cabin in the forest. Climbing on the roof, he gazed down through the smoke hole. Now at this moment Hiawatha, within, was staring into a pot of water, and he saw the face of the god reflected from its surface. He thought that it was the image of his own face that he saw, and he said to himself, "That is not the face of a cannibal." This was his moment of moral regeneration. Dekanawidah now entered the cabin and revealed himself and his mission to Hiawatha.

Dekanawidah's mission—and hereafter Hiawatha's, too—was to persuade the Iroquois to unite in a confederacy that would prohibit the usages of the blood feud among the five tribes, substituting in cases of homicide an obligatory payment of were-gild. Hiawatha now became Dekanawidah's spokesman, for the god had an impediment in his speech which prevented his ever addressing an audience (and some say he never was seen by any man but Hiawatha). Tribe by tribe, Hiawatha's eloquence persuaded the people and the chiefs to lay aside the blood feud and unite, until at last, having combed the snakes out of the shaman Atotarho's hair, he was able to bring sachems from all the tribes together into the great council at Onondaga.[9]

The deaths of ordinary people did not require such elaborate condolence procedures as those prescribed for dead chiefs, but burial and mourning rites were similarly calculated to relieve the mind of melancholy. The dead were buried in graves, frequently seated with knees drawn up under the chin, and surrounded by the goods they would need in the next world. The graves were lined with boards or bark. Because in Seneca belief the soul remained close to the body for some time after death and from time to time even re-entered it, a hole was cut in the tomb lining in order to give the soul easier access to the head. The funerals themselves were under the charge of the women, who during the procession to the cemetery near the village, and again on their return to the feast at the house of the deceased, wept and tore their hair and rolled on the ground. A woman was expected to abandon herself to despair if one of her near family died, casting herself onto the cold hearth over the grave, where ashes were thrown over her head and shoulders, to mix "with tears and drivel from the mouth and with blood oozing from many lacerations on the body." The female relatives and neighbors of the dead one, for nine more days, every morning gathered at the house of mourning to weep and lament. At last, on the evening of the tenth day after death there was held the "ten days' feast," at which the hungry soul of the departed was fed and sent on its way, and the mourners were constrained to dry up their tears and become clear-minded. The soul might, however, be reluctant to leave the neighborhood, and so occasionally for the next year food might be laid out for him. Furthermore, these haunting souls, frustrated in their longings for food and companionship, were apt to bother people in their dreams or even to plague survivors with sickness and misfortune. Such persecution by the spirits of the dead was countered by the *ohgiwe* ceremony: a night-time occasion, at which a feast is held for the ghost and the living together, and certain chants for the dead are sung. These *ohgiwe* songs were not to be profaned by being sung for no reason; if they were sung for amusement, some misfortune was bound to afflict the singer.[10]

For the dead were dangerous. The negative side of the passionate mourning for the lost loved one was an elaboration of gruesome fantasies about the cannibalistic appetites and sadistic humor of the dead. A particularly common legend was that of the vampire skeleton. Once upon a time, a man and his wife went out to hunt. The hunting ground was a two days' journey away, and on their way home, heavily laden with meat, they came to a cabin where the owner, a famous medicine man, was dead. Because it was already dark, the husband decided that they should spend the night there, in spite of the fact that the dead man's body lay on a shelf in a bark coffin. The husband gathered wood and lit a fire and then lay down to rest while his wife cooked meat and cornmeal cakes. After a while he fell asleep. The wife went about her work. Suddenly the woman heard a noise behind her, near where her husband lay; it was like the sound of someone chewing meat. She thought about the corpse on the shelf and remembered that the dead man was a witch, so she put more wood on the fire and made it blaze up, and then she looked again. She saw a stream of blood trickling out from the bunk. At once she knew that her husband had been killed by the dead man.

But she pretended that she did not notice. She said, as if speaking to her husband, "I must make a torch and bring some water." She made a torch of hickory bark, long enough to last until she could run home. Then she took the pail and went out; but as soon as she was outside the door, she dropped the pail and ran through the woods as fast as she could. She had gotten halfway home before the vampire realized that she had gone. He ran after her, whooping. She heard him behind her; the whooping came nearer and nearer. She was so scared she almost fell, but she ran on until her torch was almost out and at last reached a lodge in her village where people were dancing. She burst into the lodge and fainted.

When she revived, she told the story of what had happened to her and her husband. In the morning a party of men went to the cabin, where they found the bones of her husband, from which all the flesh had been eaten. The face and hands of the skeleton in the bark box were found to be bloody. Thereupon the chief said that it was not right to leave dead people that way. They took the bones of the vampire and buried them in a hole that they dug in the ground, and they brought the bones of the husband back to his village and buried them there also. And thereafter the dead were no longer placed on scaffolds or in shelves in bark lodges, but were buried in the ground.[11]

Beliefs about the life after death were various because any individual could, and many did, discover in a dream some new and different character for the heavenly world, and furthermore, by the eighteenth century Christian cosmology was widely known. In general, however, there was some sort of pleasant place to which, if his conduct during life was orderly and pleasing to the Good Spirit, a man would be admitted after death; and sometimes, but less commonly, there was also conceived to be a hellish place, governed by the Evil Spirit, where bad people went. An old man in a Huron village, for instance, a little while before he died, "fell into a swoon." When he came out of it, he said that he had just been to the other world, which was nothing like what the French had forecast to him (the Jesuits were accustomed to warn the heathen of the perils of hell). To the contrary, he had met several of his own departed family and other relatives, who welcomed him kindly and told him that they had been waiting for him for a long time and were preparing many "fire dances and feasts" in his honor. He was so confident of this dream's validity that in order to be able to present himself in the same magnificent dress and accouterments as his heavenly kinfolk, he had his whole face painted red, had brought and placed over him the finest articles he had, was given his plate and spoon—and thus he died. This man was reputed to have been one of the most respectable and virtuous men of the whole country, because he was peaceable, did no harm to anyone, and "greatly delighted in merrymaking and in giving feasts."[12] Other men after similar visions in illness reported that the village of souls was a mournful place like a natural village, but loud with the unceasing groans and complaints of the hapless dead. There was a story of a bridge made of a wobbly tree-trunk, which the souls of the dead must cross. This bridge was guarded by a dog, who jumped at some souls and made them fall, to drown in the torrent of rushing waters beneath.[13] Probably the conceptions of the next world corresponded with the preoccupations and wishes of the individual, as revealed to him in dreams, and only a loose framework of belief in a village of the dead, somewhere to the westward, united the opinions of the tribes.

The souls of the dead did not always rest in peace. Those who had been murdered by men of other nations could find no haven in the next world until their lust for vengeance had been appeased. Generally speaking, whatever economic or political considerations might be involved in the tensions that led to war, the actual formation of war parties was either inspired or rationalized by the obligation to avenge dead relatives. Women whose kinfolk had been killed would appear at public dances and feasts, weeping inconsolably; if this display did not succeed in arousing the warriors, the women might offer payments or accuse the lagging warriors of cowardice. Men might dream of their murdered kin and interpret the dream as the lost soul's desire for revenge; such a dream could compel the dreamer to organize a war party. Until the bereaved had "gotten even," until there had been retaliatory killings and tortures, it was as if the blood of the murdered one had not been wiped away and his corpse not covered. War-caused bereavement was a state of unavenged insult and shame (and, indeed, war parties might be organized to avenge mere verbal insults as well as killings). One might, indeed, regard the Iroquois war complex as being, psychologically, a part of the mourning process, an acting out of the paranoid resentments that were aroused by loss. But the social consequences of this propensity were momentous.

With some nations, usually distant, like the Catawba and Cherokee of the Carolinas, the Iroquois remained on terms of chronic warfare for generations. Neither side intended to exterminate or dispossess the other; the "war" consisted of occasional raids by revenge squads of ten to fifty men who at the most would burn a small camp, kill a few people, and bring back a dozen or so prisoners to be tortured or adopted. At any point in time, some family on either the Iroquois or the Catawba or Cherokee side had a score to settle, and young men seeking to validate their adult masculinity, led by the males of mourning families, sooner or later would take to the trail.

Such chronic wars, if they involved close neighbors, however, quickly reached a point of critical involvement. Separated by five hundred miles, the Seneca and the Cherokee were sufficiently insulated by distance for an equilibrium to be reached so that there was no cumulation of unavenged killings over the years. But with a neighboring tribe, physical proximity multiplied the opportunities for incidents, as well as for more diffuse economic and political tensions over such matters of competition as the fur trade. Thus feud-wars with neighboring tribes, like the Huron, the Erie, and the Susquehannocks, annually dragged more and more families into the revenge process and increased the opportunity and motivation for nonmourners to take part in a raid. Feud-wars with neighbors developed into total wars, which had eventually to be settled either by peacemaking diplomacy or by major campaigns involving hundreds of warriors. The process of involvement of a tribe in a war was like the building up of a nuclear explosion: as long as the two social masses were a long distance apart, their mutual bombardment by war parties remained in equilibrium without any cumulative increase in the rate of emission; but as the two masses were brought closer together, they stimulated each other to more and more activity, and when two sufficiently large masses were adjoining, the rate of mutual bombardment accelerated until the explosion of war occurred.

The common aim of all war parties was to bring back persons to replace the mourned-for dead. This could be done in three ways: by bringing back the scalp of a dead enemy (this scalp might even be put through an adoption ceremony); by bringing back a live prisoner (to be adopted, tortured, and killed); or by bringing back a live prisoner to be allowed to live and even to replace in a social role the one whose death had called for this "revenge." One death might be avenged several times over, in different ways; and the sentiments of the nearest (or loudest) mourner determined what disposition was to be made of a given case. In an earlier chapter was described the insatiable desire of Aharihon to kill and torture in honor of his departed brother. Other, less morbid, mourners were more humane: a woman who had lost her son might "cast her girdle" about a likely looking prisoner and adopt him as her son, a man might take a new brother, and henceforth these adopted kinfolk were regarded and treated almost as if they were the reincarnation of the dead. Whole villages might even be adopted; at times during the seventeenth century, when war casualties were heavy, as many as two thirds of the population of the Oneida nation were adoptees, and the other nations, including the Seneca, similarly depended heavily on adopted manpower. White prisoners thus adopted, as well as prisoners of other Indian tribes, apparently in many cases identified themselves thoroughly with their new roles and, in the case of white prisoners, objected vigorously to being repatriated when prisoners were exchanged. Many of the cases of reported mistreatment by returned "prisoners" (aside from deliberate torture) probably reflect either the adoptee's refusal to learn the language and accept normal native standards of living or the misfortune of being adopted by personally disagreeable relatives (a misfortune not unknown to adopted children in our own society).

Many prisoners were, however, consigned to torture, particularly during the seventeenth century; the manifest horror of the more civilized Europeans at the sight of tortures little different from those they deplored in their own societies was doubtless responsible in part for the lapsing of the torture complex during the eighteenth century. Torture was a ritual and followed a formal, predictable course, in which the victim and his tormentors were expected to play traditionally respectable roles. The victim (usually a man, occasionally a woman, rarely a child) was expected to show composure and hardihood; weaklings who were unable to perform the role, who broke down, wept, and cried for mercy, were sometimes dispatched in disgust with a quick hatchet-blow. While undoubtedly unconscious meanings, various according to the participant and spectator, attached to the torture ritual, many of the tormentors consciously were not anxious to see transports of agony and emotional collapse, but rather the reverse: they wanted to see a stouthearted man with unconquerable self-control, maintaining defiance and self-respect to the bitter end, and the torture was a test of these qualities. Since the victim was in many cases eaten afterward and had in some cases been previously adopted, he was in a very real sense being incorporated by a family and a community, and becoming a part of them, and a show of strength on his part was gratifying to those who identified with him.

The case of a Seneca man captured and burned by the Huron in 1637 illustrates the general pattern. A fifty-year-old warrior of some distinction, along with six other captives, was taken while he and twenty-five or thirty men were on a fishing expedition. The Huron council assigned him to Saouandaouascouay, a chief who had lost a nephew in a recent war. It was customary, "when some notable personage has lost one of his relatives in war, to give him a present of some captive taken from the enemy, to dry his tears and partly assuage his grief."

The prisoner, on delivery, was in bad shape as a result of mistreatment en route: one of his hands was badly bruised by a stone, and one finger had been torn off; the thumb and forefinger of the other had been half-amputated by a hatchet blow; the joints of his arms had been badly burned, and in one of them was a deep cut. The wounds were infected, stank intolerably, and were swarming with maggots; he could not lift food or drink to his lips. The villagers did everything possible to make him comfortable: he was fed solicitously, his wounds were gently cleaned and bandaged; he sang for them and they talked kindly to him. "My nephew!" announced Saouandaouascouay, "Thou hast good reason to sing, for no one is doing thee any harm; behold thyself now among thy kindred and friends." The Jesuits were impressed by the solicitude of the Hurons to the adopted captive. "To see the treatment they accorded him, you might have thought he was the brother and relative of all those who were talking to him." And so, as a matter of fact, he was.

But after a few days Saouandaouascouay changed his mind about keeping the prisoner in the family, and one morning gently explained the situation to "Joseph" (as the Jesuits had baptized him). "My nephew, thou must know that when I first received news that thou wert at my disposal, I was wonderfully pleased, fancying that he whom I lost in war had been, as it were, brought back to life, and was returning to his country. At the same time I resolved to give thee thy life, I was already thinking of preparing thee a place in my cabin, and thought that thou wouldst pass the rest of thy days pleasantly with me. But now that I see thee in this condition, thy fingers gone and thy hands half rotten, I change my mind, and I am sure that thou thyself wouldst now regret to live longer. I shall do thee a greater kindness to tell thee that thou must prepare to die; is it not so? It is [those who captured you] who have treated thee so ill, and who also cause thy death. Come then, my nephew, be of good courage; prepare thyself for this evening, and do not allow thyself to be cast down through fear of the tortures." Joseph, in a firm and confident voice, asked how he was to be tortured, and Saouandaouascouay said by fire. "That is well," said Joseph, "that is well." While this sad discussion was in progress, a sister of the dead man (and Joseph's adoptive sister) brought him some food. She was tender to him, her face was very sad, and her eyes were bathed in tears. "You would almost have said that he was her own son," observed Father Le Jeune, "and I do not know that this creature did not represent to her him whom she had lost."

At noon Joseph gave his farewell feast, "according to the custom of those who are about to die"; everyone in the village was welcome, and crowds came. Before the eating began, he strode through the middle of the cabin and announced in a loud and confident voice, "My brothers, I am going to die; amuse yourselves boldly around me —I fear neither tortures nor death." He danced and sang up and down the cabin, and after him some of the guests. The food was served, people ate, and then he was taken to the council house for the torture.

Soon after dark, eleven fires were lit down the length of the council house, and the people came, the old men seating themselves on the raised platforms and the young men crowded on the floor so tightly that there was barely room for passage. The young men, shouting with joy, armed themselves with firebrands and pieces of bark. There was a public announcement by a chief: the young men were to do their duty in this important business, which was viewed by the Sun and the God of War. They were to burn only his legs at first, "so that he might hold out until day break; also for that night they were not to go and amuse themselves in the woods."

The prisoner was brought in, amid a tumult of shouts, and forced to sit on a mat; his hands were bound; and he rose and walked around the cabin, singing and dancing. On his return to the mat, the chief took off his beaver robe and announced that it would go to a certain warrior; so and so was to have the privilege of cutting off his head; and the head, one arm, and the liver were to go to still another person, "to make a feast."

Now he began to run a circuit about the fires, again and again, while everyone tried to burn him as he passed; he shrieked like a lost soul; the whole cabin resounded with cries and yells. Some burned him, some seized his hands and snapped bones, others thrust sticks through his ears, still others bound his wrists with cords, pulling at each end with all their might, so as to cut flesh and crush bone. If he paused to catch his breath, he was forced to lie down upon hot ashes and burning coals. After making seven rounds, he collapsed on the coals and would not stir, and when a brand was applied to his loins, he fainted.

His fainting spell lasted for about an hour. The captains emptied the council house and would let no one molest him during this time; they gave him water; and at last he came to his senses again. Immediately he was commanded to sing; at first he was only able to sing in a broken and faltering voice, but he grew stronger and at last sang loudly enough for the young men outside to hear. Back into the council house they came, and the torture began again, more brutal than before, setting his feet on red-hot hatchets, burning the cords that bound him, hitting him on the head with clubs, repeatedly burning him, at first on the legs and then gradually up the body with firebrands and bark torches. Once he was forced to commit what the Jesuits called only a "shameful act."

Between the interruptions caused by his involuntary yells and groans, there was between Joseph and his tormentors a continuous interchange of jeering compliments, banter, and taunting inquiries about his welfare and comfort. Joseph never allowed himself to complain or to revile his tormentors. He was addressed, and he addressed them, with kinship terms. He was given food (roasted corn on the cob) and drink. On several occasions the priest was allowed to preach to the crowd, and the prisoner rested during these intervals. On occasion he addressed the crowd for some time, discussing the state of affairs in his own country, and describing the death of some Huron prisoners. "He did this as easily, and with a countenance as composed, as any one there present would have showed."

At dawn came the end. He was taken outside into the sunlight and made to mount a scaffold, where, tied to a post, he was burned continuously and cruelly from head to toe, and in every accessible body aperture, with hot hatchets and firebrands, until he was completely exhausted and hung motionless, scarcely breathing. At once a hand, a foot, and at the last his head were cut off and given to those to whom they had been allotted. A feast was made upon the rest of his body the same day.

Thus Joseph became a part of the Huron nation, and Saouanda-ouascouay was reunited with his nephew.[14]

II

THE DECLINE
OF THE
IROQUOIS

5

THE LAST WARS
IN THE FOREST

HANDSOME LAKE WAS BORN AT THE END OF THE ERA OF UNQUES-tioned power, respect, and prosperity for the Seneca nation. His generation saw the delicate balance between the revenge mechanism of warfare and the political structure of the League shaken and in the end destroyed. By the time he reached his forties, the Seneca would be deprived of their military ardor, reduced to political impotence, corrupted in their customs, disillusioned with their religion, stripped of their hunting land, and made to look depraved and contemptible in the eyes of their white and Indian neighbors. During his youth and early manhood, while he fought as a warrior in the last of the forest wars, he watched his society and his culture slowly crumble.

· The Play-off System ·

EVER SINCE THE LATTER HALF of the seventeenth century the British and the French had been straining to contain one another's trading empires in North America. French posts stretched in a great inland arc from Quebec to New Orleans, by way of the St. Lawrence, the Great Lakes, the Wabash, the Illinois, and the Mississippi. The British settlements crowded the Atlantic coast from New England to Florida and extended inland up the Hudson, Delaware, Susquehanna, and Potomac rivers and many other smaller streams. Between the two lines of settlement was a territory of disputed political sovereignty: the so-called "Ohio country," including the land between Lake Erie and the Ohio River, bounded westward by the two Miami rivers in the present state of Ohio, and coastward by the Allegheny Mountains. To this region the Iroquois laid claim on the basis of ancient conquest, their continuing use of it for hunting, and the location on it of tribes politically dependent upon them. This claim both French and British recognized. Thus the Six Nations were able to use the Ohio country as the fulcrum in a game of playing off one side against the other that kept both the French and the British perennially off balance.

This successful system of aggressive neutrality had originated at the beginning of the eighteenth century. In the summer of 1701 the Iroquois confederacy, aware of the fruitlessness of a longer continuance of the beaver wars and desirous of avoiding further involvement in the skirmishes between the British and the French, made two treaties, almost simultaneously, at Albany and Montreal. These treaties together inaugurated a new era of Iroquois policy, which survived in principle until 1795: a policy of peace toward the "far Indians," of political manipulation of nearby tribes, and of armed neutrality between contending Europeans. This policy led to commercial profit and to the seizure of a balance of power between the French and the British. It was a policy that required of the Iroquois as much duplicity in diplomatic dealings with the Europeans as the Europeans practiced toward them; its success is measured by the fact that both the British and the French alternated constantly between the conviction that the Iroquois were on their own side and the conviction that they had turned to the enemy. In consequence, the basic policy of both French and British toward the Iroquois was to secure Iroquois neutrality by making political and economic concessions to them. Only secondarily, and occasionally, did either aspire to their full and exclusive alliance; and these aspirations were almost invariably dashed.

The maintenance of this balance of power, however, depended upon Iroquois capacity to make credible threats, or promises, of military action. The system did not require that both French and British be equally powerful in the area, but rather that the Iroquois should at any time be considered able, by shifting their weight, to make up the difference. Any actual or apparent rigidity (induced either by in-decision or by insufficiency of resources) in Iroquois policy would threaten this system because it would permit one side or the other to anticipate decline to a point where it could no longer afford to pay the price for the necessary support. Such a point of critical im-balance could also be reached if, as a result of any outside circum-stance, one side or the other thought that a power differential existed which no degree of shifting of Iroquois support could rectify.

This point of critical imbalance came in the 1740's, when the Iroquois gave the English too-extensive trading privileges in the Ohio country. In the Ohio Valley a lesion had over the years been slowly widening in the play-off system: the Iroquois hunters domiciled there, known locally as Mingoes, had increasingly turned, along with the Delaware, Wyandot, and other tribal groups in the region, to the English for trade. In 1744 they brought the Miami—hitherto prevail-ingly French in trade connection—to Lancaster, where an under-standing was established between them and the English and an alliance worked out between them and the Six Nations. British trade-posts were built, with Iroquois sanction, on the Miami, Sandusky, and Cuyahoga Rivers, and George Croghan and other English traders and agents penetrated extensively into the Ohio. The Six Nations formal-ized their long-standing dominance over the Ohio area by appointing local "half-kings" and by allotting specific tracts to the dependent tribes.

This event compromised the ingenious policy of neutrality that the Iroquois had developed for coping with the European colonies on their flanks. The Six Nations probably did not expect the trans-actions to upset the French as much as they did. In fact, however, they impressed the French with the sense of a power deficit so extreme that in their opinion (and probably the opinion was correct) it ex-ceeded the range of Iroquois capacity to redress it. The French, therefore, set out to destroy the play-off system itself. In 1749 Celoron made his celebrated voyage down the Ohio, burying his lead plates and claiming the land for King Louis. In 1752 French forces sacked the British-Miami trading post at Pickawillany and killed and ate the pro-English, pro-Iroquois Miami chief there, Old Britain. In 1754 French troops seized the post that the Ohio Company was construct-ing at the confluence of the Allegheny and the Monongahela and replaced it with Fort Duquesne. The British retaliated with Washington's move to the Great Meadows, and then with Braddock's expedition against Fort Duquesne, both of which failed catastrophically; and the French and Indian War was on.

The Six Nations, during this conflict, attempted to salvage the old play-off system, at first by preserving a measure of neutrality, and then by fighting on both sides—the Seneca, in particular, joining the war parties of pro-French Indians, while the Mohawk joined in British campaigns on other fronts. They explained their policy in a belt given to one of their dependent allies, a Delaware leader named Teedyuscung, who recited the policy in a treaty council. "You see," he said, "a Square in the Middle, meaning the Lands of the Indians, and at one End the Figure of a Man, indicating the English; and at the other End another, meaning the French; our Uncles [the Six Nations] told us [the Delaware], that both these coveted our Lands; but let us join together to defend our Lands against both, you shall be Partakers with us of our Lands." But the situation was largely out of their control, for now the British too were uninterested in maintaining the old play-off system, but wanted rather a firm alliance (in which they would be the dominant partner). The end of the war found the French expelled, British troops stationed at Fort Duquesne, Sandusky, Detroit, Venango, Le Boeuf, Presqu' Isle, Niagara, and Oswego in the Iroquois domain as well as in posts outside the Iroquois sphere of influence, and a new spirit of economy pervading Indian affairs. No longer were Iroquois promises bought with tons of hardware and dry goods; "presents" now were limited. The old free trade was likewise curtailed, there were fewer traders, and powder and lead were sold only at government factories by surly public servants. The introduction of rum into the Indian country was officially prohibited. In 1761, in order to block the Ohio Company's plans for settlement of the Ohio lands, Colonel Bouquet at Fort Pitt promised that no white homesteaders would be permitted west of the Alleghenies; but still, British troops were not going to leave the forts. The play-off system was out; a bargaining system was in.[1]

· Pontiac's Conspiracy ·

SENECA REACTION to the new dispensation was hostile. In 1761 a group of Seneca including Guyasuta, a maternal uncle of Handsome Lake, carried a red wampum belt from the Onondaga council to Detroit, and under the nose of the British commandant exhorted the Delaware and Shawnee of Ohio and the Ottawa, Huron, Chippewa, and Potawatomi of Detroit to join the Six Nations in a simultaneous surprise attack on the British posts at Detroit, Pittsburgh, Presqu' Isle, Venango, and Niagara. Although the Ohio Indians refused to join in the plot and revealed its content to the British commandant at Detroit, the scheme was revived in the spring of 1763. Two more Seneca war belts were sent out: one passed among the Delaware and the Shawnee on the Ohio and the Miami on the Wabash; the other went to the Detroit Indians.

The war began in due course. The Seneca plan was not followed in detail, but the Seneca proposal to drive the English out of the Iroquois and Ohio country was certainly an inspiration to the tribes who joined in that epidemic of frontier assaults that is now generally (and inaccurately) called the Conspiracy of Pontiac. Pontiac himself had not actually organized a pan-Indian uprising. That so many local assaults followed his own carefully prepared attempt to take Detroit is probably best explained as a concatenation of a number of factors: the prior circulation of the Seneca plan, which suggested the general movement as well as the specific actions; the subversive encouragements of the French, still holding out in Louisiana; the generally high level of resentment against the English, who occupied forts in Indian territory but would not open up a satisfactory trade; and the nativistic prophecies of the Delaware Prophet, a religious leader whose visions and preaching were in some respects like those of Handsome Lake a generation later. Pontiac's independent action was the spark that, falling on tinder, set the woods aflame.

The "conspiracy," which had for its aim the destruction of the British forts and garrisons and the removal of the English from the Indian country between the Allegheny Mountains and the Mississippi, was manned by the Ottawa, Chippewa, Potawatomi, Huron, Miami, Wea, Delaware, Shawnee, Mingo (Six Nations Indians resident in the Ohio country)—and by the Seneca. While the eastern members of the confederacy dallied with Sir William Johnson, lulling him and General Amherst into a false sense of security, the Seneca struck perhaps the severest blows of the war, destroying the forts at Venango, Le Boeuf, and Presqu' Isle and at Devil's Hole almost annihilating two British detachments on the newly cut road along the cliff above the whirlpool at Niagara Falls. Handsome Lake may have been involved in the taking of Fort Venango, for his uncle Guyasuta was present on the occasion and as we have seen war parties tended to recruit clan relatives. According to tradition, Handsome Lake definitely was one of the Seneca ambuscade at Devil's Hole. Another maternal uncle, Jugwesus, was also at Devil's Hole, as were some of the Venango party, and an adopted uncle, Gahnasqua, was the Seneca commander at the Hole. The ambush at Devil's Hole was a bloody piece of work. The Seneca war party, numbering upwards of five hundred men, first surprised a convoy of twenty-five horse- and ox-drawn wagons, escorted by an officer and thirty men, at that point on the trail to Fort Niagara where it wound along a narrow space between woods and chasm. A volley from cover stopped the column in confusion; then the Indians ran out from the trees and attacked with tomahawks before the suttlers and their escort could form an organized defense. Stampeding teams plunged over the precipice, drivers were tangled in the harness leather or knocked down by kicking, screaming animals. Unable to use their muskets, soldiers tried to fight hand-to-hand with their backs to the abyss. Only two men of this party escaped alive. Hearing the firing, two British companies, about eighty men in all, ran to the scene. They were met in a new ambush before they reached the Hole. They too were cut down by an initial volley and then overwhelmed by an immediate hand-to-hand assault in which muskets could not be used. Within minutes half of the relief force were dead. When the garrison from the fort finally arrived, the Indians were gone and five British officers and sixty-seven men lay dead on the trail, scalped and stripped of their clothing.

But the great scheme for burning the forts and driving British garrisons out of the Indian country was in the end a failure. Detroit, Fort Pitt, and Niagara held out; reinforcements arrived; the Indian food supplies ran low; and in the end the warriors laid down their hatchets and the councilors made peace. The Seneca settled their affairs with Sir William Johnson in July, giving up some leading offenders and ceding the portage route at Niagara to the Crown. Although the British prudently made few reprisals and exacted only minor indemnities, and although the Royal Proclamation of October 1763 had set a boundary between Indian and white territory that recognized the Indians as proprietors of their traditional lands, English colors flew still over the new garrisons in the heart of the Indian country.[2]

During the war it is probable that Handsome Lake heard indirectly of the Delaware Prophet's preachings, and he may even have been informed in some detail of the content of his doctrine. Although the prophet is not known to have made any converts among the Seneca, he did serve as the emotional catalyst of the movement. The Delaware Prophet of 1762–3 was one of the religious messiahs who about this time were beginning to appear among the disintegrating Indian communities on the frontier. This man, who lived on the Cuyahoga River near Lake Erie, had visions in which the Creator spoke to him. The Creator informed him of the peril of worldly misery and eternal damnation in which the Indians stood, and gave him a code of detailed instructions that, if followed, would enable the Indians to drive the white men out of their country, recapture the pristine happiness of the aboriginal state, and find the right road again to heaven. He, Neolin, "the Enlightened," was appointed to preach the tribes to repentence and to instruct them in the proper means of recovering the favor of the Creator.

The prophet's vision was reminiscent of the story of Moses and the Ten Commandments. He dreamed that he went in search of the Creator, and after several strange adventures—taking two false trails which led only to fountains of fire, finding at last a mountain of glass, meeting there a beautiful woman in white, disrobing, washing, and climbing the mountain using only his left hand and foot—he arrived in heaven. Here he found new wonders—a regularly built village, stockaded with a gate, and a handsome guide dressed in white, who guided him to the Master of Life. The Master of Life took him by the hand and gave him for a seat a hat bordered with gold, on which the prophet sat, rather hesitantly, to hear the Creator's words.

The Master of Life then addressed him at length, saying:

I am the Master of Life, whom thou wishest to see, and to whom thou wishest to speak. Listen to that which I will tell thee for thyself and for all the Indians. I am the Maker of Heaven and earth, the trees, lakes, rivers, men, and all that thou seest or hast seen on the earth or in the heavens; and because I love you, you must do my will; you must also avoid that which I hate; I hate you to drink as you do, until you lose your reason; I wish you not to fight one

(117)

another; you take two wives, or run after other people's wives; you do wrong; I hate such conduct; you should have but one wife, and keep her until death. When you go to war, you juggle, you sing the medicine song, thinking you speak to me; you deceive yourselves; it is to the Manito that you speak; he is a wicked spirit who induces you to evil, and, for want of knowing me, you listen to him.

The land on which you are, I have made for you, not for others: wherefore do you suffer the whites to dwell upon your lands? Can you not do without them? I know that those whom you call the children of your great Father supply your wants. But, were you not wicked as you are, you would not need them. Before those whom you call your brothers had arrived, did not your bow and arrow maintain you? You needed neither gun, powder, nor any other object. The flesh of animals was your food, their skins your raiment. But when I saw you inclined to evil, I removed the animals into the depths of the forests, that you might depend on your brothers for your necessaries, for your clothing. Again become good and do my will, and I will send animals for your sustenance. I do now, however, forbid suffering among you your Father's children; I love them, they know me, they pray to me; I supply their own wants, and give them that which they bring to you. Not so with those who are come to trouble your possessions. Drive them away; wage war against them. I love them not. They know me not. They are my enemies, they are your brothers' enemies. Send them back to the lands I have made for them. Let them remain there.

Here is a written prayer which I give thee; learn it by heart, and teach it to all the Indians and children. It must be repeated morning and evening. Do all that I have told thee, and announce it to all the Indians as coming from the Master of Life. Let them drink but one draught [of liquor], or two at most, in one day. Let them have but one wife, and discontinue running after other people's wives and daughters. Let them not fight one another. Let them not sing the medicine song, for in singing the medicine song they speak to the evil spirit. Drive from your lands those dogs in red clothing; they are only an injury to you. When you want anything, apply to me, as your brothers [i.e., the Christian whites] do, and I will give to both. Do not sell to your brothers that which I have placed on the earth as food. In short, become good, and you shall want nothing. When you meet one another, bow, and give one another the hand of the heart [i.e., the left hand]. Above all, I command thee to repeat, morning and evening, the prayer which I have given thee.

Neolin remarked that he could not read, but the Master of Life told him that on his return upon earth he should give it to the chief of his village, who would be able to read it, and teach it to him, and also to all the Indians. The prophet promised to do as he was bidden and returned silently to his village, speaking to no one until he had presented to "the chief" the prayer and the laws that had been entrusted to his care by the Master of Life.

In response to a subsequent vision the prophet drew on a piece of deerskin parchment, about fifteen to eighteen inches square, a map of the soul's progress in this world and the next. This map he called the Great Book of Writing. Neolin traveled from town to town, preaching and holding the map before him while he preached, from time to time pointing with his finger to particular marks and spots on it, and giving explanations. He wept constantly while he preached.

The burden of his doctrine was that in the beginning the Creator had given the Indians a beautiful country in which to hunt, fish, and dwell (this was the outer border of the parchment). In ancient days, entry to the heavenly regions was easy and direct; but of late, the avenue to heaven has been stopped up by the white people. "Look here!" Neolin would say. "See what has been lost by neglect and disobedience; by being remiss in the expression of our gratitude to the Great Spirit, for what he has bestowed upon us; by neglecting to make him sufficient sacrifices; by looking upon a people of a different colour from our own, who had come across a great lake, as if they were a part of ourselves; by suffering them to sit down by our side, and looking at them with indifference, while they were not only taking our country from us, but this (pointing to the spot), this, our own avenue, leading into those beautiful regions which were destined for us." Instead of the old way, now the Indians were forced to find a new avenue to heaven; but this new one was hazardous, since the wayfarer must run a gauntlet of the sins and vices brought by the white people. Besides this, now there was a great gulf over which the soul had to leap, and many failed to cross and were seized by the evil spirit and carried off to his country, "where the ground was parched up by the heat for want of rain, no fruit came to perfection, the game was starved for want of pasture, and where the evil spirit, at his pleasure, transformed men into horses and dogs, to be ridden by him and follow him in his hunts and wherever he went." In the map of the heavenly regions, accordingly, the prophet drew a fat, well-fed deer or turkey, but a scrawny image in the Evil Spirit's.

"Such is the sad condition to which we are reduced," he would explain. "What is now to be done, and what remedy is to be applied? I will tell you, my friends. Hear what the Great Spirit has ordered me to tell you! You are to make sacrifices, in the manner that I shall direct; to put off entirely from yourselves the customs which you have adopted since the white people came among us; you are to return to that former happy state, in which we lived in peace and plenty, before these strangers came to disturb us, and above all, you must abstain from drinking their deadly *beson* [poisonous, bewitched "medicine," i.e., liquor], which they have forced upon us for the sake of increasing their gains and diminishing our numbers. Then will the Great Spirit give success to our arms; then he will give us strength to conquer our enemies, to drive them from hence, and recover the passage to the heavenly regions which they have taken from us." He made various other moral exhortations, too. In order to rid themselves of sin—the first necessity—the Indians were first to take emetics and to abstain from sexual intercourse. They were to quit the use of firearms; fire should be made by rubbing two sticks together, not by striking flint and steel, which was a white contamination. They were to learn to live again without trade with the whites, clothing and supporting themselves in the ancient way. In a word, they were to revive in a body their ancient customs and to live as they had before the white people discovered their country. And he prophesied (in 1762) that after a period of negotiation with the whites, there would be a war.

Actually, of course, despite his emphasis on a revival of the past, many of Neolin's recommendations were not traditional at all: he was advising the abandonment of many old cultural elements, such as "medicine songs," war rituals, polygyny; and he was introducing various quasi-European concepts, such as a high-god common to both whites and Indians, written prayers, and a written "Great Book." His code was a syncretism of native and white elements.

But nonetheless these teachings made a great sensation. The Prophet sold copies of his spiritual chart (he said it should be owned by every family) for one buckskin or two doeskins apiece. Copies were soon to be found far and wide, and disciples preached his doctrine in many villages. Indians traveled for miles to hear him speak. His suggestion of a cultural boycott was so effective that a Pittsburgh trader in 1762 wrote that the Delaware "mostly . . . have quit hunting any more than to supply nature in that way." And Pontiac himself became a convert to Neolin's doctrine and used it as supernatural sanction for his conspiracy.[3]

A similar doctrine, perhaps inspired by Neolin's, was preached by an unnamed Onondaga prophet, who about 1762 was told in a vision by the Great Spirit that "when He first made the World, He gave this large Island to the Indians for their Use; at the same time He gave other Parts of the World beyond the great Waters to the rest of his creating, and gave them different languages: That He now saw the white People squabbling, and fighting for these Lands which He gave the Indians; and that in every Assembly, and Company of Governors, and Great Men, He heard nothing scarce spoke, or talk'd of, but claiming, and wanting, large Possessions in our Country. This He said, was so contrary to his Intention, and what He expected wou'd be the Consequence at the time when the white People first came, like Children, among Us, that He was quite displeas'd, and would, altho their Numbers were ever so great, punish them if They did not desist."[4] With this revelation, too, Handsome Lake was no doubt acquainted.

· *A Dark and Bloody Ground* ·

HANDSOME LAKE, said his nephew Blacksnake in later years, was "much engaged in war prior to and during the American Revolution." Following the collapse of the Pontiac movement, in 1765 Handsome Lake betook himself with Giengwahtoh or Old Smoke, the famous Seneca war-captain of the Turtle Clan, and about one hundred other Seneca warriors, on an expedition against the Cherokee and Choctaw. This was a celebrated foray, remembered nearly a century later for the loot of scalps and other trophies with which the triumphant warriors returned. Giengwahtoh, a heavily built man over six feet tall, and sixty-some years of age, was then, or soon became, a principal civil chief of the Seneca. Handsome Lake was to see much of him during the Revolution.[5]

But although individual warriors might still find glory on the warpaths that led south and west from the Seneca country into the Ohio Valley during the thirteen years between the Conspiracy of Pontiac and the American Revolution, that valley and its Indian residents were rapidly being lost to the Iroquois. The Mingo and the dependent Delaware, Shawnee, Huron, and other tribal remnants who lived there under Iroquois hegemony had once turned confidently to the Great Council at Onondaga for support and intercession with the French and the English when they were threatened in their villages and hunting grounds. But now British garrisons were in possession of the soil and controlled the trade. And the Iroquois themselves, no longer able safely to play off the French in Canada against the English, could not risk a major war in which they would have to fight without a European ally.

The immediate result of the impasse was the Treaty of Fort Stanwix in 1768, by which the Iroquois surrendered their own and their tribal dependents' claims to the lands south of the Ohio and Susquehanna rivers. The Ohio lands in particular were then used for hunting by, and occupied by villages of, Mingo, Shawnee, and other dependents of the Six Nations. The Iroquois, claiming to represent all the occupants and users, negotiated the sale and kept all of the proceeds. One of the principal negotiators was Guyasuta. By this stroke, the Iroquois thought to get rid of a source of frontier friction between the English and themselves, by opening up all of Kentucky and a large area in western Pennsylvania and West Virginia to settlers. But the result was opposite to the intention, for they had sold off—in Kentucky—the principal hunting grounds of their erstwhile allies and dependents, the Shawnee. And the Shawnee, suddenly dispossessed and unrecompensed, secretly joined with the western Indians in a rival western confederacy to resist white colonial expansion.

Iroquois diplomacy, after the Treaty of Fort Stanwix, had an impossible task to perform: to please, and retain the friendship and alliance of, both the Shawnee and the British. The British, taking a legalistic point of view, felt that they had bought the land from the true owners, the Iroquois, who had acquired it by conquest; and now they expected the owners to evict the old tenants to make way for Daniel Boone and the rest of the settlers. But the old tenants, the Shawnee and others, taking an equally legalistic viewpoint, pressed the Iroquois to live up to the obligation to protect their interests, which the Iroquois had assumed when they invited them to live on Iroquois-owned land. Iroquois credit with the British now depended upon their ability to control other tribes, and the Iroquois knew it; but Iroquois ability to control other tribes also depended on their ability to protect them from the British. Far from being able to play off two sides against one another, the Iroquois were now being squeezed. Iroquois negotiators trod a narrow course of equivocation in council, urging peace and restraint on all sides, but finding themselves unable to take decisive action either to chastise or to join the increasingly rebellious Shawnee warriors in their guerrilla warfare with the advancing settlers.[6]

Individual Iroquois warriors, however, and particularly among the Seneca, were clearly sympathetic to the western Indians. Chafing under the eyes of the British garrisons, they watched with sullen resentment the rowdy whites of the frontier crowding in upon their own borders. At last in 1774 many of them joined the Shawnee, Delaware, and Wyandot in the brief and bloody Lord Dunmore's War— a war that soured the temper of the tribes of the Ohio and almost irritated the Six Nations into a general attack on the English frontier. Lord Dunmore's War was symbolic of the deterioration in relations between the whites and the Indians, and for that matter, of the internal order of both white and native societies. The white colonial culture was breaking down as fast or faster, if for different reasons, than the Indian cultures, and one of the symptoms of its decay was an inability of colonial officials to deter individual invasions of Indian lands.

That brief orgy of irresponsibility, cruelty, and despair that was Lord Dunmore's War began in the spring when one Michael Cresap and a company of land jobbers were exploring some of the lands south of the Ohio, bought from the Six Nations at Fort Stanwix in 1768. Missing some of their horses one day, they blamed the Shawnee Indians still hunting in the territory for stealing them and impulsively slaughtered a peaceful hunting party camped by the river. Among the dead were some of the family of Captain John Logan, a Cayuga Indian born on the Susquehanna but emigrant to the Ohio, where he had a Shawnee wife. This was Logan, the Great Mingo, a son of Shickellamy, the famous old Iroquois half-king at Shamokin, and a staunch defender of the whites among his own people. A few days later, a small party of white men, unprovoked, invited a group of Indians across the Ohio to the Virginia side, on pretense of friendly parley. They made them drunk and then killed most of them, including a brother and a pregnant sister of Logan. This stroke wiped out all of

Logan's close relatives. Some more Indians from the other side tried to cross the river to save their fellows; these were shot down in their canoes.

Logan was obligated to avenge his family. Accordingly during the summer he and eight warriors annihilated a small settlement of white families who had located on Indian lands on the Muskingum. Men, women, and children were killed; Logan is said to have refused to countenance torture. As the summer wore on, other settlements were attacked, too. The smoldering frontier along the Ohio again burst into flame.

Seneca warriors from the Genesee joined the Ohio bands. The Seneca were exasperated by the peculiarly gruesome killing of Bald Eagle. Bald Eagle was a Seneca warrior who spoke English well and lived with the Delaware at Salt Lick Town. He was known as a "good hunter" and as "a very kind, good" man who gave no one any trouble. During the winter he had gone alone up the Monongahela to hunt, and on his return downstream in the spring he was shot by a white man. The murderer tore the scalp from the old man's head, propped the body upright in the canoe, and set it adrift. The corpse in the canoe was seen by many who thought it was Bald Eagle, alive, returning down the river with his peltry.

Lord Dunmore, Governor of Virginia, while recognizing the provocation to the Indians, felt obligated to call up militia to punish Logan's outrages. Several thousand "Long Knives" and Indians met in the Battle of Point Pleasant. The outnumbered Indians—Shawnee, Delaware, Mingo, Wyandot, Seneca, Cayuga, and others—were beaten in a bloody struggle. The Six Nations at Onondaga, despite the fact that many of their warriors were already in the field, at the last refused to give official sanction to the war. The Onondaga council was utilizing the occasion as a means of punishment of the refractory Shawnee, who objected to the Six Nations' sale of the hunting grounds in Kentucky, who had attempted to organize a competing confederacy, and who were now demanding aid from the Iroquois in a war into which their own refusal to accept Iroquois land cessions had plunged them. Cornstalk negotiated a peace with Lord Dunmore; and Logan, acquiescing, made the famous speech recorded by Thomas Jefferson:

I appeal to any white man to say if he ever entered Logan's cabin hungry, and he gave him not meat; if ever he came cold and naked, and he clothed him not. During the course of the last long and bloody war, Logan remained idle in his cabin, an advocate for peace. Such was my love for the whites, that my countrymen pointed, as they passed, and said, "Logan is the friend of the white men." I had even thought to have lived with you, but for the injuries of one man. Colonel Cresap, the last Spring, cold blood and unprovoked, murdered all the relations of Logan, not even sparing my women and children. There runs not a drop of my blood in the veins of any living creature. This called on me for revenge. I have sought it; I have killed many; I have fully glutted my vengeance. For my country, I rejoice at the beams of peace; but do not harbour a thought that mine is the joy of fear. Logan never felt fear. He will not turn on his heel to save his life. Who is there to mourn for Logan? Not one.

Logan, after the defeat at Point Pleasant and the negotiated peace, became melancholic and declared that life was a torment to him. Once in a drunken frolic he knocked his new wife down. Thinking that he had killed her, he fled to Detroit, while his wife, thus abandoned, returned to her own people. Along the trail Logan accidentally met a party of Indian men, women, and children, including his nephew Todkahdohs, "the Searcher," a Seneca who lived on the Allegheny and was a kinsman of Logan's wife. Logan, ridden with guilt, thought his nephew was pursuing him to take vengeance for having murdered his wife, and he recklessly announced that he was going to kill the whole party. As he dismounted, gun in hand, Todkahdohs cut him down with a shotgun blast.[7]

The old ways of honor now led, for many men, to dishonor, loneliness, and despair. The Six Nations had seduced their dependents and allies twice into lost campaigns, in 1763 and 1774, to drive out the whites, and had still preserved the semblance of their own neutrality. But the old way of playing both ends against the middle was becoming difficult and more dangerous. It was to become catastrophic as the American Revolution unfolded.

· *The Iroquois and the Revolution: The Neutrality Policy* ·

FRONTIER INCIDENTS like Lord Dunmore's War were the backwoods expression of a chronic, restless resentment of the Crown's authority that by 1775 had become epidemic in all social classes in the British colonies. While groups of stubborn frontiersmen, defiant of law, carried on the illicit trade in liquor and furs and settled their families on Indian lands west of the Proclamation Line, the provincial capitals were stirring with the other conspiracies to subvert the military establishments, the new taxes, and the new trade regulations that an English Parliament was imposing on an increasingly expensive empire. Since 1772 committees of correspondence had been generating opposition to British measures, and mobs had been terrorizing officials of the colonial administration; and in September 1774, while Dunmore's war and its train of negotiations were still in progress, colonial representatives met in the First Continental Congress to formulate grievances and to concert a boycott of British goods. In the spring of 1775 blood was shed at Lexington and Concord, and a Second Continental Congress met, in less temperate mood, to create an army. The tide of opinion was running rapidly to the left; conservative loyalists were already under persecution by local committees of patriots; by summer, the King's officers in America realized that they faced an armed rebellion.

The Continental Congress early considered what role the Iroquois, probably the most formidable single body of fighting men in the colony of New York, should play in the developing war. In July 1775, the Congress passed an act dividing the Indian country into three departments, with three commissioners for the northern department and one each for the others. The Continental policy, like that of the British in the years before the French were defeated, was to secure, if not the assistance, at least the neutrality of the Six Nations and their dependents. Continental Indian agents accordingly represented the struggle as a family quarrel among the white people, in which the natives had no interest. The Christian Stockbridge (Mahican), who had been enlisted as allies of the Congress after aiding the patriot cause around Boston in 1775, were moved to Oneida as propagandists of the Americans, to convince the Oneida of the justness of the colonists' cause and to deter them from joining the British in case of open conflict. Samuel Kirkland, the doughty old missionary to the Oneida, appealed to them for their neutrality. In consequence of these pressures, the Oneida, and the Tuscarora and Stockbridge who lived with them, early declared their intention to stand aside from the conflict.

The Mohawk also were quickly subjected to pressure. Kirkland sent them messages advising a neutral course. In May 1775, they were addressed by delegates from Albany who reassured them that the patriots really had no evil designs on loyalist Colonel Guy Johnson, Sir William's successor as Indian Superintendent, despite mutterings and threats by lively malcontents. Colonel Johnson thereupon departed for the western Iroquois nations, to advise them of the events of the hour. On his return Johnson found popular white sentiment in the Mohawk Valley congealing into the suspicion that he and his Mohawks would plot, spy, and if need be, take up arms against their rebel neighbors. He departed again for the Indian country, holding councils with the Six Nations in Oswego and Montreal. Report had it that in these councils he urged the warriors to war against the rebels, but actually he simply urged them—as the Congress was doing—to mind their own affairs quietly, avoid frontier incidents, and not to listen to evil birds. Taking him literally and maintaining the classic Iroquois neutrality policy, at Oswego the eastern tribes of the Iroquois agreed that they would permit neither British nor American troops to pass through their country.

In August 1775, the Continental commissioners met with the Iroquois at Albany, where they explained at length, and most pathetically, the moral justifications for the colonists' recourse to arms, and said again that this was a family quarrel between them and Old England, in which the Indians were not concerned. They did not want the Iroquois to take up the hatchet against the King's troops but rather urged them to remain at home, not joining either side and to keep the hatchet buried deep. The Six Nations replied, through Little Abraham, the notable Mohawk speaker, in clear language: "the determination of the Six Nations [is] not to take any part; but as it is a family affair, to sit still and see you fight it out."

But the Six Nations, by no means naive in this sort of diplomacy, set certain conditions upon the agreement to remain neutral. Specifically, the military activities of the Continentals should be confined to the coast. The free passage of Iroquois hunters from fort to fort, from trading post to trading post, within their wide country, was not to be interrupted (rumor had it that the road to Fort Stanwix was to be closed by Continental troops). Further, Sir John Johnson, an outspoken loyalist, was not to be disturbed, nor was the Reverend Mr. Stewart, the loyalist missionary among the Mohawk, although both of them were being threatened with reprisals by the patriots. The Six

Nations also made the satisfaction of their generations-old land claims against New York a part of their understanding of the agreement— an interpretation that was not so far-fetched as might appear, since the commissioners had made much of the renewal of the old covenant between the people of Albany and the Six Nations, which was celebrated on the occasion.

The suspicions so quietly expressed by Little Abraham were not ill-founded. Doubt of Albany people had been traditional among Iroquoians for a century, and for good reason; and now the reply of the commissioners was equivocal and therefore ominous. Congress would give no assurance that their territory would not be invaded. The missionary to the Mohawk was assured of his security (actually, he was forced to flee into Canada). An open trade was promised at Albany and Schenectady. And in answer to the request for settlement of ancient Mohawk land claims, the commissioners asserted that "the accusation is groundless," and anyway was a matter for the Albany people to discuss. To this Little Abraham replied evenly, "In case I was to answer that part of your speech, it might perhaps draw us into an argument." He went on briefly to advise the commissioners that Sir Guy's advice at the western and northern councils had been "not to take any part in this dispute, as it was a quarrel between brothers."

And "We are very glad," said Little Abraham, "that your language and Colonel Johnson's so well agree."[8]

Thus it appears that the settled policy of the Six Nations, in response to the official requests for their neutrality made both by Johnson and the Continental commissioners, was to wait and watch. Hotheads there were, like Joseph Brant, who argued for an early involvement on the British side; a few high-spirited warriors committed themselves to minor campaigns, some (primarily Oneida and Stockbridge) on the American side, some (primarily the Caughnawaga Mohawk in Canada) on the British. But in the main, at first, the Six Nations avoided military alliance. The neutrality was, however, conditional upon the contending parties refraining from encroaching upon their trade, their travel, or their land. The tribes had, in effect, implemented the classic play-off policy again; they would fight *against* whoever first invaded their territory, interfered with their trade and travel, injured their people, or demanded their alliance, and *for* whoever had not upset the *status quo*.

It was not easy for the Indians who lived near rebel communities to stay neutral. The Mohawk soon found it necessary to leave their homes. Colonel Johnson had left the Mohawk Valley in 1775 with a goodly number of Mohawk for his tour of councils. He had been previously threatened with seizure by a patriotic committee, and his response had been to fortify his house and assemble a private army of Mohawk defenders. He did not choose to return to New York, nor did many of the Mohawk who left for Ontario with him. The remaining Mohawk population of the valley gradually melted away. An epidemic swept through the villages shortly after the return of the ambassadors from Albany, and the Indian community at Schoharie was almost exterminated. Some of the survivors are reported to have conceived (possibly with the aid of the Reverend Mr. Stewart) the belief that the pestilence had been sent by the Great Spirit as punishment for not having declared for the King; in any case they too left the valley and followed their fellows westward. A few of these Mohawks from New York aided the British in the defense of St. Johns, Newfoundland, and Oswego; some Caughnawaga Mohawks, on the other hand, aided the temporarily successful Americans in the capture of Montreal and the abortive siege of Quebec. When the remaining Mohawk in the Mohawk Valley learned of the imprisonment by the Americans of two of their "debauched" brethren, however, they petitioned for their release and argued that it was after all the Americans who had spilled blood on the path of peace (by seizing Oswego), and that thereby the Americans had broken the Albany agreement.

The official policy of the Iroquois was still neutrality when, in the fall of 1775, a council was held at Pittsburgh between the Congressional commissioners and the Seneca, Wyandot, Shawnee, and Delaware. The commissioners wished to obtain from these western nations a firm commitment to neutrality. Guyasuta, the old Seneca half-king, speaking for the dependent nations, promised neutrality; and although the leader of a Delaware faction, White Eyes, defiantly announced the independence of the Delaware, the council as a whole agreed in an intention to remain neutral. Guyasuta promised to use his influence on the confederate council of the Six Nations to endorse the neutral policy. Handsome Lake's brother Cornplanter, and his young nephew Blacksnake, were present at this meeting; very likely Handsome Lake was there too. In July 1776, at Fort Pitt, another council was held, and Guyasuta again announced the policy that the Six Nations had formulated at Oswego and expressed at Albany: they would be neutral, but neither British nor Americans were to be permitted to pass through the territory of the Six Nations. "I am appointed," he said, "to take care of this country, that is of the nations on the other side of the Ohio, and I desire you will not think of an expedition against Detroit, for I will repeat, we will not suffer an army to pass through our country."

It was inevitable that the Americans would sooner or later break with the Six Nations, however, for they were revolutionaries attacking the established system and could not tolerate a neutrality that maintained the *status quo*. Patriotic fervor, indeed, sometimes verged on the paranoid, interpreting almost any sort of detachment or verbal disagreement as evidence of conspiracy. A loyalist Mohawk sachem, Peter Nickus, was wounded and then hacked to pieces by patriotic white swordsmen about 1775—the first war casualty in the valley. In 1775 the Americans had seized Oswego, in defiance of the Six Nations' warnings at Albany, and captured some Mohawk warriors. In 1776, on the basis of perjurous accusations, General Schuyler besieged and imprisoned Sir John Johnson (son of the old friend of the Mohawk, Sir William Johnson), after brushing aside Mohawk objections that the Albany treaty provided for his freedom and that this same treaty prohibited the "closing of the road" with armed men. The accusation on which Johnson's arrest was based was that he was secreting a small arsenal for a loyalist campaign against the patriots. Although this accusation was proven false, the arms not being found where the informer swore they were hidden, Johnson was not exonerated but was placed on "parole." A few months later General Schuyler, who suspected, no doubt sincerely but almost certainly mistakenly, that Johnson was attempting to persuade the Indians to massacre the patriots, sent men to seize and imprison him. Johnson, presumably considering this to be a violation by Schuyler of the parole agreement, thereupon gathered together his friends, and various official records and papers and in May 1776, fled through the forests to Canada. He was declared by the Continentals to have broken his parole, his estates were confiscated, and his wife, Lady Johnson, was seized and held as a hostage in Albany. Johnson thereafter became a militant antirevolutionary, a colonel commanding Indian and ranger detachments. Handsome Lake was to serve under him in several campaigns.

The Six Nations, who had in fact kept steadfastly neutral, took

Johnson's seizure and other events of that order as a sure sign that "the road was closed," in violation of the Albany agreement. More and more of the Mohawk slipped away from the Mohawk Valley; a few remained for a time, nervously guarding their homes and wondering how soon the patriots, now throwing off all restraints, would serve them ill. On May 20, 1776, some of the Mohawk, led by the firebrand Joseph Brant (who was acting without general Six Nations' sanction), fought against the Americans at the Battle of the Cedars, in which the American forces retreating from their invasion of Canada were disastrously beaten. Lurid, if false, atrocity stories were circulated concerning this affair, and Congress denounced the British for their outrageous use of Indian troops. At the same moment, however, and before news of the Cedars could have reached Philadelphia, Congress itself was preparing to use Indian troops. On May 25 Congress resolved that "it was highly expedient to engage the Indians in the service of the United Colonies," and authorized the Commander-in-Chief to recruit two thousand paid Indian auxiliaries. This resolution flatly contradicted the neutrality injunctions issued at Albany the year before, and news of it no doubt reinforced a growing Iroquois sense of the undependability of the Continental Congress. Indeed, this resolution was passed one day after an Iroquois deputation, then in Philadelphia, was exhorted to remain neutral. Few Indian warriors ever joined the American army, however, and most of those few were Oneida, Tuscarora, and Stockbridge, from the Reverend Mr. Kirkland's congregation.[9]

· *The Oswego Council* ·

THE FIRST STEP toward an official abandonment of the neutrality position by the warriors of most of the Six Nations and their allied tribes was taken at a grand but secret council at Niagara in September 1776. Most of the Seneca were there, including Handsome Lake and his brother Cornplanter, Red Jacket, Old Smoke, and Farmer's Brother. The Seneca, Cayuga, Onondaga, and Mohawk declared their adherence to the King's government, come what may; the "props" of the confederacy—Wyandot, Mississauga, Delaware, Nanticoke, and Conoy (all from Ohio) and the "Squawkies" (Fox domiciled in Seneca country)—joined in with the declaration; and a strong appeal was dispatched to the erring Oneida and Tuscarora to quit the Boston men and join their brethren. This action, although it was not yet a taking up of the hatchet, severed the chain of friendship with the Continentals and split the confederacy, for the Oneida and Tuscarora were now defined as a dissenting body.[10]

The actual decision to take up the hatchet, however, was postponed until 1777, when internal disagreement, American untrustworthiness, and British solicitation made the continuance of a policy of military neutrality impossible. The breakdown of the neutrality policy was assisted by an unexpected disaster. In January 1777, the council fire at Onondaga was extinguished: three sachems there, and eighty-seven others, perished in an epidemic, making political decisions impossible until the condolence ritual could be performed. This was at best difficult in midwinter, almost impossible in unsettled and divisive times, and so at this critical juncture there was no federal civil council; affairs of peace and war now rested with the warriors and the separate village and national councils.

The die was cast irrevocably by the warriors at a council with the British at Oswego in the early summer of 1777. At this fort and trading post on the south shore of Lake Ontario, hundreds of Seneca men, women, and children joined with the people of the other tribes of the confederacy (except the Oneida and Tuscarora) to hear the British agents at last make the formal request that the Six Nations take up the hatchet against the rebels. After plying the Indian delegates generously with food, rum, and gifts of clothing and hardware, the British commissioner outlined the origin of the rebellion: the Americans were described as being disobedient children who had violated the laws and challenged the government of their father and who therefore required "a Dressing and punishment." "Now here is your father," he went on (as Blacksnake later recalled the speech); "[he has] offered you to take his axe and Tomahawk to hold against American and here is the Buckenknife and Bowisknife that you will also take for to take the American lock and scalps and my father will pay much Each one scalps in money. . . ." He explained that the Americans were poor and had no regular government and would be easy to defeat. "First we will go from here to take all the forts Belonging to Americas. The Fort Stanwix we will take first and Wyoming &c. These two forts that Shall take will be Sufficients to Show our fathers strength. . . ."

Decision had now to be reached by the Indians whether or not to take up the hatchet. The chief warriors agreed to take the matter under consideration in private council that afternoon. (This was not a matter for deliberation by the sachem-chiefs from the confederate council, but by the warriors who were to do the fighting.) The warriors' council, however, came to no consensus. In the morning Joseph Brant rose first and spoke for taking up the hatchet, urging that neutrality could ultimately lead only to disaster: "if [we] shoul[d] lie down and sleep and we shoul[d] be liable to cut our throat by the Red coat man or by America. . . ." Red Jacket and Cornplanter, however, urged that this was a family quarrel among the white people, that the Indians did not really know what it was all about, and that interference might be a mistake. Brant called Cornplanter a coward, and the meeting broke up in some confusion. The people, warriors, and women divided into two parties, and there was heated discussion of the issues in private Indian councils. The Seneca generally supported Cornplanter's cautious view that it was better not to take sides in a civil war among white people. "Gi-en-gwah-toh & Co-ne-di-yeu [Handsome Lake] spoke strongly against it—thought they had better remain neutral," recalled Blacksnake; and so did Guyasuta and Red Jacket. But Brant and his Mohawks called all the pacifists cowards, and the Seneca warriors "can not Beared to be called coward," as Blacksnake put it. At last, by dint of this sort of moral exhortation and British openhandedness with rum and dry goods, and the display of a wampum belt purported to be the ancient convenant between the Six Nations and the Crown, the majority of the warriors agreed that they were after all obligated to defend their kind and indulgent father. A majority of the warriors passed a resolution to accept the King's hatchet, and "the mothers also consent to Regard to it. . . ." Cornplanter, taking his political defeat gracefully, accepted the decision and exhorted the warriors to unity. "Every Brave man Show himself Now hereafter for we will find an many Dangerous times during the action of the war, for we will see a many Brave man amongst the America Soldiers whicth we Shall meet, with their sharp adge tools, I therefore Say you must Stand like good Soldier against your own white Brother Because just as soon as he fined you out that you are against him he then will Show you his wit no mercy on you an us, I therefore Say Stand to your Post when is time come Before you

But agreed yourselves. . . ." The resolution became unanimous, and the next day Brant announced to the British commissioners that the Six Nations had taken up the hatchet against the Americans.[11]

· The First Battles ·

THE IMMEDIATE OUTCOME of the Oswego council was the enlistment of several hundred Iroquois warriors in Colonel Barry St. Leger's motley little army then assembling at Oswego. This task force was to sweep down the Mohawk Valley, while Burgoyne swept down the Hudson, to a triumphal meeting at Albany. The joint force then would proceed down the lower Hudson River to New York. But the campaign was hurriedly arranged. There was inadequate artillery; the troops were a miscellany of a few hundred each of loyalist guerrillas, Hessian mercenaries, Acadian militia, British regulars, and Indian volunteers; there was neither discipline nor training sufficient for execution. The force was stopped in its tracks by the moldy palisades of old Fort Stanwix (recently renamed, patriotically, Fort Schuyler) and its ill-trained garrison of some seven hundred and fifty men. The siege, the sanguinary battle at Oriskany nearby, and St. Leger's sudden withdrawal from the ground, not merely contributed to the failure of the grand strategy that was signaled by Burgoyne's later surrender; it also largely determined the nature of future Iroquois military tactics in the Revolutionary War.

The American fort, at the beginning of the summer, was not a very substantial obstacle to a British advance down the Mohawk River. Its surrounding ditch was filled with rubbish and debris; the outer pickets were rotten and falling down; the garrison had too small a supply of powder; the "bullets did not match the muskets"; they did not even have a flag! But at the end of June small parties of Indians, including a group of Seneca under Handsome Lake's venerable captain, Old Smoke, began sniping at the Americans and occasionally killing and scalping stragglers from the fort. This harassment stirred the patriots to rebuild their defenses. St. Leger's twelve-hundred-man force, arriving on August 3, found the fort in improved condition and a garrison prepared to defend itself. The patriot commander haughtily refused a summons to surrender, and the British forces encamped near the fort laid siege, and prepared to cut off any reinforcements.

The reinforcing provincial militia approached three days later, on August 6, and, somewhat against the advice of their aging commander, General Herkimer, at once impetuously hurled themselves into the midst of the ambush carefully prepared by Joseph Brant and his Indians and by Colonel Butler and Sir John Johnson and their New York loyalists. The American force of about nine hundred men, however, was too large to be annihilated in a few volleys. The skirmish turned into a bloody afternoon-long hand-to-hand contest with muskets, knives, bayonets, and tomahawks, which ended only when the Indians and British left the field to protect their encampments from a successful sortie from the fort. The American reinforcements retreated down the valley shortly thereafter, with their mortally wounded commander. From two to four hundred of Herkimer's men were killed, and several hundred others were wounded or captured, or fled at the first alarm. About one hundred of the Iroquois, and perhaps an equal number of the loyalists, also died. Both sides claimed the victory: the British, because they had inflicted such heavy losses and had prevented reinforcements from reaching the fort; the Americans, because their survivors remained (temporarily) on the field of battle.

The major blow, however, had fallen on the Indians. Thirty-six warriors of the Seneca alone, including several sachem-chiefs serving as common soldiers, were killed on the field or died later of wounds; many others were injured; and their encampment was sacked by the sortie from the fort. Others lost substantially in reputation: Red Jacket and three others fled at the sound of gunfire and went home to the Genesee. (Blacksnake recalled this as "cowardice" seventy-three years later, but said that because it was Red Jacket's first war experience, "nothing was done or said to him.") Since all of the Seneca leaders who had been at the Oswego council were present at the Oriskany battle, it may be presumed that Handsome Lake also was present.

A few days after the battle the British officers told the Seneca—and probably the other Indian allies as well—"to go home and see [their] families." Mary Jemison, then living along the Genesee, described the disillusioning return of the survivors, who had gone to Fort Stanwix expecting to look on peacefully smoking their pipes while the Americans surrendered to the British, and instead had borne the brunt of the heaviest fighting of the war to date. As Mary Jemison put it, "Our town exhibited a scene of real sorrow and distress, when our warriors returned and recounted their misfortunes, and stated the real loss they had received in the engagement. The mourning was excessive, and was expressed by the most doleful yells, shrieks, and howlings, and by inimitable gesticulations."

Two weeks after the battle the British themselves, failing further reinforcements from Canada, unable to count any longer on their shattered Indian allies, and alarmed by rumors (largely true) spread by the "neutral" Oneida that a major American relief force under General Arnold was advancing upon them, were forced to lift the siege and to withdraw hastily across the lakes. Some embittered Iroquois warriors who had remained with St. Leger plundered the fleeing British and went home too in disgust.[12]

War was largely a summer and fall occupation among the Iroquois; in winter, warriors became hunters and family men. As Blacksnake explained, "We than Retreated for the winter . . . we Replace ourselve, at Near home for our hunting till Spring, Some of those which ware family went on home But when we got Ready and hunt Deers & Bears and Elks and others garms—for Provisions for the Next for to play upon, and for our childrens and for the old folks, whicth we have to provide for, all their wants, whicth we always maken preparation for them before we leave them."[13] Thus the winter of 1777–8 was a quiet one insofar as Indian warfare was concerned; Congress even took heart to appeal again to the four hostile tribes (Seneca, Cayuga, Onondaga, and Mohawk) to join their alliance, claiming (optimistically) that the Delaware, the Shawnee, and other western tribes were friends of the United States. But the quietness of the frontier did not mean peace: Brant's Indian emissaries and the three notorious Tories who had escaped from their Pittsburgh prison—McKee, Elliot, and Simon Girty—were busily recruiting warriors for next summer's campaign. Rumor had it that Indians from twenty-two nations were going to join Butler's Rangers in an attack on New York that would lay waste all the settlements west of Schenectady. The white frontiers passed the winter in fear.

War came again with the spring. The first attack of the season fell on Springfield, a settlement at the head of Otsego Lake: the little fort was burned, some of the men were killed and some captured, the women and children were left unharmed.

This assault set the general style of the attacks by the organized Iroquois raiding parties during the war: the first objective was the seizure or destruction of property, and the expulsion of the rebel inhabitants; if men resisted, or seemed prepared to resist, they were killed or captured; women and children were usually either left alone or taken as prisoners. There were no instances of torture (except for the case of some soldiers captured during Sullivan's Campaign) and no wholesale massacres, for the organized war-parties acted under instruction from British officers and were often accompanied by British officers, who firmly insisted on the Indians obeying the rules of civilized warfare. Brant, the Mohawk leader, was a college-trained man who consciously attempted to combine the idea of the English officer-gentleman and the Iroquois warrior-diplomat. Individual and isolated atrocities were committed, usually by independent bands of banditti who were bent solely on plunder, revenge, or sadistic enjoyment. But responsible British officers like Johnson and the Butlers, and Indian leaders like Old Smoke and Brant, wanted to prevent orgies of cruelty like those in which the Iroquois had indulged themselves in the seventeenth century. These were acculturated and, in some cases, like Brant's, "civilized" Indians, sensitive to the contempt of Europeans and anxious to acquit themselves with dignity in the eyes of a larger world.

While several additional raids were made under Brant's leadership during the summer on the settlements in the Mohawk Valley, chiefly destructive of property, the first major event of the 1778 fighting-season was the famous battle at Wyoming. Handsome Lake, as a "common warrior," participated in this battle, along with Blacksnake, Old Smoke, Farmer's Brother, and most of the other distinguished Allegany and Genesee Seneca. Following the plan announced at the Oswego council of the previous year, several hundred Tories under Johnson and Butler, and most of the Seneca warriors, were outfitted for the campaign at Niagara and early in July appeared before the Forty Fort, the rebel stronghold in the valley of Wyoming. On July 3, about 400 militia and regulars sallied forth from the fort and confronted the Indians and Tories. The two sides were arranged in a regular skirmish-line; the Indians managed to outflank the Americans, who fell back in disorder; the retreat became a rout, and 340 of the 400 were killed. The Seneca lost, according to Blacksnake, only five men. Next day the fort, under Colonel Denniston, surrendered. The settlements in the valley of Wyoming were thereafter burned and looted, and most of the inhabitants fled into the mountains. Although there was neither massacre nor torture of prisoners, the fleeing survivors spread lurid tales of atrocities; indeed, Wyoming became a symbol of Indian rapacity. Queen Esther, daughter of old Catherine Montour, was reputed to have tomahawked helpless prisoners with her own hand; the "monster Brant" (who was not even at Wyoming, being occupied with the relatively bloodless raids on the Mohawk Valley at the time) was accused of murder; tales of the slaughter of whole families by their black-sheep Tory sons made frontier blood run cold. The Seneca returned to Niagara with fifteen prisoners, whom they surrendered to the British; they received each a suit of clothes and some money, and went home, unaware that the military success of their mission was earning them an undeserved reputation for wanton savagery.

A year had now passed, during which Iroquois warriors had participated as brothers-in-arms with British troops in two major and strictly military engagements, at Oriskany and Wyoming. They had successfully raided and destroyed a number of small settlements in Pennsylvania and New York. Although as yet no retaliation had been offered by the rebels, the humiliating defeat at Wyoming, inflated in retrospect by atrocity stories, and the raids on frontier settlements in the Mohawk Valley were now beginning to spur action. Brant's summer camps for refugee Tories and refugee Mohawks, at Oquaga and Unadilla on the Susquehanna, were suspected of being the headquarters of the Iroquois raiders. Already in June he had been reported to be fortifying his post there, and the people from Cherry Valley nearby were sending out patrols and issuing challenges and threats to castrate Brant. After the Wyoming affair Congress resolved to speed its plans to chastise the Six Nations. A grandiose project for an expedition against Detroit was reduced to a program of building a string of pitifully undersupplied (and eventually abandoned) forts in the Ohio country, and the main attention was directed instead to the Susquehanna, on whose upper waters the Unadilla River lay. In September a task force of regulars and rangers from Schoharie assaulted the then-abandoned Indian towns at Oquaga and Unadilla and burned them to the ground, including in the fire the gristmill and sawmill, then the only mills of their kind on the upper Susquehanna. About the same time, some two hundred militia under colonels Hartley and Denniston drove up the Susquehanna from Wyoming, burning deserted Indian towns at Sheshequin, Tioga, and Queen Esther's Town. At Tioga, on hearing that Butler's force was nearby, they turned about and retreated toward Wyoming. They were forced to beat off an attack by Butler's Indians on their way down the river.

The consequence of these comparatively ineffectual threats was the hardening of Iroquois determination to protect their territory, which they conceived now to be in immediate danger of invasion and seizure by ruthless, land-hungry frontiersmen. Big Tree, the Seneca chief who had for a year held out against Seneca participation in the war and had continued to negotiate through the Oneida with the Americans, cast his lot with the warriors' party. In revenge for the attacks on Oquaga and Unadilla, the Iroquois attacked Cherry Valley, an old settlement founded in 1739. About one hundred of Captain Butler's rangers and perhaps two hundred Indians under Brant made up the party. Handsome Lake was one of them. (So also, for a time, was Red Jacket; but at the rendezvous he and three others turned back, complaining that the season was too far advanced for fighting. This was his second desertion.) As in the other attacks on settlements, the tactic was to immobilize the armed militia in their fort, capture a small number of men, women, and children, drive off the horses, cattle, and oxen, and take whatever movable plunder might be carried. The soldiers were kept busy in the fort answering sniping fire from the Tories, while the Indians killed people, burned barns, houses, and haystacks, drove off horses and cattle, and looted goods. A number of men, women, and children were killed in the fighting, and thirty or forty captives, mostly women and children, taken with the party on its departure. Most of these were released after a few miles' walk; others were held as hostages for the release of the wife and family of Walter Butler, who in turn were being held by the Americans as hostages for the return of Butler himself (although he was then under sentence of death). Eventually the exchange of the Cherry Valley prisoners for Walter Butler's family was arranged.

Cherry Valley was now added to Wyoming as the subject of atrocity stories; and this time the stories were more nearly true. At Cherry Valley some thirty-odd civilians, including women and children, Tory and rebel sympathizers alike, had been killed despite the efforts of Butler and Brant to maintain the disciplined behavior that had prevailed at Wyoming, where only men under arms lost their lives. In the course of an acrimonious correspondence with generals Schuyler and Clinton, Butler denied any widespread killing of women, children, and prisoners and explained the occasional killing of civilians as revenge for atrocities committed by Americans. But denials and excuses did not avail; the work of rumor made the atrocities even more enormous. The Iroquois were charged with ripping open and quartering the women and hanging their bodies on the trees, and with seizing infants from their mothers' breasts and knocking their brains out against posts. Such rumors as these had the twofold effect of sending the frontier settlements into panic and of building up in the frontier population a vindictive hatred for and contempt of the Iroquois that would later cost that people, and the British, dear.[14]

In the spring of 1779, after the winter's lull while the warriors hunted to feed their families, the Indian raids upon the frontier began again. Brant and his Mohawk and upper Susquehanna Indians burned settlements and cut to pieces pursuing militia, from the Mohawk River as far to the south as the Delaware River at the Minisinks. The Seneca and Cayuga captured Fort Freeland, near Sunbury on the Susquehanna, and looted and burned in the neighborhood; this series of raids locally was renowned for the fact that the Indians released all women and children and killed few men, although they took about thirty soldiers prisoner. Other miscellaneous bands made scattered attacks on small settlements and isolated farms all the way along the frontier from the Susquehanna to the Monongahela and the Allegheny about Pittsburgh.

Although the loss of life in these raids was relatively small, their effectiveness in destroying economic and military resources, in disorganizing the militia, and in reducing the local will to fight was very great. They were major blows to the American mobilization effort. In Brant's raid, for instance, on German Flats—one of the richest and most productive agricultural settlements in the Mohawk Valley—nearly 70 farms, including 63 houses, 57 barns, 3 gristmills, 2 sawmills, and crops in the field and furniture in the buildings were totally destroyed by fire, and 235 horses, 229 horned cattle, 269 sheep, and 93 oxen carried away. One hundred square miles of farmland were put to the torch while the several hundred inhabitants of the valley, cowering in their little forts—which were not even fired upon—watched in dismay. Only two white men were killed.

The raids by the Seneca and Cayuga on the towns along the Susquehanna were equally, if not more, disorganizing. After thirteen men were killed at the taking of Fort Freeland, the whole of the country was panic-stricken. A letter from Sunbury struck a note of hysteria: "The situation of Northumberland Country, beyond description distressing, not a single Inhabitant north of Northumberland Town. . . . I need not ask you what is to be done, Help Help; our whole Frontier laid open, and the Communication with Gen. Sullivan's army is cut off."[15] Local petitions were circulated for the recall of General Sullivan's army (whose mission was to force the Indian war-parties to withdraw to protect their families); court proceedings against the general were demanded; the forts were evacuated; the local militia refused even to leave their homes to defend the countryside. A lieutenant colonel of the militia reported to the president of Pennsylvania's revolutionary council that "Our Country is on ye Eve of Breaking up . . . there is nothing to be seen but Disolation, fire & smoak, as the inhabitants is Collected at particular places, the Enimy burns all their Houses that they have evacuated. . . ." Indeed, as the inhabitants themselves noted, it was like the French and Indian War of twenty years earlier all over again. Even the same desperate remedies were suggested: surveyor William Maclay reinvented Franklin's earlier (1755) suggestion of hunting down the Indians with dogs.[16]

· *Sullivan's Raid* ·

THE EFFECTIVENESS of the Iroquois and Troy raiders in laying waste a fifty- to one-hundred-mile belt of frontier land, from the Monongahela River to the Mohawk, thus was by now a matter of major concern to the Continental commanders. During the winter Washington had been laying plans for a blow against the hostile Indians; this campaign was to be the main American military effort of the year. In fact four American invasions of the Iroquois country took place during the summer of 1779.

The first move was a strike against the Onondaga, who had been attempting to straddle the issue of war, some of their men taking part in Iroquois forays and others, particularly the responsible chiefs, loudly proclaiming neutrality in various conferences at Albany. Three Onondaga villages were burned, twelve Indians were killed, thirty-three were taken prisoner, and considerable military equipment (including the cannon installed at the council-house) was taken or destroyed. (It is noteworthy that orders were issued by General

Clinton on the occasion of this campaign to emulate his notion of Iroquois treatment of prisoners: "Bad as the savages are, they never violate the chastity of any women, their prisoners. Although I have very little apprehension that any of the soldiers will so far forget their character as to attempt such a crime on the Indian women who may fall into their hands, yet it will be well to take measures to prevent such a stain upon our army."[17]) The immediate consequence was the alienation of the Onondaga, their commitment to the cause of British arms, and cries of outrage from the Seneca at seeing their neutralist brethren so treacherously attacked. Within the month three hundred Onondaga warriors—virtually the entire adult male population of the tribe—descended upon the little settlement of Cobleskill, east of Schoharie. Only two prisoners were taken; a fort was burned and twenty-two soldiers killed, and the whole settlement was burned and plundered.

The second, third, and fourth attacks, formulated and carried out in concert, were mounted by substantial armies under generals Clinton and Sullivan and Colonel Brodhead. Clinton with 1,500 men on 220 flatboats floated down the Unadilla River from Otsego Lake, on the crest of a flood formed by breaking a dam at the mouth of the lake, to join General Sullivan's army at Tioga. The flood ruined the Indian cornfields, and the army burned three Tuscarora villages below Oquaga and miscellaneous small Indian settlements still farther down on the Susquehanna. The passage downstream occupied Clinton's army from August 9 to 22. Sullivan took command of the combined army of about 3,000 men.

Sullivan's orders were to destroy totally the villages of the Iroquois, to take as many prisoners of all ages and both sexes as possible, and to cut a swath of terror to Niagara. A smaller force under Colonel Brodhead was simultaneously to move up the Allegheny River. Sullivan, a methodical New Hampshire lawyer, like effective anti-guerrilla fighters before and after him, was careful to maintain discipline, to bring up supplies and cannon, and to send out Indian (Oneida) spies and scouts to prevent ambuscade. Furthermore, he had the advantage of surprise: the British and the Iroquois were not expecting so massive an assault and had not assembled adequate forces for defense. The main battle, such as it was, was over almost before Sullivan's main march began: on August 29 a hastily assembled force of about 500 Indians under Brant and 250 Tory rangers under the

Cornplanter, by F. Bartoli (circa 1796). Courtesy of The New-York Historical Society, New York City

Red Jacket, by Robert W. Weir (1828). Courtesy of The New-York Historical Society, New York City

Joseph Brant, by George Catlin from the original by E. Ames

Henry Abeel (Cornplanter's son),
by Charles B. King (circa 1828).
Courtesy of the National Museum,
Copenhagen

"The Chief Read Jaret" (probably
Red Jacket), by Baroness Hyde de
Neuville (1807). Courtesy of The
New-York Historical Society, New
York City

Charles and William Abeel (sons of Cornplanter), from a photograph taken prior to 1868. Courtesy of Warren County Historical Society, Pennsylvania

Peter, a Seneca from Tonawanda, by Baroness Hyde de Neuville (1807). Courtesy of The New-York Historical Society, New York City

The fair indian
of the buffalo tribe
drawn to canisteo ? ...
1808

"The Fair Indian" of Canisteo (perhaps one of Mary Jamison's sons),
by Baroness Hyde de Neuville
(1808). Courtesy of The New-York
Historical Society, New York City

Seneca Woman and Child, by
Baroness Hyde de Neuville (1808).
Courtesy of The New-York His-
torical Society, New York City

Squah of Seneca tribe with his papus.
aout. 1808.

*An Indian Family (probably Oneida), by Baroness Hyde de Neuville
(1807). Courtesy of The New-York Historical Society, New York City*

*"Mary, Squaw of the Oneida Tribe," by Baroness Hyde de Neuville
(1807). Courtesy of The New-York Historical Society, New York City*

"An Indian and His Squaw" (probably Oneida), *by Baroness Hyde de Neuville (1807). Courtesy of The New-York Historical Society, New York City*

First White Settler's Cottage at Angelica (near Allegany Seneca Reservation), by Baroness Hyde de Neuville (1808). Courtesy of The New-York Historical Society, New York City

Butlers and the Johnsons, without artillery, fighting from foxholes and behind thin breastworks screened with shrubbery, were badly beaten by Sullivan's army at the Indian village of Newtown on the Chemung River. Sullivan had artillery and sprayed the enemy with shrapnel; his men outnumbered their opponents three to one and turned their flank. The Indians and Tories, although they contested the field in hand-to-hand fighting, were forced into flight, and they did not re-form until they had passed the Genesee, where they prepared to resist Sullivan again. But the second battle never took place; Sullivan, traveling with only a few cannon and with his men on half-rations, stopped at the Genesee and then prudently retraced his steps to Tioga.

Although Sullivan's army did not inflict many military casualties, it succeeded in laying waste all of the surviving Indian towns on the Susquehanna River and its tributaries, all the main Cayuga settlements, and most of the Seneca towns. Sullivan proceeded about his work on precisely the same principles as did the Iroquois raiders, burning all houses and outbuildings, chopping down orchards, firing fields of ripe corn and other vegetables, and driving away the inhabitants. He captured few Indians, for the villagers fled before the army. The roster of destruction is a long one (and it earned Washington the name of Town Destroyer): three towns on the Chemung River; three towns on the Tioga River; all of the dozen or so Cayuga and Seneca towns on Cayuga and Seneca lakes; the half-dozen Seneca towns on the route westward to the Genesee River; and the complex of settlements at Geneseo itself. The army missed the towns on the upper and lower Genesee and several small settlements west of the Genesee Valley. Meanwhile Colonel Brodhead, with his force of four hundred men, was marching from Pittsburgh toward the Seneca settlements on the upper Allegheny. He burned the town at Jenuchshadago and the smaller settlements (already deserted) below it, but did not reach the large villages on the oxbow. The process was much the same again: one or two light skirmishes with Seneca warriors, much burning of houses and cornfields, no natives captured.

As a final fillip to the work of annihilation Sullivan even had a small detachment descend upon a small settlement of Mohawk who had remained at the lower "castle" in the Mohawk Valley. Surrounded by white neighbors, they had been at peace; but now they were taken prisoner, and their houses and farms turned over to white refugees. Although they were later released with apologies, it is not known that their farms were restored.

Thus, with the conclusion of the summer of 1779, the four pro-British Iroquois tribes were in as difficult a situation as were the white frontiers like the Mohawk Valley and the Susquehanna. The Mohawk, Onondaga, and Cayuga towns had all been destroyed or abandoned; the towns of their dependents on the upper Susquehanna and its tributaries had been obliterated; all but two of the larger Seneca towns had been razed. The Oneida towns, being regarded by the Americans as the homes of allies, had as yet not been touched; but because of the Oneida and Tuscarora service to the Americans both during Burgoyne's Campaign and later, the British and vengeful pro-British Iroquois now destroyed them in turn. Some time in the winter of 1779–80 a mixed force of Tories and Mohawks under Brant swept down on the Oneida settlement, burned the fort, the houses, and Kirkland's mission church, and drove the Oneida themselves to seek protection among the whites. They were, in fact, forced to take refuge at Schenectady until the close of the war.

Before the Revolution, the Six Nations and their dependents had lived largely in some thirty thriving villages scattered from the Mohawk River to Lake Erie and the Ohio country. Of all these towns, by the spring of 1780 only two survived undamaged. The others were in ashes or empty, moldering in rain and wind. A few people struggled to survive on the ruins of their old homes, but most were dispersed, some crowded into the undamaged settlements, many more camped in flimsy cabins on the banks of the Niagara River, where they had access to rations from the British garrison. Cold, hungry, racked by scurvy and dysentery, many dying, they waited for spring to replant, rebuild and gain revenge.[18]

· *The Final Campaigns* ·

ALTHOUGH THE AMERICAN RAIDS of 1779 were to have a secondary impact whose effects would be felt by the Iroquois for generations, their immediate consequence was not a taming but a stimulation of the warriors. The winter of 1779–80 was a quiet one: the unusually deep snows and bitter cold of that season, and the necessity of caring for the hundreds of displaced Indian families at Niagara, kept most of the warriors at home. But in the spring they were out again, in larger numbers than ever before. By July Guy Johnson at Niagara was able to write, "The Number of Men of the Six Nation Confederacy [exclusive of their people to the Southward] is about sixteen hundred, about twelve hundred of whom are Warriors, and of the latter, eight hundred and thirty are now on service agst the frontiers, and more in readiness to follow them, which far exceeds what has ever been out at one time without the army, few, or none remaining, but those necessary to assist in planting, and providing for their families. . . ."[19] The war parties, moreover, were on the move unusually early in the spring, some 390 having marched from Niagara in March. Others came down from Lake Champlain and Crown Point, and some (allies of the Iroquois) from Detroit and Sandusky.

The 1780 raids devastated settlements in a great arc from the Mohawk Valley south to the Catskills and the Delaware and Susquehanna rivers and west to the Ohio. Handsome Lake was one of three or four hundred Seneca warriors who took part in the raid in Canajoharie (where Cornplanter's father, John O'Bail, had his farm). They laid waste the south bank of the Mohawk for miles, burning fifty-three houses, fifty-three barns, a gristmill, two small forts, and a church. Some fifty or sixty prisoners were taken, including Cornplanter's aged father, the onetime Genesee peddler. The capture of Cornplanter's father was something of an embarrassment to his Seneca relatives. Cornplanter apologized for burning his house in ignorance of its owner's identity and offered as amends to take him to the Indian country, there to support him as long as he lived. When the old man demurred, a council was held, at which, according to Blacksnake, "it was agreed to let old O'Bail & most of the other prisoners go free—which was accordingly done, as a compliment to Cornplanter." After the burning of Canajoharie a smaller party of thirty Seneca, including Cornplanter, Blacksnake, Handsome Lake, and others, probably many of them kinsmen, drifted southward toward the Susquehanna, killing and plundering.

But the major campaign of the year 1780 was the notorious Schoharie Valley expedition, led by Sir John Johnson himself. Handsome Lake was a member of this expedition, too, along with Brant, Cornplanter, Red Jacket, Farmer's Brother, Old Smoke, Little Beard, Jack Berry, and the rest of his Seneca friends and kinfolk. This expedition was comparable in size and destructiveness to Sullivan's of

(145)

the year before. Tory Rangers and Indians, converging from north, west, and south, met to make up an army of 1,500 men, well armed and even carrying mortars. This formidable force marched unopposed down the Schoharie Valley to its confluence with the Mohawk and then proceeded up the Mohawk, burning everything in its path. This raid, culminating three years of incendiary incursions, virtually wiped out all white settlement in the Mohawk Valley west of the environs of Schenectady. But Blacksnake's most vivid memory of the campaign was of hunger, and of gorging himself when they finally reached the first Schoharie settlement. "Cornplanter, Blacksnake, Connediyeu [Handsome Lake], & five others, making a party of 8, went into a house—found breakfast all set on the table ready to be eaten—& the people fled; the Indians helped themselves—didn't wait to sit down, says Blacksnake—snatched & devour'd what they wanted to satisfy the cravings of hunger—the first food they had tasted for two days."

The next two battle seasons, of 1781 and 1782, passed in much the same manner: raids into the Mohawk Valley, raids along the Hudson River itself, raids at Frankstown, Hannastown, and other places in New York, Pennsylvania, Virginia, Ohio, and Kentucky, burning and pillaging, generally leaving the garrisons bottled up in their little forts, skirmishing with the occasional parties of militia who blundered into their path or who pursued them too closely.

The effectiveness of the Iroquois frontier campaign cannot easily be exaggerated. Although the individual raids did not in themselves constitute major threats to the military forces of the colonies, in cumulation they produced economic impotence and paralyzed morale in a vast belt of settlements between the Mohawk and the Ohio. A thousand Iroquois warriors and five hundred Tory rangers were able to lay in waste nearly 50,000 square miles of colonial territory. Valley by valley, contemporary observers tell the story.

The valley of the Mohawk and its southern tributaries was the most severely damaged. From Fort Stanwix to the Hudson River, and south almost to the borders of Pennsylvania, that region was a shambles. Of a 2,500-man militia enrolled at the beginning of the war in Tryon County, by 1781 only 800 remained; of the rest, a third had been killed or captured, a third had deserted to the enemy, and a third had fled the country. There were in June 1783 said to be 300 widows and 2,000 orphaned children in Tryon County. The five

New York regiments had been reduced to two; Fort Stanwix was abandoned in 1781, and the other forts in the valley were difficult to supply because of Indian ambuscades on the supply trains; and the militia were insubordinate and deserting. Rebel leaders in the population, fearful lest invasion bring about a wholesale defection to the Crown, were witch-hunting for suspected Tories, removing suspects to concentration camps south of the river, expropriating their property, and burning their houses (spared by the Tory rangers).

The valley of the Susquehanna, in Pennsylvania, was in little better condition. As early as 1779 it was reported that "All the Houses along this River have been burnt and the Gardens & Fields the most fertile I ever beheld grown over with weeds and Bushes." By 1780 militia were refusing to stand to arms when summoned by their officers, rumors of Indians in the neighborhood were bringing all the settlers above Sunbury flooding down the river, and the local militia commander reported that "without some speedy assistance being Ordered here, I am afraid the County will break up intirely."[20]

The western parts of Pennsylvania were equally distraught. In 1780 a series of spring raids "drove the greatest part of the County on the north of Yohgeny River into Garrison." The officers of the Continental garrison at Fort Pitt—"reduced to about 300 Rank & file, many of which are unfit for the Service"—could not even buy food from the local civilians because their paper money was regarded as worthless. For five days in the fall of 1780 both officers and men at Fort Pitt—the entire garrison—were without bread. Efforts to impress cattle merely led the frontiersmen to take up arms against their own army. Rumor had it that half the population were Tory sympathizers.

A further effect of terror on the frontiersmen was to render them incapable of distinguishing between friendly and hostile Indians. Colonel Brodhead, after strenuous diplomacy unsweetened by gifts and unsanctioned by supplies, force, or kept promises, was able in the fall of 1780 to persuade a portion of the Delaware Indians at Coshocton on the Muskingum to take up the hatchet against the Seneca; but when he assembled one hundred of their warriors at Fort Pitt to help protect the neighborhood, he was forced to use soldiers from the garrison of Fort Pitt to protect the Indians. His diplomatic persuasions had been at last successful. "But as upwards of forty men from the neighborhood of Hannah's Town, have attempted to destroy them whilst they considered themselves under our Protection, it may not be an easy matter to call them out again. . . ." It was not easy; in fact, the Delaware now turned to the British. In 1781, in response to information that the Delaware had abandoned him, the enterprising Brodhead took his militiamen on the notorious "squaw campaign" to destroy the hostile Delaware towns on the Muskingum. Brodhead's troops refused to cross the Muskingum to fight the Delaware warriors, but burned the towns, destroyed the cattle, seized eighty thousand pounds' worth of plunder, and murdered almost all of their fifty prisoners—men, women, and children—before the troops reached Fort Pitt. One of them also managed to kill a Delaware chief as he stood talking over peace terms with Brodhead. The western militia next year slaughtered a band of ninety unarmed, pro-American, Christian (Moravian) Delaware at their settlement on the Muskingum, whither they had come from their bleak camps on the Sandusky to obtain food.

The revenge obtained by the Seneca and Delaware was substantial: the defeat of Crawford and Irvine on the Sandusky, and Crawford's celebrated torture; the devastation of Westmoreland County; the assault on Wheeling; and the defeat of the American militia at the Blue Licks in Kentucky.

Indeed, the war was still going well for the Iroquois warriors when the British had had enough. After the summer campaign of 1783 Blacksnake and other Seneca visiting at Fort George were told that Washington had surrendered. The news of the imminent British capitulation finally filtered through the screen of official denials to the few warriors at Fort George and to the three thousand men, women, and children at Niagara; but it was slowly that the Iroquois came to believe that the rebels had actually defeated the Great Father and that a peace was being made between them in which Iroquois interests were not mentioned.[21]

➯ 6 ⬸

THE COLLAPSE
OF THE CONFEDERACY

THE IROQUOIS DID NOT REGARD THEMSELVES AS A CONQUERED PEOPLE
in 1784, and their warriors were prepared to continue fighting.
But since the Americans were not openly threatening an attempt at
territorial conquest and since their own ally and source of supplies,
Great Britain, had made a peace with the Americans, it seemed sensible to end the bloodshed. And so the Iroquois and their allies among
the tribes to the westward entered into the preliminary negotiations
for a treaty at Fort Stanwix in the naive expectation that it would be
an honorable peace, a laying down of hatchets by the warriors of
both sides.

But the realities of politics had placed the Iroquois in an unstable
position. It would be thirteen years before their position was re-
defined; and during those thirteen years they would lose over the
council table the lands and the political sovereignty that white armies
had been unable to seize by force. That they retained anything, even
their reservations, after those thirteen years, was determined solely
by the opinion of the members of the Continental Congress, despite
the belligerent public language of American negotiators, that complete military expropriation would cost more in blood and money
than the new country was willing to pay.[1]

During these years of disastrous negotiation Handsome Lake, as

(149)

one of the chiefs of the confederacy, was in all likelihood present at most of the sequence of councils and helped to preside over the collapse of the confederacy.

· Federal and State Indian Policies and the "Conquest Theory" Treaties ·

ALTHOUGH THE AMERICANS in 1784 had no stomach for an Indian war, they still wanted the Indian lands. Both the states and the Continental Congress had come out of the war with heavy debts and poor credit; the troops had been paid, when funds were available, in a rapidly depreciating currency, and many had not been paid in full or at all; and the new government was faced with further outlays that demanded both public credit and a reasonably stable currency. The solution to these problems lay in the public lands. Public land could be used to stabilize an unstable currency by exchanging it for that currency; public land could be donated to officers and soldiers in lieu of back pay; public land could be sold to meet the debts and expenses of government. Thus from the standpoint of rational legislators and administrators the acquisition of Indian lands appeared to be an absolute necessity in order to finance both the war and the peace. But the pressure to acquire Indian lands was augmented by two other forces: the greed of land speculators, who saw the possibility of vast profits to be made from the sale, to thousands of individual settlers and entrepreneurs, of virgin timber and agricultural land, of waterways, mill sites, trading locations, harbors, town sites, and so on; and the vengeful hatred of the frontiersmen, who had lost so heavily in goods, in kinsmen, and in self-respect from the successful Indian forays.

The conflict of these interests led immediately to a scramble for advantage in Indian land purchase among the states and the Congress (now functioning only under the feeble Articles of Confederation). The Articles provided that the Congress had the sole right to regulate "Indian" affairs—that is, affairs with Indians "not members of any of the States, provided that the legislative right of any State, within its own limits be not infringed or violated."[2] The determination of the boundaries of the several states and the disposition of their overlapping claims, arising from the vague language of the British charters, at once assumed critical importance, because Indian lands within state boundaries would be public lands of the state, not of the nation. Thus Massachusetts and New York fell at once into dispute over the sovereignty and ownership of the lands of the Iroquois; Pennsylvania quarreled with New York over their mutual boundary through Iroquois territory; Virginia and Pennsylvania continued their long argument over the ownership of the Ohio Valley, to parts of which the Iroquois still claimed sovereignty; and so on *ad nauseam*. These various states'-rights assertions conflicted with the similar interests of the Congress itself. The matter, in the areas involving the Iroquois, was eventually settled by reserving to the United States the sovereignty over public lands south of the Great Lakes and west of the present state boundaries of New York and Pennsylvania, and by various specific accommodations, which need not be examined in detail, among Pennsylvania, New York, Massachusetts, and the United States about their respective rights to tracts east of that line.

The method by which the land was to be acquired was diplomacy. And that diplomacy was based on an impromptu legal theory: that the United States had not only won a war with Great Britain but had also conquered Britain's Indian allies and that therefore the Treaty of Paris of 1783 gave the United States and its several member states not only political sovereignty over, but also ownership of the soil of, all Indian territory south of the Great Lakes and the St. Lawrence River and east of the Mississippi River. Treaties of peace, of course, were still to be made with the Indian tribes, who had not been mentioned in the Treaty of Paris, but these treaties were to be considered as unilateral actions by which the United States "gave" peace to already conquered tribes and "gave" them such tracts of land as it, or its member states, might out of humanitarian motives wish to allot from the public lands. If the Indians were unwilling to surrender on these terms, the war would (theoretically) be continued until they were either annihilated or expelled.[3]

The Treaty of Fort Stanwix of 1784 was ostensibly to have been the peace treaty with the whole Iroquoian confederacy, led by the Six Nations and including the Delaware, Shawnee, Wyandot, Chippewa, and other western allies and dependents. But as a settlement of differences it was a failure. The Americans refused to recognize the

Iroquoian confederacy; negotiations were held at gunpoint; hostages were unexpectedly demanded and taken by the United States for the deliberate purpose of coercion of the Indian delegates; the tone of the Continental commissioners was insulting, arbitrary, and demanding; and two Indians given up by the Seneca to be punished according to white law were lynched by a mob shortly after the treaty. Some of the Indian delegates, including Brant, left in disgust before the peace treaty was signed. There was real question as to whether it could be considered legally valid from the Indian standpoint, even as a peace treaty, let alone as a cession of land. As Brant remarked before his departure, "we are sent in order to make peace and . . . we are not authorized to stipulate any particular cession of land." Yet by this treaty the Six Nations, under the threat of continued war, made peace and "yielded" to the United States their lands west of New York and Pennsylvania and received a reservation in New York. And on the same occasion, although in a much more amicable transaction, the Seneca sold to Pennsylvania their lands in Pennsylvania west of the line of 1768.

Two years later the Six Nations publicly repudiated the treaty, asserting that they were sovereigns of their own soil and "equally free as you or any nation under the sun." At a meeting of the League council the actions of the delegates and the language of the treaty were reviewed by the chiefs, and it was decided that the treaty was unacceptable. Rather than give up their right to the soil, they would continue the war. Furthermore, as an Iroquois speaker observed in denying the validity of the sale, "it is not the Six Nations only that reproach those Chiefs that have given up that country. The Chippewas and all these Nations who live on those Lands Westward, call to us and ask us, Brothers of our Fathers, where is the Place you have reserved for us to lie down upon?" But despite their protests the Iroquois were unwilling to renew hostilities, and the Fort Stanwix treaty was tacitly allowed to stand by default.[4]

The United States now proceeded to coerce "representatives" of the occupants of the Ohio lands into making peace under the conquest theory. In 1785 a similar treaty was held at Fort McIntosh by the U.S. commissioners and a group of the Wyandot, Delaware, Ottawa, and Chippewa of Ohio, who in return for peace received a reservation between the Maumee and the Cuyahoga, south of Lake

Erie to a line between the site of Pickawillany and the Tuscarawas-Cuyahoga portage. This treaty also was repudiated by the tribes concerned, on the grounds that the Indian signers were unauthorized and drunk. But on the strength of it the Northwest Territory was organized. In 1786 a third treaty was held, with the Shawnee, at Fort Finney at the mouth of the Great Miami. This "allotted" to the Shawnee a tract adjoining the Wyandot-Delaware reservation. It too was soon repudiated. By these treaties, all held under the conquest theory, the United States asserted that it had completed the title to the lands in Ohio and western Pennsylvania that had been acquired in 1783 from Great Britain. The Indian residents, on reservations, were to remain on sufferance.[5]

Soon the citizens of New York and Massachusetts, hungry for soil, were gnawing at the Iroquois homelands. The few Mohawk remaining in the valley of the Mohawk River had been driven off during the war; but west of the Old Line of Property of 1768 lay the lands of the five other tribes—the Oneida and Tuscarora, and the Onondaga, Cayuga, and Seneca. The Oneida and Tuscarora in 1785 sold the first parcel of land; by 1789 New York State had purchased all of the Oneida, Onondaga, and Cayuga lands, except for small reservations.[6] Almost all of the Seneca lands, however, lay west of longitude 77° W. —the so-called "preemption line." West of this line Massachusetts had the right to assert or acquire title to the land although New York retained political sovereignty. Fear of Iroquois military resistance meant that the land could not be settled without at least the forms of a real-estate transaction. A scheme was conceived by various New York politicians and financiers to subvert the constitutions of both New York and Massachusetts by acquiring in 1787 a private 999-year "lease" of *all* remaining lands of the Six Nations west of the 1768 Line of Property, including the Seneca lands. The Iroquois repudiated the fraudulent agreement[7] and the conspiracy of "Livingston's Lease" was quashed by the New York State legislature, which threatened to use force to keep out Livingston's settlers. The grand scheme died in a last feeble, failing effort by Livingston to establish a secessionist state west of the Genesee River.[8] Thereafter, in 1788, a land company acting under the Massachusetts right and advised in Indian affairs by the missionary Samuel Kirkland (who had also acted for Livingston) bought a third of the Seneca territory for $5,000 and an annuity to the tribe of $500 per annum.[9] This "Phelps and Gorham" purchase, as it was called, brought white settlements up to, and in places beyond, the ancient Seneca citadels on the Genesee River.

· The Rise of the Western Confederacy ·

To ADD TO THE DISCOMFITURE of the Iroquois, their allies and tributaries in the Ohio country were deciding that the Six Nations could no longer be depended upon to protect them in war or even be trusted to represent them in peaceful negotiations. The old Iroquois confederacy had already begun to crumble; by the close of 1784 it was no longer an effective organization. As we have seen, the western Indians had had some experience with independent action in organizing their parts of the conspiracy of Pontiac in 1763, although the initial stimulus had been provided by the Iroquois. After the failure of this effort to drive out the British, the Iroquois had left the western Indians to their fate, selling their lands out from under them at Fort Stanwix in 1768 and refusing to support them officially in Lord Dunmore's War. From about 1770 on, therefore, the Shawnee, Delaware, Wyandot, Ottawa, Potawatomie, Chippewa, Miami, Cherokee, and other western Indians had been organizing their own confederacy overlapping the Iroquois-centered confederacy. The disappointing performance of their Iroquois representatives at Fort Stanwix in 1784 spurred these western Indians to complete the separation of their confederacy from that of the Six Nations.

The Northwest Territory of the United States was still in 1784 inhabited by dozens of Indian tribes, some of them ancient dependents of the Six Nations and others ancient enemies, and all of them contemptuous of American pretensions to empire. Within the Ohio country, where Iroquois influence had been most weighty, were the Delaware, the Miami, the Wyandot, the Shawnee, and a few Ottawa. These tribes had observed from afar the humiliation visited upon their "uncles" the Six Nations in 1784 and had experienced at first hand the arrogance of the American commissioners at Fort McIntosh and Fort Finney, where paper cessions of land had been extorted from incompetent negotiators under the guise of the "conquest" theory. Their reaction, unlike that of the more vulnerable New York Iroquois, was not dismay but resolute determination to fight for their property.

The first general meeting of the new western confederacy was held at Detroit in the fall of 1785. It was intended to forestall a piecemeal buying-off of individual tribes whose lands had been weakly deeded away by the Iroquois in 1784. The confederacy promptly issued a demand that the United States recognize its existence and treat with it rather than with the individual tribes.[10] By next fall, however, the Americans had concluded the two treaties with the Ohio tribes and claimed to own the whole country, apart from the reservations. The confederacy now, in the fall of 1786, formulated a four-point policy, denying the validity of the conquest theory and declaring that the three treaties of Fort Stanwix, Fort McIntosh, and Fort Finney were invalid, that the Ohio River was the boundary between the Indians and the United States, and that a new treaty between the western confederacy and the United States was required.[11]

But the United States, hoping to exploit the tenuous political advantage it believed itself to have secured at the three treaties of 1784, 1785, and 1786, ignored the new confederacy. A series of laws was being enacted, culminating in the Northwest Ordinance of 1787, by which most of Ohio was opened to settlement. Extensive tracts of land were granted to military personnel in lieu of pay or in gratitude for extraordinary services during the Revolution. Companies like the Ohio Land Company, the John Cleves Symmes Associates, and the Scioto Land Company bought up land on speculation, hoping to sell it to waiting settlers. It was as much to protect the interests of the land companies as to safeguard the rights of the still-resident Indians that stringent regulations prohibited entry into the territory without license. Some squatters crossing the river had since as early as 1781 been following the frontier tradition of making deals with local Indian families and preempting land to be purchased officially only years later. Others did not even bother to purchase privately, but simply occupied desirable tracts and defended them with guns.

The western confederates responded with violence to these incursions. An ugly border warfare, ever renewed by outrages and atrocities committed both by whites and Indians, contained the initial beachheads of settlement within narrow limits north of the Ohio River. The United States was unable to wage either war or peace to expand these beachheads. Federal control of frontier territories was, at the time, largely nominal: the Articles of Confederation made concerted action difficult in the face of the pressures from an unpaid soldiery, from the land companies, from squatters, from secessionist adventurers, from states' righters in the Congress. The Indians, on the other hand, presented a tolerably united front. The western confederacy had high morale and had the moral encouragement of some of the Iroquois and of the British, still ensconced in their old lakeside forts, who reassured them that the conquest theory, so pompously announced at the earlier treaties, was an empty bluff and that the Indians had only to hold their ground in order to secure their rights. The British agents do not seem to have promised the Indians outright military support, but undoubtedly many Indians, including Joseph Brant, hoped and half believed that such help would be forthcoming in the event of crisis. It was obviously in the British interest to see the western confederates maintain a buffer zone between the aggressive United States to the south and the Canadian provinces to the north, a buffer state, indeed, that could continue to supply British traders with peltries. The Indians were also encouraged by past military successes, for they had defeated George Rogers Clark and his band of land-hungry Virginians in their efforts to seize the Ohio country and had virtually paralyzed American arms north of the Ohio River during the Revolution.[12]

· *The Treaty of Fort Harmar* ·

BY 1787 THE UNITED STATES was becoming aware that it could not depend on the treaties of Fort Stanwix, Fort McIntosh, and Fort Finney to ensure the peaceful occupation of the Ohio country. Further and more liberal negotiation would be required, perhaps based not on the conquest theory at all, but on an admission of Indian ownership of the soil. Plans were accordingly laid to convene a general council with the Indians. At this council an acceptable, but even larger, cession of the lands required would be obtained by a new combination of over-the-table concession and under-the-table subversion.

But communication was slow and chronically distorted by "evil birds" who scrambled messages; and to make the task of organization still more difficult, the United States presented many faces to the Indians. American policy was uncoordinated: while official minds moved toward conciliation, land companies sent in surveyors, settlers built cabins, and mounted frontier militia ravaged Indian settlements. As a confederate spokesman observed sadly, the white governments had their problems, too, and yet these problems of civil order among the whites only made war the more likely:

> If the great men of the United States have the like principal or desposition as the Big knifes [i.e., frontiersmen, not merely Virginians] had, My nation and other Indians in the East would been long ago anihilated. But they are not so, Especially since they have their liberty—they begin with new things, and now they endeavour to lift us up the Indians from the ground, that we may stand and walk ourselves. . . . [But] the United States, could not govern the hostile Big knifes, and . . . the Big knifes, will always have war with the Indians. The Big knifes are independent, and if we have peace with them, they would make slaves of us.
>
> . . . The reason the Big knives are so bad, is this because they have run away from their own country of different States, because they were very mischivous, such as theives and robbers, and murderers and their laws are so strict these people could not live there without being often punished; therefore they run off in this contry and become lawless. They have lived such a distance from the United States, that in these several years the Law could not reached them because they would run into the woods. . . . But at length the people of the United States settle among them.[13]

The confederacy even modified its policy to allow minor relinquishments of land west of the Ohio River to accommodate some existing settlements and to encourage, by making a few concessions, a more reasonable attitude on the part of the United States. [14]

There is no doubt that the western confederacy was an effective political entity; and eventually, both in council and in the field, the United States recognized its authority. But American policy in preparing for the treaty of Fort Harmar was weak because it was motivated by fear: fear of conceding too much and fear of conceding too little. If too much were conceded, the United States would lose what little color of right it still had to the Ohio lands. If too little were conceded, a cruel and costly Indian war was inevitable. A compromise solution was embodied in the instructions to General St. Clair, the governor of the Northwest Territory, the principal American negotiator. He was to go only so far in concession as to recognize, by making some payment for the lands, the unsatisfactory nature of the three treaties about which the Indians were now complaining, and to answer the confederacy's request for a peace treaty by proposing a general council. But he was to seek a compensating advantage by confirming, and even if possible enlarging, the previous cessions, by sowing seeds of discord within the confederacy and by avoiding any formal question of the earlier treaties' validity. Meanwhile, in January, 1788, the western confederacy was summoning its members, including the Six Nations, to a final meeting. The confederacy was also tiring of half measures. Since no reply had been received from the United States, the decisions made in 1786 would have to be implemented by the members. "Decisive measures" would be the subject of this council. There was still some disposition to compromise. When the American invitation to a treaty was received, the confederates were not informed of its land cession aspects. But they were suspicious nonetheless. At a summer's council in 1788 there was disagreement over whether the confederacy should go to the treaty at all. The Wabash and Miami Indians at last unceremoniously refused to attend. Shawnee attacks on surveyors and supply trains in the neighborhood of the falls of the Muskingum forced the Americans to remove the treaty grounds from that site to the mouth of the river, where negotiations might be held under the protective guns of Fort Harmar. In the fall the compromise-minded Joseph Brant and his Mohawks decided at the last moment not to attend, disgusted by the discovery that the Americans were assembling militia and were still sending surveyors across the river.[15]

The council at Fort Harmar, when it was finally held in January 1789, was a fiasco. Of the confederates, only Detroit-area Indians appeared—a few straggling Wyandot, Delaware, Ottawa, Potawatomi, and Chippewa, together with some misplaced Sac refugees (the Sac tribe itself lived far away, on both sides of the Mississippi). According to well-informed observers, of all the Indian signatories only four were chiefs of any sort: two Potawatomi, one Delaware, and one Chippewa; and none of these were "great chiefs" qualified to transact important business.[16] This rump council in effect confirmed the earlier treaties of Fort McIntosh and Fort Finney. Certain "sachems and warriors of the Six Nations," headed by Cornplanter, also transacted two treaties, one with the United States, renewing the cessions of land previously made at Fort Stanwix; and another with

Pennsylvania, ceding to the state the Erie Triangle but reserving to the Six Nations the Seneca-occupied lands east of the Conewango Creek and Chautauqua Lake (which Cornplanter and white officials alike mistakenly believed to be west of the line sold earlier).[17] The quality of the negotiations may be judged from Indian agent George Morgan's remark that "Few of the natives attended and none were fully represented; here the treaty was negotiated and speeches and explanations to the Indians made by our superintendent in the French language through a Canadian interpreter who had to guess at his meaning for he can neither write nor speak the language so as to make himself understood in any matter of that importance . . . he could find no other medium."[18]

· *The War for the Northwest Territory* ·

THE IMMEDIATE AFTERMATH of Fort Harmar was a series of diplomatic and military catastrophes for the United States. The United States at first cherished the rosy delusion that with the Six Nations, Delaware, and Wyandot pacified, it remained only to conclude a peace with the Wabash and Illinois Indians or, if they refused a peace, to chastise them into good behavior.[19] Accordingly Governor St. Clair was ordered to send emissaries to invite them to a treaty. These emissaries brought back disquieting word that not merely the "lawless banditti" who had refused to attend at Fort Harmar, but the "pacified" Delaware and Wyandot also, denied its validity and doubted the sincerity of the American intentions. At another council of the western confederacy to be held in the fall, it was rumored, the treaty of Fort Harmar was to be publicly condemned, and the hostiles were sending out war belts among the tribes, including the Iroquois, proposing a common war with British support to drive out the Americans.[20] Depredations along the frontiers were continuous, the hostiles raiding on both sides of the Ohio (by now, as Brant complained, they were "so much addicted to horse-stealing that . . . that kind of business is their best harvest")[21] and the frontiersmen and militia retaliating with massive mounted forays that indiscriminately burned the hastily emptied villages of both hostile and friendly Indians. These exchanges culminated, however, in a series of pitched battles. In 1790 the Americans lost about 190 and the Indians about 120 casualties in an engagement on the Maumee. And in 1791 a serious defeat was inflicted on an American army. Sickly General St. Clair—an officer of minimal foresight even in health— allowed his combined force of regulars and militiamen to be surrounded and ambushed in Indian country. The surviving militiamen and camp followers fled all the way to Pittsburgh; the regulars, who stood their ground, suffered some 600 fatal casualties, amounting to about two thirds of the entire regular army of the United States.[22]

While human relations deteriorate on frontiers, wisdom accumulates in capitals. In 1789 Henry Knox, as secretary of war, formulated a new and more rational federal policy, which under the newly adopted constitution could be executed with less interference from the states. It was essentially a return to the old British policy that an inexperienced revolutionary bureaucracy had temporarily forgotten. It was recognized that in order to secure possession of the Indian lands for settlement in the future, two means were available: war and negotiation. War would be prohibitively expensive to a nation which could summon for any campaign no more than a few hundred trained men, and might end in the United States actually losing the Northwest Territory. Furthermore, war without prior negotiation would be unjust. Hence a policy of negotiation was, for the time being, the only proper one. Such a policy would have to be based on a reversal of the conquest theory; it must be explicitly recognized that the Indians "possess the right to the soil." Good relations between the Indians and the white citizens of the United States could be expected to develop *pari passu* with the civilization of the Indians, which, in accordance with the currently popular doctrine of progress, was inevitable as a stage in the general "process of society, from the barbarous ages to its present degree of development." Knox suggested the importance of introducing "a love for exclusive property" as the fundament of such a march toward civilization. He also recommended the appointment of missionaries of excellent moral character to live among the Indians, and the establishment of well-stocked and well-equipped model farms.[23] Knox's formulation of federal policy was endorsed by George Washington; and one of its first practical consequences, as we shall see, was the establishment of the Quaker mission to the Allegany Seneca Indians.

But there were difficulties in the "conciliatory" policy recommended by Secretary Knox. One of these was, of course, the intransigence of the western Indians, many of whom refused to abandon their demand that the Ohio River be a permanent boundary between the races. Another was the continued presence of armed British garrisons in several forts in the Indian country. At Niagara and Detroit, in particular, British agents continued to supply Indians with hunting equipment and political advice. This advice, as understood by Joseph Brant, was in fact to make some territorial concessions for the sake of preserving peace and the bulk of their lands. But in American eyes, a British lion lay crouched in the forests of Canada, panting from past exertions but waiting only for an opportune moment to spring forth to recover the Crown's lost colonies. Thus Indian resistance was interpreted as part of a British conspiracy to destroy the new nation in its hour of birth. In such an atmosphere "conciliation" sounded to many ears like "appeasement" of united empire loyalism. And finally, to frontiersmen the platitudes of the enlightenment about the inevitability of progress and the natural equality of all men were meaningless. The frontiersmen were interested in freedom for profitable and safe exploitation of Indian land, and this goal was easier to rationalize by a doctrine of manifest destiny than by "impractical" theories about the perfectability of mankind. A conciliation policy was unenforceable on the frontiers, which instead demanded and eventually got (in 1792) a militia act and which supported the preparations for St. Clair's and Wayne's campaigns even while peace negotiations were underway.[24]

The Indians had their own troubles in developing coherent policy. By 1789 the western confederacy had split into two factions: the hostiles (Shawnee, Miami, Wea, Piankeshaw, Kickapoo of the Wabash, and various renegade Cherokee); and the moderates (Brant's faction of the Six Nations, the Wyandot, the Delaware, and the Ottawa, Chippewa, and Potawatomi in the area). The intransigent Shawnee after 1789 were the acknowledged leaders of the confederacy. The chiefs of the Six Nations in New York at first sympathized with the moderates under Brant; but the apparent profits of the play-off policy enticed them too, in 1792, into the arms of the United States. The gradual defection of the New York Iroquois put Brant into the uncomfortable position of being a moderator between extremists as well as the proponent of his own moderate policy. He played this dual role with dignity, resisting threats and refusing bribes and blandishments. The United States once offered him 1,000 guineas down and double his British military pension and, when he refused that, preemption rights to land worth £20,000 plus an annuity of $1,500 per annum, which he also refused, merely to "use my endeavours to bring about a peace." Steadily he insisted that the rational and honorable solution was a general settlement in which the United States would retain only the lands east of the Muskingum and south of a line from the Muskingum-Cuyahoga portage to Venango. But Brant's policy, although the United States would have eventually agreed to it, did not please the Shawnee, who, rashly confident after the victory over St. Clair, abandoned hope of peace in 1793. The end was inevitable: the Battle of Fallen Timbers in 1794 and the Treaty of Greeneville in 1795, by which the Indians made peace and accepted the political sovereignty of the United States and by which the United States officially recognized the Indian right to the soil. The western confederacy became a cipher (although meetings continued for years at Brownstown), and American garrisons sealed off the New York Iroquois from their western and northern brethren.[25]

· The Splitting of the Iroquois Confederacy ·

THE WAR FOR THE NORTHWEST TERRITORY was the rock on which the Six Nations finally foundered. Brant and his Mohawks since 1784 had been established in Canada, and the British Crown eventually granted them a reservation at Grand River. For a time Brant hoped to draw the remainder of his people from New York into Canada. And as the successive land cessions dispossessed more and more of the Oneida, Tuscarora, Onondaga, Cayuga, and Seneca, many of the refugees did move into Ontario, most of them to Grand River. But others re-settled in New York, especially at Buffalo Creek, and the chiefs there refused to move their council fire again.

Brant's Iroquois, as we have seen, allied themselves with the western confederates, within whose councils Brant took a relatively moderate position, advising the Indians to resist but to offer to concede land already occupied by settlers in return for a recognition by the United States of Indian rights to the soil. The Iroquois in New York, however, did not identify themselves with the British and the moderate wing of the western confederacy, but rather with the United States. They favored much the same way of resolving the conflict that Brant was urging on his allies, to be sure, but their apparent identification with American interests made the rift with Brant's group and with the western Indians a deeply emotional one.

It was not that the New York Iroquois liked the frontier Americans. Among the warriors there was hatred and contempt for white men and strong sympathy for the plight of their red brothers in the west, who were fighting desperately for survival against the invasion of a horde of coldhearted surveyors and settlers. On their own frontiers, too, rowdy white men stole, cheated, and murdered luckless Indians whenever opportunity offered; they knew that for every acre sold, a hundred became uninhabitable. Within Cornplanter's own connection, for instance, a nephew and the husband of his wife's sister were killed by white frontiersmen while out hunting.[26] Surveyors were already marking off the boundary lines of the Phelps and Gorham purchase and of the State of Pennsylvania; another quantity of land would be lost when the Erie Triangle was surveyed. Threats and rumors that the Iroquois, including the Allegheny Seneca, were about to take the warpath, both in New York and Pennsylvania and in Ohio, rumbled continuously through the woods during the period of the western troubles.

The tragedy of the situation for Cornplanter's band was the bitter and open contempt that was visited upon them by the western Indians, who saw them as degenerating from stalwart warriors to conniving cowards. The first snarls of contumely came in 1789, when the embattled Shawnee called upon the Seneca "to go to War to secure them a Bed to lie upon."[27] When the western Indians learned that Cornplanter planned a unilateral conference with Washington in Philadelphia, "the Shawanese brought a Virginia scalp and insisted on our seizing the scalp, or they would treat us the same way as the Big Knife."[28] By 1791 the threats of the western Indians had become so ominous that the Delaware from the Allegany River and the Mississauga from Conneaut, on Lake Erie, both on the borders of the Cornplanter band, were frightened off and had to be assigned new places to live, the Delaware at Cattaraugus and the Mississauga at Buffalo Creek.[29] Both of these bands eventually emigrated to the Grand River.[30] And at the council with the western confederacy at Buffalo Creek that winter, the hostiles declared that they were determined to reduce Fort Franklin and to "shake the Cornplanter by the head & sweep this [Allegheny] River from end to end."[31] Such threats as

these for a time threw Cornplanter's band and the whites in his neighborhood into an alliance of necessity. If Cornplanter's people were
unable to reach Pittsburgh, they would be cut off from supply; therefore in self-defense they had to protect white settlements and garrisons
in French Creek Valley by providing intelligence, scouts, and even
war parties against the hostile Indians.

But in 1791 Cornplanter began to gain some support from the
chiefs at Buffalo Creek. Although the chiefs were still reluctant to
lend themselves to a pro-American policy, Cornplanter achieved a
political triumph by requesting, as chief of the warriors of the confederacy, that the women be consulted in an issue so grave as war.
The matrons favored peace in the west and a "friendly" attitude
toward the Americans. This alliance of warriors and women forced
the chiefs to accept the Cornplanter policy and, perhaps against better
judgment, they agreed to accompany American officers on a peace
mission to the western Indians.[32]

The mission to the west in 1792 was the nadir of Iroquois diplomacy. To begin with, there were two missions, both carrying messages
from the United States, one headed by the Oneida Captain Hendrick,
which reached the Maumee in July, two months before the confederate nations assembled, and another headed by Cornplanter, Red
Jacket, Farmer's Brother, and various other chiefs from Buffalo
Creek. Under the great council elm at the Maumee, Hendrick was
hooted and laughed at as he spoke. Red Jacket, the Six Nations'
speaker, praised the United States as a strong, honest "new father"
and advised the western Indians to accept their new father's proposals:
i.e., to make peace and to accept the lines established at Fort Harmar
in 1789. But the Shawnee, as titular heads of the western confederacy,
threw the document containing the American offer into the fire and
called the Six Nations of New York "very coward Red men." The
conference concluded with the Six Nations of New York being assigned the role of mere intermediaries between the western Indians
and the United States in the arrangement of the never-to-be-consum-
mated council of 1793. Cornplanter's party felt fortunate to get away
without a fight and on the return trip were in such haste to make
their escape that they subsisted on dried venison and stopped only to
sleep.[33]

Next year, in 1793, the year when Wayne began organizing the
slow campaign that would end the Indian resistance, Cornplanter and

a few comrades more brave than wise undertook a final peace mission westward. They set out late in the spring, before the formal correspondence between the commissioners at Niagara and the confederates at Miami had begun, but not before General Wayne began active preparations for the invasion of the Indian country. Cornplanter complained of this duplicity to no avail; plans for the invasion continued; bids were taken in Philadelphia for military rations to be supplied at the Maumee Rapids—the seat of the confederacy! When his party reached the western encampments on the Sandusky River, they were (according to a Seneca legend that was still current a hundred years later on the Cornplanter grant) seized, held prisoner, and threatened with death. The western confederacy refused to meet the American commissioners. Released at last, the Indian emissaries were offered food; Cornplanter and a few others, fearful of being poisoned, refused to eat and fasted all the way home. During this homeward trip a number of men died—poisoned, according to Seneca belief.[34]

This disaster concluded the relations of Cornplanter's band with the western Indians; and with the battles and treaties of the following year the rest of the New York Iroquois in effect resigned from that grandly designed confederacy which their forefathers had built up on the foundation of their own League. An era had ended; and Handsome Lake and his fellow chiefs of the League might well chant in the condolence ceremony the mournful lines:

Hail my grandsires! Now hearken while your grandchildren cry mournfully to you—because the Great League which you established has grown old. . . .

The final repudiation of the Iroquois by most of their erstwhile allies and dependents in 1794 was accompanied by the further growth of dissension among the Iroquois themselves. The war of the Revolution had brought the Oneida to blows with their confederate brethren. Now the war for the Northwest Territory set Seneca against Seneca, and Seneca against Mohawk, in a civil discord whose wounds gaped wider with the years. Despite the peaceful policy of both Cornplanter's faction and the chiefs' faction during the years of warfare in Ohio, many individual Iroquois took up arms and fought against the Americans. Some of Brant's Mohawks, a few of the New York Indians, and probably numerous "Mingo," who before the wars had lived among the Delaware and Miami, fought effectively in the campaigns against Harmar, St. Clair, and Wayne. At the end of the wars many of these people remained in the Ohio country, living on the Sandusky and Miami, later drifting westward to Oklahoma, and in some instances emigrating as far as the Rocky Mountains. Others who did not emigrate retaliated, by threats, killings, and kidnappings, on their white neighbors along the Allegheny and the Genesee. Probably many of these incidents were perpetrated in obligatory revenge by Indians whose kinfolk had been killed by white frontier hoodlums.[35]

These disgruntled Iroquois, unwilling to accept the "official" policy of friendliness toward the United States, were contemptuous of Cornplanter, and as the situation deteriorated, some of them became his declared enemies. It is said that sometime after the Fort Harmar treaty an unsuccessful effort was made by some Seneca to break him of his war chieftaincy; he was defended against his critics by, among others, Big Tree.[36] The Seneca criticism of his policies continued, however, and gradually focused on his cession of the Presqu' Isle (Erie Triangle) area in 1789 and 1791. In point of fact, these "cessions" of Cornplanter's were merely quit-claims in favor of Pennsylvania to part of the lands already ceded at Fort Stanwix; they represented not a new loss of territory, but actually a gain, since the United States simultaneously was dropping *its* claims to Seneca lands along the Lake Erie shore east and north of the Erie Triangle. But these intricacies were not understood by the Seneca, nor at that time were the boundaries of the Triangle clearly known. Thus, between 1792 and 1794 Pennsylvania's efforts to survey and settle the Triangle were met with violent Seneca opposition.

After Pennsylvania began to occupy the area with surveyors, troops and settlers in the spring of 1794, attacks were planned on the forts at Venango, Presqu' Isle, and Le Boeuf, and finally a small settlement on French Creek was assaulted and the settlers forced to flee to Fort Le Boeuf.[37] Cornplanter was probably forced by political necessity to assume an antiwhite posture. He proclaimed that his "sale" of Presqu' Isle had been only a conditional cession anyway, not binding on other Seneca without their consent, and since that consent had not been given, the intruders must be removed. If they were not removed, he announced, there would be war. At a council on the Allegheny he struck the war post, bragged about his past exploits in combat, and offered Adlum, the surveyor, a pair of moccasins to wear in the field against the Indians when war came. In all this the bare bones of the play-off policy showed through: this last gesture so encouraged the British at Niagara that when he returned thence to the Allegheny in June, 1794, he came loaded down with presents; and in the fall, at Canandaigua, in order to settle the Presqu' Isle and other matters, the Americans loaded him and the rest of the Six Nations with still more presents and increased annuities, earmarked for the "civilization" of the Six Nations.[38]

The pulling and hauling of the New York Iroquois, their frantic maneuvers to please the Americans without losing their allies in the west, their internal disputes over cessions and presents, was complicated by another issue. This was the subject of the adoption of white customs. As yet it was not a prominent issue, but the division of opinion was already evident. It came to the surface in 1791, when Brant was in Philadelphia and Red Jacket at Newtown Point were almost simultaneously announcing diametrically opposite accultura-tion policies. Brant and Cornplanter wanted the Indians to give up liquor and to plow, to erect flour- and sawmills, to build frame houses, to spin and weave, to read and write.[39] Red Jacket declared that it would be a matter of "great time" before the Indians gave up their beloved ancient customs and became educated and civilized.[40] This division of opinion was destined to recur in the following years.

Brant and his Canadian settlers on the Grand River were sorely disillusioned by all of these examples of what they chose to regard as Seneca avarice and deceit. As early as 1788 Brant observed in disgust, "As for the Five Nations, most of them have sold themselves to the Devil—I mean to the Yankeys. Whatever they do after this is must be for the Yankeys—not for the Indians or the English. We mean to speak to them once more . . . and will show our example of getting together ourselves; also, we shall know who is for the Yankeys and who is not."[41] Although Brant and his people never ceased to speak to the New York Iroquois, the division between the two groups be-came sharper with the years, and by the end of the wars in 1794 relations were strained. Brant refused to attend the treaty at Canan-daigua in 1794, where the New York Iroquois settled their differences with the United States, and instead made a separate settlement of Mohawk land claims in New York in 1797.[42] The past defection of the New York Iroquois and the intermediate role that Brant had been forced to play alienated the western Indians even from him and virtually ended his influenec with the dissolving remnants of the western confederacy. His further efforts to bring the New York Indians into Canada failed. And within a few years, in 1803, the New York chiefs deposed Brant and the few members of the League council who resided in Canada, and replaced them by New York residents. Although the Grand River Indians refused to abide by this action, its consequence was a separation of the two groups into politically autonomous entities whose relations were inter- rather than intratribal. There were henceforth to be two council fires, one at Onondaga in central New York (after its removal from Buffalo Creek) and one at Ohsweken, on the Grand River in Canada.[43]

· *The Establishment of the Cornplanter Seneca* ·

WHILE BRANT'S PEOPLE were moving northward from Buffalo Creek into Canada and the refugees from the ceded lands were settling at Buffalo Creek, Cornplanter and his band of Seneca were establishing themselves in a cluster of little towns along the Allegheny River above and below the Pennsylvania boundary.

Cornplanter's band was composed of families displaced by Brodhead's sacking of the Allegheny River towns and by Sullivan's burning of the Genesee towns in 1779. Thus some of them had been Allegheny residents before the war and were now coming home. Among these old settlers the most prominent was Cornplanter himself. Some of the newcomers were relatives of his: Guyasuta, the old viceroy, whose sister was Cornplanter's mother, had lived in many places, but most recently on Cattaraugus Creek,[44] and Handsome Lake, his half brother, who had lived at Canawaugus on the Genesee. This repopulation of the upper Allegheny probably commenced shortly after the invasion of 1779 but took many years to complete; the new population probably did not become substantial until 1784 or 1785.[45] By 1792 the Seneca in and around Cornplanter's settlement on the Allegheny numbered about 350 souls, which was a sizable proportion of the approximately 1,800 Seneca of that day.[46] By 1792 one of the main villages was "Cornplanter's Town," also known as Jenuchshadago or Burnt House, on the west side of the Allegheny River just below the state line on the site of one of the towns burned by

Brodhead. Until they were moved north to Cattaraugus about 1792, a group of about 150 Delaware dependents of the Seneca lived at Hickory Town, some thirty or forty miles downriver.[47] Upriver from Cornplanter's Town were a substantial settlement at Genesing-huhta and a smaller one at Ichsua. Westward were small groups at Kiantone, on one of the tributaries of the Conewango, at Cussawago, on the upper waters of French Creek, and at Conneaut, on Lake Erie. These and a miscellany of one-or-two-family settlements scattered along the main streams tended to consolidate as time went on, their residents moving to the larger settlements at Cornplanter's Town and Genesinguhta or to other large Seneca villages at Cattaraugus, Tona-wanda, and Buffalo Creek.[48]

But the Allegany Seneca were in a vulnerable location. Their position liberated them from the pressures associated with nearness to Brant's faction at Grand River, the British garrison at Fort Niagara, and the neutralist chiefs at Buffalo Creek. But it also placed them in a location where they were dependent on the American traders at Pittsburgh and under the watchful eye of American soldiers at Fort Franklin. This fort, garrisoned by regular troops, was constructed in 1787 along the Allegheny at the mouth of French Creek, the tradi-tional southern limit of the Seneca tribal territory. Fort Franklin guarded the white settlements springing up in the neighborhood of the Indian towns and stood athwart the hunters' access to the traders in Pittsburgh, upon whom much of the Seneca livelihood depended. Fort Niagara and its British traders and troops, upon whom the Iro-quois at Buffalo Creek could call for supplies and, in case of need, asylum, was a difficult hundred miles to the north. And anyway, of all the Iroquois, the Allegany Seneca—late of Geneseo, perpetrators of the Devil's Hole massacre, holdouts against taking up the British hatchet in 1777, traditionally less devoted to British interests than the eastern band—had least assurance of British support if they were attacked by Americans. Nor could they depend in either negotiation or in armed combat on the united support of the Six Nations, for Brant's followers were now streaming into Canada, and the chiefs of of the confederacy at Buffalo Creek, including the eastern Seneca, were seemingly unable to agree on a common positive program. Thus, both economically and militarily the Allegany Seneca were an or-phaned band, dependent upon their enemies for economic support and bereft of the military backing of their allies and confederates.

This situation, and the growing conviction of Cornplanter that only by a rapprochment with the United States could the Seneca survive, probably led Cornplanter's band into adopting its leading role in the effort to end the war for the Northwest Territory.

Cornplanter, a vigorous war-captain and eloquent council-speaker, was attempting to find the best way out of a difficult situation for himself and his band. He saw no advantage in refusals to compromise and was not given to rigid adherence to the language of past rhetoric. As one of the leading war-captains of the Iroquois in the late war he had been a principal speaker at the treaty at Fort Stanwix because war captains were responsible for the public ceremony of laying down the hatchet. Although he had initially demanded that the Americans respect the existing boundaries of the Six Nations, he had not made the speech accepting the American ultimatum (this dubious honor fell to the Oneida Good Peter) and had only promised to lay the dictated treaty, in which lands were ceded, before the confederate chiefs' council for approval or disapproval, his name stood on the document. Thus Cornplanter personally received much of the blame when the chiefs' refusal to ratify the treaty was blandly ignored by the United States and when Cornplanter's protestations in 1786 resulted only in promises to make minor boundary adjustments. Feeling against the speakers at Fort Stanwix rose high. The fact that the terms had never been proposed by him, were not personally agreeable to him, and could not be accepted or rejected by him alone did not cancel the fact that he was there at the time of the catastrophe.

It is impossible to know in detail how Cornplanter analyzed the situation in which he and his band found themselves; but some inferences are possible from his behavior. During the next several years, from the time of his return from New York until the treaty at Fort Harmar in 1789, he played a passive and unobtrusive role, avoiding any challenge to the Americans. When surveyors came up to Fort Franklin to lay out the donation lands, it was not Cornplanter, among the Indians who were hunting in the vicinity, but two other "chiefs" who halted the surveyors and politely warned them to proceed no farther. In 1787 Cornplanter failed to accompany a delegation of Seneca, including his nephew Blacksnake, who visited Albany to protest the extension of New York's sovereignty at the Niagara strip and on the borders of Pennsylvania. In 1787 he signed Livingston's infamous lease and, according to report, used his influence, in return for a substantial bribe, to persuade other "chiefs" to sign it. In 1788 he signed the deed of Phelps and Gorham's purchase, by which the eastern half of the Seneca lands was alienated. Seneca hearts despaired after the Phelps and Gorham purchase; one chief is said to have declared that he would fight rather than give up his homeland, another to have asked to be "put out of his pain," and a third to have prepared to eat the "fatal root." Cornplanter's life was threatened for this betrayal.[49] And all the while, despite the glowering of the warriors, surveyors from Pennsylvania and New York quietly proceeded to mark out the state boundaries and to lay out towns and farms in the midst of the Allegany Seneca hunting grounds. It would seem that Cornplanter had decided that the New York Iroquois would have to get along with the Americans and make the best of a bad bargain.

Of all the participants in the ill-fated treaty at Fort Harmar, only Cornplanter and his delegation of Allegany Seneca (who constituted virtually the bulk of the "Six Nations" present) derived any advantage. He and his associates confirmed the language of the Fort Stanwix land agreement (it was the Senate of the United States that refused to confirm the proceedings) and concluded the sale of the Erie Triangle to Pennsylvania (recovering in the process part of the lands lost at Fort Stanwix).[50] For all this his people received a bundle of moth-eaten blankets, the concession of lands on the Conewango, and in all likelihood various goods and monies at the treaty ground (which may have been a substantial trove, for nearly two hundred Allegany Seneca were present). Cornplanter himself achieved more personal rewards. At the treaty ground he was promised by a land company a tract of 640 acres in Marietta itself; the deed to this tract was, however, according to Indian tradition, stolen from him in some frontier town on the way home when the Indians were drunk. And the grateful Commonwealth of Pennsylvania assembly, in order to reward him for his services and "to fix his attachment to the state," gave to Cornplanter in fee simple 1,500 acres of land "in this tract or country on Lake Erie." This land was surveyed under Cornplanter's direction in three tracts along the Allegheny River in 1795, and a patent was issued in 1796. Two of the tracts, "The Gift" at Oil City and "Richland" at West Hickory (the latter including the site of the Delaware town abandoned about 1792), he sold: Richland in 1795 to General John Wilkins, who established a farm there; and "The Gift" in 1818 to two partners whose failure to complete the title has left the ownership of

"The Gift" unclear to this day. The third tract, encompassing about 750 acres, included the site of the old Seneca town of Jenuchshadago and two nearby islands in the river.[51]

· *American Concessions to the New York Iroquois* ·

THE NEW YORK INDIANS, however, under the leadership of Corn-planter, Red Jacket, and Farmer's Brother, were also able to salvage something more general than presents and private land-grants from the debacle. During a series of at least seven major conferences with American officials between 1790 and 1794, the Iroquois spokesmen demanded—and received—promises of correction of abuses in the context of not too subtle, but also not too sincere, warnings of defection to the enemy. Thus Cornplanter in 1790 on the occasion of an address to the Congress of the United States observed quietly that: "When last Spring they [the western Indians] called upon us to go to War to secure them a Bed to lie upon, the Senecas entreated them to be Quiet until we had spoken to you. . . ."[52] And the chiefs on the Genesee in the same year took occasion to remind Pennsylvania, apropos of the murder of two Seneca hunters on Pine Creek, that this was the latest outrage in a series of eleven killings of Seneca by Pennsylvanians. The bereaved families wanted vengeance or reparations:

> Brothers, you must not think hard if we speak rash, as it comes from a wounded heart, as you have struck the hatchet in our head and we can't be reconciled until you come & pull it out; We are sorry to tell you, you have killed Eleven of us since peace. . . .
>
> Brothers, it is our great brother, your Governor, who must come to see us, as we will never bury the hatchet until our great brother himself comes & brightens the chain of friendship, as it is very rusty—Brothers, you must bring the property of your brothers you have murdered, and all the property of the murderers, as it will be great satisfaction to the families of the deceased. Brothers, the Sooner you meet us the better, for our young Warriors are very uneasy, and it may prevent great trouble. . . .[53]

These muted threats, coupled with offers to polish the chain of friendship, had great effect in thrusting together in amicable conference the leading dignitaries of both societies. George Washington, Henry

Knox, Timothy Pickering, and dozens of other American officials met Cornplanter, Red Jacket, Blacksnake, Joseph Brant, Farmer's Brother, Handsome Lake, and hundreds of Iroquois warriors and matrons in a series of negotiations. The history of these negotiations —the climax of a political generation during which "Indian Affairs" was the major public business of an entire nation—would make a fascinating volume; and some day a student of the period will tell the story in all the dramatic detail that it deserves. Here, however, we can only outline and summarize the course and significance of these events. Each of these conferences was preceded and followed by the long journeys, private councils, secret visits, exchange of letters, and so forth that made diplomacy an almost continuous theme in the daily lives of the Indian participants. Handsome Lake's half brother and his nephew, Blacksnake, were principal actors in the matter, and Handsome Lake himself probably attended the last and most impressive council of the series: the Treaty of Canandaigua in 1794.[54] Although his name was not recorded at other conferences, it is likely that he was intimately acquainted with the course of events.

At one time or another during these meetings thirteen demands were made upon the United States by the Indian speakers, who were usually Cornplanter and Red Jacket (for Joseph Brant, having retired to Canadian soil, could act only occasionally, and then chiefly as an intermediary). These demands concerned:

1. *The Treaty of Fort Stanwix.* The Six Nations denied the validity of the cessions of land extorted at Fort Stanwix in 1784. Their speakers claimed that the cessions had been made under duress by unauthorized representatives who had given up more land than the Six Nations would have willingly relinquished under any circumstances. The United States was requested to annul this treaty and to negotiate a new cession acceptable to the Six Nations, and particularly to the Seneca, who had been most directly injured.[55]

2. *The Phelps and Gorham Purchase.* The Six Nations claimed they had been cheated by Phelps and Gorham. These "land-jobbers" had initially revealed their bad intentions by trying to move the treaty site from the proper council-fire at Buffalo Creek to Canandaigua, had insisted on a larger tract of land than the Indians had intended to sell, had held the talks late at night, and had misled the Indians into thinking the conveyance was a lease, not a purchase. The final blow was altering the text of the papers of

cession so as to reduce the cash payment from $10,000, as promised, to $5,250. The annuity of only $500 per year amounted to about a shilling apiece when it was paid; and in order to collect the annuity, the Seneca each year had to spend the annuity itself, and all their silver ornaments besides, to buy bread in Canandaigua.[56]

3. *The Erie Triangle.* The Erie Triangle, including the lake port of Presqu' Isle, had technically been a part of the lands ceded at Fort Stanwix. Before the United States sold the land to Pennsylvania in 1792 in order to provide the commonweath with a port on Lake Erie, the commonwealth "quieted the claims" of the Seneca at Fort Harmar in 1789. Since the Triangle had not been surveyed, the Seneca believed that it would engross lands on which some of their people had villages, and they resisted surveying and settlement in the area until 1794, despite a second quit-claim Cornplanter made in 1790 upon receiving assurances that Half Town, Big Tree, and his own people would not be disturbed.[57]

4. *Other Land Grievances.* Miscellaneous other grievances over lands still rankled: e.g., fears that Livingston's lease might be upheld by legislature and courts; complaints that lands in Virginia and Pennsylvania still had not been paid for by white occupants.[58]

5. *The Conquest Theory.* Fortified by advice from British agents, the Six Nations denied the correctness in international law of the American assertion that Britain had ceded to the United States the right of soil in Indian lands. Britain, the Six Nations argued, had acquired only political sovereignty and consequently could relinquish only that.[59]

6. *Frontier Outrages.* After the peace of 1784 (which was the feature of the Fort Stanwix treaty to which the Iroquois did not object) Indian and white were, theoretically, to live amicably side by side. But the Indians were subjected to continuous outrages by frontiersmen and town dwellers alike whenever they met whites. By 1790, when the notorious Pine Creek murders were committed, at least eleven Seneca and an unknown number of others from different tribes had been killed, including two kinsmen of Cornplanter's. There were also thefts of horses, hunting gear, and personal effects, frequently from murder victims, and even more commonly attacks that did not end in fatalities: e.g., Cornplanter's party was fired on on its return from Fort Harmar, the chief Big Tree was shot in the leg in Philadelphia in 1790 during the state visit, and an assassin tried to kill Brant in New York in 1792. In 1794 occurred the famous "Brady's Beaver Blockhouse" affair, in

which a hunting party of nine—five men, a woman, and three children—were attacked and robbed by a band of twenty-seven white hunters. Four of the Indians were killed, one was wounded, and the survivors lost their horses and gear.[60]

7. *Unilateral Justice.* When whites suffered outrages at Indian hands, white courts convicted the Indian culprits (if they were found) and punished them; but little or no attention was paid to preventing or punishing informal retaliation by frontiersmen, which was not always discriminating in its object. White men guilty of crimes against Indians were either not apprehended or not tried, or if tried were neither convicted nor punished. Indians were prohibited from seeking personal vengeance, which was defined by whites as "war" or "massacre" (as in the celebrated case of Logan in 1772).[61]

8. *Security of Land Tenure.* The loss of hunting grounds and the general depletion of game in the Northeast had made it plain to the Six Nations that they would have to turn even more heavily to farming (including both crops and livestock) for subsistence. But such an investment of labor, material, and social organization required that the Six Nations receive assurances that further arbitrary seizures of land, like those first extorted at Fort Stanwix and still being imposed on the western Indians, would not be made either by the states or by the federal government.[62]

9. *Private Land Grants.* Land was the currency of Indian bargaining. Thus Indians, like Cornplanter and Big Tree, sought to obtain as "rewards" for their concessions land titles guaranteed by the whites; and they sought also to pay their faithful white friends, like interpreter and trader Joseph Nicholson, in grants by white governments from ceded lands.[63]

10. *Traders, Agents, and Whiskey.* Far from desiring unrestricted trade and occasional official communication, the Six Nations wanted traders to be licensed, in order that unscrupulous whiskey-sellers and other undesirables could be excluded from the Indian country; and they wanted a system of official, recognized Indian agents close to their borders with whom they could conveniently communicate as needed.[64]

11. *Technical Assistance.* The Six Nations generally recognized that the great changes taking place in their relations to the land and to the white society required that they invest heavily in new cultural equipment: the implements of plow agriculture, of animal husbandry, of spinning and weaving, of lumber milling, etc.; and in

the knowledge and skills necessary to use this equipment efficiently and to have confident intercourse with white men. Cornplanter in particular requested capital goods, rather than a dole of food and clothing in hard times, and schoolteachers, resident farmers, and missionaries to teach them.[65]

12. *Illegitimate Half-breeds.* The offspring of temporary unions of white men and Indian women were frequently abandoned by their fathers. They were a burden to an Indian community. Six Nations spokesmen requested that they be adopted by white society or, at least, that the white society contribute to their support and education.[66]

13. *The Western Indians.* No doubt prompted both by sympathy with their ancient dependents, allies, and kinfolk and by the needs of policy, the Six Nations' spokesmen—principally Joseph Brant—urged that the United States be moderate in its demands on the western Indians who were objecting to a set of treaties precisely comparable to the Treaty of Fort Stanwix; to Iroquois eyes, these objections were valid.[67]

The response of the State of New York, the Commonwealth of Pennsylvania, and the United States of America to these requests was, at least officially, friendly and in the main favorable. Why this should be so, despite the bitter, unquenched hatred of Indians by a large proportion of the people of the frontiers, is easily understood. Those elements of the population who hated Indians most were at this time least effectively represented in the seats of government, not only in Indian affairs, but in various economic and political issues as well. This was the period, the reader will recall, of the Articles of Confederation, of the Whiskey Rebellion, and of various secessionist movements inspired or directed by such figures as Aaron Burr, George Morgan, Philip Livingston, and other ambitious and sometimes disaffected men of wealth. The Federalists were, by and large, eighteenth-century intellectuals who sought to direct the interests of natural man into the channels of natural law; they preferred order to anarchy, commerce to virtuous isolation, and negotiation to war; they tried to pursue in all affairs a policy of enlightened self-interest. From the Six Nations they hoped to secure at least neutrality and at best their services as intermediaries. Their major fear was that the Six Nations would go over wholly to the enemy (the British and the western Indians). And the Six Nations, both through their demands in council and by their violence on the frontiers (for Iroquois warriors did their share of murder, kidnapping, mayhem, and theft) conscientiously kept alive this fear. Thus, irrespective of frontier passion, it was self-evidently to the interest of the United States to take such measures as would most effectively secure the neutrality, and eventually the allegiance, of a neighboring Indian people. And therefore a number of significant concessions were made:

1. *The Conquest Theory.* It was Indian insistence, expressed both by the Six Nations and by the western Indians, that caused the United States to reverse its interpretation of the Treaty of Paris and, between 1787 and 1793, publicly to declare that the Indian tribes had the right of soil to the lands that they occupied within the territorial limits of the United States. Although the United States maintained political sovereignty, it recognized the right of an Indian tribe to continue to occupy its lands forever if it so pleased. Specifically, it secured the Six Nations from arbitrary expropriations of lands by individuals, states, or the federal establishment, within the boundaries established at Fort Stanwix in 1784.[68]

2. *Specific Concessions on Land Grievances.* Although the validity of the Fort Stanwix cessions was upheld against Six Nations objection, several actions by various parties—individuals, states, and the federal government—had the effect of minimizing the hardships it imposed. These actions included: a promise of federal protection of Indian land rights (including supervision of any cessions); grants to individual Indians (specifically, to Cornplanter and Big Tree); assurances that Half Town and his people would not be disturbed in their villages (and the line of the Erie Triangle, as eventually run, did indeed leave them undisturbed); nullification of Livingston's lease; and postponement of plans for the settlement of Presqu' Isle and for the purchase of Seneca lands in western New York.[69]

3. *A Technical Assistance Program.* Acting on the principles that Indians were as capable of civilization as white men and that civilized Indians would be friendly neighbors, the federal government and various private agencies responded enthusiastically to Seneca and Oneida requests for technical assistance. Washington in 1790 promised to secure federal funds to support educational and capital investment programs. In 1792 Six Nations annuities were increased (to $1,500) for this purpose. In 1794 at Canandaigua annuities

were raised to $4,500, and benefits worth $10,000 were granted, for civilizing the Six Nations. Later missionary teachers were being sent to the Cornplanter Seneca and to the Oneida, a smith was established on the Genesee to work for Indians only, and Cornplanter's sons were brought to Philadelphia for education. A regular Indian agent for the Iroquois was appointed in 1792; he distributed annuities and managed various other matters.[70]

4. *Equal Justice*. An improvement was made in the handling of civil and criminal complaints by the Six Nations. The murderers of Indians were brought to trial, Indian victims or their families were indemnified for their losses, and access to the courts of white men was promised by Washington himself.[71]

These concessions were far from being mere verbal assurances; they became the basis of a new, if somewhat demoralizing, Indian way of life—the reservation system. From the United States standpoint, they were worth the cost, for the Iroquois never did turn to the aid of the western Indians, even during the anxious summer of 1794. From the Six Nations standpoint, they established Cornplanter and his people firmly on lands that their descendants occupy to this very day and made it possible for the Iroquois generally to remain one of the few Indian peoples east of the Mississippi who still live in territory that was theirs before Columbus. Furthermore, the concessions included the abandonment of the conquest theory—and this change in the Indian policy of the United States affected the future of the continent. And they gave the Six Nations a head start in the process of technical acculturation so that their villages were for a time somewhat more civilized settlements than those of the frontier whites that surrounded them.

But these were advantages slow to mature, and they had been purchased at a fearful price: the collapse of the confederacy. For while these favors were being secured by a temporary coalition of factions pursuing the ancient play-off policy, the choice of the play-off policy rather than of war at the side of the western Indians was making certain the conquest of those western Indians; and on their continued independence the play-off policy itself depended. When the western Indians were defeated in 1794, and Jay's treaty in the same year soothed the mutual fears of Canada and the United States, there were no more bargains to be made. The Six Nations had at last been outflanked. No more respect could be extorted from the United States; the confederacy itself, whose white roots of peace once under-girded half a continent, was like a great pine dying on a flood-torn hillside.

· *The Treaty of Big Tree* ·

THE SLOW PROCESS of political disintegration, which had begun with the failure of the neutrality policy in the 1750's and had culminated in the disastrous treaties of the 1780's and 1790's, left the Iroquois with a shrunken homeland, a reduced standard of living, and a demoralized society. The Seneca alone had preserved a major part of their tribal territory for themselves and other Iroquois refugees; but within a few years this too would be gone, and the reservation system, in squalor exceeded only by the surrounding frontier settlements, would impose a new way of life.

In 1797, at the Treaty of Big Tree, the Seneca administered the *coup de grâce* to themselves: they sold their lands. With the exception of a few reservations, all of the Iroquois territory in New York east of the Genesee River had already been sold. The Mohawks had gone from the valley of their name, and only a few still clung to a marginal settlement along the St. Lawrence River at St. Regis, opposite Caughnawaga; the Oneida, Onondaga, and Cayuga occupied only their tiny reservations (and the Oneida and Cayuga would soon lose these entirely); the Seneca had given up everything east of the Genesee. But west of the Genesee there remained a substantial region in which stood many of the old Seneca towns and hunting grounds and, at Buffalo Creek, whole villages of Seneca, Cayuga, Onondaga, and Tuscarora. This last vestige of ancient glory they now proceeded to sell.

The legal right to purchase these western lands was held by Robert Morris of Philadelphia, a financier of the American Revolution who now hoped to make a fortune out of speculation in frontier real estate. Morris quickly sold his preemption right to the Holland Land Company, a coalition of Dutch bankers who were in a better position than Morris to finance the actual opening of the territory to settlement (an expensive process involving long-term administration, surveys, and even the construction of roads and buildings). A condition of his receiving payment, however, was that he negotiate the purchase of these Seneca lands from their Indian owners. At first this seemed like an easy task. But Morris was delayed in the project by the war in the Northwest Territory. When in 1795 peaceful conditions were restored, he was hampered by the financial depression of that year. His creditors hounded him. He became increasingly desperate to quiet the Seneca title, for only by doing so could he claim credit from the Dutch bankers and thereby stave off bankruptcy and debtor's prison. As he told his son, "I must have it."[72]

Morris had to move fast. Against the advice of his friend Washington (who had in earlier years speculated in the very Ohio lands that had been finally secured only after thirty years of warfare) he applied for the appointment of a federal commissioner, who was now required by law to oversee any purchases of land from Indians. Morris was a gambler: "I can never do things in the small," he declared, "I must be either *a man or a mouse*." With a commissioner appointed, he hastened to seduce the Seneca into selling. The old reliable Cornplanter was brought to Philadelphia, wined and dined, and persuaded to agree that "it will promote the happiness of his Nation to sell at least a part of their lands and place the purchase money in the Public funds so as to derive an annual income therefrom." But by the time appointed for the treaty at Big Tree on the Genesee River in the summer of 1797, Robert Morris was a prisoner in his own mansion, unable even to answer the door lest he be arrested and jailed for debt. His son Thomas therefore conducted the actual preparations for the treaty, laying in stores of food, clothing, hardware, powder, and whiskey—the latter calculated at twenty-five gallons a day for thirty days. The whiskey, however, was not to be provided at once, but paraded before the thirsty Indians with the promise that it would be given them when the sale was made. Special presents of clothing were prepared for the women, and funds for bribery of the men were set aside at the outset. Red Jacket, Farmer's Brother, and Little Billy were offered life annuities of sixty dollars. Little Billy, a widely respected war chief, was a good target for bribery. Almost blind, he lived in poverty with his mother; he had a few years before been very ill, and he and his mother had been "stripped by doctors and conjurers, in order to effect his cure." The canny Red Jacket demanded a bond for the annuity at once, but the equally canny Morris refused.[73]

Seneca anxiety mounted. The year before Red Jacket had requested that the Congress issue no license to Morris to purchase Seneca lands, saying of the corpulent banker, "We are much disturbed in our dreams about the great Eater with a big Belly endeavouring to devour our lands. We are afraid of him, believe him to be a conjurer, and that he will be too cunning and hard for us. . . ." The Seneca sachems—probably including Handsome Lake, who was present— were at the outset of the conference officially and publicly opposed to any cession. Red Jacket, the official speaker for the chiefs, after a drunken spree at the start of the conference declaimed nobly against the proposal that the Seneca sell their sacred homeland: they were respected, he claimed, by the western tribes only because they owned lands on which lesser peoples could take refuge; they had no desire to become ignoble broom- and basket-makers like the Oneida. And when Thomas Morris refused even to consider the Indian offer to sell one township six miles square at a dollar an acre near the Pennsylvania line, Red Jacket leaped to his feet and shouted, "We have now reached the point, to which I wanted to bring you. You told us when we first met, that we were free, either to sell or retain our lands; and that our refusal to sell, would not disturb the friendship that has existed between us. I now tell you that we will not part with them; here is my hand. I now cover up this Council fire!" The Indians whooped and yelled and upbraided Thomas Morris for having tried to cheat them.

But bribery had done its work too well; a deliberate plot to subvert the decision of the chiefs had been in the making for months. In May Cornplanter informed Thomas Morris through one of his sons that he had called "a general Meeting of all the Warriors and Chiefs of Warriors at which no sachem was to be present, that his Intention was to induce the Warriors to insist upon a division of the property and to sell their proportion of it."[74] Red Jacket, who by day as professional orator was rejecting Morris's offers, at night sent messages to Morris saying that his negative speeches were made only to please some of his people and were not his own sentiments, and that if Morris persevered he would gain his purpose. Before Red Jacket covered the fire, Cornplanter asserted publicly that the warriors did not agree with the chiefs. On the day after Red Jacket covered the fire, the commissioners were called to a council of the warriors. There Cornplanter (who had been bribed) announced that this meeting was to smooth over the difficulties of yesterday. Little Billy (also bribed) apologized for Red Jacket's speech. Farmer's Brother (also bribed) declared that since Morris, not Red Jacket, had lit the council fire, only he and not Red Jacket could extinguish it. Furthermore, he said, "It is an ancient custom that when a difference arises among us that it should be referred to the Warriors as being the greatest number. We the sachems have therefore referred this business to the Warriors & head women and hope they will give an answer that will be satisfactory to all parties." The same day, Morris made his offer to the chief women, declaring that the $100,000 he offered for the Seneca territory would particularly alleviate the distresses of the women and children: they would be able to hire white men to plough their fields, and buy good clothes and liquor.[75] He handed out baubles and trinkets. He appealed to the women's resentment of their neglect by men: "I . . . informed them of the offers that had been made to their Sachems; I told them that the money that would proceed from the sale of their lands, would relieve the women from all the hardships that they then endured, that, now they had to till the earth, and provide, by their labour, food for themselves and their children; that, when those children were without clothing, and shivering with cold, they alone, were witness to their sufferings, that their Sachems would always supply their own wants, that they fed on the game they killed, and provided clothing for themselves, by exchanging the skins of the animals they had killed, for such clothing, that therefore the Sachems were indifferent about exchanging for their lands money enough, every year, to lessen the labour of the women, and enable them to procure for themselves and their children, the food and clothing so necessary for their comfort."[76] The Seneca women capitulated to this verbal assault and declared themselves ready to sell. For several days thereafter, little knots of women and warriors might be seen arguing and discussing the matter. The warriors wanted reservations around the villages. Morris agreed. Handsome Lake insisted on adding to the list of reserves a tract at Oil Spring, just north of the Allegany Reservation. This "spring" was a natural flow of petroleum, which the Seneca used to gather and use for a liniment to treat rheumatic pains and old ulcers. Handsome Lake's interest in the place may have arisen from his practice as shaman. In addition to the reservations, private concessions were made to individual signers:

Cash grants

Red Jacket	$600
Cornplanter	300
Hotbread and other sachems	1,000

Annuities

Cornplanter	$250
Red Jacket	100
Farmer's Brother	100
Young King	100
Little Billy	100
Pollard	50
Little Billy's mother	10

The nation as a whole received the sum of $100,000, to be invested in bank stock for the use of the Seneca; the "crop of money" amounted annually, for more than fifteen hundred Seneca residents in New York State, to less than four dollars per person. The deed was signed on the evening of September 16, 1797, by some fifty Seneca, including Cornplanter and Handsome Lake.[77] Handsome Lake's name stood third on the list of signatures.[78]

Thus the embers of the old confederacy guttered out in a welter of liquor, bribery, and high-pressure salesmanship. The name of the Great League still remained; but its people were now separated, one from another, on tiny reservations boxed in by white men and white-men's fences. For the Seneca in New York there remained only their eleven reserves surrounding the main villages, whose total land area amounted to 311 square miles, or about 200,000 acres:

1. *Canawaugus*, on the Genesee River, 2 square miles;
2. *Big Tree*, on the Genesee River, 2 square miles;
3. *Little Beard's Town*, on the Genesee River, 2 square miles;
4. *Squawky Hill*, on the Genesee River, 2 square miles;
5. *Gardeau*, on the Genesee River, 2 square miles;
6. *Oil Spring*, on Cuba Lake, 1 square mile;
7. *Caneadea*, on the Genesee River, 16 square miles;
8. *Buffalo Creek*, on Lake Erie; and
9. *Tonawanda*, on Tonawanda Creek, together 200 square miles;
10. *Cattaraugus*, on Lake Erie, 42 square miles; and
11. *Allegany*, on the Allegheny River, adjacent to Cornplanter's private tract, 42 square miles.[79]

7

SLUMS IN THE

WILDERNESS

THE RESERVATION SYSTEM THEORETICALLY ESTABLISHED SMALL asylums where Indians who had lost their hunting grounds could remain peacefully apart from surrounding white communities until they became civilized. It actually resulted, however, in the creation of slums in the wilderness, where no traditional Indian culture could long survive and where only the least useful aspects of white culture could easily penetrate. The Iroquois, even those of the relatively prosperous Cornplanter band, had lost much to the ravages of war, hunger, pestilence, and disease. But more damaging to the spirit, perhaps, than these objective losses was a loss of confidence in their own way of life, a lessening of respect for themselves, which resulted from their confrontation with the white man's civilization. Facing now at close range this vast and intricate machine, they experienced the dilemma that all underdeveloped societies suffer: how to imitate superior alien customs while reasserting the integrity of the ancient way of life.

· Cornplanter's Town ·

LIKE THE OTHER RESERVATIONS Cornplanter's Town was a slum in the wilderness. But in a way it was a unique slum. It was a kind of mountain fortress, a shabby Shangri-la hidden from alien eyes in the forests of the Allegheny Mountains where by tradition no white man could enter. Here, insulated from alien presence, Indian and white alike, the Allegany band of Seneca could maintain a greater measure of autonomy than the Iroquois living near Buffalo and Niagara and along the Genesee.

Most of the members of the Allegany band were in 1798 living in the old town of Jenuchshadego, or Burnt House, within the grant; the smaller towns upriver in the reservation proper, and on the smaller tributaries, were nearly deserted. The grant was, in effect, a sheltered sliver of fertile bottom-land, bounded on the east by the river itself, a hundred and fifty yards wide and up to six feet deep, and on the west by steep, ravine-cut, green cliffs that climbed five hundred feet to a razor-backed ridge. The cliffs swept in to within a few feet of the river above and below the grant, effectively sealing it off from unwanted horsemen and foot travelers. The principal way of access to the grant was an awkard Indian trail that cut north across the razor-back hills, up and down the ravines, from the mouth of Conewango Creek. From Cornplanter's Town the trail proceeded up the west bank of the Allegheny River to the Indian towns in the reservation at Genesinguhta and Ichsua. Pinched in between cliffs and water, or scaling steep ravine slopes, this path was often blocked by snow and mud and rock slides in the winter and in the spring and summer by swamps, fallen trees, and underbrush. Here was one of the few areas in the craggy, forested Allegheny mountain country where an Indian town and its cornfields could be maintained.

There were in 1798 only three or four whites permanently residing within fifty miles of the grant (although dozens of migrants on their way west, land prospectors, and surveyors passed through the region every summer). Fifteen miles down the river at Warren, at the mouth of the Conewango, was the Holland Land Company's local storehouse, to which supplies were brought upriver for the surveyors, the two or three hardy settlers who had bought land in the area, and the local Indians who bought goods and whiskey on credit. The storekeeper had arrived in 1796; he was joined in 1798 by two brothers-in-law. In 1800 their parents, wives, and children arrived to increase the settlement to a size of about fifteen or twenty. Warren, the best of the upper-river town sites, was nevertheless discouraging to early settlers. In the miasma-conscious nineteenth century it had the reputation of being a place "where the health-destroying clouds . . . bank upon the ground in the valleys at nightfall, and remain until eight or nine o'clock each morning for seven months in the year."[1] But it was a site easy to clear and map, for it was an old Indian town; furthermore, in the winter of 1795 a severe storm had blown down much of the timber, and a forest fire a few years later burned up the windfall. Settlement proceeded slowly in Warren County, and in 1806, ten years later, there were still only about two hundred taxable settlers, In that year also the county had seven sawmills, two gristmills, 169 cows, 75 horses, and 53 pairs of oxen. Lots in the town itself moved slowly too; in the same year there were only the company storehouse, four dwelling houses, and a licensed tavern (also used as a school) run by the local magistrate (a temperate man, it is said, who died as a result of being bitten on the thumb in the course of keeping law and order). Some lots in town were sold as investments to Allegany Seneca Indians (including three to Handsome Lake).

Outside of Warren, there was no other white town within fifty miles of the grant. Sixty miles west of Warren was Meadville; King's Settlement, a Quaker family village, was just being established on the headwaters of the Allegheny, to the east. To the north, in New York State, there was nothing within a hundred miles; by the year 1800 there would still be only twelve taxable white persons in the whole of the Holland Company purchase. A substantial influx of settlers, emigrants, riverboatmen, and loggers would not be seen for another decade in the remote corner of the Allegheny Mountains where the Cornplanter band had taken refuge.[2]

The town lay between the bank of the river and a bend of a little stream—Cornplanter Run—that ran down from the cliffs. The run was a lonely and mysterious spot, associated with ghosts and snakes. On its banks and in the adjoining groves of pine and hardwood grew all kinds of medicinal plants. In such richness did the run supply a shaman's pharmacopoeia of medicinal teas and poultices that the Indian doctors of this band were widely famed as herbalists. On a summer day's excursion the doctor could find white boneset (for colds), purple boneset (a diuretic), *cicuta maculata* (a liniment—and also a poison for suicide), angelica (for pneumonia), mint (for colds and bilious attacks), elder (for heart disease), plantain (for stomach trouble), wire grass (for warriors and ball players to use as a muscle tonic, an emetic, and a liniment), white pine and wild cherry (for cough syrup), *Prenanthese altissima* (for rattlesnake bite), aspen (for worms), sumac (for measles and sore throat), Christmas fern (for consumption), and many others. Handsome Lake was an herbalist and no doubt collected plants along the edges of the run. Up the river above the narrows was another mysterious spot: a narrow, deep ravine extending straight up the hill, "the place where the snake slid down the cliffs." Local mythology had it that here the Thunderer discovered a giant horned serpent two or three hundred feet long. He threw bolt after bolt of lightning at it and forced it to escape by sliding down the hill, gouging out the ravine in its way. Then it slithered down the river and dug the deep bottom at the eddy. In the smooth backwater of this eddy, just opposite the town, the Indians now collected fish in organized drives.

In the uninhabited, pine-forested hills around the valley the men and boys hunted for bear, deer, elk, and turkey. There was little small game. Hunters traveled on foot and in the winter used snow-shoes. Farther down the river, most easily reachable by canoe, were the maple groves where the Indians brought their big kettles and camped in the spring to make sugar. Still farther down the river was the place for spearing fish in the rough water at the mouth of Kinzua Creek. Behind the peaks lining the river was the best hunting country, well known by the hunters and trappers, who knew the location of every salt lick. Northward, on both sides of the Allegheny, pine-forested hunting grounds stretched as far as the divide between the waters of the Genesee and Allegheny. But for the past ten years game had been noticeably scarce, the fur trade was limited, and meat was becoming a rarity.[3]

The town itself consisted of about forty houses scattered in an irregular line in the meadow thirty yards or so from the water's edge. In the middle of the village stood the famous statue of Tarachiawagon, the ritual center of the community, where the ceremony of burning the white dog was performed. Nearby stood Cornplanter's house, a pair of cabins joined by a long roofed porch, close to the medicine spring where Handsome Lake drew water—always in the direction of its natural flow—for the preparation of teas, emetics, and liniments. Cornplanter's house served on occasion as the council-house. The burial ground lay between the houses and the bank of the river.

The population of the town was about four hundred persons; thus each house was occupied, on the average, by five to fifteen people. It is difficult now to establish the rules governing residence. Cornplanter's town had been the home of Cornplanter's wife, and in this very loose sense he was living matrilocally; but the composition of his own household suggests that a combination of matrilineal and affinal kinship ties, health, and economic and political power determined the actual choice of residence. Living in Cornplanter's house at this time were fourteen people or more, including at least two households: Cornplanter's and his brother Handsome Lake's. Cornplanter and his wife had five daughters and at least one son living with them. This son was retarded and was known as "the idiot." From time to time daughters brought husbands to stay there. Two other sons, Henry and Charles, also lived in the settlement. Henry was the only Seneca who could speak English. He had lived in Philadelphia and New York as a youth, in the period 1791 to 1796, and had boarded with Christian families and gone to school. He could read and write English and could speak it well enough for broken conversation but not well enough to serve as a professional interpreter. Handsome Lake, a daughter, her husband, her children, and perhaps his other daughter lived in the second half of the house. Other close male kinfolk of Cornplanter and Handsome Lake occupied several of the other houses: their nephew Blacksnake, and Blacksnake's sister, the matron of the Wolf Clan and leading woman of the community; until his recent death Cornplanter's uncle, the ancient Guyasuta, who had a sister and six sons; Handsome Lake's own son; his grandson, James (Jemmy Johnson); the old war chief Canawayendo; Captain Decker, another nephew of Guyasuta. These other kinsmen of the two brothers, with their wives, children, and assorted relatives, many of them members of the Wolf Clan, probably occupied another half-dozen of the houses and made up, together with the Cornplanter–Handsome-Lake household, a good twenty per cent of the village's population. The names of many of the other distinguished men of the Allegany community, men of middle and old age, the chiefs and noted warriors who would sit on the platform at the council, have been recorded; each of these men probably was associated with a separate household, and in many cases their patrilineal descendants still live on the Allegany Reserve: Wundungohteh, who later moved to Cattaraugus, the chief who temporarily replaced Cornplanter a few years later; Bucktooth; Captain Crow; Peter Crouse, a white man who had been captured and adopted as a boy and now was married and a father; two white men married to Indian women, Elijah Matthews and Nicholas Demuth, who served the community as interpreters; Chief Half Town, who practiced the dreaming of gifts of rum and pork on unwary white visitors; Captain John Logan, the matrilineal nephew of Logan the Great Mingo; Captain Hudson; Redeye; Chief New Arrow; Chief Skendashowa; the Black Chief, husband of one of Sir William Johnson's daughters who was one of the leading women, and by her the father of ten children; Broken Tree, frequently employed as a messenger between the town and the white settlements lower down the river. These twenty or so men were elite members of the community, although not all of them were residents of the town itself. They regularly participated as chiefs and chief warriors in council meetings and carried the burden of community relationships with whites and other Indian groups, as speakers, messengers, and interpreters. They were all veterans of the wars in the forest, all husbands and fathers, most of them heavy drinkers on occasion, and all hunters and traders who traveled up and down the river, and into the mountains, to help support their women and children. In many of their households there were also younger men, common hunters and warriors who either because of youth and inexperience or lack of the capacity for responsible leadership were not numbered among the elite.[4]

The houses were not large. Cornplanter's, the biggest, was a full 64 feet long by 16 feet wide and consisted of two apartments, one 24 and the other 30 feet in length, separated by a roofed 10-foot porch that served as an entryway and a place to store wood and pound corn in the big wooden mortar. The other houses were one-room structures about 16 feet square with attached woodshed. They were nearly all built of logs, sometimes chinked with moss, with sharply peaked roofs of chestnut or hemlock bark, sheets of which could be seen lying about pressing flat under their own weight. (A few small cabins sheathed entirely with bark stood in the village, but this older type of construction was usually reserved for the temporary camps at the maple groves.) A single door at one end opened into each house. There were no windows, but the smoke hole in the center served as a skylight. The floor was earth. The fire burned constantly in the center of the room on the floor below the smoke hole. On either side of the room ranged two tiers of bunks four feet wide, one a foot off the ground and spread with deerskins on which people slept, and the other at a five-foot level, which served to store brass kettles, wooden bowls and ladles, blankets, deerskins, the leather sack of bear's oil, guns, traps, clothing, ornaments, and baskets of corn and other vegetables. At a height of six feet from eave to eave ran rafters, and between the two center rafters a pole was laid, from which a large kettle hung over the fire by withes and wooden hooks. Enormous quantities of firewood were required for heating and cooking in this cool mountain climate, where frosts were expected from September to May. The task of collecting the firewood belonged to the women and girls of the house. They spent much of their time in the summer hauling wood from distances up to half a mile, carrying it in large bales on the back supported by a belt around the forehead, splitting it into short, narrow lengths, and storing it all neatly in a pile or shed next to the house. Trash and garbage was simply thrown out of the door into a pile near the house, where it rotted and fed swarms of flies. There were no outhouses or public latrines; people relieved themselves in the privacy of woods or brush away from the houses. There was no soap, and lice infested hair and clothing.

The economy of the village depended upon the women, who owned it collectively. All land was "national" land; users had private rights to its produce only. An area of about two hundred acres surrounding the houses had been fenced in to protect it from the deer, bear, wolves, and other hungry animals. Within the fence the ground had been fairly well-cleared of trees and brush, although bushes and patches of grass remained. The women of each household, from old women to little girls, sick or well, all took part in the cultivation of the fields. One old gray-haired woman whose feet had been frozen was a notable sight in the village, for every day in the summer she hobbled on her knees about the meadow doing her household tasks— carrying wood, making the fire, fetching water from the river, and hoeing the corn in her field two hundred yards from her house. The garden plots were small, interspersed among the bushes, and the total area under actual cultivation was only about sixty acres. Each household, on an average, gardened less than a couple of acres. The females of individual households worked the plots in parties of four or five; each household kept its own garden produce. They raised corn, squash, pumpkins, cucumbers, beans, melons, potatoes, and tobacco, cultivating the individual corn hills, each up to a foot high, with the hoe throughout the growing season and supporting the beans on sticks. The men regarded the gardening strictly as women's work and did not participate in it in any way except to split the rails for the community fence. Men did however build and repair the houses. Except for dogs, there were few domestic animals: in all of the Allegany band, a total of three horses, fourteen cows, one yoke of oxen, and twelve hogs. The cattle and hogs supplied some fresh meat and so also did the hunt, which was the male's contribution to the food quest; but the hunt now procured only a small supply of venison, bear's meat, wildfowl, and fish. Both meat and vegetable foods, including blackberries, strawberries, and whortleberries, were whenever possible dried and preserved for the winter and spring. Dried corn was pounded in huge wooden mortars by triads of women using heavy pestles up to four feet long. The meals served in the households were generally soups made of corn and all available vegetables with small chunks of meat thrown in if any was to be had. It was served in wooden bowls and supped with wooden ladles. Like the other food, it was unsalted. Corn dumplings, dipped in bear's oil or sweetened with maple sugar and dried berries, were a special delicacy. For traveling, hominy cakes were made of pounded meal-corn mixed with beans and maple sugar.

Physically the Allegany Seneca were a mixture of Indian types with white parentage visible in a few. Skin colors ranged from light tan through copper to dark brown; faces from the round-faced, flat-nosed, to the narrow, hollow-cheeked, aquiline-nosed Mongoloid types. Except for moccasins they clothed themselves entirely in brightly colored cloth. The basic garments for both men and women were tight blue or scarlet leggings, worn below the knee by women and up the thigh by the men; a breechcloth supported by a belt and hanging down fore and aft; and a ruffled calico shirt reaching to the hips. The women also wore a loose blue skirt made of a couple of yards of cloth looped over a string tied around the waist. In cold weather this basic wardrobe was amplified by waistcoats, jackets, and overcoats of blanket cloth, by blankets loosely draped around the shoulders, and by a loose hood of blanket cloth for a cap. The men still pulled out all the hair on the head except for the scalp lock on the crown; the women tied their long black hair in a pony tail and liberally oiled it with bear fat. The men frequently wore nose- and earbobs and rings of silver, and some chose singular ear ornaments, such as silver crosses, a pair of padlocks hanging from one ear, or a watch. The clothing of both sexes was liberally decorated with silver brooches, and the women decorated their garments with needlework of beads and porcupine quills. On occasions of ceremony this dress was still further elaborated by special head-ornaments of feathers and animal tails. In general, both clothes and hands were dirty by white standards, for people seldom bathed and made no soap.

The people of Cornplanter's Town were trying to survive by the old ways, with such modification as the press of need and opportunity dictated. The physical modifications were obvious: their dress was cloth and ornamented with metal; their houses were sometimes made of log rather than bark (an innovation made practical by the steel hatchet) and were too small in most cases to house whole lineages; they used steel knives, brass kettles, and guns; they buried their dead in pine coffins. Socially, too, there had been changes: the confederacy was no longer a sheltering tree, and Cornplanter—eloquent speaker, successful war-captain, and adroit politician—had become a local leader more powerful than tradition would have allowed. He had acquired personal capital from the whites, which he administered somewhat arbitrarily on behalf of the band: the land of the grant, a sawmill up the river, and credit enough to pay in cash for such favors as the release of jailed Indians in Pittsburgh. But the old town council system still remained, with the twenty or thirty chiefs and captains, the half dozen or so leading women, and the common warriors and women all lobbying with each other over public issues according to old principles. The women still claimed to own the land and had the right to urge or restrain the warriors in war matters independently of the chiefs' policies; a great man like Cornplanter, if he became too arrogant, might be deposed or even assassinated by his own relatives in the public interest.

And the ancient religion still brought the people together for the annual calendar of ceremonies and prompted the crisis rituals on occasions of death, illness, or danger. The religious center of Cornplanter's Town was still the huge painted wooden statue of a man standing on a pedestal carved from the same block, near the council-house. This statue represented Tarachiawagon, the Good Twin and Creator of the Indian way of life. At Green Corn and New Year's the statue was lavishly decorated with skins, handkerchiefs, ribbons, and feathers, and the white dog was hung on it, strangled and waiting to be burned. The drummers sat on a deerskin at the foot of the statue, and up to two hundred men, women, and children moved round it in a large circle in the Worship Dance. The ritual speaker still thanked the spirit forces and exhorted the people to live virtuously. The members of the Society of Faces still ministered with rough kindness to the sick and cavorted for the entertainment of the people in the council house. The people still burned tobacco to the Thunderer in time of drought and for good luck kindled their new fires with splints of wood from a lightning-riven tree and saved stone bolts believed to have been slung to earth by the Thunderer in his hunting of snakes. The souls of the dead were still fed at the death feasts.

On the surface, then, the old way of life seemed to be intact. The several hundred survivors of the wars, the epidemics, the famines who now made up the Allegany band of Seneca were able to maintain the ancient marriage customs, the old religious rituals, the traditional economy from year to year with only marginal change. But although they were protected from intrusion, their situation was now a precarious one even by their own spartan standards. The population was small and isolated both politically and geographically. The game was becoming scarce, and this meant little meat and also little hardware and dry goods. The river from which they took their cooking and drinking water periodically flooded the banks of sandy loam on which the fields were laid and washed away not only the year's supply but the seed corn for next year (the circumstance which had brought all the people together at Cornplanter's Town in 1798). Sometimes, in spring flood, the river washed out whole stretches of bank, eating at fields and the cemetery. In the winter and spring, the trails by which they could reach refuge with other Iroquois to the north were made almost impassable by snow, swamps, and fallen timber. In the summer, the lightning-struck forests burned for days around them until the whole village was obscured by smoke.

And the people liked to drink. They preferred not to drink alone but in large convivial groups. In the spring, hunters took their peltries to Warren, got drunk by scores, and brought more liquor home with them; at other seasons, they were able to get credit for liquor from the Holland Company factor. Raftsmen taking logs from Cornplanter's sawmill downstream to the white towns as far south as Pittsburgh spent their money on whiskey. Bringing liquor back to the grant, returning travelers sold the whiskey at retail and buyers threw all-night parties where, plied with liquor, groups spent whole nights singing, dancing, drumming, and quarreling. Women could be seen after such routs, lying in stupor beside the paths to their homes. And in the late morning the sodden households woke sometimes to find a member dead, or cut in a brawl, or frozen in the snow outside.[5]

· Depopulation ·

THE DEMOGRAPHIC CONDITION of the Iroquois of New York and Pennsylvania had deteriorated continuously during the twenty years from the beginning of the American Revolution to the Treaty of Big Tree. The net effect was to reduce the Iroquois population approximately by half.

Despite the fact that they were still able to wage an effective guerrilla war at the end of the Revolution, casualties were severe. Approximately two hundred warriors were killed in the fighting, about two or three per cent of the total population and ten per cent of the able-bodied adult males.[6] These men were not merely professional soldiers but also husbands, sons, and fathers whose labor as hunters and traders was important to the survival of nearly two hundred households. Relatively few adult male captives were taken and adopted to replace them. A small number of women and children were doubtless also lost during the fighting and perhaps as many as fifty men, women, and children by murders, both at the hands of whites and of drunken Indians, in the ten years after the war. Nevertheless, by 1788, when Samuel Kirkland made his household census of the New York Indians, the proportions of adult males and females were nearly equal. Among the Seneca, Kirkland then counted 423 females to 409 adult males.[7] These figures suggest that there was no very significant underproportion of males resulting from combat losses.

Even more damaging than direct combat casualties were the economic losses resulting from Sullivan's, Van Schaick's, and Brodhead's famous raids in 1779. The American armies, waging total war, systematically destroyed all the Indian settlements that they reached. Houses were burned, apple and peach orchards chopped down, caches of corn, squash, cucumbers, beans, and tobacco and dry fields of ripe corn, hay, and other vegetables were put to the torch. Five hundred Indian dwellings in two dozen settlements were reduced to ashes; nearly a million bushels of corn were incinerated.[8] Some of the refugees, after the armies had gone, returned to their burned-out villages along the Allegheny and Genesee. But the winter of 1779–80 brought a new catastrophe: cold. That winter was the most severe within living memory. New York Harbor froze over solidly enough for cannon to be wheeled across it. Snow covered western New York five feet deep; vast numbers of deer and other animals died of starvation, and their carcasses were found under the snow in the spring. The Indians who had returned to the burned villages were unable to secure even enough food "to keep a child one day from perishing from hunger." Another famine winter occurred in 1887–8.[9]

And still another apocalyptic horseman was riding in the sky: pestilence. About two thousand Iroquois refugees were settled after 1779 in a line of "poorly constructed wigwams" for eight miles along the road leading to Fort Niagara; according to Blacksnake many died from "salt food and exposure," and according to another Indian report three hundred died of dysentery.[10] In 1794 the Seneca and Oneida parties who visited the western Indians brought back with them an epidemic of dysentery and spread it on the reservations. Forty Oneida died; and six months later Cornplanter reported that he and Guyasuta were still sick and that now the disease had become very bad among his people as well. In 1795 an epidemic of measles killed a number of Oneida and probably of the other tribes.[11] An epidemic of smallpox had cut down the Onondaga in the winter of 1776–7, when some ninety persons had died in their principal village.[12] In the winter of 1781–2 smallpox struck again, this time among the wretched and panic-stricken survivors on the Genesee. According to an eyewitness, "The Indians appealed to the commandant of Niagara who sent English surgeons, the sick were separated from the well, huts were prepared outside the village to serve as hospitals, and as soon as symptoms appeared the individuals were sent to these rude retreats. Few persons on the upper Genesee escaped the contagion. Many died and were immediately buried. Only those who had recovered from the plague could be prevailed upon to care for the sick and the reckless indifference of some of these unwilling attendants was such that several persons were buried alive when it appeared probable they could not recover."[13] It may be presumed that the epidemic was not confined to the Genesee but spread, that same winter or later, among the rest of the susceptible Iroquois in their shabby, hungry camps at Niagara.

One cumulative consequence of the multiple disaster—combat and invasion, hunger and cold, and disease and pestilence—was a substantial reduction of the total population of the Iroquois. As early as 1779, a few months after Sullivan's raid, their British agent at Niagara observed somberly that "their number is now reduced to 2,628."[14] While this number is unduly low, it is evident that the population was declining. By 1794 no more than about 4,000 Iroquois remained: some 3,500 in New York and about 500 in Canada.[15] This figure contrasts sadly with Sir William Johnson's estimate of nearly 2,000 warriors in 1763—a figure that implies a total population of between 8,000 and 10,000 souls and that was probably close to the correct figure at the beginning of the Revolutionary War.[16] Evidently the losses through combat, murder, starvation, exposure, and disease had in the twenty years following the onset of the war cut the population of the Six Nations approximately in half.

· Loss of Confidence ·

MORE DAMAGING TO THE IROQUOIS than the actual loss of population was their declining confidence in their ability to survive as a people. A pessimistic view was maintained both tacitly and publicly by many American whites, despite official plans to "civilize" the "savages," and it reinforced in Indian thinking the somber evidence of recent experience. Benjamin Lincoln, Revolutionary War hero, one of the commissioners to the abortive treaty of 1793, and a person with whom the Iroquois had done business on several occasions, wrote piously that ". . . to people fully this earth was in the original plan of the benevolent Deity. I am confident that sooner or later there will be a full accomplishment of the original system; and that no men will be suffered to live by hunting on lands capable of improvement. So that if the savages cannot be civilized and quit their present pursuits, they will, in consequence of their stubbornness, dwindle and moulder away, from causes perhaps imperceptible to us, until the whole race shall have become extinct, or they shall have reached those climes about the great lakes, where, from the rocks and the mountainous state, the footsteps of the husbandman will not be seen."[17] The depression produced by such attitudes was vividly expressed in 1794 by an Allegany Indian named John Logan. A man of about fifty, he lived by himself in a bark camp near the American fort on French Creek. Logan was widely known as the man who had killed his uncle Logan, the Great Mingo. But when surveyor John Adlum encountered him unexpectedly, he was "astonished to see the tears rolling down his manly cheeks very copiously." When Adlum, through an interpreter, asked why he looked so sorrowful and whether there was anything he could do, Logan explained that it was "a disease of the mind." He was worrrying about the prospect of a frontier war in which the Iroquois would be inevitably destroyed. And almost echoing Lincoln and the other "savagist" white philosophers of Indian doom, he declared, "It appears to me that the great Spirit is determined on our destruction—Perhaps it is to answer some great and now incomprehensible purpose, for the better And whatever his will is I will bear it like a man."[18]

Not only did whites and Indians doubt the survival of the Iroquois: The moral value of their culture was persistently attacked. In 1784, for instance, in order to press the diplomatic attack more effectively, the federal representatives adopted a conscious policy of destroying Iroquois self-esteem, corrupting their leaders, and subverting their political system. James Duane, who had been lately a delegate to the Continental Congress and a member of its Committee on Indian Affairs, in advance of the treaty advised the Governor of New York to break down Iroquois morale at Fort Stanwix by every device of psychological warfare available to his commissioners. "They assume a perfect equality," he wrote; this attitude was to be broken by constantly treating them as inferiors, as a dependent minority group. It had been the custom of New York, Pennsylvania, and Crown commissioners for a hundred years to follow Indian usage in councils. Now these rituals were to be abandoned. "Instead of conforming to Indian political behavior We should force them to adopt ours—dispense with belts, etc." Their very existence as a political unit was to be denied: "I would never suffer the word 'Nation' or 'Six Nations,' or 'Confederates,' or 'Council Fire at Onondago' or any other form which would revive or seem to confirm their former ideas of independence, to escape . . . they are used to be called Brethren, Sachems & Warriors of the Six Nations. I hope it will never be repeated. It is sufficient to make them sensible that they are spoken to without complimenting twenty or thirty Mohawks as a nation, and a few more Tuscaroras & Onondagas as distinct nations . . . they should rather be taught . . . that the public opinion of their importance has long since ceased." Spies and provocateurs were sent among them to bribe compliance and sow dissension: "If you find that any Jealousy of, or Envy to, Brant, prevails; you will try to discover who are most jealous or envious of him, and promote it as much as You prudently can. . . ."[19]

This policy was put into effect at Fort Stanwix, where the initial Indian speakers were cut short in their delivery, informed that Great Britain had given their lands to the United States, and ordered peremptorily to sign articles of submission and cession. American spokesmen pointed their fingers at the Indians to emphasize each instruction: ". . . it made the Indians stare. The speech was delivered . . . in a language by no means accommodating or flattering; quite unlike what they used to receive." The credentials and authority of the chief Indian spokesman—a Mohawk warrior authorized to make peace on behalf of the Six Nations and all their allies and confederates, including the Ottawa, Chippewa, Huron, Potawatomi, Mississauga, Miami, Delaware, Shawnee, Cherokee, Choctaw, and Creek—were impugned, and the very existence of such a confederacy was denied (although its reality was assured enough).[20] And behind the whole proceeding lay a pose of withering contempt on the part of the white delegates, many of whom were slaveowners and only too ready to regard the Indians as lesser breeds. Washington, himself a slaveowner, about this time compared "the savage" to "the wolf" as "both being animals of prey though they differ in shape."[21] And Washington, like many another American official, had before the Revolution become an investor in abortive schemes to acquire the same Indian lands whose final relinquishment was a prime object of the treaties at forts Stanwix, McIntosh, and Finney.[22]

The Iroquois were at this moment ill-equipped to rebut, to their own satisfaction, these assaults upon their self-respect by any coordinated movement toward reform. But various individuals and groups were taking public positions that were relevant to the renaissance when, under Handsome Lake's guidance, it did develop. Against the intensification of race prejudice, some spoke for a pan-Indian resistance. When the western confederacy met in 1786, for instance, the proposal was made that *all* the nations "of our colour" unite and be of one mind. There it was urged, "Let us then have a just sense of our own value and if after that the great spirit wills that other colours should subdue us let it be so."[23] Cornplanter and others vehemently denied the popular stories of Indian atrocities and accused the whites of being more cruel than the Indians. Thus individual men of eloquence were able to reject the challenges to self-respect and to cast them back upon their enemies in the destructive dialogue of identity. But most of the time, for many of the Iroquois, the doubts remained: Were they going to survive? Were they worthy to survive?

· *Social Pathology: Alcohol, Violence, Witch Fear, Disunity* ·

THE MOST CONSPICUOUS social pathology was a great increase in the frequency of drunkenness. In earlier days, indeed, Iroquois Indians had been accustomed on occasion to drink heavily (witness Zeisberger's graphic account of a Seneca orgy in 1750). But these had been brief and periodic sprees in which whole towns indulged. Chronic individual alcoholism had long been known among the Delaware, who had lost their lands two generations earlier;[24] but until now it had been rare among the Iroquois. Now, added to the periodic drunken saturnalia, drinking became a serious social problem. Many of the most distinguished men among the Six Nations became notorious drunkards, including Red Jacket, Hendrick Aupaumut, Young King, Logan (the Great Mingo), Skenandoa, and Handsome Lake. The few leaders, like Cornplanter and Brant, who generally avoided over-indulgence were by that very fact made notable.[25]

Contemporary descriptions by white men of Iroquois drinking behavior are seldom written in a tone of amusement. Thus a surveyor noted at the Tonawanda reservation in March, 1801, "Some drunken Indians here; but this is hardly worth recording, as these people are seldom sober when whiskey can be had in sufficient quantity to make them otherwise."[26] The schoolteacher at Oneida in June 1793 (just after the annuity monies were paid, and also not long after his house burned down), wrote desperately to the Indian agent, "Since the Indians received their money this place has been almost a little Hell on earth. Wish you at least to write orders that no one white man in the place shall either sell rum or lend it to the Indians on any pretence whatsoever."[27] At Newtown Treaty in 1791 drunken warriors boasting of their exploits at the Full Moon Ceremony had to be prevented from killing one another by Fish Carrier, the Cayuga chief. One of the luminaries at that occasion was the Oneida Peter Otsequette, otherwise known as French Peter. He had been taken to

France as a youth by Lafayette and had lived there for seven years. He learned French perfectly and could recite Corneille and Racine. But "He had not been many months restored to his nation, and yet he would drink raw Rum out of a brass kettle, take as much delight in yelling and in whooping as any Indian, and in fact become as vile a drunkard as the worst of them." (He died a year later on a visit to Philadelphia and was buried with military honors at a public ceremony attended by the clergy of all denominations, the secretary of war, and a detachment of light infantry. His wife was consoled with a "present" and the return of his black silk handkerchief, leggings, black cloth mantle, and breechcloth.)[28] And the Treaty of Big Tree in 1797 saw one whole day lost to demon rum, when "Red Jacket & many of the Indians . . . from intoxication fell to fighting in groups, pulling Hair biting like dogs were ever they could get hold. . . ."[29] The prevailing mood of drunken Indians was an explosive, indiscriminate hostility that vented itself in fighting even within the family. Young Isaac Brant, the drunken ne'er-do-well son of Joseph Brant, attacked his father with a knife at an inn and suffered in return a scalp wound from which he eventually died.[30] Two drunken brothers from the Allegany band quarreled during a hunting excursion, and the elder killed the younger.[31] Mary Jemison's son Thomas in his drunken fits threatened to kill his mother for having raised a witch (for so he regarded his brother John) and was at last killed by this same brother. John later killed another brother and finally was killed himself by two Indians from Squawky Hill in the course of a drunken brawl.[32] Drunken persons, "aged women, in particular . . . were often seen lying beside the paths, overcome by [liquor]." Additional evils flowed from the drinking: skins and furs that might otherwise have been used or traded for meat and vegetables, dry goods and hardware, were spent on whiskey, which Indian women brought up to the villages and there retailed among the Indians themselves.[33] In 1796 the agent to the Iroquois wrote a discouraging report to the secretary of war: "The Indians of the Six Nations . . . have become given to indolence, drunkeness and thefts, and have taken to killing each other, there have been five murders among themselves within Six months—they have recd their payments and immediately expended it for liquor & in the course of a frollick have killed one or two. . . ."[34]

When sober, the Iroquois tended to be depressed and even suicidal. A sympathetic missionary at Buffalo Creek summarized this aspect of the problem: "Indians, as has been observed, bear suffering with great fortitude, but at the end of this fortitude is desperation. Suicides are frequent among the Senecas. I apprehend this despondency is the principal cause of their intemperance. Most of the children and youth have an aversion to spirituous liquor, and rarely taste it until some trouble overtakes them. Their circumstances are peculiarly calculated to depress their spirits, especially these contiguous to white settlements. Their ancient manner of subsistence is broken up, and when they appear willing and desirous to turn their attention to agriculture, their ignorance, the inveteracy of their old habits, the disadvantages under which they labor, soon discourage them; though they struggle hard little is realized to their benefit, beside the continual dread they live in of losing their possessions. If they build they do not know who will inhabit."[35] An unusually strong tendency for the humiliated Iroquois to commit suicide during this period is not easy to document with specific cases. One instance, however, was the suicide of Big Tree, who stabbed himself to death in Wayne's camp during the winter of 1793–94. Apparently he had felt publicly dishonored: He had been pro-American during the Revolution, had been an associate of Cornplanter's thereafter, had urged the western Indians to accept the American terms, and at the last was reputed to have become melancholic and deranged.[36]

Suspicions of witchcraft, to which disappointed Iroquois had always been vulnerable, was another expression of the fundamental demoralization of Iroquois society. The literature of the period is rife with witchcraft accusations: Cornplanter charging that his party was "poisoned" on the Maumee; Mary Jemison revealing that not only was she called a witch, but that her murderous, and eventually murdered, son John was called a witch by the first brother, whom he killed; a woman suspected of witchcraft being burned to death on the Genesee flats in 1798; and Mary Jemison, enlarging on the subject of witchcraft, noting that the Indians believed witches to be, next to the author of evil, "the greatest scourge to their people . . . more or less who had been charged with being witches, had been executed in almost every year since she has lived on the Genesee"—which was in 1798 no less than thirty-five years![37]

Many of the Indians blamed the whites for all this. The white people had once seemed a noble, virtuous, honest people; but they had brought the Indians five things: "a flask of rum, a pack of playing cards, a handful of coins, a violin, and a decayed leg bone." And the Evil Spirit had laughed and said: "These cards will make them gamble away their wealth and idle their time; this money will make them dishonest and covetous and they will forget their old laws; this fiddle will make them dance with their arms about their wives and bring about a time of tattling and idle gossip; this rum will turn their minds to foolishness and they will barter their country for baubles; then will this secret poison eat the life from their blood and crumble their bones."[38]

· *Paths to Salvation* ·

IN RESPONSE TO THE DILEMMA of civilization two points of view developed among the Iroquois, one advocating the assimilation of white culture and the other the preservation of Indian ways. We may call their proponents, for want of better terms, the progressives and the conservatives.

The progressives are better known to us today because their spokesmen were either literate, like Brant, and left written record of their policies, or else were at least in frequent contact with sympathetic white men. Cornplanter among the Allegany Seneca, the Mohawk Brant at Grand River, Captain Hendrick at Oneida, Sturgeon among the Oneida: these men, and their associates, favored extensive adoption of white customs. The two most successful of the reformers were Brant and Cornplanter; and of the two, the more radical was Brant.

Joseph Brant was a devout Episcopalian, and his acculturation policy was Episcopalian, too. This was hardly remarkable, for resident missionaries from England had been converting and educating Mohawk Indians in the Christian religion for two hundred years. A good proportion of the migrants to Canada were already baptized Christians, literate enough to read in Mohawk the New Testament and the Book of Common Prayer; and many, like Brant, spoke English well. On his trip to England in 1786 Brant had collected funds for an Episcopal church, and a church was built as soon as he reached home, with Brant himself hanging the bell in the steeple. It was a substantial building, sixty feet in length and forty-five in breadth, built of squared logs boarded on the outside and painted, with pews, pulpit, reading desk, communion table, and even a small organ. Literate Indian curates and schoolteachers supervised the flock between visits from peripatetic missionary clergymen like their old pastor John Stuart from the Mohawk Valley. But Brant's plan went beyond evangelism. Recognizing that the reservation was too small for hunting but larger than necessary for the agricultural support of the population, he proposed that lands be held in severalty and that the men take up farming on a white model. Parts of the excess reservation land could be sold off to whites and the proceeds invested in capital equipment, like plows, livestock, and a flour mill; other parts could be leased out in order to gain an annual tribal income. Brant also spoke out strongly against the evils of strong drink. But Brant was outdistancing the people he wished to lead, with his literary tastes and European dress and his plans to learn Greek in order to prepare a Mohawk translation from the original Scriptures. Before he died (in 1807) he was to see the development of a conservative faction that went so far as to attempt to impeach him for his efforts to allot lands in severalty to Indians and to sell or lease parts of the reservation to white people.[39]

Cornplanter's progressive policy was not based on a Christian rationale, for neither Cornplanter nor any of his band (with the possible exception of a few white captives who had been adopted into Indian families) was a professing Christian. Cornplanter had much respect for the members of the Society of Friends whom he had met on several occasions at Philadelphia and at Canandaigua; but this respect was based on personal liking rather than religious admiration. His policy, nevertheless, had much in common with Brant's. As we saw earlier, he was anxious to establish a secure tenure for Seneca landholdings as a basis for economic reorganization involving male agriculture with plow and cattle. In his several eloquent appeals to Washington during the winter of 1790–91 he observed: "The Game which the Great Spirit sent into our Country for us to eat is going from among us. We thought that he intended that we should till the ground with the Plow, as the White People do, and we talked to one another about it. . . . We ask you to teach us to plow and to grind Corn; to assist us in building Saw Mills, and supply us with Broad Axes, Saws, Augers, and other Tools, so as that we may make our Houses more comfortable and more durable; that you will send Smiths among us, and above all that you will teach our Children to read and write, and our Women to spin and weave. . . . We hope that our Nation will determine to spill all the Rum which shall hereafter be brought to our Towns."[40] And again like Brant, Cornplanter favored the idea of selling a part of the Seneca lands in return for an investment of tribal funds, which by guaranteeing an annuity in cash would ensure a continuing income usable for capital improvements and for emergencies like legal expenses.[41] Furthermore, Cornplanter was ready to discard ancient and revered customs if they seemed to impede the Indians in dealing with the whites, on one occasion even proposing that the rule of unanimity in consensus and the traditional female veto over warfare should be treated as mere "superstitions" and disregarded.[42] About 1792 he arranged for the Quakers to educate two of his sons in Philadelphia.[43] In 1795 he was writing to inquire about his son, saying that he wished "to hear from my son and what progress he is making in his learning, and as soon as he is learned enough I want him at home to manage my [sawmill] business for me." Cornplanter put great importance on his sawmill, which he built "in order to support my family by it," and his correspondence included negotiations for the sale of boards as early as 1795. This was five years before the white men got around to constructing the first sawmill on that part of the Allegheny that was a generation later to become a great lumber route![44]

The most prominent expositor of the conservative position at this time was Red Jacket. Red Jacket was a professional council-speaker, and thus not all of his public utterances were consistently conservative, for he was, when he spoke on behalf of a council, obliged to represent that council's views, conservative or progressive. But being resident at Buffalo Creek and commonly chosen as speaker for the Seneca sachems there, he was frequently the man who put into words the conservative policies of the council. His personal attitude toward the whites does not seem originally to have been so much nativistic as competitive. He regarded Colonel Pickering—the Indian expert whom Washington had sent to Newtown Point in 1791 and later chose to be superintendent of Indian affairs, who had organized the Treaty at Canandaigua in 1794, and who became Postmaster General and eventually Secretary of War—as his opposite number among the whites and delighted in vexing him with superior rhetoric. When he learned that Pickering had become the Secretary of War, Red Jacket remarked sadly, "Ah, we began our public career about the same time; he knew how to read and write, I did not, and he has got ahead of me; but if I had known how to read and write, I would have been ahead of him."[45] But Red Jacket's response to this frustration of a natural equality of talent was, paradoxically, an increasingly bitter defense of the old Seneca ways. At Newtown Point in 1791 he declared in regard to the "civilizing" of the Indians by teaching them to read and write and so forth that "it would be a matter of great time before they would give up their ancient customs."[46] In 1800 to a missionary who visited Buffalo Creek he declared that he and Farmer's Brother "cannot see that learning would be of any service to us; but we will leave it to others who come after us, to judge for themselves." Farmer's Brother in support of this view observed that some years ago he had sent one of his grandsons to Philadelphia to be educated. But on a visit to that city he found his grandson successively in a tavern, in a gambling den, in a brothel, and dancing.[47] Red Jacket's nativism found its most eloquent expression in 1805 in his celebrated reply to the Reverend Mr. Cram, who came to Buffalo Creek to tell the Six Nations that there was but one true religion— his own. After reviewing the traditional Indian history of inter-racial relations (at first you were weak, and we were kind; now we are weak, and you are merciless), he declared the official chiefs' policy:

> Brother, our seats were once large, and yours were very small; you have now become a great people, and we have scarcely a place left to spread our blankets; you have got our country, but are not satisfied; you want to force your religion upon us.

> Brother, continue to listen. You say that you are sent to instruct us how to worship the Great Spirit agreeably to his mind, and if we do not take hold of the religion which you white people teach, we shall be unhappy hereafter; you say that you are right, and we are lost; how do we know this to be true? We understand that your religion is written in a book; if it was intended for us as well as you, why has not the Great Spirit given it to us, and not only to us, but why did he not give to our forefathers the knowledge of that book, with the means of understanding it rightly? We only know what you tell us about it; how shall we know when to believe, being so often deceived by the white people?

> Brother, you say there is but one way to worship and serve the Great Spirit; if there is but one religion, why do you white people

differ so much about it? why not all agree, as you can all read the book?

Brother, we do not understand these things; we are told that your religion was given to your forefathers, and has been handed down from father to son. We also have a religion which was given to our forefathers, and has been handed down to us their children. We worship that way. It teacheth us to be thankful for all the favors we receive; to love each other, and to be united; we never quarrel about religion.

Brother, the Great Spirit has made us all; but he has made a great difference between his white and red children; he has given us a different complexion, and different customs; to you he has given the arts; to these he has not opened our eyes; we know these things to be true. Since he has made so great a difference between us in other things, why may we not conclude that he has given us a different religion according to our understanding; the Great Spirit does right; he knows what is best for his children: we are satisfied.

Brother, we do not wish to destroy your religion, or take it from you; we only want to enjoy our own.

Brother, you say you have not come to get our land or our money, but to enlighten our minds. I will now tell you that I have been at your meetings, and saw you collecting money from the meeting. I cannot tell what this money was intended for, but suppose it was for your minister, and if we should conform to your way of thinking, perhaps you may want some from us.

Brother, we are told that you have been preaching to white people in this place: these people are our neighbors, we are acquainted with them: we will wait a little while and see what effect your preaching has upon them. If we find it does them good, makes them honest, and less disposed to cheat Indians, we will then consider again what you have said.[48]

And as we shall see, Red Jacket's cultural nativism became more and more uncompromising as the years went by.

It is evident, then, that the ground was well stocked with the nutrients of factional strife between progressives and conservatives. Beyond agreement on a generalized sense of cultural inferiority and of the need for separateness from the wicked among the white people, the Six Nations were divided. Each little reservation had its own progressive and conservative faction. These factions worked against one another, as we have seen, both in political maneuvering at crucial council meetings and at treaties with the whites. And at times the struggle became violent. In 1787, for instance, the Onondaga war-captain named Sturgeon was murdered by a fellow tribesman. It was reported that two motives combined to make the murder: Jealousy of Sturgeon's despotic pretensions to leadership, and resentment of his progressive policies. Sturgeon "began to adopt the Dress and customs of the United States, and introduced them into his own Family—this gave great umbrage." He also planned to send his son to Baltimore to receive an English education. The friends of the murderer paid were-gild to the amount of £375 in order to save his life.[49]

In a world as confusing as this, it might be expected that other solutions would be offered, less rational than those formulated by the avowed progressives and conservatives. Minor prophets began to emerge, their words bursting like bubbles over a boiling cauldron. The best-known of these was a Mohawk at Grand River, a young man of "unblemished character" and of "a sedate and reflecting mind." In the fall of 1798 he fell into a trance for a day or more. During this time he dreamed that he had an interview with the great Tarachiawagon himself. Tarachiawagon complained grievously of "the base and ungrateful neglect of the Five Nations [the Seneca excepted] in withholding the homage due to him and the offering he was wont to receive from their fathers, as an acknowledgement for his guardianship. Many were the evils which had come upon them in consequence of this neglect. Sickness, epidemic disorders, losses in war, unfruitful seasons, scanty crops—unpleasant days." The popular response at Grand River was enthusiastic, and even Joseph Brant agreed to allow the renewal of the sacrifice to Tarachiawagon, provided it did not take on an anti-Christian tone. The sacrifice was the white dog ritual, which had fallen into disuse among all the Iroquois except the Seneca (among the Oneida, it had not been celebrated for thirty years).

News of the revival of the white dog ceremony at Grand River traveled fast. It reached the Oneida in New York in the spring of 1799. Blacksmith, the only surviving pagan priest and a son of Good Peter (one of the unlucky envoys to the Western Indians), celebrated the white dog ritual and was joined by a large number of the community. Blacksmith, after the eating of the white dog, delivered a little sermon warning the communicants not to drink any rum for ten days or they would pollute the rest of the ceremony. He also discussed the relation between the white dog sacrament and the Christian Mass, saying that eating the flesh of the roasted dog "was a transaction equally sacred and solemn, with that, which the Christians call the Lord's feast. The only difference is in the elements, the Christians use bread and wine, we use flesh and blood." Again the following May the white dog was sacrificed to the accompaniment of sermons against drinking. This time liquor was prohibited to communicants for four days before the ritual; abstinence for ten days thereafter was strongly recommended; they expected "a full blessing, a rich and ripe harvest next fall." And he spoke kindly of Christianity, exhorting "with great earnestness the whole of his disciples to exercise candour and gentleness towards their brethren, the Christians; never to tantalize or insult them for the path they had chosen. Lastly, he told them that as the religious rites of their ancestors did not require them to meet every Sunday, as the Christians do, they were at liberty, whoever so minded, to attend the Sabbath worship of the Christians and learn what good they could there."

Poor pastor Kirkland feared that the Oneida would unanimously accept the new paganism, whose potency for evil, he believed, was only magnified by the uncommon "solemnity and order" of its religious festivals and by the civility, sobriety, and philanthropy of its votaries, who drank not one twentieth as much as the Christian Indians and who included a number of apostates from his own congregation.[50]

· The Ragged Conquerors ·

DURING THE LAST FEW YEARS of the eighteenth century and the first decade of the nineteenth, the Seneca reservations were being gradually encircled by a peculiarly dilapidated and discouraged brand of European culture brought by hopeful speculators, by hungry farmers fleeing the cold and rocky hillsides of New England, and by hard-drinking Scotch-Irish weavers driven from Ulster by high taxes and the new weaving machines. The men came with golden dreams, but the dreams quickly faded. Villages were built and abandoned, roads were cleared and then grew up in brush, and the clearings were taken again by the forest. These pioneers were almost a lost legion, more primitive in material standard of living, and perhaps socially as well, than the Indians on their reservations. Even as late as 1814 there were not many more white men in Warren and Cattaraugus counties (in the center of which lay Cornplanter's tract and the Allegany Reserve) than Seneca Indians. The small, isolated farmer, up to his ears in debt to some land company, scratched the soil with a hoe, planted an acre or so of corn and potatoes, shot a few deer, and then sat back helplessly to watch his horses and cattle run away and flood, frost, windstorm, and drought ruin his crop. Dietary deficiency diseases were common: goiters plagued the settlers about Pittsburgh, rickets and jaundice were common, complexions were pasty; fleas infested the cabins, flies bred in the refuse about the yard, mosquitoes spread an endemic malaria; skin diseases, respiratory diseases, cholera, and typhoid epidemics came and went with the seasons. Witches were blamed for illness by whites as well as Indians; the bloodletting, purgatives, and emetics of the few professional doctors were probably inferior to the folk remedies, many of them herbal recipes learned from the native inhabitants. There were almost no schools; a schoolteacher, when hired, was "hired at the lowest wages, and generally one who could get no other employment." A general spirit of apathy inhibited the construction of public works; "they built no bridges, and would leave a tree accidentally fallen across the road, to lie there until it rotted." In 1816 a traveler in the region "south and west of Meadville" (i.e., in the white settlements most nearly adjacent to Cornplanter's lands) recognized the area as blighted. "An almost total want of energy prevails. Many small farms, which had been cleared some years ago, including fruit trees of handsome growth, are completely deserted; and the solitary buildings, or the burnt spots where they stood, fill the passenger with melancholy reflections. Even the improvements of former years, now occupied, are retrogressive. The chief part of the remaining inhabitants reminded us of exiles; and if they escape the ravages of famine, they must be nearly estranged to the common comforts of civilized life. . . . [The] road, indeed, only deserves the name of a track. It is little used and less repaired. . . . To increase the measure of disaster, provisions of every kind are scarce. . . ."[51]

Thus, although a Seneca Indian might still not see a white man more often than once or twice a week, after 1797 he was no longer able simply to withdraw into his own country and there, sheltered behind a wall of forests, ignore these contemptuous, quarrelsome, pushing people. For now the reservations were little islands in a slowly rising sea of white men—islands, indeed, lying so low in the flood that they were constantly awash. And, as the Indians could readily observe, many of the frontier whites were as demoralized as the natives on their reservations. There was little to emulate, even in technology, in the most immediately accessible examples of white culture.

The reasons for the difficulties of the early white settlers in the Seneca country were partly technological and partly administrative. The central technological problem seems to have been that the available cereal grains, particularly wheat, were not yet adapted to the short, cool summers and harsh winters of the regions chosen for initial settlement. The importation of non-adapted cereal strains, together with the inadequacy of the roads and an insufficiency of agricultural equipment, made the establishment of a substantial family farm a precarious enterprise. The administrative problems grew from an inefficient and often corrupt mingling of governmental and financial interests in the development of the region. The pyramid of debt, from government down to the individual settler, in effect reduced the philosophy of settlement from a capital investment program to a vast real estate promotional scheme. Because the disorganized character of the surrounding white settlements encouraged a somewhat negative Seneca response to white civilization, it is worth examining in some detail the process by which the white communities too were being made into wilderness slums.

The exploitation of the area was not conducted on an impromptu plan. It was organized and reorganized, by government first and by land companies second, each taking opportunity to lay down conditions and to take its profit. By the time the common "pioneer" himself arrived, the land had been explored, bought from the Indians, garrisoned, pacified, partially surveyed, mapped, and picked over by land companies, public officials, and private speculators seeking the most probable localities for quick profit.

Three separate regions in New York and Pennsylvania, each with its own set of Indian communities and its own topographical and climatic features, were chosen for initial development. The regions were the lush and gently rolling lower valley of the Genesee River, the flat, cold, and forested shorelands bordering on lakes Erie and Ontario and hinging on the so-called "Niagara frontier," and the mountainous and heavily forested upper Allegheny. On the Genesee were the little Seneca reserves, from Canawaugus on the north to Caneadea on the south, strung like pearls on a string, and soon to be snatched away forever. On or near the lake shore were the Cattaraugus, Buffalo Creek, Tuscarora, and Tonawanda reservations. And southward on the Allegheny was Cornplanter's band. The Genesee was the most immediate target of exploitation, for Sullivan's army and the early settlers of the Phelps and Gorham purchase had brought home bright tales of its hardwood-forested uplands, proud in oak, ash, and elm, its fertile meadows, its rich supplies of limestone. Especially famous were the Genesee flats, where the Seneca themselves had for many years concentrated their villages and where the soil was "a black, vegetable mould [overlying] a deep stratum, formed by the finer particles of loam, washed from the hills surrounding the headwaters of its tributaries, and floated down and deposited, by the river. . . ." The Genesee headwaters, however, were a harsher, colder land of steep hills, shale soil, and conifer forests.[52] Similarly severe was the Allegheny country to the south and west. But in both these regions were many fertile bottom-lands and many stands of fine hardwood and pine timber; and the Allegheny, besides, was a navigable stream and therefore a potential artery of commerce and travel. The Niagara frontier was a strategic site for commerce, being situated at the crossroads of the lake traffic and of the international ferry.

Pennsylvania's problems came immediately to the surface. By act of March 12, 1783 (while the country was still in a fervor of patriotic gratitude), the state reserved most of the land west of the Allegheny for the reimbursement of the long-unpaid officers and men of the Pennsylvania line. This action was taken before the Iroquois title was quieted at Fort Standix. The southern part of this reserved tract, the "depreciation lands," were to be sold for the now depreciated currency with which the Continental troops had been paid, thus at once rewarding the soldiers and stabilizing the currency; while the northern part of the tract, the "donation lands," were to be given away by lottery to officers and men according to rank and service. When few veterans took advantage of their opportunities to settle the wilderness parts of the state, an "actual settlement act" was passed, in the spring of 1792, opening the territory for sale. Any enterprising homesteader, veteran or not, could now acquire land: he could either pay for and have his four hundred acres of land surveyed first, then improve and settle, and finally complete title, or he could settle and improve first, and have his four hundred acres surveyed and complete title last.

There was a loophole in this law, however, that made it appeal to the enterprising speculator: he could buy for a few shillings apiece hundreds of warrants taken up by hundreds of straw men. Government officials leaped to share the spoils of one of the most profitable land grabs in the state's history. On the day the act was passed, the Surveyor General picked up eight hundred acres at a likely mill and town site on Beaver River; practical surveyors, who had explored the western lands and knew the best locations, snapped up large tracts and then resold them to Dutch bankers who, in order to avoid the law prohibiting aliens from holding lands, assigned the warrants to cooperative citizens; and the Comptroller General of the commonwealth became the president of the board of managers of the Pennsylvania Population Company, whose members included General Irvine, the surveyor and manorial neighbor of Cornplanter, George Mead, another neighbor at Cussawago on French Creek, Aaron Burr, and various other prominent men. Between 1792 and 1794, when the assembly plugged the loophole by prohibiting warrants except on the basis of prior settlement and improvement, the Pennsylvania Population Company acquired in the neighborhood of 450,000 acres, engrossing nearly the whole of the Lake Erie region west of the upper Allegheny, and the Holland Land Company engrossed about 1,000,000 acres there and to the east of the river. These two companies and a few private speculators thus managed to seize a middleman's title to nearly the whole of northwestern Pennsylvania.[53]

The consequences of speculative investment in the Pennsylvania public lands were in the long run disastrous for the region. Although the land companies cut timber, opened roads, laid out towns, built houses to be sold or even given to settlers, erected gristmills and sawmills, and opened stores where food and hardware could be bought on extended credit, they failed. They were unable, in part because of the roughness of the land and in part because of the independence of the frontiersmen, who did not like to owe money to eastern financiers, to improve and settle their lands within the legal limit of two years after the ending of the Indian Wars. The assembly, after 1799 dominated by western delegates who favored the small farmer, declared the land company claims void and encouraged independent settlement and improvement. The land companies brought suit, shots were fired, the commonwealth became embroiled in a state's rights controversy in the United States Supreme Court. The companies continued to organize settlement, but for years no settler knew whether his title was good. In the opinion of one historian of the period, "The uncertainty of title which so long prevailed in western Pennsylvania . . . seriously delayed the full and natural development of that region since the intelligent and most desirable type of settler passed by it to Ohio and northwestern New York where his title would be good."[54]

In western New York, in contrast to their situation in Pennsylvania, the land companies—particularly the Holland Land Company—were in control from the first. Land companies, not the state, had purchased the land directly from the Indians; land companies conducted the surveys of the reservations, of the towns, of the country estates. Land companies sold or leased the lands to the farmers. The Holland Land Company did not maintain so elaborate an organization as the Pennsylvania Population Company, finding it less necessary to improve the land in order to sell tracts in the fertile northern valley of the Genesee, where old Indian towns, clear fields and meadows, and well-worn trails made the task of development less severe, or in the city of Buffalo, which the Company laid out into lots. In the Phelps and Gorham purchase, however, attempts were even made to draw settlers by building good roads, hotels, and racecourses.[55] And again, as in Pennsylvania, the land companies were able to make use of public officials. General Israel Chapin, Sr., for instance, the federal Indian agent from 1792 until shortly before his death in 1796, was an old army friend of Oliver Phelps, the purchaser of the Seneca lands east of the Genesee. Both men were from Massachusetts. After the purchase in 1788, Chapin became the paid agent for the Phelps and Gorham Land Company and its business partner in land dealings in the new purchase. Phelps was attentive to Washington's tastes (ordering for instance a yoke of beef for his table) and it was very likely on Phelps's and Gorham's recommendation, directly or indirectly, that Chapin, and later his son, became an Indian agent. (Robert Morris, the Pennsylvania financier, also used his influence later to secure Chapin's son's appointment to that post.) Even after his appointment as Indian agent, Chapin was still on

Phelps's payroll, taking instructions in such duties as the care of the financier's horses and receiving promises of proper reward. A similarly equivocal relationship is apparent in the arrangement of the treaty at Big Tree, which we have already discussed: the United States commissioner, by law appointed to supervise that transaction in order to ensure fair and honorable dealings to the Indians, was none other than Jeremiah Wadsworth, perhaps the largest land speculator in the Genesee Valley. The white negotiators stayed in the house of William Wadsworth, Jeremiah's cousin and the agent in charge of selling off the elder Wadsworth's Genesee lands. Israel Chapin, Jr., was of course present as Indian agent (and it was Chapin who had notified the secretary of war, after Thomas Morris had promised bribes to the Seneca chiefs at Buffalo Creek, that the Seneca had offered to sell a part of their lands to Robert Morris). And Commissioner Wadsworth himself advised Thomas Morris on the strategy by which the Seneca were to be brought to terms, threatening that if young Morris didn't take his advice, he would leave the grounds and go home.[56]

And in New York, again as in Pennsylvania, but more slowly, agrarian discontent developed as farmers began to resent their lingering obligations to impersonal absentee landlords. Eventually rumors circulated that titles procured from the land companies were worthless, farmers refused to pay for their lands, law suits multiplied, there was gunfire. In New York, however, when the mobs formed, the government supported the land companies by calling out the militia. But nonetheless, by 1835 only about half of the Big Tree purchase had been sold off.[57]

Frequently one great company, rather than waiting for years to dispose of its land lot by lot, would sell it off to lesser companies in parcels of tens or hundreds of thousands of acres, and these companies in turn would sell to still smaller companies and to private speculators, so that by the time the theoretically intended ultimate purchaser, the small emigrant farmer, was reached, the price of the land had increased beyond his capacity to pay.[58] Actual settlement, surprisingly hesitant everywhere, was very slow in the southern Genesee and the upper Allegheny country, which remained virtually a wilderness while regions far to the westward were becoming agriculturally prosperous and even urbanized. A few taverns, some land company storehouses, and a half a dozen small and isolated settlements, whose nucleus usually was an extended family consisting of a father, his sons, and their wives and children,[59] were scattered here and there in the Allegheny country after 1794; but it was fully twenty years before settlement in substantial numbers, or even extensive lumbering, began. The watershed of the upper Allegheny and the upper Genesee was a backwater. In 1801 three Quaker visitors to the Allegany Seneca remarked, "It is not probable these Indians will have any white settlers near them soon. In all directions excepting south, we believe none are nearer than sixty miles and very few so near, and south of them there is about twenty miles of barren ridges not inviting to settlers."[60]

The land companies were placed in a desperate situation by the failure of settlers to take up the lands. Various remedial schemes were attempted: long-term credit was offered, in some cases up to fifteen years, in others indefinitely, provided taxes were paid; high-pressure advertising was circulated by the public press in handbills and at town meetings in depressed areas farther east; the transport of whole groups to planned communities was offered; great manorial estates were created (particularly by the Wadsworths on the Genesee) on which lands could be leased by tenant farmers. But none of these schemes was fully successful along the Allegheny. The cold, windy climate and the soil conspired against the raising of wheat at most locations (except those already preempted by the Seneca); the spring floods wrecked the mills, and the cutting of the timber lowered the water level and stranded them; great towns failed to materialize at strategic harbors, fords, and highway intersections. The early settlers who had enough money moved quickly on to better land in the west; the poor, trapped by debt and despair, clung to their cabins in the woods until they starved or became sick; the wise avoided the region entirely. Hundreds of thousands of acres in the central and southern portions of the tracts remained largely unsettled for generations.[61]

Thus the difficulties of the early settlers in the Seneca country were not merely the first-year sufferings of pioneers in a new land. To the inevitable hardships and disappointments of frontier life had been added the misery of irredeemable poverty. It is not surprising, therefore, that across this dark and barren country a wave of religious enthusiasm began to swell, stretching in a wide arc from the hillsides of New England, across the lonely marches of the land company tracts, down into the back country of the south. New sects sprang up;

and old denominations, their members congregating in great camp meetings, poured their sorrows into the first Great Revival.

The most lurid events of the revival occurred outside the immediate environs of the upper Allegheny region, however. In the Genesee Valley and about the Finger Lakes, where the settlers were New England Congregationalists, the wave struck in 1799–1800; the waters of faith did not flood until 1802 in western Pennsylvania south and west of Pittsburgh, where Lutherans and Presbyterians predominated. The upper Allegheny was a mission area late to be served by the joint efforts of the Presbyterians and Congregationalists, who had divided the region between them as far as church organization was concerned but who cooperated in missionary enterprise. Not until 1801 was the Presbytery of Erie organized to serve the needs of the people who lived north and west of the Ohio and the Allegheny. The first missionary is said to have reached Cattaraugus County in 1810. Thus, in religion as in economy, the Allegheny was a depressed area.[62]

But throughout the adjacent regions, in the period 1798 to 1802, and of course later, white men in hundreds communed with God. These orgies of communion laid the seed, especially in the "burned-over district" of western New York, for that territory's traditional hospitality to sectarianism, spiritualism, and millennarianism. For this was to be the country of Joseph Smith and the golden tablets of Mormon; of Jemina Wilkinson, the reincarnation of Christ; of the Millerites and the end of the world; of the Shakers at Sodus Bay; and of many other exotic flowers of religious enthusiasm that grew in the hearts of dour and drunken men. It was in these times that the camp meeting was invented, where hundreds of persons of all ages would gather over a period of several days to worship and experience religious ecstasy. Self-appointed evangelists rode the circuits of the forest, striving to save sinners from hell.

Events at these camp meetings generally followed a predictable course. An evangelistic preacher would speak vividly of hellfire and damnation. Hundreds of people were quickly seized with hysterical symptoms. A contemporary observer described the scene: "when a person begins to be affected, he generally sinks down in the place where he stood, and is for a few minutes overwhelmed in tears; he then makes a weeping noise—some person near lays hold of him—he shrieks aloud—and discovers a desire to be on his back—in this he is indulged—and a friend sits down and supports the head of the person in his lap. Every tear now leaves his eye and he shouts aloud for about 20 minutes. Meanwhile the features of his face are calm and regular. His voice becomes more and more feeble for about 20 minutes more. By this time he is speechless and motionless, and lies quiet perhaps an hour. During this time his pulse is rather lower than the usual state,—the extremities are cold, the skin fresh and clear, the features of the face full, the eyes closed, but not so closed as in sleep. Speech and motion return in the same gradual manner; the features become more full than before. Pleasure paints the countenance as peace comes to the soul, and when faith is obtained the person rises up, and with most heavenly countenance shouts—'Glory to God.' This ecstasy abates in about a quarter of an hour and the person is generally led away by a friend to his tent. Calm, mild, sedate pleasure marks the countenance for several days; and those who have been often exercised in this pleasing manner, show sweet mixture of love and joy which no tongue or pen can describe." Some victims suffered from "the jerks," in which the whole body was seized with violent contortions. Some danced for hours, others ran, some turned cartwheels endlessly. In Kentucky groups of people ran about on all fours, barking, snarling, and baring their teeth like dogs.

· *The Friendly People* ·

IN THE LAST YEARS of the eighteenth century the official policy of the United States was to confine the Indian tribes to small reservations around their villages and there to promote their civilization. It was not until years later that the removal policy, rationalized by the popular theory that Indians were savages incapable of civilization, came into official sway in the hands of the frontier politicians like Andrew Jackson and his secretary of war, Lewis Cass.

The policy of civilizing the Indian natives was embedded in a solid matrix of treaties. For the Iroquois the controlling treaties were, of course, Fort Stanwix (1784), Fort Harmar (1789), Canandaigua (1794), the Treaty of Greenville (1795), and Big Tree (1797). These agreements recognized the political sovereignty of the United States over the Indian tribes, defined the legal boundaries of the Indian communities, specified the annuity payments, and guaranteed to the

Indians certain services and immunities and to the United States certain privileges. The Iroquois boundaries we have already discussed. Their annuities amounted to: $4,500 per annum forever, payable to all the New York Iroquois by the United States under the Treaty of Canandaigua; about $8,000 paid by the State of New York to the Oneida, Onondaga, and Cayuga for lands purchased; the interest from $100,000 per annum forever, payable to the Seneca under the Treaty of Big Tree; special annuities for the Oneida and their associates who had been loyal to the United States during the Revolution; and the personal annuities of Cornplanter, Red Jacket, Farmer's Brother, and other chiefs and captains. Services guaranteed to the Indians included a superintendent (and his agents) appointed by the president of the United States, authorized to disburse annuities and to transmit Indian requests and complaints to the federal establishment. Indians were free to pass the border between the United States and Canada without such hindrance as customs duties on personal baggage. The United States reserved the right to build certain roads, to pass freely through Indian lands, and to make free use of rivers, harbors, and emergency landing places.[63] Supporting and carrying into effect these treaties were various acts of Congress and administrative regulations. Trade with the Indians was controlled by a system of licenses with heavy penalties for infractions. Land sales were to be made only at public treaties held "under the Authority of the United States." Equal protection of the criminal law was extended over both Indians and whites, even in Indian territory.[64]

The civilization policy was implicit in the eighteenth century's doctrine of progress, which regarded it as natural that, as Secretary of War Henry Knox put it in 1789, every people should pursue the same path in "the process of society from the barbarous ages to its present degree of perfection." Knox in his early formulations suggested that it was important to introduce "a love for exclusive property" as "a happy commencement of the business" of civilizing the Indians. Knox also recommended the appointment of missionaries as resident teachers of both the academic and domestic arts, and the provision of model farms, livestock, and other capital goods. His plan was endorsed by Washington and other prominent figures.[65] A few years later Timothy Pickering also offered a "plan" to Washington for introducing the arts of husbandry among the Indians instead of taking away a few Indian youths for education among white men.[66] This practice, common among the French and the British, was now almost universally regarded as bad by the Americans because the return of the native to his village so frequently produced only "the most bitter mortification. He is neither a white man nor an Indian" and met with disdain in both societies. Such a marginal man "will take refuge from their contempt in the inebriating draught; and when this becomes habitual, he will be guarded from no vice, and secure from no crime. His downward progress will be rapid, and his death premature."[67] Washington was so well impressed by Pickering's plan that he offered him the post of Superintendent of the Six Nations; and Pickering did later become secretary of state and the negotiator of the Canandaigua Treaty. The Federalists' thinking in these matters was doubtless also stimulated by the exchange of views between Cornplanter and Washington in 1790 and 1791. Cornplanter, it will be recalled, had asked for a technical aid program, and Washington in reply had promised that the United States would teach the Indians how to keep domestic animals and to ll ("the only Business which will add to your Numbers and Happiness") by sending "one or two sober Men to reside in your Nation," to maintain model farms and to serve as schoolmasters.[68]

This initial federal effort to "civilize" the Indians was not confined to the Iroquois; it extended to the southern Indians (e.g., the Creeks), who were encouraged by their agent Benjamin Hawkins to plow, fence, spin, weave, and raise cattle and hogs.[69] The funds came from federal annuities intended for "purchasing for them clothing, domestic animals, and implements of husbandry, and for encouraging useful artificers to reside in their villages."[70] But in the Iroquois case the federal program was not notably successful: a large proportion of the very limited funds went for consumer goods (food, ornaments, powder and lead, dry goods, and miscellaneous household hardware). Each of the Iroquois villages was in 1792 to be given one set of carpenter's tools. A schoolmaster was to be supplied the Oneida and a smith installed with them and one on the Genesee.[71] But even with the supplemental funds afforded by other treaties, as at Canandaigua in 1794, the amounts of money and of enthusiastic personnel were too small to make a successful program. The federal establishment therefore turned to religious denominations for assistance, for here were groups of American citizens already dedicated to the improvement, either spiritual or temporal, and sometimes both, of their Indian brethren.

The one organization that responded with an active interest in the Seneca was the Philadelphia Yearly Meeting of the Society of Friends. The Pennsylvania Quakers had for a hundred years, since the founding of the commonwealth, advocated a policy of peace and friendship toward the American Indians, and during the French and Indian Wars had exerted themselves (not always wisely) to see justice done the Delaware, whose hostility they laid to past iniquities (committed, as they argued, by the Quakers' political competitors) in land transactions.[72] The Friends had received Cornplanter and his associates with warm professions of love on their visits to Philadelphia after the Revolution, and members of the Society's "Meeting for Sufferings" had attended the treaty at Newtown in 1791, the negotiations at Sandusky in 1793, and the Canandaigua Treaty in 1794 as observers interested in guarding the interests of the natives. In November 1795 a "committee . . . for the civilization & real welfare of the Indian natives" was appointed by the Philadelphia Yearly Meeting. This Indian committee immediately consulted with Timothy Pickering, the secretary of state, and (probably with his advice) formulated a plan of action. Pickering then in February 1796, wrote officially to the Six Nations, describing and recommending the Quaker plan to introduce plow agriculture and animal husbandry among them. He also wrote to Jasper Parrish, their erstwhile captive and trusted interpreter, and to Israel Chapin, Jr., their agent, asking that they support "the plan" by recommending it heartily to the Indians when their advice was asked. He pointed out that the Friends had no ulterior motive beyond "the happiness of their fellowmen." They did not intend to proselytize nor to teach "peculiar doctrines"; nor did they or the agents whom they would employ expect any economic gain for themselves and would in fact expect to operate at a loss, since the money would be raised by themselves and not by the government. Their plan, in essence, was simply "to introduce among them . . . the most necessary arts of civil life . . . useful practices: to instruct the Indians in husbandry & the plain mechanical arts & manufactures directly connected with it. This is the beginning of the right end, and if so much can be accomplished, their further improvement will follow, of course."[73]

"The plan" went forward with remarkable dispatch. In April a letter was received from the Stockbridge Indians, signed by Hendrick Aupaumut, in response to the Quaker offer of aid. The Stockbridge (a band of Mahican domiciled with the Oneida) had conferred and "were willing to unite in endeavours towards their improvement." They asked for a number of tools and other necessaries. In June 1796, seven Quakers set out for the Oneida and Stockbridge, preceded by a shipment of tools. In June also the Onondaga replied to the Quaker offer of farmers, teachers, blacksmiths, and carpenters with an enthusiastic note of acceptance.[74] Three months later the committee sent a shipment of tools to Benjamin Hawkins to aid him in his program with the Creeks, and shortly thereafter tools were being sent to the Cherokee, Chickasaw, Shawnee, Wyandot, Delaware, Potawatomi, Ottawa, Chippewa, and Miami to the west, the Cherokee, Chickasaw, and Choctaw to the south, and the Onondaga, Cayuga, and Oneida to the north. By the beginning of 1797 the Indian committee had inaugurated technical aid to a large proportion of the Indians of the eastern United States.

In March 1797, the committee voted "to assist and encourage any suitable friends who may feel their mind drawn to go into this country . . . of the Seneca Nation of Indians . . . for the purpose of instructing them." A year later, in March 1798, three young men— Halliday Jackson, Joel Swayne, and Henry Simmons (who had already lived among the Oneida and Stockbridge)—volunteered to "spend some time" among the Seneca. And in May 1798, the Seneca mission, including the three young volunteers and two older friends, John Pierce and Joshua Sharpless, set out on their trip to the Allegany Seneca. In 1799 the Seneca mission was expanded to include the Cattaraugus band. And a year later still, in 1800, the Oneida having learned sufficiently in the mechanical arts to justify the experiment, the Oneida mission was closed in order to "make tryall" of Indian abilities to proceed alone. Thereafter the Seneca mission, with headquarters on the Allegheny River, was the focus of the Philadelphia Yearly Meeting's efforts to civilize the Indians.[75]

The five Quakers reached Cornplanter's village of Jenuchshadago ("Burnt House") on May 17, 1798. They found that a large part of the Allegany Seneca, about four hundred hungry people in all, were now settled here, many of them having in the last year or two deserted the upper settlement at Genesinguhta nine miles up stream, apparently as a result of severe floods that destroyed their corn. The visitors from Philadelphia had come at a time poorly calculated to yield them the most favorable image of the Seneca. Their first contact was with a band of drunken Indians at the land company store at Warren. This was the season when the men could not hunt or fish and when last year's food was almost exhausted; thus they saw no more than a few pounds of venison in weeks and were unable to buy meat at all. Cornplanter explained that last year's spring flood and early frost had damaged their corn harvest and left them now in near famine. The women were now very busy planting the fields, "while the men were standing in companies sporting themselves with their bows and arrows and other trifling amusements."

The Quakers first explained to the Seneca the purpose of their visit. At a public council convened the day after their arrival, Cornplanter introduced them to his people and apologized for their poverty and the primitiveness of their houses. The Quakers read the letters from the Philadelphia Yearly Meeting and from General Wilkinson at Pittsburgh, which served as their credentials. (Cornplanter's educated son Henry, fresh from school in Philadelphia, served on this occasion and henceforth as their faithful, if not too skillful, interpreter.) Then they got down to business, advising the Indians that they had left loving families and comfortable houses solely for the sake of improving the lot of the natives. They were come among them to teach "the works of the handy workman"[76] and not to secure any profit to themselves. The Indians were exhorted to "stillness & quietude and an attention to the Good Spirit in their own hearts." Finally, the Quakers, who were sophisticated in the theory of cultural progress, adroitly insinuated that the changes in way of life that they were urging on the Seneca were changes that their own ancestors had had to make in times past. They advised them to "guard against discouragements that might present in their looking forward towards a change in their manner of living, for we did not doubt but there might be many difficulties in their way, and their progress might be slow; yet there are accounts among the writings of the white people of a people who lived beyond the great waters in another island, who many years ago lived much like they do now, yet were by industry and care become very good farmers and mechanics of all kinds and from that people many of those fine leggings with the other striped and nice clothing they had on, came."

They told the Indians that plow-irons, hoes, axes, shovels, spades, and various carpenter's, mason's, and cooper's tools were on their way in a boat from Pittsburgh, and that the Quakers while they stayed would lend them out, and when they left would leave them with the Indians. And they concluded by stating their faith that the mission was pleasing in the sight of Him "whose regard is toward all the workmanship of his hands."

Cornplanter responded next day. After apologizing for the inadequacies of his son as an interpreter, he went on to give the views of the council, which had deliberated over the Quaker message:

Brothers, We take great pains to settle the proposals you made to us but we differ in opinions and we must take great pains to have everything complete—

Brothers, We suppose the reasons you came here was to help poor Indians some way or other, and you wish the chiefs to tell their Warriors not to go on so bad as they have done, and you wish us to take up work like the white people.

Now Brothers some of our sober Men will take up work & do as you say, & if they do well then your young Men will stay longer; but some others will not mind what you say—

Brothers, We can't say a Word against you, it is the best way to call Quakers

Brothers, you never wished our lands, you never wished any part of our lands, therefore we are determined to try to learn your ways & these younger Men may stay here two years to try, by that time we shall know whether Morris will leave us any Land & whether he will pay us our money; for last Summer we sold our Land & we dont know yet whether we shall get what we reserved, or whether we shall get our Money; but by that time we shall know & then if they like it, & we like it your young Men may stay longer

Brothers, If your young Men stay here we want them to learn our children to read & write.

Brothers—Two of you are going home again, if they hear anything about our Land or our Money they must write to these young Men here & they must tell us, if we are like to be cheated.

Brothers—This is all I got to say at present.

The next day was "First Day" (Sunday), and the Friends held their own religious meeting. Several sober Indian men, including

Cornplanter, sat with them during their meditations, and Cornplanter, who was extremely anxious to make a good impression, again apologized to the Friends, this time because the Indians did not keep the Sabbath: "We are ignorant, & can't read & write, besides we are poor & have work & our Men are often out ahunting. . . ."

On Monday the twenty-first Cornplanter and the Friends paddled up the Allegheny to Genesinguhta, the abandoned town on the reservation proper, in order to seek out a suitable place for the Quakers to live and build their demonstration farm. The neighborhood of Jenuchshadago, while more convenient to the population, was disqualified because it was on the Grant. Quaker improvements there, such as the house and barn, would after they left have legally belonged to Cornplanter personally rather than to the Seneca tribe. The site they chose consisted of about 150 acres of fertile flats, now much grown over with brush and covered with fallen timber; only three or four Indian families still remained. The Friends bought the cabin of an old Indian woman and her daughter for twenty dollars and moved in two days later with assurances to Cornplanter that they were not buying the land and would vacate it eventually, leaving the improvements to the Indians. The cabin that they secured was a typical Seneca house made of unchinked logs, twenty feet long by fourteen wide, with a shed before the door and a bark roof. Two rows of bunks and shelves extended along the sides; deerskins with the hair on served as mattresses. No boundaries were stated for the Quaker tract; Cornplanter told them that they were free to go anywhere and to hunt, fish, and cut timber at will. By the end of the week the Friends were physically established.

On Monday, May 28, the Quakers at their own request met the Indians in a second council at Cornplanter's. This time, their planting done, the women were present, including five or six of the important "respectable old women." After expressing their gratification that they and the Indians "seem to agree like Brothers, having but one mind in everything we do," the Friends expressed the hope that "some of your sober young men will settle by ours, and fence off Lots, as they see our Young Men fence off theirs; and our young Men will be willing to instruct & assist them a little about working their lots." If the community raised substantial quantities of corn and wheat this summer, the Quakers would supply half the money to build a gristmill, and the Indians could supply the other half out of their annuities. The Quakers also announced a four-year plan of individual cash awards to encourage men and women to learn the "works of the handy workman":

> Brothers, We will give to every Indian Man, living on this river, who shall raise 25 Bushel of Wheat or Rye in one year, on his own land, not worked by white people, the sum of two Dollars.
>
> 2. For every 50 Bushel of Indian Corn raised by any one Indian Man, in like manner aforesaid the sum of two Dollars.
>
> 3. For every 50 Bushel of Potatoes raised by any one Indian Man, in like manner aforesaid, the sum of two Dollars.
>
> 4. For every 2 Tons of Hay raised as aforesaid, and put into a stack or Barn, not being mown or drawn in by white people, the sum of two Dollars.
>
> 5. For every 12 yards of linen Cloth, made by any Indian woman, out of flax raised on her own, or her husbands land, & spun in her own house, the sum of two Dollars to be paid to the Woman.
>
> 6. For every 12 yards of woolen Cloth, or linsey made by any Indian woman, out of the wool of her own, or her husband's sheep, & Spun in her own house the sum of two Dollars, to be paid to the Woman.

A little added pressure toward sobriety was applied by denying an award to any person who had been "intoxicated with strong drink" at any time during the preceding six months.

The overt reaction of the town council was divided. Some, "particularly the women," appeared, in the Quaker phrase, "solid"—that is to say, gravely thoughtful and seriously concerned. But by far the larger number seemed to regard the proposals with levity. They retired to hold a private discussion; on their return an hour later Cornplanter spoke the group sentiments. These sentiments were, in effect, a very conditional agreement to the Quaker suggestions. The Friends themselves were personally acceptable. They had come a long way to help the poor Indians, who had been cheated out of their lands, "to become as white people." But although the consensus was that "we will try to learn your way," the community was not confident of success. For one thing they weren't sure their annuity monies would yield the required four hundred dollars for the gristmill, an essential ingredient in the plan. Furthermore, there were "some bad people" and some irresponsible young warriors among the Seneca, and indeed a certain generalized bitterness over being cheated out of their lands, which distracted their attention, "makes us bad, and our minds uneasy" and unable to "think upon the good Spirit" as they might if they were "rich people & had plenty of everything." The fact that Cornplanter had allowed the Seneca to be cheated out of their lands now made many of the young men scornful of his advice to adopt white customs: "some of my warriors wont mind what I say to them, but will have their own way, because they know I have been often cheated by the white people. If I had never been cheated, then my warriors would believe me, & mind what I say to them, but now they wont mind." And finally, the lack of tools, such as hoes and axes, and the ever-present need for the men to continue to hunt and therefore to conserve part of their money for repairing and replacing the guns, would slow down the process.

The Quakers responded to these reluctant excuses with the firm statement of two rational principles: first, that it was simply "unreasonable" (i.e., inefficient) to "suffer their women to work all day in the fields & woods with the hoes & axes, whilst the Men & Boys were at the same time playing with their bows & arrows"; and second, that the Good Spirit had endowed the Seneca with faculties and opportunities precisely equal to those of their white brethren. Thus "the great disparity, which they so frequently spoke of between them & the white people, with regard to plenty & poverty was the natural result of the different plans pursued in the obtaining the blessings of this life, and that, as their ground was equally good, with that possessed by the white people, it would also be equally productive, if the same Industry & methods of farming were pursued."[77]

A few days later the boat from Pittsburgh arrived, carrying the long-awaited hundred and twenty pounds of bacon and the plows, saws, and other equipment, and the Quakers were able to begin the demonstration farm. The older guides and mentors, Joshua Sharpless and John Pierce, departed on June 7. The three young Friends hurriedly plowed and fenced several fields, in the hope, although the season for planting corn was nearly past, to get in some kind of crop for subsistence during the winter. They were constantly visited by Indians "in great Numbers" from the lower settlement at Jenuchshadago and from the upper settlement at Cold Spring. Again the women, as they had been at the councils, seemed particularly interested. The Indians were visibly impressed at the ease with which the plow, in comparison with the hoe, prepared the ground for seed. A lively barter developed, the natives supplying the Quakers with venison, fish, strawberries, and other foods, and the Friends distributing needles, thread, scissors, combs, spectacles, and bandanna handkerchiefs. A number of Indians borrowed the carpenter's tools and even some few the farming equipment. The Quakers instructed the men in the use of the woodworking utensils. "Several of them constructed in the course of the summer, much better houses than they had been accustomed to, and manifested a considerable share of ingenuity in the use of carpenter's tools." Nor were all the men abashed by farm work. While the white men were in the fields, "the Indians would frequently come about them and sometimes take hold of their tools and work a little—some of the lads were pleased with driving the horses." Early in the fall the Friends completed their own house and stable. The house was "a comfortable two Story hewed House 18 feet by 22 Covered with White pine Shingles & Cellared underneath, with a chimney composed of Stone & clay." It was larger than any of the Indian dwellings, and when they moved in, on October 6, "the Heathen flocked about us" and expressed great admiration for the dwelling.

That winter Henry Simmons, the one of the three who had had previous experience in establishing an Indian school at Oneida, moved into the village at Jenuchshadago and set up a school for Indian children, as Cornplanter had asked. The school was only a partial success: at one time or another "nearly twenty children attended, and made some progress in learning to spell and read; but as their parents had little control over them, they were very irregular in their attendance, and no great progress in learning was made."

In general, it would seem, the responses of the Allegany Seneca was friendly. Nowhere do the diaries of the Friends record an instance of hostility, verbal or physical; the only negative reactions would seem to have been the somewhat defensive "levity" and "indifference" reported at councils. There seems to have been very determined support from the community's elite: Cornplanter and his family, who not only provided official backing but practical assistance (Cornplanter's wife sold the Friends milk and butter); the teetotaler chief who lived near them at Genesinguhta; and the clan matrons. The women, in general, seem to have taken their message to heart most deeply; only a few men tried their hand at carpentry and farm work. The annual cycle of village activities proceeded undisturbed; the men went out on summer hunts in July and August, then the women harvested their corn and other vegetable products, and in December, after the first snows, nearly the whole population went off to the hunting grounds. "Game was now plentiful. Some of their best hunters killed near one hundred deer, and some even more than that number; taking off the skins and leaving much of the meat scattered about in the woods." The women as usual packed the venison on their backs, through snow and ice, across hill and dale from where it was killed to the camps. And the ritual cycle continued unchanged as well. The False Faces had made their rounds in the spring when they arrived; the Green Corn was celebrated late in the summer, and Midwinter about the end of January.

Perhaps the most significant change was the reduction of drinking. Whiskey had been constantly available at Cornplanter's mill from the millwright who sold it to obtain food and other necessities from the Indians. But Jackson remarked, "The use of whiskey and other strong drink . . . considerably decreased among the Indians, in the course of the . . . year [1798], and many of their chiefs seemed desirous of preventing its introduction in the village."[78] It was a good augury for the coming year.

· The Cruel Spring ·

CORNPLANTER'S TOWN had been peaceful and prosperous during the fall and winter of 1798; but, paradoxically, the success of the winter hunt turned the village into a little hell on earth in the following spring. Handsome Lake contributed to this denouement. Late in the fall, after the Harvest Festival, Handsome Lake with a party of hunters and their families had left the village and drifted down the Allegheny to hunt. They set up their first camp at the mouth of the Conewango Creek, near Warren, where the Holland Company had its store. Then they hunted on down the Allegheny, moving camp southward from time to time as the weather and the game demanded, probably returning to the village for the Midwinter Festival, but going back to their growing cache of skins and dried meat. Probably about the middle of April the men left their wives and children and went on to Pittsburgh, where they bartered the skins, furs, and fresh and dried meat for various goods, including several barrels of whiskey. Then they lashed their canoes together into a raft and began the long journey northward to Cornplanter's village. The men in the middle canoes, where the whiskey was stored, were free to drink, and they yelled and sang "like demented people." They picked up their wives and children at the rendezvous and pressed on, homeward bound, in roistering good spirits, and oblivious to the tensions that were developing in the village during their absence.[79]

While Handsome Lake and his fellow hunters were on their excursion down the river, tensions were building up rapidly at Cornplanter's Town, where Henry Simmons since November had been teaching Indian children to read and write English. (The other two Friends were busy at the farm, making and mending tools for the summer's work.) Simmons' presence precipitated a crystallization of opinion among both the conservatives and the progressives. He was teaching in the house of Cornplanter, where community meetings were held and where the major religious rituals were celebrated. And before his very door stood the wooden statue of Tarachiawagon, the Good Spirit, the symbol of the traditional way of life. His school was daily a challenge to the village to take sides for or against the white man's customs and ideas.

The dissatisfaction of the conservatives grew, and at last one Sunday morning in the beginning of February young Simmons was put to the test. A dozen chiefs and warriors demanded that Simmons tell them "how the World and things there in were Created at first." Simmons knew that this was a trial on whose outcome the success of the mission might rise or fall and "immediately apply'd [his] Heart with fervent breathings to the Lord for His Aid and support." Then he launched into an account of the Christian cosmogony, as revealed by "a certain good Book, Called the Holy Scriptures," which came miraculously close to recapitulating the Seneca cosmogony. He told "of the World being made (and of all the living creatures both in Water and on Land) by the great Spirit, and also the first man & Woman whom the great Spirit created of the dust of the Earth, and breathed into them the breath of Life, and they became living Souls, who had two Sons, one of them was a good Man, and the other Wicked who killed his brother, because he was more righteous than himself." Here Seneca listeners may well have been reminded of their own myths of the primordial Good Twin (Tarachiawagon)

(229)

and Evil Twin (Tawiskaron), whose contests for power (translated into the present by the Great World Rim Dweller, whom the False Faces personified, and the still immanent Tarachiawagon, whose statue stood in the village) formed the moral structure of their universe. Simmons then went on to ask them "if they did not see it so now a days; that wicked people envy'd good ones, and at times were ready to take their lives." This too must have struck an answering chord, for "wicked people"—i.e., witches—were indeed believed to be precisely those persons who in a communal society would kill for spite. But Simmon's remark had a further implication: it pinned the label of wickedness on precisely those who opposed, out of jealousy for his prominence and wealth, Cornplanter himself, the chief proponent of white civilization and its Quaker representatives. Then Simmons went on to point out that every person experienced the presence of the good spirit, "pricking at there Hearts, and telling them not to do so . . . when they thought of doing something which they ought not to do." When Cornplanter and others of the chiefs owned that it was so, he told them that "it is the Devil that urges us to do it" and the great spirit "that tells us not to do so." Finally, he pointed out that "there would be an advantage to their Children, in learning to read, as the great Spirit pleased to enlighten their understandings and make them Sensible of this good Book; as well as many other benefits which will be likely to attend their Children, thus being Educated."

The results were gratifying. His inquisitors told Simmons, after some consultation, that they all approved of what he had said and suggested that he mention it to the rest of the people, "as there was some of them, who were averse to their Children being educated." And after this meeting the school "was much Larger than before," counting now between twenty and thirty pupils, several of them grown men, "and some of them anxious to learn, though many of them very tedious."

A week later another trial was imposed on Simmons: a runner arrived in haste from Buffalo Creek, saying "that one of their little Girls had Dreamed, the Devil was in all white people alike, and that the Quakers were doing no good among them, but otherwise, and it was not right for their Children to learn to read and write." The little community of Jenuchshadago held a council on this dream ("many of them put great confidence in their Dreams"), and a number of the people were frightened. Cornplanter, however, made fun of the story, saying that "he did not believe it, and had got very tir'd of hearing so much noise about their Dreams," and urged Simmons not to be discouraged. Simmons promptly and publicly branded the report as the whispering of bad white people and the work of the Devil. But the Devil, after all, was powerless against the plans of the Great Spirit. He therefore denounced such dreams as "nonsensical" and declared that he would "continue teaching them that would come." "The School was a little smaller for one day. But afterward was Larger than it had been at all."

Simmons was a forthright and sincere man who, when on the subject of religion, was apt to speak both bluntly and with passion. Two weeks later he became thoroughly exasperated with the "Danceing Frolicks" that were carried on to the din of tortoise-shell rattles almost every other night. These parties were the occasion of social dances at which "Men and Boys" danced and shouted "in such agitation" on account of a forthcoming dance that he could scarcely teach them anything next day. Simmons burst unannounced into Cornplanter's house and announced to the chief and his astonished family and friends that these frolics were "the Devils works" and that before he would suffer such doings in *his* house, he would "burn it to Ashes & live in a cave." Next day, when Simmons went to teach school, he found that the schoolroom was occupied by a formal council, to which, at last, and "in much fear," Simmons was summoned. But the apprehensive Simmons was much relieved to discover that he had won again! Cornplanter informed him that they had been counciling on the subject of these frolics, and had concluded (although they did not all see alike) to quit them, "for some of them thought it must be wicked, because they had Learned it of white people, as well as that of drinking Rum and Whisky & getting Drunk, which they knew was Evil." But the dances at their religious ceremonies they intended to continue.

Then they asked Simmons some questions on race relations: first, whether he "thought it was right for Indians & White people, to mix in marrying"; and second, whether "Indians & White people, went together to the same place after Death." To the first question, Simmons said, "It might be right for some to marry so, but thought it would not be right for me." The Indians then told him "of one of their Women who had a child by a White Man who then resided at

Pittsburgh, and never came to see any thing about his Child they thought the Great Spirit intended that every Man should take care & maintain his own Children." To the second question, Simmons declared "there was but two places, a place for the Good, and a place for the Bad, of all Nations of People," and when asked "whether all would be of one Language, When there," he answered "yes." "They seemed satisfied." Simmons then stood up and made a long speech denouncing "the Evil of many customs prevailing among them particularly that of Dancing, & Shouting, in such an hideous manner." He broke down in tears in the course of his peroration.

To support Simmons in his evangelical role there now emerged an unexpected ally—a young Seneca man who had had, a few nights before when out in the woods hunting, a prophetic dream. This dream he recounted to the council:

He thought an Indian Struck him twice with a Knife, when he fell, and thought he must Die, but soon appear'd to asscend upwards, some distance along a narrow path, in which appeared many tracks of People all going up some barefoot and some not; at length he came to a house, and the Door opened, for him to go in, which he did, where he beheld the beautifulest Man sitting that ever he saw in his Life; Who invited him to sit down, which he endeavoured to do, but could not, and tried to stop, & to talk. So passed on, out at a Door opposite to the one he came in at, when out, he heard a great noise and after travilling some distance he came to another building, which had an uncommon Larg Door, Like a Barn Door, in which a man met him, who looked very dismal, he Mouth appear'd to move in different shapes, from one side of his Face to the other, this person conducted him in, where he beheld numbers like Indians who seemed to be Drunken & very noisy, and looked very Distressed, some of whom he knew, who had been Dead several years.

Amongst them was one very old white headed Woman, whom they told him was dying, and when she went, the World would go too. There appeared to be a fire place on the ground, although he could not discern any thing but smoke & Ashes, of which their hair on their heads were Covered, He soon found he could sit and talk fast enough in this House, which he could not do in the other.

The person who conducted him in, who appear'd to be their officinator, gave him some stuff to Drink, Like melted Pewter, which he told him he could not take, but he insisted he should, by telling him he could Drink Wiskey & get Drunk, and that was no worse to take than it, he then took it, which he thouht burnt him very much, He then took a chain & bound round him, he asked him what that was for, he told him to prevent him from going after Women & other Men's Wives, He then told him to go strike a Woman, who was sitting there, which he attempted to do, but could not for his arms were off, He told him the reason of his loosing his arms, was because he had often been guilty of striking his Wife, And if he would entirely quit that practice, he should have his arms made whole again, and if he forsook all other Evil practices which he had been guilty of, he should have a Home in the first House which he enter'd. He was then bid to go home, when he awoke he found himself Crying, & could not tell his Dream for some time after, for Crying, for he knew it was true, And confest in the Council that he had been guilty of all those actions above mentioned.

And he added that "he intended to try to do better than he had done, and intended to learn to read."

Simmons, who in this case was willing to endorse dreaming, declared that it was his opinion that "his Dream was true," and pointed out to the Council that the old gray-haired woman in the dream was "the Mother of Wickedness who was Dying from among them, and when she was dead, the Worldly Spirit would go too." Cornplanter added piously, "The Devil would Die, if they tryed to do good."

And thus matters stood in the spring of 1799. Cornplanter and his family and a growing number of other Indians ranged themselves behind the Quakers, promising to send "a number of Boys, & some girls" to school, where Simmons should "do by them, as I would by my own Son, . . . to learn them to work, and correct them as they deserved." This group dominated the councils. But there remained a stubborn band who refused to see and think as Cornplanter did, who believed that the Quakers were up to no good, and who resented his high-handed interference with the traditional Seneca way.[80]

Handsome Lake's band of drunken hunters burst into this arena of tense and sober social consideration about the middle of May. They were probably unaware of the changed atmosphere. Cornplanter and his friends had been babbling for years about farming, and education, and temperance, but most of them had not been taking it seriously. All that they had seen was last summer three young men building a

model farm nine miles north of the village. Handsome Lake's later
memory of the time was lurid:

> Now that the party is home the men revel in strong drink and are
> very quarrelsome. Because of this the families become frightened
> and move away for safety. So from many places in the bushlands
> camp fires send up their smoke.
>
> Now the drunken men run yelling through the village and there
> is no one there except the drunken men. Now they are beastlike
> and run about without clothing and all have weapons to injure
> those whom they meet.
>
> Now there are no doors in the houses for they have all been kicked
> off. So, also, there are no fires in the village and have not been for
> many days. Now the men full of strong drink have trodden in the
> fireplaces. They alone track there and there are no fires and their
> footprints are in all the fireplaces.
>
> Now the Dogs yelp and cry in all the houses for they are hungry.[81]

And Simmons' contemporary diary confirms Handsome Lake's account:

> About the middle of the same [May], the Indians returned from
> Pittsburgh, with a quantity of Wisky, which caused much Drunk-
> enness amongst them which lasted for several weeks and was the
> means of some of their deaths. One old Woman perrished out of
> doors in the night season with a bottle at her side; numbers of them
> going about the village from morning till evening and from eve-
> ning until morning, in a noisy distracted condition sometimes fight-
> ing each other, and entering into the houses in a detestable manner,
> ready to pull others out of their Beds, even in the very house where
> I lodged myself, in the dead of the night also.

Simmons was not one to permit such a situation to prolong itself.
He summoned his colleagues and the Seneca community, where (feeling himself to be "divinely favoured to communicate some pertinent
& juditious Counsel to them on various Subjects, to the furtherance
of Civilization and their future well being") he spoke out vehemently
against "the great Evil of Strong Drink and of the many abominations
it wrought in the Earth." The Seneca council deliberated for several
days before delivering its answer through Cornplanter's mouth. But
the answer, when it came, was a declaration of national reform:

They had made enquiry and conversed with each other about us, and said they could not find any fault with us, but found we were just and upright in all our ways of proceedings amongst them Etc. and that the fault and bad conduct lay on their own side, and wished us to be easy in our minds, for they would take our advice and try to learn to do better, they had concluded with a resolution not to suffer any more Wisky to be brought amongst them to sell, and had then Chosen two young men as petty Chiefs, to have some oversight of their people in the promotion of good among them, and that they intended to take up Work, and do as we said, would assist their Wives & Women on the Labour of the Field etc.

The village now began more seriously to undertake the work of reform, which had for so long been advocated by Cornplanter and others. The Indians who were settled near to the Friends' farm at Genesinguhta early in the spring set to work splitting rails and fencing in parcels of land. The Friends plowed a number of these lots for these enterprising Indian men. Other Indian males, unburdened with family responsibilities, hired themselves out to the Friends, "and seemed capable of doing as much in a day as the generality of white people." Meanwhile, at Jenuchshadago, the Indians had as early as March offered to assist the Friends in building a more commodious and convenient school, and in June the work of construction was well started at a site about half a mile from Cornplanter's house.[82]

Handsome Lake, however, did not participate in any of these activities. After the abrupt termination of the carousal in the middle of May, when the whiskey ran out and the council announced the temperance policy, he became sick and took to his bed in the cabin of his daughter and son-in-law. It may be that he was suffering from delirium tremens induced by the long carousal and by the inadequate nutrition that so often accompanies prolonged drinking (a particularly likely thing, since this was the hungry season anyway, with little to subsist upon but dried corn and traders' flour). Handsome Lake's mind was filled with thoughts of death. The spring performance of the Corn Planting Ceremony, and its attendant Death Feast, was conducted late in May, and the dead person whose soul was the subject of concern was none other than Cornplanter's daughter, who had died about February after a lingering six months' illness. Handsome Lake, whenever he could commandeer a bottle, sang the sacred songs to the dead, the *ohgiwe* cycle—a group of songs properly never sung except at the Feast of the Dead.

Witch fear began to preoccupy the village. It was suspected that Cornplanter's daughter had died by witchcraft at the hand of an old woman who had a reputation for poisoning the families of her enemies. Now she was said to be threatening the life of a baby just recently born into Cornplanter's household. This old woman even Simmons "took . . . to be a bad Woman." When Cornplanter heard of her threats, he ordered three of his sons to kill her. On June 13 they found her working in a field and in full view of the community stabbed her to death and buried her. A drunken Indian the same day had to be physically restrained by Simmons and another Indian from beating his wife "in a cruel manner" with his fists. The village was now considerably upset, and a chiefs' council was held to deliberate the slaying of the witch. The decision was that justice had been done and that in order to put away evil from the people, "those of familiar Spirits" must be driven out of the land.[83]

III

THE

RENAISSANCE

OF THE

IROQUOIS

PREACHING TO
REPENTANCE:

The First, or Apocalyptic, Gospel

WHEN THE MISERY OF POVERTY AND HUMILIATION IS COMBINED with a hope of moral and material salvation, the resulting mixture is explosive. Along the Allegheny, where the Quakers were busily stirring these ingredients, an emotional explosion did occur, and the sparks that ignited it were the prophetic visions of Handsome Lake. Beginning with his first vision in June 1799, and continuing for years thereafter, Cornplanter's brother articulated the dilemmas in which the Iroquois were trapped and prescribed both religious and secular solutions. His first preoccupation, expressed in his visions and teachings from 1799 to 1801, was with apocalyptic themes: sin, damnation, and the destruction of the world. He condemned in particular the drinking of whiskey and the practice of witchcraft and magic, and urged his people to confess their sins, abandon their evil ways, and achieve salvation before it was too late.

· *The First Vision of Handsome Lake* ·

IN THE SPRING OF 1799 Handsome Lake lay on his bunk, bound in sickness by "some strong power," and pondered the cause of his illness and the disturbed state of his people. He feared that he would soon die. Part of the time he was depressed and melancholy and thought that he must appear "evil and loathsome" in the eyes of the Creator. At other times, when he had whiskey, he would get drunk and in defiance of custom sing sacred songs. Then in remorse he would resolve never to touch alcohol again. At night, he would pray to see another day; with the dawn, he would feel gratitude to see the sunshine and hear the singing of the birds, and in proper Iroquois fashion would give thanks to the Creator. He brooded over the witches who had killed his niece. He was, in fact, suffering from the classic Iroquois bereavement syndrome compacted of depression, bitterness, and suspicion.

And then, on the morning of June 15, when the Strawberry Festival was due to be held, Handsome Lake had the first of the visions. Henry Simmons and Cornplanter were about half a mile from Cornplanter's cabin, Cornplanter directing some men in building him a new house, and Simmons and Joel Swayne busy constructing the schoolhouse, when a runner came to say that Handsome Lake was dying. This was not entirely unexpected news, for he had been "on the decline of Life for several years." Cornplanter left at once and found a number of people, including his nephew Blacksnake, assembled at Handsome Lake's cabin. The old man's daughter reported that they had been sitting outside the house in the shed, cleaning beans for the planting. The sick man had been within, alone. Suddenly through the open door they heard him exclaim, "Niio!"—"So be it!" Then they heard him rising in his bed, and heard him walking across the floor toward the door. Then the daughter saw her father, who was "but yellow skin and dried bones," coming out of doors. He tottered, and she rose quickly and caught him as he fell. They thought he was dead or dying, and so the husband ran off to fetch first Blacksnake and then Cornplanter, Handsome Lake's closest male relatives.

Blacksnake was the first to arrive. He asked, "Is he dead?" but no one answered, so he examined the body as it lay in the shed. There was no perceptible breathing or heartbeat, and the body was cool to the touch, so he went next door and got the neighbors to help him carry the body into the house, where they straightened it out. But in handling the body Blacksnake discovered a "warm spot" on the chest. Cornplanter, when he arrived, also found the spot of warmth. After about half an hour breathing began again, and then the pulse recovered, the "warm spot" spread, and at last, after two hours,

Handsome Lake's eyes opened and his lips began to move as if he wanted to speak. Blacksnake asked, "My uncle, are you feeling well?" And Handsome Lake answered, "Yes, I believe myself well."[1]

Then, after a pause, he began to describe his vision, which, as recorded at the time by the Quakers and remembered in oral tradition, was as follows. Handsome Lake heard his name called and left the house. Outside he saw three middle-aged men dressed in fine ceremonial clothes, with red paint on their faces and feathers in their bonnets, carrying bows and arrows in one hand and huckleberry bushes in the other. Handsome Lake collapsed from weakness, but the angels caught him and let him down gently. They told him they were sent by the Creator to visit Handsome Lake, whose constant thankfulness had earned him the right to help from his sickness.

After instructing him in the choice of medicine men (the appointed herbalists were his sister and her husband), he was told to join his kinfolk next day at the Strawberry Festival and report what the Creator had to say about how things should be on earth. He was to say that the Strawberry Festival should always be held and all the people must drink the berry juice. If he did not preach the message, he, like another reluctant prophet, would be buried in a hot, smoking place in the hollow between two hills visible across the river to the southeast. The message was contained in four "words" that summarized the evil practices of men about which the Creator was sad and angry. The four evil words are whiskey, witchcraft, love magic, and abortion-and-sterility medicine. People who are guilty of doing these things must admit their wrongdoing, repent, and never sin again, and a ritual was prescribed by which moderate sinners were to confess privately to Handsome Lake. The relatively innocent could confess in public; the most wicked of all were to confess alone to the Creator. The angels referred with approval to the recent execution of the witch but said a male witch still lived in the village. Handsome Lake himself they charged only with sometimes getting drunk and singing sacred songs while intoxicated; suffering, however, excused him. After threatening him that he must not drink even in private ("for the great Spirit knew not only what people was always doing but even their very thoughts"), the messengers left with the promise to return.

At the end of his narration Handsome Lake requested his brother Cornplanter "to Call his People in Council, and tell them what he had said to him, and if they had any Dried Berries amongst them, he wishes all in the Council might take if it was but one apiece." It was accordingly done, the same day, and "a large[r] number of them assembled with shorter notice than ever I had seen them before, men Women & children." Cornplanter related his brother's visions (for Handsome Lake was too weak to address the company), and Simmons and Swayne were present at Cornplanter's request and heard the vision recited through their interpreter, Henry. Simmons recorded the vision in his diary.

The relating of this vision produced a profound effect on its audience. Simmons, ever ready to empathize spiritually with others, observed that many of the Indians appeared to be "Solid and weighty in Spirit," and he "felt the love of God flowing powerfully amongst us." He was so moved that he was impelled to speak to the council. His message evidently was laudatory of the words of Handsome Lake, for it was well accepted and the prophet's sister came over after the meeting ended and thanked Simmons for what he had said to them.[2]

This was the beginning of the new religion.

· The Sky Journey ·

HANDSOME LAKE REMAINED in a generally poor state of health after the first revelation. He told Cornplanter that the three angels had said there was a fourth angel who had not been with them on their first visit but whom he would see subsequently. On the night of August 7 he dreamed that the fourth angel ("who appear'd like the Great Spirit") manifested himself and declared that he was now come to take him along, if he were willing, out of pity for his sufferings. Handsome Lake gave the angel no answer, but in the morning when he awoke he put on his best clothes and sent for Cornplanter. Cornplanter stayed with him through the day. About evening he fainted away briefly. On recovering his senses, he told Cornplanter that he must go, but not forever, for his people wanted him. He told his brother not to dress him for burial or to move him even if he appeared to be dead. After a little while he said that he was now going, but would return, and expected to see his son who had been dead several years and his brother's daughter who had been dead about seven months. And then he fell into a trance that lasted, he claimed later, about seven hours. His arms and legs were cold, his body warm, his breathing imperceptible.[3] During the trance Handsome Lake had the vision of the sky journey. Led by a guide who carried a bow and arrow and was dressed in sky-blue clothes, he traversed heaven and hell and was told the moral plan of the cosmos. This second vision would become the core of the new religion's theology.[4]

The course of the sky journey can be reconstructed from Henry Simmons' account, which was written down on August 10, two days later, probably from Handsome Lake's own lips (he "had then much recover'd of his sickness"), and from Parker's version of the later Code.[5] It began with Handsome Lake, the guide, and the other three messengers standing together on earth. "Suddenly as they looked, a road [the Milky Way] slowly descended from the south sky and came to where they were standing. Now thereupon he saw the . . . tracks of the human race going in one direction. The footprints [the individual stars] were all different sizes from small to great. Now moreover a more brilliant light than the light of earth appeared." This road, which they soon were treading themselves, was the path by which human souls ascended into the afterworld. On it could be observed, in various situations, many different types of people striving heavenward, and from its vantage point a vast panorama of the human scene could be observed below.

The vision took the form of a series of discrete visual scenes, upon each of which the guide made a moral commentary, rather like a lecturer running through a set of colored slides. The tour thus merely provided a rationale for the presentation of loosely connected thoughts. The tour began with a miscellany of images. They saw a fat woman, unable to stand; she represented the sin of stinginess and preoccupation with material things. They saw a large group of people divided into three sections, one large, one middle-sized, and one small; they represented, respectively, the unrepentent, the lukewarm, and the true believers in Handsome Lake's message. They saw a jail, and within it a pair of handcuffs, a whip, and a hangman's rope; this represented the false belief of some that the laws of the white man were better than the teachings of *Gaiwiio*. They saw a church with a spire and a path leading in, but no door or window ("the house was hot") and heard a great noise of wailing and crying; this illustrated the point that it was difficult for Indians to accept the confining discipline of Christianity. They saw two great drops of liquid hanging in the eastern sky, one red and one yellow, threatening to drop and spread death over the earth; they represented the danger from which Handsome Lake and the angels were trying to save mankind. Similarly they saw a large white object revolving in the sky near the setting sun; it regulated the air on the earth, and it too was under the control of the messengers of *Gaiwiio*. They met George Washington, sitting on the veranda of a house with his dog, halfway to heaven; he was the good white man, who at the Canandaigua Treaty told the friendless Iroquois to live happily in their own villages as long as the sun shines and the waters run, "for they are an independent people." They met Jesus, bearing nail scars on his hands and feet, and on his breast a bloody spear-wound. Jesus reported that his people had slain him in their pride and that he would not return to help them "until the earth passes away." He asked Handsome Lake how the Indians received his teachings. When Handsome Lake said that half his people believed in him, Jesus declared, "You are more successful than I for some believe in you but none in me. I am inclined to believe that in the end it will be so with you. Now it is rumored that you are but a talker with spirits. Now it is true that I am a spirit and the one of him who was murdered. Now tell your people that they will become lost when they follow the ways of the white man."

The second phase of the journey was a set of encounters at the fork in the sky road where human souls were directed, by judges stationed there, onto the narrow road that led to heaven or the wide road that led to hell. They saw that it was mostly children who were directed to heaven. They saw a repentant woman directed heavenward, and the messengers explained that each human being was given three chances to repent and follow *Gaiwiio* and that even a deathbed repentance was efficacious. And they saw a man's breast with a bullet hole in it hanging by the road as a sign to the unrepentant to turn left onto the wide, rough road to hell.

The third phase of the journey was a tour of the domain of the Punisher. In this Indian inferno were kept under eternal torture the souls of those who had committed great sins and failed to repent. Here Handsome Lake learned, in more vivid detail than in his first vision, the nature and punishment of evil. The Punisher was a protean monster of continually changing shape who occasionally took the form of the Christian devil with horns, tail, and cloven hoofs. He ruled a vast iron lodge, longer than the eye could reach, which they first viewed from a distance through a magnifying crystal. As they approached, they felt heat radiating from the lodge and nearly suffocated in the blasts of hot wind. Within were firepits and the damned, vainly stretching out their hands for help and shrieking ceaselessly in pain. The Punisher delighted in devising sadistic torments to fit the crimes of his prisoners: the drunkard was forced to swallow molten metal; the witch was alternately plunged into a boiling cauldron and chilled on the floor by its side; the wanton woman, who had been used to attract men with love powders, was forced to expose herself naked, gaunt, with rotting flesh and serpents writhing in her body hair; the wifebeater was forced to strike a red-hot image of a woman; a quarrelsome couple were compelled to dispute till their eyes bulged from their heads, their tongues protruded, and flames shot from their genitals; a promiscuous woman was made to fornicate with red-hot penes, white, red, and black; a violin player sawed away on his own arm with a glowing iron bar; card-players handled red-hot iron cards.

Having seen the tortures of the damned, the prophet and his guide now turned back to the fork in the great sky-road and began their journey again, this time up the narrow road that led to the lands of the Creator. They hurried along, smelling the flowers and admiring the delicious fruits by the side of the road and the birds flying in the air. They refreshed themselves at a spring whose clear water, once placed in a bottle, could not be exhausted. Handsome Lake met his dog, whom he had sacrificed at the white dog ceremony last New Year; it was still decorated as for the ritual, and when it saw Handsome Lake, it wagged its tail and sprang upon him. Shortly after this Handsome Lake met his own son and infant grandson and his niece, Cornplanter's daughter, still great with child. They, like the guide, were dressed in clear blue raiments. They all embraced, and then Cornplanter's daughter expressed her sorrow that her father and her brother Henry so often argued and became angry at each other, "her brother thinking he knew more than his father, and would not take his advice, but must have his own way, which was very wrong." And she told Handsome Lake to carry this message and bid the brothers to cease disagreeing with their father.

The allusion to the controversy between Cornplanter and his son Henry implied more than a domestic squabble between an unruly youth and an aging patriarch. Henry, the Philadelphia-educated son, was an extreme protagonist of "civilization" who went even farther than his father in advocacy of the white-man's technology and regarded "native" customs, including the ancient religious traditions, with outspoken contempt. He was a rash and angry young man who proposed to find salvation by simply abandoning Seneca culture for white. And so now the guide launched gradually into an extended lecture on the things that the prophet, and the Indians generally, must do and must not do in order to achieve personal salvation from torture in the house of the Punisher above and collective salvation from physical annihilation on the earth below. The guide first told Cornplanter's daughter to stop "and said it was true what She said about her brother abusing his Father, for he ought to obey him, as long as he lives." Next Handsome Lake's son spoke, regretting that his father had suffered so much and that his other son then living had taken so little care of him and had even avoided him in his worst illness for fear of having some trouble. The guide, agreeing, declared, "every Son ought to do good for their father."

The guide now went on to lecture Handsome Lake. He praised him for reporting his vision to the people, repeated the warnings against alcohol and witchcraft, and deplored the human tendency to confuse dreams inspired by the Great Spirit with those instilled by the Devil. He advised Handsome Lake that the dispute among the Allegany Indians over letting the Quakers instruct them in white ways was bad; everyone should agree, one way or the other. And he warned again that even though many people denied it, the Great Spirit "sees & knows all things and nothing is hid from Him!" And he threatened that unless the people mended their ways, thought more about the Great Spirit, and immediately conducted the white dog ceremony, a "great sickness" would come upon the village. Handsome Lake himself was advised that if his people took care of him and gave him medicine, he might soon be well. He was not to expect to see the angels again until his death, which would come when the hair on his head was half gray. Then, if he had done "right and good as long as he lived," he would be escorted to heaven by the angels once more, this time to stay.

The guide and the prophet took up their journey again but went only a short way before they stopped and the guide said, "We have arrived at the point where you must return. Here there is a house prepared for your eternal abode but should you now enter a room you could never go back to the earth-world." And so they parted, Handsome Lake returning to his people in the little village on the banks of the Allegheny River.[6]

On his recovery the prophet recited to his brother the events of the vision, and Cornplanter at once summoned a council to meet next morning. Henry Simmons, who was invited to attend, heard them discuss Handsome Lake's second vision. Simmons was asked whether he "believed it to be true"—for if the vision were "true," it bore major implications for Seneca behavior. Simmons's reply was encouraging. He told them that white people, too, including Quakers, sometimes had visions of heaven and hell and that he believed they were true revelations. Since Indians and whites were "all of one flesh & Blood made by the Great Spirit," he saw no reason why Handsome Lake's vision should not be valid, although, "perhaps, as there was so much of it, the man might not have recollected so as to tell it exact as he seen or heard it."

The Indians were pleased with Simmons's reaction, which confirmed their own, and in the afternoon of the same day they celebrated the Worship Dance, which the guide had recommended so strongly as a prophylaxis against the great sickness that threatened to end the world. They "prepar'd a White Dog to eat, and burnt his Skin to ashes During which time it was burning a number of them Circled around the Fire, Singing, Shouting & dancing greatly; after which they all partook of their Delicious dish, of Dog Meat Etc."

Next day Simmons went to Cornplanter's house "in order to make a note of the Sick Man Saying," and while there "the old Chief" (probably Cornplanter) fell into conversation with Simmons. Cornplanter felt obliged to advise Simmons of how his thinking now stood on acculturation as a result of his brother's visions: "The old Chief said he liked some ways of the white people very well, and some ways of the Indians also, and he thought it would take some length of time, to lead them out of all their own Customs, & as to their Worship Dance which they hold twice a year, they intended to keep it up, as they could not read, they knew of no other way of Worshiping the great Spirit, if they declined that they would have no manner of Worship at all. further said it was the white people who kill'd our Saviour how he had heard about our Savior I know not, but it seems he had." Simmons was quick to retort that it was the Jews who killed Christ, and perhaps the Indians were descendants of the Jews, in view of the similarity between some of their customs and those of the ancient people of Israel. But be that as it may, "we were all still, Crucifying & Killing Him, while we were doing Wickedly." Cornplanter meekly replied that "that was very true, very true."[7]

· *The Third Vision* ·

THE NEXT VISION of Handsome Lake took place six months later, on February 5, 1800. Since his health was now improving notably, the prophet related this vision himself in a council on March 2. The burden of this third revelation was that the Great Spirit was still troubled over the condition of the Indians. The three angels asked Handsome Lake whether the Indians had given up witchcraft and whiskey, and Handsome Lake said he did not know. They deplored the fact that the whites had taken away so much of their land and were so arrogantly sure that the mind of the Great Spirit was in their books. Handsome Lake was advised to have his revelations "written in a Book" so that the Indians could remember them always. The children were to be raised in the teachings of *Gaiwiio*. Cornplanter should visit all the towns of the Six Nations and try to bring unity among the chiefs. The people were to "keep up their Old form of worship . . . and must never quit it," particularly the Midwinter Ceremony, and the ritual leader known as "the Minister" must not despair or turn to drink. Handsome Lake was advised to devote half his life to his family and half to his mission.

By the time of this third vision Handsome Lake had gained the strong support of the one woman and the two men who were probably the most necessary adherents: his half sister Gayantgogwus, who, with her husband, was "the best of the medicine people"[8] and a power in the community, appearing at councils and speaking on behalf of the women; his brother Cornplanter, the political leader of the community; and the Minister. The three angels had appointed Gayantgogwus to make the medicines that cured the prophet. Cornplanter's role in publicizing the visions, in summoning councils to have them discussed, and in attesting loudly to their validity has already been noticed. The role of the Minister is more obscure to us now but was probably no less significant. It would appear from Henry Simmons's account that among the Allegany Seneca (and perhaps in other Iroquois communities as well) there was an individual who functioned as a part-time priest. No doubt he was the senior of the two male Headmen. In May, 1799, at the Worship Dance held at seed planting time, this Minister functioned as a master of ceremonies and moral adviser: "After they had taken two heats at dance, their minister (who was a very lusty Indian) said it was enough, and thanked them, and shortly after addressed them with a long speech by way of advice, after which they concluded the business with eating. . . ." Again in August, at the Green Corn Company, this same religious functionary played a prominent role in the Worship Dance: "At certain intervals, of their dances, some of the fore rank of men made Speeches to the company, by way of Preaching, especially one who was particularly called their Minister." And at the end of Green Corn, after the Bowl Game was concluded, the Minister led the salutation of the sun: "They were then closing the Scene which was done by Shooting Guns, about 50 men stood in a Longitude direction opposite their Wooden Image & shot twice or thrice up towards the Sun, their Minister Shot first, and so on."[9] It is tempting to suspect that this Minister was none other than that later disciple of the prophet, Joiise, who followed Handsome Lake in his hegira to Tonawanda and who was celebrated in the Code, after his death, as the "faithful and good" man with "commanding voice" who called the people together for the Great Feather Dance.[10] And to this man, as to Cornplanter, Handsome Lake's revelation of the Creator's concern for and about his human creatures came as a deeply felt reassurance.

· *The Apocalyptic Gospel* ·

WITH THE ANNOUNCEMENT of the third vision in the spring of 1800, Handsome Lake's first gospel had been essentially completed. This first gospel was apocalyptic and contained three major, interrelated themes: the imminence of world destruction; the definition of sin; and the prescription for salvation.

World destruction fantasies were pervasive. In addition to the threat of the great drops of fire and of the veil-over-all, Handsome Lake formulated other images of cosmic catastrophe. Although some of these additional prognostications are contained in sections of the Code that cannot be identified with revelations occurring on specific dates, we shall include them here because of their consonance with the predominant theme of this phase of the prophet's teaching. It is also possible that some of these apocalyptic fantasies were revealed during the journey over the great sky-road. They added up to a vivid account of how the world would end after a period of three generations. Signs of the coming apocalypse would be disagreements among the civil chiefs, among the Faithkeepers, and even among the Headmen. False prophets would arise. Crops would fail, and an inexplicable plague would kill many people. Witch women would boldly perform their spells in broad daylight and boast openly of how many they had slain. The poisonous creatures from the underworld would be released to seize and kill those who did not believe in *Gaiwiio*. The true believers would be spared the final catastrophe, simply lying down to sleep and being taken up to heaven by the Creator. At the last, the Creator would suspend all the powers of nature, and the earth would be enveloped in flames; the wicked would perish in the fire. Some other contemporary accounts of the prophet's teaching also emphasize the end-of-the-world theme. Thus an anonymous correspondent of the *Evangelical Intelligencer* in 1807 reported:

This prophet says, he has repeated visions, in which he sees three spirits or angels, who make communications to him. Sometimes in dreams or visions, he pretends to have seen devils flying, and hovering over their new town, Canadesago, seeking some place to light, but could find none, because the people were now orderly, temperate, and industrious; he saw them then fly to Buffalo Creek, and light among the whisky casks. Sometimes, he says, he has seen idle, drunken Indians, clothed in rags and filth, in old worn out canoes, on lakes at a distance from shore, clouds gathering in thick and black, with awful thunder, lightning and tempest. . . . He has stated to the Indians, that great judgments would follow them, if they disobeyed the commands of the Great Spirit, such as floods, droughts, &c. . . . He is deeply impressed with the opinion that judgments are coming on the nations, unless they reform.[11]

The second theme was sin. It is noteworthy that in most of these forecasts of universal disaster and individual damnnation it was specified that only the sinful and unrepentant would suffer. The all-encompassing sin, of course, was refusal to believe in and follow *Gaiwiio*, the gospel, which Handsome Lake was revealing. Belief in *Gaiwiio* was important, however, not because of the efficacy of pure faith, but because of its exclusive power to dissuade men and women from committing the great sins: witchcraft, love magic, abortion, drunkenness, and the various other evil practices specified in his description of hell. The listing of these sins constituted the second theme of the apocalyptic gospel. The definition of sin, of course, also constituted the groundwork for the second, or social, gospel.

The third theme of the early *Gaiwiio* was salvation. Men and women could preserve themselves from personal damnation and perhaps even delay the destruction of the world if they but believed in and followed the practices recommended by Handsome Lake. This meant, of course, first of all, confession and promise to sin no more by witches, purveyors of love magic, and abortionists; second, strict temperance; and third, the performance of correct ritual, pleasing to the Creator. Except for solitary confession, only public communal ritual, performed in the course of the great ceremonies of the annual calendar devoted to the Good Spirit, was permissible. And to these traditional observances he gave general sanction. Four rites were singled out as having particular virtue: the Worship Dance, which included the burning of the white dog; the Thanksgiving Ceremony, including the Great Feather Dance; the *adowe*, or individual sacred songs of thanksgiving; and the Bowl Game. Furthermore, the old organization of the Headmen and Headwomen, a man and a woman from each moiety, and of the Faithkeepers was endorsed and the people urged to obey these religious leaders.

Handsome Lake was thus not introducing a radically new religion; he was endorsing and reviving the old. He fully supported the ancient calendar of ceremonies, and his pantheon was isomorphic with the old, for the Creator of Handsome Lake's revelation was simply the ancient culture-hero Tarachiawagon, whose wooden effigy stood outside the council house; the Punisher was but Tawiskaron, the culture-hero's Evil Twin; and the four angels were in all likelihood the Four Winds of ancient belief. These deities were, of course, now revealed to have unsuspected powers and sentiments, but the revelation of these qualities and desires and the propriety of using new names in reference to old divinities was not upsetting to a people who were prepared for such progressive revelation by the customary usages of name change and by their theory of dreams. The idea of a cosmic struggle between the Good Twin and the Evil Twin had in the old mythology been relegated to the origin myth. Now it was

made a salient issue in contemporary life, with the two beings contesting for power over the minds of men on earth and ruling the
dead in heaven and hell. The principal cosmological innovation was,
in fact, the notion of heaven and hell itself. This had not hitherto
been a general belief among the Seneca, and some of his hearers
questioned the conception. Handsome Lake had this to say to them:

> Now it is said that your fathers of old never reached the true lands
> of our Creator nor did they ever enter the House of the tormentor,
> Ganos ge'. It is said that in some matters they did the will of the
> Creator and that in others they did not. They did both good and
> bad and none was either good or bad. They are therefore in a
> place separate and unknown to us, we think, enjoying themselves.

But Handsome Lake did propose several major ritual changes. One
of these had to do with the old medicine societies. Each of these honored a different animal spirit and called upon the power ("medicine")
of its tutelary to cure disease, chase witches, and divert natural catastrophes like tornado and drought. Their members often met in secret
and sometimes livened their proceedings with alcohol. Their membership was restricted to those who had been treated by the society.
Handsome Lake wished these secret medicine-societies to disband,
particularly the Society of Faces, whose wooden masks were made in
the image of the very being who in his theology was the Creator's
archenemy, the Punisher. Furthermore, secret meetings gave off to
his nostrils an odor of witchery, a taint of evil use of nature's powers.
And in the uncontrolled performance of these privately owned
rituals ardent spirits—the Punisher's principal weapon against virtue
—were freely employed. And so he commanded that all the medicine-
societies disband. But the people objected to the banning of the
medicine-societies and attributed the prevalence of illness to their
discontinuance, and eventually Handsome Lake compromised, sanctioning the rituals of the medicine-societies if strong drink was not
used. Furthermore, the societies should hold their feasts only on one
of the "great days" of the annual calendar, under the supervision of
the Faithkeepers, in public where all the people could see and
benefit.

A second major ritual change was the introduction of confession
as a major sacrament. The prophet believed although the earth-

world was full of sin, if all men would but repent "the earth would become as new again." He repeatedly emphasized the possibility of individual salvation through repentance even up to the point of death. In the old days, forcing a witch to confess under threat of death had been a traditional means of ending her power; but coupled with the notion of repentance as a condition of salvation and as the symbol of the acceptance of *Gaiwiio,* it gradually became a customary act even for those whose sins were less heinous. When the "Six Nations meetings" were devised after the prophet's death, a regular occasion for public confession was provided for every one.

The third major ritual change that Handsome Lake proposed— probably with little effect—was the elimination of anniversary mourning ceremonies. The prophet felt that too much attention was being paid to death and that the traditional ten days of mourning, followed by the funeral ceremony, was enough. Protracted grief merely added to the sorrows of the dead.

In all of these proposed ritual innovations it is noteworthy that Handsome Lake was minimizing the traditional ceremonial opportunities for cathartic relief of the unsatisfied wishes of the soul. He disapproved of the False Faces and of other old and new medicine-societies that had been formed in response to dreams; he deplored the indulgence of romantic fancies by the use of love magic; he grimly opposed any use of alcohol; he wished to do away with prolonged mourning. He demanded the repression of desire rather than its ritual satisfaction and offered in place of human beings the more abstract images of the Creator and the Punisher, of heaven and hell, and of the prophet as the objects of strivings for dependency.

His own role in the pantheon Handsome Lake cast at first in modest terms: he was merely a preacher, a messenger of the messengers. But within the year, as we shall see, his role as leader of the new religion was to become dictatorial and even grandiose; and on one occasion at least he presented himself as divine. This arrogation of personal supernatural power was based on revelation, too. In the fall of 1800 he was persuaded by the messengers that he was clairvoyant, able to see down into the earth as deep as the elm's root, and that it was his personal responsibility not merely to preach the gospel but also "to judge the earth and cure diseases." It was no mean responsibility, for as a shaman, with the messengers as his tutelaries, he had the power to diagnose witchcraft. And apocalyptic fears led him to use this power to launch the great witch hunt and to assume, for a short time, the unprecedented role of dictator of the Iroquois.

· The Great Witch Hunt ·

IROQUOIS SHAMANS practiced divination by several techniques. One was to drink a bowl of tea made from various roots and herbs while chanting an invocation to their guardian spirits. Then, by breathing on the sick person's head, chest, and body, the shaman could render it transparent and thus directly locate and identify the malady.[12] A second method was to interpret the dreams of the patient, for in the patient's dream, either manifestly or concealed in symbols, was often expressed the identity of the supernatural being or of the witch controlling the illness. A third method—known also among northern Algonquian hunters—was for the diviner to hide his head under a blanket until in dream or reverie the nature and cause of the illness was revealed. This was Handsome Lake's own method, and it was described as follows by a contemporary observer: "Sometimes sick persons send a shirt or some other article of clothing, to the prophet that he may prescribe a cure. In such a case, he takes two handfuls of tobacco, puts their ends to the fire on the hearth, lies down and covers himself with a blanket, after he has arisen he prescribes for the disease."[13] In many cases the diviner recommended the services of the appropriate medicine-society and the performance of the proper ritual (e.g., the Eagle Dance). In cases in which a witch was at fault several courses of action were open. One was to treat the "poison" itself. Witches were able magically to project into the body of their victim various irritating objects—splinters of wood or bone, a ball of hair, a worm, and so on. If the diviner or a colleague was able to extract this malefic article by putting fire ashes on the afflicted part and "drawing" it out into the poultice, he could then burn it or cast it back into the witch's body, injuring or destroying her. Or the witch could be attacked directly (even after the death of the victim) for purposes of revenge and for the protection of the rest of the community. If the witch could be brought to confess and to repent, by threats or physical torture or by such magical devices as burning the living heart of a blackbird, the witch's power would be broken. And as a last resort, the witch could be killed. Witches were believed to be jealous and hypersensitive persons who were likely to revenge themselves on people who offended them, not by poisoning the enemy himself, but by attacking his children and relatives. Thus the cure or death of a bewitched person did not imply an end of the matter; the real target of the witch's spite was, presumptively, still living, and he and all his kinfolk were still in danger.[14]

Handsome Lake professed reluctance to practice as a diviner. As soon as he announced that the angels had promised to make him a clairvoyant, his brother Cornplanter came running with tobacco for an offering and said, "Why, having the assurance of powers, do you not commence now. Come prophesy! My daughter is very sick." But Handsome Lake refused, claiming that final permission to use his powers had not yet been granted. Again Cornplanter made his request, more earnestly than before. This time when Handsome Lake refused, people began to say that Handsome Lake "would not respond to the cry of a brother and had no hearing for the voice of a brother." A third time Cornplanter came, asking that Handsome Lake use his clairvoyant power, and with him "the people," urging that, in the terms of his own vision, "Have we not something to say to you as well as the messengers of the Creator?" The reluctant diviner then was forced to admit that he did have an obligation to the people, and he promised, despite the lack of complete authorization from the angels, to do what he could. He went into a deep sleep (using the dream method of divination), and when he awoke he reported that in his vision he had learned that *ohgiwe* should be sung for the sick woman.

But Handsome Lake's niece—a young unmarried woman who had recently born a daughter—did not improve in health. By October she was gravely ill. The failure of *ohgiwe* to cure her was explained as the result of an incorrect performance of the ritual. Handsome Lake claimed that not only Jiiwi's illness but an epidemic of unnamed disorders was being abetted by the Seneca refusal to close the secret societies.

Other Seneca argued that the epidemic was the result of Handsome Lake's own interference with the traditional medical rituals. The mysterious illness of the young woman dragged on. Handsome Lake was persuaded to examine her; after examining her, he gave it as "his opinion" that she was "bewitched by several of those Muncy [Delaware] Indians combined together for that purpose," and that "the principle Muncy Chief" was one of the witches.[15] It seems that a young chief named Silver Heels (another account gives his name as John Logan) lived at the Delaware settlement at Cattaraugus. This was the small band of about thirty cabins, containing one hundred and sixty souls, who had moved here from their old village at West Hickory on the Allegheny about 1791. In the fall of 1799 Silver Heels had come down to Cornplanter's settlement to ask permission, as was the annual custom, for Delaware hunters to use the winter hunting grounds on the Allegheny, and as usual the Allegany Seneca had agreed. During his week's visit he stayed at Cornplanter's house, and he and Cornplanter's daughter Jiiwi slept together. Then the hunting party left, and the young chief with it. When the hunters returned, probably during the Midwinter festival period, the Delaware chief and the Cornplanter girl resumed their relationship. After a while the Delaware hunters went home to Cattaraugus. Cornplanter's daughter was pregnant; she gave birth; and then she became ill. Rumors began to circulate that a Delaware witch had poisoned the girl to save young Silver Heels the trouble of taking her as wife.[16]

The accusation against the Delaware was rendered plausible not only by the circumstances of the case but by the reputation that the Delaware held among the Iroquois for witchcraft. There had been trouble of this kind before: Back in 1749, on the Susquehanna, the granddaughter of the Cayuga viceroy Shickellamy had died, and then Shickellamy himself. Shickellamy's daughter-in-law and his sons accused a Deleware "conjuror," and next year a Delaware shaman was killed for "conjuring" several Indians to death.[17] Cornplanter's people, placing full reliance on Handsome Lake's judgment (he "is esteemed by us for his sobriety and knowledge in many things superior to any of our nation"), sent several messages to the Delaware, entreating them "to remove the cause of the woman's illness that peace and harmony might again resume its place between us." At last one of the principal persons accused came to Cornplanter's village. He was unable to effect a cure. Cornplanter's people therefore held him prisoner, a hostage for the woman's life. By about January it appeared that poor Jiiwi would not long survive.

A terrible dilemma now presented itself. The prophet had declared the illness to be a case of Delaware witchcraft. The Delaware denied the charge even though they had provided the services of one of their medicine men in an effort to help the sick woman. If the woman died, and if the Seneca in retaliation killed the hostage, war between the Seneca and the Delaware would be inevitable. Yet if they failed to take revenge, the authority of Handsome Lake and the sanctity of tradition would be violated. A council was held at Jenuchshadago to deliberate the matter, with both chiefs and warriors present and the Cattaraugus Seneca represented by two principal chiefs. The council could not agree on whether or not the hostage's life should be forfeited if the woman died. Handsome Lake's advocates demanded death; others refused to sanction such an act and questioned Handsome Lake's wisdom. The council did agree, however, to ask for advice from the white people.

The Quaker missionaries at Genesinguhta were not eager to give advice. Sophisticated Quakers had long since given up their forefathers' beliefs in witchcraft and magic and censured any of their own members who fell prey to such ignorant superstitions. But they were hardly in a position to intervene in a local dispute or dissuade the Seneca from a belief that had just been emphasized by a prophet whose other preachings, such as temperance, they endorsed. Preoccupied by the "frequent meetings, councils, dances &c," the people did not send their children to classes and the grammar school had to be closed down for want of pupils. The Friends were forced to be careful and guarded in their actions. "The subject has afforded us much exercise from time to time," they eventually reported, "but so intricately situated as to require much caution had we interfered . . . the distempered state of their minds through the enthusiasm and artful contrivance of their director exceedingly obstructed any counsel or advice being profitably received. The difficulty originated from an apprehension of injuries sustained by witchcraft are not uncommon for these poor Natives to be annoyed with."[18]

At last a desperate letter[19] imploring advice was dispatched to the nearest substantial white settlement, that of David Mead and his fellow pioneers at Cussawago, on the upper waters of French Creek. The chiefs did not know what to do if the woman died. Should they take life for life, "as it has been our custom"? Or should they spare the prisoner? They were sure that Handsome Lake, "The man we confide in that professes to search into these things tells us the truth as far as he sees." They were satisfied that he was "fully capable of explaining how they [i.e., witch's spells] were contrived and executed and tell us of many of those dark inventions which is the presant cause of our trouble." But still, some of the council did not believe that they should execute the prisoner if the woman died or that other persons accused of witchcraft by Handsome Lake should be subject to the same punishment. These liberal chiefs questioned explicitly whether the use or efficacy of witchcraft could be proven by the methods employed by Handsome Lake.[20]

The settlers at Meadville held a council of their own and hastened to reply to Cornplanter and his people, advising them not to kill the suspected witch even if Cornplanter's daughter died, but taking care not to cast aspersions on Handsome Lake's good intentions. David Mead then proceeded in haste to Lancaster to deliver Cornplanter's letter to the Governor of Pennsylvania. Word also was sent to the Indian superintendent at Canandaigua that the Seneca were threatening war against the Delaware unless they discontinued their witchcraft, and this news was duly reported to the office of the Secretary of War in Washington.[21]

By April the Delaware at Cattaraugus had heard of the Cussawago settlement's efforts to intervene in the matter, and wrote on their own account to David Mead and his friends, requesting aid and blaming the trouble all on Handsome Lake. "The Accation of this great dispute is on account of Cornplanters Brother who says he has conversed with God the Great Spirit—We are accused of witchcraft which our people is entirely strangers to and puts no belief in. Also our Brothers the White people we think is of the Same Oppanion." This letter too was discussed at a council at Cussawago and then was sent posthaste to the Governor at Lancaster. The Delaware at Cattaraugus also appealed to their fellow tribesmen in Ohio, and as a result "a number of Indians of the Muncy and other tribes to the amount of about two hundred, are collected in New Connecticut near the line of Pennsylvania, that they, have left their families behind and are prepared for war, waiting to join their Brethren in case the existing dispute should not be amicably settled."

By May the Quakers in Philadelphia had learned from the Governor of Pennsylvania of the threatening conflict and prepared a message to both the Seneca and the Muncy, advising them both to hold back from bloodshed and denying that there was any such power as witchcraft. In a companion letter to the Muncy, also enjoining peace, the Friends observed that the Bad Spirit had been at work "among some of the Seneca nation" and that they had written to the Cornplanter Indians "to take the dust out of their eyes" so that they could distinguish between the promptings of the Good and the Bad Spirit.

Although Cornplanter's daughter clung unexpectedly to life, the controversy generated by her illness was transformed by Handsome Lake into a wider problem. A general council of the Seneca was convened at Buffalo Creek in June 1801, at which delegates from all Seneca villages, including those in Canada, for three days discussed both the Delaware witchcraft case and the issue of witchcraft in general. Handsome Lake had by now articulated the general thesis (already implicit in Iroquois culture) "that most of their bodily afflictions and disorders arose from witchcraft," that he was authorized by the Creator "to tell the Individuals who are afflicting these disorders on other Individuals," and "that the Whiskey is the great Engine which the bad Spirit uses to introduce Witchcraft and many other evils amongst Indians."[22] At the council at Buffalo Creek he accused "sundry old women & men of the Delaware Nation, and some few among [his] own nation" of the sin of witchcraft. The council deliberated, it is said, for three days on the question of punishment and at last determined "that those persons accused of Witchcraft should be threatened with Death, in case they persisted in bewitching the People."[23] One of those whom he accused was none other than his nephew Red Jacket, the speaker of the Seneca nation.

The confrontation between Handsome Lake and Red Jacket was precipitated by an argument over land. One of the issues brought to discussion at the Buffalo Creek council in June 1801, was the proposed sale of a strip of land along the Niagara River (the Black Rock corridor), which, as a favorite fishing place of the Seneca, had been left unsold in 1797 but was now desired by the white people for the security of their road to Niagara Falls from the head of navigation on Lake Erie.[24] Many Seneca objected not only to the idea of a sale to New York, but even to the present situation, which allowed the whites to maintain a fort at Black Rock to protect the road through their territory and to encroach by the road on their fishing ground.[25] And of those who objected, Handsome Lake was foremost, basing his opposition on the grounds of a special revelation he had received from the four angels.[26] Red Jacket (possibly representing the council) favored the sale. According to later report Handsome Lake publicly denounced Red Jacket "at a great council of Indians, held at Buffalo Creek, and [Red Jacket] was put upon his trial." Red Jacket, however is reported to have exculpated himself, speaking in his own defense for three hours and accusing Handsome Lake of manufacturing his visions and his charges of witchcraft for the purpose of restoring the fallen fortunes of his discredited brother Cornplanter. The sympathy of a small majority of the council lay with Red Jacket, and he was exonerated, although the council did endorse the prophet's opposition to witchcraft.[27] Handsome Lake's response was to immortalize, in dubious color, his rival Red Jacket in the Code. In a vision Handsome Lake saw Red Jacket in torment in Hell:

> Then the messengers pointed out a certain spot and said, "Watch attentively," and beheld a man carrying loads of dirt and depositing them in a certain spot. He carried the earth in a wheelbarrow and his task was a hard one. Then he knew that the name of the man was Sagoyewatha, a chief. Then asked the messengers, "What did you see?" He answered, "I beheld a man carrying dirt in a wheelbarrow and that man had a laborious task. His name was Sagoyewatha, a chief." Then answered the messengers, "You have spoken truly. Sagoyewatha is the name of the man who carries the dirt. It is true that his work is laborious and this is for a punishment for he was the one who first gave his consent to the sale of Indian reservations. It is said that there is hardship for those who part with their lands for money or trade. So now you have seen the doom of those who repent not. Their eternity will be one of punishment."[28]

According to Seneca tradition, Handsome Lake's "slanders" against Red Jacket, both at home and in Washington, for a time cost him his status as Seneca tribal speaker and ultimately prevented his elevation to a sachemship.

The major action of the council was to prohibit the use of liquor and to appoint Handsome Lake "High Priest, and principal Sachem in all things Civil and Religious."[29] In the Code it is recorded that "all the people assembled and with one accord acclaimed that Ganio'dai'io' should lead them and that they should never murmur." As one of the chiefs expressed it, Handsome Lake had been "deputed by the four Angels to transact our business" and the people "have perfect confidence in Handsome Lake are willing to lend an Ear to his instructions and yield Obedience to his precepts. To him they have entrusted all their Concerns to be governed by his direction, wisdom and Integrity."[30] Cornplanter, presumably satisfied that the Delaware witches had repented, told the Munsee that "He had swept their beds clean, that they might lie down in peace—that he had swept clean before their doors, that they might go out and in without molestation."[31] The Delaware band, however, was so disillusioned by the whole episode that they migrated en masse to the more tolerant atmosphere of Buffalo Creek and later to the Grand River Reservation in Canada.

Handsome Lake's position now was virtually, if only briefly, that of a dictator. He could claim that the Cornplanter girl's survival and the relaxation of tension between the Seneca and the Delaware were the result of his forthright stand against the witches. He prepared, therefore, to destroy the power of witchcraft among the Seneca, with virtually full approval, or at least acquiescence, of the entire Seneca nation. The virulence of Handsome Lake's hatred for witches was unbounded. He believed that, as the angels told him, witches were the agents of the Evil Spirit, responsible for almost all sickness and disease and working to destroy the world itself. If they were not checked by good men who believed in Handsome Lake's message, the world would come to an end. Although no one as yet, since the killing of June 13, 1799, had been executed for witchcraft, according to tradition Handsome Lake now proceeded to hunt out the witches. There are, however, no specific, documented accounts of executions during Handsome Lake's sojourn at Jenuchshadago, and in all probability not many women (for Handsome Lake's charges were generally made against women) were killed there. Local legend recalls one execution, but this case is sufficiently reminiscent of the killing of June 13, 1799, to be possibly a distorted recollection of that event. According to the story Handsome Lake diagnosed the illness of a woman as being the result of witchcraft. He accused an old lady who lived by herself and did her own planting. When Handsome Lake and his cohorts visited her and voiced the charge, she merely replied, "How do you know?" He took her hand and pointed to a mark on it that indicated that she was a witch. Then she asked him, "What do I use to bewitch people? You are a prophet. Show me plainly so that I can see." He could only repeat, "You *are* a witch." So he told his men to kill her. There was a fierce struggle, for she was a big woman and could fight like a man; she seized the blade in the hands of her executioner and her hands were cut. At last they killed her.[32] The probable reason for the rarity of such events was that Handsome Lake's revelation allowed witches the opportunity to confess and repent. Thus accused persons or persons who feared accusation could publicly, or privately before Handsome Lake, "confess" their sin and receive his absolution.

9

THE POLITICS OF

EVANGELISM:

The Second, or Social, Gospel

BEGINNING IN THE FALL OF 1801 AND INCREASINGLY IN THE YEARS
thereafter until his death in 1815, Handsome Lake presented a
second gospel, which emphasized the value in daily life of temperance, peace, land retention, acculturation, and domestic morality. His
ideas on these subjects were drawn in part from the progressive, pro-
acculturation faction among the Allegany Seneca, in part from the
federal officials who backed his movement, and in part from the local
Quaker model. The social gospel was something of a departure from
his first, extremely conservative position, however, and it earned him
the opposition of the conservatives. In the end his own political
situation became precarious as his demand for dictatorial power
alienated the progressives, the Quakers, the federal establishment, and
even conservative Indians, and he was even forced for a time to leave
Cornplanter's band. But although his political fortunes failed, he and
his disciples continued to carry the good word to other Iroquois
reservations, and even other tribes, and initiated a dramatic renaissance of Iroquois society.

· *Concessions to the Progressive Faction* ·

ALTHOUGH IN PIOUSLY CONDEMNING WITCHCRAFT and alcohol Handsome Lake was in tune with traditional Seneca morality, people from

the beginning had questioned the wisdom or even the rightness of particular executions. He had aroused criticism by his ambivalence about the adoption of European arts. Cornplanter had long favored extensive acculturation. Henry O'Bail, his son—the only "educated" man among the Seneca—had taken the Quaker advice seriously to heart and was now a sober man, owner of a herd of "eleven horned cattle." In the fall of 1801 O'Bail was found by the visiting Friends' committee splitting rails for an acre of cleared land on which he intended to plant wheat. He had moved from Jenuchshadago to the neighborhood of Genesinguhta and planned to build a house next spring. Henry O'Bail had been at the great witch council at Buffalo Creek along with his brother Charles Halftown and some others of the men who had been friendly with the Quaker visitors. At this council, despite the weight of the chiefs' opinion in favor of Handsome Lake, Henry O'Bail and four other young warriors had spoken out publicly against his advice. Handsome Lake had declared "that they should not allow their children to learn to read and write; that they might farm a little and make houses; but that they must not sell anything they raised off the ground, but give it away to one another, and to the old people in particular; in short that they must possess everything in common." On his return to Jenuchshadago Henry told his father Cornplanter that "he thought it would be much better for them to hold Councils about making fields than about witchcraft & dances & such things."

This kind of opposition enraged Handsome Lake's more ardent followers, for opposition was in itself a sign to them of evil, perhaps even of witchcraft. One of the "younger" men was quickly brought "under trial for some disrespectful expressions relating to the business." Cornplanter himself was caught neatly in the middle. His brother had to a degree usurped his former power and now was undoing much of the work of civilization that Cornplanter so laboriously had nourished, particularly in the area of education. He had been, apparently, somewhat uneasy about the Delaware witchcraft case and came back from the Buffalo Creek council with a less than cheerful countenance. For two months the two men seem to have maintained a silent struggle. The denouement was finally precipitated by the renewed request of the Friends that the children and young men be instructed in reading and writing. In October 1801, a council to discuss the matter was held, at which Cornplanter—whose "mind was become quite different from what it was two months ago"—spoke in favor of education. Handsome Lake opportunely conceded that "the white people were going to settle all around them; that they could not live unless they learned to farm, and follow the white people's ways, etc."[1]

Handsome Lake had little choice. Whatever their religious feelings, the majority of the Seneca favored technical acculturation. The strategy of the majority of the Seneca chiefs was to secure grants in aid of civilization in return for making certain minor adjustments in the boundaries of the reservations to accommodate the government or the land companies. Although Handsome Lake was opposed to land sales on principle and had a distaste for the white man's customs, the credibility of his role as political leader would be compromised if he maintained a minority opinion before the councils. To be sure, he had been publicly appointed to be the censor of the Seneca nation. But the Seneca were not accustomed to censors and were not prepared to obey a dictator against their own better judgment.

And so Handsome Lake acceded to the proposal, announced by Red Jacket as chief speaker of the Seneca nation at a council at the Genesee River in November 1801, to exchange various minor bits and pieces of land in New York for reforms in the annuity system and for a federally supported program of technical aid. The Iroquois were willing to sell the strip of land at Black Rock that had occasioned the bitter dispute between Handsome Lake and Red Jacket earlier that year. They would surrender to the Holland Land Company the small reservations along the Genesee River in return for adjustments in the boundaries at Cattaraugus and Buffalo Creek. They wished to have their annuity goods paid henceforth in coarse warm cloth like flannel rather than fine broadcloth, in order to keep the old men, women, and children from the cold winds and snow of winter; and they wanted all the cash annuities from the various treaties regularly deposited in a national fund in the Bank of the United States rather than diffused in useless small payments to individuals. And they wanted to be civilized (although not Christianized). Specifically, they requested oxen to plow the ground ("which would relieve our women from digging"), pigs, sheep, cows to provide milk, butter, and cheese, farming equipment to raise wheat and other grain, and spinning wheels. Neither Handsome Lake nor his rival Red Jacket was inclined toward Christianity, and the Christian party had not yet formed.

· The Visit to Washington ·

In order to press this proposal further, in the winter of 1801–02 representatives of each of the Six Nations, excepting the Mohawk, made plans to visit the new seat of the federal government in Washington, D.C.[2] This visit would increase the pressure on Handsome Lake to support the progressive faction by acquainting him directly with the President of the United States and his interest in the civilization of the Indians. It also focused his attention on the need to concern himself with other social issues, particularly the unsettled land issues. A preliminary letter was written to President Jefferson in January, and Jefferson replied with a cordial invitation to come to the seat of government to discuss land questions and technical assistance. The leader of the Seneca delegation was Handsome Lake, and with him traveled Cornplanter, the Tonawanda chief Blue Sky, and several warriors. Some of the young men, the Delaware in particular, enjoyed a gay time on arrival in Washington, and their Quaker hosts remarked that "their Conduct has been such as we very much disapprove in various Aspects."[3] The general purpose of the visit was to secure from the United States the promise of technical aid; and in this the visit was successful. Plows, oxen, yokes, chains, milch cows, sheep, carding and spinning equipment, were ordered to be distributed among the several reservations, and the Congress appropriated $15,000, to be renewed annually, to "civilize" the Indians of the United States.[4]

But Handsome Lake's plans reached beyond the securing of material aid for the nation. He made this visit the occasion for securing the blessing of the government of the United States on his new religion and his pretensions to leadership of the Seneca. Such an endorsement would, if obtained, not merely constitute additional validation of his mission; it would also serve to block his rival, Red Jacket, from obtaining federal support in the internecine struggle. Furthermore, he wanted the Oil Creek Reservation assigned to him as a personal estate.

Handsome Lake's first address to the President was, significantly, couched in egalitarian terms. "Brother," he began, "I thank the Great Spirit above that I have a very bright day to talk with the Great Chief of our white Brothers. It is the Great Spirits doing." Having thus pointed out how the Great Spirit favored his enterprises even in small details like the weather, he went on to explain his divine commission: "The Great Spirit has appointed four Angels and appointed me the fifth to direct our people on Earth. I thank the Great Spirit that the Great Chief of my white Brother is well and hearty. This is the first year since the Great Spirit appointed me to guide my people and give them knowledge, good from bad. He directed me to begin with my own people first and that is the Reason why I have been so long in coming to my white Brother."

He next took note of the problem of intergroup relations, pointing out that whisky and land cessions were the root of the troubles. Both parties were at fault. "I am very much troubled," he observed, "to find that my Brothers and my White Brothers have gone astray." The guilt of the Indians lay in drunken quarreling. Drink was the reason why whites and Indians did not live like brothers. "I have now come forward to make us love one another again with your assistance." The white people, for their part, were guilty because of their seizure of the Indians' land, and "the Great Spirit has told me to come and tell them of it." He asked for "a Writing on Paper for it, So that we can hold it fast." Handsome Lake also pointed out to the President that there was some urgency to his demands. "If we do not Settle all our business that we are now on, the Great Spirit will send a Great Sickness among us all. But if we can Settle all our Business, Health and Happiness will come and the Seed of the People and the Fruit will come forward."

Having thus let President Jefferson know in outline what the Great Spirit expected of him, Handsome Lake went on to expound his apocalyptic doctrine further. His revelation, he explained, was by no means intended only for Indians: it was the duty of all the people of the earth to attend carefully and to obey, on pain of divine punishment. The President of the United States, as leader of a great nation, had a special obligation to heed the prophet's requests and to negotiate only with those persons appointed by him as the "fifth angel" and the director of mankind:

Our lands are decaying because we do not think on the Great Spirit, but we are now going to renew our Minds and think on the great Being who made us all, that when we put our seeds in the Earth they may grow and increase like the leaves on our Trees. The four angels appointed with me to direct the People on Earth to tell me that if any Man whatever he may be will look on the Great Being above us all and do his will on Earth, when his days are out and the angels find he is a good man they will grant him more days to live in the World and if he lives a good Man, doing no Evil in those days, when these days are out the Great Being will take him to himself. The like of this was never known before these four angels empowered me to relieve any man of any wickness whatever it may be, if he be a good man, who looks up to the Great Spirit above but if he be a bad man and does not look up to the Great Spirit, I cannot relieve him and he cannot be helped if he be fond of liquor.

Dear Brother, the Lord has confidence in your people as well as ours, provided we can settle all our Business. He will take care of us first, and you afterwards if you will Take Notice of the voice of the Angels. The four Angels desired me to pick out two young men of my people, that I know to be sober, good young men, to take care of all our Public business. They are Charles O Beal and Strong. Here is my Brother Captain Cornplanter. He is cried down by the Sachems of Buffalo Creek which you very well know. But it is not my wish for I very well know that he has done his Endeavour for the Benefit of our nation. He is a Sober man and endeavours to make all our young men Sober and good—the Sachems at Buffalo Creek are all drunken men and dislike him. I, who am now Talking to you, would wish you to know, that half of my Spirit is here on Earth yet, and the other half is with the Great Spirit above and I wish you to consider my Business and my Nation well, that we may Continue friends and Brothers and when that takes place I will be thankful to the Great Chief of my white Brothers and to the Great Spirit above us all. We will be good friends here and when we will meet with the Great Being above we shall have bright and happier Days. Dear Brother, that is all I have got to say because I know you have got the Word of the Great Spirit among you.[5]

The President's reply was conveyed by his secretary of war, Henry Dearborn, on March 10. Dearborn began by telling his "Brothers"—Handsome Lake and the Seneca and Onondaga delegations—that their "father and good friend, the President of the United States," had thought over their message carefully "since you took him by the Hand three days ago." The President declared that if all the red people followed the advice of their friend and teacher Handsome Lake and were "sober, honest, industrious and good," there was no doubt that the Great Spirit would make them happy. He accepted the admonitions of the prophet concerning the evils of strong drink and reported that the Congress was considering a law to prohibit the use of alcohol by Indians resident within the United States. And he agreed to provide a "writing on paper" that guaranteed that their land could not be taken by anyone except by their own consent.

Encouraged by this friendly and cooperative response, Handsome Lake and his colleagues went on to more particular issues in a second address, delivered two days later. These issues chiefly concerned land, and Handsome Lake now revealed the increasing anxiety that he felt about the territorial security of the Iroquois. "The Four Angels have directed," he announced, that the Indians should receive "separate Deeds" for each reservation. An existing deed to the Cattaraugus and Allegany reservations and a map showing the survey lines had been lost, and he wanted a copy lest the occupants, unable to prove ownership, be dispossessed. He wished to be given a personal deed to the Oil Spring Reservation, "of ten miles square for the exclusive use, benefit and comfort of myself." The Great Spirit himself expected him to be "importunate" about securing the territory of the Indians. But if the matter could be satisfactorily concluded, then "the remainder of our days will be devoted to agriculture and such other pursuits, as are calculated to render life comfortable to ourselves and pleasing in the sight of the Great Spirit."

The President's second response, again communicated to the prophet and his associates by the secretary of war, was equally friendly. He proclaimed officially that all Seneca and Onondaga reservations established by treaty, convention, or deed of conveyance were Indian property, protected by the laws of the United States, and that the Indians could, if they wished, hold them "forever." He promised to look into Handsome Lake's claim to the Oil Spring Reservation (and eventually it was secured to the Seneca).

The Seneca party now set off on their return to the Allegheny, armed with copies of the speeches by the secretary of war, the territorial guarantee, a civil and military passport, one hundred dollars, and an order on the commandant of Fort Pitt to supply the travelers with money, provisions, and a shirt, axe, and hoe to each and every Indian.[6]

But Handsome Lake's anxieties about the territorial security of the Seneca were still active when he reached home. Some time late in the summer he wrote a letter (unfortunately now lost) through the local subagent, Callendar Irvine, to the President, again complaining about whiskey and iniquitous land sales of the recent past, particularly the sale of parts of the Oneida, Cayuga, and Onondaga reservations. The Secretary of War replied at once with praise for Handsome Lake's temperance program and with defense of the cessions, pointing out in the latter connection that it "must be presumed that your Chiefs would not have sold any part of your land unless they were satisfied that the sale would meet the approbation of the majority of the nation."[7] And a week later, on November 3, 1802, President Jefferson himself wrote to Handsome Lake on the matter:

Washington, November 3, 1802. Brother Handsome Lake: I have received the message in writing which you sent through Capt. Irvine, our confidential agent, placed near you for the purpose of communicating and transacting between us whatever may be useful for both nations. I am happy to learn you have been so far favored by the Divine Spirit, as to be made sensible of these things which are for your good and that of your people, and of those which are hurtful to you; and particularly that you and they see the ruinous effects which the abuse of spiritous liquors have produced upon them. It has weakened their bodies, enervated their minds, exposed them to hunger, cold, nakedness, and poverty; kept them in perpetual broils, and reduced their population. I do not wonder then, brother, at your censures, not only on your people, who have voluntarily gone into these fatal habits, but on all the nations of white people who have supplied their calls for this article. But these nations have done to you only what they do among themselves. They have sold what individuals wish to buy, leaving to everyone to be the guardian of his own health and happiness. Spirituous liquors are not in themselves bad. They are often found to be an excellent medicine for the sick. It is the improper and intemperate use of them, by those in health, which makes them injurious, but as you find that your people cannot refrain from an ill use of them, I greatly applaud your happiness to place the paltry gain on the sale of these articles in competition with the injury they do you; and as it is the desire of your nation that no spirits should be sent among them, and I am authorized by the great council of the United States to prohibit them, I will sincerely co-operate with your wise men in any proper measures for this purpose which shall be agreeable to them.

You remind me, brother, of what I have said to you when you visited me the last winter, that the land you then held would remain yours and should never go from you but when you should be disposed to sell. This I now repeat, and will ever abide by. We, indeed, are always ready to buy land; but we will never ask but when you wish to sell; and our laws, in order to protect you against imposition, have forbidden individuals to purchase lands from you; and have rendered it necessary, when you desire to sell, even to a state, that an agent from the United States should attend the sale, see that your consent is freely given, a satisfactory price paid, and report to us what has been done, for our approbation. This was done in the late case of which you complain. The deputies of your nation came forward in all the forms which we have been used to consider as evidence of the will of your nation. They proposed to sell the state of New-York certain parcels of land, of small extent, and detached from the body of your other lands. The state of New-York was desirous to buy. I sent an agent in whom we trust, to see that your consent was free, and the sale fair. All was reported to be free and fair. The lands were your property. The right to sell is one of the rights of property. To forbid you the exercise of that right would be a wrong to your nation. Nor do I think, brother, that the sale of lands is, under all circumstances, injurious to your people; while they depended on hunting, the more extensive forests around them, the more game they would yield. But, going into a state of agriculture, it may be as advantageous to a society as it is to an individual who has more land than he can improve, to sell a part and lay out the money in stocks and implements of agriculture, for the better improvement of the residue. A little land, well stocked and improved, will yield a great deal more [than] without stock or improvement. I hope, therefore, that, on further reflection, you will see this transaction in a more favorable light, both as it concerns the interest of your nation, and the exercise of that superintending care which I am sincerely anxious to employ for their subsistence and happiness. Go on, then, brother, in the great reformation you have undertaken. Persuade our red men to be sober and to cultivate their

lands; and their women to spin and weave for their families. You
will soon see your women and children well fed and clothed;
your men living happily in peace and plenty, and your numbers
increasing from year to year. It will be a great glory to you to
have been the instrument of so happy a change, and your children's
children, from generation to generation, will repeat your name
with love and gratitude forever. In all your enterprises for the
good of your people you may count with confidence on the aid
and protection of the United States, and on the sincerity and zeal
with which I am animated in the furthering of this humane work.
You are our brethren of the same land; we wish your prosperity
as brethren should do. Farewell!

Th. Jefferson[8]

This correspondence—copies of which were treasured and displayed—was of supreme importance to Handsome Lake and to his
followers, for it proved the sanction of his mission by the highest
authorities of the land.

· The Quaker Model ·

THE QUAKER MISSIONARIES maintained a silent pressure on the prophet
and on the rest of the Seneca by constantly presenting both a model
of impeccable personal conduct and an example of economic and
intellectual enterprise whose practical advantages were vividly manifest. This Quaker program the prophet adopted almost—but not
quite—in its entirety. It was consistent and cumulative. Friends
rigidly adhered to a policy of refusing any opportunity to profit
personally from their transactions, giving much equipment and instruction gratis and lending or selling other items at cost. Rather than
take up Indian land, they bought a tract off the reservation for the
model farm. This absence of economic self-interest, together with a
general discreetness in their criticism of native religious beliefs (including the belief in witchcraft), made more palatable their forthright opposition to other areas of custom, such as drunkenness, social
dances, illiteracy, and inefficient technology. The core of the program was presented in 1798 and remained constant; new elements
and additional rationalization were offered as needed. This program
may be analyzed as follows:

1. Presentation of the model of an advanced white rural community

The major part of the energy spent by the Quaker mission was devoted to constructing and operating a model farm (at first at Genesinguhta, on the reservation, and then, from 1803 on, nearby at Tunessassa on land purchased from the Holland Land Company). The farm was self-supporting to the extent that the occupants lived on their own produce; but it maintained economic relationships with the surrounding white and Seneca communities, particularly in buying hardware and cattle from white traders down the river and dispensing surplus farm produce and equipment to the Seneca. In order to facilitate this local trade, the Quakers advised the Indians to construct serviceable roads. Furthermore, the Quakers established various special facilities and services essential to a rural white community: a sawmill and a gristmill at Tunessassa, a spinning and weaving shop, and a smithy. At the farm the Quakers maintained barns, stables, and a complete set of farm equipment, including not only field tools but carpenter's, mason's and cooper's tools as well. They lived in a well-constructed two-story, pine-shingled, painted dwelling-house with cellar, stone and clay chimney, and glass windows. There the Indian visitor could see, handle, and feel the material apparatus of white rural life: scythes, bar iron, nail rods, cartwheels, sickles, felling axes, drawing knives, mill picks (to make grindstones), shoemaker's tacks, dishcloths, camp kettles, towels, soap, plow irons, augers, spinning wheels, looms, beds, chairs. . . . Furthermore, they could observe the Quakers as they went about their various tasks: the men felling trees, building fences, plowing, sowing, reaping, caring for livestock, making and repairing equipment, keeping written accounts; the women dairying, cooking and preserving foods, making soap, laundering, housecleaning, knitting, spinning and weaving, repairing clothes; the children (after a few years) doing their chores. They were able to see the apportionment of these tasks to those properly responsible, according to the seasons of the year and to the appropriate times of the day, and to note at close range the personal habits of cleanliness, sobriety, punctuality, and orderliness that were virtues in this way of life.

(273)

2. Keeping a formal school of the three R's and the manual arts

In the winter of 1798–9 Henry Simmons opened a grammar school in one of the rooms of Cornplanter's house at Jenuchshadago. In 1799 a separate schoolhouse was built near the village, but it was abandoned as a school at the time of the Delaware witchcraft crisis and apparently was never reopened, the building being used thereafter by the Indians as a council-house. Simmons's early-winter class of elementary pupils ranged from twelve to twenty-five persons, including several adults, but seasonal movements, suspicion of education as an alienating influence, and the practical inconvenience that school attendance meant for the families of the pupils combined to make formal English education the least successful of the Quaker enterprises during early years of the mission. In 1802 the Indian committee in Philadelphia, at Seneca request, offered to educate four boys, taking them at about age fifteen and returning them to the reservation at twenty-one, to live near Philadelphia in Quaker farmhouses. Here, it was thought, they would learn the rudiments of formal education and the trade of farmer or other useful country occupations, but "the chief object of our undertaking their education will be to bring them up in habits of industry as our Children are in well ordered families in the country." Although formal schools for Indian pupils were reopened at Tunessassa in 1814 and at Cold Spring in 1816, the hiatus in schooling lasted during most of the remainder of Handsome Lake's life along the Allegheny. The farm at Tunessassa did, however, establish a program of training in the manual arts, taking Indian boys as boarders for periods of up to six months and teaching them farm trades, and holding regular instruction sessions for girls and women in soap-making, spinning, and weaving.

3. Technical assistance in specific Seneca projects

Various Seneca individuals, and the Allegany community as a whole from time to time, wished to make improvements in their manner of living that required either capital or instruction or both. The Quakers initially offered to help the Seneca on such occasions and did in fact spend much time and large amounts of money in this way. Part of the program was devoted to giving out small hardware, such as needles

and thread, scissors, combs, spectacles, and other consumer goods
that were already known to the Indians but in short supply. Indian
women were allowed to keep the soap and cloth that they manufactured while learning the arts on Quaker equipment at Tunessassa.
But the major part of the technical assistance was directed toward
improvements: house construction, field clearing and fencing, plowing and seeding, roadbuilding, sawmill construction, the building of
a council house at Cold Spring. For these large jobs, the Quakers
provided tools, seed, paint, and livestock as required, helped with the
labor, and instructed the interested Indians in how to use the tools
and carry on the work. At first, the tools were presented to the
Indians after the initial job was done; later, in order to curtail an
increasingly dependent and demanding attitude, a store was set up
at which the Quakers sold hardware at cost. The most impressive
consequence was the abandonment of the old fenced settlement at
Jenuchshadago and the construction of new painted frame houses
with hung doors and glass windows in a more dispersed settlement
pattern. By 1805 three new communities had been developed: one
south of Jenuchshadago, one around the first Quaker farm at Gen-
singhuta, and a third at Cold Spring. Individual Indian households
cleared, plowed, and fenced their own fields, no longer in the
communal fenced area, but in association with the homestead. The
community built a road upriver under the cliffs from Jenuchshadago
to the tribal reservation in New York and constructed a sawmill on
a better millsite north of the state line. New crops were introduced
including wheat, hay for the cattle, and flax for cloth. And the
Indians were advised to invest tribal and individual income from
annuities in useful and productive materials, such as clothing, livestock, and plow irons, rather than in economically useless items such
as cheap jewelry and whiskey, and to enlarge their income by increasing production rather by selling off any more of their only
remaining major capital asset, the land.

4. Preaching of the Protestant ethic

The Quakers did not come to the Seneca to convert them to Christianity and enroll them in an Allegany Yearly Meeting. Hence
they did very little in the way of reciting Christian dogma and
history, reading from the Bible, or threatening sinners with damna-

tion. The general tolerance of Seneca religious belief and custom was based on the Quaker conviction that every human being, not merely the Christian, entertains an inner light that evinces itself as the voice of natural conscience. Since this inner light is the mystic presence of divinity in every man, the Seneca were in no danger of damnation if they but heeded the voice. The conscience, of course, in true eighteenth-century fashion was assumed to represent universal human values, and many of these values were intimately connected with what has been called the Protestant ethic. This ethic emphasized sobriety, marital fidelity, observance of contract, hard work, orderliness, a respect for equipment and livestock, cleanliness, the duty of patiently helping back to duty those who strayed from the path of virtue rather than killing or otherwise retaliating upon them with violence. With considerable sophistication the Quakers understood that the construction, maintenance, and growth of a self-supporting democratic rural community of small independent farmers depended very largely on the widespread acceptance of precisely these ethical values and thus addressed themselves from the outset to awakening or reinforcing them in the Seneca. It was, in the Quaker view, axiomatic that these values were expressed by the inner light and thus needed only to be drawn to the Indians' attention rather than implanted afresh. But it was also understood by the Quakers that because of the fabric of private vested interests, institutions could not be changed overnight. The consequence of this dual conviction—that Indians were human beings of the same moral stature as white men, and that when local politics was involved, it was best to work quietly—was a unique method of approach. Where no major political interests appeared to oppose them, the Quaker representatives were bluntly forthright in denouncing what they regarded as bad practice. Thus they roundly condemned even cherished local customs, such as the social dances, the traditional sexual division of labor, and the spending of relatively large sums of money on vain personal finery, and they became almost fiery in their exhortation of idolaters, whiskey drinkers, and gamblers. But where politics was involved, as in the Seneca opposition to a public school and in the witchcraft issue, they remained remarkably silent, waiting for a more opportune season to press their convictions and contenting themselves in the meantime with partial measures. On some matters, even where political opposition was not an obstacle, these preachments failed; they were unable, for instance, to persuade the Seneca, either by instruction or example, to observe the weekly day of rest ("First Day"). Their success was most marked in those areas of behavior where there already existed, on a high level of generality, an influential body of opinion consonant with their own, as was the case with respect to economic reorganization and temperance. In such areas, once agreement was established on the major abstract goals, Quaker advice on the technical necessities for attainment was apt to be readily accepted, even if it required wholesale abandonment of custom, as was the case with regard to settlement pattern and sexual division of labor. The Quakers were always careful to insure that superficial and playful imitation was not substituted for deep learning, and thus they emphasized both the communication of concepts, rather than mere rote procedure, and the assurance of rewards of praise and of substance. Prizes were given in cash and kind for successful accomplishment, and the Indians were encouraged to keep the finished products of joint labors (thus Indian women were given the cloth woven by the Quakers from the flax or wool that the Indians had spun on the Quaker wheels).[9]

· *The Social Gospel* ·

THE THEME OF THE FIRST VISION of Handsome Lake had been preeminently apocalyptic, and the immediate aim of the prophet was simply to rescue souls from the storm of judgment. Thus, although worry about the welfare of Seneca society no doubt played a role in inspiring the first vision and prompted the classification of sins given in the early revelations, the fear of imminent doom at first had diverted attention from the long-term problem of establishing an enduring society and directed it toward the immediate necessity of ritual purification of a world on the brink of annihilation. But the principles of what may be called a social gospel, particularly as it concerned temperance, were latent even in the primary vision, and they became increasingly manifest during the period from 1801 to 1803. After 1803 most of the prophet's pronouncements concerned social matters. The main values that the social gospel inculcated were temperance, peace and unity, land retention, acculturation, and a revised domestic morality.

Temperance remained a prime concern throughout Handsome Lake's mission. The social disorders other than witchcraft to which whiskey contributed were matters of daily recognition both by Handsome Lake and by other responsible Seneca. The prohibition of whiskey thus came willy-nilly to have meaning as social policy in addition to its significance in Handsome Lake's eschatology, and it therefore may be regarded as the first tenet of the strictly social gospel. Handsome Lake was not content merely to condemn drinking as a sin; he went to some pains to explain just what were the social evils attendant upon drinking: family quarrels, mistreatment of children, lowered economic productivity, and mayhem and murder at drinking parties. He used logical argument as well as his religious authority to convince the skeptical of the evils of drink:

> Good food is turned into evil drink. Now some have said that there is no harm in partaking of fermented liquids.

> Then let this plan be followed: let men gather in two parties, one having a feast of food, apples and corn, and the other have cider and whiskey. Let the parties be equally divided and matched and let them commence their feasting at the same time. When the feast is finished you will see those who drank the fermented juices murder one of their own party but not so with those who ate food only.

The second tenet of the social code was peace and its correlate, social unity. Handsome Lake deplored the tendency for chiefs to bicker, for the result was disunity among the people, and spoke out against the factional tendency in matters of politics and religion. In the vision of the sky journey he had been told that "all the Chiefs of the Six nations should put their minds together and all be of one mind."[10] In 1800 he was still talking about the problem of unity, complaining to the Quakers that "I always try to instruct the chiefs and others to do right and to be of one mind and it is the will of the Great Spirit that all people should be of one mind but some of them will not listen to what I say. . . ."[11] This concern for unity was, of course, given institutional form in 1801 when he became the moral censor of the Seneca nation and principal leader of the Six Nations. Furthermore, he came to disapprove of capital punishment and publicly expressed regret for having caused the death of two women convicted of witchcraft, for "the Creator has not privileged men to punish each other."

Another aspect of the tenet of peace and amity was the preservation of good feelings toward the whites. The whites were pictured as neither good nor evil in themselves, but simply different from Indians. Thus, for example, whiskey was permissible for white men, for whom it had been created to use as a medicine and to strengthen themselves after work. Indians, to whom it was injurious, ought not to be jealous of the white man's freedom to drink.[12] He willingly accepted Jesus as his counterpart among the white people and considered the teachings of Jesus to be the equivalent of his own but intended for whites.[13] In fact, Handsome Lake apparently was willing for Indian converts to Christianity to remain with their new faith, provided they were conscientious in obeying its prescriptions. The Oneida pagan priest, Doctor Peter, in August 1806, reported that in a conversation he had recently had with the Seneca prophet, "the man of God" said "that we who have ministers of the written holy book must attend to their instructions and obey them, for that these ministers derive all their knowledge from the written holy book, and that he [i.e., Handsome Lake] receives his from the same source from which that originated." Doctor Peter therefore warned those Indians who "had had water sprinkled upon them in the name of the white people's more immediate Savior, strictly to observe all the precepts pertaining to water baptism, or they would miss their way and finally perish." And he advised all the Indians "to live in peace and love one another and all mankind, white people as well as Indians."[14] Handsome Lake reassured his people that their fears of extermination by the whites were groundless; their doom would be brought upon them by their own sins.[15] Throughout his mission he spoke well of and encouraged the Quakers. It would then appear that he was anxious to cool the angry passions of those who hated and blamed the whites for all the ills of the Indians, recommended love and understanding between the races, and counseled mutual respect for the differences that (apart from technological acculturation) had been ordained by the Great Spirit. Each race had now had its own savior, commissioned by the same God: Jesus for the whites, Handsome Lake for the Indians; each savior had a message for his own race, but one that it was well for the other race to heed. Men of good will among whites and Indians could make their joint occupancy of the earth a happy time, but, he felt, the white men were even more commonly alienated from their own savior than the Indians from theirs.

The third tenet was the preservation of the tribe's land base. This principle seems not to have become articulate as part of the prophet's message until the third vision (February 1800) but the sources of his concerns are easily enough discerned in historical perspective. He was the outstanding proponent of an embargo on further extensive cessions. But he was not opposed to profitable exchanges of land. He favored a general consolidation of Indian land holdings into large reservations and was willing to sell or trade the smaller tracts on the Genesee for equivalent land next to the big reservations at Buffalo Creek and Cattaraugus (including his own lands at Cuba Lake). He was motivated in this by a desire to bring the dissolute Indians on the small reservations, exposed to equally dissolute white settlements, under the control of the larger village communities. This would both promote moral reform and reduce the likelihood of piecemeal alienation of Seneca land.

The expansion of the social gospel to include as its fourth major tenet a pro-acculturation policy required that the prophet take a firm position on issues about which at first he had been indifferent or ambivalent. By 1801 he had made up his mind that English schooling was desirable for at least some of the children. In that year and again in 1811 the prophet and Cornplanter joined in requesting that the Quakers reopen the school (unsuccessfully, for the school was not opened again until 1814). In 1803 he is reported to have opposed a mission school at Buffalo Creek, objecting to "the building of the house, receiving any books from the white people for the instruction of their children, or hearkening to the gospel and maxims of civilization." But on the other hand, he is also reported to have finally agreed, albeit reluctantly, to the building of the school and the instruction of the children, provided they were not prevented from celebrating the Seneca religious festivals at Midwinter and Green Corn.[16] The Code itself asserts, concerning "studying in English schools,"

Now let the Council appoint twelve people to study, two from each nation of the six. So many white people are about you that you must study to know their ways.[17]

It would appear, in the final analysis, that Handsome Lake recognized a value in formal English schooling, but a value that was limited: the protection of the interests of the tribe from white lawyers and officials whose documents the Indians must be able to read for themselves in order to avoid being cheated.

With respect to the learning of white farming and domestic technology, Handsome Lake had little problem, and when his attention turned to these matters in the summer of 1801, he saw no difficulty in advising the people "that they might farm a little and make houses; but that they must not sell anything they raised off the ground, but give it away to one another and to the old people in particular in short that they must possess everything in common." In October he and Cornplanter announced that they saw the white people were going to settle all around them; that they could not live unless they learned to farm and follow the white people's ways.[18] During the trip to Washington in 1802 he openly endorsed a pro-acculturation policy. In 1803 he spoke on behalf of all the Allegany Seneca in urging the Quakers not to remove their settlement from Genesinguhta, and he added significantly, "I myself have been advising our people to pursue the course of life you recommend to us and we have fully concluded to follow habits of Industry, but we are only just beginning to learn." He went on to ask that the Quakers sell them the tools and clothes necessary for the new way of life.[19] In 1807 the *Evangelical Intelligencer* reported that the "Seneca Prophet" was adjuring his followers to "cultivate their lands" and to "live industrious lives."[20] The Code itself unambiguously praised the abundant harvests, animal labor, and warm houses that white technology could provide and urged the people to learn the white man's ways in these matters (providing only that there be no pride in material wealth). Thus, there can be no question that the prophet gave emphatic encouragement to the transformation of the Seneca economic system from a male-hunting-and-female-horticulture to a male-farming-and-female-housekeeping pattern.

But on the other hand, Handsome Lake was not in favor of pell-

mell, indiscriminate acculturation. The educational and technological customs of the whites were to be integrated into a Seneca society
that retained as a social value the village communalism, reserved
land title to the nation itself, and depended upon traditional reciprocal gift-giving rather than commercial sale as the mechanism
of internal distribution. The moral restraints of modesty and of
kindness to animals were levied in such a way as to preclude, in
theory at least, the development of the profit motive and rural capi-
talism. Furthermore, many white culture traits were proscribed in
the Code: whiskey, mixed social dancing to the music of the violin,
gambling with cards, and punishment of evildoers by the state
(symbolized by handcuffs, whips, the hangman's rope, and prisons).
And of course religious and ethnic identity were to remain Indian.
Thus the society envisioned by the prophet was to be an autonomous
reservation community, using white technology, but retaining its
Indian identity, rejecting the centralization of police powers and the
private profit motive as social evils, and condemning the more conspicuous vices of white society (drunkenness, the sexual promiscuity
to which he felt mixed dancing by couples led, and gambling). He
had nothing to say about the fate of those aspects of white technology that had long ago been adopted by the Seneca (e.g., metal
household containers to replace pottery, guns to replace the spear
and the bow and arrow, metal knives and axes to replace stone, etc.):
these were by now an integral part of the Iroquois way of life and
were not singled out as alien because of their ultimate origin in
another land. Indeed, it would seem that Handsome Lake's attitude
toward acculturation was remarkably rational, in the sense that he
saw no peculiar virtue either in cultural nativism or cultural assimilation and made decisions about acculturation without the dogma-
tism that was aroused by such issues as whiskey, witchcraft, and
land sales.

The fifth major tenet of the social gospel was a revised domestic
morality. Like many reformers, Handsome Lake felt that personal
salvation, social betterment, and postponement of the apocalypse all
depended upon the establishment and pursuit of certain principles of
personal behavior. If these principles were followed, then all good
things would be realized. Most of the Code, both in early versions
and later ones alike, was devoted to explicating these principles of

personal morality and to describing the torments in the afterlife of those who violated them.

The earliest principle of the moral gospel to be enunciated by Handsome Lake was the duty of sons to obey their fathers. He expressed this principle in his second vision in August, 1799, in allegorical form, describing the angry dispute between Cornplanter and his son Henry and the neglect of Handsome Lake by his own son.

The second principle of domestic morality to be emphasized by the prophet was the duty of mothers not to interfere with their daughters' marriages. Handsome Lake was deeply concerned by the fragility of the classic Iroquois nuclear family and devoted much of his preaching to homilies on domestic tranquility. The "Great Message" contains, in Parker's published version of the Code, about 130 sections. The first four sections define the four cardinal sins: drinking whiskey, practicing lethal witchcraft, using magical charms, and using medicines to sterilize a woman. Three of these four bear directly on the nuclear family, for drunkenness led to quarrels between husband and wife, the magical charms included love charms that facilitated promiscuity, and sterility unnaturally limited not only the numbers of a woman's descendants but also the number of children in the household. In the latter case, Handsome Lake singled out the mother-daughter relationship as the central problem. He condemned the mother who ignored her child's warnings against wrongdoing and who advised her married daughter to abort and become sterile or to leave her husband. "The Creator," he said, "is sad because of the tendency of old women to breed mischief." These cautions, together with the implication that older women were particularly apt to practice witchcraft and to influence their daughters to do the same, amounted to a direct challenge to the primacy of the kind of exclusive mother-daughter relationship that was essential to the old quasi-matriarchal system.

The third major principle of domestic morality was the sanctity of the husband-wife relationship, which in Handsome Lake's thought now took precedence over other kinship ties. By 1806 his disciple at Oneida was reported by Kirkland to have "spoken upon the duties of husbands and wives, and the great sin of divorce."[21] In 1807 he himself was reported in the *Evangelical Intelligencer* to insist to his followers "that they put not away their wives."[22] And in a number of undated revelations he delineated his conception of how the members of the nuclear family should and should not behave. He condemned the man who deserted a series of women in order to avoid the responsibilities of fatherhood. He condemned the woman who was jealous of her husband's love for his children. He condemned quarreling between husband and wife. He condemned scandalous gossip about the misbehavior of wives while their husbands were away hunting. He praised the wife who forgave her husband who strayed, but condemned the erring husband. He condemned philandering men. He condemned the punitive mother. He condemned the drunken father. He urged the childless couple to adopt children of the wife's sister rather than separate. He condemned gossiping women who spread rumors that a woman's husband was not the father of her child. And he urged grandchildren to care for aged and helpless grandparents.

The remainder of the Code contains a number of admonitions concerning the reciprocal social and economic roles of men and women. A woman should be a good housewife: generous, serving food to visitors and neighbors' children, never a petty thief, always helping the orphaned of the community, and avoiding gossip. A man should "harvest food for his family," build a good house, and keep horses and cattle.

In review of Handsome Lake's moral admonitions, it is plain that he was concerned to stabilize the nuclear family by protecting the husband-wife relationship against abrasive events. A principal abrasive, in his view, was the hierarchical relationship between a mother and her daughter. Mothers, he believed, were all too prone to urge their daughters toward sin by administering abortifacients and sterilizing medicines, by drunkenness, by practicing witchcraft, and by providing love magic. They set their daughters' minds against their husbands, condoned mothers' severity to their children, and were above accepting advice from their own offspring. Thus, in order to stabilize the nuclear family it was necessary to loosen the tie between mother and daughter. Furthermore, men were supposed to assume the role of heads of families, being economically responsible for their wives and children and not frittering away their energies on strong drink, gambling, dancing, and philandering, nor on mother-in-law trouble. Although he did not directly challenge the matrilineal principle in regard to sib membership or the customs of nominating sachems, he made it plain that the nuclear family, rather than the maternal lineage, was henceforward to be both the moral and the economic center of the behavioral universe.

· *Political Defeat* ·

THE YEAR 1803 began auspiciously for the prophet. A general council of the Seneca nation was held in January at Jenuchshadago, or Cornplanter's Town, with chiefs and warriors from all the villages represented, amounting to about two thirds of the whole adult male population. Acting on the basis of the policy formulated at the Buffalo Creek council of 1801, which had made Handsome Lake the supreme leader of the Six Nations, this group announced "that the Great Council fire for the Six Nations is now opened at this Place which is to Continue while they are a Nation, the old fire at Buffalo Creek to be intirely extinguished." Nicholas Rosencrantz and Henry O'Bail were appointed official interpreters, and delegates were dispatched, with Handsome Lake's approval, to Philadelphia and Washington to secure economic aid for the Seneca at Tonawanda and to rescind the recent sale of the lands at Black Rock.[23]

This effort to move the council fire of the Six Nations was perhaps the high-water mark of Handsome Lake's political fortunes. At Jenuchshadago he was supported by kinsmen who functioned as administrative chiefs: his brother Cornplanter, the local political "boss"; his nephew Charles O'Bail, and his fellow clansman Strong, two "sober, good young men" whom he had appointed "to take care of all our [i.e., the Allegany band's] publick business";[24] and another nephew, Henry O'Bail, who had just become an official interpreter. Of the sixteen to twenty chiefs of the local band, no less than four, including himself, were members of the Wolf clan (the others being Cornplanter, Blacksnake, and Strong) and four more were members of the Snipe clan of Cornplanter's wife (including Henry and Charles O'Bail, his nephews). Thus nearly half of the local chiefs were closely associated by kinship with the prophet, and a number of others were solidly in his favor.[25]

But there were those who did not support the move. Brant and his Mohawks and the other Iroquois tribes at Grand River in Canada claimed that the council fire was at the Onondaga village there; the principal chiefs at Buffalo Creek insisted that it was still at Buffalo Creek. Agent Chapin claimed that although the warriors and women supported the prophet, the chiefs opposed him, and he started the rumor (which became widespread in later years) that the whole movement was a scheme of Cornplanter's "to take the lead of the Nation." He insisted that Buffalo Creek was the place of business for the Six Nations. And Handsome Lake himself traveled to Buffalo Creek in May with Cornplanter's son John to collect the annuities for the Allegany band. (And so he did in the spring and summer for many years thereafter.)

The issue as to where the council fire really was, insofar as the Seneca were concerned at least, was settled once again in August 1807, when a large council of the chiefs of the Six Nations (presumably including Handsome Lake) met at Buffalo Creek to revitalize the confederacy. According to the official report of the local Indian agent the meeting was called principally by the Seneca chiefs "for the purpose of renewing and confirming, the former confederacy of the six Nations." More Iroquois chiefs from all the tribes assembled than at any time since the Treaty of Canandaigua in 1794. The meeting was a success. "They have," said the agent, "according to their own antient customs, have pledge themselves Nationally to each other, to be United let what will happen, peace or war." Thus Handsome Lake was able to see the realization, in one institution at least, of his dream of unity—but it came at the expense of his own political interests. One chief could not dominate the confederacy. The great council fire had burned fitfully at Jenuchshadago; now it burned again even brighter than before at Buffalo Creek, where Handsome Lake's rival Red Jacket held sway.[26]

The prophet's dominion at Cornplanter's Town now also came rapidly to an end. In the fall of 1803 he presided over the local council meeting where the removal of the Quaker farm from Genesinguhta was discussed. The Quakers wanted to relocate it at Tunessassa, a few miles away off the reservation. Handsome Lake made a warm reply to this proposal. Speaking as "the united voice" of the chiefs, the warriors, and the women, he praised the Quakers as peaceable and honest people and urged them not to move too far away. "We want you to be near us," he said, "that you may extend further assistance and instruction."

Friends Tewastie—I myself have been advising our people to the course of life you commend to us as we have fully concluded to follow habits of industry but we are only just beginning to learn, and we find ourselves at a loss for tools to work with, we now request you to bring on plenty of all kinds you think will be usefull, then such of our peoples as are able will buy for themselves and such as are poor, we wish you to continue to lend and they shall be returned to you again—we also want you to bring on usefull cloths, and sell to us, that we may get some necessary things without having to go so far for them—In looking forward we can limit no time for you to live beside us, this must depend on your own judgement. . . .

The prophet also requested that the blacksmith who was teaching the men remain a while longer because he was the best smith they had ever seen and they wished to learn more from him. In a secondary role Cornplanter backed up the statements of his brother. It was an amicable meeting with the Quakers, and the relocation of the farm and various other questions were agreed on easily.[27]

But a few months later Handsome Lake and Cornplanter quarreled, and Handsome Lake and his adherents moved from Jenuchshadago to build a new town at Cold Spring, on the reservation in New York. The underlying source of the trouble was personal jealousy of the "old chief" by Handsome Lake and some of the younger men, particularly Blacksnake, who for some time had resented the high-handed manner in which Cornplanter had managed the affairs of the Allegany band. But the immediate issue was land and money. Cornplanter had built his private sawmill at a bad place; much of the year it was useless, either flooded or dry. He proposed to move his sawmill to a site within the reservation where he would lease it as before to a white man and take the profits himself. Many of the Indians thought this was unreasonable and refused to sanction the arrangement. Cornplanter in a rage declared that if the tribe refused to let him use the national land (the reservation), he would not let them use his private land (the grant), and he ordered everyone off. The band's response to this was to displace him from the office of chief, to lease the sawmill site in question to one of Cornplanter's white millwrights (for a rental of sixty thousand board feet of lumber yearly, payable to the band), thus setting up a competing sawmill at a better location than Cornplanter's, and to leave the grant. The leaders in the move were nominated to serve on the council. Cornplanter, reduced to the status of a common warrior, was left to sulk with a few loyal families at Jenuchshadago.[28]

Having thus lost his most powerful political ally, Handsome Lake now began to lose credit with the Quakers. They wanted the Indians to give up the old way of living in small villages and to disperse among the fields in the settlement pattern typical of rural white America, with houses built up to a mile apart, each surrounded by its own fenced fields and woods. But Handsome Lake, to the Friends' considerable annoyance, rejected this advice and persuaded most of the Indians to construct a new, tightly organized village on four acres of wooded knoll close to the river at the mouth of Cold Spring Creek. The men worked in gangs, cutting the timber off the village site and opening a prospect to the river, constructing log houses of rough-hewn lumber with clapboard roofs and earth floors. (Chimneys, paneled doors, and glass windows were added later.) Individual households were allowed to choose their own fields around the village to raise corn and build cabins in the summer. The prophet's reason for insisting on this settlement pattern was religious. In order to carry on "their yearly dances & sacrifices . . . they must build a town to live in, in winter seasons." The Quakers opposed this manner of proceeding as not being "the nearest road to distinct property" but only a few families followed their advice and built separate farmsteads along the bottom lands up the river. After all, they had found that at least five members of the council—Blue Eyes, Mush, Silver Heels, John Snow, and Henry O'Bail—were living apart from Cold Spring and had to be called from their homes by the blast of a horn. "To these," said the Quakers, "our advice flows freely & generally acceptable to them. the other party that are huddling together (are Indians yet) are not beginning right in our view."[29]

The result of these events was a division of the Allegany band into three mutually resentful fragments: a few families, kinsmen of Cornplanter, remaining with him on the grant; a number of Quaker-influenced families, more progressive than Handsome Lake's policy allowed, settled on the other side of Cold Spring; and the Handsome Lake faction, by far the largest, composed of an uneasy combination of progressives and conservatives, "huddling together" in the

village at Cold Spring under the leadership of the prophet and Blacksnake, whom he had "for his privy Counsellor."[30] It was an unstable
situation, which Handsome Lake was unable to control. The Quakers
covertly criticized his judgment in regard to the Cold Spring settlement and openly objected to the dirty, flea-infested Indian houses
there. Some of the people felt that Cornplanter had been unjustly
treated and favored bringing him, now that he behaved contritely,
back as chief. In 1806, when a Quaker delegation from Philadelphia
visited Cold Spring, Handsome Lake was still presiding over the
council, and Blacksnake was full of laudatory remarks; the settlements were prospering with new houses, new fields, a new road
along the river. But the Quakers sensed an undercurrent of dissatisfaction and experienced "some apprehensions that one or two of
their young Ambitious chiefs was a little uneasy in their minds. . . ."
There were rumors of whiskey being brought onto the reserve again.
Some of the speeches had been a trifle sarcastic. Handsome Lake
was also on edge, saying plaintively, in response to the Friends'
exhortation to eschew whiskey and gambling, that some of the people would not obey him. Anxious now to find support from the
Quakers, he was in the forefront of those greeting the visitors. He
concurred in the Quaker plan to send two Indian youths every six
months to live on the farm at Tunessassa "to be instructed in the
farming business or learn to manage the Mills." And Blacksnake
gave a short speech recommending him to their favor:

> All the Indians and white people know that the Great Spirit talks
> with our Prophet it is now Seven years since he began first to
> talk with him, & he tells the Indians they must leave off drinking
> whisky, & they have declined the use of it. . . .
>
> Brothers you must tell your friends, when you go home to make
> their minds easy, for we are determined never to let the whisky
> rise again and also to persue habits of industry and never decline
> it—Your young men and us are like one, when we want anything
> Done we Consult them and they assist us—and our Profit tells us
> what to do, and we get instructs from both. . . .[31]

While difficulties for Handsome Lake were accumulating along
the Allegheny, further political intrigue against him was maturing
among the chiefs at Buffalo Creek. Led by the eloquent and loqua-
cious Red Jacket, the Buffalo Creek sachems spread rumors among

both Indians and their white confidants that Handsome Lake was a false prophet.[32] It was not that these chiefs disagreed with the policies that he proposed. They all agreed with him, in principle at least, about the evils of whiskey, all believed in the traditional religion, all opposed Christian evangelism, all desired that the benefits of an English education and white technology should be made available to the Indians. But even though the Great Council had appointed him supreme leader, his earlier witchcraft accusations and his current pretensions to authority created bitter resentment. Red Jacket deliberately planted rumors that the prophet was a fraud perpetrated upon the Indians by Cornplanter, who "having lost the confidence of his countrymen, in order, as it is supposed, to retrieve his former standing, . . . persuaded his brother to announce himself as a prophet, or messenger from heaven, sent to redeem the fallen fortunes of the Indian race." When Handsome Lake appointed conjurors to designate witches and sentence them to death, the sachems insinuated that the witch hunt was "an artful expedient to render his enemies the objects of general abhorence, if not the victims of an ignominious death."[33] Personally, he was characterized as "formerly a great drunkard despised by the Indians themselves, as an ignorant, idle, worthless fellow." (His standing as one of the forty-nine chiefs of the council was conveniently passed over in these slanders.) After his reformation it was conceded that he appeared to be "meek, honest and innofensive" but "those best acquainted with him" were said to report that he was "deficient in intellect." "He converses but little. His countenance does not indicate much thoughtfulness. When questioned, however, his answers are pertinent and his public speeches are sensible. . . . At the meeting of commissioners with the Senecas, for the purpose of purchasing a tract of land at the Blackrock, this Indian was present, and opposed the sale of their lands. He related the communications, which he said he had received from the Great Spirit. Some of the communications he could not recollect, and asked his brother Cornplanter. When asked how he could forget such communications, he said at the time the Great Spirit told him these things, he related them to his brother: and that he was told so many things, he did not remember all. . . . To one, who expressed his doubts of his having such communications, and used some arguments to show him he had not, he replied with his usual simplicity, 'I think I have had such communications made to me!' " And even after the break with Cornplanter became known, the suggestions that he was merely a front man for a family conspiracy continued. The alleged conspirators now were his nephews Blacksnake and Henry and Charles O'Bail, who, being both "sensible" and "men of great renown . . . use their influence in his favour." Indian agent Chapin reported in 1807 that Handsome Lake was "consulted as the principle chief of the nation; but Red Jacket, a cunning and subtile chief at Buffaloe Creek, does not believe in him, but in his public transactions he pays him respect, as he is popular with the nation. He observed to the agent for the Six Nations, that when the prophet made his speeches, his nephews sat contiguous to him on the right and left. On a certain occasion he had taken care to place some others next to the prophet, and he was not able to say any thing."[34]

Handsome Lake was aware of a current of opposition in the Allegany band and of the enmity of Red Jacket and the other chiefs at Buffalo Creek. His tendency was, when in difficulty, to imagine that its origin lay in the malevolence of witches, and now, when he found himself in trouble at Cold Spring, he began to think about witchcraft again as the explanation. One of his opponents at Cold Spring, a mentally ill man who had on at least one occasion stood in the doorway of the council-house and, in the classic Indian gesture of disrespect to a speaker, farted at the conclusion of the prophet's homily, wandered off alone into the forests. A search party found him after three days, lost in a swamp across the river. He was sitting on a nest of branches, devouring snakes. "He was not in his right mind," the prophet concluded. They took him home, but he died soon after.

The prophet proceeded to blame the man's insanity for his disrespect to the prophet's teaching and to blame the insanity on witchcraft. He accused a Cattaraugus woman and her daughter of secretly administering poison. The chief's council met and decided to punish the women by whipping them, one stroke to be given by each chief. (There were from sixteen to twenty chiefs.) Handsome Lake agreed with this judgment after consulting with the four angels, believing (or at least so he later claimed) that they would survive the lashing. The women were whipped, and they both died as a result of it.[35]

People began to murmur. In 1807 Cornplanter was restored to his position as a member of the chiefs' council.[36] And soon after that a religious dispute began to develop over the restrictions the prophet had placed on the medicine-societies. In 1807 there was, according to tradition, an epidemic that caused a number of deaths. Many people secretly believed that the outbreak of illness was the result of a neglect of the medicine-company ceremonies. Handsome Lake, when asked the cause of the epidemic of deaths, according to oral tradition is reputed to have declared (perhaps cautiously) that a large underground animal was causing the deaths (such subterranean monsters were a common Iroquois belief). If the people would go to a certain place across the mountains and dig there, they would find the animal. A group of men, planning to kill the monster, went to the prescribed spot and dug a huge hole. But they found no animal. The people continued to die, and at last Handsome Lake declared that it must be witchcraft. Several oral traditions agree that a council was held at which many people were present. Handsome Lake pointed the finger at at least one old woman, who was killed on the spot. But the woman had dissatisfied relatives; and that night at a council of chiefs and dissidents charges were aired: that Handsome Lake was killing off only those who did not believe in him; that those whom he accused were not guilty; that it was not witchcraft, but neglect of the medicine ceremonies, that was the root of the difficulty.[37]

Handsome Lake now was convinced that although the people revered him, the chiefs were in a witch-inspired conspiracy against him, and he confided this belief to his disciples. One of these disciples, "one of the most distinguished of their young men," told a white man that "the prophet would yet be persecuted and put to death, as the wicked put to death the Lord Jesus Christ."[38]

The denouement came in 1809; and again the issue was witchcraft. Cornplanter was absent when an Onondaga woman accompanied by her husband and a few relatives arrived at Cold Spring for trial as a witch. Handsome Lake's supporters convened in council. "It was a very small Council but on looking into her hands she was pronounced Guilty of the Charge by Connudiu." An aged chief named Old Fatty now declared, "If he was a young Man & able for war as he once was he would put en End to her—on which Sun Fish immediately caught up an Axe & knocked her in the Head & among them they compleated the Massacre." According to tradition, the stunned woman survived the first blow of the hatchet, recovered consciousness, and groaned; then her throat was slit. But the woman's relatives at Onondaga were not satisfied that she was a witch: "the Relatives of the Woman threaten revenge (Blood for Blood) if ever they catch Sun Fish." When Cornplanter returned and learned of the affair, he privately told people that he disapproved of it.[39] When a Quaker committee arrived a few months later and also disapproved of the killing, he stated publicly in council, "I hope we shall be careful in future how we take the lives of any for witchcraft without being sure that they are guilty, and he thought it very difficult to prove it." Later he voiced the opinion that it would be better to invoke the death penalty against a chief for selling any more land than for witchcraft, because the one could be proved and "the other he had his doubts about."[40] And Henry O'Bail, one of Handsome Lake's chiefly nephews, now also openly took sides against the prophet. Earlier, in 1802, he had with the council's permission tumbled the rotting wooden statue of Tarachiawagon into the Allegany River; in this he had been supported by the Quakers, who regarded it as an example of "idolatry." Handsome Lake, perhaps preferring to be himself the central object of religious respect, had not objected. More recently Henry O'Bail had been among those who publicly objected to the burning of the white dog. This was one of the sacred rituals and was annually being practiced at Cold Spring under Handsome Lake's direct supervision. Now he was publicly stating that "Witchcraft . . . does not exist."[41]

Handsome Lake was now virtually without friends among the Allegany band. The Quakers were against him. His brother Cornplanter and his nephew Henry were against him. The local kinsmen of the witches whom he had accused were against him. The witches not yet discovered were against him. He secretly pondered escape. But where could he go? He could not go to Cattaraugus Reservation because there lived members of the Delaware band whom he had accused of witchcraft. He could not go to Buffalo Creek because there lived Red Jacket and the chiefs who were conspiring against him. He could not go to Onondaga because there lived the kinfolk of the woman whom he had just executed, and they were vowing revenge. He could go to Tonawanda, but that was a poor and demoralized community. He began to think again of death. At last he had another vision. As he told it later,

Now it was that when the people reviled me, the proclaimer of the prophecy, the impression came to me that it would be well to depart and go to Tonawanda. In that place I had relatives and friends and thought that my bones might find a resting place there. Thus I thought through the day.

Then the messengers came to me and said "We understand your thoughts. We will visit you more frequently and converse with you. Wherever you go take care not to be alone. Be cautious and move secretly."

Then the messengers told me that my life journey would be in three stages and when I entered the third I would enter into the eternity of the New World, the land of our Creator.[42]

And so, in the late fall or winter of 1809, Handsome Lake suddenly left Cold Spring, accompanied by a few faithful disciples, including the minister Joiise.[43] The departure was dramatic and is remembered even today among the Indians at Cold Spring and Cornplanter's Town. At Tonawanda he found refuge and a base from which he could continue his evangelical work. But he had no local political power. And so after tempers cooled, he returned to Allegany, more quietly than he had left. There he found that the chiefs' council had officially resolved "to take no more lives under a suspicion of witchcraft."[44] He remained a member of the chiefs' council, but his brother Cornplanter resumed the position of presiding chairman, which Handsome Lake had held. In 1811 he, along with ten other chiefs of the council, signed a letter replying to the Quakers that they did indeed wish to have their children taught in a school. The council had, in fact, conducted a house-to-house survey questioning parents about their views, and the community there, as well as the council at Buffalo Creek, was favorable.[45]

The prophet's last political stratagem to counteract the influence of Red Jacket and Cornplanter was only partially successful. He undertook the role of "peace prophet" during the War of 1812. During the years preceding the war the New York Iroquois had been repeatedly solicited by representatives of the revived western confederates, under the leadership of Tecumseh and his brother the Shawnee Prophet (the "war prophet"), to join them and the British in a frontier campaign to recover their lost lands. The New York chiefs unanimously opposed joining any such conspiracy, and in a council at Jenuchshadago in the summer of 1812 the chiefs of the

Allegany band, including Cornplanter and Handsome Lake, specifically reassured the whites from Warren and Meadville of their intentions to remain at peace.[46] Officially the United States also encouraged the Iroquois to remain neutral. But a number of Brant's Mohawks from Grand River did enlist in the British forces. This action prompted the United States to solicit "volunteers" to the number of 150 to 200 warriors. The Indian agent at Buffalo Creek argued, "I know of no Instance where Indians have ever lain still when war came near them" and he expressed fear that if the United States did not recruit the warriors, the British would. The Six Nations Council at Buffalo Creek tacitly permitted the recruitment. But Handsome Lake now intervened, organizing a council of the Iroquois of New York "at their ancient council fire at Onondaga." This council, attended by representatives of the Oneida, Onondaga, Stockbridge, Tuscarora, and Seneca, sent to the President of the United States a speech complaining "that a few of the Indians got together at [Buffalo Creek] and were invited to take up the hatchet —this they say is contra to the advice of Genl Washington and contra to the Wishes of their great Prophet, who attended this Council." They suggested that any request for military services by the Indians be addressed to councilors of the League at Onondaga.[47]

This action did not deter the United States from recruiting Indian volunteers. During the two years of war from 1812 to 1814 the muster roll of New York Iroquois who enlisted in the war in defense of what many of them now called "our country" numbered over six hundred officers and enlisted men. Some twenty were eventually given commissions, including Handsome Lake's chief disciples Blacksnake and Henry O'Bail and other Allegany council chiefs, among them Cornplanter, Black Chief, and Strong.[48] But Handsome Lake nonetheless had a measurable effect in slowing down the mobilization of the Iroquois, and federal officials resented his meddling. When Handsome Lake visited Buffalo Creek on his way back from the meeting at Onondaga, he insulted agent Erastus Granger, who signed up the volunteers, by failing to call on him. "If I can see him before he goes home," wrote Granger, "I shall tell him to stay at Alleghany till the War is over."[49] Against the wishes of federal Indian agents, the Onondaga warriors who were recruited in 1812 insisted on stopping off on their way at Allegany. The agent told them "not to call on the Old Prophet, for he must not interfere with the wishes of our great chiefs. The chiefs [said] that they *would* go that way; but it was for a religious purpose; they should stay there but a short time, and then go on to Buffalo." By the summer of 1813 the two reservations under Handsome Lake's greatest personal influence—Allegany and Tonawanda—had still turned out a total of only seven warriors; at Buffalo Creek nearly all the men had already taken up arms. Next year the chiefs from Allegany and Tonawanda were still reported to be reluctant about the war.[50]

The peace council at Onondaga did have another effect. It represented a temporary victory for Handsome Lake in his continuing effort to move the Six Nations council fire away from Buffalo Creek, far from the influence of his rival Red Jacket. Although the fire remained officially at Buffalo Creek until the reservation itself was sold a generation later, the fire did at long last come back permanently to its old hearth at Onondaga.

· Evangelical Triumph ·

IN THE POLITICS OF THE CHIEFS' COUNCIL, despite the eminence of his titles, Handsome Lake failed, mired in personal jealousies and tribal factionalism and unable to call upon an efficient bureaucracy for the administration of his policies. Such a failure, indeed, was in a sense ordained by Iroquois culture, for a correlate of the theme of freedom was an extreme sensitivity to issues involving personal dominance. Pretenders to greatness, like Logan and Sturgeon, were sometimes assassinated on behalf of an offended community faction by members of their own family (a procedure which aborted the revenge process); leaders like Cornplanter, Red Jacket, and Brant were apt to suffer rejection or assault; factionalism was pervasive; and the intense ambivalence about dominance was traditionally expressed in the polarity between the politeness of day to day encounters and the violence that erupted in drunken brawls, witchcraft accusations, and, in older times, the torture rituals. The prophet thus, by his very success in achieving the role of moral censor, guaranteed his own political defeat.

But as an evangelist Handsome Lake was a triumphant success. In the intensely personal but stereotyped relationship between him and his followers, he played his role with skill and grace. His head-quarters were at Cold Spring, except for the brief sojourn at Tona-wanda, and there at the big council house and in his dwelling a few yards away he had his visions, consulted with Indian visitors from tribes for hundreds of miles around, and on occasion made speeches. In person he made a vivid figure on ceremonial occasions. In 1809 he was described as he presided at a council meeting: "Old Conudiu had a blaze of vermillion [paint] from the Corner of each Eye—his ears were cut round in their manner & extended a considerable length, on each Ear were two silver quills, one about 3½ & the other 2 Inches. The erect one having a tuft of Red Feathers tuck in the lower end—part of his forehead & on big Crown were also painted red & being nearly bald & a very grave countenance, he looked venerable—on his arms were wide silver bracelets—his leggings were of Red Cloth & his covering a Blanket over all—which he threw off in Council & took up his long Pipe. . . ."[51] And from Cold Spring he regularly set off on foot, accompanied by a few disciples, on an annual circuit of visits to other reservations and to the Great Council at Buffalo Creek, preaching, inquiring into local circum-stances, and castigating sinners.[52]

The calendar of visits to the prophet at Cold Spring begins with the great Six Nations Council in 1803. In the spring of 1804 he re-ceived a delegation of men and women from Onondaga, who re-ported on their progress in the new religion.[53] In the same year an Indian woman came from the Mohawk and Seneca towns at San-dusky, Ohio, and heard the word; she took it back to the pagan Sandusky Indians, advising them to continue their old worship of "the Warrior god" Tarachiawagon, whose red-painted statue stood in their village beside the council-house. (They told a Christian missionary then visiting that "they do not consider it a God, but have it there to put them in mind of their God."[54] In 1806 he him-self visited the Wyandots at Sandusky, darkly warning that "judg-ments are coming on the nations, unless they reform." His fame as a foreteller of doom had recently been given widespread popular con-firmation by the disastrous flood along the Allegheny in the spring of 1805, which washed away many of their improvements.[55] By 1807 the agent Granger reported to Dearborn, the Secretary of War, "the old Seneca Prophet, whom you once saw in Washington, strange as it may appear, has acquired an unbounded influence over the Six

Nations—his fame has long since reached some of the western Indians, and for two years past they have been sending Messengers to him, requesting his personal attendance in their Country, that they might hear the words of the Great Spirit from his mouth." In 1807 a delegation from the west, "consisting of Shawonees & others," even asked him to return directly with them, but the prophet "declined going at present."[56] Next summer a delegation of Seneca and Wyandot came from Sandusky. And later the same summer, in pursuit of a plan concocted by Granger to use him as a peace prophet ("the old man if managed right might be made subservient to the interest of the United States"), Handsome Lake did head a delegation of chiefs of the Six Nations on a visit to the western Indians. He was accompanied by Red Jacket, Cornplanter, and eight other distinguished Seneca chiefs from various reservations, and a large number of warriors. Handsome Lake kindled a fire and held a council with the western Indians at Sandusky, advising peace between them and the United States. Granger, not knowing of the prophet's earlier trip or his plans to visit the western Indians again, and failing to anticipate the prophet's opposition to the participation of his fellow tribesmen in a war on the side of the United States, congratulated himself on the success of his intrigue to use Handsome Lake as a peace prophet.[57]

Among the Six Nations the prophet's evangelical journeys were frequent but he chose carefully which places to visit. To Buffalo Creek and nearby Tonawanda he came annually from as early as 1801 for both evangelical, financial, and political purposes, for here the annuity moneys were paid and here meetings of the Seneca chiefs and of the Six Nations Council were held. He avoided Tuscarora, where a mixture of Christian and pagan Indians, the latter led by a female prophet, were developing a syncretic religion.[58] But Buffalo Creek had the disadvantage of being both the home of his political enemies and close neighbor to a white village where much whiskey was sold. Onondaga he visited annually from about 1803 and 1804, and in 1809, as we saw earlier, Onondaga delegations visited him at Allegany. "He harangued and exhorted them continually, and became distinguished among them for his powers and abilities. Business transactions were conducted under his direction and advice. On all occasions of difficulty, he was looked up to as the only individual who could restore things to a proper degree of order."[59]

There is no record of his having ever visited the Oneida and Stockbridge Indians. The people of this band were divided into a Christian faction headed by the missionary Samuel Kirkland, and a pagan faction inspired by the Mohawk prophet who had moved there from the Grand River and instituted a modified form of worship of Tarachiawagon that substituted a deer for the white dog. Knowing of the presence of these two religious movements, which agreed with his views on the importance of temperance, universal love, and domestic tranquility, and even expressed sympathy for each other, he advised these Indians "to listen to the instructions of the missionary" and follow the Bible. The missionary, in turn, was careful never to condemn Handsome Lake in public, although privately he was critical of his reputed tendency, whenever he wanted "a new revelation, to answer any particular purpose," to "cover his head with a bear skin for an hour or two, then lay it aside, muse awhile," and then disclose a heavenly message. A garbled version of Handsome Lake's teaching was circulated at Oneida. The prophet was said to have been in a trance three days and three nights and to have asserted that even one swallow of whiskey was a deadly sin if not repented of, although it was all right for white people to drink it, and Indians should not feel jealous or resentful of them because they used it so freely. "It was God who made rum, and made it for the white people to use as a medicine to strengthen them after labor." The prophet, it was said, urged them to love one another, whites and Indians alike; husbands and wives must love one another; and divorce was a sin. The pagans at Oneida adopted the Christian sabbath, meeting in church from nine in the morning to four in the afternoon, when they required confession and absolution and made speeches. "They are careful" said Kirkland, "to mention the prophet and refer to him frequently in every speech, seldom mentioning his Indian name, which is Kanyadaligo (a beautiful lake). The titles by which they honor him are Kawegago, Saongwida, God's man and God's friend; and Soyadadogeahre, the holy man, Sagwakonwanea, our chief man."[60]

By 1806 Handsome Lake considered his evangelical program well established at Cold Spring, Cattaraugus (which was nearby), Onondaga, Oneida, and Tonawanda. The trouble lay at Buffalo Creek and on the small reservations along the Genesee River. The Genesee was notorious as the resort of "bad Indians." The proximity of white settlers selling whiskey and exploiting the Indians economically, and the absence of substantial Indian communities that could exercise any restraint, had made of these places the scene of the kind of unrestrained drinking, brawling, and murder which Mary Jemison, who lived on one of them, described in her autobiography. In 1801 and 1802 Handsome Lake had taken part in negotiations to trade off these little reservations (including his own at Cuba Lake) for equivalent areas annexed to Cattaraugus and Buffalo Creek and, in spite of considerable Indian resentment, had personally signed the deeds to change the boundaries at Cattaraugus and to sell Little Beard's Town. But most of the little reserves remained. In the summer of 1806 he decided to evangelize them and led a company of his followers from Allegany to the little towns on the Genesee, preaching industry and temperance. The mission to the Genesee concluded at a general religious council on the Genesee River. The presence of so many Indians in one place prompted a rumor that the Indians were plotting to massacre all of the white settlers in the Genesee. The nearby Indian agent attended and found that the settlers' fears were unfounded; on the contrary, it was a very peaceful occasion, as he reported to the secretary of war:

> I have constantly attended this counsil every day, from the time of their first meeting, until they dispersed, and so little cause is there for alarm, that I never, on any former occasion observed them so quiet and peaceably disposed.—the object of their meeting was to agree on some mode and form of religion, and some other internal regulations, among themselves. this council was called by the prophet (a half Brother to Corn Planter), who is religiously engaged in endeavoring to inculcate certain religious doctrines amongst the Six Nations and to prevent them from drinking the use of ardent spirits three days was set apart by the Indians to confess their sins, of their past lives to the prophet, who has become their confessor. these were the only matters of consequence that took place at the late council. The Chiefs sent a runner to me requesting me to attend their council, the principal business with me was to solicit my influence in preventing the merchant tavern keepers and other persons from selling whiskey to the Indians.[61]

But despite the success of the Genesee revival, the long-term results were disappointing. Next fall the prophet and his disciples declared to the Quakers, "We have extended a great deal of labour towards our neighboring Indians, to persuade them to leave off the use of whiskey, and though *our* young men have generally declined it, yet we are almost discouraged about our Brothers at Buffalo and Genesee River."[62]

As the years went by, a clear pattern began to emerge: Handsome Lake, despite his position as a chief of the League, a member of the Allegany council, and the declared leader of the Six Nations, was not able to control the actions even of those chiefs who subscribed to his gospel. He was widely popular as an evangelist among many chiefs, warriors, and women, and his influence was particularly great at Allegany, Cattaraugus, Sandusky, Onondaga, and Tonawanda. He was not widely followed at Buffalo Creek, where Red Jacket, without visions and in avowed opposition to the prophet's pretensions, supported a similar program of religious conservatism coupled with secular progress. At Oneida a garbled mixture of his teachings, those of the Mohawk prophet, and Christianity held sway. Tuscarora also was partly Christian and under the influence of one of Kirkland's converts from Oneida. Through the declining years of his life, therefore, he concentrated his missionary energies on visiting those communities which liked him best and followed his teaching most closely. Every summer he left his house by the council building at Cold Spring and trudged to renew the warm fellowship of *Gaiwiio* in the dark, wooded hollows at Tonawanda and Onondaga. Here he met devotees, personal converts who had undergone intense emotional experiences in the course of conversion, had been strengthened to forsake whisky and other sins, and looked to Handsome Lake as their personal savior.

These conversions were not casual matters. The Indians traversed the same mystic path to *Gaiwiio* as white converts to Christianity; and the converts retained an intense devotion to the prophet who gave them the strength to achieve salvation. "One of the Onondagas, when asked why they did not leave their drunken habits before, since they were often urged to do it, and saw the ruinous consequences of such conduct replied, they had no power; but when the Great Spirit forbid such conduct by their prophet, he gave them the power to comply with their request."[63]

But Indian converts to Christianity were less sure of their power. The Oneida and Tuscarora reservations were unhappy places, for the Christian converts could not, as Handsome Lake's could, hold to temperance. And the Christian group at Sandusky, bedeviled by the witch-hunting and war prophecies of the Shawnee Prophet on the one hand and inspired by the preaching of Handsome Lake on the other, were a troubled people. A tragic account was given of a Christian convert named Barnet at Sandusky. In 1806 he was appointed one of the executioners of four women accused of witchcraft. They were "four of the best women in the nation" and the executioners refused to perform the task. Nor could he accept the teachings of Handsome Lake. In 1810 he came to the Christian mission and said that he was "much troubled about his relatives; in particular about four of them who listened to the Seneca-prophet, and are led astray by him. He had tried to convince them of their error, and to persuade them to forsake the prophet; but finds that he can have no influence on their minds. They appear in his view, to be bent on their own destruction. He is at a loss to know whether he should say anything more to them or not." Barnet became so sick and uneasy in his mind that he could not hunt, and his wife and children were in danger of perishing for want of warm clothing. They told the missionary that "it is his trouble about sin, makes him sick." Barnet was baptized a Christian in 1811 and was so happy that he could not sleep for joy. But next year he was depressed again and said he could "compare it to nothing, but to two constantly fighting within him." He feared that he would die.[64]

To Handsome Lake's converts, by contrast, came a feeling of peace, confidence, and strength. It is no wonder, as the Christian missionaries enviously said, that he was "held in great veneration by the people."[65]

➔| 10 |⟵

RENAISSANCE

Handsome Lake's preaching was remarkably effective. Inspired by their prophet and taking advantage of the educational and technological aid offered by religious and government organizations, the Iroquois quickly began to implement the recommendations of the social gospel. A true renaissance occurred on many of the reservations in the years between 1799 and 1815. This renaissance affected the lives of the Iroquois most conspicuously in matters of temperance, technology, and religious observance.

Thus, long before his death in 1815 Handsome Lake was able to see both a spiritual and a profane reformation among his people. But the political strife that had plagued his own career continued and intensified after his death. It was not until after a generation of political disorder that his old disciples, sickened by the endless contention and threatened by the aggressive proselytizing of the Christian missions, collated and revived his words and made them into the code of a new religion, a religion that survives today as *Gaiwiio*—The Old Way of Handsome Lake.

· *Temperance* ·

The implementation of the prophet's demand for temperance was not left to individual conscience. The political structure of the several communities and of the Great League itself was mobilized to exact conformity to the discipline of sobriety. As we have seen, village, tribal, and League councils early met to discuss the prophet's Code and uniformly supported the condemnation of alcohol. At Allegany it was said that "they . . . seldom held a council without some animadversions of their baneful effects" (i.e., of spiritous liquors).[1] At many of these councils Handsome Lake appeared to exhort the people to follow the Code, but his presence was not necessary for his views were widely known and his revelations constantly cited. The Quaker journals and letters and the minutes of their meetings with the Indians were filled with formal declaration of the intention of the chiefs and principal men and women of individual communities to oppose the drinking of liquor. These council resolutions did not, to be sure, have the force of law in the European sense, for there were no police or courts to enforce the resolution; but the council members made it their business to harass nonconformists into sobriety. If the chiefs found out that someone had gotten drunk "when they were out in the white settlements, they were sharply reproved by the chiefs on their return, which had nearly the same effect among Indians, as committing a man to the workhouse among white people."[2]

The temperance program moved ahead most rapidly, of course, in the Seneca towns along the Allegheny River, where drunkards were continually under the watchful and reproving eye of Handsome Lake himself. The Quaker reports provide a year-by-year monitoring of the situation there. In May 1799, even before Handsome Lake's first vision, a council in Cornplanter's settlement had resolved not to permit any more whiskey to be imported into the town, and two young men had been appointed "petty chiefs" to enforce the resolution. By the month of September, after the vision, Cornplanter was able to report that the Allegany Seneca "now drank much less than formerly." By 1801 it was reported that "the Indians," including Handsome Lake himself, "now became very sober, generally refraining from the use of strong liquor, both at home and when abroad among the white people. One of them observed to Friends, 'no more get drunk here, now this two year.' "[3] By 1802 under the pressure of the charge that "the Whiskey is the great Engine which the bad Spirit uses to introduce Witchcraft and many other evils amongst Indians," sobriety was "in some degree spreading to other settlements of the Seneca Nation."[4] In 1803

Handsome Lake was praised as being principally responsible for curing the Seneca of "the misuse of that dreadful manbane, distilled spirits."[5] When the Quakers visited the Allegany in 1806, they learned that the surrounding white settlers were amazed by the fact that the Seneca would "entirely refuse liquor when offered to them. The Indians said, that when white people urged them to drink whiskey, they would ask for bread or provisions in its stead."[6] Blacksnake informed the Quakers that the Indians still refused to drink whiskey and were "determined never to let the Whisky rise again."[7] Next year the Allegany chiefs, including Handsome Lake, reported again that their young men had generally given up the drinking of whiskey.[8]

The profit motive, however, which the Quakers were endeavoring to encourage, had mixed effects in regard to the general question of drinking. Two young chiefs in 1807 bought some whiskey and hid it, not for their own use, but for the purpose of selling it to the white people." But this conduct was "much disapproved by the Indians generally."[9] In 1809 it was reported by Allinson that an enterprising white trader, who succeeded in making a number of Seneca drunk on cider royal, was driven away from the Indian settlements: "A White Trader about 5 Months back had bought a Load of Goods up the River and among the rest some Cyder and Cyder Royal—stopping at Cold Spring he offered them for sale and the Indians not aware of the effects of Cyder-Royal many of them purchased & Drank particularly a few of their chiefs who collecting in their council Houses alarmed many of the Sober Indians—who threatened to Stave his Casks & let out the Liquor if he did not go away—they however thought it best first to come & advise with Friends & with this View several of their Warriors Came down to Tunassasa—on their Representation Joel Swain & Jacob Taylor went with them to their Town but the Trader probably alarmed with the threats of the Indians and removed his Canoe Further up the River where it is expected he disposed of his Liquors among the White People." Allinson included his observations on Allegany Seneca drinking in 1809 on a positive note: "The Indians of this Settlement generally abstain from the use of Spiritous Liquors so that it has become very rare to see one of them Intoxicated—since which they seldom quarrel or fight among themselves but live in Harmony together—this disposition they endeavour to Cultivate among the

Children & hence they rarely differ as is very common with Boys.
... They are naturally avaricious and saving & not being so liable to
Imposition as when they drank Spirits, some of them are growing
rich."[10]

Indian storekeepers continued to contribute to backsliding from
temperance for many years, and Handsome Lake was unable completely to suppress the traffic in liquor. His prophecies of doom and
damnation were used to good effect in reducing it to minor proportions, however. In the fall of 1811 the prophet had been issuing grave
warnings of divine retribution "if they fell into their former bad
practices." During the winter several earthquake shocks were felt
along the borders of Lake Erie and the Niagara frontier "which
gave the Indians such alarm that they believ'd the predictions of
their prophet was going to be fulfil'd upon them. . . . They believ'd
it to be the voice of the great Spirit, that he had now spoken so
loud as to be heard and that some great event would follow." Resolutions against whiskey-selling were immediately reasserted. And in
1814 one of the principal Indian whiskey-sellers died of a lingering
illness. He had kept a "kind of store" where "from the love of gain"
he kept liquor to sell. "In a time of great affliction of body, and distress of mind, he acknowledged that Selling whisky and other bad
practices had brought him to that situation—this with the more
thoughtful part of the Indians had a serious effect, and in consequence thereof many of their leading characters became again animated to discourage the use of strong drink among them."[11]

On other Seneca reservations, particularly at Cattaraugus and
Tonawanda, the temperance movement was also notably successful.
In 1801 Red Jacket, as "Chief Speaker of the Seneker Nations," declared that "we have all agreed to quit the use of liquor which you
must be in some measure convinced of from what you see at the
present meeting" (which was for the purpose of receiving the
annuities, and was held at the Genesee River).[12] At Cattaraugus the
Quakers were told in 1806 that the chiefs' council "had taken up
strong resolutions against the use of Whisky and Strong drink & that
all that was then present were Chiefs & each of them kept a daily
watch over the rest of the Indians to caution them against drinking
Whisky playing ball or other Bad practices which they believ'd
was not pleasing to the Great Spirit—but were of the mind that the
Great Spirit was better pleas'd when they took hold of the ax or the

hoe and set to work—that since they had got their eyes open to see they were sensible that strong drink had done them a great deal of mischief and kept them poor but now they had got hold of it and was determined never to let it rise again & that they were in hopes that the Indians of the Six Nations would in time become master of it."[13] Even more direct was the information given the Quakers at the same settlement in 1809: the Cattaraugus Seneca "had done with the use of spiritous liquors every man, but there were yet three women who would sometimes become intoxicated, yet they did not intend to cease labouring with them till they became reformed."[14] At a council of Seneca from various reservations held at Jenuchshadago in January 1803 it was announced by a chief from Tonawanda that his people too had renounced the use of strong drink.[15]

The other tribes also joined in temperance, inspired by Handsome Lake. In 1803 a missionary reported of the Onondaga that they had "for two years greatly reformed in their intemperate drinking. . . . The Impression he made was so powerful, that different tribes held several councils on the subject, and finally agreed to leave off the intemperate use of strong liquors."[16] The effect of the prophet's preaching on the Onondaga is vividly described in the recollections of a trader and whiskey-seller named Webster. One day eighteen of the principal chiefs and warriors of the Onondaga nation called at the trading post saying that they were just setting out to attend "a great council of the six nations, to be held at Buffalo." Mr. Webster treated them to a drink all round, and they left in high spirits. In due time the delegates returned and again stopped off at Webster's trading post. The trader put a bottle of liquor before them, but to his "utter astonishment . . . every man of them refused to touch it." At first he thought that this was a sign of hostility and feared for his life, "for he could imagine that nothing short of the most deadly resentment (or a miracle), could produce so great a change." But he was quickly reassured. "The chiefs explained, that they had met at Buffalo, a Prophet of the Seneca nation, who had assured them, and in this assurance they had the most implicit confidence, that without a total abstinence, from the use of ardent spirits, they and their race would shortly become extinct; that they had entered upon a resolution, never again to taste the baneful article, and that they hoped to be able to prevail on their nation to adopt the same salutary resolution. Many at this early day adopted the temperance principles, it

is said at least three fourths of all the nation; and of all those who
pledged themselves to the cause, not an instance was known of
alienation or neglect; but to a man, they religiously adhered to their
solemn pledge. The consequence was, that from a drunken, filthy,
lazy, worthless, set of beings, they became a cleanly, industrious,
sober, happy, and more prosperous people. At this period, it was
considered one of the most temperate communities in the land; only
a very few of the nation indulging in the intoxicating cup, and these
were treated with contempt by their more sober companions."[17] On
another occasion an Onondaga, on being asked why they had not
abandoned their drunken habits before (as they had often been urged
to do by white missionaries and others, and which they knew to have
ruinous consequences), explained that earlier "they had no power
but when the Great Spirit forbid such conduct by their prophet, he
gave them power to comply with his request."[18] In 1809, Quakers
reported, the Onondaga "had totally refrained from the use of
ardent spirits for about 9 years, and . . . none of the natives will touch
it."[19]

The effect on the Oneida was equally striking. The Oneida had
for many years been served by a harried schoolmaster, by Quaker
missionaries, and by Samuel Kirkland, who had formed a congregation of more or less loyal Christians. In 1799, as we remarked earlier,
the Oneida had been swept by a revival of the pagan religion recommended by a Mohawk prophet from the Grand River. But by
August 1806, the full import of Handsome Lake's revelation had
been communicated to them, even to the Christians, by a member of
the Christian congregation, the Reverend Mr. Kirkland's Oneida
helper, Doctor Peter. After Kirkland's sermon Doctor Peter stood
up and spoke about "the late revelations from the Seneka prophet, or
man of God, as they stile him." Doctor Peter spoke "with great zeal
and eloquence. "

He said the prophet enjoined the strictest temperance and sobriety upon all Indians, and commanded them to abstain from the
use of ardent spirits, which was never made for Indians; and for
any Indian to drink a single glass or one swallow would be a
deadly sin if not repented of. (Here in his great zeal he over-
stepped the mark, and this bold assertion was apparently displeas-
ing to many.) He then exhorted them to live in peace and love

one another and all mankind, white people as well as Indians. He then spoke upon the duties of husbands and wives, and the great sin of divorce.

The pagans, according to Kirkland, although they became converts to Handsome Lake's Code, were not overly successful in their adherence to the rule of temperance; but Kirkland's flock of Christians were not always sober either. In any case, the Seneca prophet was quoted in December 1806, as insisting that total temperance was necessary to salvation. "He forbids their feeling envious or resentful towards the white people because they so generally and freely use it, forbids them to reproach the white people with being the inventors of rum. This would be very offensive to the Great Spirit, for it was God who made rum, and made it for the white people to be used as a medicine to strengthen them after labor!" But he reported that fewer among the pagan Oneida were temperate than among the Onondaga. Despite the uncertainty of their sobriety, however, even Kirkland certified that the pagan party "absolutely forbid the use of rum, and assert that no Indian can be a good man who takes even a spoonful."[20]

The temperance movement was least effective at Buffalo Creek, at Tuscarora, and on the Genesee, where Iroquois settlements were closest to major white population centers. Buffalo Creek, furthermore, was the headquarters of Red Jacket, who although a defender of the old pagan religion of the Iroquois and an opponent of demon rum, was not favorably disposed toward the pretensions to power of Handsome Lake. Red Jacket himself drank, and so did Young King, another Buffalo Creek resident, one of the most influential of the Seneca chiefs, before his conversion to Christianity in the 1820's. In 1807 Handsome Lake and other Allegany Seneca leaders declared, "We are almost discouraged about our Brothers at Buffalo and Genesee River," on account of their persistence in intemperate habits.[21] And in 1809 Allinson on his visit to Buffalo said: "There are several Indian Towns with in a few miles & the Indians are too often here to give hope, on National Ground, of their general reformation from the use of Spiritous Liquors, & yet we were told that many of them have abandoned this Destroyer & stand firm against Temptation." At Tuscarora nearby, where by 1809 the chiefs had committed the nation to Christianity, the council declared "we mean to keep sabath, and hear Gospel, and try to persuade all our Nation not Drunk Whiskey—we shamed any of our People get Drunk."[22]

The overall impression provided by many observers between 1800 and 1810 is that the Iroquois in New York had substantially reduced their consumption of alcohol. In 1806 Halliday Jackson was able to sum up his impressions to this effect: "I . . . have noted with satisfaction that in the course of our travels among all the Indians on the Allegheny River, or either of the Villages at Cataraugus we have not seen a Single individual the least intoxicated with Liquor—which perhaps would be a Singular Circumstance to Observe in traveling among the same number of white Inhabitants."[23] And Jacob Taylor in 1809, when he was at Buffalo Creek to attend a meeting of the Council of the Six Nations, remarked, "I think I never saw so many Indians together before that conducted with so much propriety— the number could not be well ascertained, but it was thought there were about One Thousand, and I dont remember to see one Drunken Indian amongst them."[24]

· Technology ·

BY 1799 THE IROQUOIS had for a generation been living in a state of economic limbo, unable any longer to hunt extensively or even very effectively to continue the traditional agriculture. During the war years, they had been largely dependent upon military stores for rations, clothing, and equipment; after the war, they had relied heavily on handouts from Indian agents and missionaries and on the annuities paid to the tribes and to individual chiefs. Now, and suddenly, they embraced the rural technology of the white man and became a nation of farmers. The effective causes for this cultural transition were, as in the case of the relinquishment of alcohol, certainly multiple. Advice and general example had been provided for many years, but agriculture by men had been resisted as an effeminate occupation with the women themselves taking the lead in ridiculing male farmers as transvestites. "If a Man took hold of a Hoe to use it the Women would get down his gun by way of derision & would laugh & say such a Warrior is a timid woman."[25] The final realization of the irrevocability of reservation life, occurring simultaneously with Handsome Lake's explicit sanctioning of the farmer's role for men and the provision of tools and instruction in their use by Quakers and other whites, made the change possible.

The Quaker observers provide anecdotal, and sometimes even statistical, measures of the pace of agricultural reform among the Iroquois. The initial approach of the Allegany Seneca to the proposed new methods was cautious and sometimes even rigorously scientific. "It was in the spring of 1801, that the Indians first began to use the plough for themselves. They took a very cautious method of determining whether it was likely to be an advantageous change for them or not. Several parts of a large field were ploughed, and the intermediate spaces prepared by their women with the hoe, according to former custom. It was all planted with corn; and the parts ploughed (besides the great saving of labour), produced much the heaviest crop; the stalks being more than a foot higher, and proportionably stouter than those in the hoed ground."[26] The support that the chief women at this time gave to Handsome Lake and to the Quakers was indispensable, for it released the men from the embarrassment of being called effeminate when they worked in the fields. By the end of the year 1801 the agricultural revolution along the Allegheny was well underway. Individual fields were being fenced (about 18,000 fence rails were sawed and split in that year alone). Instead of clusters of cabins near the river, now there were well-made log houses with shingled roofs scattered among the fields and meadows. The trail along the river was widened, and soon some twenty miles of roads, usable by wagons, connected all settled parts of the reservation. The tinkling of cowbells could be heard in all directions, and corn fodder and mown hay were stored to feed the cattle through the winter. In 1801 thirteen or fourteen new farming lots were laid out, and in 1803 some seventeen new houses were constructed. By 1806, when a Quaker inspection team arrived to survey the work of the preceding eight years, they found that both the settlement pattern and house type had dramatically changed. Now the Allegany Seneca lived in a hundred or so log cabins, of which about thirty were concentrated at Cold Spring village and the rest distributed among approximately one hundred individually fenced farms. Many of the houses were roofed with shingles and had panel doors and glass windows. A number of these farms had barns and were equipped with carts and wagons. The fencing was a good eight to ten rails high. The carpentry work had been mostly done by

Indians, including the corner-notching of the logs; "scarcely a vestige remained of the cabins they occupied when Friends first settled among them [in 1798]."[27] Standards of cleanliness had improved, and there was some modern furniture. The Quaker inspection team was entertained in the house of Cornplanter's son Henry. It was the local showpiece: "It was a good house and well finished with a Piazza in front pallisaided round, and altho' its internal furniture still bore some marks of Indian housWifery, they were furnished with a good feather bed enclosed with Callico Curtains."[28] The Minister's house, up the river from Cold Spring, was painted red and white and surrounded by a red paling fence "& at a Distance looks very smart."[29] Many of the chiefs at both Allegany and Cattaraugus built two-story houses. The council-house, at the center of Cold Spring village only a few yards from Handsome Lake's house, was forty feet long by twenty wide and the largest structure in the town. It was built of boards. All dwelling houses, however, still had earthen floors and were infested with fleas, bedbugs, and other insects, and dogs and pigs wandered through the open doors.

In 1826 the total Seneca population of 469 persons in the Allegany band was assigned by the Quakers to one or another of 80 "families" (presumably meaning nuclear households); thus the average family size was approximately six persons.[30] This suggests that the combined effect of the new settlement pattern dictated by the needs of rural technology and of the social gospel preached by Handsome Lake, emphasizing the focal moral importance of the nuclear household, had within a generation been able to complete the transition from the ancient matrilineal household to the nuclear family. Eventually, also, these families became patrilineal with respect to name and inheritance, the Indian men taking on an English name, or an English translation of an Indian name, as a surname, and transmitting this name, along with inheritance rights to real estate, in the white style.

The new agriculture was productive and diversified. By 1801 the yield of corn had been increased tenfold. Spring wheat was planted between 1801 and 1806, and by 1806 the Indian farmers were adding to the traditional staples (corn, squash, beans, and tobacco) such other new crops as oats, buckwheat, potatoes, turnips, and flax. Grain was ground at the Quaker mill; the old wooden mortars fell into disuse. The production of flax was tied to the arts of spinning and weaving, which took hold firmly about 1807; by 1813 many of the Indian women were operating their own spinning wheels and producing over the winter sufficient thread to keep two Indian weavers busy making some two hundred yards of cloth, including both linen and wool, from which they made blankets and other useful cloth; some surplus was even sold to whites off the reservation. So profitable were the farms that some Seneca were able to invest in livestock. By 1803 there were well over a hundred head of cattle and by 1806 over a hundred horses; by 1810 there were at least five yoke of oxen available for heavy farm labor, such as hauling firewood and clearing fields of stones and stumps; by 1814 there was a considerable stock of swine being kept. By 1816 all but four families had "horned cattle," and the number of such cattle in the community reached four hundred. The Indians were learning to tan hides and salt the beef. Sheep still could not be managed because of the incursions of wolves.

Inevitably, various cultural consequences flowed from the fundamental new economic transformation. Progress in public health measures was an early effect. By 1805 the Indian women were learning to make soap, and standards of personal and household cleanliness were rising. During the War of 1812 the Quakers were able to avert a threatened epidemic of smallpox by vaccinating over a thousand Seneca at Allegany and Cattaraugus.[31] The Quakers emphasized the virtue of cleanliness so strongly that some of the Indian women, when white visitors approached "would immediately begin to sweep their houses, and appear somewhat disconcerted if friends entered their doors before they got their apartments in order." But the absence of surgeons to mend broken bones and stitch cuts and the general inability of both Indian and white medicine of the day to cope effectively with infectious and degenerative diseases meant that there were relatively large numbers of older people whose bodies bore the scars and deformities of a lifetime without effective medical care. Battered, aging hulks, half blind, or lame, or crippled in hand or foot or disfigured from the lack of minor surgery, they nonetheless worked as their infirmities allowed.

A specialization of labor among Indian artisans developed, with individual Indian men setting up shop as weavers, blacksmiths, shoemakers, and carpenters. Some Indian farmers were said to be getting rich, and others, who for a time had clung to hunting as their means of support, had with the decline of the small remaining local fur trade about 1810 been forced to hire themselves out as farm laborers to the well-to-do. A few of the men were adding to their income by renting out their land and by working part time as smiths, carpenters, and shoemakers, and everyone, of course, had access to timber and grazing meadows on the "national land," which was held in common by the tribe and could be used by anyone so long as he did not interfere with anyone else's use. Some of the Indians even complained of the pace of work and resented the comparative leisure of their domestic animals. "An Industrious Indian" at Cattaraugus testified that "he had become very uneasy on thinking he had so much to do to provide for his horses and that they had done nothing to assist him that he had lost considerable of Sleep on the occasion and was determined in future to make them assist him work."[32] The Quakers were well pleased with the progress made at Allegany, and in 1814 observed that "their improvements rather exceeded, in divers respects, those made in some new settlements of white people on the frontiers, in the same length of time."

The economic structure of the Indian farm household was described in detail in 1820 by the Quaker historian of the Tunessassa mission. He compiled individual data on a sample of thirty-five families (nearly half of the community). His figures showed that the average Indian family had cleared and fenced ten acres of ground, putting four in corn, two in oats, one in potatoes, and using the rest for meadow, orchard, or vegetable garden; owned a plow and either a pair of horses or a yoke of oxen; and kept five cows and eleven pigs. Only four households had less than five acres of cleared ground and only three more than fifteen. By 1826 the eighty families at Allegany were working 699 acres of improved land, raising thereon corn (239 acres), oats (116), hay (70), potatoes (42), wheat (38), besides a quantity of buckwheat and various vegetables. These families possessed 479 head of cattle, 58 horses, and 350 hogs. The agricultural revolution had become the way of life for the next generation.[33]

Although the Quaker vocational school, conducted in the Seneca language, thus was remarkably effective in transforming the economic basis of Seneca society, comparable progress was not made in academic instruction. The Friends had in the winter of 1798–9 opened their school to instruct Indian children—in English—in reading, writing, and arithmetic, and although about twenty pupils had attended on and off, they proved irregular scholars. The project of academic, as opposed to vocational, education, was abandoned for ten years, and instead a few—perhaps half a dozen—Indian youths were sent from time to time to live with Friends in Philadelphia for several years, there to absorb English letters, Quaker values, and the manual arts. In 1810 a census of the households revealed that most of the parents wanted their children to attend a summer school. But still very few of the Allegany Seneca spoke English, and instruction in reading, writing, and arithmetic could be conducted only with great difficulty. A Quaker school at Tunessassa was not firmly established until 1822. Throughout the period from 1799 to about 1825, despite the occasional presence of a schoolmaster, not more than twenty children were regular pupils at any one time, and it may be doubted whether the schools accomplished much more than rudimentary instruction in English speech. As the Quakers observed about 1811, "very few of them had yet acquired the English language so as to be able to understand what they did learn."[34]

Technological progress was faster at Allegany, which received the concentrated attention of both Handsome Lake and the Quakers, than it was on the other reservations. But all were moving in the same direction. The Quakers frequently visited Cattaraugus and donated mill irons and plows; the Cattaraugus Seneca soon were building two-story board houses, fencing their farms, and keeping livestock. The Quakers also gave sawmill irons to Red Jacket for building a mill at Buffalo Creek, and they and Kirkland's mission had earlier helped the Oneida. And Handsome Lake was urging economic acculturation everywhere. Allegany was merely the spearhead of the movement to abandon the traditional technological and economic structure and to adopt the white man's customs.

· Religious Observance ·

HANDSOME LAKE DID NOT CONSIDER that his revelations and the gospels that issued from them constituted a new religion. He believed rather that he was commissioned to revive in a pure, full, and correct form the traditional religious observances of the Iroquois and thereby to guide his people toward a better life in this world and salvation in the next. Although later his disciples, in codifying the prophet's teachings, did in effect create a new religious institution, during his lifetime such innovations as he proposed were added to the body of Iroquois belief in the spirit of free incorporation of dream-inspired religious observance that was characteristic of Iroquois culture. At no time, despite his difficulties in political affairs, did he have to confront a conservative *religious* opposition except in the matter of the medicine-societies.

The religious renaissance among the Iroquois thus was essentially a renewal of popular observance of the traditional communal religious rituals. The major innovation in belief—the idea of divine judgment and an afterlife in heaven or hell—was readily palatable and quickly and widely accepted because it was similar in form to the old belief in the cosmic bargain between the Good Twin and the Evil Twin. There were few important innovations in ritual adopted as a result of the prophet's teaching. The old annual calendar—including the white dog ceremony—was celebrated without any modification except, at Allegany, the abandonment of the statue of Tarachiawagon.[35] The old medicine-societies—including the False Faces—continued their rituals despite the prophet's qualms about them.[36] His emphasis upon the four sacred ceremonies—Thanksgiving Dance, Great Feather Dance, Personal Chants, and Bowl Game—did not imply that all other observances should be abandoned; it was merely an endorsement of the central themes in existing ritual. The pantheon remained unchanged except for the addition of a new scene of action for the struggle between the creative and destructive principles, represented traditionally by the Good Twin and the Evil Twin, Tarachiawagon and the Great World Rim Dweller, in the domain of heaven and hell, where the same protagonists bore different names (Haweniyu or the Great Spirit, and Ganosge' or the Tormentor). The ritual of confession, which later became a central feature of the religion of Handsome Lake, was in his own time simply an application of the traditional practice of requiring confession of a suspected witch, and Handsome Lake's central role as accuser and confessor was an amplification of the old responsibility of the shaman. The prophet directly supported the Minister at Cold Spring who for years had been calling the people together for the ceremonies, and he indirectly supported any other traditional religious leader whom he could find. Even his own temporary position as great leader was an extension of custom, for in times of crisis the Iroquois were used to the nomination of powerful war-captains or political leaders (like Brant among the Mohawk and Cornplanter among the Seneca) who were made responsible for mobilizing the village, tribe, or League to action.

Thus, in the first decades of the nineteenth century, when the Quaker missionaries and Mary Jemison, the white captive, described the religious rituals among the Seneca and Kirkland wrote his accounts of the pagan ceremonies of the Oneida, they delineated a ceremonial and belief system already hundreds of years old with minor modifications of content, emphasis, and terminology recently suggested by Handsome Lake. Furthermore, each Iroquois tribe, and even each band or reservation community, maintained its own more or less variant form of this general system. Handsome Lake, under the circumstances, simply could not introduce a new religious system standardized for all the reservations. As we shall see, it was not the prophet but the prophet's disciples who created the new, relatively uniform institution known as the Longhouse Religion or the New Religion of Handsome Lake, with its own unique beliefs, rituals, organization, and ceremonial paraphernalia, and who determined the relation this new institution should have to the old religion that Handsome Lake himself had practiced.

There was, for a time, some religious doubt expressed by various critics of the prophet who, as he put it, would say, "We lack an understanding of this religion." Most of this doubt did, as one might expect, focus on the introduction of the concept of divine judgment and an afterlife in heaven or hell. Handsome Lake answered the critics who asked why no one had known these things before by suggesting that not everything was known even to the angels, who told him, "even we, the servants of the Creator, do not understand all things." When asked where the ancestors had gone, he replied,

Now it is said that your fathers of old never reached the true lands of our Creator nor did they ever enter the house of the tormentor, Ganosge'. It is said that in some matters they did the will of the Creator and that in others they did not. They did both good and bad and none was either good or bad. They are therefore in a place separate and unknown to us, we think, enjoying themselves.[37]

But rather than propose new ritual, Handsome Lake applied these new principles of belief as sanctions for the observance of old custom. It was, he said, man's duty to follow the traditional ceremonies; it was the Evil Spirit who kept him away from the performing the ancient religious observances of the Iroquois.

Thus the religious innovations of Handsome Lake were modifications of belief whose function was to ensure the dedication of the people to conservative ritual. He was in his own eyes as the messenger of God, necessarily the defender of the faith. And at his behest hundreds of lukewarm pagans and half-converted Christians returned to the council-house to hear once again the prayers of thanksgiving, to burn the white dog, to tell their dreams, and play the Sacred Bowl Game—the cosmic game of chance forever being renewed in the endless and balanced struggle between the Spirit of Good and the Spirit of Evil.

· The Death of Handsome Lake ·

HANDSOME LAKE DIED on August 10, 1815, while on a visit to Onondaga. He had for some time had intimations of approaching death. In the spring at Allegany he had had a vision:

> The day was bright when I went into the planted field and alone I wandered in the planted field and it was the time of the second hoeing. Suddenly a damsel appeared and threw her arms about my neck and as she clasped me she spoke saying, "When you leave this earth for the new world above, it is our wish to follow you." I looked for the damsel but saw only the long leaves of corn twining round my shoulders. And then I understood that it was the spirit of the corn who had spoken, she the sustainer of life. So I replied, "O spirit of the corn, follow not me but abide still upon the earth and be strong and be faithful to your purpose. Ever endure and do not fail the children of women. It is not time for you to follow for Gaiwiio is only in its beginning."[38]

That summer he went again on his annual visit to the other reservations, walking first the seventy-five miles to Tonawanda, where he received a formal invitation from Onondaga to visit there and preach to the people. Again he had a vision foreboding death.

The prophet was depressed, and his thoughts were muddled with voices and frequent visions. "I must now take up my final journey to the new world," he thought, and he "longed for the home of his childhood and pined to return." In response to a command from the angels he called together the children and told them that he would die. They pleaded with him not to go. Then the prophet "rose and exhorted them to ever be faithful and a great multitude heard him and wept." He started out afoot on the 150-mile trip to Onondaga accompanied by a number of followers. At Canawaugus, on the Genesee River, the place where he was born, they stopped and here performed the Thanksgiving Address. Then he spoke to his followers, saying, "I have had a dream, a wondrous vision. I seemed to see a pathway, a trail overgrown and covered with grass so that it appeared not to have been traveled in a long time." The company stopped again at the head of Seneca Lake, and again Handsome Lake performed the Thanksgiving Ritual and reported another dream: "I heard in a dream a certain woman speaking but I am not able to say whether she was of Onondaga or of Tonawanda from whence we came."

When they came near the Onondaga Reservation line, they stopped to eat lunch. After they had entered the reservation and were near the council-house, Handsome Lake discovered that he had lost his knife. He was disturbed and announced, "I have forgotten my knife. I may have left it where we stopped and ate last. I can not lose that knife for it is one that I prize above many things. Therefore I must return and find it." He went back alone along the trail to find the knife while the others went on to the council-house to wait for him.

He became sick while he was searching for the knife and with great difficulty struggled back to the Onondaga village. He was not able to reach the council-house "for he was very sick and in great distress," and took refuge in a small cabin some distance away, along a creek at the foot of the hill. The formal council was canceled; without the prophet the meeting was, to use the old form of words, "only a gathering about the fire place." The prophet remained in the cabin, ill and in pain, for several days. The chiefs sent a messenger to bring Henry O'Bail from Allegany. The people tried to amuse him by playing a game of lacrosse in his honor. "It was a bright and beautiful day and they brought him out so that he might see the play. Soon he desired to be taken back in to the house."

Near the end he addressed the crowd gathered about the cabin: I will soon go to my new home. Soon I will step into the new world for there is a plain pathway before me leading there. Whoever follows my teachings will follow in my footsteps and I will look back upon him with outstretched arms inviting him into the new world of our Creator. Alas, I fear that a pall of smoke will obscure the eyes of many from the truth of Gaiwiio but I pray that when I am gone that all may do what I have taught.[39]

He died soon after this, before his nephew could reach him, but attended by three persons who swore to keep the details of his last moments a secret. The story was given out by his three attendants that when he died, "he said he was going home, & then passed away without sickness."

The body of Handsome Lake was buried in the center of the council-house. In due course the ceremony of condolence required by his office as a chief of the League was performed, and his successor to the title—probably a fellow council chief from Allegany named Snow[40]—was installed. The news of his death reached Buffalo on August 27, when Indian agent Erastus Granger, his old rival, wrote vindictively, "You say the prophet is dead, and I say amen."[41] But the death notice in the *Buffalo Gazette* of October 3 was more charitable:

... died ... at the Onondaga Castle, in the 66th year of his age, the Allegheny Chief, known throughout the Indian territories as the *Peace Prophet*, to distinguish from *Neemeser*, the brother of Tecumseh. Until fifty years old he was remarkable only for his stupidity and beastly drunkenness.—But about eighteen years since he fell in a fit—continued insensible for several hours; and was considered dead. He, however, recovered and exclaimed, "*Don't be alarmed. I have seen Heaven: call the nation together that I may explain to them what I have seen and heard.*" The tribe was collected, and he told them he had in his trance seen four beautiful young men, sent by the Great Spirit, and who addressed him thus: "*the Great Spirit is angry with you, and all the red men, and unless you immediately refrain from drunkenness, lying and stealing, you shall never enter the beautiful place which we will now show you.*" He then said, he was conducted to the gate of Heaven, which was open, but which he was not allowed to enter: that it was beautiful beyond description, and the inhabitants perfectly happy:—that he was then brought back, and the young men on taking leave promised to pay him a visit yearly to witness the effect of their mission. The chief immediately abandoned his habits, visited the tribes,—related his story—which was believed, and the consequence has been, that from a filthy, lazy, drunken set of beings, they have become cleanly, industrious, sober, and happy. The Prophet continued, he says annually to receive his celestial visitants: annually made his visits to the tribes: and was on one of them when he deceased.[42]

· *The Years of Trouble* ·

THE THIRTY YEARS between the death of the prophet and the formation of a new church dedicated to his name were a new time of continuously mounting pressure for the New York Iroquois. The time of trouble culminated in a disastrous land sale and the division of the nation into Christian and "pagan" factions. The pressures upon the Indians took three forms: white settlement and economic penetration, white missionary activity, and the purchase of Indian land.

After the War of 1812 the frontiers of western New York were rapidly occupied by white farmers and entrepreneurs. All the northerly reservations were encircled by settlements, and even the old asylum along the Allegheny, which except for the area actually occupied by the Seneca was little suited for farming, was gradually surrounded by little villages and individual farms located on the isolated tracts where by hard work a family could scratch out a living. Sometimes these people pastured their cattle on Indian lands, to the considerable irritation of the Indians. Others, taking advantage of the vast stands of white pine, about this time began the logging industry, floating big rafts down the river past the village at Cold Spring to the sawmills at Warren. Although the Indians used their own sawmill for squaring logs and cutting boards for their own use, and had sold small quantities of cut lumber, they too began now to cut the big pines and float the rafts down to sell at the mills. All of these activities, coming so soon after the war, tended to expose the Indians again to whiskey and to contemptuous white men and somewhat to distract them from the process of reform that the Quakers and the prophet had launched. And in 1830 the first steamboat anchored at Cornplanter's village on its way upstream.[43]

Even more threatening to the integrity of the reservation communities was the intrusion of Christian evangelists. The social gospel of Handsome Lake had prepared the Iroquois to cope with the economic problems of life on the reservations. It had not, however, equipped them to deal successfully with the challenge of missionaries who sought to make converts. The religious people they had admitted into their communities—the Quakers at Allegany and Cattaraugus and Jabez Hyde, a Presbyterian schoolmaster at Buffalo Creek—from 1811 to 1818 had acted only as secular advisers and teachers and had not attempted to convert the Indians to Christianity. But the evangelical missionary movement, springing up in the first decade of the nineteenth century, began seriously to turn its attention to the native Indians of New York in the second. By 1814 other and more sanctimonious Christian denominations than Quakers were taking an interest in the Seneca Indians. In that year Cornplanter, resentful of Quaker criticism of him for taking up drinking, invited the Western Missionary Society to set up a school on the grant. This school lasted from 1814 to 1818 and served as the entering wedge for evangelism, for circuit preachers appointed by the society annually visited the settlement during those years to bring the word of God to the heathen.[44] In 1816 the Reverend Mr. Timothy Alden, representing the Society for the Propagation of the Gospel among the Indians of North America, visited Cornplanter's Town and the school there. He found that the schoolmaster had already succeeded in persuading the seven households still located on the grant to discontinue the annual calendar of religious ceremonies and no longer to profane the sabbath "by hunting, amusements, nor any kind of labor. Such already is the happy effect of the example set by Mr. Oldham and his family." Next year, when Alden returned to preach in Cornplanter's house, with Henry O'Bail as interpreter, he found that the schoolmaster was holding religious services every Sunday. Cornplanter told him that he was convinced the Christians must be right "because you have the words of the Great Spirit written in a book." Alden that year also visited Cold Spring and preached to the Seneca farther up the river; he gave a sermon to Red Jacket and some of the chiefs at Buffalo Creek. In 1818 he preached again at Cornplanter's Town, Cold Spring, Buffalo Creek, and Cattaraugus. In 1820 he preached at Cattaraugus and Tonawanda.[45]

About this time, at the other end of the Seneca country, the

United Foreign Missionary Society, taking over responsibility for the Seneca field from the New York Missionary Society, which had succeeded only in maintaining a school, began an aggressive campaign of evangelism. At Buffalo Creek some of the Indians were persuaded in 1818 to accept a "preacher of the Gospel," and Hyde's day school became a boarding school where the pupils would be safe from pagan influences. This Buffalo Creek missionary group fanned out quickly, dispatching a schoolteacher to Tuscarora and a missionary to Cattaraugus, and including Allegany on the annual circuit of the missionaries regularly assigned to Buffalo and Cattaraugus. A Baptist missionary was already established at Tonawanda (although he was physically ejected in 1822). The Oneida and Tuscarora were already nominally Christianized. Indian churches were organized at Buffalo in 1823, at Cattaraugus in 1827, and in 1830 at Allegany. The Allegany Christian congregation grew apace, and by 1844 it had grown to 144 members in regular standing. In 1829 the Gospel of Luke, the Sermon on the Mount, and several hymns were printed in the Seneca language. In 1831 the Reverend Mr. Asher Wright commenced his mission at Buffalo Creek and transferred it to Cattaraugus when the Buffalo Creek Reservation was abandoned in 1845. He and his wife learned Seneca and were able to maintain both a church congregation and a distinguished boarding school, the Thomas Indian School.[46]

The third source of pressure was the demand that the Indians of New York sell their reservations. In 1810 the Holland Land Company had sold to the Ogden Land Company the preemption right to the Seneca reservations. After the war the local agents and shareholders of this company, who included such prominent landowners as James Wadsworth of the Genesee and General Peter B. Porter of Buffalo, congressman and later Secretary of War, worked to persuade the Indians to sell their lands and move to the west. By 1817 the Seneca were seriously discussing such a move and even sent a delegation to Sandusky to investigate the possibility of joining their kinsmen in Ohio. But the advantages of such a removal appeared to be slight, and few if any of the Indians wished to leave New York, where there appeared to be every prospect of peaceful relations with the surrounding white community and of continuing advance in their material welfare. Nonetheless, by bribes, threats of dire punishment for refusing to obey the supposed wish of the United States government for such a move, and deliberate misrepresentation of the facts to federal authorities, Seneca and other Iroquois chiefs were brought unwillingly to sign treaties by which some of the reservations were sold to the Ogden Land Company and the State of New York. In 1821 part of the Oneida reserve was lost, and many of the pagans removed to Wisconsin. In 1826 the Seneca sold to the Ogden Land Company all five of the remaining Genesee River reservations, most of Tonawanda, about a third of Buffalo Creek, and a fifth of Cattaraugus. Pressure to remove the Indians entirely west of the Mississippi now began to form in Washington, and despite bitter complaints about the 1826 treaty almost half of the chiefs of the Indians of New York residing on the Seneca reservations in 1838 were persuaded to sign another treaty, by which they agreed to emigrate to Kansas and vacate the reservations. A party of nearly two hundred did go to Kansas, where nearly half died; nearly all of the survivors returned, complaining about the climate, the lands, and the hostility of the Indians already resident there. So much resentment was aroused by this treaty, and so many whites, including Quakers, worked to negate it, that it was finally renegotiated in 1842. By the terms of 1842 the Seneca were left in possession of Allegany, Cattaragus, and Oil Creek reservations. Buffalo Creek was evacuated in 1845, the residents finding refuge at Cattaraugus and Allegany, and at Grand River. The Tonawanda Seneca simply refused to move, and after prolonged litigation they were confirmed in possession of a small part of their original reservation. And the Onondaga, whose lands were not involved in the interests of the Ogden Land Company, also remained on their reservation.[47]

The combined effect of the pressures of settlement, missionary work, and land negotiations was to split the Seneca into two factions: the "Christian" party and the so-called "pagan" party. The missionaries had an immediate and surprising success in making converts and by 1830 probably had secured the adherence, in sympathy if not by baptism, of half the population. Probably the ratio of occasional but convinced church attenders to baptized converts was on the order of ten to one—an unfavorable ratio, from the missionary standpoint, but not an important distinction to many Seneca, who were not accustomed to think in terms of exclusive church "membership." At Allegany alone in 1819 several of the chiefs favored the gospel; by 1828 there were about 180 "Christians," including five chiefs.[48] The Christians were no more eager to sell land than the pagans, for they could not look forward to any improvement in either spiritual or material condition if they removed westward, away from their missionaries, into rough and turbulent frontier regions. The missionaries on their part sought earnestly to protect their charges, both Christian and pagan, from eviction. But the Christian Indians were apt to be more conformist, trusting, and submissive in the face of demands from land agents and government officials, who claimed to be fellow Christians. And at the urging of their ministers, who were evangelists seeking to make converts, they were also less tolerant of the pagan party in religious and political matters than the pagan party was of them.

The leader and chief spokesman of the Christian party was a Buffalo Creek chief named Young King. Young King was the maternal nephew of Old Smoke and, like Handsome Lake, was regarded among white men as a "heavy, dull, unambitious, but honest man." He was a big man physically and a respected warrior who had been wounded by a musket ball in the leg during the War of 1812. He was also a heavy drinker and in 1815, in the course of a drunken brawl, had lost an arm when a white man swung at him with a scythe. As early as 1815 he had been willing to have some Indian children educated in school and instructed in the Christian religion. During the 1820's he became an avowed Christian sympathizer and a temperance advocate; pointing to his arm, he would say, "Look what whiskey has done for me." He formed a temperance society (such societies were the Christian counterpart of Handsome Lake's admonitions), helped to support the church at Buffalo Creek by cutting wood, favored an English education for the young, and fenced and plowed on his own farm. In 1832 he and his second wife joined the Church. He died in the cholera epidemic in 1835 at the age of sixty-nine.[49]

There was, in fact, not much to distinguish the Christians from the pagans individually in regard to gross circumstances of personal history or tribal standing. All had been brought up in the old religion. All stood for similar policies in regard to temperance, education, land retention, and material progress. The difference probably lay in the fact that, for one reason or another, the Christians tended to seek assurances of worth from powerful and apparently benevolent white men like ministers and Indian agents, and the pagans aggressively rejected white men as a source of emotional support, insisting upon retaining their native identity and referring their conduct to native models. Thus Captain Pollard, another of the leaders of the Christian party (he had joined the church in 1824), asserted in council that his party "were meek & humble—the other proud and stubborn." He rejected the pagan party's citing of the prophet's advice against selling land without sanction from the Great Spirit, saying sarcastically, "The other side declared that they should dispute all power to sell their Lands, until the Claimants, should show that they had been to Heaven with their flesh on." And looking toward the future, he declared that his party "will obey & follow his [i.e., the white man's] advice because it is good. For when those who are in active life shall have passed away, their posterity will be more closely allied to the White man—they will assimilate to him in language conduct & Religion & the Gate of Heaven will not be closed against them."[50]

This trusting identification with white men was bitterly resisted by most of the leaders of the pagan group, who clung to the fact that they were Indians and sought for the most part to find in the memory of Handsome Lake a figure with whom they could identify. Red Jacket was now the recognized leader of the pagan party, for despite his earlier (and perhaps continuing) jealousy of Handsome Lake as a man, he firmly insisted that the Iroquois retain their own religion. Although, as he said, like the Christians he "believed in *One God*" and in heaven and hell, he had found little understanding on the part of the Christian missionaries, who after all were "dressed and fed by White men," and he alluded contemptuously to the ignorance of Indian religion by the ministers. "He has attended meeting," he reported, "when the stripling Priest has represented him as not knowing whether a cat or a dog was his God." Red Jacket was still reputed to be an overly ambitious man, and a story was circulated that in attempted imitation of Handsome Lake he announced that "the Great Spirit had made known to him in a dream, that their Nation would never prosper, until they made of him a Sachem." He would attribute epidemics, land sales, and "all the Misfortunes of the Nation" to the persistent failure of the Seneca to recognize him as a chief of the League. His Christian wife left him, and in 1827 the Christian chiefs deposed him as chief; but in 1828 he was reinstated as "the head Sachem of the Wolf tribe." Nonetheless, Blacksnake, the old "privy counselor" of Handsome Lake, thought well of him and was reported to have "more reverence for Red Jacket than for any other Indian" (except the prophet).[51]

Blacksnake was the leader of the pagan party at Allegany. Less hostile to the whites than Red Jacket, he strictly followed "the principles of Con-ne-di-yeu," urging temperance, morality, education, and adherence to the old religion.[52] But others of the Allegany pagans were, like Red Jacket, motivated as much by resentment against overbearing white ministers as by devotion to the old religion. Cornplanter in particular had for years been inspired by mingled and confused feelings of jealousy of both Handsome Lake and Red Jacket and even of the Quakers and Presbyterians—whom he himself had invited to Allegany. But in 1818, disturbed by the rumors of land cessions, he began to oppose all Christians and to reidentify with the pagan group. At first his program was rational. He proposed seriously that the Indians on the Allegany Reservation abandon the old system of usufruct holdings and divide their lands into private farms and that these holdings be secured by legal deeds valid under federal jurisdiction, thus at once precluding the sale of the reservations by the chiefs and advancing the agrarian reform already underway. But the women objected because their garden plots were widely scattered, and many of the young men objected because they wished to cut pine logs on the tribal lands and feared that private lots would not contain sufficient timber. At the last minute, with the surveyor on the ground, the old chief changed his mind, and the council refused to permit the division of the land into private lots.[53]

Gradually Cornplanter became morose and withdrawn. In December, 1820, he experienced the first of a series of visions. The Great Spirit told him that he was to have nothing further to do with white people or with war. He announced that "the white people were crazy, and the Indians were doing very wrong to follow their customs; he said it was wicked for the Indians to have cattle, cows, and hogs; cows in an especial manner were very injurious to the Indians: their children drinking the milk when they were very young, caused them to have misfortunes, and prevented them from being a useful people."[54] He was commanded to burn all his old trophies of war, including his captain's commission, a flag, medals, belts, a military hat, and a highly prized sword, which he immolated on a huge pile of logs. Many of his revelations were repetitions or echoes of the teachings of Handsome Lake: liquor had not been created for Indians, and they were commanded not to drink it; war and scalping were evil and had been introduced by the whites; the Indians were the true owners of the land, and the whites "should always consider that they live on borrowed soil"; Indians should sell no more land; Indian men should take care of their wives and children and were ordered "not to lust after any woman but my own"; Indians need not observe the sabbath; Indians must observe their old religion, for "if we would quit our old way we should get into confusion and something would happen or befall us so that we should lose our lives." But the old man was constantly disturbed by personal disappointments. As he said, "his wife . . . is now settling with her old husband on the Allegheny in distressful circumstances," a result of the wars brought by white men. He felt guilty about killing seven men in battle: "I was a great sinner to kill so many persons." He worried about the future of his idiot son and wanted him "to go with me and it seemed to be granted [by the Great Spirit] that we should both go together"; he vowed to take this son with him on all his journeys. He felt that his obedience to the Great Spirit had added ten years to his life. The most bizarre feature of his code was the claim that cow's milk had been cursed by Jesus. "When the Savior was on the Earth he was slain by wicked high tempered people and after his death he put his revenge on the cows milk and wicked man and woman that quarrel and fight when they use this milk then the milk and their bad temper puts them out of their senses." He claimed to be the only true living prophet of God. "I mean to be governed by the great man that speaks to me from above and no other person can hear or understand him and I am a mind to do as he tells me for I believe *him* to be my Maker and if he tells me wrong I cannot help it and he tells me not to pay any tax or have anything to do with law or war or Sabbath Days." When the tax collector arrived, Cornplanter met him with a bodyguard carrying guns. In deference to his past services to the state, the legislature agreed to exempt his lands from taxation. But the Indians thought he was deranged. They declined to close the Quaker school at his demand or to give up keeping chickens and selling eggs for cash. When he sang his speeches at council meetings, at the command of the Great

Spirit, to a tune of his own composing, the audience laughed. He changed his name to Nonuk—"Cold" or "Dead."[55]

But the derangement proved to be temporary, and his mind cleared. At the time of his death in 1835 he was still an awesome figure—like Young King, a battered wreck of a man. Nearly six feet tall, gray-haired, bearded, with one eye missing and the empty socket covered by the drooping brow, a limp hand rendered useless by a severed tendon, one earlobe torn and hanging down on his shoulder like a rag, he stood like a scarred oak among saplings. He lived in poverty on the grant in a decaying two-story log house without household furniture except wooden benches covered with deerskins and blankets and a few wooden spoons and bowls. Around him, however, lived fifty of his kinsmen in eight or ten houses.[56] In the year of his death he took his farewell of the Seneca nation at annuity time at Buffalo Creek. Just before the fire was covered, he stood up and solemnly made his last speech.

[He] recounted the principal events of his life, as connected with the interests of his nation. He said he had endeavored conscientiously to discharge his whole duty to his people. Whatever errors he might have committed were errors of judgment and not of the heart. If he had done any wrong or in any way given offence to anyone present, without just cause, he desired the aggrieved party to come forward and be reconciled. It was his wish to be at peace with all men . . . and he added "When I leave this place, most of you will have seen me for the last time." He then gave them advice and counsel for the future; went from one to another and took them by the hand, saying a few parting words to each; passed out of the door, mounted his horse, called his traveling companions, and left, never to return.

When Cornplanter died, the old team of Cold Spring council members, who had, along with Handsome Lake, been managing the Allegany renaissance between 1804 and 1809, was already dispersed and divided. It had been a kind of primitive Camelot, dedicated to the salvation of a people and the defense of the faith. Now, of the prophet's fifteen original colleagues, some were dead and some had moved away; some remained faithful to the old religion, some had forsaken it for Christianity. From the Wolf clan, Handsome Lake and Cornplanter had died; Blacksnake still lived along the Allegheny and was a chief and the leader of the pagan party; Strong had moved to Cattaraugus, where he was a leading figure in the Christian party. From the Bear clan, John Pierce and Halftown remained as chiefs at Cold Spring but were members of the Christians, and Crow had moved to Cattaraugus. From the Snipe clan, Henry O'Bail had died. He had remained a pagan, but because of his "bad practices" his father had disowned him and sent him to live with his mother along the Genesee; he died in a drunken fall. Charles O'Bail, a pagan, still lived at Allegany on the grant. From the Turtle clan, Blue Eyes still lived at Allegany where he was one of the Christian chiefs; Mush had died. From the Crane clan, Silver Heels had joined the Christians. The replacements for the dead and the living who had moved were divided; the old unity was no more.[57]

· *The Formation of the Handsome Lake Church* ·

ALTHOUGH TEMPERANCE and the economic reforms enjoined by Handsome Lake's gospel endured as commonly accepted norms by almost all of the New York Iroquois, his hopes for political unity and for domestic tranquility were not fully realized during his lifetime nor in the years after his death. Indians, Quakers, and evangelists alike deplored the still too common Indian custom of "putting away their wives." And as we have seen, the rise of the Christian party stimulated bitter factional dispute. At Allegany the quarrel became so intense that the pagan party, against its own better judgment, for a time opposed the Quaker school at Cold Spring and forced its closing. There was talk among the pagans of separating from the Christians and living on a different part of the reservation or even of emigration to the West. About fifty in number, the Christian faction were driven from Tonawanda and took refuge at Buffalo Creek; the hundred Christians at Onondaga fled to Allegany. Old loyalties were broken: Strong, a member of the Wolf clan, who had been one of the two young men appointed by Handsome Lake to oversee the people at Jenuchshadago and who had become a member of the council at Cold Spring, turned Christian. Another of the prominent men at Allegany, James Robinson, also joined the Christians and for a time was presiding chief of the Seneca tribal council.

The strong feelings generated by this division into parties reached their peak between 1818 and 1822. At that time emotion drove many of the members of the pagan party into extremely nativistic positions. Since the missionaries were demanding the abandonment of an Indian identity and calling the conservatives by the opprobrious term "pagan," some of those who chose to retain pride in being Iroquois felt forced to oppose everything any missionary proposed —not merely psalm-singing and sabbath-keeping, but also secular schooling and even further material improvements. Although the Quakers themselves opposed the evangelists, they too were resented in the general wave of nativistic feeling. Bizarre antiwhite prophecies began to circulate, which violated both the word and the spirit of Handsome Lake's preaching. Cornplanter, as we have seen, for a time appeared as a nativistic prophet. Farther up the river another Allegany prophet, Ganaego, had visions in which the Great Spirit instructed the Indians not to send their children to school and foretold disaster for those who did. Among other things he predicted that a great snake would go down the Allegheny River and make the water unfit to drink.[58] Fear of witches became more intense among the pagans, and women were executed at Buffalo Creek and at Tuscarora. Whites and Christian Indians called this murder, and when a pagan chief's children at Tuscarora died, they said it was in punishment for this sin.[59]

The responsible leaders of the pagan group disapproved of this panicky retreat into nativism. Blacksnake at Allegany, Jemmy Johnson at Tonawanda, Red Jacket at Buffalo Creek, took measures to restore balance to the adherents of the traditional religion. They were concerned not merely to retain the loyalty of the people to the old way, but also to counteract the increasingly nativistic tone of the new pagan prophets. A policy of uncompromising refusal to accept *any* white customs would be destructive for its adherents, would deepen the schism within the tribes, and would drive many reasonable people into the hands of the Christian faction. As the Tonawanda pagans succinctly put it, the Indians needed more education, not less.[60]

Beginning in 1818, therefore, leaders of the pagan party undertook to define the form and spirit of the old religion. In order to do so they called upon the memory of the great prophet, Handsome Lake, whose position with regard to religion had been firmly traditional but who had also been in favor of education, of economic progress, and of social harmony, and who had refused to condemn Christianity, hoping for mutual tolerance and respect among people of different faiths. Their effort to consolidate the old religion by appealing to the well-remembered teachings of the prophet gradually produced between 1818 and 1845 a new religious institution—a church—devoted to the preservation and propagation of the prophet's message.

The first step in this process was the convocation of a two-day religious council at Tonawanda in the summer of 1818. It was held in an old council building, fifty feet long and twenty wide, furnished exactly in the old longhouse style with two layers of bunks on each side, furnished with skins and blankets below and peltry, corn, and hunting gear above. The ceremonial fire and an outside temperature of ninety degrees kept the room oppressively hot. As an introductory ritual a form of Handsome Lake's confessional was held. Anyone who had done anything wrong was invited to come forward and confess his faults. The only one to step forward was a little girl ten or twelve years old. She stood before the chiefs and said she had done something wrong. "What is it?" asked one of them. She replied that one day she was in the trader's store and stole a paper of two rows of pins from the counter. She had never done anything bad before and was sorry she stole the pins. The chiefs decided that she should pay the trader four cents for the pins, and so the girl went to the trader and gave him four cents.

But the main purpose of this council was "to revive the moral instructions formerly received from GOSKUKKEWAUNAU KONNEDIEUY, the prophet, Kiendtwokhe's half brother, who died about the year 1815. The Indians seem now to think much of these instructions, and are desirous of having them recalled to mind, and redelivered for the benefit of the rising generation." Many speakers repeated the lessons of the prophet and urged their importance upon the listeners in the crowded building. Two of the most impressive speakers were John Sky, who spoke for three hours in a voice so loud "that every word might have been distinctly heard at a distance of a quarter of a mile." At great length he repeated the moral truths taught by Handsome Lake, emphasizing the duty of parents to set a good example to their children and expatiating on the evils of "drunkenness, lying, cheating, stealing, and other pernicious practices." He concluded eloquently: "You must not do anything bad; you must not think anything bad; for the Great Spirit knows your thoughts, as well as your words and actions. *This* is what the prophet taught us. You know it—and this is according to the word of God! . . . ."

The other principal speaker was a minor prophet who gravely recounted a vision confirming the apocalyptic preachings of Handsome Lake:

I have had a dream, which in my sleep, I was directed to relate in council. I dreamed that the sun in the firmament spoke to me. He told me to go to the Indians, and to tell them that the Great Spirit is very angry with them for their wicked ways. Tell them, they must repent of their wicked ways and forsake them, or the judgments of the Great Spirit will come upon them. If they do not repent and forsake their wicked ways, when the corn is in the cob, this year, there will be a storm, which will lay their corn flat on the ground and destroy it. If they do not then repent and forsake their wicked ways, next winter, there will be such a rain as they never saw before. The flood will be so great as to bury their houses in the water.[61]

Although the consolidation of the pagan views at this and perhaps other similar meetings tended for a time to sharpen the line of division between the Christians and the pagans, in the long run it reduced antagonism. More secure in their faith, and focused upon the image of the prophet as their great leader, the pagans were less sensitive to slight and more tolerant of their Christian neighbors. The Christians, particularly at Allegany, developed their own versions of the life and teaching of Handsome Lake, stories that grew more lurid and distorted with every year. He was accused of having slaughtered as many as one hundred suspected witches at one meeting; of having gotten his whole message from the Bible, either translated for him by his nephew Henry O'Bail or read to him by a mythical gray-haired missionary hermit in the woods across the river; of having recanted and professed Christianity during his last agonizing hours at Onondaga, while he bit through his lips to keep from screaming in pain, and steam came from under the blankets. But the pagans, increasingly secure and tolerant—more tolerant than the Christian converts— smiled and went their own way.

Throughout the twenties and thirties the followers of Handsome Lake cherished and repeated his sayings. The ministers harangued the people at Green Corn and New Year's with recitals of the prophet's moral commands. The validity of his visions was confirmed by two prophets, one at Tonawanda and one at Buffalo Creek, who received annual visits from the four angels. During the emigration crisis, when there was a proposal to move the Iroquois to the plains of Kansas, the angels took the Buffalo Creek seer on a tour of hell. "He passed over an immense prairie & at the distant end beheld an enormous stone ediface, without doors or windows, but the guide who accompanied him being a special messenger from the Great Sp[irit] knocked against the wall & instantly an opening was made from which issued a blaze that ascended hundreds of feet above the roofs, & he beheld within huge potash kettles, filled with boiling oil & moulten lead, & there were the wicked rising & falling & tumbling over in the bubling fluids & ever & over as the heads of some were thrown above the top of kettles they gave a horrid yell & down they plunged again. There he was told would be punished all the chiefs who advocated emigration." This vision virtually repeats Handsome Lake's earlier image of the domain of the Tormentor. The Tonawanda prophet, also echoing Handsome Lake, said that "there are four angels which are annually sent to him by the great spirit whose special duty it is to take charge of the Seneca Indians & that they inform him of what errors the Indians fall into, the vices they indulge in & the crimes they commit & what it is necessary for them to do to please the great spirit, & present the calamities which will befall the nation unless there is a reformation of conduct. He has recently told the Tonnawanda Indians, that a terrible sickness was coming from the rising sun, which would exterminate them unless they had a great feast & dance & all took a particular kind of medicine, which he had been instructed how to prepare. This has been done & the Indians are now safe from the disastrous evils, with which they were threatened."[62]

By the 1840's the constant recitation of the prophet's teachings and the accumulation of confirming dreams and visions by minor prophets had produced a large body of legend and text, more or less accurately recounting events in the prophet's life and his various visions and moral lessons. Individual preachers who knew this material well were able to recite versions of this Code in detail and were called upon at the two great annual festivals to serve as preachers. One of these men was Blacksnake, now an old man, still living at Allegany. Blacksnake in the mid-1840's had formulated a specific version of the Code, beginning with an account of the first vision and going on to organize the prophet's moral teachings in the form of twelve commandments prohibiting whiskey, witchcraft, love magic, divorce, adultery, premarital sex, refusal of the wife to live with her husband's parents, failure of parent to discipline unruly children, unwillingness to love all men, enmity, and gossip.

Farther north, at Tonawanda, a fuller and somewhat different version of the Code was developing, and it was here that the church took definite form. Here Jimmy Johnson, Handsome Lake's grandson Sosheowa, was the preacher in the 1840's. Annually in October he recited the Code of Handsome Lake on the mornings of four days, in a version very close in form and details of content to the later-published *Code of Handsome Lake*.[63] The Tonawanda version was to become the standard by which other speakers' versions were judged, and it was this version that was carried from village to village in the fall of each year in the Six Nations Meetings. It was at Tonawanda that the architectural form of the church building was defined, modeled after the old longhouse, but with wooden benches substituted for the two-tiered bunks, and wood stoves instead of earthen hearths. Here was kept the wampum belonging to Handsome Lake (probably the official belts and strings associated with his office as sachem in the League, for the current holder of the title remained the custodian). Here the annual ceremonial calendar, including the burning of the white dog and dream-guessing, was carried on conscientiously, along with the other major rituals recommended by the prophet. And here, on the most pagan of all the reserves, the chiefs refused to join the rest of the Seneca in the republican form of government adopted after the debacle at Buffalo Creek, preferring to stand by old political customs. Thus, from Tonawanda in the 1840's, under the guidance of Handsome Lake's grandson Jimmy Johnson, spread a new renaissance of traditional Iroquois religion. Now, however, it was crystallized in a new ritual form, the Six Nations Meeting, and invoked the prophet himself as the spiritual guide of the followers of the old religion. A renewed assertion of the sacredness of the family, expressed in heavy emphasis on those parts of the social gospel that condemned adultery, separation, and the other domestic vices, reflected the concern of the Seneca to complete the last major social reform that the prophet had urged upon the people. But now, in addition to its manifest content, the new religion of Handsome Lake conveyed a second message: that the Great Spirit, through his messenger Handsome Lake, supported and loved those who wished to remain Indians. The Indians on the reservations in New York and Canada who attended the Six Nations Meetings and the recitation of the Code at the major annual ceremonies were gaining membership in a group that, in contrast to the Christian denominations, supported identification with Indians rather than with whites.

The forms of the Handsome Lake Church were set about 1850 and have changed little since then. The dream-guessing rites and the white dog sacrifice, which aroused the indignation of white people, were gradually left out of the annual ceremonies and were no longer performed by the early part of the twentieth century. But these are not essential to the institution. Now the adherents of the Old Way are sometimes called conservatives or old-time people. What was revolutionary in the prophet's day is now, one hundred and fifty years later, the extreme of traditionalism. Today most of the men support their families by wage work in various mechanized industries: the railroads, the gypsum mines, the great industrial complex at Buffalo, high-steel work all over the country; the women, when they work outside the home, may serve as schoolteachers, secretaries, factory operatives, domestic servants. Housing, except for a few old structures, is modern. All children go to the state-supported schools. And the transformation of domestic life, which Handsome Lake promoted by teaching the virtues he felt essential to the nuclear domestic unit, has long been completed: the family names are English and are transmitted patrilineally, the man is the provider, and the old clan-and-lineage system, while not extinct, is blurred and not essential to most social relationships.

Thus the Old Way now contains little that can be pointed to as distinctively white and modern; the *Gaiwiio* today refers to values and beliefs that, whatever their ultimate origin, are now traditionally Iroquoian. Furthermore, with the fading away of the sharp antagonisms between Christian and pagan, the Christian denominations and *Gaiwiio* bear a relationship not unlike that in white society between Protestant denominations and Catholicism. Being a follower of Handsome Lake today is an expression of a somewhat nostalgic and deeply emotional identification with Indianness itself, with the group of "real" Iroquois people, as opposed to identification with white men and white-dominated organizations, and in some cases of a desire for the personal spiritual salvation achievable by renunciation of sin and acceptance of the leadership of Handsome Lake and the Great Spirit.

Now, along the Allegheny, the river rises high behind the new dam at Kinzua and covers the sites of the old towns at Jenuchshadago and Cold Spring, where Handsome Lake preached. The people have moved away to prefabricated bungalows on higher ground. No longer do the old gray houses stand among the patchwork of pale green fields and dark green forest, with thin smoke spires rising above and the lacy web of paths and roads running among them all. No longer do the flies buzz in the long grass down on the flats, or the elms and walnut trees wave softly in the wind that flows gently down from the hills. But the words of Handsome Lake still resound in the longhouses, for as the prophet said, "Gaiwiio is only in its beginning."

BIBLIOGRAPHY

AND

NOTES

Notes and References

CHAPTER 1: THE OLD WAY OF HANDSOME LAKE

1. The following description of aspects of current religious practice among followers of the Old Way of Handsome Lake refers to the Allegany Seneca specifically and is based largely on my field notes recorded in 1951 and 1952 at Cold Spring Longhouse.

2. Parker, 1913 (reprinted, with an introduction by W. N. Fenton, in Fenton, 1968). The version printed by Parker was written down in the Seneca language by Chief Cornplanter (Sosondowa), a Handsome Lake preacher on the Cattaraugus Seneca Reservation, about 1903 and was translated by William Bluesky, the native lay preacher of the local Baptist church. Sosondowa's version is embedded in Cattaraugus tradition and is supposed to have descended from Chief John Jacket's version of about 1863. There are at least three untranslated versions of the Code filed with the BAE: a Grand River Onondaga text, BAE MS 449, dated *c.* 1889; a Grand River Mohawk text from Seth Newhouse, BAE MS 3489, dated *c.* 1880; and one or more New York Onondaga texts, BAE MS 2585, dated *c.* 1908. There is also an untranslated text from the New York Onondaga at the Syracuse University Library, copies of which are held by the BAE and APS. Historical sources provide several abridged or shortened versions: an Allegany Seneca version recorded by the Christian Benjamin Williams, probably from Governor Blacksnake, Handsome Lake's nephew and apostle, *c.* 1846 (SHSW, DC, Brant Papers, 16 F 266); a Seneca version of Jimmy Johnson, as recorded by Ely Parker for L. H. Morgan, at Tonawanda in 1845 (Parker, 1919); and another version of Jimmy Johnson, as recorded in several drafts by Ely Parker for L. H. Morgan, at Tonawanda, October 1848 (Fenton, 1951; Morgan, 1951). A new version of the Code is being recorded and translated by Wallace Chafe.

3. The following description of the confession is largely drawn from an already published account: A. Wallace, 1952b.

Part I: The Heyday of the Iroquois
CHAPTER 2: THE SENECA NATION OF INDIANS

1. NYHS, OR, Vol. XV, d3 (recollections of Thomas Morris).

2. Beauchamp, 1916, pp. 67–84.

3. Jackson, 1830b, p. 19.

4. This section is drawn from a paper entitled "Handsome Lake and the Decline of the Iroquois Matriarchate," which was read at the Wenner-Gren symposium at Burg Wartenstein, Austria, on Kinship and Behavior in the summer of 1966. The concept of dominant kin relationship is developed in Hsu, 1965.

5. Kenton, 1927, Vol. II, pp. 78–80.

6. Seaver, 1824, p. 104–6.

7. Kenton, 1927, Vol. II, pp. 87–8.

8. SHSW, DC, 16 F 227 ("Cornplanter's Talk").

9. SHSW, DC, 16 F 32 ("Life of Governor Blacksnake").

10. Hamilton, 1953, p. 320.

11. Lafitau, 1724, Vol. I, p. 393.

12. Jackson, 1830b, p. 20.

13. *Ibid.*

14. *Ibid.*

15. Fenton, 1940, p. 429.

16. Kenton, 1927, Vol. II, p. 90.

17. Jackson, 1830b, p. 19.

18. Kenton, 1927, Vol. II, p. 90 n.

19. The description of the local council and its relation to the "tribal" councils is based on Seneca data recorded by the Quakers and federal officials in the first half of the nineteenth century. The dependence of the tribal council on the village councils becomes clear in the name lists of both, e.g., Bonsall's 1803 and Atkinson's 1809 lists of the Allegany Seneca chiefs (CL, Bonsall Journal, 1803, and HAVC, Allinson Journal, 1809) and the lists of treaty participants and signatories of the period (7 STAT. and ASPIA).

20. The sketch of the maturation of the Seneca child and youth is drawn from several sources; and not all of the instances are specifically Seneca, some being based on Huron data and others on Onondaga and Mohawk. The general cultural similarities of all these Iroquoian-speaking tribes, however, are sufficient to make possible the crosstribal use of most sorts of general information. Particularly useful sources were: Carse, 1949; Fenton, 1941b and 1951; Hamilton, 1953; Jackson, 1930b; Kenton, 1927; Morgan, 1851; Murdock, 1934; Parker, 1913; Pettitt, 1946; Quain, 1937; Randle, 1951; Speck, 1945; Wainwright, 1947.

21. The structure, function, rituals, and origin myth of the League of the Iroquois have been discussed at length in Morgan, 1851; P. Wallace, 1946 (from whose work the quotations in this section are drawn); and Thwaites's edition of the Jesuit Relations. There exists a large literature on the political history and institutions of the Iroquois; the principal studies are cited in the bibliography.

The classic study of Iroquois polity is of course Lewis H. Morgan's *League of the Ho-de-no-sau-nee, or Iroquois,* first published in 1851 (Morgan, 1901). Later researches have not substantially changed his description of the formal organization, but they have shown that its efficiency as a decision-making assembly, especially in matters of war, was not so high as Morgan's respect for the Iroquois had led him to believe.

CHAPTER 3: THE RITUALS OF HOPE AND THANKSGIVING

1. The major sources from which the foregoing brief and synthetic account of the Seneca annual economic and ceremonial cycle was drawn are: Fenton, 1936; Jackson, 1830b; Shimony, 1961; Chafe, 1961; Morgan, 1851; Murdock, 1934; Quain, 1937; Speck, 1945; and the author's own field notes, particularly those taken at the Midwinter Festival at Cold Spring (Allegany Seneca) in January and February, 1952. This summary necessarily presents a modal portrait to which the events of any given year in any given village did not necessarily conform. The ceremonies, for instance, varied not only from one community to another (or at least they do today) but also from one year to another in the same community, in response to dream-required innovations and to the pressure of circumstances, such as food supply, war, and the presence or absence of particular persons.

2. Jackson, 1830b, p. 28.

3. Fenton, 1953, p. 126.

4. HL, Parker Collection 1802–46, Ely S. Parker MS. (no date) on Medicine Men and Indian Dances.

5. This section is reprinted with minor changes from the author's article by the same title, published in the *American Anthropologist,* 1958, Vol. LX, pp. 234–48. Except where otherwise noted, the data and quotations are taken from the selections of the Jesuit Relations reprinted in Kenton, 1927, particularly the relations of Fathers Fremin, De Carheil, Ragueneau, Jouvency, Le Mercier, Le Jeune, De Quen, Bressani, Lalemant, and Bruyas. See also Blau, 1963.

CHAPTER 4: THE RITUALS OF FEAR AND MOURNING

1. NYHS, OR, Vol. XV, Thomas Morris to Richard Morris, September 9, 1796.

2. Hamilton, 1953, p. 317.

3. SHSW, DC, 16 F 107–219 ("Life of Governor Blacksnake").

4. W. Stone, 1838, Vol. I, p. 28.

5. Data on Iroquois witchcraft is contained particularly in BAE, Gatschet MSS., 1883–5; BAE, Goldenweiser MSS., 1912–13; BAE, Hewitt MSS., 1880–90; Morgan, 1851; Erminie Smith, 1883; Decost Smith, 1888 and 1889; and Shimony, 1961.

6. The Iroquois creation myth exists in numerous texts and summaries. Each of these differs from the next, sometimes not only in minor detail. Some of the differences are tribal: the Huron legends of the seventeenth century are not quite the same as Seneca and Onondaga, for instance. Versions differ also according to the particular informant's idiosyncrasies of emphasis and innovation and according to the patience and thoroughness of the ethnographer, interpreter, or historian. The version recited here is based on the brief "Cornplanter's Talk" of February 1821 (SHSW, DC 16 F 227) and on the long text, in very bad reservation English, recorded by the Seneca Benjamin Williams about 1846, probably from the words of Blacksnake or Brooks Redeye (SHSW, DC, 22 F 23–44). The Williams version (which recapitulates and expands Cornplanter's) is no more nor less authentic than any other; but it is almost certainly the version that Handsome Lake knew. It has been paraphrased by this writer, and some repetitious passages have been eliminated or briefly summarized. Supplementary data were taken from J. N. B. Hewitt's articles "Tawiskaron" and "Teharonhiawagon" in Hodge, 1906; from Hewitt, 1903, 1928; and from Curtin and Hewitt, 1918, since the Williams version skimps the creative activities and rivalry of the twins. The legend that identifies the giant prototype and progenitor of the Faces is found (again with minor variation) in Speck, 1949, p. 71; Fenton, 1941a, pp. 418–19; and in my own field notes at Grand River Reservation, December, 1946 (interview with the Cayuga sachem, Deskaheh). Deskaheh explicitly identifies the Great World-Rim Dweller as the Evil Twin, and this identification of the False Face with the Evil Twin is implied in all versions by their common interest in disease, windstorm, witchcraft, and winter; in their common desire to be recognized as the Creator; in their shared antipathy for the Good Spirit; in the fact that

in some versions the Evil Twin, defeated in battle by his brother, is transformed into the mountains, while in others the giant says he comes from the mountains. One version of the creation myth, however, has the False Face as the *father* of the twins. All efforts to "identify" the characters in myths by making this sort of logical equation are, in one sense, wasted, because myths are like dreams not only in their fantastic content but also in their variability from one version to the next. Nevertheless, the functional identification of the prototypical False Face with Tawiskaron, the Evil Twin, is in my opinion substantial enough to require pointing out. One might speculate that this is a syncretism: that the Iroquois, in a sense, invented *two* evil spirits, first the Evil Twin and then the False Face, and have only recently felt the need to relate them to one another.

7. BHS, Box "Indians," Parker gift, pencil notes by Asher Wright.

8. The quotations from the condolence ritual are taken from Hewitt and Fenton, 1944, and Fenton, 1946. The Iroquois Condolence Council has been extensively described in other sources, including Morgan, 1851; Hale, 1883 and 1895; Shimony, 1961; and Beauchamp, 1905.

9. The form of the Dekanawidah myth, which like other myths exists in several versions, used here is drawn from the interpretation of P. Wallace, 1946, and my own reinterpretation in terms of revitalization movements in A. Wallace, 1958.

10. Jackson, 1830b; PHC, Skinner MSS.

11. Curtin and Hewitt, 1918, pp. 458–9.

12. Relation of Father Le Jeune, 1639, in Kenton, 1927, Vol. I, p. 389.

13. Relation of Father Le Jeune, 1636, in Kenton, 1927, Vol. I., pp. 257–8.

14. Relation of Father Le Jeune, 1637, in Kenton, 1927, Vol. I, pp. 336–48.

Part II: The Decline of the Iroquois

CHAPTER 5:   THE LAST WARS IN THE FOREST

1. The play-off system and its interruption by the French defeat in the French and Indian War are detailed in the many records of commercial, diplomatic, and military relations between the whites and the eastern Indians for the period 1701–63. See particularly Sullivan, 1921–65; P. Wallace, 1945; Downes, 1940. The description of Teedyuscung's belt is to be found in A. Wallace, 1949, pp. 111–13.

2. The general material on the Pontiac Wars of 1763 is taken from Peckham, 1947. The information on the traditionally known role of Guyasuta and others of Handsome Lake's kinfolk in the affairs at Fort Franklin and the Devil's Hole, and Handsome Lake's participation in these events, comes from the testimony of Seneca informants interviewed by Lyman C. Draper in 1850 (SHSW, DC, Draper's Notes, 4 S *passim*).

3. The account of Pontiac's role in the conspiracy of Pontiac and the revelations of the Delaware Prophet is taken from materials given in Peckham, 1947, pp. 98–100, 101, 112–16, 120, 187–8; Heckewelder, 1819, pp. 291–3; Schoolcraft, 1839, Vol. I, pp. 239–48.

4. Sullivan, 1921–65, Johnson Papers, Vol. X, pp. 505–6.

5. SHSW, DC, 4 S 58–73. See also Mary Jemison's and L. S. Everett's accounts of the Devil's Hole massacre in Seaver, 1824, pp. 63–4, 154–8.

6. The Iroquois negotiations at Fort Stanwix in 1768 and their subsequent diplomatic difficulties are summarized and documented in Downes, 1940. Many of the primary documents are to be found in the Johnson Papers, Sullivan, 1921–65, and Thwaites, 1904.

7. The account of Logan and Lord Dunmore's War is taken from W. Stone, 1838, Vol. I, pp. 38–48, and from materials in SHSW, DC, 4 S 67, 98–9. Further materials on Lord Dunmore's War and Six Nations' unofficial participation in but official avoidance of it are to be found in Thwaites, 1904, in the Kirkland Papers at Hamilton College, and in Sullivan, 1921–65.

8. The material on the various negotiations with the Six Nations, culminating in the Albany Council of 1775, is taken largely from W. Stone, 1838, Vol. I, Chs. iv and v and App. No. 12 (Proceedings of the Albany Council). See also Mohr, 1933, and Harmon, 1941, pp. 1–2.

9. The maintenance of the neutrality position from 1775 until the fall of 1776 is documented in W. Stone, 1838, Vol. I, Chs. iv, v, vi, and vii, and in the narratives of the councils at Fort Pitt and Albany given by Blacksnake to Lyman C. Draper (SHSW, DC, Brant MSS., 16 F). Guyasuta's pronouncement is quoted by Sipe, 1927, pp. 402–3. See Savelle, 1932, for an account of the Fort Pitt councils.

10. The abandonment of the neutral position at Niagara in 1776 is noted in Mohr, 1933; W. Stone, 1838, Vol. II, pp. 3–4 n.; and the Draper MSS., 4 S 16. The preceding events are described in W. Stone, 1838, Vol. I, Chs. vi, vii, and xiii.

11. The council at Oswego is described briefly in W. Stone, 1838, Vol. I, pp. 186–8, and at some length in accounts by Blacksnake, who was there,

recorded by and for Draper (16 F, 4 S 17, 73). Its date apparently was in May (Beauchamp, 1905), p. 354.

12. The account of the Oriskany battle is based on Seaver, 1824, pp. 76–7; W. Stone, 1838, Vol. I, pp. 209–64; and SHSW, DC 16 F, Blacksnake memoirs I and II and 4 S, Draper's notes of February 11, 1850.

13. SHSW, DC, 16 F (Blacksnake memoirs).

14. The account of the 1778 campaign is based on W. Stone, 1838, Vol. I, and on the Blacksnake memoirs in SHSW, DC, 16 F.

15. PA, first ser., Vol. VII, p. 593.

16. The spring campaign of 1779 is described in W. Stone, 1838, and in PA, first ser., Vol. VII.

17. W. Stone, 1838, Vol. I, p. 404.

18. Sullivan's raid has been copiously described in W. Stone, 1838, Vol. II, and Brodhead's expedition in Downes, 1940, and Deardorff, 1941. Blacksnake gives some incidents of these campaigns in his memoirs in SHSW, DC, 16 F.

19. Brodhead, 1857, p. 797.

20. Norris, 1879; PA, first ser., Vol. VIII, p. 157.

21. The campaigns of 1780 to 1783 and their effects on the frontier settlements are generally described in W. Stone, 1838, Vol. II; PA, first ser., Vol. VIII; DRCHNY, Vol. VIII; Downes, 1940; and in the Blacksnake and Bucktooth memoirs in SHSW, DC, 16 F and 4 S respectively.

CHAPTER 6:   THE COLLAPSE OF THE CONFEDERACY

1. Ford, 1904, Vol. XXV, pp. 680–91 (October 15, 1783).

2. Harmon, 1941, pp. 2–9.

3. The conquest theory is outlined in PA, first ser., Vol. X, pp. 53–4, 126; W. Stone, 1838, Vol. II, pp. 240–3; Hough, 1861, Vol. I, p. 74; SHSW, DC, 16 F, Blacksnake memoirs (account of Fort Stanwix treaty); Ford, 1904, Vol. XXV, pp. 680–91. The various treaty journals and correspondence of 1784, 1785, and 1786 also contain explicit assertions of the theory. For a general review, see Mohr, 1933.

4. For events of the Treaty of Fort Stanwix in 1784 and its subsequent repudiation, see accounts in SHSW, DC, 11 F 7 (Commissioner Lee to

J. Reed, October 1784); Hough, 1861; Mohr, 1933; W. Stone, 1838; and Blacksnake's detailed account in SHSW, DC, 16 F.

5. The negotiations at these three treaties are described in a number of sources: Harmon, 1941; Mohr, 1933; ASPIA; Manley, 1932; MHS, Pickering Papers; SHSW, DC, 23 U; Hough, 1861; Ketchum, 1865; Evans, 1941.

6. The numerous cessions are recorded in Hough, 1861.

7. SHSW, DC, 23 U, Butler to Spt. Genl., August 3, 1788.

8. Hough, 1961, Vol. I, pp. 119–28 *et passim;* Flick, 1933, Vol. V, p. 156; NYHS, OR, 15 d 3.

9. Hough, 1961, Vol. I, pp. 160–2; NYHS, OR, Vol. V, p. 92 and 15 d 3; ASPIA, Vol. I, pp. 211–15.

10. W. Stone, 1838, Vol. II, p. 249; Shipman, 1933; SHSW, DC, 23 U 27–31. The organization of the northern confederacy is revealed in the speeches of Indian participants. See particularly SHSW, DC, 23 U 41–2, 51, 66–73, 172–87, Aupaumut, 1827, entry of September 17, 1792; Cruik-shank, 1923–31, Vol. I, p. 219.

11. NYHS, OR, Vol. V, p. 77; W. Stone, 1838, Vol. II, pp. 265–9; Shipman, 1833; SHSW, DC, 23 U 38–51.

12. Several monographs treat the tricornered conflict of interests in Ohio among Indians, British, and Americans: Mohr, 1933; Downes, 1940; Shipman, 1933; Harmon, 1941; W. Stone, 1838.

13. Aupaumut, 1827, pp. 127–8.

14. NYHS, OR, Vol. V, p. 88; Stone, 1838, Vol. II, pp. 273–9; SHSW, DC, 23 U 173.

15. Details of preparations for the Fort Harmar Treaty are given in Ford, 1904, Vols. XXXIII and XXXIV; NYHS, OR, Vol. V, p. 86; Shipman, 1933; and W. Stone, 1838, Vol. II.

16. John Heckewelder as quoted in Shipman, 1933, pp. 40–5, from Pickering Papers in MHS.

17. 7 Stat.; ASPIA, Vol. I, pp. 4–12; Kappler, 1904, Vol. III, pp. 698–701.

18. Quoted in Mohr, 1933, pp. 135–7.

19. NYHS, OR, Vol. VI, p. 16.

20. Shipman, 1933, pp. 46–55.

21. W. Stone, 1838, Vol. II, p. 278 (quoting Brant to Langan, October 7, 1788).

22. See Wildes, 1941, and Shipman, 1933, for a summary of political and military events in the war for the Northwest Territory.

23. NYHS, OR, Vol. VI (Knox to Washington, June 15, 1789; ASPIA, Vol. I, pp. 53–4; Harmon, 1941, pp. 10–19).

24. W. Stone, 1838, Vol. II; Shipman, 1933, p. 56.

25. Brant's activities in the affairs of the western confederacy are most fully described in W. Stone, 1838.

26. Schenck, 1887, p. 102.

27. Hough, 1961, Vol. I, p. 165.

28. Schenck, 1887, p. 98.

29. ASPIA, Vol. I, p. 158.

30. Field notes, Grand River Reservation, Ontario, winter 1947–48.

31. PA, second ser., Vol. IV, pp. 569–70.

32. Colonel Proctor's journal, 1791, in ASPIA, Vol. I, pp. 159–60; PA, second series, Vol. IV, pp. 569–70.

33. There are four major accounts of this extended meeting: Hendrick Aupaumut's journal of his mission on behalf of the U.S. (Aupaumut, 1827); Blacksnake's narrative (SHSW, DC, 16 F); reports in the Simcoe Papers (Cruikshank, 1923–31, Vol. I); and correspondence and report of the Six Nations emissaries, November 1792, NYHS, OR Vols. VIII and IX. It should be noted that the date "1793" given on the published version of Hendrick's journal is incorrect; Hendrick's mission was made in 1792.

34. PHC, Skinner MSS., pp. 121–2.

35. NYHS, OR, Vol. VIII, p. 45, and Vol. IX, p. 34; W. Stone, 1838, Vol. II, pp. 295, 313, 405, and App., pp. xiii–xxvi; PA, second ser., Vol. IV, p. 557. Today the descendants of these emigrants are known as the Seneca-Cayuga of Oklahoma.

36. SHSW, DC, Blacksnake Papers, 16 F, pp. 68–9, 117–21.

37. Rossman, 1952; NYHS, OR, Vol. X, Docs. 31, 35, 40, 41, 43, 50, 54, 57; W. Stone, 1838, Vol. II, pp. 378–9.

38. W. Stone, 1838, Vol. II, pp. 378–9; NYHS, OR, Vol. X, Doc. 31; PA, first ser., Vol. VI, p. 819.

39. Hough, 1861, Vol. I, pp. 168–71.

40. HSP, MS. Division, Journal of John Parrish to the Treaty at Newtown Point, Am 565.

41. W. Stone, 1838, Vol. II, p. 275.

42. NYHS, OR, Vol. X, p. 69; 7 STAT., p. 61.

43. W. Stone, 1838, Vol. II, pp. 394–424, and App., p. xv. Stone's assumption that Brant remained "at the head of the Confederacy, until the day of his decease" is not justified by the evidence. The council at Niagara evidently was held on Canadian soil and amounted to a rejection by Brant and his people of the claims of the New York Iroquois to control of the lands in Canada. Brant did, however, remain at the head of the Grand River Iroquois, who have continued to maintain a separate roster of League chiefs and conduct independently their own condolence and installation ceremonies (cf. Fenton, 1946).

44. SHSW, DC, 4 S, 109–11.

45. *Ibid.*, 4 S 117–21 (conversations with Charles O'Bail, Cornplanter's son).

46. NYHS, OR, Vol. VIII (Chapin's copy of Pickering's Census of the Six Nations, November 12, 1792).

47. ASPIA, Vol. I, pp. 153–4 (Proctor's Journal of 1791).

48. The locations and periods of occupation of the Allegany Seneca after the Revolution must be inferred from scattered primary sources. The following have been of particular use: Proctor's 1791 Journal in ASPIA, Vol. I, pp. 149–62; Pickering's Census of 1792 in NYHS, OR; Draper's Notes and the Blacksnake Papers in SHSW, DC, 4S and 16 F; Kirkland's 1789 Census of the New York Iroquois, HAMC; and various maps, particularly John Adlum's 1798 map of the Seneca towns in the Record Room of the Philadelphia Yearly Meeting.

49. Hough, 1861, Vol. I, pp. 110–28, 160–63; Flick, 1933, Vol. V, p. 156.

50. PA, second ser., Vol. VI, pp. 782–3.

51. The definitive history of Cornplanter's private real-estate transaction is given in Deardorff, 1941.

52. Hough, 1861, Vol. I, p. 165.

53. NYHS, OR, Vol. VI (Seneca Chiefs to Governor of Pennsylvania, August 12, 1790).

54. Schenck, 1887.

55. Cornplanter in Philadelphia was most eloquent about Fort Stanwix. The story of his visit is given in PA, fourth ser., Vol. IV; NYHS, OR, Vol. VI, August 12, 1790, Doc. 33, Vol. VIII, Doc. 3, Vol. XV, Doc. 3d; Hough, 1861, Vol. I, pp. 110–16, 161–76; and SHSW, DC, 16 F, Blacksnake memoirs. Objections had also been made in 1784, 1785, 1786, and

1787. The whole matter of the Fort Stanwix lines was not settled until the Treaty of Canandaigua in 1794 (7 STAT., pp. 44–7).

56. NYHS, OR, Vol. XV, Red Jacket to Pickering, November 25, 1790; Hough, 1861, Vol. I, pp. 160–3.

57. PA, ser. 2, Vol. VI; Meginness, 1887; Rossman, 1952, p. 233; ASPIA, Vol. I, pp. 521–2.

58. NYHS, OR, Vol. VIII, J. Parrish to I. Chapin, November 27, 1792; Hough, 1861, Vol. I, pp. 161–8.

59. Hough, 1861, Vol. I, p. 161.

60. NYHS, OR, Vol. VI, Seneca Chiefs to Governor of Pennsylvania, August 12, 1790; Schenck, 1887, pp. 99–102, 105; PA, second ser., Vol. IV, pp. 546–7; W. Stone, 1838, Vol. II, pp. 326–31.

61. Hough, 1861, Vol. I, pp. 161–71.

62. *Ibid.*

63. PA, fourth ser., Vol. IV, p. 160–4; Deardorff, 1941.

65. *Ibid;* but see also Red Jacket's lack of enthusiasm for culture change, as recorded by John Parrish in his journal of the 1791 conference at Newtown Point (HSP, MS. Division, Am 565).

66. Hough, 1861, Vol. I, pp. 168–71.

67. NYHS, OR, Vol. VIII, Chiefs of Six Nations to "General" Chapin, August 1792, and Vol. IX, Minutes of Council at Buffalo Creek, October 8–10, 1793; W. Stone, 1838, Vol. II, *passim;* Cruikshank, 1923–31, Vol. I, p. 219.

68. This reversal of policy is stated clearly in Knox's memorandum to Washington on Indian affairs of June 15, 1789 (NYHS, OR, Vol. VI), and culminated in the abortive treaty negotiations of 1793 (see Shipman, 1933).

69. Hough, 1861, Vol. I, 165–71; PA, fourth ser., Vol. IV, 160–5; Deardorff, 1941; PA, ser. 2, Vol. VI ("Papers Relating to the Establishment of Presqu'isle"); NYHS, OR, Vol. XV, Doc. 3 (Concerning delay in Morris's plans to purchase western New York); 7 STAT., pp. 44–7 (Treaty of Canandaigua, 1794); ASPIA, Vol. I, pp. 140–215.

70. PA, second ser., Vol. IV, pp. 549–50, and fourth ser., Vol. IV, pp. 109–10; Hough, 1961, Vol. I, pp. 165–8; 7 Stat., pp. 44–7; NYHS, OR, Vol. VIII, July 7, 1792, November 1797 (correspondence of I. Chapin concerning punishment of white murderer and indemnification of his victim's family). N.B. also the provisions of the laws governing the

Northwest Territory and the system of licensing under bond traders and other entrants into Indian territory.

71. PA, fourth ser., Vol. IV, pp. 109–10; Hough, 1861, Vol. I, pp. 165–8; 7 STAT., pp. 44–7.

72. NYHS, OR, Vol. XV, R. Morris to T. Morris, August 1, 1797.

73. Ibid.

74. NYHS, OR, Vol. XV, T. Morris to R. Morris, May 29, 1797.

75. NYHS, OR, Vol. XV, pp. 54–68 (Journal of Treaty of Big Tree).

76. NYHS, OR, Vol. XV, Doc. 3, Memoir of Thomas Morris.

77. Except as otherwise noted, the account of the Big Tree negotiations is taken from Wilkinson, 1953 (which is based largely on NYHS, OR, Vol. XV).

78. 7 STAT., pp. 601–3; Royce, 1899.

79. Specification of the reservations and their sizes from 7 Stat., pp. 601–3; Royce, 1899; NYHS, OR, Vol. XV, List of Reservations, September 16, 1797; and Oil Spring Reservation, Cat. Co., pp. 81–2, and Congdon, 1967.

CHAPTER 7: SLUMS IN THE WILDERNESS

1. Schenck, 1887, p. 332.

2. The history of early frontier settlement in the Allegheny Mountain area surrounding the Cornplanter grant is derived from a number of local histories, particularly those concerned with Warren County, Pennsylvania, and Cattaraugus County, New York. See in particular Schenck, 1887; Cattaraugus County, 1879; and Warren Centennial, 1897.

3. A detailed description of place names and related activities of the Cornplanter Seneca is in Fenton, 1945–46.

4. The names and reputations of most of the chiefs, warriors, and leading women of the Allegany Seneca at this time are provided principally by Adlum, 1794 (as edited and annotated by Kent and Deardorff, 1960); by John Decker in his recollections for Draper, preserved in the SHSW, DC, 4 S; and by the Quaker diarists of 1798 and thereafter, particularly MHD, Sharpless, 1798; SC, Simmons; the several Jackson journals at SC and CCHS; and Jackson, 1830a.

5. A detailed description of the houses, the economy, the diet, the religious beliefs and observances, and the alcoholic excesses of the Allegany Seneca in 1798 is given in MHD, Sharpless, 1798; SC, Simmons Letter Books, 1798–99; and Jackson, 1830b. Their accounts are based on personal observation during visits to the town in 1798 and 1799.

6. No precise casualty figures are available, of course, but an examination of W. Stone's (1838) life of Brant and of Draper's interviews with Blacksnake and other Seneca informants (SHSW, DC, 4 S and 16 F) reveals that the Six Nations lost heavily in the Oriskany battle and various numbers at the many subsequent engagements both major and minor. Two hundred fatal casualties is probably a conservative estimate when one considers the difficulties of the time in treating infections of various kinds in casualties at first reported merely as wounded, or perhaps not even reported.

7. HAMC, Kirkland Papers, Census of the Five Nations (filed with correspondence under date of October 20, 1789).

8. For details of the destruction accomplished by Sullivan, Brodhead, and Van Schaick, see W. Stone, 1838, Vo. II; PA, first series, Vol. VII; R. Stone, 1924; and any of several other accounts of these expeditions including the various journals of officers and men.

9. Seaver, 1932, p. 75; Harris, 1903, p. 423. See W. Stone, 1838, Vol. II, p. 54; Ketchum, 1865, Vol. II, p. 1; Hough, 1861, Vol. I, p. 133; and PA, first ser., Vol. VIII, p. 152, concerning the weather.

10. SHSW, DC, 16 F, Blacksnake memoirs; Turner, 1849, p. 281.

11. NYHS, OR, Vol. IX, p. 46 (August 12, 1793) and Vol. X, p. 5 (February 1, 1794); Collections of the MHS, first ser., Vol. V, p. 28.

12. W. Stone, 1838, Vol. I, p. 176.

13. Harris, 1903, pp. 433–4.

14. Brodhead, 1857, p. 780.

15. MHS, Pickering Papers, Vol. LXII, p. 250; NYHS, OR, Vol. VIII, census of November 12, 1792; Vassar College, Parrish Papers, No. 55; HAMC, Kirkland Papers, census of the Five Nations (filed with correspondence under date of October 20, 1789); Morse, 1822, App., p. 76.

16. Sullivan, 1921–65, Vol. IV, pp. 240–1; Beauchamp, 1903, p. 342. Total population is generally calculated as four or five times the number of warriors.

17. Quoted in Pearce, 1953, p. 69.

18. Kent and Deardorff, 1960, pp. 265–324, 435–80.

19. Hough, 1961, Vol. I, pp. 21–5. See also Ford, 1904, Vol. XXVI, pp. 152–5.

20. The behavior of the white delegates at Fort Stanwix is described by Evans, 1941, and in Manley, 1932, and Shipman, 1933. Blacksnake was present, and his account documents the discomfiture of the Indians at being confronted with the American policy (SHSW, DC, 16 F).

21. Manley, 1932.

22. Fitzpatrick, 1925, pp. 400–4.

23. SHSW, DC, 23 U 42.

24. Cf. A. Wallace, 1949.

25. Evidence for serious alcoholism among prominent Iroquois of this period is to be found in many sources, such as NYHS, OR; SHSW, DC, 4 S and 16 F; Deardorff, 1951; W. Stone, 1838; Parker, 1912; ASPIA.

26. Ketchum, 1865, Vol. II, p. 149.

27. NYHS, OR, Vol. IX, Calking to Chapin, June 20, 1793.

28. *Ibid.*, Vol. VIII, p. 70, and Vol. XV, Doc. 3.

29. *Ibid.*, Vol. XV, pp. 54–69.

30. W. Stone, 1838, Vol. II, pp. 464–6.

31. SC, Jackson Journal, 1800, pp. 4–5.

32. Seaver, 1824, pp. 97–101 119–22, 127–34.

33. Jackson, 1930b, p. 34.

34. NYHS, OR, Vol. XII, p. 33 (Chapin to secretary of war, September 4, 1796).

35. BHS Publications, Vol. VI, p. 245.

36. SHSW, DC, 4 S and 16 F; Wildes, 1941, p. 411. Fenton's study of Iroquois suicide (Fenton, 1941b) does not record any cases during our period.

37. PHC, Skinner, MSS., pp. 121–5; Seaver, 1932.

38. Parker 1913, pp. 17–18.

39. Brant's acculturation policy is described in W. Stone, 1838, Vol. II, pp. 287–9, 398–405, 430–45, 489; and in Lydekker, 1938, Chs. VII and VIII.

40. Hough, 1861, Vol. I, pp. 165–71.

41. NYHS, OR, Vol. XII, pp. 21, 45–45A.

42. Kent and Deardorff, 1960, pp. 465–6.

43. PYM, Indian Committee, Vol. I, Cornplanter to Brother Onas, n.d. but *c*. 1791.

44. Sipe, 1927, p. 465; Warren Centennial, 1897, claims that the first (white) sawmill in Warren County was built on Jackson Run in 1800 and that the first raft of lumber floated down the Allegheny was sawed there. Cornplanter's mill was farther upstream, just above the New York State line.

45. NYHS, OR, VOL. XV, Doc. 3 (T. Morris's recollections of Red Jacket).

46. HSP, MS. Department, John Parrish' Journal at Newtown Point, 1791, AM 565.

47. BHS Publications, Vol. VI, No. 4 (Letters of Holmes from Fort Niagara, 1800).

48. S. Drake, 1837, pp. 98–100.

49. Mathews, 1908, pp. 62–63.

50. Kirkland's account of the revival of the white dog ceremony at Grand River and Oneida is at HAMC, Kirkland Papers, February 26, 1800, and May 30, 1800. See also Blau, 1964, and Tooker, 1965.

51. The depressed condition of the south-west New York and north-west Pennsylvania frontier is amply described in several printed collections and digests of primary source materials, particularly Harpster, 1938; Buck, 1935; Buck and Buck, 1939; Wright and Corbett, 1940; BHS Publications, Vol. V.

52. NcNall, 1952, pp. 3–5 (citing Dwight's Travels of 1804).

53. Agnew, 1887; PHC, Pennsylvania Population Co., MS.; Harpster, 1938, pp. 267–70.

54. Henderson, 1936, p. 159, *et passim*.

55. PHC, Pennsylvania Population Co., MS.; McNall, 1952, pp. 18–21; "Andrew Ellicott" in the Dictionary of American Biography. See also Turner, 1849, and Ketchum, 1865.

56. The relationship of the Israel Chapins, Sr. and Jr., to Phelps and Gorham is developed in NYHS, OR, Vol. V, Docs. 1, 5, 14, 33, 38, 40, 94, 98; Vol. VI, Docs. 2, 3, 4; Vol. VIII, Doc. 17, and Phelps to Chapin, November 3, 1792, and in various other documents scattered through O'Rielly's notebooks. These relationships among the principal white men at Big Tree are also revealed in O'Rielly's notebooks, particularly NYHS, OR, Vol. XV, Doc. 3, and in McNall, 1952.

57. Cattaraugus County, 1879, pp. 45–51.

58. *Ibid.*; PHC, Pennsylvania Population Co., MS.

59. The extended family system of settlement is made evident in the local histories. See Schenck, 1887, and Cattaraugus County, 1879.

60. NA Letters received by secretary of war 1812–15, December 3, 1801.

61. McNall, 1952.

62. The distribution of missionary effort is described in Cross, 1950; Buck and Buck, 1939; Hotchkin, 1848; Cattaraugus County, 1879.

63. The major treaties and agreements are published in 7 STAT., and Hough, 1861. See also Kappler, Vol. II, p. 1027 for date on the original annuity of 1792.

64. Act of January 4, 1790.

65. Harmon, 1941, pp. 10–19.

66. NYHS, OR Vol. VI, p. 36.

67. MHS, Collections, ser. 1, Vol. 5 (1798), "Report of a Committee, Who Visited the Oneida and Mohekunuh Indians in 1796," p. 30.

68. Hough, 1861, Vol. I, pp. 48–69, 165–8.

69. Cotterill, 1954, p. 124.

70. Kappler, Vol. II, p. 1027.

71. NYHS, OR, Vol. VIII; "List of Goods delivered . . . November 1792"; Vol. IX, p. 37.

72. See A. Wallace, 1949.

73. PYM, Minutes of Indian Committee, 11 month, 3rd 1795 to 3rd month 8th 1796.

74. NYHS, OR, Vol. XII, Doc. 17.

75. The chronicle of Quaker preparations recited above is based, except as otherwise noted, on the Minutes of the Indian Committee, found at PYM, Friends Book Store.

76. This is the phrase used by Jackson (in A. Wallace, 1952a) to describe the arts and crafts taught by the Quakers.

77. The initial negotiations between the Cornplanter Seneca and the Quakers are described in MHD, Sharpless, 1798, and PYM, Pierce and Sharpless Journal, 1798, May 18.

78. The events of the fall and winter are described in Jackson, 1830a, and SC, Simmons Letter Books, 1798–99.

79. Parker, 1913, p. 20. According to legend Handsome Lake had been bedridden for four years when in June 1799, he had his vision. Although he may not have been in good health, it is highly improbable that he was bedridden earlier than a few weeks before his vision. The evidence for this conclusion is as follows. First, the Code (in Parker, 1913) begins with a description of a winter's hunting trip down the Allegheny in 1798 and a drunken return in the spring of 1799—not just a description of a drunken orgy *after* the return of the hunting party. The language suggests a participant's recollections. The allusion to "four years of sickness in bed" in Parker's (1913) Code is attributed to Handsome Lake's daughter and son-in-law. Blacksnake's memoir of the first vision (SHSW, DC, 16 F 226) begins with the words: "The year [1799] Certifies that from a personal Aquanted called good lake that year he was sick confined to his bed. . . ." Jackson's journal (in A. Wallace, 1952a) merely says: "in these days [i.e., spring of 1799] . . . one of the Heathen (the Brother of Cornplanter the Chief lay upon his bed sick. . . ." Simmons (in A. Wallace, 1952a) asserts that at the time of the vision, Handsome Lake "had been on the decline of life for several years . . ." but does not claim he had been bedridden throughout that time. Additional information is available, moreover, about Handsome Lake's official role. In July 1795, the surveyors at Presqu' Isle were escorted by "one . . . who belongs to the Nobility, he is a nephew to King Guia Shuthongn and stepson to Chitteaughdunk!" (Mathews, 1908, pp. 120–1). The only official "Nobility" among the Iroquois were the *royaner*, or League chiefs, one of whom held the title Handsome Lake, and the only League chief who was also a nephew to Guyasuta, to my knowledge, was *this* Handsome Lake. A Handsome Lake also signed the Big Tree Treaty in 1797 and later a message to the government of New York State drafted at Geneseo on November 21, 1798 (NYHS, OR, Vol. XIII, p. 34). While any man who held this League chieftainship would bear the titular name Handsome Lake, it is probable, because of the early reference to Guyasuta's nephew, that this Handsome Lake was the bearer of the name between 1795 and 1799. If Cornplanter's brother *was* Handsome Lake by 1795, then he cannot have been bedridden for four years, because he was present at Presqu' Isle in 1795, at Big Tree in 1797, and Geneseo in 1798. On the other hand, even if he was not made a League chief until after 1795, he would have had to be in sufficiently sturdy health to be capable of participating in the condolence ceremony and of qualifying as a chief, and the "four years bed-ridden" legend is again disqualified.

80. The foregoing account of Simmons's work in the late winter and spring of 1799 is taken from his second diary, which commences February 3, 1799. A copy of this diary was made by Mr. M. H. Deardorff,

and I have used this copy. The original was owned by Mr. Robert S. Ewing of West Grove, Pennsylvania, and it is now in the possession of Swarthmore College Library. Parts of this diary are reprinted in A. Wallace, 1952a.

81. Parker, 1913, pp. 20–1.

82. The increased interest in acculturation in the spring of 1799 is described in SC, Simmons Journal; in Jackson, 1830a, p. 35; and in SC, Simmons Letter Books, 1798–99, Simmons *et. al.* to the Indian Committee, March 24, 1799, and June 16, 1799.

83. SC, Simmons Journal; Jackson in A. Wallace, 1952a.

Part III: *The Renaissance of the Iroquois*
CHAPTER 8:   PREACHING TO REPENTANCE:
The First, or Apocalyptic, Gospel

1. The external circumstances of the vision are given by several sources: Parker, 1913, pp. 22–4 (the Handsome Lake traditional code); Blacksnake's own recollections in SHSW, DC, 16 F 226; and the Simmons and Jackson diaries and notes printed in A. Wallace, 1952a. These sources do agree on the essential course of events, but disagree on the duration of the trance (Blacksnake says four days, Simmons two hours) and the severity of his prior illness (as we have seen, the Code in Parker, 1913, implies in one interpretation that he was bedridden for four years, but the early material and Simmons suggest that he had been declining for some time but not that he was bedridden). The text of the Code clearly implies that Handsome Lake, sick or not, had been a member of the drunken hunting party that came back from Pittsburgh in May. Blacksnake claimed (years later) to have seen the three angels talking with Handsome Lake when the latter came out of the door. Possibly he (and Handsome Lake) misperceived Handsome Lake's daughter and her husband.

2. SC, Simmons Journal, entry of "Sixth Month 15th," and Jackson, in A. Wallace, 1952a, give almost identical versions of the vision and the subsequent events.

3. Simmons in A. Wallace, 1952a.

4. *Ibid.*

5. The vision of the sky journey is described at length in one section of Parker's version of the Code. A comparison of this Code with Simmons's contemporary account demonstrates, first, that the assemblers of

the Code, who were piecing together the recollections of the prophet's disciples, placed some of the revelations acquired during this vision of August 8, 1799, out of context in other parts of the Code (a process of randomization evident in other topics as well); and second, that Handsome Lake cautiously avoided telling Simmons about that part of the journey in which the prophet toured the domain of punishment for sinners (doubtless fearful of offending the sensibilities of white men, who frequently criticized Indians for torturing prisoners). The reconstruction given is cast as much as possible in the language of the sources that purport to quote the prophet: i.e., the Code (in Parker, 1913) and Simmons's journal (in A. Wallace, 1952a).

6. Parker, 1913.

7. Simmons in A. Wallace, 1952a.

8. Parker, 1913.

9. SC, Simmons Journal, entries under "5th Month" and "8 Mo. 28th."

10. Parker, 1913.

11. *Evangelical Intelligencer*, Vol. I (1807), pp. 92–3.

12. HL, Parker Collection, MS. of Ely S. Parker concerning Indian medicine men, n.d. (from microfilm at APS).

13. *Evangelical Intelligencer*, Vol. I (1807), pp. 92–3; Speck, 1935, pp. 159–60.

14. Parker, 1913, pp. 27–30, n. 3; pp. 49–50, n. 2.

15. Parker, 1913.

16. HSP, Penn MSS., Indian Affairs, Vol. IV, p. 56 (Cornplanter *et al.* to Mead *et al.*, n.d. [c. January, 1801]); PYM, Pierce Journal, 1801, D 10 A.

17. There are several accounts of this affair, both traditional and contemporary, from which the account given in the text is derived. See Fenton, 1946, pp. 52–5; HL, H. M. 20461 (Mead to O'Bail, February 2, 1801); Jackson, 1830a, pp. 42–3; and personal communication from M. H. Deardorff, based on his work with Seneca informants.

18. P. Wallace, 1945, p. 299.

19. PYM, Indian Committee, Box 1, Baylor, Swayne, and Thomas to Indian Committee, June 28, 1801.

20. HSP, Penn MSS., Indian Affairs, Vol. IV, p. 56.

21. NA, WD, LR, C-51(1), April 14, 1801.

22. Jackson, 1830a, p. 42; PYM, Pierce Journal, 1801, Department of Records, D 10 A; HSP, Logan Papers, Vol. XI, p. 70 (unsigned letter from Friends at Genesinguhta, January 18, 1802).

23. BHS Publications, Vol. XXVI, pp. 122–3 (Joseph Ellicott's Letter Books).

24. BHS Publications, Vol. XXVI, pp. 122–3.

25. NA, WD, LR, C-73 (1) and C-83 (1).

26. *Evangelical Intelligencer*, Vol. I (1807), pp. 92–3.

27. Clinton, 1812, pp. 39–40.

28. Parker, 1913, p. 68.

29. PYM, Pierce Journal, 1801, D 10 A; NYHS, OR, Col. XIV, p. 12 (Council of November 12, 1801).

30. Jackson, 1830a, pp. 42–3.

31. HSP, Logan Papers, Vol. XI, p. 76 (Handsome Lake *et al.* to Dearborn, March 15, 1802).

32. Fenton, 1946.

CHAPTER 9:   THE POLITICS OF EVANGELISM:
The Second, or Social, Gospel

1. PYM, Pierce Journal, 1801, D 10 A.

2. NA, WD, LR, C-29 (1), C-34 (1), C-38 (1), C-124 (1); Ibid., SW, RBIA, LS, Vol. A, pp. 164–6.

3. PYM, Indian Committee, Box 1 (March 9, 1802).

4. NYHS, OR, Vol. XIV, p. 14; Cotterill, 1954, p. 226.

5. HSP, Logan Papers, Vol. XI, p. 74 (Handsome Lake to President of United States, March 10, 1802).

6. Parker, 1919, 250 App.; NA, RBIA, SW, LS, Vol. A, pp. 193–4.

7. NA, RBIA, SW, LS, Vol. A, p. 286.

8. W. Stone, 1841, pp. 447–9. A draft copy of this letter is in HSP, Daniel Parker Papers, Box 2, and it was referred to in an accompanying letter to Callendar Irvine of November 5, 1802, a copy of which is in NA, RBIA, SW, LS, Vol. A, p. 289.

9. The synoptic description of the strategy and course of the Quaker mission on the Allegheny is taken from a number of sources. PYM contains

a number of valuable manuscripts bearing on the mission, particularly Records of the Indian Committee, Boxes 1 and 2; the sixteen volumes of "Indian Records"; Indian Notes, 1791–1878; and the journals of Joshua Sharpless and John Pierce to the Seneca in 1798 and 1801 respectively. The Haverford College Library holds the Journal of William Allinson to the Seneca in 1809. The Chester County Historical Society, in West Chester, Pennsylvania, has a number of useful documents, including Halliday Jackson's "A Short History of My Sojourning in the Wilderness" (published in *Pennsylvania History*, Vol. XIX, 1952, pp. 117–147, 325–49, under the title "Halliday Jackson's Journal to the Seneca Indians, 1798–1800"), journals of Halliday Jackson and others to the Seneca in 1806, 1814, and 1817, a tabulation of Seneca "improvements" from 1810 to 1818, and miscellaneous correspondence between the missionaries among the Seneca and their families and friends in the Philadelphia area. Swarthmore College Library has the Henry Simmons journal and letter books and Halliday Jackson's "Some Account of My Residence Among the Indians," 1800. Among the privately owned materials, copies of which were loaned to the author by Mr. M. H. Deardorff, were Joshua Sharpless's journal to the Allegany Seneca in 1798 (owned by Dr. W. T. Sharpless of West Chester, Pennsylvania) and the letters and journals of Henry Simmons, 1796–99 (owned by Mr. Robert H. Ewing, West Grove, Pennsylvania, and now in the possession of the Swarthmore College Library). Among published works, of course, the most valuable primary source is undoubtedly Jackson, 1830a.

10. A. Wallace, 1952a, p. 344.

11. PYM, Journal of John Philips to the Seneca, 1806, entry of September 16, p. 31.

12. HAMC, Kirkland Papers, Journal of December 27, 1806.

13. Parker, 1913, pp. 67–8.

14. HAMC, Kirkland Papers, Journal of August 3, 1806.

15. Parker, 1913, p. 35.

16. Covell, 1804.

17. Parker, 1913, p. 38.

18. PYM, Pierce Journals, 1801, entries of October 16, p. 42, and October 21, p. 60.

19. PYM, Records of the Indian Committee, Box 2, Speech of Handsome Lake to Friends, August 30, 1803.

20. *Evangelical Intelligencer*, Vol. I (1807), pp. 92–3.

21. HAMC, Kirkland Papers, Journal of August 3, 1806.

22. *Evangelical Intelligencer*, Vol. I (1807), pp. 92–3.

23. PYM, Indian Committee, Vox 2, Letter of Handsome Lake, January 1, 1803.

24. HSP, Logan Papers, Vol. 9, p. 74.

25. The membership of the Allegany Council is listed for 1803 in CL, UM, Isaac Bonsall Journal, 1803, and for 1809 in HAVC, William Allinson's Journal.

26. The dispute over the location of the council fire is mentioned in W. Stone, 1841, Vol. II, pp. 408–29, and App., pp. 39–44. Handsome Lake's signature is found on annuity receipts in NA, RBIA, SW, LR, and Parrish's letter to Secretary of War Dearborn in NA, WD under date of September 3, 1807.

27. PYM, Indian Committee, Box 2, Letter of Handsome Lake and Cornplanter, August 20, 1803.

28. The removal to Cold Spring and the deposing of Cornplanter are described in three letters from Friends at Tunessassa to the Indian Committee in Philadelphia, dated March 24, June 9, and August 29, 1804 (PYM, Indian Committee, Box 2). See also Jackson, 1830a, pp. 49–50.

29. PYM, Indian Committee, Box 2, Letter of March 24, 1804.

30. PYM, Indian Committee, Box 2, Letter of June 9, 1804.

31. The Quaker visit of 1806 and the councils at Cold Spring on that occasion are described in CCHS, Jackson Journal, 1806; SC, Jackson Journal published by Snyderman, 1957; and CL, UM, Isaac Bonsall Journal, 1806–07.

32. Red Jacket's personal opposition is mentioned as early as 1803. See Cram's Journal, April 2, 1803 (*Massachusetts Missionary Magazine*, Vol. I (1804), pp. 68–9.

33. Clinton, 1812, pp. 39–40. See also NYHS, OR, Vol. XIV, Doc. 19, Chapin to Dearborn, July 6, 1802, for an early reference to the Handsome Lake-Cornplanter conspiracy theory.

34. *Evangelical Intelligencer*, 1807, Vol. I, pp. 92–3.

35. Parker, 1913, pp. 40–7.

36. Jackson, 1830a, p. 53.

37. The circumstances of Handsome Lake's exodus from Cold Spring are not given in any of the Quaker records that I have seen, nor are they described very fully in Parker's version of the Code. The account of the

difficulty concerning the epidemic is based on PHC, Skinner MSS., interview with S. C. Crouse, a nephew of Blacksnake, from whom Crouse claimed he got the story; from M. H. Deardorff's notes of conversations with Eber L. Russell, March 2, 1950; and from W. N. Fenton's notes of conversation with Henon Scrogg, September 5, 1935.

38. *Evangelical Intelligencer*, 1807, Vol. I, pp. 92–3.

39. HAVC, Journal of William Allinson, September 17, 1809; SHSW, DC, 4 S, interview with Benjamin Williams; Turner, 1849, p. 509.

40. PYM, Box 2, Journal of Lee, Brown, Stewardson, and Allinson, September 25, 1809.

41. HAVC, Journal of William Allinson, Book 2, p. 15.

42. Parker, 1913, p. 47.

43. Parker, 1919, p. 18.

44. CCHS, Jackson Journal, 1810–18, pp. 14–15, 51.

45. PYM, Indian Committee, Box 2, Letter of June 4, 1811.

46. Schenck, 1887, pp. 136–7.

47. Ketchum, 1865, Vol. II, pp. 419–35; NA, WD, LR, G-147 (6), letter of September 10, 1812; Vassar College, Jasper Parrish Collection, No. 36, Granger's Letter of October 24, 1812.

48. Vassar College, Jasper Parrish Collection, No. 23, Military census of February 14, 1814.

49. Vassar College, Jasper Parrish Collection, No. 36, Granger's Letter of October 24, 1812.

50. Ketchum, 1865, Vol. II, pp. 419–35.

51. HAVC, Journal of William Allinson, Book 2, p. 44.

52. The annual circuit is specifically mentioned by Clark, 1849, pp. 103–109 and may be inferred from the frequency with which he is recorded as being at Buffalo Creek, Onondaga, Tonawanda, and the Genesee.

53. PYM, Indian Committee, Box 2, Letter of March 24, 1804.

54. *General Assembly's Missionary Magazine*, 1805, Vol. I, pp. 401–6.

55. *Evangelical Intelligencer*, 1807, Vol. I, pp. 92–3; Jackson, 1830a, p. 50.

56. Babcock, 1927, pp. 23–4.

57. Schenck, 1887, p. 136; Babcock, 1927, pp. 23–5; Stone, 1866, pp. 298–9; PYM, Indian Committee, Box 2, Letter of April 25, 1806.

58. *Massachusetts Missionary Magazine*, 1804, Vol. I, pp. 68–9.

59. Clark, 1849, Vol. I, pp. 103–9.

60. HAMC, Kirkland Papers, Journal for 1806.

61. HL, Parrish Collection, Letter of July 29, 1806; NYHS, OR, Vol. XIV, p. 7.

62. PYM, Indian Committee, Box 2, Letter of November 6, 1807.

63. *Evangelical Intelligencer*, 1807, Vol. I, pp. 92–3.

64. *Connecticut Evangelical Magazine*, 1811, Vol. IV, pp. 315–19.

65. *Evangelical Intelligencer*, 1807, Vol. I, pp. 92–3.

CHAPTER 10: RENAISSANCE

1. Jackson, 1830a, p. 51.

2. Jackson, 1830a, pp. 45–6.

3. SC, Simmons Journal, entries under "5th Month" and "9 Mo. 11th," 1799; Jackson, 1830a, pp. 35–44.

4. HSP, Logan Papers, Vol. XI, p. 70 (unsigned letter from a Friend at Genesinguhta, January 18, 1802).

5. LC, British Archives, Gilbert's Journal.

6. Jackson, 1830a, p. 51.

7. CCHS, Jackson Journal, 1806; SC, Jackson Journal (published in Snyderman, 1957), September 16, 1806.

8. PYM, Indian Committee, Box 2, Speech to Indian Committee by Conudiu *et al.*, November 6, 1807.

9. CL, UM, Isaac Bonsall Journal, 1806–07, entry of September 18, 1807.

10. HAVC, William Allinson Journal, Vol. I, p. 26, 38–9, (September 17, 1809).

11. CCHS, Jackson Journal 1810–18, pp. 14–15, 41.

12. NYHS, OR, Vol. XIV, p. 12 (Council at Genesee River, November 12, 1801).

13. CCHS, Jackson Journal, 1806; SC, Jackson Journal (published in Snyderman, 1957), pp. 60–6.

14. HAVC, William Allinson Journal, Book 3, p. 7, September 29, 1809.

15. PYM, Pierce Journal, 1801, entry of October 16, p. 42; and Indian Committee, Box 2, 1803–15, Letters of August 30, 1803, and June 4, 1811.

16. *Massachusetts Missionary Magazine,* 1804, Vol. I, pp. 68–9.

17. Clark, 1849, Vol. I, pp. 103–9.

18. *Evangelical Intelligencer,* 1807, Vol. I, pp. 92–3.

19. *The Friend,* 1844, p. 163.

20. HAMC, Kirkland Papers, Journal for August 3 and December 27, 1806.

21. PYM, Indian Committee, Box 2, Speech to Indian Committee by Conudiu *et al.,* November 6, 1807.

22. HAVC, William Allinson Journal, 1809, Book 2, pp. 34–5, and Book 3, p. 20.

23. CCHS, Jackson Journal, 1806; SC, Jackson Journal (published in Snyderman, 1957), p. 72 (September, 1806).

24. HAVC, William Allinson Journal, Book 2, p. 32 (letter of September 19, 1809).

25. HAVC, William Allinson Journal, 1809, Book 1, p. 42.

26. Jackson, 1830a, pp. 43–4.

27. Jackson, 1830a, p. 52.

28. CCHS, Jackson Journal, 1810–18, p. 54.

29. HAVC, William Allinson Journal, 1809, Book 1, p. 35.

30. Jackson, 1830a, p. 89.

31. Parker, 1919, p. 297.

32. CCHS, Jackson Journal, 1910–18, pp. 37–8.

33. The statistical information about Seneca agricultural technology and other aspects of their economic transformation is given in systematic and detailed form in Jackson, 1830a, pp. 85–9 *et passim.*

34. CCHS, Jackson Journal, 1810–18, pp. 11–13.

35. Although the white dog is not burned today by Handsome Lake followers, and some of them say that he disapproved of it, the sacrifice was still being carried out under his direct sponsorship at Allegany in 1809 (HAVC, William Allinson Journal) and was continued in the "pagan" communities in New York and Canada until it died out under the pressure of white disapproval late in the nineteenth and early in the twentieth centuries.

36. Again, although the prophet criticized the conduct of the societies and purged them of their ritual use of alcohol, their ceremonies were

publicly practiced under his eyes at Allegany in 1809 (HAVC, William Allinson Journal) and have been continued by his followers ever since.

37. Parker, 1913, p. 56.

38. *Ibid.*, p. 47.

39. *Ibid.*, p. 79–80.

40. Treaty of Buffalo Creek, August 31, 1826, in Records of the U.S. Senate (RG 46) Sen 19B-C6, 19th Congress, second session.

41. Vassar College, Jasper Parrish Papers, E. Granger to J. Parrish, August 27, 1815.

42. *Buffalo Gazette*, October 3, 1815.

43. The progress of settlement and the increasing involvement of the Seneca with whites are detailed in the country histories, particularly Schenck, 1887, and also in the Quaker records, particularly Jackson, 1830a; CCHS, Jackson Journal, 1817; CCHS, Jackson MS. 1818; and PYM, Indian Committee, Box 3.

44. PHC, transcript of the Original Records of the Western Missionary Society.

45. Alden, 1827.

46. The history of the missions to the Iroquois in New York is summarized in Howland, 1903. Original missionary narratives are published in Severance, 1903, and Asher Wright's own summary of this work is printed in Fenton, 1957.

47. The treaties of 1826, 1838, 1842, and 1857 are to be found in, respectively: Records of the U.S. Senate, RG 46 Sen 19B-C6, 19th Congress, second session; Peters, 1856, 7 STAT. 550; Peters, 1856, 7 STAT. 586; anl 11 STAT. 735. The Quaker records after 1817 record the political intrigues as they involved the Allegany Seneca in great detail. Journals and correspondence concerning these land negotiations throughout the period are retained in NA, RBIA, RG 75. See also Ellis, 1879.

48. J. Hyde in Seeverance, 1803, p. 269; Morse, 1822, App., pp. 83–4; NA, RBIA, RG 75, LR, "Report of Council of Seneca Indians with R. L. Livingston, June 25th, 1828."

49. NYHS, OR, Vol. XIV, d3; PHS, Publications, Vol. III, pp. 81–2; BHS, Box "Indians" (Parker gift); Vassar College, Jasper Parrish Papers, E. Granger to J. Parrish, July 20, 1815; *Buffalo Gazette*, April 16, 1816.

50. NA, RBIA, RG 75, LR, "Report of Council of Seneca Indians with R. L. Livingston, June 25th, 1828."

51. *Ibid.;* Manley, 1950.

52. SHSW, DC, 4 S.

53. The plan to allocate the Allegany Seneca lands in severalty is chronicled in PYM, Indian Committee, Box 3.

54. *The Friend,* Vol. XXII, p. 374.

55. Cornplanter's visions and their reception by the Indians are recorded in several versions, which agree in essentials: SHSW, DC, 16 F 277; Sipe, 1927, pp. 467–8; Alden, 1827; PHC, Index of Indian Records, pp. 215–22. Other materials cited on his nativistic period are contained in *The Friend,* Vol. XXII, p. 388, and Deardorff, 1841.

56. Schenck, 1887, pp. 149–50.

57. The fate of all the members of the 1809 Council cannot be determined. Materials used come from SHSW, DC, Draper's Notes (4S), and from treaty signatures and treaty journals in the 1826–38 period.

58. PYM, Elkinton Journals; PYM, Indian Committee, Box 3.

59. *Niagara Journal,* May 8, 1821; Tuttle, 1834, pp. 40–62.

60. PYM, Indian Committee, Box 3, Letter of November 21, 1824.

61. Alden, 1827.

62. Dearborn, 1904, pp. 55, 90–1.

63. The Tonawanda version of the 1840's was recorded by Ely S. Parker on two occasions, in 1845 and 1848, and his unpublished notes were used by Lewis Henry Morgan as the basis for his published account of the Handsome Lake religion in 1851. Parker's notes were later published by his descendant, Arthur Parker (Parker, 1919) and by W. N. Fenton, 1951. The Tonawanda version agrees remarkably well in many details with the Allegany-Cattaraugus version, which was formulated, according to tradition, at a council at Cold Spring about 1860, at which all speakers of the Code came together to compare versions and decide on an official one. This version was published by Parker in 1913. The quotations used in this book came largely from the Parker 1913 version. No explicit attempt has been made here to reconcile discrepancies or to label parts of the various published and unpublished versions of the Code as later additions and interpretations, but the author has not quoted or cited certain sections that apparently were added to the Code by speakers who did not always distinguish between the words of the prophet and their own historical and editorial comment. Thus the existing Code includes both the words of Handsome Lake and exhortations, historical introduction and commentary by later speakers, and miscellaneous interpretations, applications, and perhaps new prophetic material.

Bibliography

MANUSCRIPT COLLECTIONS

ALLEGHENY COLLEGE
  Timothy Alden Papers

AMERICAN PHILOSOPHICAL SOCIETY
  Ely S. Parker Collection

BUFFALO HISTORICAL SOCIETY
  Box: "Indians"
  Indian Papers 1811–1893, Erie County, Niagara County

BUREAU OF AMERICAN ETHNOLOGY (SMITHSONIAN INSTITUTION)
  Manuscript Collections

CHESTER COUNTY HISTORICAL SOCIETY
  Halliday Jackson Journals, 1806, 1810–1818, 1814, and 1817

CLEMENTS LIBRARY, UNIVERSITY OF MICHIGAN
  Journals of Isaac Bonsall, 1803 and 1806–1807

MERLE H. DEARDORFF
  Transcripts of Henry Simmons's Journals and Letter Book, Joshua Sharpless' Journal, 1798, and other privately owned manuscript materials

HAMILTON COLLEGE
  Samuel Kirkland Papers

HAVERFORD COLLEGE
  William Allinson Journal, 1809

HISTORICAL SOCIETY OF PENNSYLVANIA
  Logan Papers
  Daniel Parker Papers

HISTORICAL SOCIETY OF WESTERN PENNSYLVANIA
  Methodist Collection

HENRY E. HUNTINGDON LIBRARY
  Parrish Collection
  Parker Collection

MASSACHUSETTS HISTORICAL SOCIETY
  Henry Knox Papers
  Pickering Papers

MUSEUM OF THE AMERICAN INDIAN, HEYE FOUNDATION
  De Cost Smith, field notes, Onandaga, 1889

NATIONAL ARCHIVES
  War Department Records: Bureau of Indian Affairs

NEW-YORK HISTORICAL SOCIETY
  O'Rielly Collection
  Baroness Hyde de Neuville's Sketches of American Life, 1807–1822

PENNSYLVANIA HISTORICAL COMMISSION
  Transcripts of the Records of the Western Missionary Society (copy
    of thesis by Edward I. George)
  Transcripts of Indian Records
  Skinner Manuscripts

PHILADELPHIA YEARLY MEETING, ARCHIVES (located at Friends' Book Store)
  Indian Committee Collection (10 boxes)
  Joseph Elkinton Journals, 1810–1828
  John Pierce and Joshua Sharpless Journal, 1798
  John Pierce Journal, 1801
  John Philips Journal, 1806
  Miscellaneous boxes of Indian material

PRESBYTERIAN HISTORICAL SOCIETY (Philadelphia)
  Early Missionary Magazines

STATE HISTORICAL SOCIETY OF WISCONSIN
  The Draper Collection (microfilm copy at Princeton University
    Library)

SWARTHMORE COLLEGE, FRIENDS' HISTORICAL LIBRARY
  Monthly Meeting Records
  Halliday Jackson Journal, 1800
  Henry Simmons Journal, 1798–1800
  Henry Simmons Letter Books, 1798–1799

VASSAR COLLEGE
  Jasper Parrish Papers

PUBLICATIONS

Early Magazines and Newspapers

The Adviser or *Vermont Evangelical Magazine*
Buffalo Gazette
Connecticut Evangelical Magazine
The Friend
General Assembly's Missionary Magazine or *Evangelical Intelligencer*
Massachusetts Baptist Missionary Magazine
Massachusetts Missionary Magazine
The Mental Elevator
New York Missionary Magazine
Niagara Journal
Pittsburgh Gazette
Western Missionary Magazine

Published Primary Historical Materials

ALDEN, TIMOTHY *An Account of Sundry Missions Performed Among the Senecas and Munsees, in a Series of Letters with Appendix.* New York, J. Seymour. 1827

ALLEN, ORLANDO "Personal Recollections of Captains Jones and Parrish, and of the Payment of Indian Annuities in Buffalo." *Buffalo Historical Society Publications,* VI: 539–46. 1903

AMERICAN STATE PAPERS, INDIAN AFFAIRS

ASHE, THOMAS *Travels in America, Performed in 1806, for the Purpose of Exploring the Rivers Allegheny....* London. 1808

AUPAUMUT, HENDRICK "A Narrative of an Embassy to the Western Indians." *Memoirs of the Historical Society of Pennsylvania,* II: 61–131. 1827

BADGER, REV. JOSEPH *A Memoir of Rev. Joseph Badger, Containing an Autobiography and Selections from His Private Journal and Correspondence.* Hudson, Ohio. 1851

BEAUCHAMP, WILLIAM M., ed. *Moravian Journals Relating to Central New York, 1745–66.* Syracuse, Onondaga Historical Association. 1916

BLAIR, EMMA HELEN, ed. *The Indian Tribes of the Upper Mississippi Valley and Region of the Great Lakes.* 2 vols. Cleveland, Arthur H. Clark Co. 1912

BRODHEAD, JOHN R. *Documents Relative to the Colonial History of the State of New York.* E. B. O'Callaghan, ed. Vol. VIII. Albany, Weed, Parsons & Co. 1857

CENSUS, BUREAU OF *Heads of Families: First Census of the United States, 1790.* Vol. VII: State of New York; Volume VIII. State of Pennsylvania. Washington. 1908

CLINTON, DEWITT *Discourse Delivered Before the New-York Historical Society, at Their Anniversary Meeting, 6th December, 1811.* New York, James Eastburn. 1812

COVELL, LEMUEL *A Narrative of a missionary tour through the western settlements of the State of New York and into the southwestern parts of the province of upper Canada . . . in the fall of 1803.* Troy, New York. 1804

CRUIKSHANK, E. A., ed. *The Correspondence of Lieutenant-Governor James Graves Simcoe, with Allied Documents Relating to his Administration of the Government of Upper Canada.* Toronto, Ontario Historical Society. 1923–31

DEARBORN, HENRY A. S. "Journals of Henry A. S. Dearborn." *Publications of the Buffalo Historical Society*, VII, 1904. 1838

ELKINTON, JOSEPH "Journals at Tunessassa, 1815–64" (extracts). *The Friend*, XXII, XXIII. 1827–49

EVANS, GRIFFETH "Journal of Griffeth Evans, Clerk to the Pennsylvania Commissioners at Fort Stanwix and Fort McIntosh, 1784–85." *Pennsylvania Magazine of History and Biography*, LXV: 202–33. 1941

FENTON, WILLIAM N., ed. "The Hyde de Neuville Portraits of New York Savages in 1807–1808." *New-York Historical Society Quarterly*, XXXVIII: 119–37. 1954
"Seneca Indians by Asher Wright (1859)." *Ethnohistory*, IV: 302–21. 1957
"The Journal of James Emlen Kept on a Trip to Canandaigua, New York . . . 1794." *Ethnohistory*, XII: 279–342. 1965

FITZPATRICK, JOHN C., ed. *George Washington, President of the United States, Diaries 1748–1799*, 4 vols. Vol. I, 1748–1770. 1925

FORD, W. C., et al., eds. *Journals of the Continental Congress*, Vol. I–XXV, 1774–84. Washington. 1904

HAMILTON, MILTON W., ed. "Guy Johnson's Opinions on the American Indian." *Pennsylvania Magazine of History and Biography*, LXXVII: 311–27. 1953

HARPSTER, JOHN W., ed. *Pen Pictures of Early Western Pennsylvania.* Pittsburgh, University of Pittsburgh Press. 1938

HECKEWELDER, JOHN *History, Manners, and Customs of the Indian Nations. . . .* Philadelphia, Historical Society of Pennsylvania, 1876. 1819

HOUGH, FRANKLIN B., ed. *Proceedings of the Commissioners of Indian Affairs. . . .* 2 vols. Albany. 1861

JACKSON, HALLIDAY *Civilization of the Indian Natives.* Philadelphia, Gould. 1830a
Sketch of the Manners, Customs, Religion and Government of the Seneca Indians in 1800. Philadelphia, Gould. 1830b

KAPPLER, CHARLES J. *Indian Affairs: Laws and Treaties.* 3 vols. Washington, U.S. Government Printing Office. 1904

KELLOGG, LOUISE P., ed. "Frontier Advance on the Upper Ohio." *Wisconsin State Historical Society Collections,* Vol. XXIII. 1916
"Frontier Retreat on the Upper Ohio." *Wisconsin State Historical Society Collections,* Vol. XXIV. 1917

KENT, DONALD H., AND MERLE H. DEARDORFF, eds. "John Adlum on the Allegheny: Memoirs for the Year 1794." *Pennsylvania Magazine of History and Biography,* LXXXIV: 265–324, 435–80. 1960

KENTON, EDNA, ed. *The Indians of North America.* 2 vols. New York, Harcourt, Brace. 1927

KETCHUM, WILLIAM *An Authentic and Comprehensive History of Buffalo.* Buffalo, New York, Rockwell, Baker & Hill. 1865

LAFITAU, JOSEPH *Moeurs des sauvages Americains.* 2 vols. Paris. 1724

LA POTHERIE, BACQUEVILLE DE *Histoire de l'Amerique septentrionale.* Paris. 1722

LINCOLN, GENERAL BENJAMIN "Journal of a Treaty Held in 1793, with the Indian Tribes North-West of the Ohio, by Commissioners of the United States." *Collections of the Massachusetts Historical Society,* Ser. 3, V: 109–176. 1836

MASSACHUSETTS HISTORICAL SOCIETY. *Collections,* Ser. 1, Vol. V. 1798

MEGINNESS, JOHN F., ed. *Journal of Samuel Maclay, while surveying the west branch of the Susquehanna, the Sinnemahoning and the Allegheny Rivers, in 1790.* Williamsport. 1887

MORSE, JEDIDIAH *A Report to the Secretary of War of the United States on Indian affairs, comprising a narrative of a tour performed in the summer of 1820.* New Haven. 1822

NORRIS, MAJOR "Journal of Sullivan's Expedition." *Buffalo Historical Society Publications*, I: 217–52. 1879

O'CALLAGHAN, E. B., ed. *Documents relative to the colonial history of the state of New-York.* Vols. VIII, IX. Albany, Weed, Parsons & Co. 1853–87

PENNSYLVANIA ARCHIVES Ser. 1, Vols. VII, VIII, X, XI, XII; Ser. 2, Vols. IV, VI (Papers Relating to the Establishment at Presqu' Isle). 1874–1935

PETERS, RICHARD, ed. *The Public Statutes at Large of the United States of America.* Volume VII, *Indian Affairs 1778–1842* ("7 Stat"). Boston, Little, Brown. 1856

PITTSBURGH GAZETTE "Letter of January 16 concerning economic conditions in western Pennsylvania in 1790." Reprinted in 1933 in *Western Pennsylvania Historical Magazine*, XVI: 48–52. 1790

PROCTOR, COLONEL THOMAS "Narrative of the journey of Col. Thomas Proctor to the Indians of the North-West, 1791." *Pennsylvania Archives*, 2nd ser., IV: 551–622. 1876

SCHERMERHORN, JOHN F. *Report respecting the Indians, inhabiting the western parts of the United States.* Boston, Massachusetts Historical Society Collection, Ser. 2, Vol. II. 1814

SCHOOLCRAFT, HENRY ROWE "Algic Researches: Comprising Inquiries Respecting the Mental Characteristics of North American Indians." *Indian Tales and Legends*, Ser. 1, 2 vols. New York. 1839

SEAVER, JAMES E., ed. *A Narrative of the Life of Mary Jemison, the White Woman of the Genesee.* New York, New York Scenic and Historic Preservation Society, 1932. 1824

SEVERANCE, FRANK H., ed. "Narratives of Early Mission Work on the Niagara Frontier and Buffalo Creek." *Publications of the Buffalo Historical Society*, Vol. VI. 1903

SHARPLESS, JOSHUA "A Visit to Cornplanter in 1798: Extracts from the Diary of Joshua Sharpless." Published in 1930 in Warren, Pennsylvania, *Times-Mirror* (original MS. owned by W. T. Sharpless, West Chester, Pennsylvania). 1798

SLOANE, JAMES "Early Trade Routes: Adventures and Recollections of a Pioneer Trader with an account of his share in the building of Buffalo Harbor." *Buffalo Historical Society Publications*, V: 215–37. 1902

SNYDERMAN, GEORGE S., ed. "Halliday Jackson's journal of a visit paid to the Indians of New York (1806)." *Proceedings of the American Philosophical Society*, CI: 565–99. 1957

STERN, B. J., ed. "The Letters of Asher Wright to Lewis Henry Morgan." *American Anthropologist*, XXXV: 138–45. 1933

SULLIVAN, JAMES, *et al.*, eds. *The Papers of Sir William Johnson.* 14 vols. Albany. 1921–65

THWAITES, REUBEN GOLD, ed. *The Jesuit Relations and Allied Documents . . . 1610–1791.* 73 vols. Cleveland, Burrows. 1896–1901
Documentary History of Dunmore's War, 1774. Madison, State Historical Society of Wisconsin. 1904

TUTTLE, SARAH *Letters and conversations on Indian Missions at Seneca, Tuscarora, Cattaraugus, in the State of New York, and Maumee, in the State of Ohio.* Boston, Massachusetts Sabbath School Society. 1834

WAINWRIGHT, NICHOLAS B., ed. "The Opinions of George Crogham on the American Indian." *Pennsylvania Magazine of History and Biography*, LXXI: 152–9. 1947

WALLACE, ANTHONY F. C., ed. "Halliday Jackson's Journal to the Seneca Indians, 1798–1800." *Pennsylvania History*, XIX: 117–47, 325–49. 1952a

WRAXALL, PETER *An Abridgement of the Indian Affairs . . . in the Colony of New York, 1678–1751.* C. H. McIlwain, ed. Cambridge, Harvard University Press. 1915

WRENSHALL, JOHN "The manuscript autobiography of John Wrenshall, early Pittsburgh merchant, trader and Methodist leader, in 1803." *Western Pennsylvania Historical Magazine*, XXV: 81–3. 1942

Primary Ethnographic Documents

BEAUCHAMP, WILLIAM M. "The New Religion of the Iroquois." *The Journal of American Folk-Lore*, X: 169–80. 1897
Civil, Religious and Mourning Councils and Ceremonies of Adoption of the New York Indians. Albany, New York State Museum, Bulletin 113. 1907

CHAFE, WALLACE L. *Seneca Thanksgiving Rituals.* Washington, Bureau of American Ethnology, Bulletin 183. 1961
Seneca Morphology and Dictionary. Washington, Smithsonian Press. 1967

CURTIN, JEREMIAH, and HEWITT, J. N. B. *Seneca Fiction, Legends, and Myths.* Washington, Bureau of American Ethnology, 32nd Annual Report. 1918

FENTON, WILLIAM N. *An Outline of Seneca Ceremonies at Coldspring Longhouse.* New Haven, Yale University Publications in Anthropology, No. 9. 1936

"Masked Medicine Societies of the Iroquois." In Smithsonian Institution Annual Report, Publication 3624: 397–430. 1940

"Tonawanda Longhouse Ceremonies; Ninety Years after Lewis Henry Morgan." Bureau of American Ethnology, Bulletin 128: 140–66. 1941a

"Iroquois Suicide: A Study in the Stability of a Culture Pattern." Bureau of American Ethnology, Bulletin 128: 80–137. 1941b

"Place Names and Related Activities of the Cornplanter Senecas." *Pennsylvania Archaeologist*, XV: Nos. 1–4 and 1946; XVI: No. 2. 1945

"An Iroquois Condolence Council for Installing Cayuga Chiefs in 1945." *Journal of the Washington Academy of Sciences*, XXXVI: 110–27. 1946

"Seth Newhouse's Traditional History and Constitution of the Iroquois Confederacy." *Proceedings of the American Philosophical Society*, XCIII: 141–58. 1949

The Roll Call of the Iroquois Chiefs: A Study of a Mnemonic Cane from the Six Nations Reserve. Washington, Smithsonian Miscellaneous Collections, III: No. 15. 1950

The Iroquois Eagle Dance: An Offshoot of the Calumet Dance. Washington, Bureau of American Ethnology, Bulletin 156. 1953

FENTON, WM. N., ED. *Parker on the Iroquois: Iroquois Uses of Maize and Other Food Plants; the Code of Handsome Lake, the Seneca Prophet; the Constitution of the Five Nations.* New York State Study Ser., II, Syracuse University Press. 1968

GOLDENWEISER, ALEXANDER A. *On Iroquois Work.* Summary Reports of the Geological Survey of Canada, 1912 and 1913. 1914

HALE, HORATIO *The Iroquois Book of Rites.* W. N. Fenton, ed. Toronto, University of Toronto Press, 1963. 1883

"An Iroquois Condoling Council." *Proceedings and Transactions of the Royal Society of Canada*, Ser. 2, I: 45–65. 1895

HEWITT, J. N. B. *Iroquoian Cosmology.* Washington, Bureau of American Ethnology, Annual Reports 21 and 43. 1903–28

"The Requickening Address of the Iroquois Condolence Council." *Journal of the Washington Academy of Sciences*, XXXIV: 65–85. 1944

MORGAN, LEWIS H. *League of the Ho-De-No-Sau-Nee or Iroquois.* New York, Dodd, Mead & Co., 1901. 1851

Systems of Consanguinity and Affinity of the Human Family. Washington, Smithsonian Institution. 1871

MYRTLE, MINNIE *The Iroquois: or the Bright Side of Indian Life.* New York. 1855

PARKER, ARTHUR C. "Secret Medicine Societies of the Seneca." *American Anthropologist*, XI: 161–85. 1909

The Code of Handsome Lake, the Seneca Prophet. Albany, New York State Museum, Bulletin 163. 1913
The Constitution of the Five Nations. Albany, New York State Museum, Bulletin 148. 1916

RANDLE, MARTHA "Iroquois Women, Then and Now." In W. N. Fenton, ed., *Symposium on Local Diversity in Iroquois Culture.* Washington, Bureau of American Ethnology, Bulletin 149. 1951

SCOTT, DUNCAN C. "Traditional History of the Confederacy of the Six Nations." *Proceedings and Transactions of the Royal Society of Canada,* Ser. 3, V: 195–246. 1912

SHIMONY, ANNEMARIE A. *Conservatism Among the Iroquois at the Six Nation's Reserve.* New Haven, Yale University Publications in Anthropology, No. 65. 1961

SMITH, DE COST "Witches and Demonism of the Modern Iroquois." *Journal of American Folk-Lore,* I: 184–93. 1888

SMITH, ERMINIE, ed. *Myths of the Iroquois.* Washington, Bureau of Ethnology, 2nd Annual Report.

SPECK, FRANK G. *Naskapi: The Savage Hunters of the Labrador Peninsula.* Norman, University of Oklahoma Press. 1935
Midwinter Rites of the Cayuga Long House. Philadelphia, University of Pennsylvania Press. 1949

Secondary Sources

AGNEW, DANIEL *A History of the Region of Pennsylvania North of the Ohio and West of the Allegheny River. . . .* Philadelphia, Kay & Brother. 1887

ALVORD, CLARENCE WALWORTH *The Mississippi Valley in British Politics, A Study of the Trade, Land Speculation, and Experiments in Imperialism Culminating in the American Revolution.* 2 vols. Cleveland, Ohio. 1917

BABCOCK, LOUIS L. *The War of 1812 on the Niagara Frontier.* Publications of the Buffalo Historical Society, 29. 1927

BEAUCHAMP, WILLIAM M. *A History of the New York Iroquois.* Albany, New York State Museum, Bulletin 78. 1905

BERKHOFER, ROBERT F. *Salvation and the Savage: An Analysis of Protestant Missions and American Indian Response.* Lexington, University of Kentucky Press. 1965

BLAU, HAROLD "Dream Guessing: A Comparative Analysis." *Ethnohistory*, X: 233–49. 1963

"Function and the False Faces: A Classification of Onondaga Masked Rituals and Themes." *Journal of American Folk-Lore*, LXXIX: 564–80. 1966

BRISTOW, ARCHIE *Old Time Tales of Warren County*. Meadville, Pennsylvania, Tribune Press. 1932

BRYANT, WILLIAM C. "Orlando Allen: Glimpses of Life in the Village of Buffalo." *Buffalo Historical Society Publications*, I: 329–71. 1878

BUCK, ELIZABETH HAWTHORN "Social Life in Western Pennsylvania as Seen by Early Travelers." *Western Pennsylvania Historical Magazine*, XVIII: 125–38. 1935

BUCK, SOLON J., and BUCK, ELIZABETH HAWTHORN *The Planting of Civilization in Western Pennsylvania*. Pittsburgh, University of Pittsburgh Press. 1939

CAMPBELL, WILLIAM W. *Annals of Tryon County; or, the Border Warfare of New-York, During the Revolution*. New York, Harper. 1831

CANFIELD, W. W. *The legends of the Iroquois told by "The Cornplanter."* New York. 1802

CARSE, MARY ROWELL "The Mohawk Iroquois." *Bulletin of the Archaeological Society of Connecticut*, XXIII: 3–53. 1949

[CATTARAUGUS COUNTY] *History of Cattaraugus County, New York*. Philadelphia, L. H. Levers. 1879

CLARK JOSHUA V. H. *Onondaga; or Reminiscences of Earlier and Later Times....* 2 vols. Syracuse, Stoddard and Babcock. 1849

CLEVELAND, C. C. *The Great Revival in the West, 1797–1805*. Chicago, The University of Chicago Press. 1916

CONGDON, CHARLES E. *Allegany Oxbow: A History of Allegany State Park and the Allegany Reserve of the Seneca Nation*. Little Valley, New York, Straight Publishing Co. 1967

COTTERILL, R. S. *The Southern Indians: The Story of the Civilized Tribes Before Removal*. Norman, University of Oklahoma Press. 1954

CRAIG, NEVILLE B. *The Olden Time*. Pittsburgh. 1846–48

CRIBBS, GEORGE ARTHUR "The Frontier Policy of Pennsylvania." *The Historical Society of Western Pennsylvania*, II: 5–35, 72–106, 174–98. 1919

CROSS, WHITNEY R. *The Burned-Over District*. Ithaca, Cornell University Press. 1950

· Bibliography ·

CRUIKSHANK, E. A. *The Employment of the Indians in the War of 1812.* Annual Report of the American Historical Association. 1895

DAHLINGER, CHARLES W. "Old Allegheny." *Western Pennsylvania Historical Magazine,* I: 161–223. 1918

DEARDORFF, MERLE H. "The Cornplanter Grant in Warren County." *Western Pennsylvania Historical Magazine,* XXIV: 1–22. 1941
"Zeisberger's Allegheny River Indian Towns: 1767–1770." *Pennsylvania Archaeologist,* XVI: 2–19. 1946
"The Religion of Handsome Lake: Its Origin and Development." In W. N. Fenton, ed., *Symposium on Local Diversity in Iroquois Culture.* Washington, Bureau of American Ethnology, Bulletin 149. 1951

DONEHOO, GEORGE P. *A History of the Indian Villages and Place Names in Pennsylvania.* Harrisburg, Telegraph Press. 1928

DOWNES, RANDOLPH C. *Council Fires on the Upper Ohio: A Narrative of Indian Affairs in the Upper Ohio Valley until 1795.* Pittsburgh, University of Pittsburgh Press. 1940

DRAKE, BENJAMIN *Life of Tecumseh, and of his brother the Prophet, with a historical sketch of the Shawanee Indians.* Cincinnati. 1841

DRAKE, SAMUEL G. *Biography and History of the Indians of North America.* Boston. 1837

ELLIS, FRANKLIN *History of Cattaraugus County, New York, with Illustrations and Biographical Sketches of Some of its Prominent Men and Pioneers.* Philadelphia, L. H. Everts. 1879

EVANS, P. D. *The Holland Land Company.* Publications of the Buffalo Historical Society, 28. 1924

FENTON, WILLIAM N. "Problems Arising from the Historic Northeastern Position of the Iroquois." *Smithsonian Miscellaneous Collections,* C: 159–251. 1940
"Seth Newhouse's Traditional History and Constitution of the Iroquois Confederacy." *Proceedings of the American Philosophical Society,* XCIII: 141–58. 1949
"Iroquois Studies at the Mid-Century." *Proceedings of the American Philosophical Society,* XCV: 296–310. 1951
The Iroquois in History. Paper read at Wenner-Gren Symposium, Burg Wartenstein, Austria, August 7–14, 1967. 1967

FERGUSON, RUSSELL J. "A Cultural Oasis in Northwestern Pennsylvania." *Western Pennsylvania Historical Magazine,* XIX: 269–80. 1936

FLICK, ALEXANDER C. *History of the State of New York.* 10 vols. 1933–37

GIPSON, LAWRENCE HENRY *The British Empire Before the American Revolution.* 13 vols. New York, Knopf. 1954–67

HALE, NELSON R. "The Pennsylvania Population Company." *New York History,* XVI: 122–30. 1949

HALSEY, FRANCIS WHITING *The Old New York Frontier: Its Wars with Indians and Tories, Its Missionary Schools, Pioneers and Land Titles 1614–1800.* New York, Charles Scribner's Sons. 1912

HARMON, GEORGE DEWEY *Sixty Years of Indian Affairs.* Chapel Hill, University of North Carolina Press. 1941

HARRIS, GEORGE H. "The Life of Horatio Jones: The True Story of Hoc-Sa-Go-Wah, Prisoner, Pioneer and Interpreter." *Publications of the Buffalo Historical Society,* VI: 383–514. 1903

HENDERSON, ELIZABETH K. "The Northwestern Lands of Pennsylvania, 1790–1812." *Pennsylvania Magazine of History and Biography,* LX: 131–60. 1936

HODGE, F. W., ed. *Handbook of American Indians North of Mexico.* Washington, Bureau of American Ethnology, Bulletin 30. 1906

HOTCHKIN, JAMES H. *A History of the Purchase and Settlement of Western New York, and of the . . . Presbyterian Church in that Section.* New York. 1848

HOUGHTON, FREDERICK "History of the Buffalo Creek Reservation." *Publications of The Buffalo Historical Society,* XXIV: 3–181. 1920

HOWLAND, HENRY R. "The Old Caneadea Council House and Its Last Council Fire." *Publications of the Buffalo Historical Society,* VI: 97–124. 1903

HSU, FRANCIS L. K. "The Effect of Dominant Kinship Relationships on Kin- and Non-Kin Behavior: A Hypothesis." *American Anthropologist,* LXVII: 638–61. 1965

HUNT, GEORGE T. *The Wars of the Iroquois: A Study in Intertribal Trade Relations.* Madison, University of Wisconsin Press. 1940

IBBOTSON, JOSEPH D. "Samuel Kirkland, the Treaty of 1792 and the Indian Barrier State." *Proceedings of the New York State Historical Association,* XXXVI: 374–91. 1938

KELSEY, RAYNER WICKERSHAM *Friends and the Indians 1655–1917.* Philadelphia, the Associated Executive Committee of Friends on Indian Affairs. 1917

LOTHROP, S. K. "Life of Samuel Kirkland, Missionary to the Indians." In Jared Sparks, ed., *Library of American Biography,* Ser. 2, XV: 137–308. Boston, Charles C. Little & James Brown. 1848

LOUNSBURY, FLOYD G. "The Structural Analysis of Kinship Semantics." In Horace G. Lunt, ed., *Proceedings of the 9th International Congress of Linguists*. The Hague, Mouton & Co. 1964

LYDEKKER, JOHN WOLFE *The Faithful Mohawks*. New York, Macmillan. 1938

MACLEAN, JOHN P. "Shaker Mission to the Shawnee Indians." *Ohio Archaeological and Historical Quarterly*, XI. 1903

MANLEY, HENRY S. *The Treaty of Fort Stanwix, 1784*. Rome, New York, Rome Sentinel Co. 1932
"Buying Buffalo from the Indians." *Proceedings of the New York Historical Association*, XLV: 313–98. 1942
"Red Jacket's Last Campaign and an Extended Biographical and Biographical Note." *New York History*, XLVIII: 149–68. 1950

MATHEWS, CATHARINE VAN CORTLANDT *Andrew Ellicott, His Life and Letters*. New York, The Grafton Press.

MCNALL, NEIL ADAMS *An Agricultural History of the Genesee Valley, 1790–1860*. Philadelphia, University of Pennsylvania Press. 1952

MOHR, WALTER H. *Federal Indian Relations, 1774–1788*. Philadelphia, University of Pennsylvania Press. 1933

MURDOCK, GEORGE P. *Our Primitive Contemporaries*. New York, Macmillan. 1934

PARKER, ARTHUR C. "The Senecas in the War of 1812." *Proceedings of the New York State Historical Association*, XV: 78–90. 1916
"The Life of General Ely S. Parker: Last Grand Sachem of the Iroquois and General Grant's Military Secretary." *Publications of the Buffalo Historical Society*, XXIII. 1919
"An Analytical History of the Seneca Indians." Rochester, New York, *Researches and Transactions of the New York State Archaeological Association*, Vol. VI, Nos. 1–5. 1926
"Notes on the Ancestry of Cornplanter." Rochester, New York, *Researches and Transactions of the New York State Archaeological Association*, Vol. V, No. 2. 1927

PEARCE, ROY H. *The Savages of America: A Study of the Indian and the Idea of Civilization*. Baltimore, Johns Hopkins Press. 1953

PECKHAM, HOWARD H. *Pontiac and the Indian Uprising*. Princeton, Princeton University Press. 1947

PETTITT, GEORGE A. *Primitive Education in North America*. Berkeley and Los Angeles, University of California Press. 1946

QUAIN, BUELL H. "The Iroquois." In Margaret Mead, ed., *Cooperation and Competition Among Primitive Peoples*. New York, McGraw-Hill. 1937

ROSSMAN, KENNETH R. *Thomas Mifflin and the Politics of the American Revolution*. Chapel Hill, University of North Carolina Press. 1952

ROYCE, CHARLES C. *Indian Land Cessions in the United States*. Washington, Bureau of American Ethnology, 18th Annual Report. 1899

RUSSELL, EBER L. "The Lost Story of the Brodhead Expedition." *New York History*, XXVIII: 252–63. 1930

SAVELLE, MAX *George Morgan: Colony Builder*. New York, Columbia University Press. 1932

SCHENCK, J. S. *History of Warren County, Pennsylvania*. Syracuse, D. Mason & Co.

SCHOOLCRAFT, HENRY R. *Notes on the Iroquois*. New York. 1846
Historical and statistical information respecting the history condition, and prospects of the Indian tribes of the United States. 6 vols. Philadelphia. 1851–57
Archives of Aboriginal Knowledge: Information Respecting the History, Condition and Prospects of the Indian Tribes of the United States. 6 vols. Philadelphia. 1860.

SHIPMAN, FRED WALDO *The Indian Council of 1793: A Clash of Policies*. Clark University, M.A. thesis MS. 1933

SIPE, C. HALE *The Indian Chiefs of Pennsylvania*. Butler, Pennsylvania, The Ziegler Printing Co., Inc. 1927

SMITH, JOSEPH *Old Redstone, or Historical Sketches of Western Presbyterianism and Its Early Ministers*. Philadelphia. 1854

SNYDERMAN, GEORGE *Behind the Tree of Peace: A Sociological Analysis of Iroquois Warfare*. Ph.D. Dissertation, University of Pennsylvania. 1948; published in *Pennsylvania Archaeologist*, Vol. XVIII, Nos. 3–4. 1948.
"A Preliminary Survey of American Indian Manuscripts in Repositories of the Philadelphia Area." *Proceedings of the American Philosophical Society*, XCVII: 596–610. 1953

SPECK, FRANK G. *The Iroquois: A Study in Cultural Evolution*. Bloomfield Hills, Michigan, Cranbrook Institute of Science. 1945

STONE, RUFUS B. "Brodhead's Raid on the Senecas." *Western Pennsylvania Historical Magazine*, VII: 88–101. 1924

STONE, WILLIAM L. *Life of Joseph Brant—Thayendanegea*. 2 vols. New York, Blake. 1838

The Life and Times of Red Jacket, or Sa-go-ye-wat-ha; being the Sequel to the History of the Six Nations. 2 vols. Albany, Munsell. 1866

THATCHER, B. B. *Indian Biography, or an historical account of those Individuals who have been distinguished among the North American Natives....* New York. 1840

TOOKER, ELIZABETH "The Iroquois White Dog Sacrifice in the Latter Part of the Eighteenth Century." *Ethnohistory*, XII: 129–40. 1965
"On the New Religion of Handsome Lake." *Anthropological Quarterly*, XLI: 187–200. 1968

TRELEASE, ALLEN W. *Indian Affairs in Colonial New York: The Seventeenth Century.* Ithaca, New York, Cornell University Press. 1960

TURNER, O. *Pioneer History of the Holland Purchase of Western New York.* Buffalo. 1849
History of the Pioneer Settlement of the Phelps and Gorham Purchases. Albany. 1852

WALLACE, ANTHONY F. C. *King of the Delawares: Teedyuscung.* Philadelphia, University of Pennsylvania Press. 1949
"Handsome Lake and the Great Revival in the West." *American Quarterly*, Summer, pp. 149–65. 1952b
"Mazeway Resynthesis: A Biocultural Theory of Religious Inspiration." *Transactions of the New York Academy of Sciences*, XVIII: 626–38. 1956a
"Revitalization Movements: Some Theoretical Considerations for their Comparative Study." *American Anthropologist*, LVIII: 264–81. 1956b
"Stress and Rapid Personality Change." *International Record of Medicine*, CLXIX: 761–74. 1956c
"The Origins of Iroquois Neutrality: The Grand Settlement of 1701." *Pennsylvania History*, XXIV: 223–35. 1957
"Dreams and the Wishes of the Soul." *American Anthropologist*, LX: 234–48. 1958a
"The Dekanawidah Myth Analyzed as the Record of a Revitalization Movement." *Ethnohistory*, V: 118–30. 1958b
"Cultural Determinants of Response to Hallucinatory Experience." *AMA Archives of General Psychiatry*, I: 58–69. 1959
"Cultural Composition of the Handsome Lake Religion." In W. N. Fenton and John Gulick, eds., *Symposium on Cherokee and Iroquois Culture.* Washington, Bureau of American Ethnology, Bulletin 180. 1961
Religion: An Anthropological View. New York, Random House. 1966

WALLACE, PAUL A. W. *Conrad Weiser, 1696–1760: Friend of Colonist and Mohawk*. Philadelphia, University of Pennsylvania Press. 1945

The White Roots of Peace. Philadelphia, University of Pennsylvania Press. 1946

"Historic Indian Paths of Pennsylvania." *Pennsylvania Magazine of History and Biography*, LXXVI, No. 4. 1952

Indian Paths of Pennsylvania. Harrisburg, Pennsylvania Historical and Museum Commission. 1965

WARREN CENTENNIAL *An Account of the Celebration at Warren, Pennsylvania . . . 1895*. Warren, Pennsylvania, Warren Library Association. 1897

WHITE, EMMA SIGGINS *Genealogical Gleanings of Siggins and other Pennsylvania Families*. Kansas City, Tiernam-Dart Printing Co. 1918

WILDES, HARRY EMERSON *Anthony Wayne, Trouble Shooter of the American Revolution*. New York, Harcourt, Brace & Co. 1941

WILKINSON, NORMAN B. "Robert Morris and the Treaty of Big Tree." *Mississippi Valley Historical Review*, LX: 257–78. 1953

WILSON, EDMUND *Apologies to the Iroquois*. New York, Farrar, Straus, and Cudahy. 1960

WRIGHT, J. E., and CORBETT, DORIS S. *Pioneer Life in Western Pennsylvania*. Pittsburgh. University of Pittsburgh Press. 1940

YOUNG, ELEANOR *Forgotten Patriot: Robert Morris*. New York, Macmillan. 1950

INDEX

(iii)

Anthony Wallace was born in Toronto, Canada, in 1923 and did both his undergraduate and graduate work at the University of Pennsylvania (Ph.D., 1950). He has been Chairman of the Department of Anthropology at the University of Pennsylvania since 1961. In addition to his present position, Mr. Wallace is Medical Research Scientist at the Eastern Pennsylvania Psychiatric Institute where he was formerly Director of Clinical Research. He has written three books, *King of the Delawares: Teedyuscung* (1949), *Culture and Personality* (1961), and *Religion: An Anthropological View* (1966). He lives in Philadelphia with his wife and their four children.

A NOTE ON THE TYPE

The text of this book was set on the Linotype in Janson, a recutting made direct from type cast from matrices long thought to have been made by the Dutchman Anton Janson, who was a practicing type founder in Leipzig during the years 1668–87. However, it has been conclusively demonstrated that these types are actually the work of Nicholas Kis (1650–1702), a Hungarian, who most probably learned his trade from the master Dutch type founder Kirk Voskens. The type is an excellent example of the influential and sturdy Dutch types that prevailed in England up to the time William Caslon developed his own incomparable designs from these Dutch faces.

This book was composed, printed, and bound by
The Book Press, Brattleboro, Vt.

Typography and binding design by
GUY FLEMING